HISTORY OF THE
WAR IN SOUTH AFRICA
1899-1902

HISTORY

OF THE

WAR IN SOUTH AFRICA

1899–1902

COMPILED BY DIRECTION OF
HIS MAJESTY'S GOVERNMENT

BY

MAJOR-GENERAL SIR FREDERICK MAURICE, K.C.B.

WITH A STAFF OF OFFICERS

VOLUME IV

The Naval & Military Press Ltd

Published by
The Naval & Military Press Ltd
5 Riverside, Brambleside, Bellbrook
Industrial Estate, Uckfield, East Sussex,
TN22 1QQ England
Tel: +44 (0) 1825 749494
Fax: +44 (0) 1825 765701
www.naval-military-press.com

In reprinting in facsimile from the original, any imperfections are inevitably reproduced and the quality may fall short of modern type and cartographic standards.

PREFACE.

This Volume comprises the account of the War in South Africa from the assumption of the command-in-chief by General Lord Kitchener, G.C.B., G.C.M.G., to the termination of hostilities. It might, therefore, be considered as dealing with a distinct phase of the campaign, even if the peculiar nature of the operations did not of themselves distinguish it from what had gone before. From December, 1900, to May, 1902, was waged incessantly guerrilla warfare of the purest type and on the most extensive scale between an army of 195,400 men on the one side and of 30,000 to 50,000 men on the other. The contest was remarkable in many respects, but in none, perhaps, more than in its duration. When it is considered that at the moment at which this narration opens the Boer forces were already beaten, inasmuch as their cause was irretrievably lost, their long-sustained effort to ward off the end requires some military explanation. It is to be found in the fact that in their expiring struggle they reverted to weapons which were peculiarly their own and precisely those in which their opponents were least practised. Casting off the trammels of formal warfare, and disintegrating into a thousand bands, they compelled the British Army to conform, and agitated the whole vast theatre of war with an infinite complexity of movement which never for a moment desisted, nor for more than a moment was marked by any distinguishable trend.

To trace in detail the components of this universal stir has been the author's task. It was necessary to do so minutely. An official historian owes a duty from which a general writer is exempt; his work would be valueless to military students if it could not be referred to for information concerning the minutiæ of the campaign, the lesser as well as the greater tactics, the work of units, and even of individual officers and men. Moreover, a campaign such as that recorded in the following pages especially calls for dissection, because it was mainly composed of a myriad of events, each so small, yet contributing to so vast a sum, that it was often impossible to determine which was greater than another, or which was worthy or unworthy of mention. The elimination of every minor operation would, in fact, have resulted in almost total silence on a whole campaign of small affairs which together composed one of the greatest feats of the British Empire and Army. As much as possible, therefore, has been briefly recorded; to record it all was beyond the power of man.

Of one deficiency in the scheme of the Volume the author is well aware, namely, the rarity of any periodical "purview" or general glance over the theatre of war. This has not been neglected because it was forgotten, but because it seemed alike valueless and impossible. Rarely was the campaign marked by any permanent development of the situation; never, until the end, by one that affected it all. If the enemy appeared few and dispirited on one day, they were numerous and aggressive on the next; the clearance of one area did but embroil its neighbour; defeats and victories of columns and commandos followed one another with a regularity in which the gradual attrition of the weaker side was scarcely to be perceived. In short, it could never be said precisely how matters stood at any given moment; those who attempted to do so from the seat of war were sadly at fault. Now, as then, only the size of the campaign can be truly stated, for shape it had none.

For the assistance of the reader it may be remarked that the work has been so designed that those desirous of following the operations in any particular province of South Africa may do so by omitting the intervening chapters which deal with other parts.

In cases where a number of officers of the same name were in the field, the initials are repeated as often as is necessary to avoid confusion.

A mass of technical material for which there was no place in the text has been incorporated in Appendices.

In conclusion, the author wishes to record his indebtedness to two officers, namely, Captain J. Bowers (Army Service Corps) and Captain L. Oppenheim (2nd Dragoon Guards, Queen's Bays), who took charge of, and extracted the essentials of the enormous and intricate mass of material from which this Volume has been written. He can say no more, and no less, than that without their services the work could not have been completed.

M. H. GRANT.

CONTENTS.

VOLUME IV.

CHAP.		PAGE
I.—Events in the Western Transvaal. December, 1900		1
II.—Events in the Eastern Transvaal. December 1st, 1900—January 30th, 1901		23
III.—Events in the Orange River Colony. December, 1900—January, 1901		45
IV.—Events in Cape Colony. December, 1900—February 28th, 1901		60
V.—Events in the Orange River Colony. (Continued from Chapter III.) February—June, 1901		93
VI.—Events in the Eastern Transvaal. (Continued from Chapter II.) January—March, 1901		111
VII.—Events in the Western Transvaal. (Continued from Chapter I.) January—April, 1901		128
VIII.—Events in the Eastern Transvaal and Natal. (Continued from Chapter VI.) April—May, 1901		139
IX.—Events in the Orange River Colony. (Continued from Chapter V.) April—June, 1901		156
X.—Events in Cape Colony. (Continued from Chapter IV.) March—April, 1901		172
XI.—Events in the Western Transvaal. (Continued from Chapter VII.) May—August, 1901		181

CHAP.	PAGE
XII.—Events in the Eastern Transvaal. (*Continued from Chapter VIII.*) June—September, 1901	198
XIII.—Events in Cape Colony. (*Continued from Chapter X.*) June—September, 1901	224
XIV.—Events in the Orange River Colony. (*Continued from Chapter IX.*) July—August, 1901	245
XV.—Events in Cape Colony. (*Continued from Chapter XIII.*) September—October, 1901	270
XVI.—Events in the Western Transvaal. (*Continued from Chapter XI.*) September—November, 1901	291
XVII.—Events in the Eastern Transvaal. (*Continued from Chapter XII.*) The Action of Bakenlaagte, October 30th, 1901	304
XVIII.—Events in the Orange River Colony. (*Continued from Chapter XIV.*) August—November, 1901	316
XIX.—Events in the Western Transvaal. (*Continued from Chapter XVI.*) November, 1901—January, 1902	339
XX.—Events in the North-West and West of Cape Colony. April—December, 1901	349
XXI.—Events in the Eastern Transvaal. (*Continued from Chapter XVII.*) November, 1901—January, 1902	371
XXII.—Events in the Orange River Colony. (*Continued from Chapter XVIII.*) December, 1901—February, 1902	382
XXIII.—Events in the Western Transvaal. (*Continued from Chapter XIX.*) January—March, 1902	406
XXIV.—Events in the Orange River Colony. (*Continued from Chapter XXII.*) February, 1902	423
XXV.—Events in the Northern Transvaal. April, 1901—May, 1902	435

CONTENTS.

CHAP.		PAGE
XXVI.—Events in Cape Colony. (*Continued from Chapter XX.*) January—May, 1902		453
XXVII.—Events in the Orange River Colony. (*Continued from Chapter XXIV.*) March—May, 1902		475
XXVIII.—Events in the Western Transvaal. (*Continued from Chapter XXIII.*) March—May, 1902		491
XXIX.—Events in the Eastern Transvaal. (*Continued from Chapter XXI.*) February—May, 1902		512
XXX.—The Conclusion of Peace		523

ILLUSTRATIONS.

Witkoppies—Views of, from the North and West
Facing page 104

APPENDICES.

NO.		PAGE
1.	SUMMARY OF SUPPLIES SENT BY THE NATAL DISTRICT FOR GENERAL FRENCH'S FORCE, GARRISONS, ETC., FEBRUARY—MARCH, 1901	567
2.	THE EVOLUTION OF THE BLOCKHOUSE SYSTEM IN SOUTH AFRICA	568
3.	LETTER FROM GENERAL C. R. DE WET TO GENERAL J. C. SMUTS, APPOINTING HIM SUCCESSOR TO KRITZINGER AND GIVING INSTRUCTIONS AS TO THE CONDUCT OF THE CAMPAIGN IN CAPE COLONY, FEBRUARY 8TH, 1902	577
4.	ORDERS BY LIEUT.-GENERAL SIR I. S. M. HAMILTON, K.C.B., D.S.O., COMMANDING COLUMNS OPERATING IN WESTERN TRANSVAAL, MAY 6TH, 1902	581
5.	NOTES ON THE SUPPLY SYSTEM IN SOUTH AFRICA, 1901—2	584
6.	NOTES ON THE TRANSPORT SYSTEM IN SOUTH AFRICA, 1901—2	598
7.	NOTES ON THE ROYAL ARMY MEDICAL DEPARTMENT IN SOUTH AFRICA, 1901—2	602
8.	NOTES ON THE ARMY ORDNANCE DEPARTMENT IN SOUTH AFRICA	617
9.	NOTES ON THE ARMY POST OFFICE CORPS IN SOUTH AFRICA	625
10.	NOTES ON THE MILITARY RAILWAY SYSTEM IN SOUTH AFRICA	629
11.	NOTES ON THE ARMY REMOUNT DEPARTMENT	650
12.	NOTES ON THE REFUGEE CONCENTRATION CAMPS IN SOUTH AFRICA, 1901—2	659

NO.		PAGE
13.	STRENGTH OF THE GARRISON IN SOUTH AFRICA ON AUGUST 1ST, 1899, AND REINFORCEMENTS, ETC., FROM HOME AND COLONIES DURING THE WAR UP TO MAY 31ST, 1902	671
14.	DRAFTS, ETC., DESPATCHED TO SOUTH AFRICA DURING THE WAR, 1899—1902	675
15.	STATEMENT SHOWING :—	
	(A.) COMPARATIVE RECRUITING FIGURES OF THE ARMY AND MILITIA PRIOR TO AND DURING THE WAR IN SOUTH AFRICA	678
	(B.) RECRUITING FIGURES DURING THE WAR OF THE IMPERIAL YEOMANRY, VOLUNTEERS, SOUTH AFRICAN CONSTABULARY, ETC.	679
16.	CASUALTIES, WASTAGE, ETC., IN THE ARMY IN SOUTH AFRICA DURING THE WAR, UP TO MAY 31ST, 1902	680
17.	STATEMENT OF CASUALTIES, BY CORPS, DURING THE WAR IN SOUTH AFRICA, 1899—1902	681
18.	EXPENDITURE INCURRED ON ARMY VOTES IN CONSEQUENCE OF THE WAR IN SOUTH AFRICA	698
19.	A LIST OF RECIPIENTS OF THE VICTORIA CROSS DURING THE WAR IN SOUTH AFRICA, 1899—1902	700
20.	STATEMENT OF BOER PRISONERS OF WAR, SHOWING HOW DISPOSED OF	704
	MONTHLY COMPARATIVE STATEMENT FOR 1901—2, CASUALTIES IN THE BOER FORCES	705
	SUMMARY, SHOWING DECREASE OF BOER FORCES	705

LIST OF MAPS AND SKETCHES.
VOLUME IV.

No. 56.   EASTERN TRANSVAAL.
No. 57.   THE ACTION OF BAKENLAAGTE. October 30th, 1901.
No. 58.   SOUTH AFRICA, *showing lines of Blockhouses, Stationary Garrisons and Posts*, May, 1902.
No. 59.   WESTERN TRANSVAAL.
No. 60.   GENERAL SIR IAN HAMILTON'S "DRIVE" IN THE WESTERN TRANSVAAL, May 6th—11th, 1902.
No. 61.   PLAN OF RAILWAY LINE. *Illustrating System of Blockhouses, etc., generally adopted.*
No. 62.   PLAN OF ROAD—MACHADODORP AND LYDENBURG. *Illustrating System of Blockhouses, etc., generally adopted.*
No. 63.   CAPE COLONY.
No. 64.   ORANGE RIVER COLONY.

MAPS TO VOLUME IV.

THE general remarks on maps prefacing Volume I. are applicable also to the maps in this Volume. Maps Nos. 56, 59 and 64 have been compiled chiefly from the four-miles-to-one-inch sheets issued by the Topographical Section of the War Office previous to the war, and these again were prepared from the Government Farm Surveys of the Transvaal and Orange Free State. Where the ground is not covered by that series, Jeppe's Map of the Transvaal has been used.

No. 57 is an enlargement made from some reconnaissance mapping done since the war.

Nos. 58 and 63 are compiled from ordinary published maps of South Africa revised in parts from special sketches made by officers.

No. 60 is from Jeppe's Map of the Transvaal.

Nos. 61 and 62 are from special sketches.

THE WAR IN SOUTH AFRICA.

CHAPTER I.

EVENTS IN THE WESTERN TRANSVAAL, DECEMBER, 1900.*

AT the moment of Field-Marshal Lord Roberts' departure from the theatre of war, and of the assumption of the chief command by General Lord Kitchener, G.C.B., G.C.M.G., the Western Transvaal seemed very little disturbed except by rumour. Of the combined Boer descent upon Cape Colony nothing had materialised except De Wet's single-handed incursion between the Orange and Caledon rivers, where that daring leader was daily becoming more deeply involved in one of the most dangerous predicaments of his career.† Botha himself was not to be seen; his foremost troops were supposed to have fallen back into the Pilands Berg. Liebenberg, near Ventersdorp, and De la Rey, known to be hovering between the Harts river and Wolmaranstad, seemed to be cut off alike from De Wet by distance, and from their Chief to the north by Lord Methuen's garrisons at Lichtenburg, Otto's Hoop, Zeerust, by Cunningham's at Rustenburg, by Douglas', Barton's, Hart's and Clements' along the Klerksdorp—Pretoria railway, and by the various columns which certain of these Generals despatched from both flanks to and fro across the Zwart Ruggens between Otto's Hoop and the Magaliesberg mountains. At the end of November, 1900, the western approaches to that range were being patrolled by Broadwood, whose nominal coad-

_{General situation in the West.}

---

* See map No. 59.   † See Volume III., pages 494 and 495.

VOL. IV.   1

jutor, Clements, was tied up in Krugersdorp ; Hart was operating in the Gatsrand. All these were under general command of Lieut.-General French, who had been placed in charge of the entire Johannesburg district,* which extended westward to Klerksdorp and southward to the Vaal river.

Yet though there was no sign of any considerable concentration of hostile forces, there were several troublesome parties in the country beyond the Magaliesberg to the west of Rustenburg. During November they had been kept moving by Broadwood, and he was in constant touch with them as he fell back for orders behind Olifants Nek in the first week in December.

Situation in the Magaliesberg.
On December 1st the reported arrival of De la Rey himself at Vlakhoek in the midst of these bands gave their presence a fresh significance, and Clements was ordered northward from Krugersdorp to join Broadwood in clearing the neighbourhood.† Clements had already arranged to do this some days earlier ; but the constant depletion of his command whilst in Krugersdorp— some of his men and guns being lent to Hart in the Gatsrand, some sent to Potchefstroom, some chained to garrison duty in Krugersdorp during Hart's absence, and at the fortified communication post at Rietfontein, whilst Broadwood himself had possession of half of one of Clements' battalions—all this had so weakened Clements that he considered himself practically immobile, and on November 27th had informed Broadwood that any joint action must be postponed for the present. The Commander-in-Chief's orders of December 1st found him in no better position ; nevertheless, they were peremptory, and on December 3rd Clements marched northward as far as Dwarsvlei with about 1,500 men and ten guns,‡ Broadwood arriving at

* See Volume III., Chapter XXI.

† Telegram No. K. 33, from Lord Kitchener to General Clements, December 1st, 1900.

‡ Composition—Two hundred and forty-two men 2nd M.I., 211 men Kitchener's Horse, 199 men Imperial Yeomanry, P. battery R.H.A. (four guns), 8th battery R.F.A. (four guns), a 4.7-in. gun and a Vickers-Maxim, 38th company R.E. (twenty-four men), 2nd Northumberland Fusiliers (560 men), 2nd King's Own Yorkshire Light Infantry (279 men).

EVENTS IN THE WESTERN TRANSVAAL.

Oorzaak, on the north side of Olifants Nek some thirty miles away, on the same date. On that very day, and almost midway between the two, the enemy struck a blow more unexpected from its direction than its weight, though it was heavy enough.

At Rustenburg, it will be remembered, Cunningham had been stationed since the re-occupation of that town in October. He had some 2,000 officers and men in the place, too few to combine the guardianship of a large depôt with field operations, especially at a post which might have to be evacuated at any time, yet numerous enough to require frequent convoys to keep them supplied. These convoys had been wont to travel along the Rustenburg—Pretoria road. It was so long since the enemy had been seen in this quarter that the track had come to be considered "as safe as Piccadilly."* To and fro throughout November the baggage trains had passed regularly without molestation, with escorts growing gradually weaker and vigilance relaxing; yet the passage was long and difficult, unguarded westward of Commando Nek, and open to sudden forays from either side. Noting these things, and being in need of supplies himself, De la Rey kept watch upon the road from the southern side of the mountains, determined to seize the first opportunity for a coup. In the last week in November a convoy of more than 260 wagons, having discharged its load at Rustenburg, proceeded eastward to refill. The journey was made in peace, and on December 2nd, the road being reported as safe as usual, the wagons once more headed westward for the return march. De la Rey saw his chance. Broadwood was still beyond the western arm of the mountains, kept there by the presence of the aforementioned patrols; Clements lay inactive on garrison duty in Krugersdorp. Stealing into the gap between, De la Rey dashed across the range by Breedts Nek, and on the morning of the 3rd was in hiding with 800 men near Buffelspoort, flanking the track of the advancing convoy. This was marching in two equal divisions, the leading half escorted by twenty men of the

* Description by an officer.

Victorian Mounted Rifles, two companies 2nd West Yorkshire regiment, twenty-one men 1st King's Own Yorkshire Light Infantry, two guns 75th battery R.F.A., the whole under command of Major J. G. Wolrige-Gordon (1st Argyll and Sutherland Highlanders). The rear portion, accompanied by twenty men of the Victorian Mounted Rifles and two companies Argyll and Sutherland Highlanders, was under Captain A. Patten (Argyll and Sutherland Highlanders). The whole train covered some eight miles of road, so that with an escort of the strength and composition detailed it was practically defenceless throughout its length, whether the troops were kept concentrated at one point or distributed in many. At 3 a.m. on December 3rd the convoy left its halting-place of the night before, near Wolhuter's Kop, and proceeded along the lower of the two tracks leading to Rustenburg, the more northerly and safer road having been rendered impracticable by a fortnight's fall of rain. Two hours later the foremost wagons were abreast of Buffelspoort, and here the scouts reported the presence of a hostile party close ahead. This was at once a surprise and a confirmation. The road had indeed been reported clear on all sides by every British authority, but a native headman, coming in to the bivouac at Wolhuter's Kop, had warned Wolrige-Gordon of De la Rey's passage of the Magaliesberg, adding, however, the misleading information that the Boer General had gone away to the northward, and had not returned. Immediately after the first discovery—too quickly to allow of the wagons being parked for defence—a hot fire-attack was delivered from the south of the road; many of the draught oxen were shot, the native drivers and conductors fled, and the head of the convoy fell into instant disorder. In the few moments at his disposal the commander of the escort made prompt preparations for defence. On both sides of the track stood kopjes some 700 yards apart, that to the south of small dimensions, but 500 feet higher than the northern hill, which was longer and divided by a depression. Seizing the former with half a company of the West Yorkshire, Wolrige-Gordon posted half a company of the same battalion on the western end of the northern kopje, and the guns and the

Loss of a convoy, Dec. 3rd, 1900.

EVENTS IN THE WESTERN TRANSVAAL.

handful of the King's Own Yorkshire Light Infantry on the nek to the east, sending back at the same time to warn the second half of the convoy, which was now some six miles in rear. It happened that at this moment the leading half of the convoy was itself divided into two parts by the intervention of a spruit. In front of the second part of the train marched another company of the West Yorkshire, which was immediately pushed forward into the bed of the spruit, whilst the wagons were parked behind it. But the company itself was first in difficulties. Dense bush, which there was no time to clear, blinded the banks of the stream; the enemy, crawling through the thickets, closed around in force, and, firing suddenly from point-blank range, shot down sixteen of the soldiers and made prisoners of the rest when their ammunition was exhausted. Before this Wolrige-Gordon, seeing the predicament of his rearguard, had signalled to Patten to bring up his men to the rescue from the rear division of the convoy. Patten, who had laagered his section of wagons at the first alarm, complied; but on approaching the spruit under heavy fire he became aware that the Boers were turning his own flanks to get at his now unguarded wagons, and he prudently fell back to protect them, leaving the company in the spruit bed to its inevitable fate. Meanwhile the troops at the head of the convoy were being hard pressed. The dispositions, of necessity hurriedly made, were all in favour of the enemy. The higher hill on the south of the road, the key of the other, was held by but thirty-five non-commissioned officers and men; they had no officer with them, and being directly between the main kopje and the enemy, who attacked from the south, had to bear the full brunt with no possibility of support by fire from their comrades behind, whose guns and rifles their position effectually masked. Nor was any assistance, except replenishment of ammunition, sent to them; and at 3.30 p.m., after having lost but four killed and wounded, they surrendered to the enemy. This placed the main defences almost at the mercy of the captured crest. From it the Boers looked down into the hastily built sangars, and, firing fiercely into them, they began an enveloping movement which it was impossible to check. Towards 6 p.m., when the kopje was practically surrounded, the Boers rushed in to carry it, directing their greatest efforts against the artillery, which with its paltry escort and bushy surroundings seemed a certain prey. Then arose a combat which General De la Rey himself, than whom there was not in the whole theatre of war a keener critic of close fighting, watched with admiration. Encircled by the enemy, the rapidly diminishing infantry shot back as fast as their magazines could be emptied and re-charged. The guns—finely commanded by Captain H. J. Farrell, R.A., an intrepid officer, who when many of his men were down armed the rest with rifles taken from the slain and laid the field-pieces himself—were run trail to trail, and with depressed muzzles shattered the front of the charge at only forty yards' distance with case shot and shrapnel fuzed to zero. The infantry around the guns showed equal valour. Of the twenty-one men of the King's Own Yorkshire Light Infantry, who formed the escort, eleven fell; but of the soldiers of this regiment it was to be known that so long as any remained alive guns were safe in their keeping. The survivors rifled the pouches of the dead for cartridges with which to avenge them. But not only here did the troops fight with resolution; over all the kopje the loss of half the defenders found the rest still resisting to the utmost, and when darkness fell the Boers had exhausted their spirit, if not their strength, for they were six to one. About 7.30 p.m. they ceased firing and fell back amongst the wagons on the encumbered road. There their booty was heavy enough to make amends for the failure to conquer the British detachment on the ridges above. One hundred and twenty-six wagons of supplies, much needed, especially by Broadwood, and 1,862 oxen were driven off or destroyed; losses to the number of 118[*] had been inflicted on the escort. Tactically, the results were that the Rustenburg communications were effectually severed, and Cunningham at that place and Broadwood at Olifants Nek were cut off alike from Pretoria and from Clements at Krugersdorp. But De la Rey, knowing how more prompt his

---

[*] Casualties—Killed, eighteen; wounded, forty-six; prisoners, fifty-four.

EVENTS IN THE WESTERN TRANSVAAL.

opponents were to avenge than avoid a disaster, had no intention of being caught with his practically beaten men between converging forces. Already troops were on the march from Rustenburg, more might be coming out of Pretoria, whilst Broadwood, though he had not yet stirred, was certain to be on the scene shortly. Moreover, De la Rey had plans afoot which rendered him particularly anxious not to hazard his force. He therefore drew off, and a relieving detachment from Rustenburg* which at 1 a.m. on December 4th reinforced Wolrige-Gordon on the kopje, had nothing to do but to conduct the surviving troops and wagons to their destination, which was reached on the 7th. Broadwood had come up soon after the Rustenburg troops; but no sooner had he arrived than he received insistent warning from Rustenburg that the Boers were now making for Olifants Nek, with the intention of attacking that key to the western Magaliesberg. Accordingly Broadwood hurried back to Oorzaak, only to be met there on the 6th by a message from Clements, ordering him eastward to begin the pre-arranged co-operation. Clements by this time was upon the Magaliesberg above Scheerpoort, and hearing only on the 5th of the capture of the convoy, he proposed marching westward along the mountain crests towards the scene of the disaster, and to meet Broadwood. Once more Broadwood set out eastward, and on the 7th at Kromrivier, to the south of Buffelspoort, gained touch with Clements, who had advanced along the Berg to Doornhoek, intending to take the joint forces on towards Olifants Nek in search of the destroyers of the convoy. But Clements had now become aware of the real nature of those marauders. Not now had he to deal with the usual gangs of freebooters such as had formerly infested the Magaliesberg; he was in the presence of a strong and aggressive force, led by one of the most able Generals of the federal armies. To search out and attack so formidable an opponent in unfavourable country with his own diminished and

Clements on the Magaliesberg.

---

* Strength—Detachment Victorian Mounted Rifles, two companies West Yorkshire regiment, and two guns, under Lieut.-Col. W. Fry, West Yorkshire regiment. This detachment had left Rustenburg at 3 p.m. on December 3rd.

almost immobile column seemed to him the height of imprudence. In any case he required reprovisioning, and concentrating his troops at Nooitgedacht on December 8th, he sent a convoy to Rietfontein for the rations, and renewed his requests both to French and to Headquarters that the rest of his proper troops might be freed from their garrison duties in Krugersdorp and despatched to reinforce him. French, not knowing where to find other guards for the important centre, refused, and so at first did Headquarters; but in the meantime Hart returned to Krugersdorp from his expedition, and on the 11th and 12th Clements, who was now stationary at Nooitgedacht, was told that his men had been ordered to proceed to him on the 13th. At this moment rumour, the will-of-the-wisp of troops in the field, spirited Broadwood from him just as he had at last got him to his side. First, Broadwood had on December 11th moved across to Elandskraal, consequent on a report that Commando Nek was in danger of a raid from the north. Here he was still in close touch with Clements; but he had halted for only a few hours when another alarm from the exactly opposite direction called him to horse again, Rustenburg once more warning him that Olifants Nek was about to be attacked from the west. Back to the Nek for the third time hurried the cavalry leader, nor could he well refrain, since to keep open the Rustenburg road was the chief of his duties in the Magaliesberg. Yet dire events were to hang largely on his departure, and what can be said of the system which allowed a brigade of cavalry to be thus abstracted from its column and led about a mountain range by the messages of friends and feintings of hostile patrols? At this time, indeed, the whole military machinery in the Magaliesberg was out of gear, largely owing to a somewhat confused delimitation of areas of command. Clements, whilst at Krugersdorp, had been under French; but that General's jurisdiction did not extend to the Magaliesberg, so that Broadwood had been always in a different sphere of command from his colleague, until Clements, having reached Nooitgedacht, became himself beyond the orders of an officer who yet retained command over the considerable portion of his force which remained behind; finally, as has been seen, Clements was unable to keep Broadwood near him for more than a few hours together. Thus doubly weakened, Clements' column lay in the mountains during the second week of December, its continued isolation carefully noted by the scouts of a Boer commander whose manœuvring had done much to produce it. For De la Rey had now, with a skill worthy of all admiration, played the opening moves of a game as well conceived as any which had been undertaken by the federal tacticians, a game, moreover, which was to be for heavy stakes. Ever since the *débâcle* at Komati Poort a cloud had hung over the Boer arms, casting a shadow all the darker because, though the disintegration of Botha's commandos had its origin in the fine encounter at Bergendal, its final stages had lacked the glamour of severe fighting. Exhaustion and bewilderment had done more than combat to scatter the Boer forces, and an army which breaks up thus is harder to mend than one shattered by defeat in a pitched battle. Botha, sheltering unmolested in Pietersburg, had worked hard to piece together his dissevered armament; and so well did he succeed that by the end of November he was ready with a scheme, which if it could not save the campaign, or even set it back greatly in favour of his side, would at least revive in his commandos the spirit of offence which was fast rotting. That it could do more than this the Commandant-General could scarcely hope, for he, almost alone amongst his compatriots, had an eye to measure the disaster which had overtaken his country. His plan was to fall upon the Johannesburg—Krugersdorp line, and to capture if possible one or both of these places, the first the mainspring of his enemy's existence in South Africa, the other the Mecca of his countrymen, where stood the monument sacred to all burghers slain by British and Zulus from 1836 to the triumph at Majuba Mountain forty-five years later. To approach this line was tactically easy by way of the Magaliesberg and the Witwatersrand, but all depended upon the strength of the British forces at those defensible ranges. All depended, too, upon the quality of the leadership, and Botha, looking about for men to conduct the enterprise, found one at his side and

<small>The Boer plans.</small>

another within easy call. At Pietersburg was General Beyers, an officer who had had need of all his great strength of character to overcome the unpopularity caused by his somewhat brusque supercession of the aged and beloved Grobelaar, the former commandant in those parts. The other was General De la Rey, a leader who in his sombre intensity of purpose, his courage, and his high sense of honour, bore witness to the Huguenot blood which preserved in him a personality somewhat foreign and aloof from his compatriots. These two would undertake the operation. At the beginning of December the situation in the Magaliesberg was as favourable as it was ever likely to be. Paget, with his efficient scouting service, had been removed to the eastward too far to be able to keep watch on the road. The garrison at Rustenburg was practically immobile; at Krugersdorp there was no sign of movement, except in the opposite direction. The only free troops in the Magaliesberg were those of Broadwood. Him it was very desirable to lure aside, and, as has been seen, De la Rey found little difficulty in doing so at will by demonstrating at the western arm of the Magaliesberg. So surely as he showed troops there was Broadwood called to the spot, a victim to the tactics which had placed a mountain range in the keeping of a brigade of cavalry. De la Rey had first tested his power in this manner on December 3rd, when, having drawn Broadwood away to Olifants Nek, he had captured the convoy a few miles behind his back at Buffelspoort. He had then retired through Breedts Nek, which was unguarded by British troops, to Boschfontein, to await the coming of Beyers from the north, only falling back a little way to Zeekoehoek when Clements and Broadwood effected their brief and fruitless union at Kromrivier and Doornhoek.

On December 6th Beyers marched from Warm Bath with some 1,600 men of the Krugersdorp, Zoutpansberg and Waterberg commandos. Moving slowly at first—he was only at Hamanskraal on the 11th—a night march of sixty miles carried him with a rush across the Rustenburg road and into touch with De la Rey. Plans were quickly made for an attack on Clements.

Boer combination in the Magaliesberg.

EVENTS IN THE WESTERN TRANSVAAL.

That General had now lain for a week in the same camp at Nooitgedacht below the Magaliesberg; every detail of his position was known, and they all seemed to favour an attack. Broadwood was away to the west; the reinforcements from Krugersdorp had not yet started; nothing was to be feared from Rustenburg, where the small garrison was shut up in strong entrenchments as. became an isolated post with the enemy in strength in the field.

Clements, in truth, had done little to discount the many disadvantages under which he laboured. Of Beyers' approach, indeed, he knew nothing; but he was aware of De la Rey's presence at Zeekoehoek, and recent events were sufficient indication that the Boer was not there for sport. So little did Clements divine the true situation that, weak and isolated as he was, on the very day of Beyers' junction with De la Rey he telegraphed to Headquarters that his presence at Nooitgedacht prevented "any combination of Boers in south joining those in valley north of Magaliesberg."

This, had it been true, were enough and good reason for his long pause at Nooitgedacht; but the General's supposition rested on no foundation. At Nooitgedacht he blocked no passage through the Magaliesberg; the nearest, Breedts Nek, he knew to be at that very moment in the hands of a strong force of the enemy,* apparently ignored by the British, though it had been and was shortly to be again a gateway of the greatest value to De la Rey. At Nooitgedacht, in short, Clements hampered the movements of no one but himself, for he lay under the Magaliesberg where they rose most sheer. His tactical position was as dangerous as his strategical. Where, at Nooitgedacht, a steep ravine indented the Magaliesberg, he had pitched his camp close against the mountain side, holding the crests of the cliffs high overhead with a line of piquets, whose chief duty was to maintain communication with Broadwood. These were found by four companies of the 2nd Northumberland Fusiliers, which were disposed, two on the height east of the ravine, and two on *Clements' position on the Magaliesberg.*

---

* Major-General Clements' report, evening of December 12th.

that to the west, which was more lofty than the other. The left front, where the crest receded and fell abruptly southward, was watched by a post of Legge's mounted infantry, whose camp lay close behind them on the western buttress of the ravine. South of this, on an isolated knoll called Green Hill, were forty men of Kitchener's Horse, their post protecting the camp from the south-west. Some kopjes which rose separately from the flat ground below the range, to the east and south-east of the camp, were held by men of the 2nd King's Own Yorkshire Light Infantry. The defects of such an arrangement from the point of view of defence were many. The piquets on the mountain could neither be reinforced nor withdrawn quickly. So steeply fell the ground behind them that the ravine constituted the only line of approach or retreat, and the use even of this narrow and difficult way depended on the integrity of the heights on both sides. Should either fall, not only would the troops on that opposite be cut off, but the camp itself and the artillery within it would lie at the mercy of plunging rifle fire, from which escape would be difficult, for the only line of retreat ran across the flat and exposed ground skirting the foot of the heights. But there were even more serious internal faults in the position. Solid rock, crowning the mountain top, rendered entrenching impossible; the ground in front of the crest either continued to rise gently or fell in rounded shoulders which hid the neighbouring hollows. The piquets, in short, could neither see nor shoot for any great distance, so that the only lines of observation and resistance were of little avail for either purpose. Finally, the eastern half of the piquets, invisible from the camp below, could only signal to Headquarters through the western section; and both portions, though divided by the nature of the ground, were under a single commander. Against this not very formidable disposition De la Rey and Beyers planned a triple attack, to be carried out by Beyers himself across the mountains against the piqueted British front; by Commandant Badenhorst, from De la Rey's contingent, against the camp itself, from under the foot of the range from the west; by De la Rey's main body from the south-west, whence he would threaten the line of retreat. A reconnaissance on the previous day had pointed to the mountain tops being but weakly held; for the piquets, though they had detected the investigation, had refrained from firing according to rule, though on this occasion, perhaps, a smart fusilade might have inspired a groundless respect for the strength of a front, the position of which was already known to the enemy. At midnight on December 12th Beyers ordered his men to saddle their almost exhausted horses, and led them out towards the northern slopes of the Magaliesberg. His plan of attack was simple and tactically perfect. The British piquets lay in a shallow line, their main body hundreds of feet below the cliff behind; their left flank, the key to the whole, in the air. This flank he intended to roll up with the Waterbergers, whilst the Krugersdorpers engaged the right, and the Zoutpansberg men, advancing up a central depression which led up to the head of the rift between the two portions of the position, would endeavour to cut the hostile line in two. He himself accompanied the Waterbergers, both because their task was the crux of his tactics, and because much depended on making connection with Badenhorst on the lower ground on the same flank. Guides from De la Rey's force, who knew the ground more intimately than the northerners, accompanied each division. Before dawn on the 13th the three commandos began to climb the slopes. The first blow at the British, however, was not to come from them. At 3.40 a.m., Badenhorst, betrayed into too great haste by his easy line of advance below the mountains, fell hotly but single-handed upon the mounted infantry post to the west and south of the piquet line. For a time he carried all before him. The mounted infantry, reinforced by a company which Legge despatched to the front at the first shots, stood firmly with the bayonet against the determined rush of the Pretoria and Krokodil River burghers; but Badenhorst had nearly 400 men, some of the posts were soon annihilated, and through the gaps thus formed the enemy darted in until the whole spur was practically in their hands. Their hold was as brief as the fight for it had been. In a few minutes Legge was upon them with every man from the mounted infantry camp; and though

The Boer plan of attack upon Clements.

The action at Nooitgedacht, Dec. 13th, 1900.

he himself fell in the forefront almost at once, his men, well handled by Colonel G. A. Cookson, and aided by two guns of P. battery R.H.A., under Lieut.-Colonel Sir Godfrey Thomas, and a Vickers-Maxim which was brought across at full speed from the main camp by General Clements in person, fairly wrested the ridge back from the Boers by hard fighting, and re-occupied it themselves, heavy losses occurring on both sides. Badenhorst was flung back westward ; not a shot had supported him from the crest ; he had struck too soon, and his opponent's impression that this had been but an ordinary attack on outposts seemed to be confirmed. Badenhorst, however, had been premature by so few moments that his discomfiture points again the old moral how with the utmost care and calculation perfect co-operation by separated units in a night attack is practically impossible except by chance. Scarcely had the echo of his rifles died away when distant shots were heard coming from the extreme left of the line of infantry piquets on the summit of the Magaliesberg. There the four companies of the 2nd Northumberland Fusiliers, under Captain C. Yatman, were not only fully prepared for but expectant of an attack. Whilst standing to arms before dawn they had heard the firing during Badenhorst's abortive attempt ; the Boer reconnaissance of the day before, the movement of lights all night about their front, had given certain warning that a hostile body was near, and every man was vigilant. The many precautions taken did not, unfortunately, include either a demand for reinforcements or the supply of a reserve of cartridges, of which there was only the normal field supply in the pouch of each soldier. An attempt to communicate with Broadwood, a matter of vital importance, was foiled by the haziness of the dawn. There was to be little opportunity to repeat it. At 4.25 a.m., quiet being restored in the camps below, the officer in command was about to dismiss his spare men from parade, when the enemy suddenly appeared in front of the extreme left of the piquet line, and advancing swiftly, speedily enveloped it, shooting rapidly the while. The troops fought well, but they were outnumbered and outflanked from the first. Group by group from the left

EVENTS IN THE WESTERN TRANSVAAL.   15

they were overwhelmed, the Boers steadily gaining both ground and prisoners as they worked eastward along the ridge towards the head of the rift behind the centre of the line of piquets. For half an hour or more there was severe fighting along this, the left, section of the Northumberland Fusiliers; but during all that time Yatman, though the rapidly swelling firing was plainly audible to him, knew nothing of the fate befalling the key of the position, for being on the eastern and lower half of the ridge, much of the ground to his left was invisible. At the first outbreak of shooting his own attention had been attracted by a strong body of the enemy who came in sight for a moment upon a patch of green grass some 1,700 yards to his front. These were fired on by his men so long as they were visible; but, riding forward, they were soon lost to view in the dead ground nearer the position, and for a time the two eastern companies had nothing to do but listen to the unaccountable uproar drawing momentarily nearer to their left flank. Whilst they stood, the Boers on their own front were making rapid and silent headway. They too heard with anxiety the heavy firing to the west, for all depended on success in that quarter. As, still unseen, they approached the crest they were given cheering evidence that matters had gone well on the right. Away from the back of the Waterbergers' position marched a band of a hundred British prisoners. A few moments later, about 6 a.m., Yatman's two companies found themselves under a warm fire from front and right and left fronts, and worse, soon from left and left rear, for the Waterbergers, having swept away the British left, had worked eastward along the ridge as far as the dividing rift, from the edge of which they commanded the remaining defenders in flank and reverse. Yatman's position was doubly lost; for even without this turning of his flank, the frontal attack which he had now to meet was many times heavier than his men could bear. The Boers, safe in their superior numbers, disdained all cover and advanced like veteran infantry, adopting as their formation that enclosing horn which at the price of many a devastated laager they had learned from the Zulu impis. The Northumberland Fusiliers faced in all directions and strove desperately to keep off the swarm of riflemen; but they had no cover from such a ring of bullets, and soon were without bullets themselves, for their furious firing all but emptied their pouches. At 6.45 a.m. came the inevitable end; when only some score out of the original 150 soldiers remained effective, the officer in command ordered the white flag to be hoisted to save the lives of the rest. About that time Clements returned to camp, from which he had been absent since Badenhorst's attack on the western piquets. He had heard the shooting on the Magaliesberg, and riding towards the front to investigate the cause, had himself come under fire; but it was not until, puzzled, he sought information in camp that he learned that the summit was in the hands of the Boers. Lieut.-Colonel the Hon. C. Lambton, the commanding officer of the Northumberland Fusiliers, who had been left in charge of camp, had earlier inkling of the situation. Reinforcements and ammunition mules which he had sent to close the lower end of the ravine had instead gone to the top; but had been unable to reach the piquets. The Fife and Devon Yeomanry lost half their numbers as they attempted to emerge from the head of the kloof, whilst a half company of the King's Own Yorkshire Light Infantry, who climbed the precipice by a goat track in single file, were shot down man by man until their officer withdrew the survivors. Then a last signal message had come down from the mountain to the effect that the enemy was within 300 yards of the piquets, which were cut off. In a few moments the worst fears were confirmed by a warm plunging fire from the crest beginning to beat at medium range upon the defenceless camp. Now in one instant every vice of his position came home to Clements. With the loss of his piquets his lines of observation and resistance had disappeared together. He had lost all chance of communicating with Broadwood; he had lost one half of his force, and it seemed as though nothing could save the other half from as summary a fate, so totally exposed was it to an unanswerable fire from high overhead. But Clements' skill was only awakened by a situation which would have confused or appalled a weaker soldier. The camp, which was becoming mixed under the searching fire, was quickly brought to order by his cool and rapid commands. Leaving the guns to bombard the crest of the Magaliesberg, he ordered the transport, hospitals, etc., to make for a hill, called Yeomanry Hill, to the south-east, where he intended to gather his troops and make a stand. The artillery in the main camp at this moment consisted of the 8th battery R.F.A. (four guns), under Major H. Chance, and a 4.7-in. gun Eastern Division R.G.A., under Major N. B. Inglefield. The four guns of the R.H.A. were with the mounted infantry on the other side of the ravine, two being in the camp there, and two in the piquet line, where they had gone to assist in the repulse of Badenhorst. All were completely exposed, and the gunners and teams suffered heavily; but, covered by a united fire, Clements gradually evacuated his camps in spite of inconceivable difficulties caused by the destruction and terror amongst his draught animals and the flight of most of the native drivers. Nearly two hours elapsed before the wagons could be got to move, and during that time nothing but the admirable practice of the guns kept the enemy from pouring down the mountain side. The danger of the situation reached its climax when it became the turn of the artillery to retire. Referring first to P. battery R.H.A., on the west side of the ravine, Lieut.-Colonel Sir G. Thomas, seeing the stir of retreat in the main camp, and finding that the enemy was gradually closing upon his two guns in the piquet line, sent them back by a circuitous track which he had fortunately discovered and investigated during the week's halt at Nooitgedacht. This track was somewhat protected; for on the knoll which marked the south-western extremity of the destroyed piquet line, Kitchener's Horse were still holding on, though the advance of De la Rey from the south-west was threatening to make their position untenable. Both guns, after coming into action again on an intermediate position, retired in safety on the main body. After their departure Sir G. Thomas hurried back to the other two guns in the mounted infantry camp close behind. He found the officer whom he had left in charge wounded; one gun was being vigorously fought by a sergeant, the other stood silent and deserted, all its gunners out of action, its last round expended. The teams of neither piece were to be seen, for they were sheltering in two separated kraals in rear; but when found they were brought up into a clump of scrub as near to the guns as the hot fire permitted. Then, by dint of crawling on the ground, Sir G. Thomas and a few volunteers contrived to make fast the ends of eighty-foot ropes to the trails, the pieces were hauled into the bush, and were driven off under the very eyes of the enemy. A little later the whole battery came into action again from near Yeomanry Hill. At the main camp, the 8th battery R.F.A., which had been firing heavily from a knoll close behind the tents of Clements' Headquarters, fell back with little difficulty by the direct route to Yeomanry Hill. There remained only the 4.7-in., and the fate of this ponderous cannon seemed certain. It stood on rising ground towards the north of the camp, in an emplacement which had at first been surrounded by scrub and brushwood. To gain a field of fire this, however, had been cleared away on all sides except the northerly, where it still grew so high and dense as to screen the weapon from view of the crest of the Magaliesberg. To this fortunate circumstance, which emphasised once more how little the mountains had been considered the true front of the position, the 4.7-in. owed its rescue. The Boers were beginning to come down from the hills, from which a fierce fire continued; the troops had departed, and but for his detachment and escort Inglefield was almost alone. His team of bullocks, which he had inspanned at the first alarm, had stampeded, and their drivers were not to be seen. To extricate so large and heavy a target seemed a forlorn hope; but after half an hour's search Inglefield collected nine bullocks, seven less than the proper team. To drive these up to the emplacement was impossible, so hot was the fire. The gun had to be dragged to them, and after one failure the five tons of metal began to move over the rough ground. The stirring of the weapon from the bushes betrayed to the Boers how great a prize was slipping from their grasp. Every rifle was levelled at the spot, and two of the detachment were wounded. But the gun, now travelling fast downhill, rolled on beyond reach; more

EVENTS IN THE WESTERN TRANSVAAL. 19

bullocks were found and yoked in, and soon Inglefield, from Yeomanry Hill, was bursting shell over the very spot whence he had so narrowly escaped, for he had barely got clear when the whole camp was in the hands of the Boers.

Scarcely had Clements concentrated the remnants of his force, some 350 rifles in all, upon Yeomanry Hill, when fresh misfortune befell him. De la Rey's advance from the southwest had been unexpectedly tardy, largely owing to the firm stand of Kitchener's Horse on Green Hill; but now he too began to draw near, and opening fire with his artillery, made as if to surround Yeomanry Hill. His two guns were quickly silenced; but not before they had almost completed the ruin of the column, for the shells, falling amongst the already terrified transport animals, sent the whole baggage-train careering in panic towards Rietfontein to the south. Bands of Boers had already been seen in that direction, others were coming in from east and west; the wagons were rushing straight into the arms of the enemy. Clements had always been famous as a horseman; his skill in the saddle was now to stand him and his troops in good stead. Galloping with a few others at full speed after the receding mob, he succeeded in heading and turning them back, a feat the difficulty of which only veteran stockriders can appreciate. So narrow was the margin of safety that his own aide-de-camp, who accompanied him, rode into the enemy in the course of the chase, and was taken prisoner. This disaster averted, Clements had now to face the multitude of dangers by which he was confronted, nay surrounded, for by this time the Boers were on all sides of Yeomanry Hill. Shortly before the stampede of the transport he had received a message from the Intelligence Department warning him of Beyers' march from Warm Bath with 2,000 men. The information, coming circuitously from Rustenburg through Paget far to the east, was late indeed; half his infantry were already prisoners to that very Boer leader; but it was not without value, for it confirmed Clements in the knowledge of the great superiority of the forces which had fallen upon him. He had previously determined to entrench and fight to the last at Yeomanry Hill;

but having lost nearly 640 men,* the warning of the numbers surrounding him rendered this too desperate a resource, and he now watched narrowly for a chance of withdrawing. For a brief moment such a chance was given. Wearied by their night's marching and the long fighting of the morning, which had cost them about one hundred men, the Boers paused in their advance. To the indignation of their officers, they lingered in the deserted British camps, looting freely, and little encouraged to advance by the shells from the batteries on Yeomanry Hill. Their bands on flank and rear were not yet formidable. Clements saw his opportunity and that it must be seized instantly or not at all. At 2.30 p.m. he gave the order to retire, and setting out three quarters of an hour later, the column marched almost unmolested, and with fine discipline, through the night, arriving at Rietfontein at 4.30 a.m. on December 14th. Clements' action at Nooitgedacht will long be remembered, but rather for his triumph over almost incalculable misfortunes than for the errors which led to them. The disaster, indeed, ought never to have been incurred; but having occurred, it should by the laws of tactics and topography have been final, so deeply had the troops been compromised. That it was not fatal was due to the presence of a commander able to collect a broken force and lead it out from the very midst of ten times its numbers.†

At Rietfontein Clements found reinforcements enough. During December 14th his own men, released at last from Krugersdorp, marched in, nearly a thousand strong, comprising

Clements retreats.

* SUMMARY OF CASUALTIES, DECEMBER 13TH, 1900.

Ranks.	Killed.	Wounded.	Prisoners and Missing.	Total.	Remarks.
Officers	9	*7	13	29	*1 died of wounds.
Other ranks	65	†179	355	609	†13 died of wounds.
TOTALS	74	186	368	638	

† For gallantry at this action Sergeant D. Farmer, 1st battalion Cameron Highlanders, was awarded the Victoria Cross.

EVENTS IN THE WESTERN TRANSVAAL.

the 1st Border regiment, 200 mounted infantry, and two guns of the 8th battery R.F.A. Here, too, he was joined by Brigadier-General E. A. H. Alderson with 800 mounted men and J. battery R.H.A. Nevertheless a critical moment had arrived, not so much for Clements as for the whole balance of the campaign in this area. The Magaliesberg were now in the hands of the enemy, for Broadwood and Rustenburg were for the moment negligible quantities, and even in extreme danger. And these mountains were the key to the Western Transvaal, indeed to the whole theatre of war, so closely did they command the most vital parts of the country. The briefest pause might confirm the Boers in possession of the range, and Lord Kitchener saw that no time was to be lost in wresting it back. Appointing French to command the whole zone, he directed him to use all the troops for the clearance of the district, at the same time bringing a brigade of cavalry across from Heidelberg to the Krugersdorp line, and summoning Paget westward towards Hamanskraal. Within three days of the repulse at Nooitgedacht the columns took the offensive to regain the lost advantage. <small>Results of the action at Nooitgedacht.</small>

December 16th, Dingaan's Day,* found French busily gathering troops into the town in which the Boers had vowed to celebrate the festival. But the place was in little danger; once more the enemy showed his incapacity to follow up a stroke or maintain a brisk offensive. The collaboration of Beyers and De la Rey failed just when it might have been fruitful, and Nooitgedacht, the first of their united efforts, was also their last. French at Krugersdorp and Clements at Rietfontein concentrated their units with little hindrance, and on the 19th joined forces at Thorndale in the Hekpoort valley. The enemy was there in strength; but Nooitgedacht seemed to have exhausted his courage as well as his energy; a very brief encounter sufficed to send 2,000 Boers " in a panic-stricken rout "† northward, through Breedts Nek, losing some fifty as

---

* An annual festival of the Boer States, commemorative of the defeat of the Zulus under Dingaan by Pretorius on Sunday, December 16th, 1838.

† Lieut.-General French's telegram, December 20th, 1900.

they ran. These were De la Rey's men, and leaving Clements to deal with them, French sent Gordon westward down the Hekpoort valley, driving Beyers before him towards Broadwood, who had been summoned southward to co-operate. Having thus effectually cut up the Boer combination, French returned to Krugersdorp, and thence to Johannesburg, where he organised a force for the complete clearance of the disturbed sub-district. The immediate danger to be met was a descent upon Potchefstroom by Beyers, who appeared to be circling southward on finding himself pursued by Gordon and headed by Broadwood. To keep him off the Potchefstroom—Johannesburg railway French decided to establish a centre at Ventersdorp, which was easily occupied on December 28th.

By the last day of December French had drawn a line of columns from Olifants Nek through Ventersdorp to Klerksdorp, thus denying to the enemy all the vital tract to the eastward, whilst Clements and Alderson in the Magaliesberg acted as a similar guard against incursion from the north. Thus, the stir in this region abated, the year closed less anxiously than had seemed probable, for undoubtedly the Boer arms had for a few hours pointed near to the heart of the British occupation of the country.

French clears up the situation.

APPROXIMATE STRENGTH STATES OF COLUMNS REFERRED TO IN FOREGOING CHAPTER.

COLUMN.	Mounted Troops.	Infantry.	Guns, including Vickers-Maxims.	Machine Guns.
December, 1900.				
Maj.-Gen. R. A. P. Clements	652	863	10	2
Brig.-Gen. R. G. Broadwood	444	344	7	2
Brig.-Gen. E. A. H. Alderson	800	—	4	—

CHAPTER II.

EVENTS IN THE EASTERN TRANSVAAL.*

DECEMBER 1ST, 1900—JANUARY 30TH, 1901.

FOLLOWING on Paget's engagement at Rhenoster Kop,† the month of December witnessed much, if somewhat unproductive activity along the eastern line. On the 1st Payne's, and on the 3rd Carleton's and Macbean's columns returned to their bases at Middelburg and Belfast, having neither inflicted nor suffered any but trifling losses. The outgoings included an expedition by Barker from Balmoral on the 3rd, and another under W. P. Campbell (1st K. R. Rifles) on the 7th, the latter being designed generally for co-operation with Paget, and specifically to close the Waterval Drift (Wilge river) to any Boers who might fall southward away from Paget's force. A week had, however, elapsed since Viljoen's retirement, and in any case that leader's command had withdrawn in good order, not south, but north to the Botha's Berg. Campbell, therefore, met but few opponents; and after communicating with Paget on the 10th—only then to be apprised of the direction of the enemy's retreat—he returned to Middelburg on the 12th, Paget remaining entrenched about Rhenoster Kop. Troops, indeed, could ill be spared from a line of communication, which, even in their presence, appeared almost at the mercy of the enemy. On the 5th, 6th, 8th,‡ 20th, 24th and 26th,§ attacks were made

Situation on the Delagoa Bay railway.

---

* See map No. 56.

† See Volume III., page 450.

‡ Casualties—Two men killed and five wounded, one officer and thirteen men taken prisoners. Near Barberton.

§ British casualties—One man killed, one officer and four men wounded. Boer casualties—One killed, seven wounded. At Pan.

on trains, rail or fortified posts, causing occasional loss of each. The series culminated on the 29th in a memorable onslaught.

Towards the end of December, General B. Viljoen removed his laager from the Botha's Berg to Windhoek in the Stenkamps Berg. Since leaving Rhenoster Kop his command had been nearly doubled by the addition of the Lydenburg and Middelburg commandos; and Viljoen, eager to use his strength, ooked for the weakest link in the chains of British posts which traversed the district. Nor was his choice easy: there were many posts; none escaped the scrutiny of his scouts, and few were numerically formidable, though all were sufficiently entrenched to demand an assault to bring them down. But in Viljoen the too elastic tactics of his countrymen were braced by a soldierly confidence in the timely use of weight of men as well as of lead; and of all the federal leaders none would have made better use than he of the steel which was missing from the equipment of his burghers. And so much more powerful is leadership than training with natural soldiers like the burghers, that, as will more than once be seen, the very presence of such a man at the head of commandos sufficed to convert them from evasive guerillas into daring and determined regiments, not afraid of close combat, though without the only proper weapon for such work. Viljoen's men, too, were in high feather from other causes. The affair at Rhenoster Kop, whether victory or rebuff, mattered little compared with cheering events outside, which, now some months old, must have worked far in their favour. In November Viljoen had received information, the egregious source of which, as is usual with good news in the field, was disregarded in the delight of the message. At a conference held at Paris, so ran the telegram, England had begged in vain of the Powers six months in which to attempt to finish the war. The German Consul at Pretoria had received instructions from Berlin to remain accredited, not to the British, but the Republican Government. As for France, she was ready to land troops in England at any moment. The Czar of Russia had received the Boer delegates at St. Petersburg as representatives of a friendly State. The Belgian monarchy was pre-

EVENTS IN THE EASTERN TRANSVAAL. 25

paring to do the same. In America the hoped-for election of Mr. Bryan to the Presidency was assured. Internally the cause of Britain was in even greater straits. Australia, India, Canada and Cape Colony were clamouring for the return of their contingents. Two thousand five hundred loyalist troops in Cape Colony had already broken with the army, had been disbanded and their arms burnt.* Such documents, the *excreta* of warfare, would not be worth recording, were they not in this case actual weapons of war in the hands of the leaders of an immured and gullible people. In the field all armies credit fair prophecies as blindly as men in the desert press on for cascades suspended in the far-off air. None were even more prone to feed on myths, or were more lavishly fed, than the Boers; and it is as difficult to measure the stimulant thus derived as to determine its morality. With his burghers in this spirit Viljoen cast about to do damage, and he soon selected Helvetia for his first blow.

This post—originally dropped, it will be remembered, by Sir R. Buller in September, as the first link of his communications with Lydenburg—was held by a mixed force of 344 officers and men with a 4.7-in. gun, under Major S. L. Cotton (King's Liverpool regiment). It consisted of four separate kopjes aligned east and west, of which the outside two, called respectively King's Kopje and Gun Hill, were somewhat distant from those in the centre, *i.e.*, South Hill and Middle Hill. All were defended by closed works and by barbed wire entanglements. In front (north) of the centre kopjes a camp was pitched for the troops of the detachment not on outpost duty. The nearest adjacent posts were at Zwartkoppies, some three miles to the north-east, at Machadodorp, the same distance to the south, and at Waterval Boven, four miles to the south-east. Well situated and defended, and adequately garrisoned, the place seemed strong enough for all contingencies; appearing especially inaccessible to the enemy on its eastern and southern sides, since these were practically surrounded by neighbouring

* Telegram from Superintendent of Telegraphs, Ermelo, to General Viljoen, November 2nd, 1900, embodying the report of a German doctor recently released from the British lines.

garrisons. The configuration and garrison of the post were well known to Viljoen, and since it was probably most alert towards the north and west he decided to assail it from the south and east.

Leaving Windhoek on the night of December 28th with some 580 men, he marched through Dullstroom and across the Crocodile, upon the left bank of which he paused to arrange the attack. Against a place so ringed in by friendly camps as Helvetia, Viljoen had to provide as much for the safety of his command as its success. But the very audacity of his plan of attack relieved him of the necessity of detaching largely in order to fend off reinforcements from adjacent garrisons. Insinuating his whole force between Helvetia and its neighbours, he ordered two field-cornetcies (120 men) to attack Zwartkoppies simultaneously with his own descent on Helvetia, whilst the main body (350 men), encircling the eastern extremity of the line of kopjes, would both deliver the assault and keep off any assistance coming from Waterval Boven. A third body of about 100 men, chiefly composed of State artillerists, serving as mounted riflemen since the loss of their guns, would act at once as a reserve and as scouts towards Machadodorp and Belfast. Viljoen fixed 3.30 a.m., December 29th, as the hour of attack.

<small>The attack on Helvetia, Dec. 29th, 1900.</small>

A thick fog descending about 2 a.m. aided the main body to take up its positions undetected, but the eastern detachment lost its way, and failed to find Zwartkoppies. Nevertheless, at the appointed time, Viljoen, who had been apprised of this mischance, gave the word, and his men, discharging a burst of musketry, ran in upon the kopjes. Gun Hill, the nearest, fell at once; and with it the 4.7-in. gun upon it and its twenty-one attendant artillerymen passed into the hands of the enemy. This, the first blow, was tactically and morally the worst for the defence; for Gun Hill commanded the other knolls, whilst the officer in command of Middle and South Hills, deprived of judgment by a severe wound in the head, thought nothing worth saving when the gun was lost, and ordered a surrender. Thus, only the isolated King's Kopje remained, and there the defenders, a half company (sixty-five men) of the Liverpool regiment,

EVENTS IN THE EASTERN TRANSVAAL. 27

under Lieutenant F. A. Wilkinson, knowing nothing of the capture of the cannon, resisted so stoutly that no effort of the enemy could reduce them. The value of this handful's tenacity appeared when at daybreak the Boers proceeded to remove their trophy and the prisoners, who numbered 235, from Gun Hill. This they began to do by way of the track running westward close below Helvetia Kopjes, and away from Zwartkoppies, which was now thoroughly alert and had brought two guns into action. But the undiminished shooting of Wilkinson's detachment effectually denied the route, and the captors of the gun, compelled to make a détour to the northward, came under the shrapnel from Zwartkoppies, which not only did execution, but forced them to abandon the only wagon-load of 4.7 projectiles, and another containing the rifles of the prisoners of war.* Viljoen then made off with his cortège towards Dullstroom, soon releasing the prisoners, but retaining the gun, which was now nothing but an unwieldy trophy, for the loss of its store of ammunition had rendered it useless.

The news of the surrender of Helvetia sent a thrill through the British army such as had not stirred it since the sombre affair at Nicholson's Nek; but its effect proved actually detrimental to the enemy. There is no better touchstone of the quality of troops who have been long in the field than their attitude after disaster, an indication by no means trustworthy with fresh and inexperienced soldiers. Over the theatre of war were scattered a multitude of posts similar to Helvetia, and liable momentarily to a like trial; and in them there served no officer or soldier who did not look again to his defences, his vigilance, and his resolution, and promise himself that such a test would not find him so easy a victim.

If on the other line of communication in the Eastern Transvaal—*i.e.*, the railway from Johannesburg through Standerton into Natal—no event had transpired of such importance as that at Helvetia, the troops thereon were incessantly employed

---

* Casualties—Killed, eleven men; wounded, one officer and twenty-eight men; prisoners, four officers and 231 men.

throughout December, and any departure from the fortified line entailed fighting or skirmishing with hostile bands. But though from Heidelberg down to Zandspruit there was scarcely a patrol or an outpost which did not exchange shots with the enemy, the absence of any notable Boer leader in these parts enabled much to be done in the way of clearance of crops and supplies from the country-sides adjacent to the railway. Especially was this the case in the northern district, where the Boers, though bolder and more numerous than in the south, were kept on the move by the constant peregrinations of Lieut.-Colonel A. E. W. Colville's mobile column of about 1,400 men of all arms, with eight guns, which was usually based on Greylingstad. Trains, the easiest prey of guerillas, were more than once intercepted, resulting on one occasion (December 9th, at Vlaklaagte) in the loss of 124 horses; but not until the end of the month did the Boers seriously take the initiative. On December 24th a foraging party from Eden's Kop, near Heidelberg, was roughly handled by a band of 100 with a Vickers-Maxim, losing sixteen out of the 150 men of the 2nd Devonshire regiment who were engaged. Two days later Colville's column was itself heavily attacked twelve miles to the west of Greylingstad. Colville's constant depredations amongst the farm-borne stock and supplies, upon which the enemy depended for subsistence, had greatly exasperated the local commandos under Buys and Trichard. The clearance of Rietvlei, south of Vlakfontein, on December 24th, had already been more strongly opposed than usual*, and when, two days later, Colville, turning southward, undertook Roodewal, the Boers were ready with a trap, which they all but closed upon the column. Having cleared one farm, not without considerable opposition, Colville moved forward to another, leaving the baggage, guarded by 150 men of the Rifle Brigade under Captain C. E. Radclyffe, with a Vickers-Maxim, some distance in rear. As the column advanced, continually engaged in front, it was reported to Colville that a body of the enemy had worked around his flanks and was closing

Events on the Johannesburg-Natal railway.

---

* Casualties—Killed, one man; wounded, two men.

EVENTS IN THE EASTERN TRANSVAAL.

in upon the baggage. He therefore ordered a retirement, which was begun at about 1.15 p.m., the Boers following too closely for much speed to be made. Before the column could come within reach, the blow which it was hurrying to avert, fell. Surrounding the transport, the enemy opened a furious fire upon the parked wagons, and were with difficulty kept off by the escort, until Radclyffe, having got the oxen inspanned, moved the train off towards the approaching column. The Boers pressed hard, the Vickers-Maxim narrowly escaped capture, and Radclyffe, as the only means of saving his charge, delivered a dashing and successful counter-attack, with very inferior numbers, which gained him a covering position 800 yards in front of the wagons. Here he was reinforced by artillery and by a company of infantry which Colville had sent in mule-wagons from his own force. The baggage was thus enabled to draw off in safety, but at a cost to the rearguard of fifty-seven casualties, including Radclyffe himself, wounded. The majority of the losses arose from the annihilation of a detached half company, which was surrounded and decimated, and forced to capitulate after firing the last cartridge. Altogether, the day's losses amounted to eighty-one*, out of a total of ninety sustained by the column during the whole month of December.

Meanwhile the troops of the Natal command had been kept uneasy by sporadic fighting, not, indeed, within the colony itself but in the south-east angle of the Transvaal, which marched with the frontier. Persistent rumours of a hostile concentration on a large scale for the invasion of Natal were afoot, and seemed to be warranted by the numbers and aggressions of the enemy, who appeared to be aiming at bases for an important movement in these parts. Thus, Wakkerstroom, Utrecht and Vryheid were centres around which revolved continually bands which were evidently anxious to test the strength of the defences. A half-hearted and easily repelled inquiry at the Vryheid outposts on December 1st was followed by a sharp skirmish outside

_{Signs and rumours of an invasion of Natal.}

---

* Casualties—Killed, eleven men; wounded, three officers, forty-seven men; prisoners, twenty men.

30   THE WAR IN SOUTH AFRICA.

Attack on Vryheid, Dec. 10th—11th, 1900.

Utrecht on the next day,* and that by a brief but warm bombardment of the Wakkerstroom lines on the 6th, when in one hour two Boer guns sent a hundred shells against the entrenchments. Then on the 11th Vryheid, despite these warnings, was surprised by night and all but lost. The defences there were as singular from their strength as their configuration. North of the village rose a high, steep hill, named Lancaster Hill, upon the flat top of which was pitched the camp of the half battalion 2nd Royal Lancaster regiment who defended it. The rim of the summit, which was roughly square, was armed at the four corners with natural bastions formed by projections of the almost precipitous faces, and upon the north-westerly and south-easterly of these, 12-pr. guns were strongly emplaced, the infantry lining the others and the "curtains" between. Five hundred feet below the sheer western side of Lancaster Hill an oval flat, called Mounted Infantry Plateau, projected like the low forecastle of a turret ship, and on this were the camp and outposts of a company of the 5th division mounted infantry, from which one small advanced post, under an officer, was thrown out upon the Utrecht road, 2,200 yards to the north of the mounted infantry encampment, and another midway between this and the north gun on Lancaster Hill. Sentries were numerous and well posted, their supports strongly entrenched. The distance of the mounted infantry camp from the infantry supports, the isolation of the weak posts at night, the presence of tents so close to the piquets, and the fact that both the officers and visiting non-commissioned officers slept in them, the exposed position of the horse lines, were nevertheless defects which were soon to be all discovered in turn.

At 2 a.m. on the morning of December 11th, the Boers gathered around Vryheid in numbers over a thousand strong. The detached post to the northward fell into their hands at once, not a warning sound reaching the camp behind. They then moved on against the plateau, rushed the line of sentries from

---

* British casualties—Killed, two men; wounded, one officer and four men; missing, three men. Boer casualties—Killed, six men; wounded, ten men; prisoner, one man.

EVENTS IN THE EASTERN TRANSVAAL. 31

end to end, and breaking into the lines, stampeded all the horses, and used the very rows of saddles on the ground as cover from which to pour a fire which threw the whole mounted infantry camp into confusion. The troops made every effort to recover possession. Time after time knots of men, hastily rallied by the officers, charged, and engaging the enemy hand to hand with bayonets and clubbed rifles, drove them out temporarily. But the attackers were in overpowering strength, and the mounted infantrymen had either to fall back or to be demolished. The Boers then closed around Lancaster Hill, collecting thickest below the gun emplacements on its opposite sides. There the garrison was ready, and denied any further advance with a girdle of musketry. An attempt to rush the northern gun at 3.30 a.m. was trapped within fifty yards of the crest by a barbed wire entanglement; the southern gun, its muzzle depressed to the utmost, defended itself by sweeping the steep hillside. At 4 a.m. Lieut.-Colonel J. M. Gawne (2nd Royal Lancaster regiment), the officer in command and District Commissioner at Vryheid, led a half company up from the village, where he was in residence, towards the scene of the fighting. High up the track he came upon a knot of mounted infantry, whom two young officers had collected and posted to keep the enemy from descending into Vryheid. The reinforcement, hotly assailed at close range, could get no further, Gawne himself being mortally wounded as he attempted to climb higher; but its presence here still further safeguarded the town. Thus the attack was everywhere held in check, and the Boers, relinquishing all further attempts at assault, settled down under cover to an aimed musketry, which lasted without intermission throughout the day. At 7.30 p.m., when Lancaster Hill had shown itself the master, and retirement was covered by dusk, they made off. The day's fighting had cost the garrison fifty-eight officers and men, and nearly all the horses.

Lieut.-General H. J. T. Hildyard lost no time in despatching troops to the eastward, Colonel C. J. Blomfield (commanding at Dundee) taking a column of all arms across De Jager's Drift on the 12th, in co-operation with a mounted force under Lieut.-

Colonel H. De la P. Gough, which hurried out from Nqutu. Though the actual attackers of Vryheid had vanished northward, Blomfield and Gough on the 14th encountered on the Schurwe Berg, to the west of that place, a strong body which they all but succeeded in catching between them, the enemy losing heavily as he galloped for safety under a searching shrapnel from the 69th battery R.F.A.* On the same day, a small column, under Major-General J. Talbot Coke, marched to Wakkerstroom. On the 16th Blomfield, warned at Vryheid that Utrecht was threatened, reconnoitred vigorously in that direction, driving the enemy over the Kambula Mountain with no loss to himself, and securing stock which brought his total captures during the two days' fighting up to nearly 10,000 head. Thereafter, nothing noteworthy occurred until December 26th, when reiterated reports of an attempt to be made on Utrecht were justified to the full.

Never in the whole course of the campaign had a British force been fore-armed with more ample information of an impending attack. There was not only a fantastic epistle from a Russian officer, who on the 24th wrote demanding supplies from the District Commissioner under menace of a descent which was actually to be made at the time threatened, but the Boers themselves seemed to have thrown to the winds their accustomed secrecy, for there were reports of speeches by their leaders promising them Utrecht in compensation for Vryheid. There was so much prophecy, indeed, that it rendered the possibility of an actual attack almost incredible in a campaign where it had become an axiom that the expected did not happen. Nevertheless, it was duly delivered, and the commander at Utrecht, profiting by his unusual good fortune, had made all ready to receive it. The force available consisted of six companies of infantry drawn from the 1st and 2nd York and Lancaster, the 2nd Royal Lancaster, and 2nd Middlesex regiments, of which two companies lay in the town, one on a hill to the east, and three, with a 12-pr. gun, two Maxims, and sixty

Attack on Utrecht, Dec. 25th—26th, 1900.

---

* Casualties—Two killed, four missing.

mounted infantrymen, on another hill to the northward, the whole under command of Major A. J. Chapman (Royal Dublin Fusiliers). To deceive the many eyes which he knew were directed on his defences, that officer practised an artifice which can never fail to mystify the most wary of adversaries. Posting his men towards evening, but in full light, as if in their defences for the night, he would transfer them as soon as it was dark to completely different positions, so that hostile scouts and spies were alike baffled to report their true situations. Remembering Vryheid, Chapman furthermore emptied his tents and manned his trenches by night, giving the troops rest in the daytime; he also removed his horses from their lines into a sheltered donga.

Against this well-prepared post the Boers advanced on Christmas night, and at 2 a.m. attacked it on every side. On the side of the town a band, shouting a battle cry of " Utrecht! Utrecht!" poured a violent fusilade against the untenanted camp and its entrenchments. Encouraged by the silence, they then rushed through both, only to be disconcerted first by the deserted state of the defences, and next by an unmistakable summons to halt from the rifles of the inner line. Here, then, a heavy interchange of lead began to stream from and to the town, the inhabitants of which, by a pre-arranged plan, had at once sought safety in the church. Meanwhile, a determined onslaught was being made upon the hill to the west. This was a kopje so broken and precipitous that it could be defended only in parts where there was room for half a dozen men to entrench, and the hill was dotted with such posts. The foremost, which lay under a low cliff, was surrounded and captured early, the Boers, who had wrapped sheepskins round their feet to deaden the sound, climbing to the verge of the overhanging cliff, whence they shot straight down upon the soldiers. But the other posts, warned by the firing, were not to be caught; and though the enemy approached within fifteen yards of the rifles—in one case cutting through a barbed-wire entanglement in their ardour to close—and though, when repulsed, they more than once came on again, the knots of British, standing firm and shooting steadily, lost not another foot of ground, and heavily punished their assailants. Before daybreak the Boers were in retreat on every side, carrying with them many dead and wounded, amongst them the before-mentioned Russian, mortally struck as he headed an attack on one of the groups of infantry. The British losses numbered but seven, of whom four were prisoners; few, indeed, and little indicative of the closeness of the fighting until it is remembered how little dangerous is a night attack when the advantage of surprise has been lost, and there is no steel to make it good. An attack on the hill to the north at the same time as that on the east hill came to nothing, owing, so said the enemy, to the cowardice of the commanders detailed to lead it.

These successes, though they by no means cleared the districts, ensured for Natal almost complete repose for a month, during which the interest of the eastern campaign again shifted to the Delagoa Bay railway.

The anxiety of the Commander-in-Chief to unlock at least a portion of the army of troops on that expensive line of communication for more active service in the open field found expression in earnest solicitations to the commanders to reduce their permanent posts and increase the strength of their mobile columns. But if no channel of supply absorbed more men per mile, none was more continually harried, and in the first week in January, 1901, an unmistakable hint was given that in the presence of an enemy who could put even strong posts, strongly entrenched, in jeopardy, weak columns in the open were scarcely to be thought of. On the 3rd and 4th of January, 1901, Commandant-General Louis Botha rode up from Ermelo with 1,200 men under Generals C. Botha and T. Smuts. Leaving the commandos on the Upper Komati, between Carolina and Belfast, Botha himself with his subordinates crossed the line east of Middelburg by night, and on the 5th summoned all his officers to receive his orders at Hoedspruit, a farm on the western slopes of the Botha's Berg. Amongst others, General Ben Viljoen repaired to the spot, receiving there the congratulations of his chief on his recent feat at Helvetia. Botha had in mind no less

EVENTS IN THE EASTERN TRANSVAAL.

a plan than a wholesale demolition of the British eastern line of communications by means of simultaneous night onslaughts on its central section from both sides, by Viljoen from the north, and by C. Botha and Smuts from the south. As the points of attack he selected Machadodorp, Dalmanutha, Belfast, Wonderfontein and Pan, with the smaller posts linking these garrisons. Such a scheme possessed radical defects which by no means escaped the criticism of Botha's lieutenants. With an available strength of under 3,000 men it contemplated an operation on a front of forty miles, and that by divided forces at night, when the advantage of darkness would be more than counterbalanced by the difficulties of timing and intercommunication. Nevertheless, the conception commended itself by its very boldness to the majority of the Boer leaders, and it was resolved to carry it out to the letter.

The night of January 7th exhibited every circumstance of vileness which is prejudicial to defence. It was intensely dark; a fine cold rain fell persistently, and a piercing easterly gale, which deadened the ears of sentries, did nothing to dissipate the driving mist which blinded their eyes. With everything in their favour the various Boer detachments gathered, and at midnight each hurled itself upon its appointed victim. But the lesson of Helvetia—a lesson which Botha himself had feared might prove a marplot*—had not been wasted. As at Utrecht, commanders of garrisons had long turned night into day for their men; the trenches were bivouacs guarded on every side by mazes of barbed wire and often by chained watch dogs; the soldiers who slept fully armed therein had been taught to anticipate a night attack as a certainty. Nor were they entirely without specific warning. A native, coming into Nooitgedacht† at dusk, had foretold a visitation that night, and the word had been passed along the posts, which, however, were now habitually prepared without it, and indeed gave little

General attack on the Delagoa Bay line, Jan. 7th—8th, 1901.

---

* General B. Viljoen, "The Anglo-Boer War," page 309.

† This place, which lies close to Pan upon the line midway between Belfast and Middelburg, is not to be confused with another of the same name situated midway between Machadodorp and Nelspruit, *i.e.*, some fifty miles to the eastward.

credence to intelligence from such sources, so often disproved. Thus each post, suddenly struck, was ready at once with a counter-blow, and all along the line arose bouts of fighting, so close, so well contested, and so disconnected, that they must be recounted, however briefly, in detail, and for convenience from east to west.

Attack on Machadodorp. Machadodorp, the headquarters of Reeves's section of the line, was attacked simultaneously by Viljoen's Lydenburgers from the north, and on the other side by the Ermelo men, under Smuts. The garrison consisted of the 2nd Royal Irish Fusiliers, with guns and cavalry, disposed on three heights, Rocky Hill, Natal Hill, and Signal Hill, all of which were separately engaged by the enemy and stoutly defended. On the first-named especially was there a remarkable combat in which ninety-three men of the Fusiliers and six artillerymen withstood and finally repulsed the onset of nearly seven times as many burghers. Natal Hill and Signal Hill, though closely beset, were in little danger from smaller commandos, and by 3 a.m. on the 8th the whole attack, decisively defeated, was withdrawn.

Attack on Dalmanutha. Dalmanutha, to the westward, was attacked at the same time, but at first from the south only. This garrison, the easternmost of Smith-Dorrien's section, was held by two companies (161 men) of the 2nd Royal Berkshire regiment, and a troop of the 19th Hussars, with a 12-pr. gun. The defences on the north side of the railway consisted of a redoubt, surrounded by smaller works, and an entrenched piquet on the line itself, the ground on the southern side of which fell sharply. The southern side, the weakest and most accessible, was selected by the enemy, who, collecting below the slope, charged suddenly up the hill, shooting from the saddle as they galloped, rode over the sentries and groups, and had lined the railway before they were checked by the fire of the entrenched piquet only thirty yards away on the other side. So hot was their reception here that the attack faltered in spite of the efforts of the Boer leaders, who shouted encouragement to their men. At 1 a.m. the burghers ceased firing altogether, hoping thus to silence the unendurable fusilade from the British trench. Meanwhile another party, working

EVENTS IN THE EASTERN TRANSVAAL.

round to the north, fell upon the redoubt and the gun-pit, their attack being accompanied by so overwhelming a recrudescence of fire from the railway that the entrenchments began to crumble, and the piquet seemed likely to be overpowered. The Boers, however, knew nothing of the effect they were producing and, being in worse case themselves, soon fell back. At 2.15 a.m. Dalmanutha was free, the losses numbering but four in killed and wounded, and a few prisoners, who were shortly afterwards released.

Belfast, the key of the line, and Smith-Dorrien's Headquarters, had a far more severe trial. Here were over 1,300 infantry of the 1st Royal Irish regiment, 2nd Shropshire Light Infantry, 1st Gordon Highlanders, 1st Royal Inniskilling Fusiliers, together with 230 men of the 5th Lancers, 180 mounted infantry, the 84th battery R.F.A., and two 5-in. guns. But this was all too small for the ground to be defended, which, extending over a perimeter of fifteen miles, cut up the force into detachments nowhere strong enough to be safe against such attacks as those which were launched against them by Botha in person. Every post, was, however, strongly entrenched, and so thickly belted round with wire that it seemed as if they must be impregnable from that cause alone. The system of defence, which was divided by the railway into northern and southern sections, was as follows: Monument Hill, to the north-east of Belfast, and about one and a half miles from it, was crowned by a fort containing a company of the Royal Irish regiment, which found piquets in subsidiary works in front. Another company, not on outpost duty and under canvas in rear, brought the numbers on the hill to ninety-three officers and men. Outside the northeast corner of Belfast the Shropshire Light Infantry, less one company on duty in the town, garrisoned a fort, which, like that on Monument Hill, was piqueted by troops in smaller works. A drift, due north of Belfast and midway between the two above-mentioned heights, was held by mounted infantry; and this completed the northern section. South of the railway a semicircular line of defences was in the keeping of the Gordon Highlanders, who maintained it by means of the two main works

Attack on Belfast.

on either flank, connected by circular fortalices of stone, the main body of the battalion lying encamped behind the centre, in support. Belfast was thus well watched on every side, but as there were neither troops nor ground for an inner line, its defences possessed the weakness common to all in which the lines of observation and resistance are compelled to be the same, namely, the liability to be ruptured by the mere surprise of an outpost. The first and heaviest stroke fell upon Monument Hill. Nowhere were the fog and drizzle thicker than here, so dense, indeed, that not only did the sentries fail to detect the approach of an enemy, but the Boers themselves, about 500 Johannesburgers and Boksburgers under Muller, saw nothing until they were through the outlying posts, which, in consequence, fell into their hands. They then broke through the entanglement, especially at one point where it was weak owing to a failure of the stock of wire, and rushed upon the fort calling upon the garrison to surrender. The soldiers, unable to stop them with their rifles, answered with defiant shouts as they met them at the parapet, and a fierce *mêlée* ensued in which bayonets and butts of rifles were freely used, some even fighting with their fists, whilst others wrestled upon the ground. Everywhere the garrison, hopelessly outnumbered, resisted desperately, their commander, Captain F. L. Fosbery, animating all by his example until he was slain. Amongst so much valour as was displayed there is room here to mention none but the most conspicuous, and that was shown by Private J. Barry (No. 3733). Seeing the regimental Maxim gun surrounded by the enemy, this brave soldier burst into the group and proceeded to smash the lock in order to render the trophy useless; and this, in spite of threats, he persisted in doing, until one of the Boers, less chivalrous than the rest, shot him dead.* For half an hour the struggle continued before the garrison, having lost thirty-eight of its number, was overpowered. Together with the fort, two officers and fifty-one rank and file, belonging chiefly to the second company on the hill, were taken

---

* For Private Barry's gallant act a Victoria Cross (posthumous) was awarded.

EVENTS IN THE EASTERN TRANSVAAL.

by the enemy, who lost thirty-four in the assault, and dared not wait for light on the scene of their triumph, which was re-occupied by the British at dawn.

Simultaneously with the above a combat, only less disastrous because on a smaller scale, was in progress at the Colliery to the westward. Here, as usual, the outlying post fell a victim, but not until it had covered itself with glory by its resistance. In the small work in front of the Shropshire fort were nineteen men under a subaltern, who were suddenly set upon by a band more than ten times their number, chiefly composed of Viljoen's State artillerymen, led by Coetzee. For an hour this handful held their own, shooting down some two dozen of their assailants before they themselves succumbed, having lost their officer and thirteen men killed and wounded. The main work behind was then threatened, but the tenacity of the annihilated post had taken the sting from the attack, and the Boers were easily driven back. A demonstration against the mounted infantry at the drift between Monument and Colliery Hills led to heavy interchange of firing, but was pressed no further.

The attacks on the north of Belfast had been in progress some time before Botha's men made their descent upon the southern section; and the Gordon Highlanders, warned by the distant uproar, had reinforced their outposts and were lying in readiness for what might befall. At 1.15 a.m. matters opened by an onslaught by 400 Boers upon the extreme right, or southwest work, which was occupied at first by twenty-five men and two officers, who were soon assisted by the approach of two companies from the supports. Severe fighting followed here. The Boers, carrying stones, built up sangars within forty yards of the parapet, and actually inside the wire entanglements, which, as at other places, had failed to keep out their determined rush. But the Highlanders kept them at bay, and at the end of two hours the Boers fled beaten, leaving their dead behind. From this spot, however, the attack of the Ermelo and Carolina men had developed rapidly all along the arc, and there was no entrenched group but had to fight its hardest to avoid destruction. Only one, a post of ten men under a corporal, somewhat exposed near the eastern flank, after losing six of its number and firing nearly 200 rounds per man, was eventually demolished by the invasion of 200 Boers. So much for the defence of Belfast, which cost the garrison 134 casualties.

Attack on Wonderfontein.

Next in order of place, though not of time—for it was one of the first to be attacked—came Wonderfontein, where separated trenches of strong profile, guarded by a continuous and complex zigzag of barbed wire, sheltered the 150 men of the 2nd Royal Berkshire regiment who formed the garrison. Here the enemy were unfortunate from the outset, themselves giving warning by a preliminary reconnaissance which was discovered by the sentries, whilst sounds of fighting from other parts had already brought the defence to arms when at midnight the Middelburgers and men of Germiston opened upon the piquets to west and north of the enclosure. The post on the railway was most heavily engaged, some 200 burghers emptying their rifles against it, striking the officer and seven of the eleven men who lay therein. But here for once the formidable wire did its work, and after attempts to get in at different spots, which lasted two and a half hours, the enemy fell back, their retirement being hastened by shrapnel from two 12-pr. guns which had been mounted on armoured trucks upon the line.

Attack on Wildfontein.

At Wildfontein, too, the soldiers had been called to the loopholes by the firing on either side. Here some 100 men of the Royal Berkshire were entrenched within an oval enclosure, having the railway as its longer axis; a detached triangular work sheltered a detachment of the 5th (Royal Irish) Lancers on the south of the line. The latter was first attacked, but the firing soon spread, until both southern and western forces were fully engaged. Matters, however, went no further, and when the enemy departed at 2.30 a.m. the British detachment had suffered but three casualties.

Attack on Nooitgedacht.

Nooitgedacht, warned as related, was as admirably entrenched as every other post held by the Royal Berkshire, a regiment which since the days of McCracken's Hill* had been notable

---

* See Volume I., Chapter XXIV.

EVENTS IN THE EASTERN TRANSVAAL. 41

for its skill in field fortification. One hundred and fifty men of that battalion, a detachment of the 5th Lancers and a section of the 66th battery R.F.A. held the place, which was a square formed of rifle pits on three faces, and on the fourth—the southern—of loopholed farm buildings of brick and masonry. It was against this side that the Boers, creeping up two bifurcating ditches, advanced in two parties. So doing—a faint moon giving some intermittent light—their heads were discerned by the sentries, who aroused their comrades. A trap was then set for the would-be surprisers. A sudden volley at close range staggered the advance and checked it once and for all, shrapnel from the field guns joined in with effect, and Nooitgedacht remained intact with but two casualties.

Finally Pan, kept by a company of the Royal Berkshire, with two field guns, had to withstand an attack from the east, a bridge guard on the railway in that direction retiring just in time to avoid capture. Secure in their strong and well-designed trenches, which formed a parallelogram about the station, the garrison easily held its own, with the loss of one man, against an attempt less determined than at other places, and at 1.30 a.m. its vicinity was clear enough for the bridge to be re-occupied. <small>Attack on Pan.</small>

Such was the memorable attack on the eastern line of communication on January 7th; and if it seem to have been dwelt upon with overmuch detail, yet too much that was creditable to the arms of both sides has been unwillingly omitted.*

Throughout the rest of the month of January, the flame, which for one night had been concentrated, spread and broke out at every spot along the eastern line which afforded it momentary fuel. On the 8th, 12th, 14th, 23rd, 25th and 29th skirmishes occurred near the line; a convoy of wagons and sheep was captured near Bronkhorstspruit Station on the 13th; on the 9th one train was wrecked, on the 17th three trains; the line being severed on several other days, on one occasion (23rd) cutting off the Commander-in-Chief from Middelburg, whither he was proceeding for an interview with Lyttelton. On the

---

* For full casualty list see end of chapter.

night of the 16th, Rocky Hill at Machadodorp was twice attacked, whilst Helvetia had to repulse attempts on the nights of both the 19th and 21st. In short the line was harried with a persistency which seemed to point to more than a desire to cause annoyance. Botha, indeed, had long been occupied with preparations from which he anxiously wished to divert attention. To that end had been inflicted every damage which the British had suffered on the line and in the field since Viljoen's affair at Rhenoster Kop. His proceedings were, however, well known to the British Intelligence Department. Every report disclosed a powerful concentration of commandos about Bethel and Ermelo, and all that was at first uncertain was its purpose. By the time that became clear, Lord Kitchener had already devised measures to avert what might have proved a grave crisis. To both the Transvaal and Free State generalissimos, as with the majority of their brothers in arms, the south still glowed with the memories of early successes. Along the Tugela, on the heights of Cape Colony, and the Modder, the campaign had once seemed so nearly won that it might perhaps still be saved there. Botha and C. De Wet had determined, therefore, to turn again that way from the disastrous north, and had planned a simultaneous re-invasion of Cape Colony and Natal, the former to be carried out by De Wet, Hertzog, the Free State judge, and Kritzinger, of Zastron, whilst Botha reserved for his own hands to grasp at the well-remembered mountains and valleys across the Buffalo. Some talk there was also of a ship to be met by Hertzog at Lamberts Bay, laden with munitions of war and mercenaries from the Europe which almost every burgher, except the Commandant-General himself,* still believed to hold his interests first in its heart. This scheme had already partially broken down by the failure of the very leader whose success had been most confidently expected. A month earlier De Wet, hemmed in by the flooded waters of the Caledon and Orange rivers, and pursued by a pack of columns, had so

Botha's fresh plans.

---

* "It is useless for us to entertain the thought of intervention, and we shall have to fight the matter out ourselves."—Letter to General C. De Wet, January 15th, 1901.

EVENTS IN THE EASTERN TRANSVAAL. 43

narrowly escaped destruction* that he was no longer to be counted on as a factor in Botha's strategy. But Hertzog and Kritzinger had fared better. They were at this moment in the heart of Cape Colony, re-opening everywhere the deepest sore in the British cause.† Such success could only be partial, but a vigorous offensive in the east might yet confirm it, and Botha persisted in his plan. Slowly—for communication was more difficult than of yore—he gathered together some 4,000 men at the places mentioned, employing part of them on January 7th in the raid upon the line which, costly failure as it had proved, might yet, he hoped, have served as a useful blind to his and De Wet's proceedings in the opposite direction.

But now, with every railway in British hands, the theatre of war had resolved itself into a series of fortified angles within one or the other of which every Boer force still in the field was compelled to operate. Thus Botha, marching southward from Ermelo, would find himself entering the narrowing tract shut in on the one side by the Swazi and Zulu borders, and on the other by the railway posts until they gave place to the forts and garrisoned drifts which screened and defended the Buffalo. Into this corner Lord Kitchener prepared to hunt him with a pack of columns to be directed by Lieut.-General French; but whilst they made ready he first, on January 25th, despatched Smith-Dorrien to Carolina with about 4,000 men of all arms and fourteen guns to try the ground. This column had to fight all the way out and back, and when it returned to Wonderfontein on the 30th had suffered fifty-five casualties at the hands of 2,000 Boers who were left close to Carolina. Smith-Dorrien then awaited on the line the approach of the great expedition in which he was to play a part, and which French had already set in motion two days earlier.

On the Heidelberg—Standerton section of the line nothing of importance had occurred during January. Only Colville in the course of his usual patrolling encountered near Vlaklaagte on the 16th another combination of some 900 Boers who attacked his

---

* See Volume III., pages 494 to 496. † See Chapter IV.

baggage and drove in the rearguard, only to be handsomely beaten by a bayonet charge, followed by a pursuing fire, delivered by six companies of the 1st Rifle Brigade which formed his main body. The enemy lost fifty men, and Colville but sixteen. At the end of the month he was as before in the neighbourhood of Greylingstad.

CASUALTIES—RAILWAY LINE OF COMMUNICATION—EAST OF PRETORIA—NIGHT ATTACK BY BOERS, JANUARY 7TH, 1901.

ACTION.	Killed.		Wounded.		Captured or Missing.		Total.	
	Officers.	Other Ranks.	Officers.	Other Ranks.	Officers.	Other Ranks.	Officers.	Other Ranks.
Machadodorp	1	1	—	11	—	—	1	12
Dalmanutha	—	1	—	3	—	—	—	4
Belfast	1	16	3	48	2	70	6	134
Wonderfontein	—	3	1	7	—	—	1	10
Wildfontein	—	1	—	2	—	—	—	3
Nooitgedacht	—	—	1	1	—	—	1	1
Pan	—	—	—	1	—	—	—	1
TOTALS	2	22	5	73	2	70	9	165

The Boer casualties numbered approximately 100, of which some thirty were killed. Commandant-General Botha returned his losses as twenty-one killed, sixty-one wounded, and two missing, but this was somewhat under the mark.

CHAPTER III.

EVENTS IN THE ORANGE RIVER COLONY.*

DECEMBER, 1900—JANUARY, 1901.

AFTER his abortive attempt to enter Cape Colony in December, 1900,† De Wet turned northward hoping to find a retired spot about Hammonia where he could prepare for another effort. His reputation and his force were alike little weakened; his numbers, indeed, were actually increased by bands which joined him upon the left bank of the Caledon, and he was soon at the head of some 5,000 burghers. Only his horseflesh had suffered greatly in the forced marches up and down the miry river banks: his passage of the Caledon alone had cost him 500 animals; more dropped out at every mile, and deprived of horses, De Wet, like every Boer, was like an engine without steam. But he had small immediate prospect of the respite he so greatly desired. His fortunate escape from a circle of floods had but delivered him into the midst of another of British troops and forts. On December 11th, when his commandos gained Helvetia,‡ Major-General C. E. Knox was so close behind that the Boer rearguard was actually engaged with the three columns of Lieut.-Colonels J. S. S. Barker, W. H. Williams and W. L. White (the latter replacing Lieut.-Colonel E. B. Herbert). Further back, in the Rouxville district, was Colonel C. J. Long

De Wet turns back from the Orange river.

---

* See map No. 64.

† See Volume III., pages 494 to 496.

‡ Not to be confused with the place of the same name on the Delagoa Bay railway.

with Lieut.-Colonels T. D. Pilcher and H. M. Grenfell advancing in front of Herbert in support at Aliwal North. Colonel Sir C. Parsons, who had relieved Major-General H. H. Settle at Edenburg on the 5th, was on the left front at Reddersburg; Colonel A. W. Thorneycroft and Lieut.-Colonel the Hon. J. Byng, brought from Standerton and Volksrust respectively, were lining up from Israels Poort through Thabanchu and Springhaan Nek to the banks of the Caledon, thus shutting off the north-east, or right front. C. Knox first manœuvred to drive the Boers upon Sir C. Parsons at Reddersburg; but De Wet, kept well informed by his scouts, edged away to the north-east, and, passing between the Caledon and Dewetsdorp, laagered at Daspoort, seven miles to the east of the latter on the night of December 13th. C. Knox and Sir C. Parsons were then only ten miles behind, with Pilcher, the foremost of Long's command, twenty-five miles in rear again.

His dangerous position. De Wet was now voluntarily entering a trap very similar to that from which, four months before,* he had escaped with his own small following, leaving the Orange Free State army fast in the toils of the Brandwater basin. He was perfectly aware of the situations of his various opponents, of the line of troops and blockhouses barring his front, the great topographical strength of their disposition, and of the exact distance of his pursuers. His haven was only to be gained by extreme good fortune or an expensive engagement, whilst failure, of which there was every chance, would mean total ruin, for half a day's march by C. Knox, in rear, would shut him up. Here, as elsewhere, indeed, De Wet, compelled to stake everything upon long odds, made it doubtful whether he did not shine brighter as an inspired gambler than as a serious leader of men. A greater than he had indeed set, at Somosierra for instance, the seal of genius upon feats of unbridled tactical licence based upon penetration as profound as it was instantaneous of his enemy's condition. But in tactics, as apart from policy, Napoleon never risked his all except once, when all was already lost; whereas De Wet, now

* See Volume III., pages 292 to 306.

EVENTS IN THE ORANGE RIVER COLONY. 47

become on his smaller scale, even more than Napoleon, the soul of his country's resistance, had to hazard on one throw the whole campaign. But he knew that his chances were better than they appeared, and neither he nor his adversaries failed to improve them. The line taken up on the night of December 12th by Byng and Thorneycroft ran, as stated, from Israels Poort to the banks of the Caledon river facing south. Thorneycroft, who was in command, assigned the right, from Israels Poort to the foot of Patchoana, to Byng, taking post himself on Patchoana, about the left centre. On either side of Thabanchu his disposition followed the course of the existing block-houses, which, indeed, the columns had been sent by the Commander-in-Chief to reinforce. These defences had the double defect of lying too far apart, and of stopping short at an important point. For example, the pair called Springhaan Post and Intermediate Post, which had been designed to command Springhaan Nek, the best outlet towards Hammonia and the north, were no less than 4,000 yards apart. Another 2,700 yards separated the latter of these from its nearest neighbour, Hut Post, the easternmost defence of the Nek, beyond which again a stretch of rideable ground extending to Patchoana Mountain was entirely unobstructed. Intervals like these over so wide a front the two commanders, who had less than 1,100 men between them, were unable to fill and at the same time preserve strength and mobility to strike from any part. It was absolutely necessary to retain the power of offensive; for though Springhaan Nek was the main entry, it was neither the only passage, nor from its very prominence that most likely to be attempted. De Wet himself had avoided it to make use of another, namely, the space between Hut Post and Patchoana, on his recent march southward to the Orange, and there was soon given another sign of the enemy's preference for this track.

Springhaan Nek.

Its importance had been by no means overlooked by Thorneycroft. Well aware of the weakness at this spot, he had already requested Byng, in whose section it lay, to make it good; but Byng could find no troops for the duty. Immediately on his arrival on Patchoana, therefore, Thorneycroft pushed out a company of his own regiment midway into the space, where it entrenched itself, an orderly being sent to the officer at the Hut Post to acquaint him with the proceeding. Soon after this man had delivered his message, and while it was still dark, a strong body of horsemen appeared in the gap, coming not from the south but the north. They rode forward with such confidence that the garrison of Hut Post, believing them to be Thorneycroft's approaching company, refrained from shooting, thereby letting Prinsloo's Bethlehem commando, some 400 strong, pass through undamaged. Descending the Nek in safety, Prinsloo pursued his way southward and joined De Wet at Daspoort. On this being reported, Thorneycroft, though he could ill spare the men, at once entrenched another company in a series of detached posts across the space, leaving himself less than 300 mounted men available for offence. Neither he nor Byng could do more for the centre, for Thabanchu on the one side and Patchoana on the other were themselves by no means unlikely to be completely turned. Thus Springhaan Nek proper, except for the inadequate defences on its widely separated flanks, remained open; and it was peculiarly vulnerable because close in front of it a height called Ngoana towered some 700 feet higher than the general line of defence, forming both a secure gathering ground for a rush upon the Nek and an excellent point from which to reconnoitre the whole of the British dispositions. This mountain, the true outwork of the passage, was left unoccupied. De Wet, as he approached the gateway, had in fact determined to win t by his former route, which would carry him outside the defending blockhouses instead of between them. Prinsloo's undisputed passage promised well, and he trusted that the troops since arrived in this quarter were too few, and had had too little time to entrench to be able to oppose him seriously. He had more fear of those in the direction of Thabanchu, whom very little delay on his part in front of Springhaan would assuredly bring down upon him, when, even if he could master them at all, it must be at such expense of time that C. Knox

EVENTS IN THE ORANGE RIVER COLONY. 49

would inevitably come up on his rear and ruin him. To keep the defence extended, then, and to pierce it quickly were vital objects, and to this end he set in motion a train of masterly tactics.

In order to contain the western troops and hold them to their position it was necessary, unless De Wet detached largely himself, to threaten them from a point which would arouse more apprehension than a merely frontal demonstration. De Wet determined, therefore, to send a small force to break through the weak centre, and to place it directly in rear of the Thabanchu section of the line. It was probable that the commander there, menaced from so unexpected a direction, would not venture to move a man to the assistance of any other quarter. For this service De Wet selected the last arrivals, the Bethlehem burghers, whose horses were fresher than his own exhausted animals, who, moreover, had but the morning before traversed in one direction the very ground over which his plans required them to return. Before light on December 14th, Prinsloo, marching well ahead of the main body, approached the gap at a point between Hut Post and the most westerly of Thorneycroft's detached outposts. He was immediately detected and fired upon; but keeping his men well together, and protected by the darkness, he charged through the narrow gap almost unharmed, indeed almost unseen, for the troops were under the impression that they had driven back the majority of the party, and so reported to Thorneycroft when he sent a patrol to ascertain the cause of the firing. In a few seconds Prinsloo was safely on the other side, when he swung north-westward, and made for the reverse of Byng's line of defence.

At sunrise Thorneycroft received a heliograph message from Wepener to the effect that De Wet and Steyn, with 4,000 men and three guns, were approaching him from the south. But he had little need of warning. Soon, from the top of Patchoana, the Boer army came full into view, marching from the direction of Dewetsdorp. Guns, transport and commandos were all plainly discernible, and warning was sent along the line to all

De Wet's tactics at Springhaan Nek.

the posts, all, that is, with the exception of Thabanchu itself, which was so thickly shrouded in mist that the heliograph was useless. As a consequence Byng, who from the first had had no very clear idea of the situation, remained throughout in partial ignorance of the significance of the ensuing events, though his uncertainty had but little effect upon the results, for he had not a man to spare.

De Wet now manœuvred to discover his best crossing place. Still bent on that immediately to the east of Hut Post, at 5.30 a.m. he sent his scouts forward to prove it. But daylight had rendered it impassable. The fire from the Post, and from Thorneycroft's western detachment covered all the space. The Boer scouts then probed further to the east, towards Patchoana; but here matters were even worse, for still Thorneycroft's men lay in front, whilst from the slopes of Patchoana the artillery joined in denying the passage. Though baulked here, the reconnaissance gave De Wet the clue to the problem before him. His old route was closed; but the disclosure of the presence of the British main strength upon Patchoana rendered Springhaan Nek itself not only his sole hope, but no bad one. The wide separation of its defending forts was known to him; it was unlikely that Thorneycroft's extension had been continued so far to the west, whilst Byng's must by this time be surely checked and contained by Prinsloo's appearance on his rear. Nevertheless, Thorneycroft was still nearer to the Nek than De Wet himself, and it was essential to pin him to his ground until the last moment. Falling back, therefore, with half his force under the shelter of Ngoana, De Wet sent the other half, nearly 2,000 strong, to threaten the outer or eastern flank of Thorneycroft upon Patchoana, feigning an intention against the difficult but almost unguarded tract between Patchoana and the Leeuw river. Whilst this demonstration was in progress, De Wet edged the wing upon Ngoana under the mountain side towards a point opposite the entry of Springhaan Nek. Thorneycroft, to whom the above evolutions were plainly visible, was now in a greater quandary than if he had seen nothing at all. It was impossible to devise

EVENTS IN THE ORANGE RIVER COLONY. 51

the enemy's real intentions. He had, as stated, a striking force of less than 300 men left under his hand; to strip Patchoana of these in order to reinforce Springhaan would be to expose his baggage, his left flank, and the ground beyond to a force six times the strength of his own. To withdraw the already entirely inadequate defences of the Nek would present the main passage as a free gift. It was impossible to summon Byng to the spot, even more so than Thorneycroft was aware.

Hidden in thick mist, Byng was at this moment preoccupied by reports of attacks from all sides, and practically isolated by the necessity of dealing with Prinsloo, who was well seconding the able tactics of his chief by his close attentions to the Thabanchu defences. Sending a Colt gun to Hut Post, and to Intermediate Post a section of Byng's mounted infantry which had joined him the night before, Thorneycroft therefore remained on Patchoana, watching keenly for the slightest disclosure of the real attack. He had not long to wait. At about 8 a.m. the commandos with De Wet, having wound around Ngoana, began to move rapidly upon Springhaan. As they advanced the body on the right inclined inwards, and refusing the front of Patchoana, swiftly closed in upon the others. Only one party of 300 men under Commandant Haasbroek of Winburg remained behind, and, turning back at Ngoana, disappeared westward down the Khabanyana river. Instantly Thorneycroft, his doubts removed, issued from Patchoana with three companies of his regiment, two guns R.F.A. and a Vickers-Maxim, and galloped for Springhaan Nek, leaving but one company to guard the baggage on the mountain. *The forcing of Springhaan Nek, Dec. 14th, 1900.*

As he debouched, the enemy also broke into a gallop, and in two compact bodies rushed for the entry. The first, led by Vice-Chief-Commandant P. Fourie, burst through almost unscathed by the hurried long-range fire from the badly placed flanking forts, before Thorneycroft came within reach. Having passed the fire zone, this party of Boers swung eastward and, facing round, took up a fire position which commanded not only the rear of the Nek, but also the flank of Thorneycroft's advance, an admirable piece of tactics which would have done much to ensure success had much been necessary. Flankers from this band soon engaged Thorneycroft's foremost troops, and, though they were driven back, the slight delay enabled the main Boer body to get through the more safely, because Thorneycroft found himself obliged to detach from his handful in order to cope with so dangerous a menace to his flank. With one united rush the second portion of De Wet's force, under Field-Cornet J. Hattingh, covered the space between the forts, the hurried and distant fire from which was again almost ineffectual. Just as all had passed Thorneycroft threw himself with his few remaining men athwart the gap, his guns shelling the receding horsemen with some effect. To pursue in force was out of the question, but a strong patrol which Thorneycroft sent out upon the line of retreat met with gratifying success. The capture of forty-two stragglers, a 15-pr. gun, a Vickers-Maxim (the former part of De Wet's booty at Dewetsdorp) and 60,000 rounds of ammunition, in some measure made amends for the loss of the main issue of the day.

De Wet's daring and lucky venture had not been made a moment too soon. By mid-day C. E. Knox, marching up on a broad front through Daspoort, W. H. Williams' column on the right, Barker's in the centre, W. L. White's on the left, had practically closed all retreat from Springhaan Nek. Haasbroek's band was actually caught at dusk by White near Victoria, and before it escaped in the darkness lost nearly forty burghers, the majority at the hands of "A" squadron 16th Lancers and a party of the Welsh Yeomanry, who, under Colonel W. Forbes, charged into the midst of the laager, taking twenty prisoners and killing and wounding as many more. At nightfall C. Knox halted on either side of Ngoana.

Pursuit of De Wet.

On the next day, December 15th, Thorneycroft, having collected his men, went in pursuit of De Wet, who had disappeared in the direction of Walspruit. On clearing this farm in the forenoon the Boer rearguard was seen falling back across Brands Drift on the Linyana Spruit, and Thorneycroft's advance parties

EVENTS IN THE ORANGE RIVER COLONY. 53

pushed on to gain touch. But they found De Wet posted too strongly to be interfered with on the heights commanding the Spruit from New Holstein down to Hoepel, with a party thrown in advance of his right flank on the mountain at Lokoala. Thorneycroft could do no more than remain in observation at Maseru Farm. About 1 p.m. the Boers ostentatiously withdrew their piquets along the whole front, and despatched their convoy down the Linyana towards Zamenkomst. Thorneycroft, suspecting that a trap was being set for his greatly outnumbered force, prudently stood fast on Maseru. His caution was soon amply justified. A pause of half an hour exhausted the patience of the enemy, who, seeing that the column was not to be inveigled, suddenly emerged, nearly 3,000 strong, from behind New Holstein, and followed their baggage northward. Still a considerable body remained concealed, and the outlying force on Lokoala was actually reinforced. But early on the 16th Thorneycroft detected both parties, and remained stationary, whilst Barker joined him at Maseru, White moved up towards his left flank, and Pilcher, who had caught up with C. E. Knox the day before, took post upon his right. This alignment was complete on December 17th, and a united movement in pursuit of De Wet was on the point of being made, when orders were received which broke up Knox's combination in the Thabanchu district. Thorneycroft, W. H. Williams, Byng and Sir C. Parsons were now to hasten to Bloemfontein to entrain for Cape Colony, where Hertzog and Kritzinger, more fortunate than their chief, were rapidly penetrating British territory by west and east.* Only Pilcher, W. L. White and Barker remained with Knox, and with these the chase of De Wet was resumed.

A three days' advance by Clocolan, Mequatlings Nek, Evening Star and Conoviam confirmed the north-easterly direction of the Boers' retreat. All three columns were constantly in touch with one portion or another of De Wet's widely extended rearguard, which on the 25th appeared to be covering a position lying between Gouverneur's Kop and Ficksburg.

* See Chapter IV.

In the last-named town much activity was apparent, and Knox sent Pilcher and Barker upon the place by way of the Caledon, whilst White moved on Hammonia. This advance into the heart of the most tangled district of the Orange River Colony promised to lead to serious fighting. But De Wet was more intent on husbanding his resources for his main strategy, a renewed invasion of Cape Colony, than on giving battle. He knew well that so long as he kept his large force together neither men nor horses would have rest from pursuit. Moreover, he was being rapidly driven into a district every town of which, Lindley, Senekal, Reitz, Frankfort, Bethlehem, was held by the troops of Sir L. Rundle, based on Harrismith, portions of whose division, under Lieut.-Colonel C. P. Crewe and Major-General J. E. Boyes, were already moving on his flank with convoys for Lindley from Winburg and Senekal. At this point, therefore, De Wet broke up his army, dispersing it, part under Assistant-Head-Commandant P. Botha, part under Vice-Chief-Commandant P. Fourie, part under Commandant Davel, to which last he also entrusted the guardianship of President Steyn. Davel's party made towards Reitz. De Wet himself, with a small guard, rode for the Heilbron district, intending there to collect, with General P. Froneman's assistance, transport and ammunition for his next attempt on Cape Colony. Thus the British columns, though unaware of the cause, found their task at once lightened and confused. Ficksburg, in spite of its strong defences, was at once yielded, whereupon Pilcher hastened to the assistance of W. L. White, whose single column at Hammonia had as much as it could manage with a considerable hostile body. On December 28th White and Pilcher advanced to Rietvlei; Barker, having destroyed the flour mills in Ficksburg, moved to Commando Nek. Next day all three turned northward upon Rexford, on the Senekal—Bethlehem road, White and Pilcher in front, Barker following to Rietvlei. The columns were now in close touch with Fourie's detachment, which was pushed through Rexford, and kept in a north-easterly direction by a movement by White on Tweepoort, and Pilcher on Luipaardsfontein, Barker halting at Rexford. This band

EVENTS IN THE ORANGE RIVER COLONY. 55

then seemed to disappear; but on December 30th another, that of P. Botha, was discovered in the other direction upon Kaffir Kop, a strong position on the northern spurs of the Witte Bergen. C. E. Knox manœuvred to surround the Kop by despatching White around the north by Lindley, Barker towards the south, whilst Pilcher moved directly against the position. The appearance of a strong line of battle on the morning of the 31st heralded an engagement, and for four hours the three columns skirmished with clouds of riflemen, who were especially thick opposite Barker on the left. But a threat of closer quarters and the practice of the howitzers speedily cleared the mountains, and the commando vanished towards the north. White then marched to Lindley, Pilcher back to Tweepoort, and Barker camped close to Kaffir Kop.

On January 1st, 1901, all three concentrated at Lindley, and on the 3rd White and Barker led the advance eastward upon Reitz. Arrived at Plesier in the afternoon, the two columns were joined by Crewe, who had been sent from Boyes' command at Winburg with 500 men of the Colonial division. (At this time both Winburg and Senekal were garrisoned by troops from Boyes' column.) Crewe arrived in the presence of disaster. It happened that some 150 men of an irregular corps from White's force, entitled the Commander-in-Chief's Bodyguard, had been sent to reconnoitre in front of Plesier towards the head of Liebenbergs Vlei. At Kromspruit this party, which regardless of rules and experience was in close formation and without even ground-scouts, fell suddenly in with P. Botha's vastly superior force, which had not been seen since its evacuation of Kaffir Kop, three days before. In a moment the patrol was completely surrounded. A desperate but hopeless combat ensued, which was maintained until forty officers and men, including the commanding and three other officers, had been killed and wounded. The remainder then surrendered, were immediately disarmed, but as quickly released, White dashing up to the rescue a few moments later.

Once more P. Botha's and every other formed body disappeared, and C. E. Knox, turning from Reitz, cast vainly northward in search of something to strike at. He began to suspect that the enemy had doubled and was now behind him. Accordingly on January 5th he concentrated his columns at Gelderland, north-west of Reitz, preparatory to a movement southward, that is, by the way he had just come. On the 6th he was at Winbult, close by his former halting-place at Plesier. Here he lost Barker's and White's columns which were ordered to Kroonstad for reconstruction and subsequent service under Bruce Hamilton, who was coming from Hoopstad to organise a force for operations against De Wet. Knox pursued his way uneventfully with Crewe and Pilcher to Senekal (January 10th) where he found Boyes, come from Winburg, together with a column of 500 horsemen, chiefly Bethune's mounted infantry, under Colonel S. C. H. Monro, which had been railed from Dundee, in Natal, to relieve Lindley at the end of December. Monro had reached Lindley on January 2nd, and two days later had joined Boyes. On January 6th, when marching together on Senekal, both had been heavily attacked in flank and rear by the ubiquitous P. Botha at Rietpan, where there was some difficulty in saving the guns, one of which was disabled, the other deprived of its horses. In the skilfully conducted rearguard action the columns lost fifteen, the Boers twenty casualties. Throughout the march such large hostile bodies were discovered in the Lindley district that, on his arrival at Senekal, Boyes was able to report the main body of the Boers in that quarter. Nevertheless, a council of war between the five commanders resulted in the decision that, in accordance with orders received from the Commander-in-Chief, Boyes should return to his proper sphere, Harrismith, and Monro into Lindley, to evacuate the perilously placed garrison of that town. C. E. Knox himself, completely at a loss amid conflicting reports and an invisible foe, marched on to Winburg, which he entered on January 12th.

Monro lost no time in undertaking his dangerous mission. For such a task as probably awaited him, his force, composed of only 400 mounted men, 100 regular and 200 militia infantry, with three guns, was totally inadequate, just such a body, indeed, as De Wet loved to discover isolated upon the veld. Fortunately the Free State leader was intent on other schemes, and Monro pushed on almost unnoticed, encountering only a weak Boer force on January 11th at Bronsfontein, midway to his object. On the 13th he entered Lindley unopposed, cleared the place of its garrison and stores, and safely gained the railway at America Siding on the 23rd.

Boyes had more trouble on his march to rejoin Rundle at Harrismith. He moved by Honingfontein and Wilansspruit, in the angle of the Senekal—Lindley and Senekal—Bethlehem roads, a route which, for a time at least, afforded some support to Monro. On the last-named of these two roads a commando was discovered, which moved parallel with Boyes as far as Rexford, and when he turned south-easterly for Bethlehem, placed itself upon his left front about Onverdacht, disputing his further advance on January 13th from a strong double position. For nine hours Boyes fought for his passage, much hindered by the enveloping nature of the enemy's dispositions, and by a 15-pr. gun which was accurately served against his troops. The key of the advance was a prominent hill some 5,000 yards in the direction of Bethlehem. Although this was unoccupied by the enemy, approach to it was difficult, because of the danger of being surrounded on the way; for the Boer riflemen lapped partly around the left rear, only awaiting an opportunity to close in. Boyes, keeping off the left attack with his guns and infantry, collected his mounted men, under Lieut.-Colonel R. B. Firman, on his right, which was protected by the Zand river at Wilansspruit, and at 3 p.m. ordered them to go forward and attempt to seize the commanding hill in front. Firman moved out boldly, and approaching the height, saw that he could do even better than secure it, for his line of advance led him with good cover actually around the enemy's left flank. He therefore circled rapidly to his left, and furiously charged the flank of the Boer first line, which instantly dissolved. In ten minutes the whole situation had been reversed. Boyes then pushed forward all his strength and carried both positions,

Action at Onverdacht, Jan. 13th, 1901.

the enemy's second line not awaiting his attack. He was no more opposed on the west of Bethlehem, which he entered on the 15th. Thence he moved to and emptied Reitz. Orders were then received from Rundle to join hands with Major-General B. B. D. Campbell at Elands River Bridge, and this, with constant skirmishing by the way, was carried out on January 23rd. Boyes' column arrived in a deplorable condition. Not only the incessant marching with columns more mobile than itself, than which nothing is more exhausting to any unit, had worn its efficiency to the last thread. A form of low fever had infected the ranks and claimed many victims. Both the commanding officer and his brigade-major were seriously ill. Out of the two battalions which composed the column 170 had already come in sick to the base. One of these regiments, which Rundle had sent out 700 strong, returned with only some 300 men able to stand on parade, and of these nearly half were reported by the medical officer as unfit for active service. The other battalion was little less debilitated. All were in rags, the majority bootless.

De Wet turns again for Cape Colony.
On the very day on which Boyes and Monro reached their respective destinations, De Wet, having completed his preparations, joined his reunited commandos on the Doornberg, and prepared to lead them once more southward to the invasion of Cape Colony. Lord Kitchener had kept in remarkably close touch with his obscure manœuvres of the previous three weeks; in closer touch, indeed, than his subordinates on the spot, whom a less elaborate intelligence service and the constant encountering with bodies of unknown strength served to bewilder beyond all hope of distinguishing the Boer main body. No sooner was De Wet on the march when Bruce Hamilton, at Kroonstad, and C. E. Knox, who had worked his way round to Leeuw Kop again, were ordered to converge upon his rendezvous and cut him off from the south. Then followed the events next to be described in connection with De Wet's second inroad into Cape Colony.*

* See Chapter IV. pages 75 to 78.

EVENTS IN THE ORANGE RIVER COLONY.

APPROXIMATE STRENGTH STATES OF COLUMNS REFERRED TO IN FOREGOING CHAPTER.

Column.	Mounted Troops.	Infantry.	Guns, including Vickers-Maxims.	Machine Guns.	
December, 1900—January, 1901.					
Lieut.-Colonel J. S. S. Barker	750	90	4	2	Major-General C. E. Knox in command.
,, ,, W. H. Williams	340	—	3	6	
,, ,, W. L. White	830	138	5	1	
,, ,, T. D. Pilcher	1,070	82	7	2	Col. C. J. Long in command.
,, ,, H. M. Grenfell	450	—	3	—	
,, ,, E. B. Herbert	386	110	5	—	
Colonel A. W. Thorneycroft	500	150	5	—	
Lieut.-Colonel the Hon. J. H. G. Byng	380	—	3	—	
Colonel Sir C. Parsons	500	—	3	3	Lieut.-General Sir L. Rundle in command.
Lieut.-Colonel C. P. Crewe	640	—	4	2	
Major-General J. E. Boyes (later Harley)	318	1,361	5	3	
,, ,, B. B. D. Campbell	342	1,393	5	2	
Lieut.-Colonel S. C. H. Monro	320	480	2	—	
Major-General Bruce Hamilton	830	752	8	3	

CHAPTER IV.

EVENTS IN CAPE COLONY.*

DECEMBER, 1900—FEBRUARY 28TH, 1901.

<small>Attitude of Cape Colony.</small>
To a commander in the field a more constant anxiety than an open foe is a wavering ally. Such a confederate must be alternately trusted and suspected ; though he may at any moment assume the offensive, he must be given no cause of offence ; his territory is sacred, yet must be watched like that of a hostile State ; the very grasp of his right hand must be received with caution, in case his left conceal a dagger. When, in addition, so doubtful a friend dwells upon the chief lines of communication, the danger and difficulty of dealing with him become doubled ; for, even should he himself be too weak or timorous to strike, he may have a welcome for enemies bolder than himself, who will ask no more than admittance within his borders. Such was the position of a large portion of Cape Colony throughout the war in South Africa.† The reasons why long years of prosperity under British rule had failed to win the loyalty of many sections of this great province have been already given ; the first outbreaks of disaffection and their suppression have been described.‡ Let it suffice to say that when, after the paltry rebellions of the spring of 1900, Sir Charles Warren ceased his punitive expeditions in July, none who knew the colony, none, indeed, who knew war, were deceived into the belief that

---

* See map No. 63.

† Roughly, the parts about Colesberg, Philipstown, Hanover, Burghersdorp, Albert, Steynsburg, Aliwal North, Wodehouse, Prieska, Kenhardt, Griqualand West, Hay, Herbert and Barkly West.

‡ Volume III., Chapter I.

the immense communications of the western theatre of war stood at last upon a firm foundation. The fear of a widespread rebellion had, indeed, become more remote. The enthusiasm of the disloyal farmers for the Republican cause had now been diagnosed. In the majority of cases it was likely to indulge itself very little further than the giving of supplies and information to the favoured side, and withholding them from the other, valuable, nay indispensable, military aids to guerilla bands, but in no way symptomatic of a universal conflagration. Moreover, the merciful measures taken by the British Government after the first rebellion had considerably dulled the edge even of that enthusiasm. Martial law has never been more leniently administered than it was upon the armed rebels of the early part of 1900, who found not only their lives, but their liberties, possessions, and even their business, preserved for them after a mere pretence at arraignment. But disaffection, in spite of all opiates, is a light sleeper; if it slumbered throughout the summer of 1900, the Boer leaders had good hopes that it only awaited the time and the call to awake. Neither were long delayed; nor could the moment for the summons have been better chosen. The early days of 1901 found Cape Colony thinly and unscientifically occupied by British troops, and stirring uneasily from its lethargy. In November, 1900, so-called " congresses," in reality meetings of conspirators, engineered by agents of the Boer Government, had been held at various centres of unrest, notably Graaff Reinet and Worcester, with no more interference by the British authorities than had been exercised with the target practice of notorious rebels in the previous year. It was a moment when something of a St. Martin's summer was beginning to revive the waning Republican cause; when their forces all over the theatre of war were being strengthened by the reappearance of hundreds of burghers, who were driven, or rode voluntarily, back from their sworn neutrality into the ranks of the commandos. The British armies, on the other hand, were in the act of depriving themselves of most of the first contingents of Colonials, whose presence had bestowed the very qualities which the regular troops most lacked and the campaign most demanded. It has been seen how, despite these advantages, the Boers' initial strategy in the contemplated double scheme of invasion went to pieces amidst the waters of the Orange and Caledon.* But this did not save Cape Colony. Two of De Wet's officers, less closely watched than their famous leader, contrived to evade both the floods and C. E. Knox's columns; and soon the disturbance of the whole colony, down to its very seaboard, was to point the lesson how that the least considered factors of an enemy's combination may, in certain circumstances, prove the most troublesome of all. On December 15th and 16th, Commandants P. H. Kritzinger and Judge Hertzog dashed across the Orange river, the former between Bethulie and Odendaal Stroom, the latter by Sand Drift, opposite Philippolis. To have foreseen this sally on the part of one at least of the invaders should have required no great gift of prophecy. For the past fortnight Lieut.-Colonel H. M. Grenfell, in the Rouxville district, and Sir H. MacDonald, reconnoitring across the Orange from Aliwal North, had been in close observation of Kritzinger, and their reports gave no uncertain indication of his designs. It was known on December 8th that the Free Stater was seeking information about the drifts over the Orange, that the whole Zastron district was covered with his parties busy collecting fresh horses. Continually, too, he edged southward, and on the 14th was at Wolve Kop, within a march of the main drift at Odendaal Stroom. Still no hint of his intentions was gathered; his refusal to be headed northward, and his long delay about Rouxville, were attributed only to the presence of C. E. Knox at Smithfield, whilst the recent repulse of De Wet rendered inconceivable a single-handed foray southward by his weakest lieutenant. Kritzinger's appearance south of the Orange, then, caused as much surprise as though he had ridden secretly 500 miles to effect it, instead of from one bank of the river to the other. Not only the audacity of these unsupported invaders showed their supreme and significant confidence in the sympathy of the British province. Their

De Wet's advanced parties invade Cape Colony.

---

* See Volume III., Chapter XX.

forces were small; Kritzinger had but 700 men, Hertzog some 1,200, nearly all of them oath-breakers.* They carried with them no wheeled vehicles of any kind; artillery would be of as little service as transport to leaders who intended to rely for success on avoiding engagements, and for provender on the innumerable friendly farms, with the names of which the sleepless agents of the Boer cause had furnished them. So disproportionate, in short, seemed these expeditions to the task of serious invasion that the British Headquarters were scarcely to be blamed if they regarded them as merely marauding bands. Though they were, in fact, little more than this, the inroad of the two Free Staters was a serious diversion, partly because it was evidently designed for the purpose of collecting horses and supplies from the rich districts within the British borders for the use of a larger force which was to follow, but still more because of its constant incentive to that large section of the people which, though it had proved alike its stupidity, timidity and egotism, was Republican to the core. However damp the powder in the barrel, the entry of sparks even so feeble as the armed bands of Kritzinger and Hertzog might provoke an explosion at any moment.

The passage of the Orange placed the two Boer forces at once in rear of the only formed body of troops in Cape Colony. This was part of a brigade of Guards under Major-General Inigo Jones, which was disposed on either side of Norval's Pont, along the Orange river. There was no second line, nor anywhere else a force in being either of foot or horse; only the militia and irregular levies under Major-General Sir H. MacDonald, who commanded at Aliwal North, and of Lieut.-General Sir F. Forestier-Walker at Cape Town were distributed in small guards along the lines of communication. There, however, they were invaluable. The possession of the railways, always of the first importance, becomes practically the sole means of coping with an adversary of superior mobility. Already the British commanders had learned how to wage guerilla warfare on the

* De Wet to Botha, dated from Smithfield, December 10th, 1900.

Importance of the railways. rails. Throughout the complicated operations which followed, the skilful employment of the railways was so constant a feature of their tactics that it will not always be especially remarked upon. For a general scheme of defence this would have been simple enough. The tracks were seldom in the enemy's hands. Their general direction towards the southern ports, through the parallel mountain ranges and desert plains which guarded them like lines of fortifications and glacis, rendered easy the conveyance of troops from the remotest garrisons in South Africa into strong positions covering the most valuable portions of the colony. Against a regular enemy the province could quickly have been rendered impregnable. Armies could have lain in the Roggeveld, the Sneeuw Bergen and the Storm Berg, covering Cape Town, Port Elizabeth and East London as securely as Lisbon was covered from Torres Vedras. But here was an enemy of a different type, one who operated from no base and towards no objective, whose victories lay in escapes, and in the length of time during which he could remain untrapped; who could never be said to advance or retire, but merely to move, now this way, now that, his tactics rendered unfathomable either by utter lack or rapid change of purpose. Against such an opponent cross railroads are the chief need, and these were infrequent in the eastern part of the colony, and altogether absent in the west. In the east, from Hopetown to Cape Town, there existed but one cross communication with the Norval's Pont—Port Elizabeth line; from that, and the Port Alfred line which joined it at Middleburg, to the Aliwal North— East London railway, but one. With what infinite resource these meagre facilities were managed will only be understood when it is told how seldom the great spaces between the lines of railway were free from the presence of roving bands, and how seldom these were unattended by columns which had been hurried into contact by train. In the west the value of the main and only line lay chiefly in its power to provide for the protection of the capital by placing troops in possession of the encircling ranges from either side. For the offensive within the vast equilateral triangle, whose sides, each 300 miles long,

EVENTS IN CAPE COLONY.

were the Atlantic seaboard, the Orange river and the railway itself, the absence of branch lines rendered it useful only as a moveable base.

A strong hold upon the railway system of an extensive theatre of war goes so far to nullify the weakness or faulty disposition of troops in any part, that the Director of Railways and his protecting troops are the real props and executive of strategy. Within a week of the violation of the frontier of Cape Colony, no less than sixteen bodies of troops were within the border and organised for the field. To Hanover Road from the Rouxville district, where they had been left by Major-General C. E. Knox after his operations against De Wet, came the commands of Lieut.-Colonels H. M. Grenfell, G. F. Gorringe and E. B. Herbert; from other parts of the Orange River Colony the columns of Colonel Sir C. Parsons, Lieut.-Colonels A. W. Thorneycroft, R. K. Parke, the Hon. J. H. G. Byng, E. C. Bethune and W. H. Williams and H. de B. de Lisle to Naauwpoort; from the Transvaal, Lieut.-Colonel W. Lowe with the 7th Dragoon Guards and Brabant's Horse; Kimberley provided a force of Yeomanry, whilst Inigo Jones immediately formed three mobile columns under Major H. G. D. Shute at Colesberg, Lieut.-Colonels E. M. S. Crabbe at Petrusville, and the Hon. A. H. Henniker at De Aar. All these were placed under the general command of Major-General Sir H. H. Settle, who had been called up from Cape Town to Naauwpoort on December 18th. His first task was to delimitate the commands. Taking himself the western area, with Headquarters at De Aar, he assigned to Inigo Jones the central, with Headquarters at Naauwpoort, to Sir H. Macdonald the eastern, Headquarters at Burghersdorp. In endeavouring to obtain a grasp of the enemy's plan of campaign a strange difficulty beset him. The closer his touch with Kritzinger and Hertzog—and he was at once in touch—the more uncertain became their motives. On December 18th Shute found Hertzog south of Petrusville; next day Grenfell touched Kritzinger near Venterstad. On the 19th Hertzog passed through Philipstown, and three days later entered Britstown, whilst Kritzinger, though he loitered below Venterstad, still pointed southward on Steyns-

Tactics of the invaders.

burg. Thus there seemed an inclination of the Boer leaders to separate rather than combine, tactics so unusual that it was some time before the British commanders, accustomed as they were to the occurrence of the unexpected in Boer warfare, could realise that bodies so weak had ventured to invade a vast hostile territory on divergent lines and unsupported. When, however, the full significance of such a movement was suspected, it increased the necessity of taking prompt measures against the marauders. Their single-handed persistence and daring left little room for doubt that De Wet himself was soon to form the body to his far-thrown wings. To manœuvre to gain time and a bloodless penetration of Cape Colony became at once the main object of Kritzinger and Hertzog; to destroy them before they could be linked by the redoubtable Commander-in-Chief of the Free State, before, in short, the disconnected forays were transformed into a real invasion, was Settle's insistent problem. Now, therefore, his campaign resolved itself into two distinct operations—the chase of Hertzog in the west, of Kritzinger in the east. By the arrangement of commands above referred to, the pursuit of Hertzog came within his own province, of Kritzinger within that of Inigo Jones and Sir H. MacDonald, and the fortunes of each must be briefly followed.

It would be an endless task to describe in detail the efforts to find and engage in a vast terrain bands whom a single hollow could conceal, who rode fast, and who were bent on nothing so much as avoiding battle. Space denies all but an indication of the toil involved, the constant scouting, marching, and entraining, the never-ceasing contest of wits on the part of the leaders on both sides, of endurance on the part of their men.

Kritzinger heads southward.

On December 26th Kritzinger, shadowed by Grenfell (in command of Gorringe and Herbert), by Colonel A. A. Garstin, who had come from Kimberley to command Lowe, W. H. Williams, Byng and Shute, suddenly headed for Stormberg, was turned back at Henning from crossing the Stormberg—Rosmead railway, and sidling first north-westward between the Zuur Berg and Kikvorsch Berg towards Colesberg, and then southward past Arundel, attacked Sherborne and Bangor on December 30th.

He then went on south, making presumably for the historic centre of Boerdom in Cape Colony, Graaff Reinet. Next day he was not to be seen, and the five columns concentrated at Middleburg and Rosmead to search for him.

At Britstown Hertzog threatened the very centre of the western system of supply, the great depôt at De Aar, and instant efforts were made to chase him thence. On December 23rd Sir H. Settle arrived at De Aar, and on the same day de Lisle, Thorneycroft and Parke marched westward. Hertzog, however, had passed through Britstown, which was occupied by Thorneycroft on the 25th, and was now reported at Strydenburg. Accordingly the columns, moving on a broad front, swung northward, the left on the Ongers river, on the banks of which de Lisle ran into the enemy near Houwater on the 26th. A sharp skirmish resulted in the Boers slipping away towards Prieska; but the encounter proved a valuable reconnaissance, for it revealed both the strength and composition of Hertzog's force, which was discovered to consist of six commandos, 1,200 strong in all, under Hertzog, Brand, Wessels, Pretorius, Theunissen and Nieuhoudt. On this day and the next Sir C. Parsons and Bethune appeared on the scene, the former detraining at Victoria West, the latter at De Aar. Both had been intended to march northward, but on the 28th Hertzog, doubling de Lisle's left flank, struck suddenly southward, arousing fears both for Carnarvon and Victoria West. Bethune was accordingly railed to the latter place, Sir C. Parsons hastened by forced marches to the former, whilst de Lisle, Thorneycroft and Parke clung closely to Hertzog through Vosburg and Brandewyns Kuil. On December 30th the commandos were within seven miles of Carnarvon, and Bethune from Victoria West prepared to turn them back into the arms of the pursuing columns.

Pursuit of Hertzog.

In this he was unsuccessful; but his movements had the effect of diverting the enemy's advance from south to west, and the occupation of Fraserburg and Carnarvon by Sir H. Settle's troops cut all communication between Hertzog and his confederates in the eastern part of the colony. The western and southern counties were still open, however, and these, the

Hertzog turns westward.

richest agricultural districts in all South Africa, were Hertzog's real object. There he could subsist in plenty for an indefinite period, requisitioning with small risk of refusal amongst prosperous farms well stocked with horses, grain and every kind of provender, and inhabited many by open, many by secret sympathisers. At present this hunting ground could hardly be denied to the marauders, and only on his possession of the railways could Sir H. Settle base his hopes of barring Hertzog from the approaches to the capital, and the raiding of the southern seaboard counties, which would turn a mere incursion into a veritable invasion.

Thus the New Year of 1901 saw the virus of rebellion running deeply into the receptive veins of the colony. The Boer plan of campaign was now more obvious than the means of confounding it. Experience had taught that to come to terms with bands like those of Kritzinger or Hertzog by fair chasing was a remote hope. They possessed mobility such as their opponents could never attain. Provided with two or three horses apiece they could always keep ahead of pursuit; made acquainted by the reports of their spies with every granary and pasture, they were sure of supplies; whilst so great was their elasticity that their usual habit was to march and forage at full speed over a front of fifteen or twenty miles, concentrating at a given point at the end of the morning or afternoon stage to receive fresh orders. The only way to deal with such an enemy is to press him hard, and at the same time to throw troops across his path. These tactics must absorb a large number of men, all, indeed, that were available in Cape Colony; and it was now more than a suspicion that Kritzinger and Hertzog were purposely drawing the British troops aside to east and west in order to leave a clear course down the centre of the colony for the expected rush of De Wet. The problem, in short, was of a complexity only to be fully understood when it is remembered on what dangerous ground it had to be worked out; ground beneath which rebellion smouldered like an imprisoned flame, ground upon which rested not only the stability of the armies manœuvring in the Orange River

Difficulties of the campaign.

EVENTS IN CAPE COLONY.

Colony and the Transvaal, but the whole British ascendency in South Africa. The loss of Cape Colony, even temporarily, or even a serious struggle within its frontiers, might transform the whole campaign. Therefore, Cape Town itself stirred uneasily on the news of the inroad of these insignificant bands; the men-of-war lying in its harbours prepared for a possible part in a campaign which had recently seemed to be dwindling far in the interior of the sub-continent towards the Tropic of Capricorn. Loyalty, which never slumbers on a bed so uneasy as Cape Colony, sprang to arms in every county. Within three weeks 10,000 officers and men were enrolled, and despatched in detachments to hold the towns and villages which stood in the path of the commandos. And as for the regular troops, they threw themselves once more into the weary task of running down an enemy swifter than themselves, who promised infinite toil before he could be caught, and little honour in the catching.

On January 1st Sir H. Settle confessed his inability to confine the raiders to the north by moving his Headquarters down to Beaufort West. Next day Thorneycroft and de Lisle, having by great exertions followed Hertzog to Spioen Berg, east of Williston, were obliged to leave him to seek supplies at the railway. Thus disencumbered, Hertzog turned due southward once more, and de Lisle and Thorneycroft were thrown hurriedly into Fraserburg; Sir C. Parsons, few of whose men had mounts, was ordered to follow. It was less likely, however, that Hertzog should trouble to surmount the difficult mountain ranges which intervened between him and Cape Town, than that he should turn them where they sank towards the western seaboard by Clanwilliam and Piquetberg. This, indeed, if done earlier, would have been a master-stroke, and it was not yet too late for the Boer to attempt it if he were really in earnest. Sir H. Settle, therefore, appreciating the fortunate trend of his communications, requested Sir F. W. Forestier-Walker at Cape Town to send a garrison for Clanwilliam by sea, whilst, in order to shut off the south, he railed portions of his own troops to Matjesfontein, whence he extended them westward, Bethune through Sutherland, and Henniker along the passes of the

[Sir H. Settle covers Cape Town.]

Roggeveld mountains, the natural outpost line of Cape Town. This last was a delicate manœuvre, the result of which hung in the balance of moments, until Henniker, by an admirable forced march from the line had made all safe at the passes. Now, therefore, was presented the singular spectacle of one set of forces hurrying southward by train, another northward upon the ocean, converging towards the critical spot at a speed beyond the utmost capacity of their opponents. But Hertzog was as quick to perceive as Sir H. Settle to utilise the dangers of the narrowing angle. He continued to sidle westward, and on January 7th de Lisle was ordered to entrain for the south at Beaufort West, and to move on Clanwilliam by Piquetberg, which was held by a levy under Major H. J. Du Cane, R.A. As Hertzog's westerly movement became more pronounced, Bethune was railed southward to Touws River to follow de Lisle; Lowe and Parke came down to Prince Albert Road; Thorneycroft, still followed by Sir C. Parsons, from Fraserburg to Sutherland; whilst at Matjesfontein, which Sir H. Settle now made his Headquarters, a mounted corps, called Kitchener's Fighting Scouts, was being raised under Colonel Colenbrander for the operations in the west. Henniker, with Du Cane on his left at Piquetberg, remained in the Roggeveld. By January 21st Hertzog found himself cut off from south and east by an advancing semi-circle traced from Sutherland through Ceres, Tulbagh, Piquetberg and Clanwilliam to the open sea itself, where H.M.S. *Sybille*, the true left flank of the British forces, was steaming up to Lamberts Bay. Hertzog immediately drew in his horns. Foraying amongst the farmsteads of Prieska, Kenhardt and Calvinia, he had let slip the moment when he might even have outrun the railway, which had now placed an impenetrable fence of columns in his way. He checked his advance on the Doorn river, and Sir H. Settle, whose chief anxiety up to now had been to save the colony from being overrun, saw that the tide had reached its height, and immediately assumed the offensive.

On January 30th de Lisle and Colenbrander, supported by Bethune, were ordered to cross the Doorn river and march on

EVENTS IN CAPE COLONY.   71

Van Rhyns Dorp and Calvinia, which were occupied on February 6th. They found their advance unexpectedly easy. Hertzog, making no pretence at resistance, fell back rapidly through Williston, and thence past Carnarvon, which de Lisle reached on the 16th. But the Boer leader retired, not in alarm, but in hope; his task in the west was completed, and he was now hastening to take his part in events of which his own incursion had been but the foreshadow. As he marched the chase grew weaker; the same causes which drew him northward with equal urgency calling off his pursuers. More dangerous game than Hertzog was now afoot. *Hertzog falls back.*

Meanwhile, it will be remembered that by the end of December Kritzinger had penetrated the eastern part of the colony as far as Middleburg. On January 1st, 1901, when Colonel D. Haig arrived to take command of the four British columns, Kritzinger was moving southward on New Bethesda, and orders were issued for Lowe and Grenfell to be railed to Graaff Reinet to forestall him by operating northward. Shute's column accompanied them to garrison this, the kernel of Boer influence in the colony, and from this time forth the place was kept quiet, if not loyal, by that officer's administration. Kritzinger, however, who was now marching fast, was first in the town, and on the 4th Haig disposed his forces so as to enclose him, Byng on the east in front of the Cradock border, Grenfell on the south between New Bethesda and Graaff Reinet, Lowe on the west, whilst W. H. Williams remained to hold the passes of the Sneeuw Bergen on each side of the lofty Compass Berg. This pressure was too much for Kritzinger, who on January 6th, finding himself checked in all directions but the west, turned that way as Hertzog had done on the other side of the colony, and for greater safety divided his forces into two parts, one of which under Commandant Scheepers moved on Richmond, the other, under his own leadership, on Murraysburg. Haig at once followed in pursuit, much hampered by the want of reliable information, always the chief difficulty of a commander in chase of separated forces. On the 13th Kritzinger and Scheepers reunited ten miles west of Murraysburg, only to move southward singly once *Pursuit of Kritzinger.*

more, the one by the Willowmore road, the other by that leading to Aberdeen. Haig then sent Lowe round by rail to Prince Albert Road, and attempted to throw Byng and W. H. Williams between the Boer columns, Grenfell falling out to refit at Beaufort West. But the enemy was travelling too rapidly to be caught; on the 18th, Haig, reaching Willowmore, found the commandos still to the south of him, and with nothing between them and the coast. Mossel Bay, Knysna and all the coast townships were in a ferment, the first-named especially, for it was now an important supply depôt for Haig's columns. The place had neither defenders, defences, nor transport until Captain W. L. Grant, R.N., arriving in H.M.S. *Doris*, by great energy succeeded in organising not only fencible forces, but a complete system of supply and communication with Haig. The subsequent appearance of H.M.S. *Widgeon*, which scouted beyond Plettenberg Bay, still further reassured the coast dwellers, who had given themselves up for lost.

On January 19th Lowe, from Prince Albert, was at Klaarstroom, watching, but by no means safeguarding, the approaches to Cape Town, whilst the Free Staters, again separating, sprayed outwards over the seaboard counties, Kritzinger towards Oudtshoorn, Scheepers towards Uniondale. Haig, now for the first time favoured by the configuration of the ground, soon had them in difficulties. Blocking the Oudtshoorn—Klaarstroom end of the Olifants River valley with the columns of Lowe and Grenfell, who had now rejoined, he despatched W. H. Williams to Uniondale, whilst he himself with Byng drove down the Olifants from the direction of Willowmore. Williams, entering Uniondale early on January 21st, all but put a summary end to Scheepers, whom he surprised at breakfast with his commando at the village inn. The Boers escaped, however, with the loss of four of their number. Haig's dispositions now had the effect of herding the enemy amongst the Kammenassie mountains, where, on January 24th, Haig proceeded to surround them by means of Lowe and Grenfell on the west, Williams from the north, Byng from the east, a fifth column—a new organisation of 500 Colonial Defence forces under Colonel G. F. Gorringe—

[margin: Kritzinger near the coast.]

EVENTS IN CAPE COLONY.

approaching from Steytlerville to co-operate. For two days Kritzinger lurked in the mountains, uncertain how to escape, for Haig's troops appeared to occupy every outlet. On January 26th he made a dash for the west by Dysseldorp, but running into Grenfell, who had artfully changed the stations of his piquets after dark, he retired precipitately. An attempt to emerge in the opposite direction near Avontuur was similarly foiled by Major H. E. Gogarty, who had come on from Willowmore with a party of details, the Boers losing five killed and several wounded. But Kritzinger, seeing that he must break out or be lost, renewed his attempt at the same spot before dawn on the 28th, and favoured by the darkness slipped by Avontuur and made for Haarlem, closely pursued by Gogarty, and threatened in front by Gorringe, who was approaching from the east over the difficult mountain ranges between Uniondale and Steytlerville. Kritzinger's commandos lost nine men in the resulting skirmishes, and broke up into small bands, which, scattering northward, fled into the Baviaans Kloof mountains, a stronghold of gorges and precipices.

Meanwhile Scheepers, instead of following his chief eastward, had left him to attempt a break-back through Zuurberg Poort towards Willowmore. The Groote Zwarte Bergen passages were here held by Parke's Yeomanry, whom Haig had especially cautioned to guard a certain footpath by which the enemy might escape. Scheepers' first attempt was frustrated, and he fell back in a somewhat perilous plight. He then heard that a party of Yeomanry was marching to block the footpath in question, which hitherto had been left unguarded. Knowing that his sole hope of safety rested on keeping this outlet open, he advanced towards the approaching troops with the intention of fighting. The Yeomanry, fifty in number, marching carelessly without the proper scouts and flankers, were completely surprised, and after a brief resistance captured; whereupon Scheepers, dashing for the footpath, got clear north of the Groote Zwarte Bergen. Now the Boer leaders, abandoning all idea of concerted action, made haste northward by widely different routes, Scheepers heading towards Beaufort West, Kritzinger in

Kritzinger turned back northward.

the direction of Aberdeen. Grenfell, clinging closely to Scheepers, harried him through Amos Poort, and on February 9th was in front of him at Letjesbosch, on the railway. Grenfell was then ordered into Beaufort West for more urgent operations elsewhere, and Scheepers had a temporary respite. Kritzinger, hunted by Lowe, and raced by W. H. Williams on the railway, made for Swanepoerls Poort, where a vain attempt was made to entrap him, thence over the railway near Klipplaat (February 7th), and north-west, as if pointing on Murraysburg. On February 10th he was at Been Kraal, amongst the headstreams of the Kariega river. Once more Haig reshuffled his cards, railing Byng up from Willowmore to Aberdeen Road for Camdeboo, Gorringe from Uitenhage to Beaufort West for Murraysburg, Lowe to Graaff Reinet to forward supplies, whilst W. H. Williams was sent to beat up the Kariega River valley from its lower end. Byng's appearance at Camdeboo on the 11th had the effect of deflecting Kritzinger north-eastward through Bassons Hoek to near Murraysburg, whence, given no rest, he circled towards Graaff Reinet. On the 16th Byng pushed him hard, whilst Lowe coming from Graaff Reinet by way of Zuurpoort placed himself in front of the commandos. Thereupon Kritzinger, swinging rapidly westward and northward, hurried across the Sneeuw Bergen directly to Dassiefontein, south-east of Richmond. There on February 17th he found the pressure unexpectedly eased by the withdrawal of three of the pursuing columns. The same urgent summons as had relieved Scheepers of Grenfell, and Hertzog of the attentions of de Lisle, Thorneycroft and all the columns in the west, now called Haig with Lowe, Byng and Williams to other parts of the colony. What that summons was Hertzog by this time knew, and Kritzinger and Scheepers could surely guess. De Wet had crossed the Orange river; he had been already a week within the colony, and the time had come for the consummation of the campaign in front of which the three Free State Commandants had scouted long and anxiously from the frontier down to the seaboards of the Atlantic and Indian Oceans.

To the Boers, Transvaalers as well as Free Staters, great

EVENTS IN CAPE COLONY.

events waited on the inroad of De Wet. Two months earlier Kritzinger had written that the Cape farmers were only waiting for the event to rise *en masse*.* Assistant-Commandant-General J. C. Smuts, when on the eve of his temporary triumphs at Modderfontein and against Cunningham in the Gatsrand,† promised to come with General Beyers and 2,000 men to aid an enterprise of which the fruits were to be a "general revolution and declaration of Independence of Cape Colony . . . the beginning, not only of the real independence of the Republics, but also the deliverance of the whole of South Africa and the union of our people into a great nation from Table Bay to the Equator."‡ But his hopes would have soared less high had he known that the Free State Chief had already lost his most trusted weapon, that of surprise. De Wet had indeed been less adroit than usual in retaining it. Lord Kitchener had suspected and fully prepared for his design from its earliest initiation in the interior of the Orange River Colony. The probability of an effort to wipe out the memory of the rebuff from the Caledon had always been recognised. The unrest in the Smithfield and Rouxville districts, and the bold perseverance of Kritzinger and Hertzog in Cape Colony tended to confirm the cloud of rumours which invariably arose whenever the invasion of British soil was in the air.

On January 22nd the Commander-in-Chief was warned that De Wet was on his way to join his commandos, the majority of which had been on furlough, at the Doornberg, north-east of Winburg. Next day the Free State leader, accompanied by President Steyn, crossed the railway near Holfontein Siding, and was traced on his way to the Doornberg, whereupon Major-General Bruce Hamilton at Kroonstad and Major-General C. E. Knox at Leeuw Kop were ordered to concentrate and engage him before he could organise his forces and set out for the south. The two British commanders arranged to attack the Doorn-

---

* Kritzinger to De Wet, December 22nd, 1900.

† See Chapter VII.

‡ Smuts to De Wet, January 20th and February 10th, 1901.

Pursuit of De Wet through the Orange River Colony.

berg on the 28th; but De Wet, who was watching as keenly as he was watched, slipped between the converging columns on the night of the 27th, crossed the Winburg branch line, and moved southward at full speed with more than 2,000 men under Commandants Froneman, Fourie and Haasbroek, two 15-pr. guns and a Vickers-Maxim. C. E. Knox, who was nearer than Bruce Hamilton, followed in pursuit at once with a twin command composed of forces under Lieut.-Colonels T. D. Pilcher (Bedfordshire regiment) and C. P. Crewe (Border Horse), whilst Bruce Hamilton hurried into Winburg and Smaldeel, hoping to be able to throw his troops by train between the Boers and the Orange river. De Wet was travelling at a great pace; but he was driving before him large flocks and herds, the food supplies for his intended campaign, and lingering to let these gain an offing, he allowed Knox to come up with his rearguard on the Tabaksberg, forty miles north of Thabanchu, on January 29th.

Action on the Tabaksberg, Jan. 29th, 1901.

The position was immensely strong, and Knox, sending Pilcher against the front, and Crewe with only 600 rifles and three field guns around the Boer right flank, no less than ten miles distant to the eastward, found his divided forces, which would have been fully employed even if acting together, almost over-matched. Pilcher, attacking doggedly, made ground with difficulty all day against a delaying action, which was dangerous from the accuracy of the shrapnel burst by De Wet's artillerymen. By the evening, with a loss of fifteen killed and wounded, including two officers, he had sent the Boer rearguard after its main body, and occupied its ground. Crewe, isolated to the eastward, fared more hardly. His appearance on the flank endangered the enemy's line of retreat, but he was too weak to push his advantage, and could barely withstand the resistance which his threatening position brought against him. Indeed, only the fine conduct of his troops, especially of the Kaffrarian Rifles, preserved him from destruction, for he was outnumbered by three to one, and it was vital to De Wet to disable him. In a fierce attack made in the afternoon the Boers got so nearly home that they actually surrounded and captured in his lines a Vickers-Maxim gun which had jammed. Crewe was then

EVENTS IN CAPE COLONY.

practically surrounded; but seizing commanding ground in the very midst of the enemy he concealed his transport below it, and entrenched himself successfully, beating off another heavy attack delivered during the night. Altogether his casualties numbered thirty-five, making fifty in both columns. The enemy lost about the same number, but they had Crewe's gun, and had kept their southward road open. On January 30th De Wet, outpacing Knox and forestalling Bruce Hamilton, reached Israels Poort, whence, hearing of no body of British troops between himself and the frontier of Cape Colony, he raced on southward and disappeared. Lord Kitchener now saw that direct pursuit was fruitless, and that De Wet could only be headed upon the same swift steed that had outstripped Kritzinger and Hertzog, the railway. Ordering well-nigh every body of troops in Cape Colony to the strategic points, and summoning the columns of Paget and Plumer from far-distant Balmoral and Brugspruit, he called in Bruce Hamilton and C. E. Knox to Bloemfontein, to entrain for Bethulie. He further withdrew all the township garrisons in the Smithfield and Rouxville districts, and transferred the forces which had been acting in those districts under Lieut.-Colonels E. B. Herbert and J. W. Hughes-Hallett from the right bank of the Orange to the left. Finally at Naauwpoort he concentrated a new mobile force, composed of the 1st (King's) Dragoon Guards and two battalions (900 men) M.I., just landed from England, the Prince of Wales' Light Horse, 3rd Dragoon Guards and G. battery R.H.A. The cavalry and horse artillery were formed into a brigade under Lieut.-Colonel E. C. Bethune; two battalions of mounted infantry with four field guns into a fresh column under Colonel T. E. Hickman (Worcestershire regiment). These and all other troops in Cape Colony were then placed under Lieut.-General the Hon. N. G. Lyttelton, who left the Pretoria—Komati Poort line of communications to take charge of the defence of Cape Colony against the oncoming Free State forces. *Preparations against De Wet's invasion of Cape Colony.*

Whilst all these measures were being prepared against him, De Wet, with singular lack of penetration or information, acquired confidence instead of suspicion from the sudden cessation of the pressure on his rear, and delayed his march upon the Orange. Not until February 4th were his scouts in observation of the river, which they found so strongly guarded on both sides of Norval's Pont that a passage there was out of the question. Thereupon De Wet, crossing the railway at Pompey Siding, struck westward, and was lost to sight at the very moment when close touch would have been most valuable. He cleverly obscured his intentions as well as his movements. Even when it was discovered that he was pointing directly upon Sand Drift, the passage by which Hertzog had entered the colony six weeks previously, the continued presence of strong commandos under Fourie, whom De Wet had purposely detached in the Rouxville district, rendered it by no means impossible that the real invasion was to be from that side, and the westward march nothing but a blind. Awaiting the resolution of these alternatives, and with insufficient troops for both, Lyttelton held his forces in readiness for either until, on February 8th, on which day Fourie followed his chief, Bruce Hamilton, reconnoitring north-eastward from the line of the Slik Spruit, found the country clear. To the west, then, the crossing would probably be made. On February 9th C. E. Knox was ordered from Bethulie to Philippolis, Bruce Hamilton to follow from the Slik Spruit, and the troops in the colony were directed towards Sand Drift.

On the 11th Knox was at Philippolis, Bruce Hamilton at Priors Siding; Plumer, passing through Colesberg, by a forced march reached Onverwacht, on the Seacow river. But these movements, admirably designed to shut in Sand Drift from both banks of the river, were two days too late. De Wet had thoroughly confused his opponents. On February 10th whilst Army Headquarters were telegraphing to Lyttelton that they still believed that the crossing place would be between Bethulie and Aliwal, the Free State leader took all his forces across the Orange by Sand Drift. On the 12th Pilcher, from C. E. Knox's column, traversed the flooded drift far behind him, followed by Bruce Hamilton who, after crossing, turned from the direct pursuit of De Wet to hasten for an intercepting position to the south of him. Then Plumer, coming down the Seacow with Cradock

De Wet crosses the Orange river, Feb. 10th, 1901.

EVENTS IN CAPE COLONY. 79

and Jeffreys in extended line, encountered the heads of the invading commandos at Hamelfontein. This was a critical meeting, for all De Wet's hopes of penetrating into the interior of Cape Colony depended on his being neither delayed nor deflected at this moment. Plumer's problem, on the other side, was of the utmost nicety. To keep the invaders from the vitals of the colony he must not only turn them, but turn them westward. The enemy's left, in short, was the strategical flank, and Plumer, though he fully recognised this was fortunately served by subordinates able to anticipate his orders before they could be conveyed across the field. It happened that the enemy was first struck into by a reconnoitring squadron of the Imperial Light Horse, commanded by Captain G. T. M. Bridges, R.A. Had this party bungled in its tactics infinite harm might have resulted; but the situation was as clear to Bridges as to his chief. He instantly sprang towards the proper flank and, establishing himself in a defensive position, successfully clung to De Wet and warned him away from the east until Jeffreys' column, coming up, finally barred the south and east, and bent the hostile line of advance in the required direction. After a sharp skirmish, in which six of Plumer's men were wounded, the Boers drew off towards Philipstown, whence another part of the Boer vanguard was beaten off by the small garrison, opportunely supported by Henniker's Coldstream Guards, after eleven hours' fighting. *De Wet is turned westward.*

De Wet now began to have misgivings. The preparedness of his adversaries, and their swift recovery from the false scent about Bethulie took him by surprise. He had intended to have penetrated the colony in three separate divisions, but forced marches had much diminished both his strength and mobility; he was already short of 600 men, many of the remainder went afoot; there were hostile columns both before and behind him. He had been compelled already to abandon his southerly incursion; but his enforced deflection might yet turn to his advantage, for Hertzog was pressing to join him with 1,500 fresh horses, the fruits of his forays amongst the stud farms of the west. On February 13th he swung back to the Hondeblafs river, and laagered at De Put, north of Philipstown. Here late in the afternoon he was unearthed by Plumer, who, drawing in his wings at Venter's Valley, had followed the trail closely from Hamelfontein. Hastily mounting, the enemy retreated westward to Wolve Kuil, Plumer, who was beset by a great thunderstorm, being compelled to call a halt at Leeuw Berg, after a march of thirty-four miles. The rain continued to fall; all that night and the next both sides halted knee-deep in water. On the 14th the Boers, anxious to give their convoy time to get away over the quaggy roads which led around the northern end of the Bas Berg, stood firmly on the strong position at Wolve Kuil. Plumer lost no time in attacking, and once more one of his officers, this time Cradock, on his own initiative anticipated his wishes by falling instantly and with vigour upon the Boer left, thus holding them up still to the westward. Contained in front by the King's Dragoon Guards and Imperial Light Horse, and turned by the 3rd Imperial Bushmen and New Zealand Mounted Rifles, after considerable resistance, which cost Plumer fourteen casualties, the Boers followed their transport around the Bas Berg, pursuit being shortly foiled by another storm which laid the tracks two feet deep in mud. Meanwhile C. E. Knox, hampered by the same causes, had not yet reached Philipstown, Pilcher, who led his advance, being still six miles short of that place, which was entered on the 15th. Then Knox, learning how closely Plumer was pressing the commandos, judged that they would soon double southward. Bruce Hamilton had already made De Aar, and Knox took his own troops towards Hout Kraal, where an armoured train and a small column composed of a company of the 3rd Grenadier Guards, two guns and 150 mounted troops under Colonel E. Crabbe had already arrived, expecting to be joined by another under Henniker, which was on the march from Philipstown. These bodies had been hastily formed at De Aar by Sir H. Settle for the express purpose of clinging to De Wet until the regular columns should arrive. At 4.30 a.m. on the 15th, before either Knox or Henniker appeared on the scene, Crabbe discovered the Boers in the act of crossing the railway four miles north of Hout Kraal. De Wet had destroyed

EVENTS IN CAPE COLONY.

the track on either side of the crossing, and the armoured train, which promptly steamed towards the spot, could only shell the rear portion of the convoy, whilst Crabbe was too weak to do more than follow in observation. About noon he was joined by Plumer, whose march in pursuit of the commandos would have been rendered intolerable by the morasses had not these exhausting obstacles held so many derelict Boer wagons as to cheer his men with evidence that the enemy's case was worse than their own. More than twenty wagons, for the most part laden with flour and ammunition, lay embedded in the mud, to be joined soon by as many of Plumer's. The night's scurry from Wolve Kuil and Plumer had indeed reduced the Boers to an abject plight. It confirmed the suspicion which had already arisen in the minds of the majority of the burghers, that their trusted leader's sole triumph in Cape Colony was to be that over the floods of the Orange river, a victory which that uncertain stream might yet avenge. They were now without reserve ammunition or the certainty of supply; horses and men were failing as rapidly as their adversaries were increasing around them. General Fourie, who had remained behind to attempt to extricate the wagons before they fell into Plumer's hands, had disappeared. At this moment their adventure threw off the last rags of the disguise which had begun to drop from it from the day of their entering the colony. Nor was there now any burgher so blind as to mistake this headlong flight for the hurry of invasion. Later on the 15th Henniker joined forces at Hout Kraal, after skirmishing his way through from Philipstown with a few casualties. Next day the chase was resumed. The enemy had pointed on Strydenburg, and Plumer, most of whose supplies were still fast in the bogs of the Bas Berg, pressed on that way to Brits Kraal, followed by Crabbe and Henniker as far as Pienaars Pan, whilst C. E. Knox pushed his leading troops through Hout Kraal to Rhenoster Vlakte. On the 17th De Wet fled northward, intending to strike for Prieska by one of the lower drifts of the Brak river.

De Wet in difficulties.

Whilst resting his weary forces at Gous Pan he was once more marked down by Plumer's efficient Intelligence Staff, conducted by Captain B. Williams, R.E., who, fastening on the spoor, and guided more than all by the receipts for commandeered horses and provender which De Wet thoughtlessly left behind him at every farm, never lost touch with the enemy during 300 miles of tortuous riding. A threat of attack sent the commandos on again, to be hunted as far as Geluks Poort, where their breaking up into various bands seemed to indicate a dissolution. But at this moment Plumer was compelled to call a halt. He was absolutely destitute of supplies; neither man nor horse had fed that day, the latter were almost immoveable from fatigue. He had run himself to a standstill at the very brush of his exhausted quarry. However, a few carts came up during the night, and Crabbe and Henniker, who closed up from the rear, shared what scanty rations they had with Plumer's starving troops, who thought themselves fortunate at receiving one biscuit apiece, with five pounds of grain for their horses, after a succession of forced marches as severe and under conditions as trying as it is possible to conceive. On February 18th the three columns pushed on, tracking the commandos by a trail of foundered horses through Elsjes Vlakte and Gras Vlakte to Krans Pan. There at 4 p.m. the troops once more came in sight of the game, just as their own force was spent and that of De Wet's men renewed by the brief rest which was the reward of their short but irreducible lead. De Wet, too, had made good a measure of his losses in horseflesh by vigorous requisitions, and this advantage he retained throughout by depleting the stables and paddocks close in front of his pursuers. Next day (February 19th) Plumer employed his last fragment of strength in struggling on to Zout Pan. Halting there, he collected the remaining crumbs of his supplies, and picking from the three columns under his command the best mounted men, he despatched them, 230 in number under Major Vialls (3rd regiment Australian Bushmen), towards the banks of the Brak to endeavour after all to deny the passage to De Wet, or at least to keep him in sight. Vialls started at 9.30 a.m. and bivouacked in the evening at Vrouw Pan, having reported to Plumer at 1 p.m. that the Boers were

EVENTS IN CAPE COLONY.

now heading south-west, that is, up the course of the Brak. To intercept this fresh direction seemed impossible, which indeed it was for Plumer. But C. E. Knox, accurately forecasting on the 18th De Wet's dash towards Prieska, and knowing that the Brak ran high, had thrown his own troops wide on Plumer's left flank in the hopes of placing them between De Wet and the river, which a few hours' fine weather would convert from a barrier to an outlet of escape. Three messengers whom he sent to Plumer, who was at that moment lying well-nigh exhausted at Krans Pan, were captured by the enemy's scouts; but Knox, though completely out of touch with his colleague, persisted in his movement, was at Springbok Vlakte on the 19th, and next day at Klip Drift on the Brak river, thus denying to De Wet all but the lower and heavier waters of the Brak. Knox even contrived to send a strong patrol under Pilcher across the raging stream to demonstrate upon the other bank towards Karabee. On the 20th Plumer, bankrupt of every form of supply, was forced to fall back on Elsjes Vlakte, bitterly regretting that—so he thought—he must yield the drifts of the Brak to a quarry who had so barely outstayed him. But Knox's tactics fully counterpoised the enforced abandonment of the direct pursuit. On the day of his appearance at Klip Drift De Wet arrived on the banks of the Brak some ten miles above its confluence with the Orange, and sought eagerly for a practicable drift. But the Brak was a torrent, "its great waves roaring like a tempestuous sea,"* and it would have been less foolhardy to brave the troops of Knox, whose approach was now reported, than the whirlpools of the swollen river. De Wet, however, had hopes of encountering neither. One way of escape still remained, if indeed that could be called escape which exchanged one peril for another, a way so hazardous that De Wet, before he threw the dice, thought proper to submit the chances to Mr. Steyn. This was to double back eastward, past the right flanks of Vialls at Vrouw Pan and Plumer at Elsjes Vlakte, and to dash for the Orange river

_{De Wet foiled at the Brak river.}

* "Three Years War," by C. R. De Wet, 1902.

below Hopetown, trusting that the main stream might have fallen. The plan teemed with dangers. To be discovered meant to be hemmed in between two rivers at present impassable; and even if undetected the Orange might remain in flood, when nothing but a miracle could deliver him. The first throw fell well. Taking advantage of a night of intense darkness, De Wet led his burghers, many of them dismounted, down a broad depression which sheltered him from Vialls' outposts, and striking north-eastward was abreast of Plumer by dawn on February 21st. By this time Vialls had discovered the evasion, and Plumer, receiving his report, hastily threw Crabbe and Henniker in the direction of the Leeuw Berg. C. E. Knox, it should be mentioned, had also anticipated this last shift of De Wet, and had done his best to close the gap between Plumer and the railway by ordering the Kimberley column, which was marching westward from Hopetown, under Major Paris, to halt between that place and Geluks Poort. Then Knox himself, learning the news, began to move north-eastward towards Zout Pan, whilst Bruce Hamilton, who was at this moment driving another band of Boers from Beer Vlei towards Knox, deflected his columns instead towards Strydenburg. De Wet was thus shut into the great loop of the Orange, where it receives the Vaal, by a semicircle of troops curving from the confluence of the Brak river through Blink Kop to Hopetown, whilst Plumer, Crabbe and Henniker, who were hurrying up by different routes to Welgevonden, were close upon him. Still closer, though De Wet did not know it, was a party of Queensland Imperial Bushmen, whom Vialls had despatched from the Brak to keep contact with the commandos. These men, in spite of the difficulty of subsistence —for they carried no supplies and were directly in the wake of an enemy who left the farms bare—never lost the trail from beginning to end of the chase, and their feat was only robbed of its full value by the difficulty of transmitting news to Plumer. For De Wet all depended on the mood of the Orange river. The frontier stream proved to be in league with the waters of the Brak against their common violator. The Orange, although falling, was still impassable. De Wet turned upstream, trying

De Wet doubles eastward.

EVENTS IN CAPE COLONY. 85

every yard for a practicable crossing, only to find each drift a cataract. At the entry of the Vaal river the ferry punts, which ordinarily were moored there, were found to be destroyed. The report that a boat had been discovered some miles higher up sent the despairing commandos cantering in that direction; and though the boat proved to be a mere wherry it was joyfully hailed as a means of escape from the dreaded colony. By the evening of February 21st 200 burghers had been transported over the river by this means, a few more in their eagerness crossing by swimming. The rest bivouacked at nightfall on the left bank, awaiting daylight to enable them to follow their envied comrades. But dawn brought news of Plumer's near approach, and De Wet hurried on to De Kalk, where he off-saddled and halted to draw breath. Here Plumer, who had marched in the dark from Welgevonden, discovered him about 10 a.m. and rushing upon him with all the force his wearied troops could muster, threw him in utter confusion past Kameel Drift, Slyp Steen and Dooters Kraal, the Boers scattering in all directions. At Slyp Steen Plumer was informed about 3.30 p.m. that De Wet's guns were close ahead, with beaten animals. The troop-horses were all but exhausted, but a mixed party of his own and Henniker's men, consisting of the King's Dragoon Guards, Victorian Imperial Bushmen, and Imperial Light Horse, pushed on, led by Colonel Mostyn Owen and Henniker's staff officer, Captain R. J. Marker (Coldstream Guards). After a three hours' chase, which foundered most of the horses, the two pieces of artillery, a 15-pr. and a Vickers-Maxim, were sighted on the road at Disselfontein, surrounded by burghers who, thinking that they had outrun pursuit, were preparing to bivouac. Every Boer immediately galloped in panic from the less than half a dozen troopers with Marker who had been able to urge their horses to the spot. By nightfall, when Plumer ordered a halt at Disselfontein, besides the guns and two ammunition carts, 102 burghers were prisoners, an unlooked-for celebration of the anniversary, the forty-seventh, of the foundation of their native State. Meanwhile, little more fortunate, De Wet and the rest struggled on upstream, hoping,

Finds the Orange impassable.

Capture of De Wet' guns.

but scarcely expecting, to be able to double by the west of Hopetown and strike across the railway below the town towards Petrusville. But De Wet's rapid countermarch from the Brak river had actually saved him, by bringing the pursuit closer on his heels. When it had become certain that De Wet, foiled at the Pont, at Mark's Drift and every other drift within the angle of the Vaal confluence, was pushing south-east up the left bank of the Orange, it became of the first importance to intercept as well as press him. Pursuit alone, the hotter it was made, could but tend to drive him the faster out of the imprisoning angle towards an outlet only partially filled by Paris at Geluks Poort. Plumer, of course, could not abandon the direct pursuit. It was his incessant harrying alone which had turned De Wet's retreat into a rout. At any moment he might run the Boer down, and he knew too well the danger of relaxing even for an hour the pressure on so elusive a quarry. It was for the commanders in rear to provide the "stops," and one of these was prompt to recognise the emergency. Henniker, marching northward from Verlaten Dam upon Welgevonden, had perceived the advantage to be gained by a change of direction; but though permission to turn eastward was given as soon as asked, it came too late. De Wet indeed had escaped but narrowly at De Kalk and Disselfontein; but he asked no more; he could at least run as fast as his pursuers could follow. As he approached Hopetown he learned that Paris' column extended between that place and Middelplaats. The discovery little dashed his rising hopes of safety. Paris' column was small, and alone. A rapid night ride would carry him around its flank with less risk than that which had led him past Plumer's associated columns at Welgevonden. De Wet's chief anxiety was for his dismounted men, of whom he was now hampered by many. These it was impossible to take with him on a march so fast and far as that which lay before him. He therefore detached this unhappy band under Commandant Haasbroek, and bade them strike by a short cross road for the banks of the Orange, where they must trust to fate for a crossing. Then with the rest he rode all night clear around Paris, passing outside, that is, to the

EVENTS IN CAPE COLONY. 87

westward of him, until, having got well to the south of Hope- De Wet passes Hopetown.
town, he turned sharply eastward and broke across the railway
above Kraankuil at 11.30 on the morning of February 24th.

Meanwhile Bruce Hamilton, by hard marching, had reached Strydenburg. At De Aar he had received orders from the Commander-in-Chief to block the west and south; and moving up the Ongers river about Houwater he had been in touch since February 21st with a strong commando, evidently not that of De Wet, which he had chased northward through Beer Vlei, until, as described, the movements both of his own quarry and of De Wet himself turned him towards Strydenburg. Bruce Hamilton soon discovered that he was on the heels of no less Reappearance of Hertzog.
a personage than Hertzog, then hurrying from the raided western counties to join his chief. On the evening of the 23rd Hertzog was still in front of Hamilton, travelling north-eastward with the evident intention of effecting a junction with De Wet above Hopetown; but, turned, as De Wet had been, by the troops at Middelplaats, he swung eastward instead, and darted in two bands for the railway. Bruce Hamilton, who was in Strydenburg early on the 24th, thus found the pursuit of both the Free State leaders temporarily in his hands alone. For the moment Plumer and C. E. Knox, both beyond Hopetown, were out of the chase. Only Paris, turning rapidly southward from his now useless Middelplaats—Hopetown line, was following the stragglers of De Wet's broken bands north of the Elands Berg. Lyttelton had already, on the 23rd, ordered Thorneycroft, who had been left in a watching position further down the line, to entrain at De Aar for the north, to attempt to intercept De Wet wherever he should strike the line. With the rest of his troops he made after Hertzog's divided commando, which he was unable to prevent from crossing the railway at Paauwpan and Potfontein. Thorneycroft went very near to better fortune. At 10.30 a.m., an hour before De Wet began to cross above him, his trains arrived at Kraankuil; but the station was so congested with transport trains that Thorneycroft did well to get his column on the march by 2 p.m., when he hurried after De Wet to Bakoven Pan. Next day, February 25th, he pressed on the trail

towards Zoutpans Drift, to learn that De Wet had turned from that impracticable passage towards Petrusville. Thorneycroft heard also of Hertzog's approach from across the railway, in strength reported as 1,500 men. Whilst he continued the pursuit up the Orange, Plumer and C. E. Knox marched into Hopetown, Crabbe and Henniker into Kraankuil, and a newly arrived column, under Hickman from Hout Kraal, to Philipstown. Of these Knox alone received some compensation for the enormous and apparently wasted exertions of the past ten days. News having been brought to him that Haasbroek's horseless unfortunates were engaged in stealing across the Orange by means of a small boat below Hopetown, Knox despatched thither the Scottish Yeomanry. Although the majority of the fugitives had crossed when the troops arrived, they secured thirty-seven burghers, killed ten, and were only prevented from doing greater damage by the jamming of the Maxim gun.

The Orange still impassable. Meanwhile, the commandos flying with De Wet were undergoing every vicissitude of hope and fear. The cheering effect of the successful passage of the railway was brief enough. The Orange was still inexorable; it ran even higher than before; Zoutpans Drift was impassable; Bosjesman's Drift, Vissers Drift, Lemoenfontein Drift, by Petrusville, were the same, and Thorneycroft chased the fugitives furiously through that town. A still greater danger than the direct pursuit was the column of Hickman, which was coming up on the flank from Philipstown; but from this the Boers were delivered by an error of tactics on the part of their opponents. Hickman had rightly intended to march straight on Sand Drift, where he might well have anticipated the commandos. Instead, he received an order to go to Petrusville, which would bring him in touch with Crabbe and Henniker, but must inevitably place him behind instead of before De Wet. As he reached De Put Hickman discovered the Free Staters hurrying out of Petrusville across his front eight miles ahead. He immediately dashed for the mouth of the Hondeblafs river; but he was too late; the enemy was already to the south of him. Meanwhile, Crabbe and Henniker reached Kalkfontein, Thorneycroft halting outside Petrusville.

EVENTS IN CAPE COLONY.

Lyttelton now rested upon the railway, the last expectation of heading De Wet, and he ordered Plumer to entrain for Colesberg, where Byng, from Haig's command, was about to detrain, whilst W. H. Williams and Lowe, from the same force, had been railed to Hanover Road, with orders to advance on Philipstown. With the Boers every hope centred on Sand Drift, and many a prayer went up that the gateway which had ushered the commandos in to the conquest of Cape Colony should now let the remnants of them out to save themselves from destruction. But here, too, the water covered man and horse, and the two burghers who tested the crossing for the rest all but lost their lives. As De Wet, his hopes nearly extinguished, turned once more upstream, he was joined at last by Hertzog and Brand with all their burghers; with them came Fourie, last seen below the Bas Berg. Such a union, effected in the very midst of encircling columns, and in the course of a disastrous flight, constituted a tactical feat as wonderful as it was now useless. Hertzog's reward for his bold entry into the zone of peril could only be to share the confusion and perhaps the capture of his general. On February 27th the British cordon began to tighten round both, though the converging movements were much retarded in the case of some of the columns by delays in the railway arrangements, of others by the length of the marches and the severe storms which ruined the marching. The neglect to post signallers on Coles Kop, whose lofty summit became visible to every column in turn, further militated against speedy communication and transmission of orders and information. On this day Hickman was in closest touch with the enemy, whom he might have shut in had the line of the Seacow been held in time. On the 28th Byng was about De Eerste Poort, intending to throw his right to the Orange at Twyfel Poort, his left towards Karee Kuil, where Lowe and Williams would link him with Hickman at Venters Valley. On Hickman's left at Riet Valley was Thorneycroft, coming down to close the Hartzen Berg from Kattegat, Crabbe and Henniker at Elands Kloof beyond, completing the circle to the river. Plumer was hastening up from Colesberg; Paris, who since the 24th had been on the trail of a wandering party in the direction of Britstown, was approaching Venter's Valley from Kraankuil. These movements, improvised by consultation between the various commanders during the morning of the 28th, were in progress when they were suddenly interrupted, about 2 p.m., by the news that De Wet had already crossed the Seacow river opposite Goede Hoep, and was two hours on his south-eastward way. Byng, who was at that time about Weltevreden, immediately threw his flankers out to Bastards Nek—Rietfontein Ridge, following with his main body to Ortlepp's Request, marching forty-five miles during the day in the endeavour to get to the Orange at Colesberg Bridge before De Wet. But his efforts were in vain. A long night march had carried De Wet across the front of the columns, and on to the bank of the Orange at Leliefontein, close to Colesberg Bridge. Here was a drift, the fifteenth which he had sounded during his flight, but one so little known and used that there seemed small chance of its proving the prayed-for means of salvation. With intense anxiety the burghers watched the progress of the few whom De Wet ordered to essay the passage. The stream still ran high; it washed over the saddles; but just as a cry of despair went up over yet another failure, the horses floundered into shallow water and emerged on the other side. "Soon," wrote the Free State leader in after days, "the river was one mass of men from bank to bank."* Thus, with psalms of thankfulness for their deliverance, the broken rabble rushed from the territory into which, a little more than a fortnight before, they had ridden to conquer. Their campaign had been but one headlong flight; abandoned guns, horses, transport, and prisoners marked their track. Their reputation amongst their adherents in Cape Colony had fallen as low as their confidence in themselves. That they, who had lost everything else, still retained their trust in their leader was on this occasion at least more to the credit of his irresistible personality than to any display of skill. De Wet's invasion had been guided by little of the tactical genius which had led, and was again

De Wet escapes across the Orange river, Feb. 28th, 1901.

---

* "Three Years War," by C. R. De Wet.

to lead, to successes which made his name famous. Truly, once on the left bank of the Orange he was guiltless of the misfortunes of his burghers. There he was crushed by superior numbers, worn down by men as inexhaustible as himself, warred against by the rivers, until his mere escape from such odds seemed a military miracle. His error lay rather in the initial strategy of his campaign; in the advertisement of his intentions by the despatch of Kritzinger and Hertzog in advance; by the delay in supporting his forerunners until his opponents had ample time alike to comprehend the warning, to reduce his detachments to impotence, and to prepare for himself. His own undisguised and dilatory march from the Doornberg had but intensified the rashness of his passage of the Orange. Not for one moment had Cape Colony been in danger; and if the exertions of the British columns in pursuit of him had been almost superhuman, it was rather in the fervent hope of capturing his person, the highest prize in all South Africa, than of foiling his campaign, the futility of which had been apparent from the first.

THE WAR IN SOUTH AFRICA.

APPROXIMATE STRENGTH STATES OF COLUMNS REFERRED TO IN FOREGOING CHAPTER.

COLUMN.	Mounted Troops.	Infantry.	Guns, including Vickers-Maxims.	Machine Guns.	
December, 1900—February, 1901.					
Maj.-Gen. Sir H. MacDonald	140	500	2	1	
Lt.-Col. H. M. Grenfell	450	—	3	—	
Lt.-Col. G. F. Gorringe	500	—	1	—	
Lt.-Col. E. B. Herbert	380	640	2	2	
Col. Sir C. Parsons	195	320	2	—	
Lt.-Col. A. W. Thorneycroft	500	150	5	—	
Lt.-Col. R. K. Parke	500	—	—	1	
Lt.-Col. the Hon. J. H. G. Byng	380	—	3	—	
Col. E. C. Bethune	130	—	2	—	
Lt.-Col. W. H. Williams	340	—	3	6	
Lt.-Col. H. de B. de Lisle	639	3	3	—	
Lt.-Col. W. H. M. Lowe	400	—	2	1	
Col. A. A. Garstin	200	300	2	1	
Maj. H. G. D. Shute	200	350	2	1	
Lt.-Col. E. M. S. Crabbe	122	360	2	1	
Lt.-Col. the Hon. A. H. Henniker	220	640	2	2	
Maj. H. J. Du Cane	220	300	2	—	
Maj. H. E. Gogarty	640	—	1	—	
Lt.-Col. T. D. Pilcher	1,070	82	7	2	} Maj.-Gen. C. E. Knox in command.
Lt.-Col. C. P. Crewe	640	—	4	2	
Maj.-Gen. B. Hamilton	400	—	7	2	
Col. S. C. H. Monro	320	480	2	—	
Maj.-Gen. A. H. Paget	100	2,200	4	3	
Col. H. B. Jeffreys	455	—	8	—	} Brig.-Gen. H. C. O. Plumer in command.
Lt.-Col. M. Cradock	503	—	2	2	
Lt.-Col. J.W.Hughes-Hallett	25	385	2	1	
Col. T. E. Hickman	880	—	5	—	
Maj. A. Paris	326	176	3	—	

CHAPTER V.

EVENTS IN THE ORANGE RIVER COLONY.
(*Continued from Chapter III.*).*

FEBRUARY—JUNE, 1901.

ON February 10th, his pinions already considerably shorn, De Wet passed out of his native country to begin that feverish rush of seventeen days over the northern portion of Cape Colony described in the previous chapter. His departure left to the Orange River Colony an interlude of comparative quiet. Only B. Campbell and Colonel G. E. Harley (who succeeded the invalided Boyes) manœuvred about Harrismith, whilst small columns, under Major W. G. Massy, Lieut.-Colonel E. C. Ingouville Williams and Major J. E. Pine-Coffin, revolved about Bloemfontein, Heilbron and the Doornberg under the auspices of Lieut.-General C. Tucker, the commander of the lines of communication. Amongst other successful performances Williams withdrew the garrisons and inhabitants of Frankfort and Ventersburg, the latter after a sharp engagement which cost eleven casualties. But the peace was short-lived. On the last day of February De Wet brought with him in his leap back to his own side of the Orange a dozen columns and a very whirl of activity. The operations at once resolved themselves into two distinct portions, *i.e.*, those to the east and west of the Bloemfontein railway. The latter, as being concerned with the immediate pursuit of De Wet, will be first dealt with.

On the day after De Wet's passage at Leliefontein, Plumer, whose columns were in Paget's command, crossed the Orange in pursuit at Norval's Pont; C. E. Knox, Pilcher and Lieut.-Colonel

<small>Pursuit of De Wet continued.</small>

* See map No. 64.

C. P. Crewe and Lieut.-Colonel E. C. Bethune crossed at Orange River Bridge, the first being thus immediately behind the fugitive, the others upon his left (western) flank. Plumer earnestly desired to find himself at Springfontein, whence it would be possible to throw himself into Philippolis and across the front of the commandos. Indeed, had his plans been carried out, he would now, even at this eleventh hour, most surely have cut De Wet off from the north, and perhaps have brought about his ruin. Plumer's two columns, Colonel H. B. Jeffreys' and Lieut.-Colonel M. Cradock's, had been entrained at Hopetown in three parties, the first comprising Jeffreys, the second Cradock, the third Plumer himself and his staff. All were on the rails in excellent time to be carried across the river past De Wet to Springfontein. But on arriving at Colesberg Plumer found to his chagrin that Jeffreys had been ordered to detrain at that place; his trains blocked the way of Cradock's and the rest, and much invaluable time was lost before the troops could be again sent on their way. Not until late on March 1st was Plumer in Springfontein, whence he hurried across to Philippolis, only to learn that De Wet had already passed on his way to Fauresmith, parting with Hertzog, whom he had deflected with 500 men towards Luckhoff. Paget, who had accompanied Plumer's columns, then returned to Springfontein, after sending orders to Massy, who happened to be well placed to the west of Edenburg to be on the alert to act as a "stop." Plumer, continuing the pursuit northward, made forced marches to Zuurfontein (March 4th) and Fauresmith (5th), but by no exertions could he gain upon De Wet, who, putting forth equal efforts, kept from eighteen to twenty hours ahead. Nor could Plumer gain touch with any friendly column until, having crossed the Riet river at Kalabas Drift, he came in signalling communication with Bethune on his left late on the night of March 5th. Bethune had crossed at Orange River Bridge on the 1st, and had only made less speed than Plumer because of the necessity of dealing with the strong flank guards which De Wet threw out as he posted northward. One of these, nearly 1,000 strong, he all but brought to action at Openbaar on the 4th and 5th, and a small wagon laager fell

EVENTS IN THE ORANGE RIVER COLONY. 95

into his hands. Both columns then pushed for the Modder river, which Plumer reached at Abrahams Kraal on the 7th, when Bethune entered Petrusburg behind him. The news of De Wet was for once authentic, but the reverse of encouraging. He was still eighteen hours ahead of the columns, a lead which there was now little hope of reducing, for Plumer was obliged to halt a whole day for supplies. When Plumer reached Hagenstadt on March 10th, De Wet had not only doubled his former advantage, but had practically thrown out the chase by turning eastward and breaking across the railway nine miles north of Brandfort. Plumer followed to Brandfort on the 11th, his last hopes of coming to terms with De Wet being there extinguished by torrential rains, which stopped all progress on the 12th. Giving up the pursuit he went into Winburg on the 15th, and four days later entrained his column for Pietersburg, having thus, in the course of a single month, performed arduous service in the remotest extremities of the theatre of war. His subsequent operations in the Northern Transvaal are elsewhere described.* At this time Major-General A. H. Paget returned to England.

Bethune found Petrusburg infested with the enemy, even before the last of Plumer's troops had quitted it. A party of thirteen men of Plumer's force, who had been left in charge of some empty wagons, had already been attacked, and when Bethune entered the place he found them disarmed, having been captured and released in the brief interval between Plumer's departure and his own appearance. When next day (8th) Bethune marched on for Abrahams Kraal, he left an ambuscade in Petrusburg; but the Boer patrols which entered the town behind his rearguard were saved by the discharge of a premature shot. The enemy, in short, appeared to be on every side. A convoy of empty wagons which Bethune despatched towards Bloemfontein was heavily attacked on this day, and only extricated by the prompt arrival of reinforcements from the column. On March 13th Bethune entered Bloemfontein, where he remained awaiting orders.

* See Chapter VIII.

The ubiquity of these small commandos was not at once to be accounted for. As he had done after his first rebuff from Cape Colony in December, De Wet had sought safety in dispersion, splitting his force into no less than twenty units, each of which, under its own Field-Cornet, repaired towards its local habitation, skirmishing with whomsoever it met on the way. Thus every column engaged in driving northward was surprised to fall in with bands which seemed to have little connection with De Wet's supposed general retirement. C. E. Knox, crossing the Orange on March 4th with Pilcher and Crewe, and marching by Ramah and Koffyfontein, found the enemy on the 8th at Venter's Poort, where one of Pilcher's patrols, advancing too far to the front, was lost, three being killed, five wounded, the rest, numbering nine men and an officer, captured. Next day Crewe, who was marching apart from Pilcher, ran down near Olievenberg, to the south of the Bloemfontein—Petrusburg road, a convoy belonging to the Petrusburg commando, which like the rest was returning to its own district. After a chase of sixteen miles Crewe secured the whole, consisting of twenty-one vehicles, and some 11,000 head of stock; but he soon had to fight hard to hold his capture. At 4 p.m. a strong body made desperate efforts to retake their supplies at Driekop, and were only driven off at dark. This, it will be seen, occurred within a few miles and hours of the passage of Plumer and Bethune. On March 11th C. E. Knox entered Bloemfontein, where Crewe left him to take part in the operations in Cape Colony. There remained but one column engaged in the pursuit on the west of the railway, namely, that of Colonel D. Haig, which had crossed the Orange from Norval's Pont three days later than Plumer. Haig made for Philippolis, and De Wet being now hopelessly out of reach, he turned instead upon Hertzog, whom he pushed in the direction of Luckhoff. Haig was then called in to the line, and moving by Fauresmith and Jagersfontein, reached Edenburg on March 10th.

Meanwhile, on the east of the railway, Lieut.-General the Hon. N. G. Lyttelton had been organising an operation of a more coherent nature than the improvised scurry after De Wet

De Wet again disperses his forces.

EVENTS IN THE ORANGE RIVER COLONY. 97

on the western side. This was a "drive" on a broad front from the Orange river to the Bloemfontein—Thabanchu—Basutoland line of posts, which was reinforced by Harley's (late Boyes') column from Sir L. Rundle's command. For this purpose Lyttelton took under his control the three columns (Lieut.-Colonels Monro, Maxwell and White) of Bruce Hamilton's command at Aliwal North, Colonel T. E. Hickman's column at Bethulie, Haig's at Edenburg, and that of Thorneycroft, who, having crossed the river at Norval's Pont on March 6th, was at Springfontein on the 9th. On March 10th Lyttelton began his advance, and for the next ten days the array rolled slowly northward, hampered at every mile by enfeebled oxen and tracks axle-deep in mud, and by an ever-increasing mob of captured cattle. The enemy's bands scattered in all directions, but few fell victims, for the enclosing lines were by no means so impenetrable as had been hoped. First Hickman, then Thorneycroft and finally Bethune fell in on the left of the line as it progressed, whilst Pilcher placed himself by Harley's side at Hout Nek to act as a "stop." On March 20th the operation closed at the defended line with seventy prisoners, 4,300 horses and an enormous mass of stock to its credit.

The columns then dispersed in accordance with a redistribution of commands which had recently taken effect in the Orange River Colony. Bethune, clearing the country by Winburg and Ventersburg, repaired to Kroonstad on April 2nd. There he came under command of Major-General E. L. Elliot, who, having recently arrived in South Africa from India, had been allotted the northern section of the province down to the line Bultfontein—Winburg—Ficksburg and west of Frankfort—Reitz—Bethlehem, beyond which Sir L. Rundle retained his jurisdiction. Thorneycroft marched into Bloemfontein on March 19th, thence on the 26th to Brandfort, replacing now the departed Crewe as a unit of C. E. Knox's sphere, which on the north marched with that of Elliot, and on the south terminated along the line Petrusburg—Thabanchu—Ladybrand. South of this Lyttelton commanded down to the Orange river, Haig proceeding to Commissie Drift on the Caledon river to strengthen

Distribution of commands in the Orange River Colony.

the watch on the frontiers of Cape Colony. Finally, Bruce Hamilton, with Hickman's in addition to his own three columns, after commencing a fresh sweep from the Basuto border towards Wepener and Dewetsdorp, was ordered to concentrate southward to intercept an expected northerly movement on the part of the invaders of Cape Colony, where Kritzinger especially seemed about to be hustled back across the Orange river.* On the last day of March Bruce Hamilton had all his columns in and about Springfontein.

The various manœuvres recorded above were not made without an immensity of labour and incident, which were not always commensurate with the damage inflicted on the enemy's fighting strength. Now, as long after, the columns, passing through almost virgin tracts of hostile territory, had strict orders to clear the country wherever they moved; and often a commander, when in not too promising pursuit of some body of the enemy, found himself in doubt as to whether he should not turn from the possibly fruitless chase to the certain profit to be gained from the teeming flocks and herds, the spreading crops, and the well-garnished farmhouses which surrounded him. The decision of leaders in such situations will commonly be in favour of the enemy, who would probably in any case escape, and against the stock and produce which cannot. There will be few willing to risk the verdict of failure which will be incurred by one whose very zeal after the foe brings him into his base with nothing to his credit, neither prisoners, nor herds, beasts and tons of farm stuffs. The duties of pursuit and clearance are always widely separated; they are actually antipathetic when fugitives so mobile and resourceful as Boer commandos lead the chase. The failure resulting from the attempt to compass both ends, and the delusive gains of a sole devotion to the less important aim were alike seen too often during the campaign in South Africa to be omitted from its history.

Massy and E. C. Ingouville Williams, their duty of blockading De Wet on the west of the railway ended by the

* See Chapter X.

EVENTS IN THE ORANGE RIVER COLONY.

Boer leader's disappearance eastward, recrossed the line on March 24th and, combined as one column under Williams, successfully swept up the neighbourhood of Heilbron until the middle of April. Similar duties about Ficksburg, Thabanchu and Vrede, the last of which was now completely evacuated,* occupied the mobile portion of Sir L. Rundle's Harrismith command, namely, the columns of B. Campbell and Harley; Pilcher, from Bloemfontein, co-operating with Harley in the more westerly operations. Finally, to complete the account of March, the doings of Major A. Paris' Kimberley column must be briefly mentioned. After playing his part in the pursuit of De Wet in Cape Colony, Paris had returned to his own district, reaching Kimberley on March 12th. From the 26th he raided between the railway at Boshof, continually and sometimes heavily engaged with bands found at Doornbult, Raadel, Kameelfontein and the adjacent farms. All of these he dispersed with the loss to his own force of six killed and a few wounded, and on April 2nd returned to Kimberley with 9,000 head of stock, having taken or destroyed some forty vehicles besides and a large amount of foodstuffs.

The early days of April, 1901, were spent by the troops in the Orange River Colony in refitting and reorganising in accordance with the scheme of redistribution above detailed. Their greatest need, however, at this time was certainly that of a definite object. De Wet's wholesale dissemination of his army had practically paralysed the initiative of his opponents, who found themselves forced to a necessity the most uninspiring to an energetic army, that of undertaking something for no better reason than the undesirability of doing nothing. De Wet, repudiate as indignantly as he might the term "guerilla,"† only failed to shine when he undertook operations which encroached on the province of legitimate warfare. None employed worse than he the arts necessary to united action for a grand purpose,

---

* See Chapter IX.

† "Three Years' War," by C. R. De Wet, page 282. The Boer leader failed to observe that the term "guerilla" refers not to a measure but a form of warfare.

such, for instance, as the invasion of Cape Colony; none better the thousand annoyances, distractions and local triumphs which are the best arms of the outnumbered partisan. Especially was he skilful in the timely use of the weapon of dispersion, to which, as has been seen, he never failed to resort when danger, want or fatigue became too pressing. Time after time he had thus in one moment torn to pieces the plans of the British Headquarters, cancelled their carefully compiled lists of his commandos, and obliterated all traces of his own much sought-for person, which certain staff officers only lived to shadow, detective like, day and night. Such an artifice as this dispersion, indeed, can seldom lead to success; but it may often atone for failure, and the commander of regular forces who finds the terrain dominated by innumerable small bands in place of a single large and tangible body will usually confess that the last state of his district is worse than the first. Confronted by circumstances such as these, the army in the Orange River Colony, in default of an enemy, had to content itself with warring instead upon the countryside on which he subsisted.

In the first week of April Elliot had partially completed at Kroonstad the organisation of a division 6,000 strong, composed of the three columns of H. de B. de Lisle, R. G. Broadwood and E. C. Bethune. On the 10th he moved out with the object of sweeping the western side of the railway up to the Vaal, travelling slowly, both to effect a thorough clearance and to acclimatise his men and animals, many of whom were fresh to campaigning. With very little incident the three columns worked northward in line, and on April 15th Bethune on the left touched the Vaal at Vlakfontein, followed next day by Broadwood in the centre to Rensburg Drift, de Lisle somewhat withholding the right at Paardekraal. At Parys, which Bethune entered on the 17th, the column of E. C. Ingouville Williams, from Wolvehoek, was met with. Since April 9th Williams had been conducting a successful raid within the quadrilateral formed by the lines Wolvehoek—Heilbron—Frankfort—the Vaal river. Putting in at Wolvehoek on the 17th, he had been ordered by Elliot to co-operate with the cavalry division on the west of the

Elliot's first "drive."

EVENTS IN THE ORANGE RIVER COLONY.

railway. A south-easterly swing then brought in Elliot's force on the 20th to Vredefort Road, where it was revictualled. Williams returned to Wolvehoek to hand over his column to Lieut.-Colonel W. G. B. Western, he himself proceeding to Pretoria to command a new contingent from New South Wales. The booty obtained by both commanders had been chiefly in the nature of supplies, and the amount brought in from the area which had been partially cleared—a mere strip bordering on the railway and the Vaal—bore testimony to the magnitude of the task of subjugating a nation of farmers by such means. Up to April 20th Elliot had secured 35,000 head of stock, forty-seven wagons and carts, 184,400 lbs. of grain. His losses in killed and wounded exactly equalled those of the enemy, namely, three killed, five wounded, but the columns had come the worst out of the trifling exchanges by the loss of a complete patrol of an officer and thirty-five men, who were taken on the Rhenoster river on the 14th, and subsequently released. Williams' two raids had resulted in the gathering of 14,500 animals and twenty-four vehicles, besides the destruction of thousands of bags of flour and of the mills which had ground it. After one day's pause Elliot disposed his troops for a second march, this time to the east of the line.

The new plan, communicated by the Commander-in-Chief on April 14th, was of greater scope. Whilst Elliot's three columns moved eastward, on the broad front Heilbron—Lindley, C. E. Knox, from the south, would drive the scattered bodies hovering between Senekal and Bethlehem in the way of the march by despatching a column towards Reitz; Western performing a similar service from the opposite flank, from the line of the Wilge river north of Frankfort. When his left-hand column should have cleared Heilbron, Elliot, pivoting his other two units on that place, would circle northwards, his right passing through Frankfort, the whole then moving upon the Vaal. During this second phase columns were to come out from Standerton and Heidelberg towards him. Finally, as a third phase, the whole line, turning at the Vaal, would sweep down the Klip river, inside the line Frankfort—Tafel Kop—Vrede to

Elliot's second "drive."

the borders of Natal, when it would have scoured the great triangle whose angles lie at Vereeniging, Heilbron and Botha's Pass.

In accordance with the first part of this scheme, from the 24th to the end of April Bethune moved eastward from Vredefort Road to Heilbron, Vechtkop, Uitkyk, Hamburg; de Lisle from Roodeval by Tulbagh, Elandskop, Kleinkop ; Broadwood from Honingspruit by Lindley and Buffelsvlei. In the neighbourhood of Reitz on the 28th Broadwood momentarily came in sight of Pilcher, from C. E. Knox's force,* who thus performed the duty assigned him under the scheme of combination.

On the 30th Elliot re-rationed his whole command in midveld from a convoy which came out from Heilbron, and next day a twenty-five mile march took Headquarters and de Lisle's column into Frankfort. At this time a few small Boer convoys flitted about the front, of which one was now and then brought in by one or other of the columns to swell the enormous booty which Elliot was accumulating. After four days' raiding, with some skirmishing, from Frankfort up to the Vaal, Elliot, hearing of the richness of the country towards Vrede, decided to traverse it. When on the point of starting Broadwood became unfitted for immediate work and was sent back to Heilbron under an escort which turned its journey into profit by capturing on the way two Boer laagers, with sixteen prisoners, thirty-five vehicles and 500 cattle. De Lisle then took over Broadwood's column, Lieut.-Colonel R. Fanshawe replaced de Lisle, and Colonel W. H. M. Lowe relieved Bethune, who was also temporarily absent. On May 7th the columns lay as follows : Lowe at Villiersdorp, de Lisle at Parys and Perth, Fanshawe at Tafel Kop. On the 9th Cornelia was cleared, and the next day de Lisle surprised and surrounded Vrede, taking seven prisoners. The curious nature of this species of warfare was seldom better exemplified than by the fact that Fanshawe, supporting de Lisle to Driespruit, that is, immediately in rear of an irresistible combination of troops, was hotly engaged through-

* See page 101.

out his march, a portion of his rearguard being at one time surrounded. Approaching De Lange's Drift on May 11th, communication was established with Lieut.-Colonel A. E. W. Colville's column from Standerton. Two days later Elliot handed over to Colville for escort to the line twenty-three prisoners, 70,000 head of stock, 106 captured vehicles and many more belonging to the refugees, who numbered 826 souls; all these were the proceeds of only ten days' operations, for the General had already sent back with the convoy returning to Heilbron thirty-three carts and wagons and nearly 9,000 stock. At De Lange's Drift Bethune rejoined the command.

The fourth phase of the operation comprised a four days' south-easterly sweep parallel to and on the west of the Klip river, on the other side of which Colville kept in line, having on his own outer flank a small column under Lieut.-Colonel F. J. Pink, from Zandspruit, which scoured the Verzamel Berg.* At every mile the country became more difficult, for not only had the columns to cross the innumerable tributaries of the Klip, but they were approaching the buttresses of the Drakensberg, which become more broken as they protrude westward and sink to the great plateau on which they are founded. On May 19th Elliot called a halt at the mouth of Botha's Pass, through which he sent his wagons to be refilled at Newcastle, and a further 22,000 head of stock, the gleanings of the Klip basin.

The increasing activity and numbers of the enemy had for some days past aroused a suspicion in Elliot's mind that he was intruding upon some secret haunt of the enemy. For example, at Vlaknek and Rietport Passes, the western posterns to the greater gateway of Botha's Pass, the Boers had strongly disputed the passage on the 18th; indeed, Lowe could scarcely have forced Rietport without the aid of de Lisle, who, having fought his way through Vlaknek, sent a detachment to open the other entrance from inside. Since then every raiding excursion had been resisted in a manner hitherto unusual, and Elliot looked about for the source of this sudden volume

* See Chapter VIII., page 154.

of opposition in so remote a corner of his district. He was not long in discovering it. Some twenty-five miles to the west of Botha's Pass a horseshoe of isolated downs, ten miles in length, arose from the High Veld, crowned with crags so sheer, and so squarely hewn by Nature, that the hills appeared to be crenellated by a parapet of Norman castles. This remarkable feature was shown upon no map; information about it was difficult to obtain; it was, indeed, a place of some mystery, and there were strange tales of miles of caves which burrowed into its depths as if eaten out by the waves of some long vanished sea.

The place was a typical Boer stronghold, and its almost unsearchable recesses had long been used as a magazine and a remount depôt for the Orange Free State commandos. At this very moment, so Elliot was informed, De Wet and Steyn were in the neighbourhood endeavouring to organise the scattered horse and cattle guards to keep him from their sanctuary. He therefore decided to search the place at once, and on May 20th manœuvred to get upon its flank and rear by despatching Bethune back through Vlaknek Pass for Boschhoek, placing Lowe upon the Elandshoek Plateau, and supporting him by de Lisle at Mowbray. This march was little opposed, though the road ran through so veritable a cañon that Lowe had actually to blast a track up to the plateau. Next day de Lisle and Lowe faced west and advanced straight upon the Witkoppies, Bethune being then at Boschhoek on the right. Only a few Boers, some 400 in all, had gathered to hold their ramparts, and these speedily broke and scattered in all directions on being shelled. Their occupation here was shown by a thousand horses which they left to be driven in by the invaders. The columns then marched over the Witkoppies, finding nothing more above ground, and not pausing to search the subterranean vaults, of which at that time rumour had scarcely reached them. Once more on the open veld, Elliot spread his columns again, sending Lowe north-westward, Bethune to the west, and de Lisle southward in chase of the dispersed commando. On May 23rd Headquarters and de Lisle entered Harrismith with

VIEW OF WITKOPPIES, LOOKING NORTH.

VIEW OF WITKOPPIES, LOOKING WEST.

[Facing page 104.

EVENTS IN THE ORANGE RIVER COLONY. 105

1,700 captured horses. Elliot then ordered a concentration at Vrede which was effected by the end of the month, all the columns loading themselves afresh with four-footed captures, and meeting with constant but ineffectual opposition on the way to the rendezvous.

The opening of the fifth and last phase of the great foray was somewhat delayed by the difficulty of obtaining supplies owing to the enormous demands being made at this time upon the depôt at Standerton. Elliot was now to return to Kroonstad by way of Reitz and Lindley, a road which never failed to afford fighting; and as a precaution he had already sent de Lisle forward with what rations he could spare, to hold Pram Kop, towards the Wilge river. From the moment of starting, on June 3rd, the enemy was in active attendance, especially on the rearguards, which they pestered not only with rifles but with miles of flames urged across the grass by a following wind. On June 5th Lowe was in contact with and took nine wagons from a commando reported to belong to De la Rey. On that evening de Lisle was on the Wilge at Schurvepoort, east of Reitz, and was there ordered to push a party across the river to search for a Boer laager reported to be in the neighbourhood. De Lisle sent 100 men of the 6th (Bedfordshire regiment and Gordon Highlanders) mounted infantry, and 100 South Australian Bushmen, under Major J. R. F. Sladen, who, early on the morning of the 6th, discovered a large convoy upon Graspan, seven miles east of Reitz. A dashing charge resulted in the capture of 114 wagons and carts and forty-five prisoners, whereupon Sladen, parking his booty, sent sixty of his Australians to regain touch with de Lisle. This party had hardly disappeared when Sladen suddenly found himself almost surrounded by a semi-circle of horsemen more than double his own strength, which with scarcely a pause bore straight down upon him.

Sladen's position lay on a spur, at the foot of which he had drawn up his captured wagons; his men lined some scattered kraals above, in one of which were immured the prisoners. In a moment the enemy was at the wagons, and dismounting there,

The action at Graspan, June 6th, 1901.

some remained under cover, others ran forward to the shelter of the nearest native huts which Sladen had been unable to occupy. Then, whilst some of those behind secured and drove off the wagons, the rest of the Boers settled down to a fire attack at less than fifty yards' range, which seemed likely to have but one end for the outnumbered and outflanked mounted infantry. Sladen had indeed fallen into a nest of hornets, and his prospects, bad as they plainly were, were even less hopeful than they appeared. Behind him de Lisle, as yet in total ignorance alike of his detachment's first success and its subsequent predicament, was being greatly delayed by a bad drift over the Wilge. Around him, even in his midst, lay a commando whose daring and promptitude bespoke no common leadership. Such was in fact the case. No lesser personages than De Wet and De la Rey led the attack, drawn to the spot by chances which will be described later. The wagons were already practically retaken, many were being fast removed, with the mass of the Boers between them and the troops. It seemed equally impossible to retain the prisoners, who lay in a hut within ten yards of the foremost of the attack, the escort consisting of but two men.* Giving up for lost the wagons at any rate, Sladen's men turned stubbornly to keeping themselves from capture, and for four hours their rifles were neither silent nor ineffective. Meanwhile de Lisle had at last made the passage of the Wilge and, all unaware of the above events, was marching towards the spot. Not until 3 p.m., when yet six miles distant, did he receive a message from Sladen, learning more soon after from a fugitive who had been captured and released by the enemy. De Lisle at once pushed on and soon arrived on the scene at the gallop. He found Sladen's detachment still holding its own, despite the loss of a quarter of its numbers. By its indomitable resistance it had even gained the upper hand.

Presence of De Wet and De la Rey.

* Sergeant Sutherland and Corporal Geddes, of the Gordon Highlanders. Both were especially commended in Colonel de Lisle's report for the way in which they prevented the escape of their forty-five charges. Sutherland performed his duty in spite of a severe wound obtained when assisting a wounded comrade outside the hut. He was awarded the Distinguished Conduct Medal, Geddes being promoted to sergeant

The losses of the attack were heavy, the burghers were disinclined to close in further, and at the sight of the reinforcements they at once broke and fled, leaving twenty dead and wounded on the field. In the pursuit which followed de Lisle recaptured all but two of the wagons and 6,000 oxen. Altogether the enemy's losses—fifty killed and wounded, including two officers, and forty-five prisoners—nearly doubled those of the troops, which numbered three officers and twenty-three men killed and twenty-four wounded. The severity of the fire may be gauged by the fact that, though somewhat covered by the kraals, nearly 150 horses were shot. The whole affair redounded greatly to the credit of all concerned, and especially, if distinctions can be made, to two young officers, Lieutenants C. P. Strong of the Bedfordshire regiment, and G. E. Cameron of the Gordon Highlanders, who both fell in the forefront.

Not their foe but their friends had brought together the chief of the Republican leaders at this unimportant spot in the Orange River Colony. Early in May the Government of the Transvaal, in a moment of weakness, had actually laid before the directorate of the sister State proposals for an armistice with a view to negotiations for peace. The spreading desolation of their country, the certainty of ultimate defeat, had so dismayed the Transvaalers that even ardent patriots like J. C. Smuts, B. Viljoen and F. W. Reitz, the last, especially, the incarnation of the spirit of irreconcilable resistance, had felt it their duty to put their hands to a document which had been forwarded to President Steyn for his consideration. But this unexpected thrust only struck fire from the leader of the Orange Free State. In an indignant reply he had repudiated on behalf of his nation all thought of yielding. If the Transvaal laid down her arms, he said, his own countrymen, who had endured the first blows of the campaign, would assuredly strike the last. He would be no party to this " National Murder,"* and even were he to be so base, he knew that his people would abandon, not their country

---

* President Steyn's reply to Secretary of State F. W. Reitz's communication on behalf of his Government, dated from the Government Offices on the Veld, Ermelo District, May 10th, 1901.

Reason of De Wet's presence.

but himself, and would continue the struggle without him. Then, fearful lest his ally should take some irrevocable step, Steyn had summoned De Wet to his side for a visit in company to the Transvaal Headquarters. At that moment De Wet himself was on the point of meeting De la Rey in the Western Transvaal to discuss plans for a joint invasion of Cape Colony, ever the *ultima ratio* of the strategy of the Western leaders. In view of the freshly arisen contingency, De Wet had then requested De la Rey to meet him instead in the presence of Steyn, and June 5th found all three in laager on the Liebenberg's Vlei, less than thirty miles in front of Elliot's returning army. Close by a large convoy of wagons laden with local families and their household effects was seeking to escape from the British troops. On the morning of June 6th Sladen's successful dash upon these wagons was reported to the assembled Boer leaders, who immediately decided upon a rescue, with the results already seen. At the conclusion of the affair the Boer officers made off for Lindley, thence to make their way by circuitous routes and with many an adventure to a momentous conference on the banks of the Waterval river, east of Heidelberg, which will be described elsewhere.*

After the affair at Graspan, Elliot, his left flank sweeping through Bethlehem, marched on Reitz (June 9th) and thence in to the railway at Kroonstad, which was re-entered on the 15th. During his seven weeks' absence he had deprived the enemy of 100 prisoners, thirty-six killed, 131,500 cattle, sheep and horses, 264 wagons and carts and an incalculable amount of foodstuffs. At Kroonstad Elliot remained a week, a pause of which advantage will be taken in a subsequent chapter to synchronise with his operations the work of the other divisions of troops in the Orange River Colony. One unit may, however be first dismissed, that of Western, which, acting as the northerly " stop " as Elliot passed Frankfort, had held the drifts over the Wilge from its confluence with the Vaal up to Leeuwbank Drift from May 1st to 6th. After raiding

* See Chapter XII.

EVENTS IN THE ORANGE RIVER COLONY.

13,000 head of stock, Western moved into Heilbron on the 8th. There he was met by a wire from Headquarters acquainting him with the presence of a laager at Buffelsvlei. He immediately took his force thither by two divergent lines of march, so as to come upon the camp from opposite sides, tactics which were most successful. At dawn on May 10th Major D. P. Driscoll with his regiment of Scouts surprised the Boers from the east, and with no loss to himself secured thirty-one prisoners, seventeen vehicles, 100 horses and more than 3,000 stock. Western then pursued his way to Vereeniging, on both sides of which he foraged until the end of the month, when he had sent into Vereeniging from the country side sixty-one carts and wagons, 7,300 animals and some 7,500 bags of grain. His next move was towards Parys, which, in the face of sharp opposition, he entered and cleared on June 4th. Two days later, reconnoitring from Vredefort, Western gained touch with his Parys opponents, 150 in number, and chased them for five miles, capturing two. Passing Reitzburg he then made for a laager at Witkopjes, which he attacked and dispersed on the 8th, taking eight prisoners, thirty-nine vehicles, 1,400 stock and a quantity of grain and ammunition. Thence he put in at Kopje Station, taking the field again on the 17th to clear the banks of the Rhenoster river down to the Vaal. A ten days' active raid brought him into Klerksdorp with eight prisoners, ten wagons and spans of oxen and 3,000 stock, having destroyed as much again on the march. Western was then attached to G. Hamilton, at Klerksdorp, thus passing out of the area under review in this chapter.

THE WAR IN SOUTH AFRICA.

Approximate Strength States of Columns referred to in foregoing Chapter.

Column.	Mounted Troops.	Infantry.	Guns, including Vickers-Maxims.	Machine Guns.	
February—June, 1901.					
Lieut.-Colonel J. S. S. Barker	750	90	4	2	⎫ Major-General
,, ,, W. H. Williams	340	—	3	6	⎬ C. E. Knox in
,, ,, W. L. White	830	138	5	1	⎭ command.
,, ,, T. D. Pilcher	1,070	82	7	2	⎱ Col. C. J. Long
,, ,, H. M. Grenfell	450	—	3	—	⎰ in command.
Colonel A. W. Thorneycroft	500	150	5	—	
Lieut.-Colonel the Hon. J. H. G. Byng	380	—	3	—	
Colonel Sir C. Parsons	195	320	2	—	
Lieut.-Colonel C. P. Crewe	640	—	4	2	⎫ Lieut.-General
Major-General J. E. Boyes (later Harley)	318	1,361	5	3	⎬ Sir L. Rundle
,, ,, B. B. D. Campbell	342	1,393	5	2	⎭ in command.
Lieut.-Colonel S. C. H. Monro	320	480	2	—	
Major-General Bruce Hamilton	400	—	2	—	
Lieut.-Colonel W. G. Massy	510	—	3	1	⎫ Lieut.-General
,, ,, E. C. Ingouville Williams (later G. W. B. Western)	459	625	4	—	⎬ C. Tucker directing.
Major J. E. Pine-Coffin	447	—	3	1	
Colonel E. C. Bethune	130	—	2	—	
Brigadier-General H. C. O. Plumer ⎫ Colonel H. B. Jeffreys ⎬ Lieut.-Colonel M. Cradock ⎭	1,522	—	10	2	⎧ Major-General ⎨ A. H. Paget in ⎩ command.
Major-General Bruce Hamilton's columns :					
Lieut.-Colonel S. C. H. Monro	290	—	3	—	
,, ,, C. Maxwell (later S. W. Follett)	650	—	6	—	Lieut.-General the Hon. N. G. Lyttelton directing.
Lieut.-Colonel W. L. White	617	—	3	—	
Colonel D. Haig's columns :					
Lieut.-Colonel the Hon. J. H. G. Byng	654	—	4	—	
,, ,, W. H. Williams	351	—	3	3	
,, ,, H. J. Scobell	639	11*	3	—	
Colonel T. E. Hickman	560	—	5	—	
Lieut.-Colonel E. B. Herbert	380	—	3	1	
,, ,, the Hon. A. Murray	185	—	2	1	
Major A. Paris	325	131	2	1	
Brigadier-General R. G. Broadwood (later de Lisle)	2,083	—	4	1	⎫ Major-General
Colonel E. C. Bethune (later Lowe)	1,411	—	5	—	⎬ E. L. Elliot in
Lieut.-Colonel H. de B. de Lisle (later R. Fanshawe)	700	22*	—	1	⎭ command.
Lieut.-Colonel W. G. B. Western	764	266	3	—	
,, ,, A. E. W. Colville	267	376	5	1	
,, ,, F. J. Pink	170	280	2	—	

* Cyclists.

CHAPTER VI.

EVENTS IN THE EASTERN TRANSVAAL*

(Continued from Chapter II).

JANUARY—MARCH, 1901.

BY the evening of January 27th eight columns, of a fighting strength of 15,000 men and sixty-three guns,† had taken stand around the fringe of the Eastern Transvaal, under the supreme command of Lieut.-General J. D. P. French. From left to right they were placed as follows :—At Wonderfontein, Major-General H. L. Smith-Dorrien with 3,000 men and twelve guns ; at Middelburg, Colonel W. P. Campbell with 1,250 men and five guns ; at Mooiplaats, Brigadier-General E. A. H. Alderson with 1,900 men and nine guns ; at Bapsfontein, Colonel E. C. Knox with 1,850 men and eight guns ; at Putfontein, Lieut.-Colonels E. H. H. Allenby and W. P. Pulteney with respectively 1,560 men and seven guns and 1,800 men and eight guns ; at Springs, Brigadier-General J. G. Dartnell with 2,600 men and nine guns ; and at Greylingstad, Lieut.-Colonel A. E. W. Colville with 650 men and five guns. The scheme had originally included the force of Major-General A. H. Paget ; but the threat to Cape Colony, the most sensitive nerve-centre of the campaign, had caused his withdrawal from the eastern theatre, and he was at this moment marching westward to entrain for service in the south. W. P. Campbell filled the gap in the arc, and Pulteney, hitherto intended to be held in reserve, came up as a unit of the first line.

<small>Positions of the columns.</small>

* See map No. 56.

† Exclusive of machine guns. The numbers quoted are of combatants only ; the whole assembly totalled over 22,000 men and 20,000 animals. For state, see page 127.

The topographical situations of the above-named columns foreshadowed the general intention. The Eastern Transvaal was to be swept diagonally; at first eastward—whilst W. P. Campbell and Smith-Dorrien barred the northern exits; then south-eastward towards the broken *cul de sac* between the Buffalo and the forbidden native border. Thither, it was hoped, the commandos of Botha would be headed, and there receive a *coup de grâce* such as Prinsloo had undergone in the Brandwater basin.

<small>The country and the plan.</small> Imagination must supplement the map if the scope of such an operation is to be grasped. Briefly, it comprehended a clearance of the High Veld, a tract 170 miles by 150 in area, destitute of all supplies save those afforded by the infrequent and impoverished townships and by the scattered farms whose produce in all which is required by armies was in inverse ratio to their acreage; a tract on which movement alone was easy, though even that grew difficult as the immense prairies, as if constricted by their narrowing political frontiers, piled themselves up into the mountains of the south-east corner. Further, as is commonly the case, facility of movement was liable to be heavily braked by the anxious question of subsistence. The columns were to start with supplies for ten days; but an army in the midst of the High Veld might be almost as isolated as one at sea, so vast the distances to be traversed, and so exposed to the enemy the routes. In one particular, however, the conditions favoured the projected manœuvre, in that the columns whilst marching away from one base would be approaching another. Their supply thus resolved itself into two separate phases. To deal with the first stage Colville was detailed to escort convoys working out from Greylingstad by a line of advance which would be daily more masked and protected as the fighting columns swung south-eastward. He, perhaps, might serve as far as Ermelo, and thereafter French must look for sustenance to Natal, where, in the quietude of January, preparations to that end had been in full progress. There is space for only a suggestion of the infinite and minute calculations which formed the basis of the Commander-in-Chief's orders under this head; computations of places, times, and

EVENTS IN THE EASTERN TRANSVAAL. 113

loads; of the comings, goings, and interchanges of full and loaded convoys; of the provision of escorts, and a thousand other details which had to be none the less exact because the weather, the roads, or the enemy, might confound them all. Truly the spirit of prophecy must inform those whose duty it is to supply armies in the field. Such was the plan, and such the material; it remains now to describe the issue.

On January 28th French struck eastward with the columns of Alderson, E. C. Knox, Allenby, Pulteney and Dartnell. The first obstruction was the line of the Wilge river, running due north and south across his front, with the commandos of General Beyers and Commandant Badenhorst watching it from end to end. Beyers was merely in observation; but skilfully utilising the long ridge, the local watershed, which runs from Bapsfontein across to Bethel, he stood in turn at Boschmanskop, Rolspruit and Rooipoort. Four days' operations and several sharp encounters threw him back on Bethel. On February 4th French, accompanying Pulteney's column, reached that village, which was found deserted. The positions of the other columns on this date were as follows :—Smith-Dorrien at Onbekend, six miles south of Carolina; W. P. Campbell at Boschmanskop, on the Middelburg—Ermelo road; Alderson, who was now in touch with Campbell, at Schurvekop, on the eastern fork of the Oliphant river; E. C. Knox at Eerste Geluk, due south of Alderson and four miles north-east of Bethel; Allenby at Rietfontein, the same distance south-east of Bethel; Pulteney, as stated, at Bethel; Dartnell, due south of Allenby, at Schaapkraal; Colville at Niekerksvlei, eleven miles out on the Standerton—Ermelo road. None had been seriously engaged except Campbell, who had fought successfully every day since leaving Middelburg, and Allenby and Pulteney, on whom had fallen the brunt of Beyers' rearguard tactics from the Wilge river until he disappeared at Rooipoort, leaving a gun in Allenby's hands. With 2,000 men Beyers fell back on Ermelo, his arrival swelling the forces there to some 6,000; and French, in Bethel, learned that Botha intended to give battle at De Roodepoort, before Ermelo. French, therefore, on February 5th, manœuvred to surround that place, and

Opening of French's campaign in the Eastern Transvaal, Jan. 28th, 1901.

Occupation of Bethel, Feb. 4th, 1901.

VOL. IV. 8

had all but got his columns into position when a blow fell upon one of them which not only dislocated his plan, but seriously affected the whole enterprise. In Botha French had an opponent in many respects resembling himself, one as quick to escape as to draw a cordon, and as sure of eye to detect a single doorway opening into or out from the midst of his enemies. The Boer General, though he already gave up hopes of marching as an invader over the southern mountains, had no intention of being driven into them, still less of being "corralled"* in mid veld, as French bade fair to do at this juncture. He determined to break loose at once, sent word to Viljoen to demonstrate strongly against the eastern railway, and looking around for the best outlet, fixed his eye on the north, and on Smith-Dorrien.

<small>Botha determines to escape.</small>

On the evening of February 5th that general's column went into bivouac at Bothwell, at the north end of Lake Chrissie. There had been little fighting during the day, and the main trend of the enemy seemed still to be in the opposite direction, for a convoy, many miles in length, had been sighted at 9.30 a.m. on the move from Ermelo towards Amsterdam, and had been pursued until dusk. Nothing, therefore, seemed less probable than an attack from the south. The night passed quietly. At 2.55 a.m. on the 6th an officer from French's Headquarters arrived, bearing orders for Smith-Dorrien relative to the converging movement upon Ermelo. As he rode into the lines, a semi-circle of fire broke like a squall against three sides of the outpost-line which fringed the bivouac, striking most heavily upon that section held by the 2nd West Yorkshire regiment.†

<small>Botha's attack on Smith-Dorrien, Feb. 6th, 1901.</small>

* As it will be found necessary frequently to employ throughout this volume similar expressions borrowed from the domain of sport, an explanation may not be found superfluous by every reader. A "corral" is a pen or enclosure into which wild game is driven for capture or destruction. "Beaters" are men whose duty it is to "flush" or arouse game from its hiding place. Their combined action in a straight or curved line, and in a given direction, constitutes a "drive." "Stops" are men or groups posted at intervals some distance ahead of or on the flanks of an advancing "drive," in order to confine the game fleeing from the "beaters" within a desired area, by turning back any attempt to break out. Though devices such as these are common to both the sporting and military arts, the latter has no terms which so adequately express them.

† For gallantry at this action Sergeant W. B. Traynor, 2nd West Yorkshire regiment, was awarded the Victoria Cross.

EVENTS IN THE EASTERN TRANSVAAL.

The piquets stood firm, but the interior of the camp fell into wild disorder. Some, thinking the enemy had penetrated, ensconced themselves amongst the bushes, and began to fire in all directions. The horses of the cavalry, lashed by innumerable bullets, wrenched themselves from their fastenings, and stampeded in a body through the outposts. Outside they were turned again by the oncoming commandos, whereupon they wheeled and galloped back the way they had come, carrying with them a knot of Boers who, hidden in the mob of animals, dashed into the camp, and swelled the promiscuous shooting from inside. Their speedy annihilation of two of the piquets opened a road for their comrades. But the rest of the outposts remained immoveable; the supports closed up, and by a furious fire shattered the rush of the Boer main body before it closed upon the camp. At 4.15 a.m. the commandos abandoned the attack and passed on, leaving thirty-three killed and wounded on the field, and filling every farm with their injured as they made off northward; for unfortunately they had not been turned, nor could anything have turned them from that direction. The British losses were eighty-two officers and men killed and wounded, and in horses no fewer than 254 killed and lost, besides a number of animals belonging to the supply column which Smith-Dorrien was conveying to W. P. Campbell and Alderson. Thus Botha, with more than 2,000 men, was free to unite with the not inconsiderable forces whom Smith-Dorrien had brushed aside, and who had harassed W. P. Campbell abreast of Carolina. Smith-Dorrien, ordered to remain motionless on the 6th, was joined by W. P. Campbell on the morning of the 7th, the two columns thenceforward working under the first-named officer's direction.

Botha breaks out of the cordon.

February 6th had not passed without fighting in another quarter. French, hopeful of securing the Boer convoys, which were on the eastern of the two roads crossing the Vaal at Witpunt and Beginderlyn, ordered Allenby to pursue. On the night of the 5th Allenby was at Vereeniging on the Kaffir Spruit, and at dawn on the 6th he pushed on for the drift at Witpunt. But the enemy, fighting a delaying action with 1,000 men at

Kromdraai, successfully covered the passage of their train which had got a start of many miles, and there was nothing for it but to resume the chase with the whole army.

<small>Occupation of Ermelo, Feb. 6th, 1901.</small>

In closing in upon Ermelo, French had bared both his own flanks. To prevent being turned by the right, he despatched Dartnell southward on the 7th by Beginderlyn to Amersfoort, which was reached and occupied on the 8th; whilst Smith-Dorrien extended eastward on the 9th to close the gap on the left. So doing, he seized a chance of damaging severely his vanished assailants of the 6th. Heavy rains had swollen the spruits and clogged the tracks, and Botha, speeding northward, had far outstripped his transport, which was labouring after him by a circuitous route close under the Swazi border. On the 9th the head of the convoy had got no further than the north bank of the Umpilusi river, where it was sighted by Smith-Dorrien's cavalry, the Imperial Light Horse, commanded by Lieut.-Colonel D. McKenzie. The convoy was strongly guarded, but McKenzie, despite the fatigue of his horses, which had already covered more than twenty miles, fell impetuously upon the column, and after a spirited encounter drove off the

<small>Smith-Dorrien captures a convoy, Feb. 9th, 1901.</small>

escort and captured some sixty wagons, 18,000 head of stock and twenty-one prisoners, with which he returned in triumph to the bivouac at Lilliburn. The Umpilusi, running high in flood, prevented any enterprise against the rest of the Boer transport which was water-bound on the south bank, nor could operations be immediately undertaken by the other columns, which were awaiting supplies from Standerton. During the night of the 10th Colville safely delivered at Ermelo 117 wagons which he had escorted from Niekerksvlei, and on the next day French, evacuating Ermelo, pushed on. Meanwhile, Smith-Dorrien's engineers had been strenuously bridging the raging Umpilusi, which he crossed to Warburton on the 10th, effecting next day a further capture of twenty wagons and 5,000 head of stock.

Pulteney and Allenby, crossing the Vaal at Witpunt and Uitspan, were next in sight of the quarry, both converging on the tail of the retiring train at Klipfontein on February 12th.

EVENTS IN THE EASTERN TRANSVAAL. 117

The Boer rearguard was brushed aside by a charge delivered by the 6th (Inniskilling) Dragoons, who, getting amongst the burghers with the sabre, accounted for many and took ten prisoners, with the loss of five troopers. The two columns camped that night at Rotterdam and Kalkoenkrans, on opposite banks of the Mabusa Spruit; E. C. Knox at Zandspruit, within eighteen miles of Amsterdam; Alderson at Sandcliff, midway between Knox and Smith-Dorrien, the last of whom, by means of an improvised bridge of sunken wagons, had crossed the Umpilusi for the second time to Busby. Dartnell being still at Amersfoort, the columns were now arrayed in an unbroken diagonal line from the Swazi border to the apex of Natal. Though a heavy booty seemed assured, it was even more certain that the most desired quarry, Botha and his force, was already at large behind them. On the 13th the army moved forward as follows :—Smith-Dorrien to Maryvale, Alderson to Kliprug, Knox to Zandspruit, Allenby to Donkerhoek, Pulteney to Taaiboschspruit, and Dartnell from Amersfoort into the Elands Berg to Mooipoort. On the 14th Smith-Dorrien entered Amsterdam, remaining there whilst General French with the columns of Knox and Pulteney occupied Piet Retief on the 16th, and Allenby made good the Slangapies Berg by the seizure of the pass at Langgewacht. A small mounted force under Rimington, detached by Pulteney to Meyershoop, kept touch between Headquarters and Dartnell. *Occupation of Amsterdam and Piet Retief, Feb. 14th—16th, 1901.*

French now turned to Natal for supplies, which were sorely needed. Throughout the month Hildyard's chief occupation had been the accumulation of enormous quantities of stores and wagons, and he had at this moment three large convoys ready for forwarding, borrowing troops from other commands to furnish the escorts.* On the 12th he had despatched the first convoy, containing supplies for 12,000 men and for 15,600 horses and mules, with a number of fresh horses, with orders to be at Lüneberg on February 16th or 17th. He had provided for the safety of its march by posting a small force under Colonel *French changes his base, Feb. 16th, 1901.*

---
* For details of supply and transport work done by Natal during February and March, see Appendix 1.

G. M. Bullock in the mountains east of Wakkerstroom. But Dartnell, arriving at Lüneberg on the appointed date to meet the convoy, found that it had not arrived, and moved on eastward on both sides of the Slangapies Berg to Marienthal. The convoy, delayed by fog, floods, precipitous gradients and muddy roads, was, in fact, no nearer than Vaalbank, outside Utrecht, on the 16th, with the barrier of the Elands Berg still before it. Not until the 19th, when it had safely surmounted the Elands Berg, did Bullock gain any communication with Dartnell, and still nearly thirty miles separated the two. Six more days elapsed before the first wagons were received by Dartnell at Marienthal. Meanwhile the troops of the columns had been enduring great privations. The rain, which had seldom ceased since the start, settled down on the 18th to a downpour of six days' unbroken duration, swelling the smallest spruits to impassable torrents, turning the roads into bogs, and placing camps and bivouacs in an indescribable state. On the 19th supplies totally failed owing to the non-arrival of the convoy, which was itself at this time contending with atrocious conditions. The columns had then to subsist upon the country, a task which armies have found difficult even in districts of fat harvests and well-stored villages, but here, on the starveling uplands, necessitating resort to shifts which recalled those of long besieged garrisons. The enemy suffered still more severely. Not a day passed but they were deprived of stock, crops, wagons and fighting men. Their heaviest loss in one day occurred on March 1st, when Colonel St. G. C. Henry's mounted infantry, in advance of Smith-Dorrien's column which was in process of sweeping along the Swazi border, fell upon the convoy of the Piet Retief commando near the junction of the Shela and Compies rivers, and took fifty-six prisoners, twenty-four wagons, and a quantity of stock. The Boer Commandant, vainly hoping to retrieve a desperate situation by a voluntary surrender, fled from the field with thirty burghers and gave himself up to W. P. Campbell, who was operating a few miles to the southward; but as the wagons had already fallen in fair fight into Henry's hands, the Boer lost both his commando and

EVENTS IN THE EASTERN TRANSVAAL.

his liberty.* On the 10th and the night of the 12th further successful enterprises by Henry resulted in the capture of twenty-six prisoners, eighteen wagons and more sheep and cattle. The positions of the various columns on March 15th were as follows :—Smith-Dorrien at Rustplaats, north-west of Piet Retief ; W. P. Campbell and Allenby on the Assegai river at Zandbank and Mahamba ; Alderson at Marienthal, midway between Campbell and Dartnell, the last-named being on the Intombie river north-east of Lüneberg. A small force under Rimington south of that place guarded the convoy road about Schikhoek, whence Brigadier-General J. F. Burn-Murdoch held the line to Utrecht. Bullock was still to the east of Wakkerstroom, and Headquarters with E. C. Knox's and Pulteney's columns in Piet Retief.

On March 6th the rain, which had given a brief respite, began again, to fall continuously for eight days, until for the troops, exposed day and night and hemmed in by cataracts, health, cheerfulness and movement seemed alike impossible. Nevertheless they remained healthy, their good spirits were never more marked, and they were kept in full activity ; for though confined temporarily within narrow limits, every column thoroughly cleared its immediate neighbourhood, and each had to make its own roads through the morasses, its own bridges and ferries across the almost innumerable streams, and its own living from the scarce and hidden foodstuffs which, as a rule, only heavy bribes to the natives succeeded in bringing to light. For a full month, from February 16th to March 16th, these conditions prevailed, and though daily surrenders and captures bore witness to the value of the work done, yet every description of ill luck had caused it to fall short of the results which the columns had set out to procure. The proper finish to the great sweep, from which so much had been hoped, seemed now to be drowning in the deluge of rain. Botha's refusal on March 16th of terms of peace proffered by the British Government at an interview with Lord Kitchener at Middelburg on *Botha refuses terms of peace, March 16th, 1901.*

* For gallantry in an outpost affair near Derby, on March 3rd, Lieutenant F. B. Dugdale, 5th Lancers, was awarded the Victoria Cross.

February 28th,* was not only in itself evidence of the indecisiveness of the campaign in the south-east, but it blew up again the flame which for a moment had seemed to flicker. The Commander-in-Chief began to be impatient for the conclusion of French's operations and for the return of troops who were urgently needed elsewhere. French, however, had still to accomplish much that only the terrible weather and the failure of supplies had prevented him from doing three weeks earlier, and Lord Kitchener left him to his task.

French changes his line of supply, March 16th, 1901.

On March 16th French abandoned the Lüneberg—Utrecht line of communications which had proved so unreliable, and, trusting to a new line *viâ* Volksrust and Wakkerstroom, and to Vryheid, which Hildyard had filled with supplies, resumed his advance. Securing the lines of the Pongola and Pivaan rivers by means of Alderson's and Rimington's columns, he directed Dartnell on to P. P. Burg, which was occupied on the 18th. Smith-Dorrien, who had absorbed Allenby in addition to W. P. Campbell, then came down into Piet Retief, relieving E. C. Knox and Pulteney, who marched southward across the Assegai. On the 25th French was in Vryheid with Pulteney, Dartnell and Rimington; Knox being at Ersterling on the right bank of the Pivaan, next to Alderson at Welgevonden. At Vryheid French had a personal interview with Hildyard, and a telegraphic conversation across 320 miles of wire with Lord Kitchener. On March 27th the last beat of the " drive " was set on foot. The tracts still to be cleared fell naturally into two triangles, each with its apex pointing eastward; the one lying between the confluent Pongola and Pivaan rivers, its central point being P. P. Burg; the other, and larger, between the converging lines of the Pongola and the Zulu border, Vryheid standing on the centre of its base. French assigned the clearance of the former to Knox, detailing for the latter Alderson, Dartnell and Pulteney, with whom he himself intended to take the field. The result of these movements could only

* See Chapter XXX.

EVENTS IN THE EASTERN TRANSVAAL. 121

be to drive the enemy against the Swazi border, and Smith-Dorrien with his own, W. P. Campbell's, and Allenby's columns was instructed to hold a blocking line from Piet Retief through Zandbank—Mahamba—Plat Nek—Henwoods to Langdraai on the Pongola. On the 27th Dartnell, with supplies for ten days, marched from Vryheid eastwards to Rietvlei, followed by Pulteney, who was to operate on his right flank, as far as Welgevonden. Alderson, who was designed to cover Dartnell's left rear, was at Express on the 28th, when Dartnell made Welkom, and Pulteney Vaal Krantz, the latter also reconnoitring towards Alderson as far as Waterval. The enemy fell back before them in such straits that C. Emmett, the principal remaining leader and a bold man, offered to surrender if he could obtain the authority of his officers. But there was no surrender. On the 29th the chase continued to Pietersrust, Toovernaarsrust and Bloemendal. On the 30th Dartnell, finding the roads becoming impassable for wheeled transport, formed an entrenched depôt at Toovernaarsrust and turned thence northward to Wonderboom, whilst Alderson drew towards him to Kruisfontein, and Pulteney moved to hold at Rietvlei the road which Dartnell had quitted. The driven Boers now began to throw themselves against Smith-Dorrien's "stops." At Langdraai an attempted passage of the drift yielded three guns, some prisoners, transport and stock to Allenby, who was there on watch; at De Kraalen, where the Piet Retief road crossed the Assegai, W. P. Campbell surprised a small Boer convoy in the act of crossing, and captured the whole. On the next day (March 31st) Emmett endeavoured to make a stand with the few men—under 500 in number—he could collect, and for a time contested Dartnell's advance at Smaldeel. But his burghers fought without heart, and allowing themselves to be outflanked, were driven away with the loss of a gun, nearly 150 wagons and carts, and some 14,000 head of stock. Dartnell then proceeded to Langverwacht, where he was joined next day by Alderson, who had outstripped his infantry and transport at Mooiklip. Having raided as far as Uithoek in company, the two columns

Various operations in the south-eastern Transvaal.

again separated on April 1st, Dartnell's going on to Wonderboom, Alderson's returning to its main body at Mooiklip. For the next few days these columns scoured this neighbourhood. Dartnell, reaching the easternmost point of the operations, Zuikerkran, on April 2nd, descended thence along the Zulu border to Morgenzon, where he turned his face homeward. On the 5th he broke up his depôt at Toovernaarsrust and marched by Welkom back to Vaalbank, near Hlobane Mountain, where he arrived on the 6th, and remained for four days awaiting the cessation of the operations. Alderson, who had preceded him to Vaalbank on the 3rd, was outside Vryheid until the 6th, when he passed through the town and took up a line through Zaaifontein to the Blood river, in preparation for an excursion down the angle between the Umvolosi river and the Nqutu wedge of Zululand. On the 7th and 8th he was on the line Tintas Drift—Strydplaats, on the 9th on Brand Kraal—Spitzkop—Wanbestuur, on the 10th at Scheeperslaagte, whence he took the road *via* Leeuwnek (April 11th) back to Vryheid, thus concluding the clearance of the lower triangle.

Meanwhile E. C. Knox, sweeping up his river-enclosed area, had seen little of the enemy until on April 5th he surprised and took a convoy and nine prisoners at Dordrecht, ten miles east of P. P. Burg. On the 10th he, too, was in Vryheid on his way to the railway at Glencoe. Pulteney had already departed the same way a week earlier; Dartnell followed on the 12th, Alderson on the 14th, and two days later French, entraining at Dundee, quitted the scene for Johannesburg.

Results of French's operations. His two and a half months' labours, though unattended by any remarkable *coup*, had not been unproductive. At a cost of 150 casualties* to his own force, he had deprived the enemy of over 1,300 fighting men, of eleven guns, of 2,281 carts and wagons, of 272,752 head of stock, and of a quantity which is not to be measured of crops and farm produce. If the operations had failed of their chief expectations by the escape of

---

* Casualties—Killed, five officers, forty-one men; wounded, four officers, 108 men.

EVENTS IN THE EASTERN TRANSVAAL. 123

Botha with nearly 3,000 of his following, they had nevertheless contributed largely to a crisis in the affairs of the Republics. Rumours of capitulation filled the air, and doubt and mistrust the burghers, who, after each day of disaster, knew well how many of their weaker brethren—even men hitherto honoured as "splendid burghers"*—were stealing away by night to give themselves up to the invaders. By the middle of March Botha, who had hurried from Lake Chrissie to join the Government at Roos Senekal, was back at Ermelo, establishing his Headquarters at Rietspruit, outside the town. There he learned of the failure of De Wet's descent upon Cape Colony. This, then, was the real end of an enterprise which a month earlier had been reported to him as opening with a triumphal march through the Orange River Colony, attended by the destruction of two British camps, and the death of General C. E. Knox, and culminating in the approach of the commandos to Cape Town—"rumour says right in the Cape."† On March 29th Botha took horse for Vrede to ascertain the truth from De Wet in person. At this moment, indeed, the Commandant-General found himself beset by a multitude of falsehoods, both of good and evil report, which gathered as numerous as his enemies in the field. Even he did not escape the universal breath of suspicion which, like a poisonous gas, had begun to creep amongst the discomfited commandos all over the southern theatre of war. His flight from the front to Roos Senekal, his pourparlers with Lord Kitchener, and even his present visit to De Wet, all met with cavilling, which, though only whispered, Botha deemed loud enough to be refuted.‡ Nor was mistrust the only foe which he had to drive from his own laagers. It was a time when many of the commandos were so untrustworthy that it was unsafe to call them from the homes to which they

Botha visits De Wet.

---

* Letter from Commandant-General to Acting State President, April 5th, 1901.

† Report from Acting Chief-Commandant C. Badenhorst, February 14th, 1901.

‡ Letter from Commandant-General to General B. Viljoen, March 17th, 1901 ; and other sources.

Depression amongst the Transvaal commandos.

had retreated*; when even such stalwarts as General B. Viljoen " emphatically urged that the war must now be brought to an end,"† when the Acting President himself evinced a gloom which, had it been universally shared, had speedily ended the struggle. "All human help," wrote Burger to his "Brother in oppression,"‡ "upon which we have hitherto relied has proved a broken reed. Europe is silent, and the enemy proceeds to destroy our people with his great force, . . . The question is, what must we, what shall we do? May we, can we, continue the struggle further?" Such despondency was not confined to high places. That sudden dejection which the historian has noted even in victorious armies, for example in the Germans marching in full career against Paris in 1870, had descended heavily upon the harried forces of the Transvaal, and the weaker spirits were yielding in hundreds to it and to their enemy. But Botha, though his military insight had long condemned him, too, to dread the issue of the struggle, saw in this wastage of his numbers the very means of making his foes pay the more dearly for their inevitable triumph. Only now, in fact, in its darkest hour, was his army undergoing that process of sloughing off the old skin of its defective system and undisciplined spirit, which, under the attrition of war, no guerilla levies can escape, which many have not survived at all, and from which few indeed have emerged so reinvigorated as the federal forces were to do. None better than Botha, none, perhaps, except he, could have safely tided over this most critical period of his country's campaign. For none knew better how indomitable a spirit lay like a core within his fast-shredding commandos, a spirit the finer in temper the less it was in touch with the influences of the old Dopper *régime*; the spirit, in short, of the young men who had grown up with himself. Yet he had been loyally silent when many had loudly declared that had this spirit of the Young Transvaal been

---

* Letter from Commandant-General to State President, March 23rd, 1901.

† Letter from Commandant-General to President, Orange Free State, April 28th, 1901.

‡ Letter from Acting-President Schalk Burger to President Steyn, March 21st, 1901.

invoked to begin instead of finish the war, under his leadership the British had long ago been driven to the sea, leaving the Republican flags floating over their territories behind them. In the breasts of men of this stamp the Acting President's cry of despair found faint echo. Not from them came the lament that the commandos moved about their ancestral veld like " the ghosts of the past in a haunted house."* Unlike the greybeards, they looked not for the miracle, but the victory which should save them, remaining in the very midst of the destitution wrought by French's columns " as cheerful as if they were living like kings."* Sustained by such a reserve, though at the lowest ebb of fortune, Botha had refused terms such as have rarely been offered by the conquerors of a province. He now sternly silenced the cry, so difficult to stifle, " We are betrayed ! " which had begun to sound in his ranks, and for long to come his followers were to show that such a raid as this of General French was but a tooth of the file required to wear them down.

On April 1st Botha returned from Vrede to his camp at Rietspruit. Two decisions had resulted from his interview with the Free State leader ; one, that owing to the shortage of small-arm ammunition operations in the open should be abandoned in favour of incessant interruption of the British communicating railways, until, perhaps, a captured train or two should have replenished the bandoliers ; the other, that a meeting should be contrived between the Governments of the two States. To the former resolve were due the fresh series of attacks on the line from Middelburg to Standerton, and as far south as in Natal, where a train was attacked and a farmstead burned below Majuba on April 7th. To effect the meeting of the Governments was a less easy task, for neither President knew on one night where his resting-place for the next might be, and an adventurous ride through hostile forces and across two closely-guarded railways lay before whichever official elected to visit the other. But Botha, assuredly grown accustomed to safeguarding his peripatetic Executive as an addition to his multifarious cares, made all

Botha returns to the Eastern Transvaal.

* Diary of a Burgher.

arrangements. On April 12th, Burger and his *entourage* were safe at Ermelo; on the 13th they set out for Vrede, and on the 16th Botha, who had escorted them, was back at Rietspruit, where on the 21st he saw Smith-Dorrien go past on his way northward to Wonderfontein.

Of all the columns engaged in the above-described operations, those of Smith-Dorrien alone returned by road. On April 12th he had drawn in his widely-extended lines, and starting northward in two divisions on the 13th, arrived at Wonderfontein on the 27th after a march which bogs, swollen streams, weak horses and a cumbersome train had hampered more than the Boers, though they were never absent. Little of importance had occurred on the Delagoa Bay railway line during Smith-Dorrien's long absence. Viljoen's somewhat feeble efforts to create diversions in favour of his hard-pressed chief had, nevertheless, the effect of drawing troops from the thinly manned line to deal with him. On February 12th two small columns of 700 and 900 men and nine guns, from Belfast and Lydenburg respectively, united under Major-General F. W. Kitchener at Zwartkoppies, near Dullstroom, proceeding next day to reconnoitre towards Roos Senekal, where Viljoen was known to be in laager. A scrambling fight ensued in which neither leader, each over-estimating the strength of the other, risked any definite course of action. F. W. Kitchener came into Belfast on the 14th and took over command of the line of communication, which Lyttelton had relinquished to proceed to Cape Colony. Nothing further transpired until the end of the month, when Lord Kitchener's fruitless conference with Commandant-General Botha took place at Middelburg. Much more blood and treasure were still to be expended to purchase the very terms then offered and refused.*

The month of March was little more eventful, being chiefly marked by a succession of blown-up trains. The losses caused thereby were set off, first by an ambush laid on the 29th near a destroyed train at Wonderfontein, which resulted in the death of seven Boers; secondly by a success at Lydenburg,

<small>Events in the north-eastern Transvaal.</small>

---

* See Chapter XXX.

where Colonel C. W. Park, of the 1st Devonshire regiment, commanding in the absence of F. W. Kitchener, surrounded a laager at Krugerspost, capturing thirty-six Boers and a quantity of stores. Equally infested was the railway along the Heidelberg section, where scarcely a day in February passed but damage was done by raiders, resulting in the loss of two complete trains, and on almost every occasion in the severance of communication. During March this section had more quiet, though attacks on cattle guards were frequent, and a train was blown up on the 22nd. These two months passed with little incident over the Standerton section, where the enemy remained as before few in numbers and very little venturesome. Finally, Colville's mobile column, busied during February in supply work in connection with French's operations to the eastward, spent the greater part of March about Standerton, and was very slightly engaged with the enemy.

LIEUTENANT-GENERAL FRENCH'S FORCE.

APPROXIMATE STRENGTH OF COLUMNS DURING OPERATIONS DESCRIBED IN FOREGOING CHAPTER.

COLUMN.	Feeding Strength (approximate only).			Fighting Strength (exclusive of R.A., R.E., A.S.C., etc.).			
	Men.	Horses.	Mules.	Mounted Troops.	Infantry.	Guns, including Vickers-Maxims.	Machine Guns.
Brigadier-General J. G. Dartnell ...	4,222	2,500	1,400	1,901	708	9	4
Colonel E. H. H. Allenby	2,000	1,600	1,000	1,079	481	7	3
Colonel W. P. Pulteney	2,956	1,600	1,200	936	878	8	3
Colonel E. C. Knox	2,572	1,900	1,300	1,362	490	8	3
Brigadier-General E. A. H. Alderson	2,674	1,600	1,000	1,348	529	9	6
Colonel W. P. Campbell	1.600	1,000	900	430	829	5	2
Major-General H. L. Smith-Dorrien	6,000	1,400	1,500	1,304	1,840	12	5
Lieut.-Colonel A. E W. Colville ...				207	440	5	1
Totals	22,024	11,600	8,300	8,567	6,195	63	27

CHAPTER VII.

EVENTS IN THE WESTERN TRANSVAAL* (*continued from Chapter I.*).

JANUARY—APRIL, 1901.

At the beginning of January, 1901, the situation in the Western Transvaal was as follows: At or near Ventersdorp were the Headquarters of the columns brought together by Lieut.-General J. D. P. French, namely, those of Major-General J. M. Babington (920 men), Colonel W. P. Pulteney (940 men), Brigadier-General J. R. P. Gordon (1,160 men), and Colonel R. G. Kekewich (980 men). Brigadier-General R. G. Broadwood was now invalided, and his brigade, handed over to Colonel E. C. Knox, was refitting at Potchefstroom. Major-General R. A. P. Clements was at Wolhuter's Kop, passing convoys to Rustenburg, where Brigadier-General G. G. Cunningham was still in command. Major-General A. H. Paget was on the march westward from north of Balmoral, arriving at Commando Nek on the 8th. Major-General A. FitzR. Hart held the railway from Welverdiend to Krugersdorp, with posts in the Gatsrand.

<small>Situation in the Magaliesberg.</small> Although the lines of communication were now protected, the Rustenburg and Hekpoort districts had been by no means cleared by the incursion of so many troops. De la Rey and Beyers were still at large, and though no longer acting in concert, were all the harder to find and deal with from their very isolation. Herein were illustrated once more two ever-present embarrassments of the campaign. In ordinary warfare to break up the enemy is a victory; in South Africa it usually only doubled the difficulty of subduing him. Again, to introduce thousands of fresh troops into an area of conflict

* See map No. 59.

EVENTS IN THE WESTERN TRANSVAAL. 129

is commonly to assure the desired result. In South Africa these troops had at once to be thinly spread over the particular line of communication threatened, and this the more urgently the smaller the bands into which the defeated or voluntarily separating enemy had broken. In short, if the defensive was difficult, an effective offensive was almost impossible, and time rather than arms had to be invoked to get the better of the enemy. Such a prospect was no new thing in war, and had for some time been evident to students of such campaigns as had had for their object the reduction of an entire nationality. The European forefathers of these very burghers had proved that the weaker people need not own even time itself as their subduer, but rather as their deliverer. The flag of peace in South Africa, then, was still below the horizon, and nowhere did it seem less likely to emerge immediately than in the Western Transvaal at the New Year of 1901.

Babington, left at Ventersdorp in command of his own, Gordon's, Kekewich's and Pulteney's columns, was early on the move towards Rustenburg, with the intention of driving northward, whilst Breedts Nek, recognised at last as the enemy's chief passage through the mountains, was blocked by Gordon. On January 5th De la Rey was come upon near Naauwpoort, between the Witwatersrand and the Magaliesberg, and was duly pushed northward, not, however, before he had inflicted a loss of forty-eight men upon the scouts of the Imperial Light Horse, who rode too eagerly into close range of his lines. On the 9th Babington was back at Ventersdorp, leaving the patrolling of the Magaliesberg and the Hekpoort valley to Paget and Plumer, who had arrived at Commando Nek the day before, to Clements on the Rustenburg road, and to Gordon south of Breedts Nek. As he marched south Beyers on his left flank did the same, and on the 8th fell in with a convoy for Gordon coming from Krugersdorp. The Boers were repulsed with loss ; but Beyers was under urgent orders to join Commandant-General Botha in the expedition against Natal, and, pushing on, he camped on the night of the 11th only ten miles north of Johannesburg. On the 12th he fell upon the railway with all his force, and after a warm bombardment broke across to the eastward, laagering that night at Bapsfontein on a position too strong for the small forces which hurried out from Springs and Germiston in pursuit. Gordon from Breedts Nek, E. C. Knox from Johannesburg, and Plumer from the Hekpoort valley were immediately on Beyers' track, Knox coming into contact with him on the 13th. But the Boer leader was travelling too fast to be caught or turned from his union with Botha at Ermelo. Knox's column therefore abandoned the chase, to resume it in a few days as a unit in the extensive operations in the Eastern Transvaal described in the last chapter.

Meanwhile De la Rey remained in the west, and Babington, his Headquarters transferred to Naauwpoort, watched him as closely as possible with the columns serving in the district. To these had been added the force lately commanded by Clements and now by Cunningham, who handed over Rustenburg to Lieut.-Colonel B. J. C. Doran (Royal Irish regiment), and marched through Olifants Nek to join the rest. So doing he was hotly attacked in the defile, and for two days was hard put to it to hold his own in the unfavourable ground. Babington's approach from Ventersdorp on the 25th eased the pressure, and getting through with a loss of fifty-seven killed and wounded, Cunningham gained touch with Babington and camped at Vlakfontein. De la Rey had now thrown detachments in all directions. One penetrated into Bechuanaland; another, more than 1,000 strong under the State Attorney, J. C. Smuts, entered the Gatsrand,

Capture of Modderfontein, Jan. 31st, 1901.

and on January 31st surrounded Modderfontein. This post, after an attack lasting forty-four hours, was literally overwhelmed by force of numbers, many of the soldiers being disarmed, as they were shooting in one direction, by Boers coming up from the other.* A convoy which arrived from Krugersdorp at the height of the fighting—the failure of the sun having made a warning heliogram impossible—became part of the enemy's booty. Cunningham, who had come down to Gemsbokfontein

---

* Casualties—Killed, two officers and eighteen men; wounded, two officers and forty-seven men; captured and missing, three officers and 190 men.

EVENTS IN THE WESTERN TRANSVAAL.

on January 31st, was immediately ordered to Modderfontein, together with six companies of infantry, under Lieut.-Colonel the Hon. U. de R. B. Roche (South Wales Borderers), which had been detailed to relieve the place as soon as its danger had become known. On February 2nd Cunningham marched southward with 2,500 men, and was quickly in touch with the captors of the garrison. But Smuts had been reinforced and was now so strongly fortified that Cunningham, after vainly endeavouring to turn his flank, was glad to be able to withdraw with no more than forty casualties, and marched back to the railway at Roodepoort, intending to try to turn the Boer position by a wide movement from the western arm of the Gatsrand. For some days, therefore, Smuts was left master of the field, and in such high feather that he wrote to De Wet proposing to join him in his descent on Cape Colony " to bring about a revolution."* A week elapsed before Cunningham was again on the offensive, working now in co-operation with a column which had been formed at Potchefstroom under Colonel G. E. Benson, R.A. Cunningham's instructions were to make for the Frederikstad area, and for the rest of February he patrolled the Gatsrand with little damage to himself or to the enemy, who was not now to be found anywhere in strength except on one occasion at Buffelsdoorns (February 13th) when he was left undisturbed. On the 28th Cunningham was back at Krugersdorp.

Meanwhile Lord Methuen had entered this sphere of operations from the west. Throughout December and January he had been manœuvring without cessation, now between Lichtenburg and Otto's Hoop and Zeerust, at all of which he left garrisons; now into Griqualand West (January 22nd), where a Boer incursion from the south caused anxiety; now at Vryburg (December 31st), and finally at Taungs, whence he garrisoned and provisioned Kuruman, ninety-eight miles south-west of Vryburg (January 16th—25th). Owing to the departure of the columns from the Krugersdorp command, and the disturbed

* Smuts to De Wet, February 10th, 1901.

condition of the country south of that place, Lord Kitchener decided to call Lord Methuen eastward. On February 5th he left Taungs, had a slight engagement at Schweizer Reneke (which he had evacuated on January 9th), and on the 13th reached Wolmaranstad. Continuing his march on the 15th he obtained information that a large laager belonging to the commandos which had hung about him since leaving Taungs lay at Brakpan, north-west of Klerksdorp. He further discovered that the Boer fighting force was lying in wait for him at Hartebeestfontein, across the direct Klerksdorp road, leaving their encampment weakly guarded at Brakpan, which they thought to be safely out of the line of march. Lord Methuen, therefore, determined to strike at the laager first, and marching at midnight on the 17th, surprised the camp guards. By noon he was in possession of the whole laager, with thirty-six prisoners, sixty-seven wagons and carts and quantities of gear of every description. He then turned towards Hartebeestfontein. Here he found himself confronted by nearly 1,500 Boers, under De Villiers and De Beers, posted on the plateau on either side of a defile which led towards Klerksdorp, and bent on resisting to the utmost the despoiler of their laager. Lord Methuen first attempted to gain the western height, but the 5th Imperial Yeomanry whom he sent thither with a Vickers-Maxim were so hotly received that they were unable to gain ground, though they were not to be shaken off all day from the spurs and flanks of the hill. Leaving them to hold the enemy there, Lord Methuen ordered the 10th Imperial Yeomanry to storm the eastern wall, covering the advance by four field guns. The attack was brilliantly delivered, and the nearer crest won with little loss; but the Boers then fell back to the more distant edge of the plateau, and the task of the Yeomanry became formidable. Not only had they to face a serious fire from the front, but the enemy on the unconquered western crest now had them in full view; a flanking fire from the left swept the summit of the plateau, whilst danger appeared in the rear in the shape of 500 Boers who approached and engaged the escort of the convoy. Reinforced by the Victorians the Yeomanry continued to gain ground, fighting like veteran troops

EVENTS IN THE WESTERN TRANSVAAL.

from one cover to another; finally, greatly relieved by detached attacks which Lord Methuen launched against prominent parts of the Boer stronghold on either flank, the whole line charged against the southern edge of the plateau and tumbled the enemy on to the plain below, where he was punished severely with a following fire. By this spirited action, which cost forty-eight casualties,* the road to Klerksdorp was opened, and on February 19th Lord Methuen marched in with all his forces and an immense mass of captured stock, forage and Boer families.

Lord Methuen, however, was not to remain long in the Klerksdorp district. After a few days of bustling operations in conjunction with Benson in the triangle Klerksdorp—Potchefstroom—Ventersdorp he again turned towards his own district in order to withdraw the garrison of Hoopstad, marching by Wolmaranstad, south of which, on March 6th, he found the local commando standing between him and Commando Drift, by which he intended to cross the Vaal river. A running fight of twenty-three hours' duration brought the column to the banks of the stream; but a high flood was in progress, and try where he would Lord Methuen was unable to find a practicable passage, though he marched down the whole length of the right bank as far as Fourteen Streams, which was reached on March 14th.

This enforced change of direction, unwelcome as it was, was perhaps fortunate, for behind Lord Methuen on March 8th there occurred at Wolmaranstad a concentration of commandos strong enough to have overmatched the British column, which it was the Boers' avowed object to pursue to Bloemhof. At Warrenton Lord Methuen was placed temporarily on the sick list, and Colonel the Earl of Erroll, who assumed command, carried out the original purpose of the march by leading the column to Hoopstad and back between March 27th and April 7th. On April 23rd Lord Methuen resumed command, and at once transferred his force to Mafeking for service against De la Rey, who *De la Rey concentrates,*

---

* Casualties—Killed, three officers, thirteen men; wounded, five officers, twenty-seven men.

had been practically unmolested in the Lichtenburg district for the past two months, since Babington's line of posts was almost powerless beyond its own piquets. De la Rey had employed his freedom to singularly small purpose, save in fermenting the country and deluding British columns into long and purposeless marches. On March 6th De la Rey, with Celliers and Vermaas, 1,500 men in all, made an attack on Lichtenburg which seemed at first certain to be successful. Penetrating the outposts, which were widely separated owing to the large circumference of the defences, the Boers surrounded each piquet in turn and cut them off from all communications with Headquarters. The piquets, however, were strongly entrenched, and fought valiantly, and the enemy could get no further during twenty-four hours, finally retiring after as singular an investment as had occurred during the campaign. The Boers lost, besides much credit, sixty-seven burghers; the troops, who were ably commanded by Lieut.-Colonel C. E. Money (Northumberland Fusiliers), had sixteen killed and twenty-six wounded, and gained great honour for their stout resistance to superior numbers. Foiled at Lichtenburg the federal combination then rushed southward, and on the 8th joined the Wolmaranstad men at their capital with the intention, as previously referred to, of cutting off Lord Methuen from his march down the Vaal. But the British commander had two days' start, and all innocent as he was of the storm gathered in his rear, was making too good speed towards Fourteen Streams to be worth following. Immediately on news of the attack on Lichtenburg reaching Headquarters, Babington, still at Naauwpoort, was ordered to the relief of the place, to be joined at Ventersdorp by Lieut.-Colonel H. P. Shekleton with a column from Rooipoort. It was fortunate that Lichtenburg was in no need of assistance, for Babington, delayed by bad weather, did not appear until the 17th. He then turned southward after the long vanished enemy, arriving at Klerksdorp on March 21st with sixty-two prisoners taken in the constant but unimportant skirmishing which had fallen to his lot.

Two days later De la Rey, with 500 men and three guns,

EVENTS IN THE WESTERN TRANSVAAL.

beset one of Babington's patrols at Geduld, within twenty miles of his Headquarters. The patrol, which was composed of men of the 1st Imperial Light Horse, was less than half the strength of the enemy, and had but one Vickers-Maxim, but it was well handled by Major C. J. Briggs (King's Dragoon Guards), and defended itself so resolutely that once more De la Rey had the mortification of seeing his men retire beaten from a field where all the odds had been in their favour. The Boers lost some two dozen killed and wounded; the British party two officers and five men killed, three officers and thirteen men wounded. Babington coming up next day drove the Boers still further northward, and on the 24th completed their rout by overtaking and capturing the whole of their guns, nine in number, including two 15-prs., a Vickers-Maxim, and six Maxims, all with ammunition complete, transport to the number of seventy-seven wagons and carts, and all the camp stuff, together with the escort of 140 men, on the banks of the Taaibosch Spruit. The action which brought about this success was a model of pursuing tactics. The enemy continually took up strong rearguard positions, out of which Babington as constantly manœuvred them by vigorous threats at the flanks, withholding a powerful and menacing front until the defence had actually begun to dissolve under the lateral pressure. The result was a series of hasty retreats on the part of De la Rey's rearguard, soon degenerating into a rout which infected the whole force and hurried it in disorder from the field. This was a heavy blow to De la Rey, whose star was now considerably obscured by such repeated terminations to forays, the first speed and spirit of which had died at the moment of action. Babington with Shekleton then made for Ventersdorp, where he halted on March 26th, Shekleton soon after handing over command of his column to Lieut.-Colonel Sir H. Rawlinson.

is defeated by Babington, March 24th, 1901.

It is necessary now to revert to Benson, who, it will be remembered, had been in co-operation with Lord Methuen for the short time that officer was in the Klerksdorp area before his departure to Fourteen Streams and Hoopstad. Benson then received orders to traverse the country east of Frederikstad, and arriving there on March 4th, marched to Kaalplaats next day. He was busily employed in clearing the farms when the news of De la Rey's attack on Lichtenburg caused him to be recalled to Frederikstad, and thence to Potchefstroom (March 9th), where he remained hemmed in by flooded roads until the 15th. Thence he proceeded to scour the country lying between the Vaal, the railway and the Gatsrand, being in constant touch with the enemy until the end of the month, when he halted on the Riet Spruit with fifteen prisoners, fifty wagons and a great herd of captured stock. On April 4th Benson marched to Krugersdorp where his force was broken up, and he and his staff transferred to another column, the eventful career of which will be followed elsewhere.*

During March Cunningham had been holding Naauwpoort since Babington's departure for the relief of Lichtenburg. On April 7th he was relieved in command by Brigadier-General H. G. Dixon, who also absorbed the column lately commanded by Benson. The command of the Klerksdorp area had shortly before been delegated to Major-General M. W. Willson, who thus found himself in control of the columns of Babington, Dixon and Sir H. Rawlinson. These he was anxious to concentrate for combined operations in the Schoon Spruit district; but the Commander-in-Chief was unwilling to relax even temporarily his hold on Naauwpoort, the key of the campaign in these parts; Dixon, therefore, remained about Naauwpoort during April, making sundry raids between that place and the railway at Welverdiend, and was finally diverted on April 28th towards Tafel Kop.

Babington, based on Ventersdorp, operated on both sides of that place during April, being at Tafel Kop on the 4th, and on the 18th near Klerksdorp, to the west of which he found De la Rey with Kemp in full strength on his old ground at Hartebeestfontein. The enemy was not pressed, however, and Babington moved by the Schoon and Taaibosch Spruits to Syferkuil, thus leaving the enemy threatening his communica-

* See Chapter XVII.

tions with Klerksdorp, on which he depended for supplies. As a result, an empty convoy which he despatched to Klerksdorp on the 22nd was attacked from all sides at Brakspruit on the Schoon Spruit by 700 Boers, who rode out of the Hartebeestfontein hills; but the skill of its commander, Major H. T. Lyle (Royal Welsh Fusiliers), and the stoutness of the escort preserved it from capture. The enemy was beaten back with the loss of more than thirty men, and the convoy proceeded in safety with the loss of eight of its guards.

Sir H. Rawlinson had for the most part co-operated in Babington's operations during April, and his movements were generally indistinguishable from those of his superior. On one occasion, however, he had an experience individual indeed. On April 13th a laager had been discovered near to the scene of Lord Methuen's capture two months earlier at Brakpan. The laager, which contained a 12-pr. gun and a Vickers-Maxim, was surprised by a night march conducted by Babington, and captured with all its contents by Sir H. Rawlinson's column. It was not until after they had lost their camp that the enemy returned from a *sauve qui peut* to fight. So close did they come in from all sides that the guns of P. battery R.H.A. had to face in opposite directions to drive skirmishers almost from their muzzles, whilst Sir H. Rawlinson, who was riding close behind the battery, found himself in the midst of a band who shot his horse and disarmed him. In the confusion caused by the short-range artillery fire he contrived to escape, and rejoining his troops, easily held the enemy for the rest of the day with the assistance of Babington, who had been marching wide on the right and now came across to reinforce. This was a most successful affair, for whilst the Boers lost, besides their guns and all their impedimenta, twenty-three prisoners and sixteen other casualties, Sir H. Rawlinson had but three men slightly wounded. These, though a host of minor incidents are necessarily omitted, were the chief events of the campaign in the Western Transvaal up to the end of April, 1901.

Affair at Brakpan, April 13th, 1901.

APPROXIMATE STRENGTH STATES OF COLUMNS REFERRED TO IN FOREGOING CHAPTER.

COLUMN.	Mounted Troops.	Infantry.	Guns, including Vickers-Maxims.	Machine Guns.	
January—April, 1901.					
Maj.-Gen. J. M. Babington	470	450	6	1	
Col. W. P. Pulteney ..	—	941	3	1	Lt.-Gen. J. D. P. French in command.
Brig.-Gen. J. R. P. Gordon	1,085	80	11	4	
Col. R. G. Kekewich ..	700	280	5	2	
Col. E. C. Knox	883	270	8	—	
Maj.-Gen. R. A. P. Clements	883	1,647	14	2	
Maj.-Gen. A. H. Paget ..	100	1,400	4	1	Maj.-Gen. A. H. Paget in command.
Col. M. Cradock	500	—	2	1	
Brig.-Gen. H. C. O. Plumer	450	—	8	—	
Brig.-Gen. G. G. Cunningham	100	1,460	6	2	
Lt.-Col. G. E. Benson ..	365	515	6	—	
Lt.-Gen. Lord P. Methuen	1,294	—	8	5	
Lt.-Col. H. P. Shekleton ..	1,500	—	8	—	
Brig.-Gen. H. G. Dixon ..	1,050	1,216	8	2	
Maj.-Gen. J. M. Babington	860	580	9	—	Maj.-Gen. M. W. Willson in command.
Col. Sir H. Rawlinson (late Shekleton's)	1,250	—	2	—	

CHAPTER VIII.

EVENTS IN THE EASTERN TRANSVAAL AND NATAL*

(*Continued from Chapter VI.*).

APRIL—MAY, 1901.

NEARLY three weeks before the conclusion of French's operations south of the Pretoria—Delagoa Bay railway, Lord Kitchener had taken the preliminary steps in a similar scheme, to be worked out to the northward of that line. On March 26th Brigadier-General H. C. O. Plumer was despatched to Pietersburg, which was occupied almost without fighting on April 8th. Plumer, who for this purpose was withdrawn from the pursuit of De Wet in the Orange River Colony,† had with him a mounted force, composed of Australian and New Zealand corps, and numbering 1,200 men with eight guns. He remained at Pietersburg until the 14th, his line of communications with Pretoria being held by the 2nd Gordon Highlanders, the 2nd Northamptonshire, and 2nd Wiltshire regiments. *Preparations for clearance of the north-eastern Transvaal.*

Meanwhile, for the projected clearance six columns had been prepared, under the command of Lieut.-General Sir B. Blood, which on the evening of April 13th were stationed as follows:

Place.	Commander.	Infantry.‡	Mounted Troops.‡	Guns, including Vickers-Maxims.	
Lydenburg	Lieut.-Col. C. W. Park	930	200	3	Under command of Major-Gen. F.W. Kitchener.
,,	Major-Gen. F. W. Kitchener	2,290	550	6	
Witklip ...	Lt.-Col. W. Douglas ...	1,280	330	3	
Belfast ...	Lt.-Col. W. P. Pulteney	800	750	8	Under command of Major-Gen. R. S. R. Fetherstonhaugh.
Middelburg	Lt.-Col. G. E. Benson	350	720	8	
,,	Maj.-Gen. S. B. Beatson	1,020	600	4	
		6,670	3,150	32	
		9,820			

* See map No. 56.   † See Chapter V.   ‡ Round numbers only.

The country to be swept was roughly a square, nearly bisected by the Steelpoort river, and bounded on the north by the 25th parallel of latitude, on the south by the railway, on the east by the Stenkamps Berg, on the west by the Oliphant river. Towards its central point—the reported refuge of the Transvaal Government at Roos Senekal—the columns were to converge from north, east, and south, the expected breakaway to the westward being blocked by the seizure of the drifts over the Oliphant by Plumer, who would thus enact along that river a *rôle* similar to that recently performed in the south-eastern Transvaal by Smith-Dorrien around the Swazi border.

Two days before the machine was set in motion the Acting President and his officials had slipped out of its reach, and were in safety by the side of Commandant-General Botha. On the very day on which Blood's columns moved to enclose Roos Senekal, the Transvaal Government body was setting out from Ermelo to meet ex-President Steyn at Vrede. Whether this timely evasion was by accident or design, the British operations in the north came as no surprise to Botha. A month earlier he had warned General B. Viljoen of the probability of such an event, and had cautioned him against being taken unawares.* It will be seen how narrowly that leader escaped, despite the foresight of his chief.

Sir B. Blood's operations in the north-eastern Transvaal.

Of Sir B. Blood's columns that of Park was the first to move. Leaving Lydenburg on the evening of April 12th, Park marched northward by Krugerspost, seeking a position whence he could block the northern exits of the Steelpoort and Waterval valleys. At dawn on the 13th he reached Vlakfontein. A commanding nek near De Grootboom, which threatened to bar his next day's progress, was seized the same evening by a party of mounted infantry under Major H. B. Walker (Duke of Cornwall's Light Infantry) who performed a forced march of thirty-five miles to gain their end. The main column followed to Klipkloof on the 13th, and next day to De Grootboom, where an attack on the

---

* Letter from the Commandant-General to General B. Viljoen, March 17th, 1901.

EVENTS IN EASTERN TRANSVAAL AND NATAL. 141

rearguard was driven off with three casualties. On the 15th Park reached Bergfontein, where he took a small laager and much ammunition. Thence he sent on a detachment to seize the Magnets Hoogte which commanded the passage of the Steelpoort. Park then moved to Rietfontein. F. W. Kitchener had left Lydenburg on the night of the 13th and come up by Boschhoek and Boschfontein, in hot pursuit of a 94-pr. gun. This piece, the identical cannon which had bombarded Ladysmith from Pepworth Hill sixteen months before, was blown up by the enemy as it was on the point of being taken. On April 17th F. W. Kitchener moved on towards Magnets Hoogte, whilst Park, remaining at Rietfontein, sent into the eastern valley-fork of the Dwars river two small columns under Lieut.-Colonel H. W. N. Guinness (Royal Irish regiment) and Major C. L. E. Eustace (King's Royal Rifles). These met with immediate success; for the enemy, chased eastward from the valley by Guinness, ran into Eustace as he lay in wait at Vygehoek, and sixty-two burghers with 1,000 cattle were the prize. The two parties remained out until the 20th, when Park, recalling them, turned his attention to the Waterval valley, which he shut up with four divisions of his command, thereby enclosing and capturing on April 25th, forty-two Boers, two guns, and much stock. He then returned to Rietfontein, where he remained until May 3rd, leaving no corner of his neighbourhood unscoured. Meanwhile F. W. Kitchener had arrived on the Magnets Hoogte on the 18th, marching the next day *via* Pokwani to Fort Weeber, where he gained touch with Plumer, whose movements in the interval must now be described.

Leaving a garrison in Pietersburg, Plumer had quitted the town on the 14th April, pointing on the Oliphant river. On the 16th, after an uneventful march, he was upon the banks of the stream, which he proceeded to hold from its junction with the Malips river to some fifty miles up stream, by means of the drifts at Port Scheiding, Tabakplaats, Oliphant's Poort, Bathfontein, to Koedoes Kop, with many lesser passages between; extending eventually (April 22nd) as far as Commissie Drift, twenty-two miles further up the river. Plumer received

Plumer on the Oliphant river.

supplies from P. P. Rust for his posts on the upper river, for those on the lower from Pietersburg. The journeys of convoys, though never interrupted, were not unaccompanied by fighting. On one occasion (April 24th) fourteen Boers were captured during an attack on an escort commanded by Lieut.-Colonel J. W. Colenbrander, at Jaskraal.

Plumer by no means contented himself with passively watching the drifts. He had early sent patrols into F. W. Kitchener's lines at Fort Weeber, and his parties wandered far afield. On April 25th Lieutenant G. E. Reid (4th Imperial Bushmen's corps), the officer at Commissie Drift, located a Boer camp fifteen miles to the south-east. This was a party resting from a twenty-four hours' flight from the 1st Devonshire regiment, of F. W. Kitchener's force. Under cover of darkness Reid surrounded it with only twenty men who at daybreak rushed in and captured the whole laager, taking the commandant, twice their own number of burghers, a Maxim gun, besides wagons, horses and cattle. On April 29th, when Sir B. Blood's operations were drawing to a conclusion, Plumer concentrated at Commissie Drift, and on the following days marched down the lines of the Elands and Kameel rivers, *viâ* Uyskraal, Slagboom, Pieterskraal to Enkeldedoorns. Beatson was at this time moving parallel to Plumer down the Wilge river towards Eerstefabrieken, whilst Allenby, fresh from the operations at Piet Retief, was out from Witbank in co-operation with the two columns which were working southward. From Enkeldedoorns Plumer detached a party under Major H. G. Vialls (3rd regiment Australian Bushmen) in pursuit of bands which were scattering across the railway about Hamanskraal from the area traversed by Beatson. Vialls, having chased them about all day, bivouacked at Haakdoornfontein in the evening, with twenty-seven prisoners, and a convoy of Boer wagons and cattle in his possession. On May 4th Plumer gained the eastern railway at Eerstefabrieken.

Whilst the " stop " on the Oliphant river was thus occupied, the main " drive " to the eastward had been in full progress. On April 14th, when Park was at De Grootboom and F. W.

EVENTS IN EASTERN TRANSVAAL AND NATAL. 143

Kitchener at Boschhoek, Douglas, trending south-west from Witklip, seized the Zwagershoek Pass, camped at Zuikerboschhoek that night, at Palmietfontein on the next, and on the 16th, after handsomely repulsing a determined attack by 700 Boers led by Muller, entered Dullstroom, which he made his centre of operations for the remainder of the month. Pulteney, who had come up along the Belfast road by Moeyelykheid, joined Douglas at Dullstroom on the 17th, whilst on the same day Beatson, who had struck north from Middelburg, and marched by Driefontein and Klipplaatdrift to Naauwpoort, fought a successful skirmish in the Botha's Berg. Benson's—the other column from Middelburg—with which went Sir B. Blood, was then at Bankfontein, facing north-east with the object of turning the Botha's Berg by the east, as Beatson meant to turn that range by the west. Thus a circle of troops some seventy-five miles in diameter had begun to compress the area around Roos Senekal, and had there been any formed bodies of the enemy therein, they must soon have been forced to a battle. But the commandos of B. Viljoen, in spite of his efforts to hold them together, had scattered into the thousand rifts and secret places of the district, until the whole country-side teemed with small groups, which lurked invisible until by chance or perseverance some were discovered and hunted from their holes. Only a minority remained around Viljoen, who began to look about anxiously for a sally-port. The cordon around him tightened daily. On April 20th Sir B. Blood was with Benson at Blinkwater, behind the Botha's Berg; Pulteney close to the eastward at Windhoek; Beatson, who had turned the Botha's Berg by Avontuur and Laatste Drift, at Leeuwfontein to the westward; F. W. Kitchener and Park being, as already described, respectively at Fort Weeber and in the act of clearing the Dwars River and Waterval valleys. On the 19th Benson had scored a signal success by the capture of twenty-nine Boers with a convoy at Klipspruit, Beatson taking a smaller number near Wagendrift. On his arrival at Blinkwater Benson was met by a body of 100 Boers desirous of surrender, most of whom

Viljoen's forces scatter.

had been previously deprived of horses and ammunition by Viljoen.

Operations next day by Benson resulted in the voluntary surrender of thirty-two more burghers and the capture of thirty-one; a Krupp gun, discovered upset in a kloof, was also secured. On the same day one of Beatson's patrols, consisting of only six men under Lieutenant J. H. Brabazon (Victorian Mounted Rifles), ranging far across the Oliphant, and even across the Moos river, chased and captured a convoy of ten wagons and fourteen Boers. Meanwhile F. W. Kitchener had cleared the country southward through Pokwani down to Paardeplaats, where he camped on the 23rd. Pulteney during the same period had moved northward from Windhoek to Klipbankspruit, and thence on the 22nd to Roos Senekal, capturing four, and accepting the surrender of sixty Boers on the way. Sixty-eight more capitulated during the next few days, which Pulteney devoted to searching the environs of the town, finding amongst other trophies a Vickers-Maxim and a 15-pr. gun, both destroyed, and a parcel of Transvaal banknotes of the face value of £50,000. Pulteney joined Headquarters at Blinkwater on April 29th, by which time F. W. Kitchener had descended to Holnek, and Beatson, working from Roodepoort, had thoroughly swept the angle formed by the sharp easterly turn of the Oliphant river at Slaghoek. Benson had joined Douglas at Dullstroom on the 28th, and on the 30th both columns, under Douglas's command, proceeded to attack a band which had gathered at Roodekranz, a position threatening the line of retreat on Belfast. In the brief engagement which resulted, three Boers were killed and two captured; and all were dislodged, though mist and the difficulty of the ground prevented an attack being pressed home. F. W. Kitchener, now on his homeward way, had come still further southward, and on April 30th held a line from Buffelsvlei, through Rooikraal to Kleinfontein on the northern slopes of the Botha's Berg; Park was still at Rietfontein; Benson and Douglas in the neighbourhood of Dullstroom; Pulteney with Sir B. Blood at Blinkwater; Beatson, whose share in the operations was now ended,

EVENTS IN EASTERN TRANSVAAL AND NATAL. 145

was about Roodepoort, whence he soon after began the march back to the line in the co-operation with Plumer which has already been referred to.

Meanwhile B. Viljoen, wandering about Mapoch's Gronden in the very vortex of the revolving columns, had been making desperate efforts to escape. On the 20th April his position had become intolerable, and Benson's success at Klipspruit warned him that but a few hours remained in which to make a dash for liberty. On that night Viljoen burnt all his transport, destroyed his few remaining guns, and stole out southward, intending to work his way down the valley of the Steelpoort to Wonderfontein, there to cross the railway and gain the freedom of the High Veld. But his scouts found Benson barring the way at Blinkwater, and Pulteney at Windhoek; and Viljoen, baffled on every side, returned before dawn to his abandoned bivouac at Mapoch's. Previous to his march a hundred of his burghers, chiefly men of the Boksburg commando, having no heart for such an adventure, had deserted him in a body, openly announcing their intention to surrender. These, as related, gave themselves up to Benson at Blinkwater. Shut in on east and south, Viljoen saw that his only hope of safety, and that a faint one, lay to the westward. As soon as darkness fell on the 22nd, he led his men across the Steelpoort at Lagersdrift, struck thence north-westward along the Bloed river, and evading Beatson's patrols and outposts reached the banks of the Oliphant before dawn on the 23rd. By sunrise he was safely over a dangerous and little known drift situated near the confluence of the Bloed and Oliphant rivers. Viljoen then gave out to the natives—the best intelligence department of his adversaries—that he was bound for Pietersburg, and for a while marched steadily in that direction. But striking the Moos river, he swung suddenly south-west along its course, and by the evening was on its headstream at Roodepoortje. Next day, turning eastward, he crossed the Wilge below Langkloof, and bivouacked at Blackwoods Camp, less than twenty miles north of Balmoral, where he hoped to cross the railway. Here, actually in rear of the columns which had hunted him for a

Viljoen's efforts to escape.

Viljoen escapes,

fortnight, he remained for several days, so confident of security that he ventured to send a detachment back across the Oliphant to attack the post at Wagendrift. In the first week in May the commando, divided into two parties, safely effected the passage of the line between Balmoral and Brugspruit. Viljoen, leaving his men to a much needed rest at Kromdraai, near the sources of the Wilge river, then rode on to join the Commandant-General at Beginderlyn on the Vaal, south of Ermelo. In this manner did Boer leaders, not once, but on many occasions, slip from the grasp of their pursuers; nor are there methods of war which can frustrate them, except by a fortunate chance. In a wide country full of innumerable hiding places, against an enemy who is acquainted with them all and has a mobility which enables him to vanish from one haunt when it becomes unsafe to the next, and again to a third or a fourth in the course of a day or a night, what art can close every outlet, or what number of troops watch every hollow and every thicket, though any one may contain the sought-for game? Under such conditions the escape of well-led fugitives even from vastly greater forces is not only practicable but easy, and few but the careless, the treacherous, or the faint-hearted will be caught.

On May 2nd, Pulteney, surrounding Roos Senekal after a night march from Blinkwater, secured a small laager to the north of the town, the Boers losing thirteen men. This was the last noteworthy incident of the operations, which were soon afterwards concluded. On May 5th Sir B. Blood returned to Middelburg, and during the next few days all his columns regained their respective bases. Three weeks of ceaseless activity had resulted in the capture of 1,439 armed Boers, nine guns, 750 rifles, half a million rounds of S.A. ammunition, 964 wagons and carts, and nearly 55,000 head of stock, besides two engines and thirty-six trucks found by Plumer in Pietersburg station.

With scarcely a pause the Commander-in-Chief now turned the tide of war from north to south of the Pretoria—Delagoa Bay railway. Once more the scattered townships of the south-eastern Transvaal—refuges which French had vainly solicited permission to raze to the ground—had begun to attract the

EVENTS IN EASTERN TRANSVAAL AND NATAL.

hunted bands who roved the country in search of rest. There was, in short, every indication of a re-occupation by the enemy; to nip it whilst yet in the bud no fewer than thirteen columns were prepared early in May.

Colonel G. M. Bullock, relieved of his supervision of French's convoys in the Wakkerstroom Hills, had come into Volksrust, and there, on April 25th, had taken over from Dartnell—whose political duties recalled him to Natal—the command of his column, with promotion to the rank of Brigadier-General. This force, in conjunction with another under Colonel M. F. Rimington from Standerton, Lord Kitchener now directed on Ermelo, whilst eleven other columns made ready to thresh out the same area. Bullock, leaving Volksrust on April 29th, marched by Amersfoort, the Riet Spruit, Tweefontein, and Vereeniging, failing to gain touch with Colville's and two other small columns which went out to co-operate from Standerton and Platrand towards Blauw Kop. On May 9th Bullock arrived at Ermelo, after several spirited skirmishes with General Botha who was here in company with B. Viljoen, the latter just come from the scene of his adventures around Roos Senekal. Rimington started from Standerton on May 14th and moved along the Ermelo road with a convoy for Bullock, whom he joined on the 16th. Thereafter the two units, raiding the country in all directions, took up a stopping line from Ermelo up to Lake Chrissie, blocking the exits from the area about to be swept by the main force. A column at Nelspruit under Brigadier-General J. Spens effected the same service at the northern outlets, playing indeed a double part, for Park was driving the country from Lydenburg down to Nelspruit *via* the Mauch Berg, and Spens placed himself to turn both Park's quarry fleeing southward, and fugitives making northward out of the Ermelo district. Now began two distinct but converging sets of operations, one by Sir B. Blood from the Delagoa Bay railway, the other by Plumer from Pretoria and the western line. These it will be necessary to describe separately.

Bullock and Rimington.

The tactics of Sir B. Blood had as their object a junction with Bullock, and a complete clearance of the zones around

Sir B. Blood's tactics.

Carolina, Steynsdorp, down to Amsterdam, much of which had been untouched by French during his raid of March and April. For this task six columns and a brigade of cavalry were allotted which up to May 12th were posted as follows :—At Middelburg, Major-General F. W. Kitchener and Lieut.-Colonel W. P. Pulteney; at Belfast, Lieut.-Colonel G. E. Benson; at Machadodorp, Lieut.-Colonel W. Douglas; at Wonderfontein, Major-General J. M. Babington with the cavalry brigade; at Nelspruit, Brigadier-General J. Spens, to be joined later by Colonel C. W. Park from Lydenburg.

<small>Sir B. Blood marches south from Middelburg.</small>

F. W. Kitchener and Pulteney marched out of Middelburg on May 13th, and sweeping the country on either bank of the Klein Oliphant river, were between its source and that of the Komati river on the 16th, camping at Groblers Recht and Witkrans respectively.* Douglas reached Uitkomst on the same date, his left flank harassed all day from Schoonwater, and his wagons impeded both by morasses and by bands whom he finally drove with loss south over Boschoek into the Komati valley. F. W. Kitchener and Pulteney reached the Carolina—Ermelo road at the source of the Vaal river on the 18th, when Benson, who had only left Belfast on the 16th, was at Bonnefoi, where he joined hands with Douglas, and co-operated with him in hunting the scattered groups of Boers who were in hiding in the Komati valley. Carolina, guarded on three sides, was now safe, and there the cavalry brigade was based on the 18th for operations to the eastward. Pulteney, échelonned on F. W. Kitchener's right-front at Goodeverwachting, made Lake Chrissie on the 19th, these two columns pushing on to Florence and Lilliburn on the 20th, next day to Weltevreden and Holnek, and on the 22nd to Jacht Lust and Pittville, whilst Benson and Douglas to the northward cleared to the banks of the Komati about Kalk Kloof and Driehoek. On the 27th Pulteney occupied Steynsdorp.

Whilst the columns circled about these areas, running down with an infinity of toil the broken handfuls of Boers who fled

---

* For gallantry on May 16th Lieutenant F. W. Bell, West Australian M.I., was awarded the Victoria Cross.

before them, or hid in their very midst, the cavalry, coming forward by Rietfontein, Silverkop and Boschoek (on the Zekoe Spruit), entered the Komati valley below Benson, and endeavoured likewise to track fugitives, drive cattle, and collect wagons and Boer families. The brigade returned to Boschoek on the 28th with but a single prisoner, with twenty-five burghers voluntarily surrendered, and a quantity of stock and wagons. Where infantry, scrupulously searching for individuals or trifling laagers over the scarred country by day and night could reap however small a harvest, cavalry might have been expected to glean more than a few ears. The total gain of all these columns by the end of May was but 142 Boers (of whom four were killed in action, and forty-four had voluntarily surrendered), about 270 wagons and carts, and some 36,000 head of stock; and both troops and commanders were mortified to discover how little their severe exertions were affecting the fortunes of the campaign. From the end of May to the middle of June, F. W. Kitchener and Pulteney beat up these districts between the Komati and Impilusi valleys, and from Lake Chrissie to the Swazi border. The cavalry worked from Silverkop, concentrating there on May 30th, when Benson returned to Carolina; whilst Douglas, after exhaustive operations around Driehoek, retouched the line at Machadodorp on June 5th. On that date also Bullock, having marched with many a foray by Beginderlyn, went into Standerton with thirty prisoners and 180 Boer wagons.

Meanwhile, Plumer with his own, Allenby's, and E. Knox's columns had been similarly employed in the western half of the High Veld area. Plumer, it will be remembered, had gone to Eerstefabrieken, after his operations on the drifts of the Oliphant. Thence he moved to Silverton, where he lay on May 13th, his coadjutors, Allenby and E. C. Knox, being at Witbank and Greylingstad respectively on that date. On May 14th all three columns started to converge on the sources of the Wilge river. At Kromdraai still rested the exhausted commandos which Viljoen had temporarily abandoned in order to join the Commandant-General at Beginderlyn. Viljoen was now on his

Plumer marches south from Silverton.

way back to his command, with a wary eye for Bullock, who was raiding to the east, and Rimington, who was making his way out from Standerton to join Plumer. Of Plumer and his trio of columns, however, he knew nothing until, arriving on the Steenkool (or Steenbok) Spruit, on the evening of the 15th, he was startled to hear first of Knox's sortie from Greylingstad. Guessing his purpose Viljoen hurriedly extricated his commando; and uniting with Commandant Mears, an independent freebooter of a type irregular even in that army of partisans, spent the ensuing period darting about in the midst of the increasing crowd of his enemies, trying at every hour every point of the compass for an opportunity to sting or a chance to escape.

On May 15th Plumer, marching by Klipkoppies, reached Leeuwpoort, where the Queensland Imperial Bushmen, chasing a knot of fifty Boers, rode them down and captured five. Allenby on the same day camped at Zaaiwater, midway between the Wilge and the Oliphant rivers; and E. C. Knox, at Paardefontein. The two former columns both searched Kromdraai on the 16th, Knox, who had been delayed, getting no further than Zondagskraal, and on the 17th to Grootpan where he communicated with Plumer. On the 18th, Allenby, after handing over a convoy to Plumer, set out *via* Cypherfontein and Bloemendal for Springs, arriving there on the 20th with eight prisoners, many Boer families, and 6,300 head of stock. At Springs he remained some days preparing to co-operate with Beatson in another series of operations which will be described later. Finding Kromdraai to be an empty nest, Plumer now pushed on to Bethel. There by way of Blesbokspruit, and on a front Kaffirskraal—Tweedraai, he arrived with E. C. Knox on May 20th, having been much pestered on the way by skirmishers who clung to his flanks and rear, but melted like mist before his van.

Plumer at Bethel.

On May 21st Rimington, on his return journey from Bullock at Ermelo, came into touch with Bethel and reported the state of the districts through which he had passed. Plumer's intention had been to send this column northward, but hearing that considerable forces still roved between Bethel and Ermelo, he detained Rimington, and arranged a joint drive by the three

Plumer continues southward.

columns in a southerly direction. By the 23rd he had drawn a line of mounted troops completely across the interval between the two towns, posting Rimington at Middelplaat, E. C. Knox at Uitzicht, his own column at Rietpan. The infantry and transport remained at Bethel, with orders to pursue the high road which led southward to the Vaal. On the 24th the line advanced to Uitgezocht (Rimington), Winkelhaak (Knox), Klipfontein (Plumer), and Witbank (transport), and next day to Drinkwater, Klipkraal and Bankhoek. Few Boers were encountered, and those chiefly by Rimington, outside the left flank. To all appearances this country, so recently ravaged by French, contained little but a few deserted families on the farms, and some fields of crops which had been overlooked. But the enemy, practised in being hunted, was not necessarily absent because he was not in front of the chase. Nor was Viljoen a leader slow to profit by an opportunity because he was being pursued; and an opportunity was soon given him. Plumer's transport, following the Standerton road, was marching outside the line of columns; and the Boers, observing this, had dogged it closely, twice attacking the rearguard since leaving Bethel. The train consisted of 120 wagons, and a large herd of stock, escorted by 650 men of the 2nd Somersetshire Light Infantry and 1st Royal Munster Fusiliers; 120 mounted men, and two guns Q. battery R.H.A., the whole under Lieut.-Colonel E. J. Gallwey (Somersetshire Light Infantry). At 6 a.m. on the morning of May 25th this column, as it left Witbank for Mooi- *Plumer's convoy* fontein, was waylaid by Viljoen, and attacked simultaneously *attacked, May* from front, right, and rear. *25th, 1901.*

The Boers fell on with spirit, rushing into close quarters time after time, in spite of the accurate practice of the artillery, and the firmness of the infantry, who beat back every attack. Soon the whole column was enveloped by flaming grass ignited by the enemy, who endeavoured to penetrate into the baggage and snatch the cattle under cover of the smoke. But every attempt was foiled by the steadfastness of the defence. A Vickers-Maxim with which the Boers belaboured the British guns and right flank was quickly silenced; the wagons, stoutly guarded, were gradually moved to a place safe both from the flames and the enemy, and after seven hours of close and anxious fighting Viljoen was beaten off with the loss of nearly forty men, that of Gallwey having been thirty-one.

Plumer regains the railway.

Immediately on hearing of this occurrence Plumer hurried westward towards the convoy, which he conducted as far as Verblyding (May 27th) whence it was passed into Standerton. The arrival of E. C. Knox north of Standerton and of Rimington at Platrand on the 28th concluded the operations, which had yielded thirty-seven prisoners and about 12,000 head of stock.

Allenby and Beatson.

Turning again to Allenby's column at Springs, May 24th saw it marching eastward towards Beatson. The last-named commander had known no rest since he dropped out of Sir B. Blood's operations around Roos Senekal. Unceasingly he had scoured the country on both banks of the Wilge river, between its junction with the Oliphant and the railway—the escaping Viljoen barely avoiding him—finally concentrating at Brugspruit on May 23rd with 166 Boers, many wagons and much stock to the credit of his troops. He immediately received instructions for a foray southward about the junction of the Oliphant river and Steenkool (or Steenbok) Spruit, where the fugitives from Bethel were reported to have collected; Allenby was to co-operate from Springs. Accordingly, Beatson was at Klippan on the 25th, and next day at Van Dyksdrift, at the confluence, where he gained touch with Allenby, who had come by Witklip, Leeuwfontein, and Hartebeestfontein, capturing on the way a small laager, eight prisoners and a Colt gun. Beatson now found himself in the midst of scattered bodies of the enemy, which during the next few days he engaged constantly and always with success, fighting at Koornfontein on the 27th, at Middelkraal on the 28th, at Rensburghoop on the 29th, and again near Koornfontein on June 1st, with loss to his own troops of ten officers and men killed and wounded, and to the enemy of twelve killed and wounded, seven prisoners, the contents of fifty farms cleared or destroyed, and more than 100 wagons and 13,000 head of stock captured. Meanwhile Allenby, working back, by arrangement with Beatson, towards the source of the Wilge, came upon many untouched farms, and considerable bands of Boers subsisting upon them. By the last day of May he had thoroughly swept a line through Middeldrift, Rietvlei, Weltevreden, Straffontein and Van Dyksput, having taken in all twelve prisoners and 21,000 head of stock before he returned to the railway at Wilge River station, *en route* for Pretoria.

Of the lines of communication during April and May there was little to record. The universal stirring of columns over the open veld in April had the effect of casting many small bands of Boers, like waves from a distant storm, up against the surrounding lines of communication. Posts on the Delagoa Bay line were frequently attacked to cover the passage of fugitives from one untenable district into the other. On the Standerton line the mounted reconnaissances from Heidelberg, and Colville—who captured a laager at Boschmanskop on the 29th—more than once met with the enemy in force, whilst, lower down, the blockhouses between Kromdraai and Volksrust dealt successfully with five different attempts to cross the railway.

The lines of communication during April.

Natal, during this month, though continually threatened from Botha's Pass and the west, had chiefly to cope with an irruption by the enemy into the Nkandhla and Mahlabitini districts of Zululand. From the former a small column under Major A. J. Chapman (Royal Dublin Fusiliers) temporarily dislodged them by a sharp attack at Babanango on the 26th; whilst the Boers, attacking in their turn the magistracy at Mahlabitini two days later, were repulsed with loss by the Natal Police, who, in the course of a stout resistance to ten times their numbers, lost seven out of the twenty men who formed the garrison. These successes, however, by no means freed the districts, which attracted the enemy by their fertility after the ruin and desolation of their own veld; and Lieut.-General Hildyard was compelled later to adopt regular methods of clearance.

In May, Spens and Park were active on the Delagoa Bay line, whilst the Standerton railway furnished several small offensive forces, notably one under Major J. M. Vallentin (Somersetshire Light Infantry) from Heidelberg on the 25th, which surprised a laager and took nine prisoners on the banks of the Vaal river.

The lines of communication during May.

The two columns mentioned previously as issuing from Standerton and Platrand to co-operate with Bullock were under Brigadier-General E. O. F. Hamilton; they returned on the 7th with five prisoners, having suffered the same number of casualties. Another force, under Colonel F. J. Pink (Queen's regiment), in co-operation with Colville—who was in his turn a flanker of a sweep by Major-General E. L. Elliot in progress along the other side of the Klip river*—made a bonfire of the Verzamel Berg, a noted place of call for wandering commandos both from the Orange River Colony and the Southern Transvaal. A feat performed during the month by an officer stationed at Gras Kop, Captain H. R. Bottomley (Queen's regiment) by name, deserves mention if only to show that the Boers were not always the layers but sometimes the victims of ambuscades. Riding out by night, and concealing himself and a few companions in the town of Amersfoort before daylight on the 22nd, this officer killed, wounded, or captured, singly, several noted Boers of the district, including the commandant of the Wakkerstroom commando; and when at last forced by the arrival of strong parties to gallop for the distant Gras Kop, took with him three prisoners whom he had snatched from the very midst of the Boer bands.

Once more Hildyard, in Natal, had had to deal with the Nkandhla and Melmoth districts of Zululand, where the Boers, though quiet after their repulses in April, had quartered themselves on the farms in such numbers that except for the few British posts they were practically in occupation of the country. Three small columns were accordingly despatched thither, under Colonel R. W. Evans (Natal Volunteers), Captain G. Capron (Vth division mounted infantry), and Major A. J. Chapman (Royal Dublin Fusiliers). A night march on May 19th by the last-named officer resulted in the capture of a complete laager in the Babanango range. Next morning Chapman was himself attacked by superior forces, and though compelled to retire into Nkandhla, extricated his party and inflicted more

---

* See Chapter V.

EVENTS IN EASTERN TRANSVAAL AND NATAL. 155

losses than he received. Chapman was then reinforced from Dundee, and the establishment of entrenched posts at various spots soon safeguarded the districts from raids.

There fell also upon Lieut.-General Hildyard at this time the preparation of columns and lines of entrenchment for stopping the western passes, to assist that operation of Major-General Elliot in the Orange River Colony to which allusion has already been made in connection with the forays of Colonels Colville and Pink on both sides of the Verzamel Berg.

APPROXIMATE STRENGTH STATES OF COLUMNS REFERRED TO IN FOREGOING CHAPTER.

COLUMN.	Mounted Troops.	Infantry.	Guns, including Vickers-Maxims.	Machine Guns.	
April—May, 1901. *Lieut.-General Sir B. Blood's Force.*					
Col. C. W. Park	200	930	3	—	} Maj.-Gen. F. W. Kitchener in command.
Maj.-Gen. F. W. Kitchener	550	2,290	6	—	
Lt.-Col. W. Douglas	330	1,280	3	—	
Lt.-Col. W. P. Pulteney	750	800	8	—	} Maj.-Gen. R. S. R. Fetherstonhaugh in command.
Lt.-Col. G. E. Benson	720	350	8	—	
Maj.-Gen. S. B. Beatson	600	1,020	4	—	
Brig.-Gen. G. M. Bullock	2,537	621	14	4	
Lt.-Col. M. F. Rimington	1,450	278	—	—	
Lt.-Col. A. E. W. Colville	250	370	4	—	
Brig.-Gen. H. C. O. Plumer	1,428	—	6	1	
Brig.-Gen. J. Spens	163	570	2	3	
Maj.-Gen. J. M. Babington	1,004	337	8	1	
Col. E. C. Knox	1,490	464	8	1	
Lt.-Col. E. H. H. Allenby	762	550	7	2	

CHAPTER IX.

EVENTS IN THE ORANGE RIVER COLONY*

(*Continued from Chapter V.*).

APRIL—JUNE, 1901.

<small>Sir L. Rundle's operations.</small>

OF the larger units in the Orange River Colony, the Harrismith command must now be dealt with. Since early in February Sir L. Rundle had seen neither of his mobile columns, Harley's being in garrison at Ficksburg, that of B. Campbell in parts still more remote. Campbell, after evacuating Vrede of all but its garrison on February 10th, had marched into Standerton to re-equip. The duty of forwarding supplies to French, who was then in the Eastern Transvaal,† detained him at Standerton, after which he paid a second visit to Vrede on March 4th. This town, which was held by the 1st Leinster regiment under Lieut.-Colonel H. Martin, had been virtually invested during the past five months, the troops suffering greatly from disease. It was now completely cleared by Campbell, who for the eight days following found his return blocked by swollen rivers. So unlikely then seemed the prospects of his being able to regain Harrismith by his former route, that the column was entrained for Ladysmith in Natal, thence to march on Harrismith by way of Van Reenen's Pass. In effecting this Campbell was still further delayed by an attack by a party of Boers on the line at Mount Prospect, near Laing's Nek, where a goods train was blown up in front of the troop trains. Not until April 10th was Campbell back in Harrismith. Harley, locked up in Ficks-

---

* See map No. 64.   † See Chapter VI.

EVENTS IN THE ORANGE RIVER COLONY.

burg, had been similarly alienated, performing, however, much useful work from that place both in co-operation with Pilcher about Ladybrand, Clocolan and Mequatlings Nek, with Lyttelton on his northerly drive from the Orange, and on his own account, for he had never ceased to radiate expeditions into the disturbed area about him.

Campbell's return enabled Sir L. Rundle to resume the offensive. He selected as his first objective the Brandwater basin, which Harley reported to be teeming with the enemy. So numerous were the bands, and so formidable their strongholds, especially the passes which led into the basin, that Rundle represented to the Commander-in-Chief the desirability of the co-operation of at least four columns in the work. Neither Elliot nor C. E. Knox, however, were at the moment available, and Lord Kitchener instructed Sir L. Rundle to conduct his expedition as a reconnaissance on the results of which future action would be decided. On April 20th Rundle took B. Campbell's reconstructed column, 2,200 strong with eight guns, out of Harrismith. Four days' incessant skirmishing, which cost eighteen casualties, brought the force to Bethlehem, where two days were spent in reorganising the garrison of Bethlehem and fitting it for the field. This set at liberty an additional battalion, the 2nd Manchester, under Lieut.-Colonel C. T. Reay, which, until April 28th, cleared the vicinity of Bethlehem in co-operation with Campbell's column. On the 29th the whole force plunged into the Brandwater basin by Retief's Nek, and on May 2nd entered Fouriesburg. For the next month Sir L. Rundle constituted this town as his base for raids in all directions.

First, two small columns under Lieut.-Colonels Reay and F. W. Romilly beat up the immediate neighbourhood of Fouriesburg, finding scattered all over the mountains patrols which, assembled, would have totalled some 800 men. These groups contented themselves, however, with long-range skirmishing from the mountain tops, and never seriously interfered with the extensive clearing operations in progress beneath them. From the 15th to the 29th Rundle had four columns out, under Lieut.-

Colonels J. L. Keir, Reay, Romilly and Colonel Harley, the latter having come from Ficksburg with a convoy of supplies. Ten days later Rundle, having destroyed everything within reach, evacuated Fouriesburg, and began a double movement upon the Roode Bergen to the east. Whilst he himself marched direct upon Naauwpoort Nek, Campbell took the road out of Retief's Nek. Campbell was escorting a convoy for Bethlehem, and he had orders to strike south-eastward when he should have delivered it, and attempt to rejoin the main body at Naauwpoort Nek. In spite of considerable opposition Campbell, who had to fight his way to Bethlehem, duly effected this on May 31st. Making a forced march back, he appeared so suddenly at the north entry of Naauwpoort Nek that a small Boer convoy of nine wagons, which was making its escape from Rundle, fell into his hands, the skirmish costing him five wounded. Sir L. Rundle was at that moment on the other side of the Nek, above Mooihoek, and moving with Harley up the valley of the little Caledon, he ordered Campbell to move by Naauwpoort Nek and sweep eastward along the Roode Bergen on the opposite or northern side, thus completely enveloping the range. Throughout the first week of June the movement proceeded, the main difficulty being the roads, or the lack of them, for the troops had practically to cut their own track, and several wagons were lost over the precipices. On the 4th both columns issued from the mountains, Campbell by Witzies Hoek, Harley by Golden Gate, both converging towards Elands River Drift, where they united on the 8th. Their joint captures amounted to 6,000 head of stock, forty-one vehicles, a quantity of Krupp shells and small-arm ammunition, and 350 tons of foodstuffs, about the same quantity having been destroyed for lack of means to remove it. The British casualties had numbered twelve killed and wounded, those of the enemy about double. Sir L. Rundle then marched for Harrismith, where he arrived on the 9th, and proceeded to refit.

C. E. Knox's operations.

Turning now to the troops of the central district, C. E. Knox's two columns, namely, Pilcher's and Thorneycroft's, like those of Sir L. Rundle, had been engaged in opposite directions in the

EVENTS IN THE ORANGE RIVER COLONY. 159

early part of April. Pilcher, it will be remembered, had been sighted at Reitz by Broadwood, on the right flank of Elliot's easterly drive, on April 28th. Three weeks earlier Pilcher had been in touch with Harley at Ficksburg on Mequatlings Nek; and when amongst the headstreams of the Vet river at New Holstein, orders had reached him to convey the mass of booty which he had acquired into Winburg. Skilfully turning the formidable Koranna Berg on April 8th, Pilcher worked his way by easy stages, and incessantly engaged, to Winburg, which he reached on April 22nd. Thence he was ordered to Senekal to resume co-operation with Thorneycroft. That officer had been as busy as Pilcher in another direction. A raid to the west of Brandfort in the first week of April had culminated in a successful night surprise of a laager at Mooiwater, where by admirable tactics Thorneycroft's seasoned regiment secured thirty-three prisoners. On April 5th Thorneycroft returned to Brandfort, to sally again two days later to the east of the railway. Another week's sweep by Landdrost Monde, and between the Vet river and Winburg, brought him into that town on the 14th, thence by Tzamen, the Tabaksberg and Verblijden on April 20th to Brandfort again, where he handed over nearly 500 refugees and 16,000 beasts. Thence by the same route Thorneycroft returned to Winburg on the 23rd, and on the next day C. E. Knox himself accompanied him towards Senekal with a view of co-operating with Elliot with both his columns. Arriving at Senekal on the afternoon of April 25th, Knox found Pilcher already in possession of the place, having surrounded it by a well-conducted night march from Doornfontein. Pilcher was then despatched towards Reitz, his task being to drive as many of the enemy as he could in front of Elliot, Knox returning to Winburg with Thorneycroft. Pilcher, as already recorded, duly reached Reitz by the difficult road on the 28th, and, having performed his part, returned almost immediately, being under orders to rejoin his Headquarters by May 2nd. On that date he reached Senekal, where he had expected to find C. E. Knox; but that General had moved to Winburg, leaving orders for Pilcher to penetrate the Doornberg from the north, whilst

Thorneycroft entered from the opposite side. Accordingly Pilcher marched to Leliefontein, and thence to Spytfontein, skirmishing all the way with a strong body which was based on Schaapplaat. On May 8th, in co-operation with Thorneycroft from Helpmakaar, the Doornberg was thoroughly scoured, after which Pilcher put in to Ventersburg Road on May 9th, and Thorneycroft to Virginia Siding.

At this time the railway both north and south of Kroonstad was infested by bands which it seemed impossible to prevent from crossing, and in many instances from damaging the line. They were especially numerous on the west, and Major J. E. Pine-Coffin's mounted infantry, which W. G. Knox, the commander of that section of the lines of communication, had despatched on May 6th to attempt to sweep the country towards Bothaville, had to return before superior numbers. C. E. Knox was therefore ordered to proceed with his two columns to this district, and on the night of May 13th he moved out with the general intention of clearing up the tract between the Vet and Valsch rivers. An attempt to compress a commando between Thorneycroft, supported by Pine-Coffin, at Kalkkuil—Kopje Alleen and Pilcher at Bloemhof—Geluk failed, though some loss was occasioned to the enemy. Thorneycroft then remained stationary whilst Pilcher circled by Alettasdraai towards Bothaville. His movements had the effect of forcing the Boers south-westward towards the drifts of the Vaal north of Hoopstad, which they endeavoured to gain. Pilcher was too quick for them, however, and seized both Commando and Hofman's Drifts, whilst Thorneycroft closed towards him to Boschrand on the 16th to cover the crossings of the Zand Spruit. Thus shut in, the enemy's bands broke up, and Pilcher was directed on Bothaville. An outpost which he had thrown across the river at Commando Drift was hotly attacked on the night of the 16th, losing fifteen horses. The detachment at Hofman's Drift was also attacked as it was withdrawing, all the captured stock being retaken by the enemy, who inflicted five casualties upon the troops. Next day this party was again attacked, the Boers coming in to close quarters. Eleven more casualties

EVENTS IN THE ORANGE RIVER COLONY. 161

resulted, but the detachment was fortunate to rejoin Pilcher with so few, for the enemy fought with determination, and nothing but the coolness of the rearguard kept them at bay.* On the 19th Thorneycroft and Pilcher united close to Bothaville, to part again next day, each in chase of separate hostile bodies which were reported to be trekking southward. Little more fighting occurred. The Boers had made good their escape out of the area, and only some fifteen vehicles fell into Pilcher's hands at Roodepoort; a patrol of Thorneycroft's, reconnoitring across the Valsch, found five more hidden in the bed of the Rhenoster river. On May 22nd Pilcher arrived at Virginia Siding and Thorneycroft at Kroonstad, their total capture amounting to twenty-three wagons and carts and 5,000 animals; the casualties numbered eighteen, as against some score amongst the enemy. Seven mills, including an important one at Alettasdraai, and a vast amount of crops had also been destroyed; but the area was too great and too well furnished to be completely cleared by the number of troops employed. At the close of May Pilcher was at Brandfort and Thorneycroft at Vet River station, whence they soon issued to co-operate with the columns of the southern section of the Orange River Colony, whose previous operations must now be described.

At the end of March Lyttelton had under his command Bruce Hamilton's three columns (Monro, W. L. White, C. Maxwell), the three under Haig (Byng, W. H. Williams, Lowe) and Hickman's. Of these, it will be remembered the first was at Springfontein, Bethanie and Edenburg; Haig was on the Caledon river, Hickman at Edenburg, all preparing to intercept the expected return of the worsted invaders of Cape Colony.† This event, however, came to nothing; Cape Colony was not relieved of a single Boer band, and Bruce Hamilton's troops were otherwise employed. News having come that a commando

Lyttelton's operations.

---

* Lieutenant and Adjutant G. H. B. Coulson (killed), King's Own Scottish Borderers (7th M.I.), was awarded the Victoria Cross (posthumous) for gallantry on this occasion.

† See Chapter V., page 97.

was in occupation of Dewetsdorp, on April 7th the three columns marched thither, and on the 9th Monro, who was leading, surrounded the town, only to find that the enemy had been warned and had just made off. The trail pointed south-eastward, and on the morning of the 11th Monro fastened upon it, and for three hours galloped in pursuit with 150 men and a Vickers-Maxim. The tracks then disappeared, obliterated by the heavy rain, and Monro, calling a halt, scouted widely. It was not long before the commando was discovered outspanned by a group of farms which, though protected in front by a deep donga, were surrounded by kopjes within rifle range. Instantly Monro's squadron leaders, scarcely waiting for orders, rushed for the points of vantage, and in a few moments every commanding knoll was in their possession. The Boers who filled the donga made a hot reply; but a dash into the hollow from both flanks awed them so thoroughly that the fifty-three burghers therein soon succumbed to half their numbers, and the farm buildings behind lay uncovered. They were defended by some thirty riflemen whose rapid firing showed that they were by no means daunted by the capitulation which had occurred before their eyes. They seemed to be in expectation of assistance, and Monro, scanning the horizon, saw that he must make haste, for the distant hilltops were dotted with approaching horsemen. An immediate assault, however, was not easy, his force being now scattered too widely around the farms to be quickly assembled. He therefore determined to try negotiation, and called for a volunteer to approach the buildings under the white flag with a demand for surrender. Thereupon Lieutenant H. H. Shott, an officer of Bethune's mounted infantry, who had already greatly distinguished himself by his initiative in the attack on the donga, armed only with a handkerchief walked up to the farmhouses, in spite of the hot fire still pouring from them. After a parley, which was attended with extreme danger to himself, Shott succeeded in inducing the defenders to yield. Monro, who had lost but five men, then marched off with eighty-three prisoners, including two officers, and many wagons and animals, and arrived at Dewetsdorp at

EVENTS IN THE ORANGE RIVER COLONY. 163

midnight, having covered forty miles since the morning. A similar expedition towards Ventershoek on the night of the 12th was less fortunate ; the party became entangled in difficult country, and owed its escape with but seven casualties largely to its being mistaken for friends by the Boers, who were met with in considerable strength.

On April 13th Bruce Hamilton was ordered to take over command of the southern area from Lyttelton, who had been granted leave of absence. He accordingly returned to the railway, whither his columns, which were now to be commanded by Monro, also skirmished their way back on the 18th, bringing ninety-five prisoners and 46,000 head of stock. The main incident of the return march occurred at the junction of the Hex and Riet rivers, where a troop of thirteen men of the 9th Lancers, of C. Maxwell's column, gallantly charging a kopje on foot, were overcome by a superior body entrenched on the top, and all but one killed or captured. A dash upon Reddersburg on April 21st, to Helvetia two days later, and into the Smithfield district on the 25th, placed Monro favourably for a clearance of the trans-Caledon area, for which orders now came from the Commander-in-Chief. Such a movement was especially necessary, because at this moment Kritzinger was actually north of the Orange, having temporarily parted from his allies in the Barkly East district in the manner described elsewhere.* For this purpose was designated also W. H. Williams, who had taken over Haig's command when, on April 8th, that officer had been ordered across the Orange river to deal with the raiders in Cape Colony. Williams brought with him, in addition to Byng, the columns of Herbert and the Hon. A. Murray, lent by Hart from Aliwal North and Bethulie, and after clearing the Elands Berg, he was at Smithfield and in touch with Monro on April 25th. A combined southerly raid on both sides of the Caledon was then arranged, Williams to move on the west of the river with W. L. White and C. Maxwell added to his own troops, whilst Monro was responsible for. the country on the opposite bank. On the 28th, when

Margin notes: Bruce Hamilton succeeds Lyttelton. Kritzinger visits the Orange River Colony.

* See Chapter X., page 176.

Bruce Hamilton repaired to Aliwal North, his columns were thus disposed from east to west: At Akel, on the Basuto border, were White and Maxwell; at Naseby, Williams with Byng; at Constantia, Herbert; at Smithfield, Monro; whilst Hickman, who had for the past week been watching the Orange about Krugers Drift to intercept an anticipated retreat by Hertzog, was nearing Bethulie for Karreepoort, where he was to commence the clearance of the fork between the Orange and Caledon. Murray was in Aliwal North, detailed to escort a convoy of supplies for the columns. By the time the foraying columns had arrived about Rouxville, a reported concentration of the enemy along the frontier near Philippolis caused Williams, with Byng and Lieut.-Colonel P. G. Wyndham (successor to Herbert), to be transported across the railway with orders to move along the right bank of the Orange towards Ramah, Bruce Hamilton taking a central position at Edenburg. Monro remained in the east, vainly endeavouring to close with Kritzinger, who was supposed to be travelling northward from the Orange.

Starting from Springfontein on May 10th, W. H. Williams was at Goemans Berg on the 12th, and two days later had a sharp affair fifteen miles south-west of Fauresmith, where two squadrons of the South African Light Horse killed and wounded three and captured fourteen burghers, including a noted Field-Cornet, Van der Merwe. On May 15th Williams was at Somersfontein, and on the 21st reached Ramah with his prisoners and tens of thousands of sheep and cattle, having found no hostile concentration, but instead an immense herd of stock which had been driven from the Fauresmith farmsteads. Williams subsequently regained the railway at the end of the month at Priors Siding, marching by Philippolis. Meanwhile Monro could get little more news of Kritzinger than a rumour, which proved true, that the Boer was on his way back to the frontier. He was in the midst of a cast around Rouxville on May 19th when he was ordered to take his column into Cape Colony, where he shortly embarked on that career of activity in the north-eastern counties which is fully narrated in subsequent chapters.* Kritzinger, doubling cleverly, had preceded Monro a week earlier, and his departure left that part of the south of the Orange River Colony east of the railway practically clear. But Kritzinger's re-entry into the British province, effected in spite of the bevy of columns around him as easily as his former passages in and out of it, added to the growing demands of the state of affairs south of the Orange. Haig had long ago gone thither; A. Murray, replaced by Lieut.-Colonel L. E. du Moulin, had rejoined Hart at Aliwal North; and now first Monro, then W. L. White, were ordered across the border, to be followed in course of time by others. The 9th and 17th Lancers were also entrained for Cape Colony, taken from the column which was now commanded by Major S. W. Follett in place of C. Maxwell, who, on May 20th, had been thrown from his horse, sustaining injuries from which, to the regret of all, he died. Finally Hickman, on his return to the railway on May 30th, proceeded to Cape Colony, leaving his column at Edenburg. These changes afforded a favourable opportunity for a reorganisation of Bruce Hamilton's forces into less unwieldy units, a measure which the Commander-in-Chief had recently enjoined. After another short expedition by three of his commanders towards the Caledon, which produced some 97,000 livestock, Bruce Hamilton prepared to resume operations on a larger scale but with smaller columns. His three remaining forces he sub-divided into seven, each about 500 strong, and placed them under command of the following officers, Colonel A. N. Rochfort, Lieut.-Colonel W. H. Williams, Lieut.-Colonel the Hon. J. H. G. Byng, Majors F. L. Banon, H. E. Gogarty and O. Harris. With these, and certain reinforcements, Bruce Hamilton now undertook a scheme of considerable dimensions.

Kritzinger recrosses the Orange river.

Bruce Hamilton reorganises his columns

For some time past all reports had tended to show that the tract between the Riet and Modder rivers provided a sanctuary for many of the fighting men and most of the stock of the Boers of the southern part of the Orange River Colony. Here, but for the hasty passages of Plumer and Bethune when in chase of

---

* See Chapters X., XIII., XV. and XXVI. on operations in Cape Colony.

De Wet, they had remained almost undisturbed. W. H. Williams had merely skirted the fringe of their preserve on his recent march to and from Ramah, but his gleanings, nearly 100,000 head of stock and seventy prisoners, seemed to be good evidence of the value to be obtained from a clearance of the richer and more secluded country to the north. In the first week of June, therefore, Bruce Hamilton, in conjunction with C. E. Knox, arranged an extensive "drive" from south to north through the district in question. Whilst Knox sent Pilcher from Brandfort and Thorneycroft from Vet River station to block the drifts of the Modder from Brandvallei to Kruger's Drift, Hamilton drew out his troops into a great semi-circle, facing northward from Kaffir River on the east, through Jagersfontein Road, Philippolis and Luckhoff, up to the banks of the Riet river south of Jacobsdal. The western section of this disposition was supplied by Major A. Paris' column from Kimberley, and by a new force under Colonel St. G. C. Henry which had just completed its organisation at Orange River station. By the night of June 5th all were in their places, and next morning the movement began. Its subsequent history was too uneventful to be followed in detail. For the next three days the wide arc of troops rolled towards Petrusburg, its approach continually heralded by the agitated stirring of herds of stock, clusters of wagons laden with women and children and household goods, and small knots of armed Boers, who darted hither and thither about the front seeking to escape. The majority of these fell into the hands of one or other of the columns; but with the formed fighting bodies, of which several were reported, Bruce Hamilton was less fortunate, for none were stopped either by the advancing troops or those watching the drifts in front.

and drives up to the Modder river.

Altogether some 600 men escaped in this way; but when Hamilton drew up on the line Emmaus—Petrusburg on June 8th, he had taken 243 prisoners and much material, including several sets of signalling apparatus belonging to Hertzog's commandos. The combination of columns was then broken up.

EVENTS IN THE ORANGE RIVER COLONY. 167

Sending W. H. Williams westward with his own and the two western columns to clear the country beyond Luckhoff up to the Kimberley railway, and Byng with two columns to do the same between Fauresmith and Philippolis, Bruce Hamilton himself returned to Edenburg with Rochfort and du Moulin and all the captures, which he increased by twenty-five prisoners taken on the way. For the rest of the month there was incessant but disconnected activity in every quarter of Bruce Hamilton's and Sir C. Knox's areas. Within the vast quadrilateral whose sides were the Kimberley and Bloemfontein railways, the Vaal and the Orange rivers, six columns fell to work. Henry forayed towards Boshof, where on the 21st he was joined by Paris, the two making Christiana by the 27th. Williams, having reached Witteputs station on June 18th, turned eastward again after refitting, and thereafter was continually in touch with small commandos which revolved about Luckhoff, daily depriving them of men and stores, but having his account somewhat lowered by the loss of an officer and thirty-two men, captured from his rearguard on the 20th. Byng performed similar services about Philippolis, both he and Williams gradually working towards Headquarters at Edenburg, which they reached on July 4th. Further north, but still within the figure described above, Sir C. Knox, withdrawing his troops from the Modder at the conclusion of Bruce Hamilton's " drive " to Petrusburg, employed his troops in scouring the country between the line Paardeberg—Bultfontein—Smaldeel and the railway, that is, to the east of the operations of Henry and Paris. Pilcher, moving by Doornlaagte, Jagtpan and Kalkfontein, surrounded Bultfontein on the 18th and took three prisoners. Next day, when reconnoitring towards Hoopstad, he had himself to beat off a determined attack made under cover of a veld fire near the town, which he did with the loss of three to his own force and seven to the enemy's. Thence by easy stages he made his way into Brandfort on June 25th. Thorneycroft worked in combination with Pilcher by Nooitgedacht, Schiedam, Gannafontein, Cyfergat and Luxemburg, skirmishing with considerable

Various operations west of the Bloemfontein railway.

bodies and finding much to clear. He, too, entered Brandfort on the 25th, the joint captures of the two columns amounting to four prisoners, 181 vehicles and more than 20,000 livestock. The casualties had been an officer and two men killed and an officer and twelve men wounded, the Boers having lost some thirty-five men.

Operations east of the Bloemfontein railway.

Meanwhile—a sufficiency of troops thus traversing the districts on the west of the railway—Bruce Hamilton employed Rochfort and du Moulin upon a fresh expedition on the opposite side. By this time W. L. White had re-entered the eastern area from Aliwal North, and moving northward by Commissie Drift, had reached Wepener on June 19th, reporting all local Boers to have gone to Dewetsdorp. Accordingly Bruce Hamilton directed his two units thither in co-operation with White. The columns found themselves at once amongst the enemy. On June 21st Rochfort fell in with a Boer convoy on the Smithfield—Dewetsdorp road, capturing the whole, with seventeen prisoners, twenty-one vehicles and a herd of horses and stock. Another convoy on the Reddersburg—Dewetsdorp road evaded him two days later, after which the three columns combined against a commando discovered at Oorlogs Poort. This party scattered southward, and in the pursuit du Moulin captured a third small convoy of fifteen vehicles and five prisoners ten miles west of Helvetia. The chase was continued towards Reddersburg, near to which, on June 28th, du Moulin's force suffered five casualties from a counter-attack delivered by the hard-pressed enemy. At the end of the month these columns were still engaged between Reddersburg and Dewetsdorp, where for the present they must be left, to turn to operations of greater scope elsewhere.

Elliot "drives" eastward from Kroonstad.

On June 22nd Elliot, having refitted his armament in Kroonstad, started out on another of those raids upon the enemy's scattered means of subsistence with which, in the absence of formed hostile bodies or definite lines of supply, the side on the offensive has to be content. Elliot now had four mounted brigades, and with Bethune on the left, Lowe at left centre, de Lisle at right centre and Broadwood on the

EVENTS IN THE ORANGE RIVER COLONY. 169

right, he swept between Lindley and Senekal, making for Springfield Drift, where he was to re-ration. A night march by the right flank on Senekal on June 25th found the town empty, the Boers having had full warning of the advancing array. On the left Bethune's frequent night raids and forced marches proved equally fruitless, and for the whole of the eastward march the enemy, whose tracks were numerous, had no difficulty in keeping well ahead of Elliot's van. On July 2nd the division drew up at the appointed spot with only 3,000 captured horses and the same number of cattle in its train. This species of warfare, cheated of the armed opponent, its proper prey, falls the more terribly upon the innocent. No fewer than 12,000 sheep were slaughtered on the march, their numbers and slowness of foot rendering it impossible to drive them on.

Meanwhile, before Elliot's departure from his base, Sir L. Rundle had been operating about the very tract over which the Kroonstad division was to pass, but from the opposite direction. A few days had sufficed to refit his columns after their exertions in the Brandwater basin, and on June 13th they were again in the field, hunting bands on either side of the Harrismith—Bethlehem road. Working towards them was a small force despatched from Bethlehem. On June 16th both columns were across the Libenbergs Vlei, about Loskop and Spitzkrans, south-east of Bethlehem. Here Rundle received notice of Elliot's impending movement, which he was first to provide with fresh supplies at Springfield Drift, and thereafter to reinforce. On the 18th Rundle occupied both sides of the Bethlehem—Harrismith road by sending Harley to Leeuwpoort, north of the first-named town, and B. Campbell to Poortje to the south-east. During the next three days he refilled Bethlehem with two months' supplies and relieved the garrison, and on the 22nd fell back towards Harrismith to prepare the mass of provender which would be required by Elliot, Campbell marching by Jollykop, Harley by Tweefontein. The last days of June were spent in forwarding the material to Springfield Drift, where it was duly taken over by Elliot on his arrival.

Sir L. Rundle marches towards Elliot.

This completed the more important affairs of June. The processions of troops which traversed the country on either side of the railway by no means rendered the guardians of the line either immune or immobile; but there is no space to record the numberless encounters which enlivened the lines of communication, whence Sir C. Tucker from Bloemfontein, Sir W. G. Knox from Kroonstad and Barker from Winburg had all frequently despatched small forces for special purposes in their neighbourhoods.*

* For gallantry during a skirmish near Thabanchu on June 15th, Serjeant James Rogers, South African Constabulary, was awarded the Victoria Cross.

NOTE.—Lieut.-General C. Tucker, Major-Generals W. G. Knox and C. E. Knox were created Knights Commander of the Bath for services during 1899-1900.—*London Gazette*, April 19th, 1901.

EVENTS IN THE ORANGE RIVER COLONY.

APPROXIMATE STRENGTH STATES OF COLUMNS REFERRED TO IN FOREGOING CHAPTER.

COLUMN.	Mounted Troops.	Infantry.	Guns, including Vickers-Maxims.	Machine Guns.	
April—June, 1901.					
Lieut.-Colonel C. P. Crewe	640	—	4	2	Lieut.-General Sir L. Rundle in command.
Major-General J. E. Boyes (later Harley)	318	1,361	5	3	
,, ,, B. B. D. Campbell	342	1,858	8	2	
Lieut.-Colonel S. C. H. Monro	320	480	2	—	
,, ,, W. G. Massy	510	—	3	1	Lieut.-General Sir C. Tucker directing.
,, ,, E. C. Ingouville Williams (later W. G. B. Western)	459	625	4	—	
Major J. E. Pine-Coffin	447	—	3	1	
Major-General Bruce Hamilton's columns:					
Lieut.-Colonel S. C. H. Monro	290	—	3	—	
,, ,, C. Maxwell (later S. W. Follett)	650	—	6	—	Lieut.-General the Hon. N. G. Lyttelton directing.
Lieut.-Colonel W. L. White	617	—	3	—	
Colonel D. Haig's columns:					
Lieut.-Colonel the Hon. J. H. G. Byng	654	—	4	—	
,, ,, W. H. Williams	351	—	3	3	
,, ,, H. J. Scobell	639	11*	3	—	
Lieut.-Colonel T. D. Pilcher	1,070	82	7	2	Major-General Sir C. E. Knox in command.
Colonel A. W. Thorneycroft	500	150	5	—	
,, T. E. Hickman	560	—	5	—	
Lieut.-Colonel E. B. Herbert (later P. G. Wyndham)	380	—	3	1	
Lieut.-Colonel the Hon. A. Murray	185	—	2	1	
Brigadier-General R. G. Broadwood (later de Lisle)	2,023	—	4	1	Major-General E. L. Elliot in command.
Colonel E. C. Bethune (later W. H. M. Lowe)	820	—	5	—	
Lieut.-Colonel H. de B. de Lisle (later R. Fanshawe)	658	22*	3	—	
Lieut.-Colonel C. T. Reay	150	480	2	—	Lieut.-General Sir L. Rundle in command.
,, ,, F. W. Romilly	150	850	3	—	
,, ,, J. L. Keir	150	160	1	—	
Colonel G. E. Harley	332	1,595	5	3	
,, A. N. Rochfort	530	—	3	—	
Lieut.-Colonel W. H. Williams	500	—	2	1	
,, ,, the Hon. J. H. G. Byng	709	—	2	—	Major-General Bruce Hamilton in command.
Major F. L. Banon	550	—	2	2	
,, H. E. Gogarty	640	—	1	—	
,, O. Harris	517	—	2	—	
Lieut.-Colonel L. E. du Moulin	184	250	3	—	
,, ,, St. G. C. Henry	642	—	3	1	
Major A. Paris	325	131	2	1	

* Cyclists.

CHAPTER X.

EVENTS IN CAPE COLONY.*

(Continued from Chapter IV.).

MARCH—APRIL, 1901.

Effect of De Wet's inroad.
THE expulsion of De Wet at the end of February left Cape Colony in a singular condition. The extinction of that chief firebrand removed all immediate danger of a general conflagration in the British province. Nevertheless, he had bequeathed a legacy of unrest which was not to be stamped out. Everywhere arose incendiaries who endeavoured to set a light to the combustible material which existed in every quarter of the colony. It became the fashion for any minor leader who possessed or could raise a following to take the field and try his skill at blowing about the sparks of rebellion. Although only the most trivial and sporadic outbreaks arose in response, yet the attempts themselves were so persistent, so widespread, and so difficult to cope with from their very insignificance, that for the rest of the duration of the war they formed the history of Cape Colony and the sole occupation of nearly 50,000 British troops, regular and colonial.

Foremost amongst these disturbers of the peace remained for a time Kritzinger, with his adherents Fouché and Scheepers, who have been traced into the Sneeuw Bergen, into which they had been chased when three of the four pursuing columns were withdrawn to join in the hue and cry after De Wet. The crumbling of the main Boer plan of campaign on the banks of the Orange, and the disappearance of De Wet and Hertzog, left Kritzinger alone in the heart of Cape Colony.

* See map No. 63.

Kritzinger had in full measure the unlimited self-reliance of Kritzinger's the Boer warrior. Deeply buried though he was in hostile movements. country, with greatly superior forces between himself and his native land, with the strategy of which he was only a factor ruined, and its mainstay falling back broken in the opposite direction, he yet showed no disposition to vanish after his receding commander-in-chief. He had occupied the period o De Wet's disastrous campaign in the north by leading Gorringe and Herbert a tortuous chase from Dassiefontein to Twist Kraal, thence to Roode Hoogte, where he burned the station, to Spitz Kop, and back into the Sneeuw Bergen on February 25th. He then rode northward to Dwars Vlei Siding, where on the last day of the month he emulated De Wet, who was then plunging across the Orange, by escaping out of all touch with his pursuers. During this adventure Kritzinger received some compensation for his desertion by De Wet and Hertzog by the arrival of Lieutenant W. Malan, an independent leader, who had contrived, whilst all eyes were turned towards De Wet, to work his way deep into the colony with some 100 burghers.

Meanwhile (February 6th to 28th), Scheepers had been similarly dragging Grenfell and Sir C. Parsons about the Klaarstroom district and up into Aberdeen.

De Wet, flying routed into the Orange River Colony, trailed after him all but two of the fourteen columns which had hunted Troops in him for the last seventeen days. Only those of Colonel E. M. S. Cape Colony Crabbe, now at Kraankuil, and Lieut.-Colonel the Hon. A. H. Henniker, about Petrusville, remained within the border, the latter scoring a success on March 1st by securing with one of his patrols thirty-three stragglers from the departed commandos on the banks of the Orange above Sand Drift. Besides these there were now in Cape Colony columns under Lieut.-Colonel H. M. Grenfell (Colenbrander and Wilson) about Nels Poort station, Colonel Sir C. Parsons and Colonel H. J. Scobell at Aberdeen Road, Lieut.-Colonel R. F. Lindsell around Sutherland, Lieut.-Colonel G. F. Gorringe, soon to be joined by Lieut.-Colonel H. de B. de Lisle and fresh levies under Lieut.-Colonel E. B. Herbert and Colonel A. E. Codrington in the Cradock district;

all these under the general direction of Major-General Sir H. H. Settle, who resumed command on Lieut.-General the Hon. N. G. Lyttelton's departure.

Now Cape Colony became the field of kaleidoscopic operations of which the space at command renders it impossible to attempt to arrest more than the main figures. On the one side were Kritzinger, Fouché, Scheepers and Malan, and many lesser leaders, sometimes united in various combinations, sometimes separate, now joined by some fresh arrival of minor standing whom they absorbed, now by officers more noted than themselves, who for the time dominated the scene; on the other side were British columns, varying from fifteen to twenty in number, pressing now this, now that commando with such tireless industry and infinite complexity of movement that the symmetrical vagaries of the kaleidoscope present actually the truest image of their activities.

Pursuit of Kritzinger.

Early in March Gorringe, marching southward through the Cradock country, refound Kritzinger and 600 men at Pearston on the 5th, and drove him towards Somerset East. Here the Boer force was headed by de Lisle who had come by train to Cookhouse station, and turned southward down the Vogel river, Gorringe and de Lisle hurrying to Darlington to intercept it.

On March 7th Kritzinger was located at Waterford; thence he dashed due eastward to Sheldon station (March 10th), and so northward into the Winter Berg, closely dogged by the columns, which reached Adelaide on the 16th. Kritzinger now doubled again, leading Gorringe to Elands Drift on the Tarka river, thence northward across the Bamboes mountains towards Steynsburg. On the 21st he crossed the railway at Henning, and threatened Burghersdorp. Now the hunt was swelled by Henniker, Codrington and Crabbe, but heavy rain covered Kritzinger's tracks and he was temporarily lost. Some reported him to have continued northward; others that he had doubled back beyond Tarkastad; nor did the discovery of a commando at Venterstad on the 26th clear up matters, for it was suspected that Kritzinger, like a stag too closely pressed, had roused a fresh quarry to exhaust the hounds whilst he himself drew breath.

Whether this was so or not, the new game showed that it was dangerous by destroying a British post at Van Tonder's Drift on the last day of March, moving afterwards on Knapdaar.

Meanwhile, close to the west, on the other side of the Fish river, Sir C. Parsons, Scobell and Colenbrander had been in chase of Scheepers and Fouché through the districts of Aberdeen, Graaff Reinet, Jansenville and Somerset East. A sharp fight on March 6th, north of Aberdeen, which cost Parsons thirty casualties, drove the Boers in disorder into the Koudeveld Bergen, where on the 15th they were engaged by Scobell, who took six prisoners. Crossing the railway at Marais Siding on the 17th, and turning south-eastward, Scheepers and Fouché then menaced Jansenville; but Scobell, by a march of forty-five miles, anticipated them there, and the Boer leaders halted undecidedly at the junction of the Bull and Sunday's rivers. Here they were joined by Malan from Poortje, south of Aberdeen, whence he had been driven by Grenfell after events to be next described. A nearly successful attempt by Scobell to surround the trio on March 20th caused the complete disorganisation of the commandos, which lost about 150 horses and many men, Scobell having only seven casualties. The combination was effectively broken up; Scheepers and Malan crossed the line at Kendrew, making for the Camdeboo hills, Fouché running in the opposite direction for Pearston, whither Scobell, who was in Graaff Reinet on the 24th, despatched a detachment under Major K. E. Warden in pursuit.

Pursuit of Scheepers and Fouché.

Malan's appearance was to be accounted for thus. Raiding alone at the head of the Kariega valley in the first week of March, he had been pushed in the rear and flank by Lieut.-Colonel A. E. Wilson from Biesjes Poort and Grenfell from Beaufort West. The former was first in touch, and Malan turned upon him at Stellenbosch Vallei before Grenfell, who was advancing to Juriesfontein, could make his movement felt. Wilson was temporarily checked; but on Grenfell coming up next day Malan made down the Kariega valley, being so hard pressed at Hartebeest Kuil on the 12th that he abandoned his march on Willowmore and turned eastward. Wilson was then recalled to Graaff

Pursuit of Malan.

Reinet, leaving the chase to Grenfell, who from the 13th drove Malan beyond Poortje and into Scobell's sphere of operations.

On April 1st Sir H. Settle established his Headquarters at Graaff Reinet and assumed immediate command of the group of columns in the midland area. Both combatants adopted fresh combinations, Grenfell departing for the Northern Transvaal, Gorringe falling out to refit, Codrington's column being broken up, whilst Crewe, Pilcher's former colleague under C. E. Knox, came into service in the northern area, and Henniker in the southern. On the Boer side the most notable variation was the junction of Fouché with Kritzinger to the south of Middleburg. Their union was brief, however. Pressed by Crewe from April 11th, the two commandos sidled eastward, crossed the railway near Fish River station, and on the 18th passed to the south of Maraisburg and thence north into the Zuur Berg. Here they separated, Kritzinger riding off to recruit in the Orange River Colony, whilst Fouché, followed by Crewe, passed eastward into the Jamestown district to await his return. Meanwhile, Scheepers and Malan, attended by Scobell and Henniker, revolved between Murraysburg, Aberdeen and Jansenville, being nearly caught at the last-named place by Scobell on April 13th.

Kritzinger visits the Orange River Colony.

About this time occurred several changes amongst the British commanders in Cape Colony. In the field, Sir H. Settle proceeded to De Aar, prior to his return to England a month later, when he handed over his office to Colonel Colin Mackenzie, Colonel D. Haig assuming direction of the operations in the midland area. On April 13th Major-General Sir H. MacDonald was ordered home, his command of the Highland brigade and the Aliwal North—Bethulie zone being added to that of Major-General A. FitzRoy Hart, who was already in charge of the lines of communication from the Orange river up to below Bloemfontein. At Cape Town Lieut.-General Sir F. Forestier-Walker embarked for England on April 18th, and handed over the command of Cape Colony to Major-General A. S. Wynne. Wynne succeeded to an office daily becoming more difficult to administer. Upon him centred with full force all the anomalies of war in a friendly, yet infected country. Situated as he was in

Administrative difficulties at Cape Town.

a city, which his Intelligence Department warned him was the headquarters of treason and rebellion, he was yet unpossessed of the only weapon, martial law, with which such foes could be encountered. Newspapers of republican sympathies issued their inflammatory sheets untouched because out of his reach. His officers looked on powerless whilst munitions of war, or what were reported as such, and mail bags containing matter little less encouraging to the enemy, were landed at his dockyards and delivered at their destinations. Suspected individuals bound to and from ports, the very names of which were certificates of hostility, came and went by steamer with impunity, because too rapidly to be waylaid by the slow and cautious process of civil law. He was in daily and necessarily intimate contact with leading men, some of whom he distrusted and others had actively to oppose, so little secret was there of their sympathy with his country's enemies; whilst even some of those with whom he had common cause were forced by the very duties of their offices to run counter to him on vital points of administration. Martial law, which had been proclaimed in many districts of the colony, stopped short at the very boundaries within which it was most needed, those of the great seaports. Cape Town, receiving none of its advantages, was nevertheless the focus of all its woes and hardships, which poured into the city, there to be bandied between the Government officers, the natural protectors of the proclaimed districts, and Wynne, their official oppressor. This became more marked when troops took the field over whom Wynne had no control, though their every misdeed amongst the farmsteads came home to him unfailingly in a swarm of complaints which grew the more numerous and bitter as columns entered the colony fresh from the ravagings of the Transvaal and Orange River Colony, and unable to appreciate immediately the niceties of dealing with countrysides which were at the same time friends to the British and magazines to the Boers. Wynne's jurisdiction was further complicated by its enormous extent, its lack of homogeneity, and the difficulty of reaching its units. Forty thousand men received his orders, but they were composed of many different organisations—regulars, militia, colonials, town guards and fencibles—and were largely locked up in the multitude of townships of Cape Colony. His chief channels of administration were the commandants of districts, officers charged with the control of large areas infested often by open, always by secret, enemies, and these in their turn had to rely largely upon magistrates, whose natural antipathy to martial law was apt to find expression in direct communication not with the military but the civil powers in Cape Town. Such were some of the disabilities under which Wynne and the Cape Legislature were to labour alike in the capital until, six months later, the proclamation of martial law in that and all the other ports removed a source of serious weakness in the conduct of the campaign in Cape Colony.

Pursuit of Scheepers and Malan.

At the end of April Scobell and Henniker drove Scheepers and Malan northward on the line Pearston—Zwagers Hoek, a wing of the Cape Mounted Riflemen, freshly arrived from the Orange River Colony under Lieut.-Colonel H. T. Lukin, assisting from the flank at Cradock ; but the Boers, breaking the cordon, doubled back by Garstlands Kloof and were next heard of across the railway at Daggaboers Nek. Chased thence by Henniker, Malan and Scheepers separated after recrossing the railway near Drennan, the former going northward past Cradock, the latter making back for his old haunts in Somerset. At Zwagers Hoek Scheepers was intercepted and severely punished by Henniker who came from Witmoss on the railway, finally escaping in a snowstorm on May 12th, much reduced in strength, by Kendrew to a stronghold at Camdeboo. Henniker, who put in to Graaff Reinet, kept touch with him during the rest of May by a detachment from his column under Colonel B. Doran. Meanwhile Scobell, finding Malan ten miles west of Cradock, handled him roughly there on May 2nd, drove him northward across the railway near Fish River, and closing upon him again on May 20th at Doorn Nek signally worsted him. Once more Malan, who had now but a handful, turned for sanctuary to the nearest of his friends whom he could hear of. He found an ally both close at hand and of reassuring strength.

EVENTS IN CAPE COLONY.

A few days earlier Kritzinger had returned across the border Kritzinger
with fresh men and horses, rejoining Fouché, who had avoided returns to Cape Colony.
Gorringe and Crewe by breaking back across the railway at
Rayner station into the Zuur Berg. The combined commandos
now numbered 1,500 men, and Haig drew every available column
towards the Zuur Berg. But the Boers, dashing past Steynsburg and across the branch railway near Thebus, moved on
Maraisburg, receiving the enfeebled Malan into their midst as
they marched southward. By rapid marching Gorringe placed
himself to the west of the enemy, Scobell and the others to the
south, below Maraisburg, effectually turning Kritzinger, who
flew off at a tangent into the Bamboes mountains. Here for
the next week he was so ruthlessly harried that, leaving behind
Malan and a commando of rebels under G. H. P. Van Reenan,
he crossed the railway at Cypher Gat on May 29th and pressed
on eastward. Still the British columns, finely handled by Haig,
met him at every turn. The 9th Lancers, detraining at Dordrecht from the Orange River Colony on June 2nd, were, with
Lukin's Cape Mounted Riflemen, placed under Scobell, who took
them at once to Toom Nek, south-east of Jamestown, to bar
Kritzinger from the east. Gorringe, with whom was a column
under Lieut.-Colonel the Hon. A. Murray, hurried north of
Jamestown and, extending his wings, joined up with Scobell on
the east, and on the west as far as Albert Junction with Crabbe,
with Lieut.-Colonel W. P. Wyndham (the 17th Lancers), who had
detrained at Burghersdorp and Colonel S. C. H. Monro's column
freshly arrived from Rouxville. Kritzinger, boldly charging the
cordon, surprised the small and somnolent garrison of Jamestown
on June 2nd, and being then turned by Gorringe, made north-
eastward down the Holle Spruit, closely pursued by Scobell and
Gorringe. Four days later Kritzinger was all but caught as he
and his men lay asleep at Wildfontein Farm, north of the Kraai
river, where Scobell, throwing Lukin's force upon him at 3 a.m.,
killed six and captured twenty-five burghers and seventy horses,
Kritzinger himself escaping on foot into the mountains. Next
day (June 7th) he was again set upon and much damaged, this
time by Gorringe, aided by a force from Aliwal North under

Lieut.-Colonel W. L. White. These were but the chief of incessant attempts to bring the evasive Boer to book, endeavours apparently profitless, but in sum so effectual that before the middle of June the constant friction had worn away two-thirds of Kritzinger's fighting strength.

Nor had Malan and his companion, Van Reenan, been left in peace. An attempt to surprise the former in the Doorn Berg on the night of June 7th miscarried, the commando getting warning and disappearing. But on the same night Van Reenan was completely scattered close to Steynsburg by the 17th Lancers, under Wyndham, whose leading squadrons, led by Captain D'A. Legard, rushed upon the farm buildings which sheltered the commando and cleared them, capturing twenty-three prisoners. Legard was seriously, and two men mortally, wounded in the affair.

APPROXIMATE STRENGTH STATES OF COLUMNS REFERRED TO IN FOREGOING CHAPTER.

COLUMN.	Mounted Troops.	Infantry.	Guns, including Vickers-Maxims.	Machine Guns.	
March—April, 1901.					
Lt.-Col. E. M. S. Crabbe	647	200	2	—	
Lt.-Col. the Hon. A. H. Henniker	427	179	2	2	
Lt.-Col. H. M. Grenfell	432	—	5	—	
Lt.-Col. J. W. Colenbrander	830	—	1	—	
Lt.-Col. A. E. Wilson	500	—	1	—	
Col. Sir C. Parsons	500	—	3	3	Major-General Sir H. Settle directing (later Colonel D. Haig assumed the direction of the columns in the midland area).
Col. H. J. Scobell	879	115	5	1	
Lt.-Col. R. F. Lindsell	—	242	2	—	
Lt.-Col. G. F. Gorringe	530	—	3	—	
Lt.-Col. H. de B. de Lisle	461	30*	3	—	
Lt.-Col. E. B. Herbert	400	122	3	1	
Col. A. E. Codrington	210	55	2	—	
Lt.-Col. C. P. Crewe	700	—	3	1	
Lt.-Col. H. T. Lukin	690	—	3	1	
Lt.-Col. the Hon. A. Murray	185	—	2	1	
Col. S. C. H. Monro	820	—	3	3	
Lt.-Col. W. L. White	648	—	3	1	
Lt.-Col. W. P. Wyndham	426	—	3	—	

* Cyclists.

NOTE.—Major-Generals H. A. MacDonald and H. H. Settle were created Knights Commander of the Bath for services during 1899-1900.—*London Gazette*, April 19th, 1901.

CHAPTER XI.

EVENTS IN THE WESTERN TRANSVAAL*

(Continued from Chapter VII.).

MAY—AUGUST, 1901.

ON May 1st Lord Methuen marched from Mafeking south-eastward in order to gain touch with Willson's columns for combined operations in the Klerksdorp district. On the 3rd he passed through Lichtenburg, and two days later came near Brakpan, where he hoped to get sight of Willson. As usual, the enemy, undeterred by their recent discomfitures on this very spot,† were in occupation of Brakpan, and a party nearly succeeded in cutting off some of Lord Methuen's transport, which had been wrongly guided behind the column. Beaten off once they continued to follow, were reinforced a few miles further on, and were only deterred by the forming up of the whole of the rearguard behind the wagons. These manœuvres were intended to distract Lord Methuen's attention from their own transport, which was making off across the British front, guarded by 500 burghers. The convoy was nevertheless espied, and the 5th and 10th Imperial Yeomanry giving chase, returned with seven prisoners, one of the British field-pieces which had been lost at Zilikat's Nek,‡ and a few wagons. The column bivouacked at Brakpan. During the day Lord Methuen was in communication with Babington, who was waiting on the Taaibosch Spruit, and plans were instantly made for combination. The object was the Hartebeestfontein hills, so long the

Operations in the Klerksdorp district.

---

* See map No. 59.   † See Chapter VII.
‡ See Volume III., page 240.

haunt of De la Rey and his lieutenants, and the troops were already well placed for a converging descent upon the stronghold by Lord Methuen, Babington, Sir H. Rawlinson, and a column under Lieut.-Colonel E. C. Ingouville Williams, which Major-General M. Willson brought out from Klerksdorp. But the carefully-laid trap, working perfectly on the 6th, closed upon nothing, nor was there the slightest intimation as to the direction the game had taken. A series of confused and profitless attempts to intercept first a possible northward, then a southward flight, concluded by Lord Methuen and Sir H. Rawlinson marching parallel, following a trail, towards the western line of railway, the former arriving at Mafeking, the latter, who took several small laagers on the way, at Maribogo on May 12th. Willson's other columns continued to operate in the Wolmaranstad area, Dixon, from Tafel Kop, coming down towards them as far as Leeuwfontein. All had fighting, but with such scattered bands as to render still more uncertain the direction in which the main Boer force had vanished. On May 8th Babington, scouting from Palmietfontein, intercepted a convoy travelling northward, and took twenty prisoners and forty-four wagons and carts. Two days later E. C. I. Williams, whilst marching for Korannafontein, came upon a considerable commando east of that place and drove it off headlong. The success of the attack was marred by the misfortune of a troop of the New South Wales Mounted Rifles, who, mistaking a party of Boers for comrades, were cut off and lost two officers and eight men as they ran the gauntlet back to their own side.

On May 14th Willson's columns were again near Klerksdorp, having secured between them seventy-six prisoners, more than 100 vehicles and myriads of sheep and other stock. The general result of the combination had been thoroughly to smoke the hive at Hartebeestfontein; but the swarm was still at large, and there is little doubt but that to scatter guerrillas of the type of the Boers is a military misfortune rather than a gain.

On May 15th Babington departed to command a brigade of cavalry, handing over the leadership of his own column to Lieut.-Colonel W. B. Hickie, whilst Major-General R. S. R.

EVENTS IN THE WESTERN TRANSVAAL. 183

Fetherstonhaugh was appointed to direct the group composed of the columns commanded by Hickie, E. C. I. Williams and Sir H. Rawlinson. The last-named was now on the march back from the western line, whence Lord Methuen was also returning. Nothing of importance occurred during the rest of May except an attack on a Potchefstroom—Ventersdorp convoy on the 23rd. The attack, which was twice repeated, was of a determined nature, and the convoy was surrounded and all but taken as it came within sight of Ventersdorp. The Boers were kept off, however, by the stubborn defence of the escort, under Major P. Palmes (Loyal North Lancashire) and Captain E. C. Purchas (South Wales Borderers), and by a gun which the Commandant at Ventersdorp, Major J. H. du B. Travers (South Wales Borderers), took out from the village with what men he had—some twenty in all—and the convoy barely escaped with the loss of six killed and thirty-one wounded amongst the escort. At the end of May Lord Methuen was at Lichtenburg with thirty-five prisoners and seventy-eight vehicles, captured in two raids between Mafeking and the Little Harts river; Sir H. Rawlinson was back at Brakspruit; Hickie and E. C. I. Williams at Klerksdorp, Fetherstonhaugh having received orders to concentrate his command consequent upon events now to be related.

Since May 8th Dixon had been moving into the area from Tafel Kop, marching by way of Putfontein on the Lichtenburg—Ventersdorp road, where he surprised and captured twenty-five of a laager of 100 Boers. From Leeuwfontein (May 10th—12th), he marched by the Schoon Spruit and Witpoortje to Welverdiend on the railway (May 17th). Hence he returned north by the direct route to Naauwpoort (May 24th), halted there one day, and on the 26th set out westward, with twelve days' supplies, to clear the Witwatersrand towards his former post at Tafel Kop. That height had been by no means deserted during the fortnight of Dixon's absence. Like Hartebeestfontein near Klerksdorp, like Kromdraai at the head of the Wilge river, like Blauw Kop on the Vaal, the Elands Berg in the Wakkerstroom district, and a number of other places of the kind, Tafel Kop provided a secure and commanding camping ground, very valuable

Boer strongholds.

in a wide and inhospitable terrain such as South Africa. At such spots the enemy was always to be found, either concentrating before an engagement, or taking rest or refuge after one. They became as well known to the troops as storm-centres to the meteorologist, and there were but few expeditions throughout the long campaign which had not one or the other of these places as their objects. So familiar were they, and as a matter of course so easily defensible—otherwise they would not have answered the enemy's purpose—that it may well be worth consideration whether such strongholds, which are the bases of all guerrilla warfare, should not be impregnably fortified and held at the very outset of campaigns like that in progress in South Africa in 1901; and for this but small garrisons would be necessary. In richer and more enclosed theatres of war such a mode of action would of course be impossible; but fortunately guerrilla warfare does not commonly occur in such theatres; if it did it would bid fair to be interminable.

Thus it happened that no sooner had Dixon disappeared from Tafel Kop on May 8th when the place began to refill with Boers from all directions. General Kemp, one of De la Rey's most dashing subordinates, had been invested with almost supreme powers of commandeering in this district, and thoroughly he exercised them. From every side appeared bands which after the manner of their kind had been resting, idling, or wandering in the neighbouring valleys and ranges, until Kemp, finding himself in command of nearly 3,000 men, began to look about for a task worthy of so imposing a force.

<small>Kemp collects a force.</small>

Dixon's return at once gave him the opportunity he sought. The British column was alone and weak, weaker indeed than it ought to have been, for 200 of Dixon's mounted men had been detained on the lines of communication, whilst some of his infantry were on convoy duty in Krugersdorp. Moving east as Dixon approached from Naauwpoort on May 28th, Kemp was in observation from Basfontein to Tafel Kop, his parties being sighted and slightly engaged by Dixon as he made for a camping ground at Vlakfontein. Not a whisper of the Boer concentration had reached the British commander. On the 29th he made a short

<small>Dixon marches from Naauwpoort.</small>

EVENTS IN THE WESTERN TRANSVAAL. 185

march to search for some guns and ammunition reported to be buried on the farms at Vlakhoek and Waterval, close to the north-west. The approaches to them from Vlakfontein consisted of two parallel ridges with a valley between. Dixon, conforming his dispositions to the ground, marched in three divisions, sending Lieut.-Colonel C. E. Duff with 100 Scottish Horse, two companies King's Own Scottish Borderers, and two guns 8th battery R.F.A. along the right-hand (northern) ridge; Major H. Chance with 250 men Imperial Yeomanry, 100 men of the Derbyshire regiment, two guns 28th battery R.F.A. and a Vickers-Maxim along the left-hand ridge; he himself followed the central depression with two companies King's Own Scottish Borderers, one company Derbyshire regiment, two guns 8th battery R.F.A. and a howitzer.

Waterval, the first farm searched, proved empty, though a large hole in the ground showed where the guns had once lain buried. Dixon then faced about to investigate Vlakhoek, east of Waterval. This wheel transferred his former left flank into a rearguard, Chance being so instructed by a message sent from Waterval before the movement began. Finding nothing at Vlakhoek Dixon ordered a general retirement to camp, and soon he and Duff were on the march towards Vlakfontein, expecting Chance, from whose direction some unimportant firing had been heard, to follow. But Chance did not appear, and there was no intimation of events on his position until Dixon, nearing camp, became aware to his amazement that shrapnel from that very ridge, and from Chance's own guns, was bursting amongst the tents. *Dixon's manœuvres at Vlakfontein.*

With an enemy in the neighbourhood Chance's position had from the first been peculiarly dangerous, for the nature of the ground rendered it well-nigh impossible to guard against surprise. Running east and west, the ridge at its western extremity fell steeply to a deep donga, beyond which a rocky and bush-covered kopje rose again athwart the general line of the ridge like the cross-piece of the letter "T." To the south another ridge ran parallel to and of equal height with that occupied by Chance, who could see little of either of these *His position at Vlakfontein.*

neighbouring heights owing to the convex nature of the contours of his own hill, on the bare summit of which his men had little or no cover. The position, in short, resembled closely that at Nicholson's Nek in Natal, where Sir G. White's detachment had met with so serious a reverse in the earliest days of the campaign.*

Chance, having previously reconnoitred the ground, had better acquaintance with its dangers than means to obviate them. The wooded kopje on the west was too distant to hold, and the donga beneath it consequently untenable. He could, therefore, do no more in this direction than throw out upon his own side of the hollow a screen of mounted men, whom he strictly ordered to halt a thousand yards short of and overlooking the donga. Behind these he placed a party in support, and in rear of these again his two guns and infantry, the left of the whole being guarded by a troop (twenty-five men) of Imperial Yeomanry, which he sent under an officer on to the parallel ridge to the south. From the very moment when Dixon's retrograde movement from Waterval on Vlakhoek and the camp converted Chance's party from flankguard to rearguard, this troop of Yeomanry, which was composed of men totally fresh to campaigning, became the most important unit in the field, for they were then rearmost of all and nearest to the enemy. Kemp, who had at once marked Chance's ridge as the vulnerable point of Dixon's whole disposition, was equally quick to discern the joint in the harness. Despatching part of his force to the southward towards the Yeomanry on the ridge, he attracted attention in the other direction by delivering a frontal attack from the woody cross-kopje across the donga up the western spur of Chance's ridge, that is, full against the screen and supports which lay in front of the guns. As they advanced the Boers lighted the dry veld grass, and coming on behind the smoke and flame, were soon upon the summit. Their attack here, which they had taken little pains to conceal, had been visible from the first, and Chance's artillery had no difficulty in bringing it to a check. It was plain, however, that in view of Dixon's retire-

Kemp attacks Dixon at Vlakfontein, May 29th, 1901.

* See Volume I., Chapter X.

ment, which was then in progress, the rearguard was now too far westward ; and, amidst considerable firing, Chance withdrew his screen, guns and infantry about a mile along the ridge, towards the camp. As he did so the detached troop on his left, which was also being smothered by the smoke of an advancing fire, retired likewise ; but instead of reporting their action to Chance, they fell back directly eastward, unknown to the rest, so that Chance knew nothing of the exposure of his flank. Kemp, on the other hand, who had been keenly watching this very spot, was instantly aware of his advantage. Rushing on at great speed behind the racing fire, the burghers swept unseen across the depression between the two ridges, and in a moment appeared in the very midst of the guns, shooting down the gunners and teams, and playing havoc with the escort. There was a brief, but for one combatant hopeless, *mêlée*, in which many gallant acts were performed by men of both sides. The few gunners who were not laid low by the first volley attempted to fire with case ; but their own magazine was ablaze and no other shells could be reached. Then the drivers, riding into the midst of the press, strove to extricate the guns : every horse and most of the riders were shot at once. In a few moments the hill was covered with dead ; and when all resistance was crushed the Boers, who had brought artillerymen with them, seized the guns and turned them towards the camp which Dixon, as related, was in the act of entering with the rest of his forces.

At about that moment a messenger whom Chance had contrived to despatch before the end of the struggle around the guns reached Dixon with news which confirmed the need for instant help on the ridge. Dixon immediately launched a counter-attack as daring as it was rapid. Some time earlier, just before falling back on camp, he had posted on a knoll at the western end of Vlakfontein two guns of the 28th battery R.F.A , the howitzer, a Vickers-Maxim, with a company of the Derbyshire regiment to act as a covering force to his own and Chance's retirement. Sending these to the front, and Duff with his section of artillery back to his former ridge, he ordered a general advance. The Boers at once turned the fire of the captured

_{Dixon's counter-attack.}

guns from the camp to the troops, shelling especially the guns of the 8th battery with Duff. But once more a victorious commando had spent its strength and spirit upon its first success. Dixon's troops, attacking by rushes which were not to be stopped by any fire, came to within 600 yards of the scene of disaster, and were about to hurl themselves over the ridge when the burghers' hearts failed. Mounting hastily they galloped away, leaving all their trophies on the field. Thus for only the second time in the campaign—the first had been at Wagon Hill—a resolute counter-stroke had retrieved the apparently hopeless fortunes of the day. Moreover, it had cost the enemy more than his so nearly won triumph. Forty-one burghers bit the dust on the spot; many more fell out of sight or were removed. The heavy losses on the British side—186 officers and men*—were chiefly amongst Chance's detachment, and the value of the lesson taught by Dixon lay in the small expense with which he had re-taken both the guns and the ground of a wing which had been annihilated.

In spite of his hard-won success Dixon could not disguise from himself that his column was not only useless, but in extreme danger in the presence of the greatly superior forces of Kemp. At any moment the tables might be turned on him as quickly as he had turned them on his adversary. After burying his dead, and allowing Kemp, who asked permission under a flag of truce, to do the same, Dixon, instead of persisting to Tafel Kop, fell back on Naauwpoort, whilst every available column moved to reinforce him. Fetherstonhaugh's already mentioned concentration at Klerksdorp was consequent on receipt of the news of Vlakfontein. From the west came Lord Methuen with orders to be at Doorn Kop, next to Tafel Kop, on June 8th; from the east Brigadier-General G. Hamilton, now in command of a brigade of cavalry at Heidelberg; whilst in Pretoria Colonel E. H. H. Allenby was held in readiness to co-operate when the projected sweep should have arrived within reach.

Concentration of columns against Kemp.

Fetherstonhaugh moved from Klerksdorp with his three

---

* Casualties—Killed and died of wounds, six officers, fifty-one men; wounded, six officers, 115 men; missing, one officer, seven men.

EVENTS IN THE WESTERN TRANSVAAL. 189

columns (Sir H. Rawlinson, E. C. I. Williams and Hickie) on June 1st; was at Ventersdorp on the 3rd, at Klipkrans next day, and on the 7th upon the scene of Dixon's engagement. With support thus at hand Dixon himself quitted Naauwpoort on the same day, and leaving to Fetherstonhaugh the area to the west of the Magaliesberg, followed the north-eastern slopes to Boschhoek, whilst Fetherstonhaugh moved on through the broken country to Kosterfontein, turning thence towards Rustenburg to Roodewal, where he captured seventeen prisoners and thirty-three carts and wagons. He then lined up his columns along the Rustenburg—Zeerust road, intending to drive the country up to the Elands river in conjunction with Lord Methuen, who had arrived at Brakfontein on the 9th. Lord Methuen, however, came no further, and Fetherstonhaugh, who was so little in need of more troops that he had dispensed with the assistance of G. Hamilton, whom he sent into Krugersdorp, proceeded to the banks of the Elands river at Bestershoek. Still no considerable body of the enemy was to be found; indeed, scarcely a Boer was seen until Fetherstonhaugh, returning southwards, came upon a moderate gathering on the old ground at Vlakhoek. His attempt to enclose it on June 13th was foiled by the dispersion of the enemy, and after a raid up the valley of the Selous river, which produced six prisoners, he returned with Hickie and Sir H. Rawlinson to Ventersdorp, leaving Dixon at Selouskraal, G. Hamilton close to Tafel Kop, E. C. I. Williams at Krugersdorp, and Allenby at Doorn Kop. *Kemp disappears.*

The last-named had been out since the 10th in the Hekpoort valley, where he had been joined by G. Hamilton from Krugersdorp on the 12th. As usual he had found the useful passage at Breedts Nek strongly held. A brisk skirmish on June 14th had temporarily cleared the pass; but Allenby, moving on westward, once more left it to the enemy, who thus still retained both a gate of escape and a sallyport for attack through the mountains. For a week after these indecisive operations there was a pause, the only movement being that of Sir H. Rawlinson and Hickie into Klerksdorp, consequent on an unfounded alarm that the town was in danger. This part of the Western Transvaal indeed

The problem of the Western Transvaal.

had become a rock in the path which was beginning to be recognised as being only soluble by the vinegar of time. All that could be done had been done; in every direction columns and groups of columns had swept until their tracks crossed and recrossed each other almost beyond the power to trace them. Still the enemy remained at about his original strength, losing it is true a few here and there, but making good his losses from the recruiting grounds provided by the lonely farms and valleys, where hundreds of recreant burghers only awaited the advent of a capable leader to take the field again for some bold enterprise. Yet scarcely a rifleman was to be found when sought for. The columns with Fetherstonhaugh might have been wandering in a wilderness haunted by a few bandits, so little had they seen of armed strength worthy to have called so elaborate a concentration from its base. What had become of Kemp and his three thousand, of Badenhorst, of De la Rey himself? Since they were neither in the north, east nor south, the western watershed remained the only undrawn covert, and on June 26th orders were issued for a general drive in the direction of Zeerust by way of the Magaliesberg valley and the Zwart Ruggens mountains. Accordingly on June 29th, E. C. I. Williams, arriving at Vlakfontein, was in touch with Sir H. Rawlinson and Hickie at Klipkrans, the three columns manœuvring next day to get into line from Roodewal through Basfontein to Rietfontein. Kemp was reported to be at Koperfontein; but only a small band was unearthed about Basfontein, which, after an attempt to capture Williams' baggage, was driven off with loss, Williams' casualties being three. Kemp himself, however, was close by, as was proved by the receipt of a flag of truce seeking permission to bury the dead. Meanwhile Dixon, who was also to take part in the expedition, had moved up to Bashoek at the western extremity of the Magaliesberg.

The country driven towards Zeerust,

On July 1st the westward march began. It would serve no purpose to follow its various stages, so destitute were they of any marked features. The columns were opposed throughout, or rather harassed than opposed, and on July 10th entered Zeerust with a few prisoners. Four days before this Lord Methuen had been in the town, coming from Mafeking on his way into the Enzelberg to the north. He was back at Zeerust on the day of its evacuation by Fetherstonhaugh, and in Mafeking again on the 16th. After taking in ten days' supplies Fetherstonhaugh's columns set out on the 12th for the return march to Klerksdorp, which was reached on the 28th. This stage was slightly more eventful than the former. On the 17th Hickie's camp at Doornbult was attacked with some determination by 200 Boers, to drive off whom some close fighting was necessary. Next day the same band endeavoured to cut off Hickie's rearguard, only to be again chased from the field with loss. Throughout these operations Dixon had been somewhat detached from the rest, though he entered Zeerust on the same day from the line of the Elands river. At the close he went to Welverdiend, and thence by the direct route northward to Naauwpoort and Olifants Nek, which he reached on July 31st, handing over command of his column shortly afterwards to Colonel R. G. Kekewich.

Whilst Dixon was thus occupied Hickie and E. C. I. Williams, leaving Sir H. Rawlinson in Klerksdorp, again took the field, heading this time due westward through Hartebeestfontein towards the Little Harts river, which Lord Methuen was also approaching from Lichtenburg. Hartebeestfontein was for once clear, but a short distance beyond it the enemy had laid an ambush which E. C. I. Williams detected in time to turn the tables by attacking the flanks of the would-be surprisers and scattering them over the veld. Four casualties resulted on Williams' side and six on the other, no fewer than thirty-two horses being shot in the affray. Thereafter both columns made straight across country, and striking the Harts river at Kopjesvlei, marched down it past Schweizer Reneke to Taungs, which was entered on August 8th with fifty-nine prisoners, and nearly 100 captured vehicles. The return journey to Klerksdorp was commenced the next day, the columns marching with their right on the right bank of the Vaal, which Hickie touched at Bloemhof on August 15th. Next day E. C. I. Williams came in touch with a Boer convoy travelling eastward. A three days' chase through Leeuwboschen and Brandewynskuil, with

and from Klerksdorp to Taungs.

a halt at Wolmaranstad, resulted in the capture of nine wagons; but these were known to be only a fragment of the fugitive train, which was now reported to have doubled westward. E. C. I. Williams hurried to intercept it at Katdoornplaat. In this he was successful. Group by group the wagons were overhauled and taken, the resistance of the escorts being summarily swept aside by the New South Wales Mounted Rifles, and on the evening of the 18th E. C. I. Williams halted at Spruitplaats with eighteen prisoners and more than 100 wagons and carts. On August 23rd both columns were back at Klerksdorp.

Lord Methuen drives from Taungs to Klerksdorp.

In this operation Lord Methuen had co-operated from Lichtenburg, and a small column under Lieut.-Colonel A. B. Scott from Vryburg. Lord Methuen had quitted Taungs in company with Fetherstonhaugh, and getting upon his left flank, swept eastward in line with him across to Klerksdorp. Approaching Wolmaranstad on August 15th, he intercepted and captured a convoy which was making off from Fetherstonhaugh's south-easterly advance, taking twelve prisoners, sixty-two vehicles, and large herds of stock. Three days later, when passing to the north of Wolmaranstad at Korannafontein, he in his turn suffered some loss by a patrol of Yeomanry falling into an ambush which deprived them of twenty-four officers and men, of whom fourteen were made prisoners. On August 22nd Lord Methuen arrived in Klerksdorp, where he stayed until the 27th.

Operations of G. Hamilton, Allenby and Kekewich.

Turning back to the other columns: during July G. Hamilton had never ceased to move about Klerksdorp, Potchefstroom, Ventersdorp and Wolmaranstad, putting in at the first-named place on the last day of the month. He had had constant skirmishing, and one brisk and successful affair on the 26th at Blinkklip, where, deceiving Potgieter by a ruse, with four casualties he captured his entire laager of thirty vehicles, with ten of the escort, the like number escaping wounded. Early in the month G. Hamilton was temporarily strengthened by Western's column from the Orange River Colony. Allenby, too, had a few days' co-operation with Hamilton, and was then ordered north into the Magaliesberg. Approaching Breedts Nek he came upon a force guarding the southern entrance, which

EVENTS IN THE WESTERN TRANSVAAL. 193

he promptly attacked on July 10th, and deprived of thirteen prisoners and their belongings. Two days later, at Nooitgedacht, the scene of Clements' engagement in the previous December, he found another laager of thirteen wagons, all of which were burnt by the flames from a dynamite wagon which had been exploded by a shell from Allenby's 5-in. howitzer. On the 31st his camp was at Boschfontein, whence he issued to assist through Olifants Nek a convoy which Kekewich was taking from Naauwpoort to Rustenburg.

Kekewich, after delivering his convoy, came back through Olifants Nek, and instead of returning to Naauwpoort turned eastward and co-operated with Allenby in an attack on Breedts Nek. The enemy abandoned it at once, and on August 7th the pass which had assisted to more than one British reverse was at last crowned with a defensive post. *Occupation of Breedts Nek.*

Whilst Allenby remained about Breedts Nek with parties out in all directions, Kekewich moved eastward along the Magaliesberg to Boschfontein and Elandskraal. Allenby, keeping touch with him, reinforced him with mounted men through the rift at Damhoek, eight miles north-east of Hekpoort, which was held by Barton's infantry. The enemy was unexpectedly numerous in these often-scoured ravines. At Elandskraal on August 10th forty-one prisoners fell to Kekewich's search parties after scarcely a shot had been fired, and cattle were to be taken at every step. After halting a while at Commando Nek, and refilling with supplies at Rietfontein, Kekewich turned north to clear the Hekpoort and Sterkstroom valleys, then south (August 24th) to Wolhuter's Kop across the Rustenburg road. There he remained until fresh orders came at the end of the month relative to a projected operation against Kemp, causing him to move to Broadwood's old camping ground at Oorzaak on the 31st. On August 19th Allenby also refitted at Rietfontein, and after accompanying Kekewich northward, returned on the 29th to Rustenburg, whence he too moved in accordance with the same instructions as had reached Kekewich, the effect of which will be described in a subsequent chapter.*

* See Chapter XVI.

About the middle of August Allenby had had another brief co-operation with G. Hamilton. That officer had marched from Klerksdorp on the 5th; and raiding northward through Geduld and across the Taaibosch Spruit, in pursuit of a commando under Liebenberg which no effort could bring to a stand, was in Ventersdorp on the 12th. Hence he moved *via* Klipkrans into the Witwatersrand at Basfontein, where he came into touch with Allenby. An attack on Basfontein made jointly with the 6th Dragoon Guards (Carabiniers) from Allenby's force on August 14th resulted in the capture of a laager of thirty-eight carts and wagons, three Boers being killed, ten captured, Allenby losing an officer and six men killed and wounded. G. Hamilton, followed by skirmishers, of whom he captured three, then reconnoitred Tafel Kop, returning to Ventersdorp on August 18th. On the 21st he came near the railway at Kaalfontein to take charge of a convoy for Rustenburg, coming from Krugersdorp. After this had been carried out without incident, G. Hamilton was detailed to join Allenby and Kekewich in the above referred to scheme, which was also about to absorb the attention of Lord Methuen, and the three columns under Fetherstonhaugh.

Minor columns.

Two fresh bodies of troops working in the neighbourhood at this time must be referred to, namely, that of Major-General Barton who was covering the establishment of a line of blockhouses for occupation by the South African Constabulary in the Hekpoort valley, and another, under Colonel Lord Basing (Royal Dragoons), which was affording similar cover to a blockhouse line building from Breedts Nek to Frederikstad, the other end of which was watched by a force under Lieut.-Colonel W. Fry (West Yorkshire). Both Barton and Lord Basing had come out from Pretoria, the former on June 24th, the latter on July 16th.

On August 5th Lord Basing was detached in pursuit of a party of Boers under P. De la Rey, which had broken south from Barton's stopping line along the Hekpoort valley. After a circuitous chase by Vlakplaats, Kaalfontein and Steenkoppies, the Boers dodging amongst the rapidly growing blockhouses,

EVENTS IN THE WESTERN TRANSVAAL. 195

Lord Basing was stopped near Olifants Nek, having fairly broken up P. De la Rey's band by incessant hunting, and picked up thirteen of his men who had fallen behind. On August 15th Lord Basing repaired to Krugersdorp, where he was entrained for Springfontein, to assist in the turning of Smuts from Cape Colony.*

Other troops new to the area were those of Lieut.-Colonel F. S. Garratt, who, starting from Springs on July 9th, had come past Vereeniging to the Los Berg. Before him fled a Boer convoy which was come up with just as it had crossed the Vaal at Lindequee on the 21st. Garratt, sending 100 men across the drift in pursuit, had surrounded the whole with little fighting when General Smuts, appearing from the west, hastened to the rescue with a strong commando. Twenty-six prisoners and fourteen wagons were nevertheless secured and brought across the river, and next day Garratt pushed out to come to terms with Smuts. That leader, however, after several rearguard actions, established himself too strongly at Buffelshoek to be disturbed, and Garratt returned to Lindequee, whilst Sir H. Rawlinson took his men out from Klerksdorp and moved *via* Potchefstroom to his assistance. On July 27th the two were in touch with each other, and also with a small column come out from Vereeniging under Brigadier-General G. G. Cunningham.

On the 28th, whilst Garratt moved down the right bank of the Vaal, Sir H. Rawlinson and the Vereeniging column fell in concert upon a commando which was laagered near the junction of the Krommellboog Spruit with the Vaal. The Boers fled before a determined attack by Sir H. Rawlinson's mounted infantry, making off so fast south-west through Vredefort that, gallop as he would, Rawlinson could not catch them. The whole of the convoy fell into his hands, however, with some score of prisoners and twenty-five wagons. On the next day Sir H. Rawlinson was called away for operations elsewhere, and Garratt, continuing alone, had just regained touch with the enemy at Schoeman's Drift when he received orders to join in the same movement which had drawn Sir H. Rawlinson away from him.

Operations of Garratt.

* See Chapter XIV.

Elliot makes a brief appearance in the Western Transvaal.

This was the passage of the three columns of Major-General E. L. Elliot's division on their way southward to carry out the great sweep south of the Vaal and west of the main railway down to the Modder river, the initiation of which is described elsewhere.* On July 23rd Elliot's Headquarters were at Klerksdorp, where he absorbed two other minor columns, those of Colonels Henry and Western, the former of whom had been working in the Hoopstad district, the latter about Bothaville and Coal Mines. Elliot made but a brief pause within the Western Transvaal. On July 28th he marched out with all his seven columns due southward to Yzerspruit and Koedoesdraai, passing at once beyond the limits of this chapter.*

In three weeks' time Garratt re-appeared in the Western Transvaal. Having acted in second line during the greater part of Elliot's advance, on August 21st he turned northward again, and recrossing the river at Wonderwater, made for Los Berg, where he expected to find parties which had broken aside from the front of Elliot's sweep. Nor was he mistaken. A laager discovered on the 23rd in the recesses of the Los Berg was easily captured, and was being removed when 300 Boers, coming south from the Gatsrand, attempted to rescue their wagons. For a time they pressed hard, but Garratt pushed them as strongly back, and after a spirited encounter drove them northward, losing four officers and men himself, and capturing eight and killing three of the enemy. Until the end of the month he remained in this neighbourhood, actively covering the construction of a line of blockhouses which was to deny this favourite haunt to the enemy. Constantly patrolling amongst the hills, he had another successful affair on August 28th, taking nine and killing one of a party of twenty-five Boers who were laagered at Enzelpoort. These were stragglers from a larger convoy which had gone on to Weltevreden, where Garratt engaged them the same evening, securing three more prisoners.

* See Chapter XIV.

EVENTS IN THE WESTERN TRANSVAAL.

APPROXIMATE STRENGTH STATES OF COLUMNS REFERRED TO IN FOREGOING CHAPTER.

COLUMN.	Mounted Troops.	Infantry.	Guns, including Vickers-Maxims.	Machine guns.	
May—August, 1901.					
Lt.-Gen. Lord P. Methuen	1,163	150	10	2	
Brig.-Gen. H. G. Dixon	1,050	1,216	8	2	
Maj.-Gen. J. M. Babington	860	580	9	—	Maj.-Gen. Mildmay Willson in command.
Col. Sir H. Rawlinson (late Shekleton's)	1,250	—	2	—	
Lt.-Col. E. C. Ingouville Williams	569	169	3	—	
Lt.-Col. W. B. Hickie (late Babington's)	849	500	8	—	Maj.-Gen. R. S. R. Fetherstonhaugh in command.
Lt.-Col. E. C. Ingouville Williams	996	168	4	—	
Col. Sir H. Rawlinson	1,279	—	8	—	
Brig.-Gen. H. G. Dixon	760	555	8	1	
Brig.-Gen. G. Hamilton	1,060	356	3	3	
Col. E. H. H. Allenby	740	729	7	1	
Col. R. G. Kekewich	576	835	4	2	
Lt.-Col. F. S. Garratt	870	296	5	1	
Col. St. G. C. Henry	666	265	3	1	
Col. W. G. B. Western	670	118	3	1	
Brig.-Gen. R. G. Broadwood	2,032	—	5	3	Maj.-Gen. E. L. Elliot in command.
Col. E. C. Bethune	991	—	5	1	
Lt.-Col. H. de B. de Lisle	967	—	5	2	
Col. Lord Basing	442	—	3	1	Maj.-Gen. G. Barton in command.
Lt.-Col. F. Hacket-Thompson	269	671	5	1	
Lt.-Col. W. Fry	40	792	2	—	

CHAPTER XII.

EVENTS IN THE EASTERN TRANSVAAL*

(Continued from Chapter VIII.).

JUNE—SEPTEMBER, 1901.

Difficulties of the campaign.
To arrest the broken bubbles of mercury were a similar task to that which at this time confronted Lord Kitchener's troops. In all parts of South Africa they were called upon daily to get sight of the invisible, to crush the impalpable, and to surround—nothing. The Commander-in-Chief clearly realised the nature of the problem before him.† His heaviest blows, though they never failed to break up the enemy, did so into fragments so numerous and full of vitality that there was not a soldier in the British forces but wished that they might re-unite into a body worth finding, worth striking, or capable of being found and struck. Few such gatherings were in the field; a dozen Boers had become a notable prize for a strong column; a field-cornetcy for a whole complicated operation; neither were often to be secured at all, and never without labour and wastage out of all proportion to the reward. Such is the triumph—prolonged perhaps, though inevitably doomed to extinction—of guerrilla warfare, and, of the belligerents concerned, only soldiers of experience and keen sight can avoid being impatient on the one side or contemptuous on the other. Not only the Boers at this juncture had doubts whether the British forces had not become but " an army of cow-catchers,"‡ when chiefly droves of stock, every thousand head of which would have been willingly

---

* See map No. 56.   † Despatches, July 8th, 1901.
‡ Diary of a Burgher.

exchanged by the captors for but a single rifleman, poured into the camps, or perished in heaps upon the veld, the useless trophies of exhausting campaigns.

Yet even the Boer supplies seemed inexhaustible. Expeditions which brought in thousands of beasts had only to sally out again to find thousands more ; conflagrations which illuminated the whole horizon seemed impotent to burn the crops ; broad belts of ransacked farms ran only like lanes of ruin through districts which still afforded not only shelter but subsistence. In short, in spite of the enormous efforts of the British columns, the Republican forces were being but slowly whittled.

Even in the much scoured region of the High Veld there still roved at least 6,000 men, and only so much territory as lay within the British outposts was conquered. Thus there was no rest for the various columns dealt with in Chapter VIII. The early days of June saw each and all of them once more in motion, until the Eastern Transvaal was again alive with bodies of troops from the Mauch Berg down to the borders of Natal. First, Plumer, E. C. Knox and Rimington, within three days of their conclusion of one set of operations, set out to undertake another —this time to the south of the Vaal river, where the country between Amersfoort and Piet Retief was reported to be as rife with the enemy as though French and his array of columns had never been. Next, Beatson, revisiting the district at the junction of the Steenkool (or Steenbok) Spruit and Oliphant river, found the enemy not only present but so aggressive that Sir B. Blood, whose forces were still busied between Carolina and Amsterdam, had to move westward with four columns to his assistance. Spens, Park, Benson and Douglas returned from a raid northward of the Delagoa Bay railway line, with captures sufficient to show how much they had met and left behind. Nor did Bullock brush fruitlessly the right bank of the Vaal eastward up to its junction with the Mabusa Spruit, and Colville the same bank westward towards Villiersdorp, nor Grey twice visit the districts of Bethel and Ermelo in vain. These were the doings in June, each of which must now be described shortly.

Operations in the south-east.

On June 1st Plumer placed his three columns in line for an advance on Piet Retief—E. C. Knox on the left at Uitkyk, north of the Vaal, his own column at Springbokspruit, that of Rimington starting one day later from Platrand. Zevenfontein—Hartebeestfontein—Strydkraal was the line on the 2nd, Transvalia—Rietspruit—Amersfoort on the 3rd, when Bullock was sighted on his way back from Ermelo to Standerton. On June 4th E. C. Knox touched the Vaal at Welgelegen, Plumer reached Familiehoek, and Rimington Kromhoek on the spurs of the Elands Berg, the last-named column becoming more closely engaged as it neared that constant haunt of the enemy. Turning the mountain range by Kalkoenskranz next day, Rimington drove aside a commando which opposed him, and reached Balmoral, whilst Plumer made Welgevonden on the Mabusa, and E. C. Knox crossed the Vaal at the well-used drift at Witpunt. On the 6th Knox drew towards the Compies river to Alkmaar, thence eastward to Zoar and Watervaldrift on the Shela, Plumer marching on his right by Rotterdam and Brereton to Breda, whilst Rimington, still in touch with the enemy, came up on Plumer's right to Driefontein. During the night of June 8th, Plumer enclosed Piet Retief on north, west and south. The Boers hurriedly evacuated the town, which was found deserted when E. C. Knox entered it at dawn; but a number who had delayed their departure until too late were cut off by Rimington, who was blocking the drifts on either side of Swartwater, and thirty prisoners and twelve wagons, with horses, cattle and sheep were taken.

Plumer now turned quickly against the Slangapies Berg, both because that range was reported to harbour several Boer laagers, and because it stood in the way of a convoy which was expected from Wakkerstroom for his own supply. Accordingly on June 12th he was at St. Helena, advancing next day to Zuikerhoek where he safely received the convoy. For the next few days his three columns searched the Slangapies Berg and the Pongola Bosch, hunting with fair success the ravines and thickets of that almost inaccessible region, in which armies might have lain hidden for weeks, and single men for ever. Only twice

EVENTS IN THE EASTERN TRANSVAAL.

did this furtive enemy take the offensive, once in a manner more worthy of brigands than of soldiers in the field. On June 16th a train of empty wagons, which was making its way into Utrecht to refill, was attacked in the Elands Berg, Rimington going to its assistance next day. On the same occasion a mounted patrol, in the course of searching amongst the gorges of the Slangapies Berg, came upon a laager deep down in a wooded crevice of the mountain, and noticing that a white flag hung from a wagon, assumed that surrender was intended, and trotted forward to accept it. Instantly a murderous fire broke out from the bush on either side; six horses fell at once, the patrol was all but hemmed in, and before it had galloped into safety, had lost an officer and ten men by bullet and capture. Plumer hurried next day to avenge the losses; but though he seized and burnt the laager, the Boers crawled scathless through the impenetrable scrub, and only three of their number were accounted for.

Between June 18th and 20th P. P. Burg was surrounded as Piet Retief had been, with the same result, Rimington again securing the only seven Boers captured as he intervened between the emptying township and the Pivaan river. Plumer then cast back to the Elands Berg, which he thoroughly cleared, concentrating around Utrecht on the 23rd. Since leaving the Standerton railway he had accounted for six Boers killed, seventy-nine prisoners, 125 wagons and carts, and a quantity of cattle. At Utrecht the columns parted company, Plumer with E. C. Knox setting out northward on June 28th for the Delagoa Bay railway, whilst Rimington remained behind to continue the clearance of the mountains between Utrecht and Wakkerstroom. Plumer marched by Pivaanspoort and Lüneberg, capturing a small laager on June 30th south of that town; thence over the eastern end of the Slangapies Berg, across the Assegai, Shela and Compies rivers, taking another laager between the last-named streams on July 4th, to pursue his way by Onverwacht to Driefontein, where another laager fell into his hands on July 6th. On the 7th Plumer was at Bothwell, on the 9th at Carolina, whence he made his way into Wonderfontein with captured wagons and stock and thirteen prisoners. Soon after he was railed to Bloemfontein to take part in a vast combination which was about to sweep across the Orange River Colony.* It must here be stated that in this, as in many other instances, considerations of space alone compel arduous marches and carefully laid plans such as those narrated above to be thus dismissed in a mere itinerary. A history such as this must largely confine itself to results; and they are frequently the feeblest colouring of a campaign. The thousand problems and trials of soldiers on the march form no part of the writer's task, nor could he, however profuse, adequately paint such detail upon a canvas so enormous as the theatre of war in South Africa. It is fitting to mention this here, because many an operation which in less crowded times would have provided material for a volume in itself, has been and will be referred to with a brevity all unworthy of the immense toil, thought, and self-sacrifice expended on its execution. Let it then be always understood that credit for such expenditure is not omitted because it was not earned, but because it is too great for inclusion.

Rimington went into Platrand on July 7th after a series of forays amongst the Elands Berg, Pongola Bosch, Slangapies Berg and Rand Berg which had effectually cleared those fastnesses of all that was visible. In conjunction with parties from Utrecht he had harried the enemy on July 2nd at Schuilhoek, and again on the 3rd and 4th, pressing him sometimes so closely that the burghers threw away their rifles and bolted for safety into the dark recesses of the surrounding bush, where only a pack of bloodhounds could have tracked them.

Meanwhile Bullock's column, which left Standerton on June 10th, was operating in the same neighbourhood as Plumer's, but neither in connection nor communication with it. Bullock had marched by nearly the same route as E. C. Knox had done; camping at Uitkyk on the 11th, Morgenzon 12th, Dorpsplaats 14th and Beginderlyn, where the Vaal was crossed, on June 16th. Thence, like Knox, he turned southward into the

* See Chapter XIV.

EVENTS IN THE EASTERN TRANSVAAL. 203

Elands Berg, aiming at Langberg on the 19th, proceeding then to clear the eastern slopes of the range as far as Roodepoort. Cattle and farms alone rewarded his efforts, both in surprising quantities in a district which had never known respite from the forays of both armies. On June 27th Bullock was recalled to Standerton, which he reached on July 4th by way of Bergvliet, Wolvespruit and Platrand, having taken five prisoners, 3,700 head of stock and fifty-nine wagons.

Turning now to the north—On June 5th Beatson, at Brugspruit, received orders to go down to Bethel in order to co-operate with the columns of Sir B. Blood, which were about to move southward from the neighbourhood of Carolina. Beatson marched next day, making once more for the junction of the Oliphant river and Steenkool (or Steenbok) Spruit, where the enemy was reported. Having cleared his way to Van Dyksdrift, he halted for several days, using this spot as a base for the despatch of reconnaissances and raiding parties in every direction. Upon one of these fell disaster. Hearing of the presence of a small commando at Boschmansfontein, on the Middelburg—Ermelo road, Beatson sent in that direction on June 10th a force consisting of 350 men of the 5th Victorian Mounted Rifles, with two Vickers-Maxim guns. Soon after their departure, he himself discovered the enemy nearer and more to the south, at Elandsfontein. He thereupon signalled to the detachment, which had found Boschmansfontein empty, to concentrate on Elandsfontein, where he intended to move next morning. Returning to carry this out, the Victorians halted for the night of June 12th at Wilmansrust. Here they were marked down by General Muller, who was in command of a portion of General B. Viljoen's force, that leader himself, with the remainder, being away on duty with the Transvaal Government, which he was about to escort westward to another meeting with the Executive of the sister State. Muller had been left with orders to attack any detachment which ventured far from its main body, and he recognised his opportunity. Surrounding the spot as darkness fell, his men approached within twenty yards before they were discovered. After a tremendous

Operations in the north-east.

Affair at Wilmansrust, June 12th, 1901.

discharge of ten minutes' duration which did heavy execution, they rushed in, and in a moment the whole camp was theirs. Of the Australians fifteen had been killed, forty-two wounded; few of those unhurt escaped capture and as many as 100 horses were shot. Muller then disarmed and released his prisoners, looted the camp, and made off with the two guns, several wagons and about 100 horses, having inflicted a blow as humiliating to the worsted as it was admirable for its lightning-like rapidity and the numerical inferiority of the force with which it was dealt.

At 1.30 a.m. on the 13th Beatson received intelligence of this disaster and at once hurried to the scene, arriving there before daylight. As his baggage left Van Dyksdrift it was dogged by a commando, and it was evident that the column was in the midst of the enemy, who was still reported in force at Elandsfontein. But Beatson, moving south, passed by that place unmolested on the 15th, when he halted ten miles north of Bethel. He then turned towards Ermelo, in order to draw nearer to Sir B. Blood, who had been ordered to his assistance. Sir B. Blood was at this time in general command of operations which stretched from the Mauch Berg down to Amsterdam, his eight columns being actively employed in every direction. Four of them, namely, Spens', Benson's, Douglas' and Park's, were engaged to the north of the Delagoa Bay railway line on a scheme which will be subsequently described. The remainder were still east and south of Carolina. They had consisted, it will be remembered, of F. W. Kitchener's and Pulteney's columns and Babington's cavalry brigade, and Sir B. Blood had now increased his mobile strength by the creation of another column out of part of the troops holding his lines of communication under Colonel W. P. Campbell (King's Royal Rifle Corps). This force had already operated independently and successfully around Carolina from June 7th—12th, clearing forty-four farms. The remainder of the lines of communication troops were placed under Colonel J. W. Hughes-Hallett, and watched the Komati valley about Goodehoop, so that Sir B. Blood now controlled nine units.

On receipt of Lord Kitchener's orders to repair to the district which Beatson had found so full of the enemy, Sir B. Blood made arrangements to draw out his four southern columns towards the west. They were widely separated; F. W. Kitchener and Pulteney being north and south of Amsterdam, W. P. Campbell and Babington about Carolina. Sending orders to the two former commanders to follow as soon as possible, Sir B. Blood, on June 16th, took the others to Vaalbank, and thence towards Ermelo to Sterkfontein, where on the 18th he was in signal communication both with Beatson on the west and F. W. Kitchener on the east. On the next day junction was effected with Beatson, the three columns camping together at Hartebeestspruit. On the 20th Sir B. Blood received intelligence that Commandant-General Botha and the members of the Transvaal Government were close to the westward. He immediately despatched a flying column under Babington towards Kaffirstad, and on receipt of news from that officer on the 21st that the enemy was moving up the Oliphant river, expected notable results. But the information, though well founded, was late. Botha and the Government with Viljoen's escort had indeed passed that way two days before. At the very time of Babington's message they were bidding farewell to ex-President Steyn, Generals De Wet and De la Rey, and the members of the Orange Free State Executive, on the farm Witbank, twenty-six miles east of Heidelberg, after a conference which had been begun the day before at Branddrift, on the Waterval river. Not without adventures had either party reached the place of meeting. Acting-President Burger, Botha and the Transvaalers had escaped with such difficulty from the Amsterdam district that they had had to abandon every vehicle; and carrying alike their personal effects and the insignia of Government upon their saddles, had wormed their way, conducted by Viljoen, through the very midst of the surrounding British columns. Steyn and his companions had only escaped destruction by a hair's breadth on their ride from Vrede. Striking the railway south of Platrand on the night of June 14th, an alert blockhouse had first to be dealt with, and its attention having been distracted by an attack, the whole party rushed across the line. No sooner had they crossed when a dynamite mine exploded a few yards behind them. Next morning the men of the blockhouse found two slain horses, a rifle, and some burnt clothing on the spot, proof that the travellers had not escaped scathless. Steyn and De Wet then made for Blauw Kop on the Vaal, and after awaiting there for three days the arrival of the Transvaalers —whilst Bullock, all unconscious of their presence, passed them by one day's march to the east—repaired to Waterval, where the meeting took place on June 20th. On that night the Boer leaders, fearful of discovery, transferred their laagers to Branddrift; nor were their fears groundless, for the British Intelligence Department had full warning of their assembly. In mid-veld, watched on every side by vedettes, the Council of War took place. There were present the following officers and officials: Acting-President Schalk Burger, ex-President Steyn, State Secretary Reitz, Commandant-General Botha, Chief Commandant De Wet, Generals Hertzog, Viljoen, Spruyt, De la Rey, Smuts, Muller, Lucas Meyer and several commandants and officers of inferior rank.

The Boers hold a Council of War, June 20th, 1901.

Of the results of the discussion the most important was the decision arrived at "That no peace shall be made, and no peace proposals entertained which do not ensure our independence, and our existence as a nation, or which do not satisfactorily provide for the case of our Colonial brethren," etc.* Beyond this the conference was chiefly confined to speeches of a general nature, in which dissatisfaction with Kruger, with his silence and the unprofitable results of his European mission, was openly expressed. The appearance at the meeting of a silken banner worked by the hands of the Boer ladies in Pretoria, was evidence alike of the spirit of the women and of the ease with which communication could still be had with sympathisers who were immured deeply within the lines of the British forces.

At noon on June 21st the assembly broke up, the Transvaalers returning eastward, whilst Steyn, De Wet and De la Rey,

---

* Report of a Boer who was present.

recrossing the line near Vlaklaagte without incident, moved down the Waterval through a district which Colville had only just quitted. Arrived on the banks of the Vaal the party separated, De la Rey proceeding down stream to cross the railway between Vereeniging and Meyerton, whilst the ex-President and his Chief Commandant entered the Orange River Colony at Villiersdorp.

In accordance with an arrangement arrived at at the Council of War, B. Viljoen, having rejoined his commando, now moved up the Oliphant river, intending to make war once more in the Lydenburg district from which he had so narrowly escaped. His adventures on the way will be related later. His were the commandos reported on June 21st and following days by Babington, who, to Sir B. Blood's disappointment, did nothing to intercept them, but remained at Kaffirstad until joined on the 24th by W. P. Campbell. By this time (June 22nd) F. W. Kitchener had come up to Tweefontein, and Sir B. Blood ordered a general concentration at Middelkraal, to be carried out whilst he himself with Beatson's column went into Middelburg to bring out supplies. Kitchener moved by Vaalbank and Bankpan—a mounted infantry patrol being cut off with the loss of an officer and two men during a reconnaissance to the south on the 22nd—and after further operations was with Campbell at Middelkraal on the 29th, where Babington, who had had skirmishing and affairs of outposts at Uitgedacht and Legdaar, arrived on the same date. Meanwhile Pulteney had gone into Carolina on the 21st, and raiding far around that place, failed to receive Sir B. Blood's orders to meet him and the convoy, and conduct them to the place of concentration. He eventually (July 3rd) made his way into Middelburg to refit. Here for the moment Sir B. Blood's southern columns must be left, whilst those to the north of the Delagoa Bay railway are followed.

Spens and Park at Nelspruit, Benson and Douglas at Machadodorp were ready on June 8th, and next day began an operation which had for its object the clearance of the country in the triangle Machadodorp—Lydenburg—Nelspruit. Spens, *Operations in the north-east.*

who was in charge of the scheme, divided the sphere of operations into two zones, namely, the country north and south of the Crocodile river respectively, basing Douglas and Benson on the Machadodorp—Lydenburg road, his own and Park's columns on Nelspruit and Alkmaar. By June 18th the northern section had been cleared, and the four columns having been refitted, turned to the southern section, which was thoroughly scoured by the 29th. The enemy's tactics consisted mainly in hiding, and the chief work of the troops lay in ferreting amongst the deep and thicketed ravines which seamed this, one of the most difficult terrains in South Africa. Twenty days' exhausting labour resulted in the accounting for sixty-five Boers, about 15,000 stock, and 266 carts and wagons, besides a quantity of rifles and ammunition, and a number of mills which were destroyed. Spens then returned to Alkmaar, Benson and Douglas to Machadodorp, whilst Park went into Lydenburg. A small column under McCracken of the 2nd Royal Berkshire regiment, which had co-operated with Spens' quartet during the last week of their operations, returned to Godwaan on June 28th.

Viljoen returns to the north-east.

Two days earlier Viljoen, having evaded Babington and all Sir B. Blood's southern columns, had made his dash across the Delagoa Bay railway. He had received with misgivings his orders at the Council of War of June 20th; the Botha's Berg district held no good luck for him, and none but the best of fortune would enable him to escape for the second time from an area so beset by columns. Merely to re-enter that area was difficult enough, and nearly proved disastrous to Viljoen and his commandos. On the night of June 26th he attacked two blockhouses one and a half miles apart between Balmoral and Brugspruit, and attempted to pass his baggage and guns across between them. But the little forts, held by a few men of the 2nd Buffs (East Kent regiment), resisted furiously; many burghers were laid low around them, and all would have gone well had not the garrison, seven in number, of one of the blockhouses, in their eagerness to get a better field of fire, rashly left the shelter inside the walls for the trench without, where they

EVENTS IN THE EASTERN TRANSVAAL. 209

were soon overwhelmed by numbers and captured. The burghers then hurriedly filled up a roadway across the ditches of the permanent way, and Viljoen with some of the men and carts passed over. But suddenly the armoured train from Brugspruit dashed into the very midst of the procession, and illuminating the scene with its searchlight, quickly cleared the vicinity with discharges from rifles and Maxim guns. Viljoen's force was thus cut in two; the party attacking the western blockhouse was beaten back with loss; some of the carts were wrecked, including that containing Viljoen's papers and personal effects, and the whole commando was in confusion. The Boers on the south of the line then drew off; not until two nights later did they manage to cross with Viljoen's assistance close to the south-west of Middelburg, and then not without adventure. Once more an armoured train, this time from Pan, descended upon them, and though a dynamite charge brought it to a stop short of the scene, its fire and that of the railway guards did much damage, and several wagons and rifles were picked up by the soldiers in the morning.

In the Standerton section, now commanded by Clements, the columns of Grey and Colville had little rest during June. Grey, leaving Standerton on the 6th with special instructions to search for guns reported to be with the commandos in the Ermelo district, surprised a laager at Rietvlei on the 11th, killing and capturing eleven Boers. Thereafter he was in constant touch with the enemy, having several brisk affairs which incurred eleven casualties before he regained Standerton on the 17th with twelve prisoners, seventeen other Boers having been accounted for in action. Colville moved in the opposite direction, and drove Buys from Villiersdorp on the 5th and 6th. He then traversed the country on the left bank of the Vaal, the Boers clinging closely to the column. On one occasion (June 8th) a determined rush against the rearguard was finely met by a counter-charge. On the 21st Colville was at Val station, where he received orders to co-operate with Grey in a sweep through the Bethel district towards the columns of Sir B. Blood which were then converging on Middelkraal. Colville, camping on the Klip Spruit, was

Raids from the Standerton line.

attacked at dawn on the 24th by a party under Commandant Alberts, the attempt being repulsed with the loss of three men to each side. Neither column succeeded in gaining touch with Sir B. Blood, and towards the end of the month both were back in the neighbourhood of Greylingstad, where Grey handed over command of his force to Colonel F. S. Garratt (6th Dragoon Guards, Carabiniers). On July 1st Colville and Garratt received fresh orders to co-operate with Sir B. Blood. On the next day they again marched northward, and on July 3rd Colville gained touch with F. W. Kitchener near the source of the Steenkool (or Steenbok) Spruit. Sir B. Blood was now nearing the close of his operation, only the angle between the Heidelberg—Pretoria and Pretoria—Middelburg railways remaining untraversed. Between July the 7th and 10th his troops gathered along the line Springs—Elandsriver station; Headquarters with F. W. Kitchener and Babington were at the former place, W. P. Campbell on the right was at the latter. All then, after sundry minor expeditions, converged on Middelburg, where Babington's column was broken up (July 18th). Colville and Garratt, who had been in touch with the left, were then detached from Sir B. Blood's sphere, Colville returning to the Greylingstad district, whilst Garratt was called away into the Orange River Colony.* On the way thither he had a smart engagement with Colville's late opponent, Buys, on the banks of the Vaal midway between Vereeniging and Villiersdorp, the Boer commander being surprised in his laager and severely punished.

Operations against Viljoen in the north-east.

Meanwhile north of the Delagoa Bay railway Spens had employed Park's and Benson's columns in the pursuit of B. Viljoen, and his own in carrying supplies to these from Middelburg. Benson pointed on Dullstroom, marching early (July 3rd) from Machadodorp in order to surprise a laager midway between the two towns. But the enemy had warning, and after a pretence at flight, turned hotly upon the Scottish Horse who led the column. In the close combat which followed the Scottish Horse patrols lost eleven out of twenty-six men engaged, the

* See Chapter XIV.

EVENTS IN THE EASTERN TRANSVAAL.

Boers one more.* Benson reached Dullstroom on the 7th, whence he pushed Viljoen westward towards Blinkwater. On the 8th he gained touch with Park from Lydenburg, whom he asked to watch his right flank about Klipbankspruit whilst he advanced against Roos Senekal, whither Viljoen appeared to be heading. A bustling chase on the 9th and 10th brought Benson to Roos Senekal, Viljoen's men scattering over the Steelpoort river with the loss of many wagons and a few prisoners. The column accounted for over thirty fighting men in the course of the raid. On the 13th Park returned to Lydenburg to refit, whilst Benson, whose wagons had been refilled by Spens, continued the pursuit of Viljoen to the banks of the Oliphant at Laatstedrift, where a sharp fight cost him ten casualties, but the Boers many more. Next day, as Viljoen still fled westward, Benson crossed the Oliphant river and pressed towards the Moos river. But the wary Boer was not to be hustled further, and turning northward, doubled across the Oliphant at Kalkfontein back into the Roos Senekal territory from which he had been so often driven. Benson who was running short of supplies had then to return to the line to replenish. On the 21st he reached Groote Oliphant River station, passing on the way a small column which Beatson had taken out for the second time during the month from Middelburg on the 12th. Beatson's previous excursion (July 7th—11th) had resulted in the surprise and capture of a small laager which had been discovered twenty-five miles north of Middelburg. His second foray closed on the 24th, when he returned to Bronkhorstspruit station. The total increment of the work of Sir B. Blood's nine columns between July 1st and 24th had been the capture of fifty-four prisoners, twenty-five surrenders, 289 wagons and carts, over 16,000 sheep, 1,600 oxen, besides rifles, ammunition and farm produce.

Brigadier-General Spens was now called away to take charge of a force for the Orange River Colony.† His column was

* For gallantry on this occasion Lieutenant W. J. English, 2nd Scottish Horse, was awarded the Victoria Cross. On the following day (July 4th) Private H. G. Crandon, 18th Hussars, performed an act of gallantry for which he was awarded the Victoria Cross

† See Chapter XIV.

therefore broken up, and on July 24th Sir B. Blood reconstituted his forces into five mobile columns under F. W. Kitchener, Park, Benson, W. P. Campbell and Beatson, and a covering body under Hughes-Hallett.

On the lines of communication in the Eastern Transvaal little of note occurred except in the southern section, where a brilliant little affair brightened the tedium of the passive but laborious duty of the troops. The Intelligence Officer at Platrand having notified the presence of a laager at a farm behind the Verzamel Berg, Brigadier-General E. O. F. Hamilton, who commanded that sub-section, despatched seventy-six men of an irregular corps called Menne's Scouts, under Captain F. C. C. Barker, to attempt to surprise it on the night of July 30th. The enterprise was perfectly successful. The Boers were surrounded asleep, and the Scouts utterly routed them, killing and wounding over thirty men, and securing nine prisoners, nearly all the horses, cattle, and camp stuff. They might have taken the whole had not a detachment sent from Zandspruit to hold a pass over the mountain been checked by a superior Boer piquet, which caused Barker to fear for his line of retreat. As it was he completely demolished the site of the laager, after which he made his way safely back to camp with his booty.

Affair near Platrand, July 30th, 1901.

In the Boer camps some stir was caused at the end of July by a deed of Assistant-General T. Smuts. Despatched to clear the Swazi border, that officer, having accomplished his mission, burned to the ground the township of Bremersdorp, which he declared had formed a focus of robbery and freebooting in this remote district. Such an act, performed at a time when bitter recriminations as to needless violence were rife between the British and Boer authorities, drew upon Smuts the anger of the Commandant-General, who promptly dismissed his subordinate from his command, and turned a deaf ear to all arguments for his reinstatement. The correspondence which ensued between the two commanders, on the one side indignant and protesting, on the other dignified and implacable, is too long for insertion; but Botha's choler at an event which leaders of far more

EVENTS IN THE EASTERN TRANSVAAL.

punctilious societies than his have regarded as a justifiable act of war, exemplifies one of the most curious traits of the Boer military character, namely its humanity and regularity of conduct, unusual products of soil so rough as that from which had risen the warriors of the Republican States in South Africa.

On July 25th F. W. Kitchener's four columns were again on the march with orders for a fresh search for Viljoen, the needle in the bottle of hay of the tangled Roos Senekal area. Pointing north-east from Middelburg, Kitchener and Campbell cast across the eastern arm of the Botha's Berg and reconnoitred towards Witpoort, where Viljoen was said to be. He was not there, however, and the majority of the reports pointed to his presence in the opposite direction, on the Bloed river, a tributary of the Oliphant river. On the 29th, therefore, F. W. Kitchener took a flying column* from his and W. P. Campbell's camps in the Botha's Berg, and had not gone far when he discovered Viljoen's convoy moving towards the Bloed river about Blaauwbank. A hot chase, consummated by a bayonet charge by the men of the 19th Hussars, resulted in the capture of a Vickers-Maxim gun and a number of wagons. Until far into the night the pursuit went on, and dawn of the 30th saw the troops again on the heels of the Boer train. But Muller now came across to the rescue of his chief from the banks of the Oliphant river, with some hundreds of men and another automatic gun, and a stiff skirmish ensued, both sides taking and losing prisoners as they fought at close quarters in the dense bush. After some hours of exciting combat the Boers withdrew, leaving six wagons in the hands of F. W. Kitchener, who next day established his men in a central camp at Diepkloof, whence he raided the surrounding country. Up to this date his gain had been fifty-seven Boers killed, wounded and taken prisoners, the Vickers-Maxim gun, forty-four wagons, and a number of animals and camp equipment. On the morning of August 4th he added to these

Operations against Viljoen resumed.

---

* 18th and 19th Hussars, West Australians, two guns 81st battery R.F.A., two guns 83rd battery R.F.A., one Vickers-Maxim, one company 1st Devonshire regiment in wagons.

214   THE WAR IN SOUTH AFRICA.

by the surprise of a laager beneath Olifants Kop, fourteen more burghers falling into his hands. Meanwhile Park, who had started from Dullstroom, had come across the Steelpoort river. Beatson, who had set out under F. W. Kitchener's orders, was supposed to be west of the junction of the Wilge and Oliphant rivers; but Kitchener, sending the 18th Hussars on August 10th to join him on the banks of the Oliphant, heard to his surprise that Beatson was not to be found. Beatson, in fact, had been recalled to the railway by the Commander-in-Chief on the 6th, preparatory to the breaking up of his column.

F. W. Kitchener thereupon decided to cross the Oliphant river himself, for Viljoen was now reported to be between the Moos and Elands rivers to the west. On the 11th his mounted troops were at Uyskraal, near the confluence of the Elands and Oliphant rivers, the drift over the latter being held by the infantry and mounted infantry, behind whom again was W. P. Campbell in an entrenched camp on the Bloed river. Viljoen was now chased first down stream towards Commissie Drift, then up stream past Slagboom, beyond which, on August 16th, he nearly entrapped the 19th Hussars who were scouting ahead of the column. The Hussars lost six killed and wounded, and twenty-six by capture, the prisoners, however, being released the same day. The 18th Hussars who came to the rescue lost three. F. W. Kitchener then returned to his base camp, having accounted in all for eighty Boers by battle and surrender, sixty-one wagons and carts, and the usual sundries in cattle and stuffs. On August 24th he moved into Pan.

Operations south of the Delagoa Bay railway.

South of the railway Sir B. Blood had accompanied Benson (July 26th) on a foray up the Oliphant river, returning himself to Middelburg on August 7th, whilst Benson pursued his way by Ermelo (August 10th) to Carolina (14th). When on the Komati river, west of Carolina, on July 29th news had been received that the wandering Transvaal Government had paused near the head of the Vaalwater, and Sir B. Blood had at once despatched Benson in pursuit. At dawn on the 30th the site of the laager was successfully surrounded, and though the Government officials had vanished, twenty-four Boers were

EVENTS IN THE EASTERN TRANSVAAL.

taken. So close was Benson to the more important object, that the Scottish Horse surprised and captured five of Botha's despatch riders who were resting in a kraal two miles from the scene. Up to his arrival in Carolina Benson had accounted for seventy of the enemy's men from all causes. Immediately on his return he received intimation of a laager to the east, at Warmbath, south-west of Hlomohlom, and at once set out again. Marching all night, the column arrived on the scene, thirty-four miles distant, before dawn on the 16th, and surprised a cluster of small encampments, capturing thirty-two Boers. Benson returned to Carolina on the 20th. Next day he received urgent orders to hurry westward to deal with Prinsloo who was reported with a following of 600 on the Bronkhorst Spruit. Accordingly Benson left Carolina on the 22nd, and after a fruitless search towards the Upper Oliphant, was at the head of the Steenkool (or Steenbok) Spruit on the last day of August. He had killed or taken over 100 of the enemy during the month. In the first week in September he moved towards the Delagoa Bay railway, reaching Middelburg on the 7th. During the latter part of August Benson had been in touch with a column from Springs, under Lieut.-Colonel R. C. A. B. Bewicke-Copley (King's Royal Rifle Corps), which had been operating between the Bronkhorst Spruit and Springs from August 17th to September 4th. Bewicke-Copley had been in touch also with Colville's column which, reinforced by the Johannesburg Mounted Rifles, had marched north from Greylingstad on August 1st on a rumour that the Transvaal Government had been marked down at Watervalshoek, twenty-six miles north of Greylingstad. Colville found the enemy west of Bethel on the 4th, and on the 5th, after a chase of seven miles, killed and captured twenty-one Boers and took forty carts and wagons and a quantity of stock from a convoy which, however, was unaccompanied by the sought-for Government. Colville then made for Standerton, whence on August 15th he marched by Müllers Pass down to Newcastle. The Johannesburg Mounted Rifles had already gone by train to Dundee with orders to co-operate with a column under Pulteney which was forming at Utrecht.

This concentration of troops on the border of Natal, of which Lieut.-Colonel C. J. Blomfield, the commandant at Dundee, assumed command, was in consequence of warnings that Botha was about to re-enter the colony. As the invader failed to appear, the columns were employed in raids through the Vryheid district, and on September 8th both were back at Dundee, Colville having returned to Standerton two days earlier. The rumours, to both sides the most stirring that could blow about the theatre of war, continued however, and they were not without foundation. Botha was indeed meditating a descent, pluming himself on the " commotion "* it would cause in the British councils. On September 2nd he was at Piet Retief, sending the fiery cross amongst the dispirited burghers of Vryheid and Utrecht. To Viljoen, whom he severely upbraided for some unauthorised parleying with Sir B. Blood at Lydenburg on August 25th, the Commandant-General wrote that he expected to be near Glencoe at the middle of the month. But rain, the arbiter of military plans in all South Africa, and especially in this part of it, fell heavily, and Botha had to postpone the movement. Meanwhile more troops converged towards Natal, for the British Intelligence Department was closely watching the barometer as it fell before the approaching storm. On September 4th Lieut.-General the Hon. N. G. Lyttelton assumed command of all the forces in Natal. On the 6th Garratt's column, summoned from the Orange River Colony, detrained at Paardekop, and promptly reconnoitred across the Elands Berg towards Wakkerstroom (September 9th—17th), whilst Colville, from Standerton, felt towards Amsterdam. Colville gained touch with F. W. Kitchener, who at Lyttelton's request was hurrying southward in company with W. P. Campbell to deal with the impending invasion, of which Garratt had now got almost certain information from a prisoner taken in the Elands Berg. On the 13th, too, Major H. de la P. Gough's mounted infantry arrived at Dundee from the Orange River Colony ; soon after Allenby from Pretoria, G. Hamilton from Klerksdorp, Spens from Kroon-

<small>Botha plans an invasion of Natal.</small>

---

* Letter to General B. Viljoen, September 12th, 1901.

EVENTS IN THE EASTERN TRANSVAAL.

stad, and Clements from Standerton were ordered to Natal, whilst Sir L. Rundle from Harrismith made arrangements to close the Drakensberg Passes, sending Sir J. Dartnell,* who now again took the field, across the mountains to co-operate actively in Natal. Finally Elliot's cavalry division was held in readiness to reinforce on the edge of the Orange River Colony. Such was the " commotion " which, as Botha had anticipated, was caused in the British camps at the whisper of a menace to Natal.

On September 16th the Commandant-General issued his orders, which were almost duplicates of those which had carried Joubert's commandos down to Glencoe at the dawn of the war, an occasion to which the Commandant-General significantly referred. Next day fortune rather than foresight enabled him to strike his first blow, and it was ominously heavy. On the 15th Gough had taken his mounted infantry, together with Lieut.-Colonel H. K. Stewart's Johannesburg Mounted Rifles, out from Dundee, bent on a reconnaissance to ascertain the true situation in the east. Having crossed the Buffalo river by De Jager's Drift, the parties pushed eastward, and were approaching the Blood river on the 17th when Gough, who was an hour's ride in front of Stewart, espied a band of 300 Boers who came from Scheepers Nek, a height which from a distance of seven miles overlooks the town of Vryheid, and apparently off-saddled at a farm. Gough determined to attack them at once. He had all available information of the strong hostile gathering in this quarter ; but the long campaign against an almost invisible enemy had lulled him into disbelief of the existence of powerful Boer forces. The commando now in sight delighted him by its unusual incautiousness, and at last there seemed a prospect of a combat on equal terms. Having made a *détour* to isolate the unwary commando, he sent a messenger back to inform Stewart of his plans, and gave the word to close. His men had scarcely got within range of the enemy when they were fallen upon by two bodies, each of five hundred Boers, one

Affair at Scheepers Nek, Sept. 17th, 1901.

---

* Created a Knight Commander of the Bath for services during the Natal campaign.

of which swooped down upon the right flank, overriding it completely and sweeping round to the rear, where they galloped amongst the guns, whilst the other bore down upon the front. After a *mêlée* of twenty minutes' duration Gough and the whole of his force were surrounded and captured. One officer and nineteen men were killed, five officers and nineteen men wounded, six officers and 235 men taken prisoners. Only Gough himself and a few more contrived to slip away when darkness and the careless guardianship of the elated burghers made escape possible. Meanwhile Stewart, who had early information of the disaster, was confronted with a difficult problem. To go to Gough's assistance would be to involve his own small force with its guns and baggage with unknown but certainly strong numbers of the enemy, and moreover would lay bare the road to De Jager's Drift and Dundee. He therefore wisely fell back on the drift, where he was joined next morning by Gough, who, after many adventures, had made his way on foot from the scene of his discomfiture.*

This reverse, if it taught once more the difficulty of dealing with an enemy against whom daring seemed as dangerous as caution was unprofitable, at least thoroughly cleared up the situation. Botha was on the borders of Natal with a muster powerful enough temporarily to destroy Natal as a line of communication even if the colony itself were in no danger of being reconquered. But the betrayal of his presence was the signal for an answering concentration, the celerity of which might well have made the Boer commander envious. He who by exhortation, by endless labour and by the most difficult correspondence with distant subordinates had been barely able to muster a few thousand fighting men, now saw arrayed against him at a few days' notice nine columns of all arms, standing across the path to Natal. At Utrecht was F. W. Kitchener, in command of his own, of W. P. Campbell's and Garratt's columns; Clements lay at De Jager's Drift, with Stewart, Pulteney and G.

_{Botha on the borders of Natal.}

---

* For gallantry on this occasion Lieutenant L. A. E. Price-Davies, King's Royal Rifle Corps, was awarded the Victoria Cross.

EVENTS IN THE EASTERN TRANSVAAL. 219

Hamilton; at Vant's Drift was Bruce Hamilton, in charge of the forces of Spens and Allenby. The Drakensberg mountains were full of Sir L. Rundle's men; Sir J. Dartnell was on the march from Harrismith. The "invasion" was checkmated ere scarce begun. Shouldered away from the Buffalo border by the imposing forces there in waiting, Botha, still seeking to achieve his purpose, edged away southward down the long tongue of the Vryheid district which penetrates Zululand between the Nqutu, Nkandhla, Entonyaneni and Ndwandwe districts, its termination pointing close to Melmoth. Near that place and to the northwest of it two small posts guarded the British frontier, namely, Fort Prospect and Itala. The former was held by thirty-five men of the Vth division M.I., and fifty-one men of the 2nd Dorsetshire regiment under Captain C. A. Rowley; the latter by 300 men of the Vth division M.I., and two guns 69th battery R.F.A., commanded by Major A. J. Chapman of the Royal Dublin Fusiliers. Towards these trifling obstacles Botha's commandos converged with the intention of sweeping them both aside.

Itala had been well fortified, but it possessed a weak spot in the point of the mountain which stood up a mile distant from the entrenchments, and could not be included in them. On receipt of warning of the Boer advance on September 25th Chapman manned this pinnacle with eighty mounted infantrymen under Lieutenants B. P. Lefroy (1st Royal Dublin Fusiliers), and H. R. Kane (1st South Lancashire regiment). At midnight the sound of an outburst of firing from this advanced post reached the main position; it ceased for a few moments, again broke out, and finally died away altogether. Shortly after, Chapman heard that the outpost had fallen to vastly superior numbers, and he took care that his own men were prepared for a conflict. About 2 a.m. he found himself surrounded by 1,500 Boers. Preceded by a whirlwind of bullets the enemy stormed close up to the stones of the sangars, only to be beaten back by the troops who stood immovably and fenced their stronghold with a ring of fire. At 4 a.m. the Boers, their first momentum spent, fell silent, and Chapman, thinking they had given back, sent out his

Attacks on Itala and Fort Prospect, Sept. 26th, 1901.

scouts to reconnoitre, and also a medical officer to tend the wounded on Itala point. But suddenly a fusilade even fiercer than the first broke upon every side of the camp. It seemed as though the defence must be shortly blown to pieces, so heavy was the storm of lead which, coming from all sides, appeared to revolve like a tropical typhoon around the restricted area of the fort. For twelve hours the Mausers poured out an almost unbroken volley, which was answered by Chapman's men as rapidly as the diminishing store of ammunition allowed. Their cover was good; but nothing could have withstood such battering, and men fell regularly. The gunners, who had at first sent shell with great effect, were ordered by Chapman to leave their pieces and take shelter when their officer and four men had fallen.* As the day wore on the position became almost untenable; but to retire from it was impossible, for L. Botha, who directed the attack by signal from a neighbouring height, had drawn an outer ring of investment. One commando lay across the southern roads; General D. Opperman with 500 burghers stood between Itala and Melmoth and also between that place and Fort Prospect, fifteen miles to the east; General C. Botha with 800 barred the west, and 600 riflemen under Commandant H. J. Potgieter held the front (north). There was, then, no way out; but Chapman had determined already to fight to a finish where he stood, for he knew every moment's resistance was invaluable to Natal behind him. As evening descended over the long day's combat, his firmness began to draw towards its reward. The enemy, disheartened by their losses, which numbered over 300, and astounded at the failure of their apparently irresistible attack, fired more and more feebly. The encircling rifles, ceasing one by one, and group by group, gave the sign, more significant to a veteran soldier than a sudden cessation, of an onslaught which had spent its force. At 7.30 p.m. the musketry had died away, and Chapman, having waited an hour in silence, once more felt all around him with scouts. He soon learned that the enemy was retiring in every direction. Then only, his task being accomplished, did he

* For gallantry on this occasion Driver F. G. Bradley, 69th battery R.F.A., wa awarded the Victoria Cross.

think of retreat. His casualties* numbered over eighty, the survivors were exhausted, their ammunition was well-nigh expended. Loading every wagon with stores he marched away at midnight and at 4 a.m. on the 27th reached Nkandhla, deriving the best assurance of his victory from the fact that the slow progress of his weak and weary force had been unmolested by the enemy.

Meanwhile it had gone hard also with Fort Prospect, surrounded and isolated fifteen miles to the east. There for each soldier inside the fort were seven Boer riflemen who strove for the mastery from 4.30 a.m. to 4 p.m. Two separate assaults were repelled at the very wires surrounding the sangars, and thereafter the enemy attempted, like their comrades at Itala, to batter the place to pieces with lead alone. With unwavering resolution the defence maintained itself, the Durham company of militia artillery, under Lieutenant R. C. M. Johnson, especially distinguishing itself at the north-west angle. During the forenoon the garrison was moved to admiration by the appearance of a posse of Zululand Native Police, led by Sergeant Gumbi, who, hearing the firing from their post four miles distant, had galloped to the scene, and broken through the surrounding Boers to the aid of their comrades. By 6 p.m. the garrison of the fort had gained the upper hand with the loss of but nine men, and Commandant Grobelaar led his dumbfounded burghers off the field.

The irresolution of the enemy—for half his numbers might have poured irresistibly over both Itala and Fort Prospect—was largely to be accounted for by the very cause which made it fatal to his plans, namely, the movement of the numerous British columns on his flank and rear. F. W. Kitchener was now near Vryheid, Clements across Vant's Drift, Bruce Hamilton

---

* British casualties—Killed, one officer and twenty-one men; wounded, five officers and fifty-four men. Boer casualties—Reliable eye-witnesses stated, killed, 128; wounded, 270 (about). Amongst their killed were Commandants Scholtz and H. J. Potgieter.

Ammunition expended by the force—Guns, sixty-three shrapnel; Lee-Metford, 70,040 rounds.

approaching Melmoth, each with the group of columns enumerated above. Sir J. Dartnell was making for Eshowe. Bullock at Wakkerstroom was busy throwing a line of blockhouses across to the Swazi border; Colville covered his working parties, expecting momentarily the return of Plumer from the Orange River Colony. From the midst of Natal itself a mounted column, 1,450 strong, under Lieut.-Colonel G. A. Mills (Royal Dublin Fusiliers), was mobilising at Greytown.

Botha, excusing his failure to his Government on the score of false information and the unfavourable weather,* ordered a general retirement, and fell back with a small following. He narrowly avoided being cut off by F. W. Kitchener and Colville, and was heard of at Amsterdam on October 8th. Thence he was hunted by columns under Colonel Sir H. Rawlinson, recently come, like Plumer, from the Orange River Colony, and Colonel M. F. Rimington from Standerton, who nearly succeeded in surrounding the Boer Headquarters, actually capturing some of Botha's personal property and papers, from which useful information was obtained. Sir H. Rawlinson went into Volksrust on October 30th and Rimington to Zandspruit. Meanwhile the main columns to the south completed the repulse of Botha's levy by a thorough scouring of the Vryheid and Utrecht districts, and on October 21st Lord Kitchener, considering their task accomplished, dispersed them in other directions. G. Hamilton, W. P. Campbell, and Allenby went to Standerton, *viâ* Dundee; Spens to Newcastle; F. W. Kitchener's columns, except Garratt's and Pulteney's, to Volksrust; Sir J. Dartnell returned to Harrismith; Plumer swept to and fro between Wakkerstroom and the Swazi border. As for Natal, the "commotion" over, it returned to its normal role of sleepless guardian of the line of communications.

* Letter to State Secretary, September 28th, 1901.

EVENTS IN THE EASTERN TRANSVAAL. 223

APPROXIMATE STRENGTH STATES OF COLUMNS REFERRED TO IN FOREGOING CHAPTER.

COLUMN.	Mounted Troops.	Infantry.	Guns, including Vickers-Maxims.	Machine Guns.	
June—September, 1901.					
Lt.-Col. H. B. Jeffrey	553	—	6	—	} Brig.-Gen. H. C. O. Plumer in command.
Lt.-Col. F. F. Colvin	496	264	—	—	
Col. E. C. Knox	1,393	452	8	3	
Lt.-Col. M. F. Rimington	1,470	278	—	—	
Maj.-Gen. S. B. Beatson	800	347	4	—	
Brig.-Gen. G. M. Bullock	1,705	545	12	4	
Lt.-Col. A. E. W. Colville	418	347	5	1	
Lt.-Col. R. Grey	879	357	5	1	
Brig.-Gen. J. Spens	120	512	4	3	
Col. G. E. Benson	1,398	808	8	—	
Col. W. Douglas	340	709	5	1	
Col. C. W. Park	130	636	4	1	Major-Gen. Sir Bindon Blood in command.
Maj.-Gen. F. W. Kitchener	800	839	7	2	
Col. W. P. Pulteney	850	861	7	4	
Maj.-Gen. J. M. Babington	400	—	3	2	
Col. W. P. Campbell	530	460	1	—	
Col. J. W. Hughes-Hallett	300	648	2	2	Lines of Communication.
Lt.-Col. R. C. A. B. Bewicke-Copley	328	859	2	1	
Lt.-Col. H. K. Stewart	800	—	3	3	
Col. E. H. H. Allenby	750	—	5	4	
Maj. H. De la P. Gough	600	—	—	2	
Brig.-Gen. G. Hamilton	820	345	5	3	
Brig.-Gen. J. Spens	1,200	—	8	—	
Brig.-Gen. Sir J. G. Dartnell	1,100	—	3	1	
Col. Sir H. Rawlinson	1,200	185	6	—	
Lt.-Col. F. S. Garratt	950	348	5	1	

CHAPTER XIII.

EVENTS IN CAPE COLONY*

(*Continued from Chapter X.*).

JUNE—SEPTEMBER, 1901.

French takes command in Cape Colony, June 9th, 1901.

On June 9th Lieut.-General Sir J. French† arrived at Middleburg, and assumed command of all the mobile columns in Cape Colony. Wynne, however, still retained the administration of the province, and jurisdiction over all garrisons, a dual control which was to result in considerable inconvenience. The operations had now reached a scale which necessitated an army in the field. Indeed a fresh source of trouble had recently arisen in the shape of a renewed ebullition of the old fountain of rebellion in the Prieska, Kenhardt, Calvinia and Namaqualand districts, where a certain commandant, S. G. Maritz, one of Scheepers' officers and a man of strong character, had been sent to consolidate the incoherent rebel bands which had sprung into activity at the advent of Hertzog and De Wet. Nevertheless, Sir J. French took over from Haig a not unfavourable situation, both tactical and administrative. Supply, transport, intelligence, remounting, communication, had all been elaborated to an admirable degree, and were fully adequate to the extraordinary demands of a campaign which consisted of nothing but the incessant gyrations of many small bodies of both belligerents.

Tactically, the outlook was more hopeful than at any time during the operations. The north-western counties, at no time disturbed by more than a few hundreds of timid and half-hearted

---

* See map No. 63.

† Created a Knight Commander of the Bath for services during 1899—1900.— *London Gazette*, April 19th, 1901.

rebels, were adequately patrolled by a small mounted column, some 500 strong, with two guns, which Sir H. Settle had fitted out at De Aar at the end of April, under Major H. S. Jeudwine, R.A.,* and which was now about Katkop. In the central area, although no Boer leader had been captured, all had been weakened, and transformed from raiders into fugitives. The chief of these, Kritzinger, together with his lieutenants, Fouché, Myburg, Erasmus, Lategan and the rebel Lotter, had been manœuvred into an *impasse*, and was at this moment enclosed within the triangle Burghersdorp—Dordrecht—Barkly East by Scobell, Gorringe, Murray, White and Monro, of whom Haig retained the direction. Wyndham with the 17th Lancers near Molteno, and Crabbe towards Knapdaar, lay in wait to intercept a break-out either southward or northward. But this promising aspect of affairs was quickly dispelled. On June 14th the Boers, breaking up into small groups, filtered southward through the cordon and gained the Bamboes mountains, west of Sterkstroom. Monro from Stormberg and Crabbe from Steynsburg promptly advanced against the mountains, whereupon Myburg and Erasmus fled eastward along the ranges and across the railway, where Wyndham came in touch with them. Kritzinger and the others, including Van Reenan, who had left Malan and rejoined his chief, continued southward, followed by Monro and Crabbe, and made towards Tarkastad. On the 17th, when still north of that place, Kritzinger was overtaken and sharply engaged, losing forty-four burghers, of whom eight were taken prisoners, and seventy-five horses, before he made good his escape past Cradock—where Van Reenan parted company—into the Tandjes Berg. There the remarkable fatality which throughout the campaign had so often promptly consoled the Boer arms for reverses enabled Kritzinger to avenge his recent mischance by capturing on June 20th a patrol of sixty men, which, coming out from Cradock, was reconnoitring about Water Kloof, north of Petersburg. Now French attempted to shut Kritzinger into the Tandjes Berg by drawing a line,

Pursuit of Kritzinger.

---

* For a brief account of this and other isolated bodies of troops in the north-west, see Chapter XX.

composed of B. Doran's column (from Aberdeen, in Henniker's command) and local defence troops, from Kendrew through Pearston to Somerset East, whilst Scobell, from Graaff Reinet, occupied Petersburg on July 1st, and Crewe was ordered to come down by Spitz Kop to Zuurfontein, where he would close the only road leading northward from the Tandjes Berg. But instead of this Crewe directed his march upon Bethesda Road; Kritzinger at once darted out by the opened door; the combination became useless, and Scobell returned to Graaff Reinet. Meanwhile Van Reenan, after leaving Kritzinger, had pursued his way due southward, hunted by Crabbe alone, Monro having returned to Molteno. A fast and ringing chase, during which Van Reenan was continually turned by the local defence troops, first from Somerset East eastward along the northern boundaries of Bedford and Fort Beaufort counties into the Winter Berg, thence northward through Tarka, sent the pursued once more into the Bamboes mountains by the end of June, and Crabbe into Tarkastad, where he refitted. On July 5th Crabbe was at Cradock, with orders to resume the pursuit of Kritzinger and leave Van Reenan to Haig.

Pursuit of Malan.

Malan, more to the west, had been pursuing an adventurous course since his evasion of Crabbe in the Doorn Berg on June 7th. Winding amongst the subsidiary ranges which branch northward from the Sneeuw Bergen, he was followed by Crewe, from Conway, who turned him out of one haunt after another. On June 23rd Malan was met in the Rhenoster Berg by a reinforcement of 120 men, whereupon he assumed the offensive, not against his pursuer, but in exactly the opposite direction. Hurrying to Richmond, he invested and fiercely attacked that place on the morning of June 25th. The garrison, who were disposed in small forts around the town, defended themselves gallantly, but seven out of the twelve posts fell with the loss of thirty-five men in a day and night of fighting, and it might have gone hard with the rest had not a small column under Captain F. T. Lund (9th Lancers), which French had fitted out at Middleburg two days before, arrived on the scene at 7 a.m. on the 26th. Malan was driven off and fell back northward,

EVENTS IN CAPE COLONY.

and at Vogelfontein, close to Hanover, was forced by Lund's close pursuit to turn and give battle. Though strongly posted he was completely outmanœuvred and his band cut into two parts which fled east and west, Malan himself accompanying the latter, and a certain Breedt the other portion. Malan's losses here and at Richmond numbered some forty men out of 220 engaged. Richmond was then regarrisoned and provisioned, and the safety of the district further assured by the arrival in the first week of July of the 16th Lancers with two guns and a squadron of Imperial Yeomanry under Lieut.-Colonel W. P. Wyndham, who had handed over command of the 17th Lancers to Colonel D. Haig. As for Scheepers, throughout the month of June, as in May, he continued to rove the Graaff Reinet district from his haunt in the Koudeveld Bergen, watched only by the weak column of Lieut.-Colonel B. Doran. His most noteworthy feat during this time was a partially successful attack on the outposts at Willowmore on June 1st. On the 23rd Sir J. French himself visited Graaff Reinet, and for two days reconnoitred Scheepers' rugged stronghold, the most inaccessible in all Cape Colony. The intricacy of the country well nigh forbade the use of artillery, and the General returned to Middleburg convinced that nothing less than three or four columns would avail. B. Doran's column was therefore merely strengthened and rendered more mobile by the addition of some newly arrived Yeomanry, and Scheepers was left to himself for the present. The Boer's confidence was supreme, and whilst marvelling at his attitude, it is necessary also to understand it, for it was that of every guerrilla leader who was at this moment in a like extraordinary military position within the border of Cape Colony.* In a long communication to De Wet, written on July 3rd, Scheepers announced his intention of wintering in the Camdeboo district, where "everything was in excellent condition, bandoliers always full," and of sallying towards Cape Town as soon as the rains should have fallen. Five-sixths of his commando, he boasted, were rebels; fresh men were daily

Pursuit of Scheepers.

---

* See remarks upon Kritzinger, Chapter X., pages 172-3.

joining him. He was in communication both with Kritzinger and with Maritz in the north-west. French, he was aware, was busy concentrating an overpowering force of 15,000 men around him, but he " awaited their arrival." This from a leader of less than 300 men, lurking in a mountain range nearly 200 miles from his own frontier, unsupported, unvictualled, and unsuccessful in all but evasion, may, by throwing light on the almost insensate valour and self-reliance of one such a man, afford a hint of the difficulty of dealing with many like him in a vast country bristling with strongholds and populated by their friends.

Scheepers is surrounded. Sir J. French now determined on a special effort to rouse this close-lying band. Early in July he began to draw around the Camdeboo area the cordon of which Scheepers had already had an inkling. His plan was, after shutting up the mountainous region from all sides, to send a column in from the north to attack the laagers. Accordingly Wyndham, from Rosmead, was ordered to Murraysburg, Crewe and B. Doran from Graaff Reinet to Sneeuw and Uitkomst respectively, whilst infantry and Yeomanry from Graaff Reinet formed a line facing westward. The extension of all these by the morning of July 13th would close every exit of the mountains, when Scobell, passing through Zuurpoort, would descend upon the Koudeveld from the north and attack the laagers which were known to be about Ossenberg. Whilst the columns moved to their appointed positions on the 12th, each side struck a blow. That of the enemy was in a direction very unexpected. At 3 a.m. a party of thirty of Scheepers' men coming from Aberdeen attacked the railway station at Aberdeen Road, burnt the buildings and stores, destroyed the telegraph material, and looted the mail bags, making off unscathed on the approach of an armoured train. A little later Scobell more than levelled the score in the mountains to the north. Leaving Zuurpoort at 1 a.m. he marched by Quaggas Drift and up the Toverwater river, skirmishing with the Boer outposts which covered Camdeboo. Contact with laagers of any importance was not to be obtained, but Scobell, hearing of a detached band outside his right flank, moved south

EVENTS IN CAPE COLONY.

and by hard galloping over difficult ground succeeded in surrounding and capturing in a kloof two officers and twenty-seven burghers. At the same time B. Doran, opposite Graaff Reinet, made prisoner a patrol of seven Boers on the Zwart river, after which he moved forward to Zeekoe Gat to tighten the hold on the Camdeboo area. On the 13th, whilst all the columns closed inwards, Scobell pressed Scheepers back to Plat Rust, where the commando came under artillery fire also from Crewe, who had moved up to the north-west of Camdeboo. All looked promising for the next day's operations, when Wyndham's troops, guarding the south-west, were moved into Aberdeen for supplies, leaving a gap on that side by which Scheepers instantly dashed for the outlet at Oorlogs Poort. Wyndham, supported by B. Doran, at once turned in pursuit, and at Been Kraal overtook the enemy's rearguard. But no mere stern-chasing could catch a Boer commando in retreat. On the 15th Scheepers hurried through the Poort, where he was joined by Malan with such remnants of his band as had survived the reverses at Richmond and Hanover. The pair were closely tracked by Wyndham, who again engaged the rearguard at Alexanders Kraal on the 18th, and kept the retreat in the desired northerly direction. But the enclosure of the Camdeboo mountains had failed, and French, who had witnessed the three days' operation from Spandouws Kop, seven miles west of Graaff Reinet, had already returned to Middleburg. *Scheepers escapes.*

On July 16th he was visited there by the Commander-in-Chief. Lord Kitchener's appearance in this remote quarter of his command signalised the extraordinary success of the insignificant marauders who had so long kept the colony in a broil, and defied the strength of an army corps to extirpate them. Their agitations had now rendered affairs in Cape Colony the most serious item of the whole British campaign and one which seemed about to become still more grave, for there were reliable reports of the approach of fresh and more powerful invaders. The continued occupation of territory of the Crown by defiant hostile bands could not fail to be universally regarded as a stigma on the British arms. So long as matters stood thus the enemy, *Lord Kitchener visits Cape Colony.*

however worsted elsewhere, need never acknowledge defeat; moreover, it was not to be forgotten that the Boers, with some show of reason, based their fondest hopes of European sympathy upon their success within British frontiers. The strangely incurable disorder which they had succeeded in fomenting in Cape Colony imposed a particularly heavy burden upon Army Headquarters at this moment. Probably at no time during the war had the Commander-in-Chief been, or was he to be, more preoccupied by every branch of his vast jurisdiction, military, political and administrative, than in this month of July, 1901, and many of his cares were such as cannot without injury disturb a General deeply occupied in the field. These, as regards Cape Colony, had mainly to do with the administration of martial law and the terms to rebels, subjects on which Lord Kitchener and the Cape Government, and indeed the Government at home, were by no means in thorough agreement.* Moreover, the members of the Cape Legislature had not hesitated to give expression to their natural uneasiness at the, to them, inexplicable continuance of the insecurity within their borders, supporting their views with a request, impossible to comply with, for the restoration to their own control of the local forces then engaged in the field.† Their complaints drew from Lord Kitchener a categorical opinion as to several matters in which the Government at Cape Town might do more to hasten the desired end. The incidence of the expense of maintaining the Colonial Defence forces, too, was a further question between Army Headquarters and Cape Town, no less than two-thirds of the entire cost of such troops in South Africa being incurred in Cape Colony. Finally, the apparent ill success of the columns in the field was a disquieting factor. They seemed quite unable to do more than push the commandos from one part of the colony to another, an endless process against an enemy who was only to be suppressed by extinction. Lord Kitchener's

---

* Correspondence between Lord Kitchener, the Secretaries of State for War and Colonies, and the Governor, Cape Colony, April 17th to July 18th, 1901.

† The Governor, Cape Colony, to Lord Kitchener, July 8th and 17th, 1901.

wonder at a demand for more troops in a certain locality when there were already "five thousand mounted men to catch as many hundred" expressed a feeling not confined to Army Headquarters, and the reply that "quality rather than quantity" was required was little reassuring, for it undoubtedly embodied the truth about the raw irregulars of whom the pursuing columns were largely composed. In short, affairs in the colony were running as little smoothly in council as in the field, and just at this moment the rumours of renewed invasion sharpened the thorn in the side. Against such an eventuality the colony, full as it was of troops, was totally unprepared. Every considerable column was already fully occupied in the midland districts, leaving almost unprotected the counties of the western seaboard, by which hostile reinforcements would find a practically open road down to Ceres and the capital. On July 19th the Intelligence Department issued warning that a double inroad by Smuts from the Transvaal and De Wet from the Orange River Colony was to be expected. <small>Warnings of renewed invasion.</small>

It became absolutely necessary to draw the bulk of the troops towards the crossings of the Orange river, and French decided to utilise the northerly trend of Wyndham in his pursuit of Scheepers by carrying out a general sweep towards the frontier between the midland and western lines of railway, using three of the four columns which the recent manœuvre in the Camdeboo district had brought together, joined by that of Lund, who was refitting at Nels Poort station, after his successful expedition against Malan. Crewe would remain in the Camdeboo district to frustrate any attempt by Scheepers to return to his favourite haunt. On July 18th then, Lund on the left was at Nels Poort; Wyndham, in close pursuit of Scheepers, was near Poortje; B. Doran was coming up on Wyndham's right, south of Murraysburg, whilst Scobell completed the line of troops between the railways at Graaff Reinet, where he remained until the 20th. The first important incidents of the advance occurred on the left flank, and amongst them was one which showed once more the amazing promptitude of the Boers to profit by the most momentary lapse on the part of their opponents. On the 18th Lund, leaving Nels Poort, moved north-eastward somewhat in advance of Wyndham's left towards Karree Bosch, where next day he encountered and drove back with loss a roving band under a certain Smit. On that day, the 19th, Wyndham was close behind Scheepers and Malan at Poortje, so that the Boers, with Lund before them and Wyndham behind, were in a dangerous predicament. On the 20th, however, Wyndham, unable to cling to his quarry, fell back to his wagons, which he had far outstripped, at Stellenbosch Vallei, and in a moment Scheepers was not only free but again on the offensive. Dashing westward for the railway, which was now uncovered by Lund's departure, he attacked and burnt a troop train a few miles north of Nels Poort on the night of the 20th, inflicting a loss of five men killed and two officers and twenty-one men wounded. He then gained an opening to the westward and disappeared. Wyndham then marched into Richmond. Meanwhile, on the other flank, Scobell, quitting Graaff Reinet on the 20th, reached Smithvale next day. He had seen little of the enemy, but hearing of a commando, 120 strong, under Lategan, at Tweefontein, twenty-five miles to the east, at the junction of the Sneeuw and Voor Sneeuw Berg mountains, he detached the Cape Mounted Riflemen, only ninety in number, under Lukin, to attempt to surprise them by night. In spite of the length of the march Lukin's men brilliantly carried out their task. Lategan's band was completely scattered; many of the Boers fell; eleven, including a Field-Cornet, with 105 horses, were captured. Scobell was then directed to Middleburg to work with Haig, his place in the combination being taken by a column under Lieut.-Colonel A. G. Hunter-Weston, R.E., who will be remembered as having performed much valuable scouting in front of Lord Roberts's advance upon Pretoria in the early months of the previous year. On July 26th French's four columns were thus placed—in front were B. Doran and Lund on the railway at Hanover Road and Rietfontein, with Hunter-Weston at Wildfontein, and Wyndham in rear at Richmond. The arrival of reinforcements, consisting of five mounted corps (5th and 12th Lancers, 10th Hussars, each with two guns R.H.A., Prince of Wales' Light Horse, Nesbitt's Horse) and the 1st Royal Berkshire regiment, materially strengthened Cape Colony. Now also the policy of blockhouse building along the Orange river, the railways and important routes, and around infested areas, was being actively pursued, the covering of the construction being entrusted to Inigo Jones.

East of the Graaff Reinet railway Kritzinger had been as active as his fellow commandant to the west of that line. He had made but a short flight after his escape from the net around the Tandjes Berg at the end of June, hovering about Garstlands Kloof, a few miles north of his former haunt. Here, after sundry false casts in the first fortnight of July, he was discovered by Crabbe, who had come across on the 6th from Tarkastad, where, it will be remembered, he had put in after his fruitless chase of Van Reenan. An attack on the kloof on July 17th drove Kritzinger southward into the hills west of Witmoss station, and Crabbe, anxious to turn him in the opposite direction, manœuvred to get to the southward of him on the 20th. So doing, he was ambushed near Zwagers Hoek by the watchful commandant. On the morning of the 21st a sudden fire from all sides stampeded 200 of Crabbe's horses, which fell into the hands of the enemy. Thereupon the Boers pressed hard on the column, which they twice summoned to surrender. But Crabbe, keeping them off all day, fell back safely under cover of darkness to Mortimer station, leaving Kritzinger to himself. The Boer leader's ascendancy in the Cradock district was shortly afterwards still further promoted by the arrival of Commandant Theron and 100 burghers who had crossed the Orange river on the 16th. On his way southward from the frontier Theron had temporarily joined Van Reenan, who was then running from kloof to kloof in the Bamboes mountains before Gorringe and the 17th Lancers, whom Haig had sent into the mountains at the end of June. The commandos soon separated, Van Reenan, with great loss of horses, escaping northward, whilst Theron pursued his way in the opposite direction to join Kritzinger. Meanwhile Myburg and Erasmus, Kritzinger's recent allies in the Bamboes mountains, easily

Operations against Kritzinger.

Crabbe is ambushed.

Arrival of Theron.

avoiding Wyndham in the Molteno district, had attached themselves to Fouché, whom they found between Barkly East and Jamestown. Since the middle of June Fouché had been resting and recruiting in the Transkei, a territory which, since the local Government had undertaken to defend it, Sir J. French had not included in his scheme of operations. Fouché, however, was left undisturbed, and occupied his time mainly in collecting fresh horses. On July 4th he moved to Rhodes, and three days later was joined by the two above-mentioned officers. Major-General Hart at this moment had two mobile forces available, one under Colonel S. C. H. Monro, based on Dordrecht, the other, a partly mounted battalion of the Connaught Rangers, commanded by Lieut.-Colonel M. G. Moore, who drew his supplies from Jamestown. These columns had taken the field immediately on the approach of the three Boer bands, Monro following Myburg and Erasmus northward, Moore, starting from Aliwal North, coming from the opposite direction to intercept Fouché. On July 12th Monro was north of Jamestown, his left flank extending to midway to Burghersdorp; Moore was at Plat Kop Drift, on the Kraai river, with a party of Lovat's Scouts, under Lieut.-Colonel the Hon. A. Murray, to the east of him at Drizzly Hill. The effect of these converging movements was to compress Fouché and his associates into the hills which close the southern angle of the Aliwal North county. On the 13th Moore moved into Zuur Vlakte in close touch with the enemy, whereupon Fouché, with good soldiership, seeing one of his opponents unsupported within striking distance, determined to strike first. On the morning of the 14th he lay in wait on a semi-circle of hills west of Zuur Vlakte. Moore, who had moved from bivouac in a south-westerly direction at 8 a.m., came in touch with Fouché's advance parties about 10 a.m. and drove them back; then, finding his march disputed, immediately parked his wagons and assumed the offensive. But he had to deal with superior numbers posted on commanding ground; a ring of fire began to encircle his men as they advanced over the level veld which footed the heights, and when the enemy began to ride boldly down the slope towards

EVENTS IN CAPE COLONY.

the column Moore saw that further progress was impossible. So also, whilst daylight lasted, was retreat, so exposed and so closely committed were the troops. From noon until dusk, therefore, the Connaught Rangers, ably handled by Moore, lay on the defensive with every disadvantage of position, and with no more cover than that afforded by the infrequent ant-hills, their heavy and well-directed shooting and that of a Maxim gun keeping the enemy at arm's length. Only on the right (west), where a section of a company watched the hills which curved around that flank, did the Boers succeed in closing, and that only because, unknown to the rest, a sentry on the exposed flank had been silenced. All this party, including the officer in command, were killed or wounded. As twilight fell, Moore began to withdraw his men, and though a heavy fusilade greeted the retirement of each unit, he soon, and with small loss, had them posted on a strong line of rocks in rear. Many of the enemy followed up the retreat, and these now found themselves upon the same open ground as the troops had lain upon all day, with the difference that now their opponents instead of themselves commanded it from cover. They began to lose considerably, and Moore was in a fair way to compensate for his day's losses, which numbered thirty-one,* when it became too dark for aimed firing. After nightfall, Moore, who had shown the greatest resource throughout a very critical action, scored the last point by recovering all his wounded by a ruse almost from the very midst of the Boer outposts.

At 5 p.m., before he began his retirement, Moore had sent off a despatch acquainting Hart with his situation. The message was received twelve hours later, and Hart at once led out a party of 230 Lovat's Scouts, arriving at the scene at 3.30 p.m. on July 15th. The Boers had disappeared westward, and touch with them was lost until on the 19th Monro discovered them attempting to break southward. They were already on the Molteno border at Roode Kloof, but Monro successfully drove them back north-east in spite of a determined attack on his

---

* Casualties—Killed, seven men; wounded, three officers, seventeen men; missing, four men.

baggage. Fouché then hurried past Zuur Vlakte, skirmishing again on the 20th with Moore, who was still there, and made towards the Kraai river. Moore followed for some miles and pitched a new camp near Vlaktefontein. Thereupon the Boers doubled back undetected to the Aliwal—Jamestown road, and on the morning of the 26th fell upon a convoy proceeding to the latter place below Limoen Kloof. The escort, which consisted of only thirty men, succeeded in holding their own until Moore, hearing the firing, galloped to the spot and cleared the ground. Proceeding to escort the wagons towards Jamestown he found the enemy so numerous and strongly posted across the narrow road that he thought it prudent to await the arrival of Monro, who had gone into Burghersdorp. On the 28th the two columns, directed by Hart in person, combined against the heights; but Fouché had vanished. On the previous evening he had re-appeared outside Aliwal North, where at 8 p.m. he delivered a vindictive attack on the refugee camp which sheltered his own compatriots of both sexes. Next day he was over the Orange river.

Fouché crosses the Orange river.

On July 29th Myburg and Erasmus, who remained behind, were joined by a fresh commando of Free Staters about Toom Nek, north of Dordrecht. Here they were severely dealt with on July 30th by Gorringe, who had come eastward after his chase of Van Reenan in the Bamboes mountains. The three commandos then fled south-westward through Oorlogs Poort, ten miles north-west of Dordrecht, and across the railway about Rayner, closely pursued by Gorringe, who for some days was never far from their rearguard. In the first week of August he came up with them in the Keesen Berg, north-east of Steynsburg. Gorringe successfully surrounded that stronghold, and although the Boers broke through his cordon at night, it was not without severe loss both in men and horses.

French "drives" to the Orange river.

At the end of July, Lieut.-General Sir J. French initiated a change of tactics. The Boer commandos in the midland districts were at this moment all to be found within controllable limits, and the unceasing harrying to which they had been subjected made it probable that they would not be able to withstand a strong impetus in any given direction. French, therefore, determined to attempt to push them bodily across the Orange river by a combined drive by all the available columns. For this purpose it was necessary first to place the troops to the southward of the enemy without arousing suspicions, and this French accomplished in the following ingenious manner. Disposing first, on July 30th, eight columns on a line Victoria West—Richmond—Middleburg—Schombie—Sterkstroom, he ordered them to march southward towards the enemy, not closed up, but maintaining wide intervals between the flanks of columns, so that the Boers, espying the gaps, as they surely would, might take advantage of them to break through in the direction most desired by French, that is, to the north of his line of columns. This plan proved very profitable. On August 3rd when the columns, after two successful skirmishes by B. Doran and Hunter-Weston on the 2nd, faced about for the return drive on the line Beaufort West—Aberdeen—Witmoss—Seymour, all the commandos but one were between them and the Orange river. The exception was Scheepers, who, recoiling southwards from Oorlogs Poort, west of Aberdeen, at the first advance of the columns, was already below Willowmore when they halted, nor could Lieut.-Colonel H. Alexander, whom French detached by train with the 10th Hussars and two guns, head him back into the net. Sending the 12th Lancers and two guns, under Lieut.-Colonel T. J. Atherton, to assist Alexander, French ordered his line to move northward on August 6th. In front of him were now seven commandos, those of Kritzinger, Malan, Lategan, Theron, Smit, Lotter and C. J. Botha. All but two, Theron's and Smit's, had moved east of the Graaff Reinet railway, and for the next three days they made desperate attempts to break through the advancing lines. On the 9th Scobell had a sharp affair at Spitz Kop with Lotter and Botha, whom he drove north-westward. Kritzinger, who attempted to support them, was intercepted by Crabbe and Lieut.-Colonel C. T. McM. Kavanagh from Maraisburg, who hustled the interloper northward nearly to Thebus. Kritzinger then made a determined effort to shake himself free. Braving the blockhouses and armoured trains which guarded the line, he threw his men across in small parties on the nights of August 9th and 10th, and on the 11th gained the Zuur Berg, where he found Van Reenan and Wessels, whom Gorringe had driven thither from the Keesen Berg. Thereupon Gorringe, from Stormfontein, joined Crabbe in the pursuit and pressed the three commandos northward past Venterstad, clear over the Orange river, on August 15th, Gorringe inflicting severe loss on Kritzinger on the 13th.* Once across the river the commandos separated. Kritzinger remained in the Orange River Colony, but Van Reenan, swinging down stream, recrossed the frontier between Hopetown and Colesberg Bridge, and once more entered British territory. On the 19th he broke across the De Aar—Orange River railway, and disappeared westward. Meanwhile the columns of B. Doran and Wyndham had been marching upon either side of New Bethesda, connected by Captain Lord W. A. Cavendish-Bentinck's squadron of the 10th Hussars from Alexander's command. Theron and Smit were before them ; the former, after being engaged by each in turn, made his escape southward, to be no more seen. At The Willows, Smit was joined by Lotter and C. J. Botha as they fled from the advance of Scobell and Hunter-Weston between the Sneeuw Bergen and the railway. An attack by B. Doran had the effect of driving them northward to Leeuw Hoek, where they separated, Smit moving westward, the other two to Roode Berg and Gryze Kop in the opposite direction. The Boers had now before them the heavily defended railway, and French promptly made dispositions to bear them against it. On the night of August 16th Doran was to the north of the enemy at Winterhoek, Hunter-Weston behind them at Paarde Vallei, Scobell south of them at Vinkfontein, and Kavanagh, who had been withdrawn from the chase of Kritzinger, at McKinnon's Post, whence he was linked by local troops from Middleburg to the railway, which was patrolled by two armoured trains. The escape of Lotter and Botha seemed impossible. On the night of the 16th they hotly attacked the blockhouses,

* Sergeant-Major A. Young, Cape Police, was awarded the Victoria Cross for gallantry on this date.

but were repulsed at every point. Before dawn next day the columns began to converge on the imprisoned commandos. With the courage of despair the Boers rode to meet them. Between Scobell and Kavanagh there was a gap, narrow, but large enough to be discovered and used by men who never lost their heads or their way. Rushing through this at full speed in the darkness they broke free, and by the afternoon were safely back in the Rhenoster Berg, leaving only a trail of dead horses and a few prisoners behind them. Sir J. French sent Kavanagh and Scobell in pursuit at once, but the Boers, passing over the Rhenoster Berg, and thence under the mountains to Spitz Kop, made no halt until they had gained the Tandjes Berg. There, at Water Kloof, north of Petersburg, they were engaged by Scobell and Kavanagh, who drove them through Garstlands Kloof, whence they doubled back to Spitz Kop. Here B. Doran, whom French had posted at Lang Kloof, intercepted them, and they separated, Botha, pursued by Doran, going eastward across the railway, Lotter once more seeking the Tandjes Berg at Water Kloof. At this moment Theron was rediscovered, and was reported to be making his way towards the southern counties. As this was at all costs to be avoided, French withdrew Kavanagh to oppose him, leaving Lotter alone for the moment, whilst Scobell and Doran devoted themselves to Botha. Driving that leader about east of Cradock they had so worn him out before the end of the month that less than thirty men remained with him, and French diverted the two columns to deal with Lotter instead. On August 30th Scobell and B. Doran put into Cradock to re-equip.

Meanwhile Smit, after parting with Lotter and Botha near Middleburg, had been shouldered north-westward by Wyndham from Richmond, and Bentinck and Lund from Hanover, the last-named coming once to close terms with him. Smit was moving on Britstown on August 18th when French was compelled by news of the concentration of a fresh body of invaders near the frontier to withdraw Lund and Bentinck to join the columns of observation which it was necessary to post along the Orange river. Wyndham, therefore, continued the pursuit of

Smit alone, and during the first week of September he chased him, inflicting daily losses, into the hills south of Sutherland. Simultaneously the other columns drove Lategan out of the country.

Pursuit of Lotter.

Lotter, at Water Kloof, thus remained the chief figure, with Scobell, B. Doran and a column of local forces under Lieut.-Colonel J. R. MacAndrew devoted to his destruction. On September 1st these three officers opened a scheme to enclose him in the Tandjes Berg. Scobell, who feigned to be marching on Bethesda, moved to Koude Heuvel, MacAndrew to close to the south of Water Kloof, whilst Doran blocked all the exits on the eastern side. On the next night (September 2nd) Scobell, fetching a compass completely around the Berg, placed himself secretly upon the south-west of the Boer laager. Thereupon Lotter abandoned his position, and endeavoured to break out in two opposite directions at once. Both attempts were repulsed with loss, but soon after, the commando, reuniting, fought a clever rearguard action which enabled it to escape into the intricate country east of Petersburg. Scobell lay on the night of September 3rd at Middle Water. He fully realised that in order to come to close quarters with Lotter he must disregard direct pursuit in favour of surprise from an unlooked-for direction. His own men and horses, as well as supplies, were nearly exhausted, but he determined on one last effort to accomplish his task. Served as well by his Intelligence Staff as by his troops, he was at once informed of Lotter's line of march, which led back in the direction of Petersburg. Throughout September 4th, by dint of incredible exertions amongst the precipitous Tandjes Berg, the column actually succeeded in outpacing the rapidly moving commando. In the evening Scobell bivouacked near the village of Petersburg, having marched completely around Lotter, who, all unconscious of his pursuer's *volte face*, had taken refuge in a secluded farm near Groen Kloof. Here he was soon " harboured," and Scobell,

Capture of Lotter, Sept. 5th, 1901.

after issuing an inspiriting order to his men, at 1 a.m. on September 5th led them out in cold and wet for a last round with the elusive rebel. Steered by first-rate guides the expedition

EVENTS IN CAPE COLONY.

found itself at dawn within striking distance of the laager. This lay close behind an isolated hill which was easily approached from the side to which the force had been conducted, but on the other, whence alone the Boers expected attack, was protected by tier upon tier of ridges. Upon the kopje overhanging the camp there was not even a piquet, though it commanded at short range two open kraals and the small farmhouse which formed the sleeping places of the burghers. Scobell, accurately informed of the nature of the ground by his invaluable scouts, quickly delivered his attack. Directly against the intervening hill went the Cape Mounted Riflemen led by Lukin and Captains J. F. Purcell and C. L. Goldsworthy. Two squadrons ("A." and "D.") of the 9th Lancers under Captains Lord D. Compton and E. Gordon respectively passed around either flank to envelop the laager behind. The Boers were thought to be in the farmhouse; but as the flankers of "A." squadron rode by the intervening kraals a shout went up from the interior, followed by a hot fire which at the closest range did execution amongst the Lancers. Lord D. Compton, nevertheless, led a party of his men at the gallop through the fire zone to his appointed place in rear of the enemy; the rest flung themselves under the very walls of the kraals, and fought it out muzzle to muzzle. Purcell's squadron of the Cape Mounted Riflemen rushed for the crest of the unguarded hill and began to shoot down into the kraals, and soon, "D." squadron of the 9th Lancers having swung completely around the farm from the side opposite to "A." squadron, the whole laager was invested by a circle of musketry. In the farmhouse itself were only five burghers, all of whom were shot as they dashed for the open. Eight more were killed in the kraals, from the walls of one of which, after half an hour's fighting, a white flag went up, signifying that Lotter and all his commando, to the number of 120 men, of whom forty-six were wounded, surrendered as prisoners of war. Two hundred ponies and some 30,000 rounds of ammunition which also fell into Scobell's hands testified to the excellence of the equipment of the bands which troubled Cape Colony. Scobell himself lost nine men killed and an officer and eight men wounded, eighteen in all, and twelve of these casualties (seven killed, five wounded) occurred in Lord D. Compton's squadron outside the kraals. To that officer, Scobell, in a congratulatory order, especially conveyed his thanks, for had he allowed himself to be checked by the point-blank fire the Boers would undoubtedly have made off over the hills in rear, where the column, which was destitute of every means of subsistence, was incapable of pursuing. But to Scobell himself, and to every officer and man in his force, was due much honour for this, the first real success in Cape Colony. Not the small numbers engaged or who fell or were taken in action were the measure of the brilliance of this feat of arms ; rather the enormous exertions and privations which preceded, and the skill and resolution which consummated it. Yet it is not to be forgotten that there were at this moment in Cape Colony, and indeed in all South Africa, a multitude of columns whose equal endurance and devotion had not procured a like result. Seldom in the history of war have soldiers been so willing as the British troops in South Africa in the last phase of the campaign against the Boers to expend their utmost strength upon objects apparently so insignificant, yet so difficult to attain. There was at this period no more striking example of this ill-rewarded energy than in the south, where Scheepers, repeating the earliest triumphs of the invasion, was scouring the southern counties from the Port Elizabeth to the Cape Town railways, bidding defiance to the utmost efforts of Alexander and Atherton to catch him. On August 15th Major-General S. B. Beatson arrived at Willowmore to take charge of the operations, and at once made plans to enclose Scheepers, who was then between Uniondale and Avontuur. But Scheepers, taking the offensive, drove back not only the squadron which had been posted at Avontuur to stop him, but also Alexander himself who moved to its support out of Uniondale on the 19th, the 10th Hussars losing sixteen casualties, including two officers, in the encounters. Atherton's 12th Lancers were then sent to Uniondale to reinforce the 10th Hussars, and both together pressed after Scheepers, who was travelling westward through

Operations against Scheepers.

EVENTS IN CAPE COLONY. 243

George county into Oudtshoorn, making for Ladismith. Before making his point Scheepers' rearguard was twice caught up by the cavalry, first at Moeras River on the 23rd and again near Calitzdorp; but he gained the town, and passing through it, turned as if for Montagu or Swellendam. Both the Cape Town and Worcester—Swellendam railways were thus endangered and at points of the greatest importance. At Swellendam, the then easterly terminus of the branch line, there were large accumulations of stores, which Wynne hastened to safeguard by despatching a company from Worcester to hold the pass of the Lange Bergen, which commanded both Swellendam and Montagu. Worcester itself contained some thousands of remounts, and in addition to men whom Wynne borrowed from a recently arrived troopship to fill the place of those sent to Swellendam, the 1st Royal Berkshire regiment was ordered from De Aar to Worcester. Beatson, who found his opponent running out of his reach, now changed his Headquarters to Matjesfontein. But before he left Willowmore the situation had been complicated by the approach of Theron, who was coming down through Prince Albert with a band of eighty men. To deal with him Kavanagh was ordered from Graaff Reinet to Willowmore, where he arrived on September 2nd, marching next day against Theron, who was then nearing Oudtshoorn. *Disturbed state of the southern counties.*

Thus the early days of September, 1901, saw a recrudescence of trouble in a part which it had been hoped had been delivered. Once more Cape Town and the sea-board communities became uneasy, wondering impatiently at the apparent impossibility of stopping the leaks by which the small, but dangerous, Boer bands trickled down upon them. The renewed disturbance in this quarter was doubly unfortunate and difficult to deal with at this moment because in the north a fresh cloud had arisen, more portentous than any which had threatened Cape Colony since the incursion of De Wet.

APPROXIMATE STRENGTH STATES OF COLUMNS REFERRED TO IN FOREGOING CHAPTER.

COLUMN.	Mounted Troops.	Infantry.	Guns, including Vickers-Maxims.	Machine Guns.
June—September, 1901.				
Lt.-Col. E. M. S. Crabbe ..	816	96	2	—
Lt.-Col. the Hon. A. H. Henniker	686	179*	2	1
Col. H. J. Scobell	1,091	12†	3	—
Lt.-Col. G. F. Gorringe ..	530	—	3	—
Lt.-Col. C. P. Crewe ..	500	—	3	2
Lt.-Col. H. T. Lukin ..	690	—	3	1
Lt.-Col. the Hon. A. Murray	252	84	2	1
Col. S. C. H. Monro ..	820	—	3	4
Lt.-Col. W. L. White ..	500	—	3	1
Lt.-Col. W. P. Wyndham ..	426	—	3	—
Maj. H. S. Jeudwine ..	370	50	2	—
Lt.-Col. B. Doran ..	668	50†	2	—
Capt. F. T. Lund ..	594	—	1	1
Lt.-Col. A. G. Hunter-Weston	468	14†	3	1
Lt.-Col. M. G. Moore ..	250	250	—	—
Lt.-Col. H. Alexander ..	604	—	2	1
Lt.-Col. T. J. Atherton ..	633	—	2	1
Lt.-Col. C. T. McM. Kavanagh	480	—	1	1
Lt.-Col. J. R. MacAndrew..	380	7†	—	—

NOTE.—Lieut.-General Sir J. D. P. French assumed command of all columns in Cape Colony on June 9th, 1901.

* Thirty-three Cyclists. † Cyclists.

CHAPTER XIV.

EVENTS IN THE ORANGE RIVER COLONY*

(*Continued from Chapter IX.*).

JULY—AUGUST, 1901.

AT the beginning of July, to sum up the situation all over the Orange River Colony, six columns had come in to the railways, namely, W. H. Williams' and Byng's, of Bruce Hamilton's command at Edenburg; Pilcher's and Thorneycroft's, of Sir C. Knox's sphere at Brandfort; Henry's and Paris', of the western area, at Christiana. In mid-veld Bruce Hamilton had Rochfort, du Moulin and W. L. White about Oorlogs Poort; Elliot and Sir L. Rundle were at Springfield Drift. The enemy was nowhere absent, yet nowhere in strength sufficient even seriously to dispute the wholesale destruction of his flocks, herds, mills and magazines, which had become the common task of columns on the march. De Wet himself was as ubiquitous as his purposely dispersed burghers. All fears of the desertion of his country by the allied State had been removed by the conference on the Waterval,† and he rode from one group of his adherents to another, exhorting them to avoid fighting and to direct their efforts mainly against the lines of communication, which in consequence had suffered continual annoyance and damage throughout June. De Wet was at this time unaccompanied by Steyn, who, parting from him after their return together from the Transvaal, had repaired to the district about

---

* See map No. 64.

† See Chapter XII., page 206.

Reitz with his political staff. Here the ex-President was within Elliot's zone of operations, and, as will be seen, went very near to being added to his booty.

<small>Elliot and Sir L. Rundle sweep north.</small>

Elliot made but a brief halt at Springfield Drift. On July 4th he was again on the march, this time in a northerly direction; his brigades, de Lisle on left, Bethune in centre, Broadwood on right, filling the space between the Libenbergs Vlei river and the left bank of the Wilge, on the opposite side of which Sir L. Rundle, with B. Campbell (16th brigade), and Harley (17th brigade), prolonged the front as far as the eastern of the two roads from Harrismith to Vrede. Rundle had now organised his division into three columns under Reay, Harley and B. Campbell, which marched in that order from left to right, Reay thus linking with Broadwood across the Wilge. The whole front covered some fifty miles of country. On the 5th Elliot threw his left flank forward by advancing de Lisle to Driehoek, south of Reitz; Bethune, with whom were Elliot and his Headquarters, moving to Rust, whilst on the right Broadwood remained at Springfield Drift, the whole of this part of the array thus facing diagonally north-eastward. Sir L. Rundle pushed on nearly to the Mill river from Constantia to Astan Drift. Next day de Lisle passed through Reitz—Steyn and his entourage evacuating in good time—to Wolfnest; Bethune moved to Vaalbank; Broadwood, after detaching Lowe to Morgenzon on the Leeuw Spruit, up to Klip Drift on the Wilge river; Sir L. Rundle made the line of the Cornelis river. On July 7th Elliot's front from left to right was Rustfontein—Vlakfontein—Mooigelegen (Lowe)—Rondedraai. Sir L. Rundle continued to conform until the 10th, when he halted on the line Leeuw Kop—Botha's Berg. Meanwhile Elliot, still keeping his left forward, had passed through :—

July 8th, Roodekopjes—Zorgvleit—Leeuwspruit.

July 9th, Paardenkraal—Leeuwkuil—Aasvogels Krans—Strijdpoort.

July 10th, Groenvlei Drift—Boschmansfontein—Vogeldraai—Rietgat.

EVENTS IN THE ORANGE RIVER COLONY. 247

With the exception of small rearguard actions by de Lisle and Bethune on the 8th there was no fighting, and the chief occupation of the troops consisted in gathering in the wandering wagons, flocks and herds, and the isolated rovers who flitted across the front. In the midst of this monotony, however, suddenly occurred an incident which, like a stroke of lightning, might have struck off one of the sturdiest limbs of the Orange Free State.

The persistence of the enemy upon his left-rear had caused Elliot to realise that he had brushed aside bands sufficiently numerous to be worth a diversion from his main line of advance. On July 9th, therefore, he had sent orders to Broadwood to carry out a night raid upon Reitz, whence the annoyance probably emanated. The message had arrived too late to be acted upon on that night, so Broadwood deferred action until the next, when, having diverted suspicion by sharing in the general advance as far as Rietgat, he suddenly wheeled 400 mounted men under cover of darkness, passed behind the brigades of the centre, and made for Reitz, calculating to surround it exactly by dawn on the 11th. Delayed, however, by the straying of one of his connecting files, he lost so much time that when day broke he was still three miles from Reitz. He therefore ordered his men to gallop, and as the sun rose bore rapidly down upon the sleeping township. Such an approach could scarcely escape detection, but its very speed all but gave it its reward. Not until the troopers thundered into the outskirts did any stir arise amongst the buildings, and then it seemed all too late to save the Republics from the most crushing blow they had yet suffered. In Reitz lay Steyn and all his military and political staff. He had re-entered the village close behind de Lisle four days before, and tracking the columns northward by means of the scouts which had attracted Elliot's attention, felt all secure from any return of the receding waves of the British advance. In this way Broadwood, bursting into Reitz with no greater hope than that of surprising a small commando, found himself in the midst of the headsprings of the resistance of the Orange Free State. There was little or no opposition. Generals A. P. Cronje and

Surprise of Reitz, July 11th, 1901.

J. B. Wessels, Commandant O. Davel, Field-Cornet Steyn (the brother of the ex-President), T. Brain, his private secretary, and twenty-four other officials were quickly made prisoners. Steyn himself was not to be found. None thought of associating the deposed leader with a solitary mounted figure which was seen galloping, coatless and unbooted, away from the opposite edge of the town and out across the veld. Two horsemen, an officer and a sergeant, were in hot pursuit, and gained rapidly on the fugitive. They drew within point-blank range, and were on the verge of overhauling the flying Boer, of whose personality they knew nothing, when their horses, which had already been ridden thirty miles, stopped beaten. Leaping to the ground the sergeant levelled his rifle at the burly form now only eighty yards distant. But the oil on the sliding bolt and striker-spring had become frozen and clogged in the long night ride, disabling the weapon. Thrice the man pulled trigger harmlessly, the quarry sped on, and when shooting and further pursuit alike became hopeless the pair turned towards Reitz, regretting not overmuch the loss of a single ordinary burgher. Thus Steyn made his escape by a miracle which was not undeserved. If he had led his countrymen into war, there was not one amongst them who fought with higher motives than he, or displayed greater fortitude and love of country. His hopes crushed, his nation sacrificed by allegiance to an ally who, once so domineering, was now to be kept in heart mainly by his own indomitable spirit; ailing, especially in his eyes, nowhere so vitally a man's outposts as in time of war and upon the veld, there was no hardship or danger which he had not shared; nor was there any despair, and this affliction Steyn, who knew better than any the hopeless state of his people, added in double measure to his trials by steadfastly concealing it. In a war not poor in striking figures Steyn will ever stand out as the man whose obduracy most nearly approached heroism.

<small>Narrow escape of Steyn.</small>

The ex-President lost everything but his liberty. Besides his staff, all his papers and his treasury, containing £11,000, fell into the hands of Broadwood, who immediately set out to rejoin Elliot. He had to skirmish all his way back, and when he

EVENTS IN THE ORANGE RIVER COLONY.

reached Grootklip on the Harrismith—Frankfort road he had covered more than sixty miles. Meanwhile, the general line had gone forward, swinging on the 11th through Groenvlei and Klipoog towards Heilbron, which was entered on the 13th, Broadwood appearing there on the next day. The whole force was back upon the railway at Vredefort Road on July 16th, bringing with it sixty-one prisoners, 54,000 sheep, 4,000 ponies, 3,600 cattle and seventy-five carts and wagons, the casualties having been only three men slightly wounded.

Sir L. Rundle had also advanced, his front on the 12th stretching from the Wilge river through Tafel Kop nearly to Vrede, south of which a commando some 800 strong was sighted but could not be brought to action. On the 13th a patrol of Imperial Yeomanry from Harley's brigade had to be rescued from superior numbers after an engagement in which the patrol had lost six wounded, but the Boer commandant, C. Botha, had been killed. Rundle then pointed on Standerton, whence columns under Colonel F. S. Garratt, Brigadier-General G. M. Bullock and Lieut.-Colonel M. F. Rimington were on the march in his direction across the drifts of the Vaal river. With little further incident Sir L. Rundle's columns entered the depôt town on the 17th, having had sixteen casualties, and taken or destroyed 46,000 sheep, 10,000 ponies, 6,000 cattle and eighty-nine vehicles, besides a mass of wheat, fodder and farming implements.

Of the three Standerton columns touched by Sir L. Rundle during the above march, Bullock soon returned to the railway. Garratt, who, with Colville, had recently been in combination with Sir B. Blood south of Middelburg,* skirmished his way along the Vaal by Vereeniging and Parys to Reitzburg, where he will be met with again in connection with events shortly to be recorded.† Rimington must have somewhat fuller mention. He had come from the Wakkerstroom district of the Transvaal, where in company with Plumer he had been engaged in the operations described in an earlier chapter.‡ Plumer and

* See Chapter XII., page 210. † See *post*, page 254.
‡ See Chapter XII., pages 199—202.

Rimington entered the Orange River Colony at about the same time, and for similar duties, but by widely different routes. Plumer, as will be seen, made for the Modder river by way of Bloemfontein. Rimington, crossing the Klip river by Steele's Drift, pointed on Vrede, coming immediately in touch both with Sir L. Rundle's columns and with the Boers. At Gemsbokhoek Berg on July 13th ten prisoners and forty-four wagons were smartly captured. Constantly engaged, Rimington reached Heilbron on the 21st, and on the night of the 23rd moved his columns first parallel to the Frankfort—Lindley road, then inwards and back towards Heilbron, a ride of sixty miles which resulted in the capture of twenty-two prisoners. Based on Heilbron, Rimington scoured the country on all sides, working in co-operation with Spens, who arrived from Heidelberg on August 5th, fresh from the arduous operations in the Lydenburg district.* Together the two commanders cleared the neighbourhood, and the end of August found both in Kroonstad with some thirty prisoners and the produce ravished from many square miles of country.

Elliot marches west. Three days' pause on the railway re-rationed Elliot's troops for another effort. This time the goal was to be Klerksdorp, the march upon this base of the British operations in the never quiet Western Transvaal having a twofold object. At this time Fetherstonhaugh was on his way back to Klerksdorp from that expedition to Zeerust which has been referred to.† Elliot hoped to intercept any commandos which might seek to avoid Fetherstonhaugh's returning columns by crossing to the left bank of the Vaal. This, however, was but a subsidiary aim. His main intention was to dispose his own columns, and certain fresh ones which he was to acquire, for a great sweep from the Vaal to the Modder, over the rich tracts which Pilcher and Thorneycroft had recently found it beyond their powers to clear effectually. On July 19th Broadwood, on the right flank, was on the Vaal near Parys, de Lisle to the south-east of Reitzburg, and Lowe (who had now succeeded Bethune) at

---

* See Chapter XII., page 211.   † See Chapter XI., page 190.

EVENTS IN THE ORANGE RIVER COLONY. 251

Wilgeboschdrift on the Rhenoster. Broadwood then got astride the Vaal, and the columns, searching every cranny as they marched, moved on down the Vaal towards the rendezvous, entering Klerksdorp on July 23rd and 24th with fifteen prisoners, 16,000 stock and fifty-two vehicles, the losses having been but two. In four days all was ready for the development of the main scheme, but before narrating Elliot's subsequent movements it is necessary to turn back to the doings of the commanders of other areas of the Orange River Colony.

Sir L. Rundle regained his own district by way of the Botha's Berg, Verkykers Kop and Maaritsdrift, Harley and Reay being detached towards the Witkoppies. Constant opposition of a trifling sort was met with, and on August 3rd Rundle was back at his base. He was met by news of a minor disaster which had occurred in his absence. On July 27th, a Boer laager having been reported inconveniently close to Harrismith, the town Commandant had promptly despatched all his available mounted men to attempt a surprise. But the party, finding the encampment to be much more distant than had been supposed, had pushed on too far, and coming upon the enemy in a strong position, had lost an entire patrol, falling back with the loss of an officer killed, six men wounded, and an officer and twenty-four men taken prisoners. *Sir L. Rundle returns to Harrismith.*

More to the south Bruce Hamilton for the first half of July resumed his double operations on both sides of Edenburg. Rochfort and du Moulin circled about Dewetsdorp chasing scattered bands first northward towards Wepener, then in the opposite direction on Helvetia. On the west of the railway W. H. Williams and Byng combined in a more detailed scheme from July 5th, sweeping defined areas, the former north and the latter south of the line Edenburg—Fauresmith—Luckhoff—Belmont, intending subsequently to cross the Riet river and beat back to Petrusburg. These affairs were in progress when on July 16th Bruce Hamilton received notice from the Commander-in-Chief that, in view of Elliot's approaching sweep towards the Modder, a general hostile movement might be expected from the Vaal southwards, and that the troops of the *Bruce Hamilton's operations.*

southern command were to be at once disposed so as to secure the Bloemfontein—Jacobsdal blockhouse line and to deny approach to the Orange. Breaking off his own operations, Hamilton called Rochfort and du Moulin to Edenburg, formed a new column under Major J. H. Damant for the protection of the railway, and issued orders in accordance with which W. H. Williams hastened with his three columns (his own and two others, commanded by Majors S. Bogle Smith and G. N. Going) to Jacobsdal, whence he reached out eastward through Kalklaagte to Emmaus. Beyond this Rochfort extended past Petrusburg to within touch of Bloemfontein, a strong line being thus formed behind the Modder. More to the south Byng went on to Ramah, du Moulin marched on Philippolis, whilst Damant took up his station at Jagersfontein Road. These movements were completed by July 21st when Bruce Hamilton proceeded to Bloemfontein and thence traversed his whole front along the Modder, being at Petrusburg on the 25th, Poplar Grove and Brandvallei on the succeeding two days, and on the 29th at Kimberley, whence the train conveyed him back into his own area at Springfontein on the last day of the month. Several minor successes had been achieved by his various detachments. On July 20th Damant, sallying eastward, attacked a band who had occupied some kopjes twelve miles from Jagersfontein Road, and after an hour's fighting captured the Commandant and twelve of his men. A few days later Rochfort, having got news that Commandant Myburgh was laagered on the Riet river, west of Jagersfontein Drift, on his way to invade Cape Colony, made a night march of twenty miles from Zwartkoppies in conjunction with a detachment from Tafelkop, under Colonel A. W. G. Lowry-Cole. Favoured by a thick mist the two parties effected a complete surprise on the morning of the 28th. Myburgh, mortally wounded, was secured with seven of his men by Lowry-Cole, Rochfort taking sixteen prisoners in addition, and killing another commandant, Erasmus. Finally, on the last day of July, Damant, making a sudden raid on Fauresmith, made prisoners of three Field-Cornets and ten burghers who were sheltering in the place. Soon after his

EVENTS IN THE ORANGE RIVER COLONY. 253

return, Bruce Hamilton received orders to co-operate with Sir C. Knox, whose previous operations must here be described.

From the 1st to the 13th of July Sir C. Knox employed his troops in raiding the mountainous country between Brandfort, Thabanchu, Ladybrand, Senekal and Winburg, *i.e.*, the area to the north of that which was being simultaneously cleared by Rochfort and du Moulin. What little fighting occurred fell mainly to Thorneycroft about Mequatlings Nek, and on the 13th and 14th Thorneycroft put into Ladybrand and Pilcher into Thabanchu with 16,000 stock and seventy-three vehicles, their joint casualties amounting to but six killed and wounded. Finding all Bruce Hamilton's units then withdrawing across the railway in accordance with the orders detailed above, Knox then decided to remain on the east of the line and embark upon a systematic clearance of the country as far as the Basuto border. This was carried out by five parties, made up from the two normal columns, and placed under Lieut.-Colonels H. d'A. P. Taylor and C. F. Minchin and Majors K. E. Lean, F. C. Lloyd and H. C. Copeman. Pilcher's detachments were reassembled at Bethulie on July 26th, Thorneycroft's at Aliwal North two days later, the casualties being nil, and the booty five prisoners, 126 carts and wagons, and nearly 70,000 stock, some of which were brought in but more destroyed. Some 350 ovens, threshing machines and other baking and agricultural appliances had also been wrecked.

From the western boundary of the Orange River Colony three columns had been active during July, namely, those of Western, Henry and Paris. The first named, returning on the 8th from his temporary alliance with G. Hamilton west of Klerksdorp,* subsequently swept both banks of the Vaal eastward, basing himself on Coal Drift, and clearing in the course of his operations Venterskroon and Bothaville. He returned to Coal Drift on July 23rd with 5,000 head of stock and sixteen carts, and was then ordered to fall in with Elliot's drive to the south. From July 1st to 12th Henry and Paris from Christiana

---

* See Chapter XI., page 192.

combined to sweep up both banks of the Vaal through Bloemhof to Hoopstad. Whilst Paris then went into Warrenton for supplies, the expected southerly Boer movement took Henry eastward to Aaronslaagte from July 18th to 24th to watch the roads leading from the drifts of the Vaal. He was there rejoined by Paris, who, on his march from Warrenton, had had a sharp little affair at Palmietpan on the 23rd. The two columns then raided the district in company, another brisk skirmish at Wolvepan on the 26th resulting in Paris completely routing his opponents, who left eight dead, and their Field-Cornet wounded on the field. Orders now came for these forces, too, to fall in with Elliot's great manœuvre, and Paris moved into Windsorton on July 31st to obtain supplies for Henry, whilst the latter marched on Hoopstad.

Drawn into these parts by the same cause now came also Garratt, as previously mentioned, and Sir H. Rawlinson from Klerksdorp,* and on July 27th, the tale of his columns being complete, Elliot gave the order to march.

The general scope of the plan on which he was about to embark had now assumed colossal proportions. In addition to the numerous columns already enumerated as coming within his jurisdiction, not only had several minor bodies, such as Pine-Coffin's from Kroonstad and Barker's from Vet River station, been ordered to strike out in co-operation with him from the lines of communication, but Plumer had now appeared from distant Carolina† to take a part, with the columns of Colonel Sir J. Jervis-White-Jervis, R.A., and Lieut.-Colonel F. F. Colvin. Railed from Wonderfontein, these fresh contingents had arrived at Bloemfontein on July 17th, and had thence made a preliminary excursion down both sides of the Modder river by Palmietfontein, Poplar Grove, Kameelfontein and Pandamsfontein, that is, directly across Elliot's projected front. Only the flanking parties were engaged, but much country was cleared, and on July 31st Plumer marched to Modder River station with eleven prisoners, having taken or

---

* See Chapter XI., page 195.   † See Chapter XII., page 202.

EVENTS IN THE ORANGE RIVER COLONY. 255

destroyed some 10,000 stock and twenty vehicles. He was now in position to fulfil his *rôle* in Elliot's scheme, and he awaited the moment to begin it.

The great quadrilateral whose sides were the Kimberley and Bloemfontein railways, and the Vaal and Modder rivers which intersected them, was now completely enclosed by troops. Across the north stood Elliot, holding in line from Klerksdorp to Vredefort the columns of de Lisle, Broadwood, Lowe, Western and Sir H. Rawlinson in this order from west to east, besides a seventh, under Lieut.-Colonel H. M. Owen, which he had recently organised and attached to Broadwood. Western and Garratt were at Coal and Schoeman's Drifts on either side of Klerksdorp; Paris and Henry lay lower down the river opposite Hoopstad. On the west was Plumer ready to extend in any direction. The east was doubly guarded by the heavily defended railway and the two light columns of Barker and Pine-Coffin. Finally the fourth side, the line of the Modder on the south, was trebly barred, first by a connected series of defensible posts which had been recently completed and manned by the South African Constabulary, secondly by the columns of Sir C. Knox which were to watch the line of the right bank of the Riet river, thirdly by Bruce Hamilton's troops, in the country on the left bank of the Riet, still further to the south. The whole area, in short, resembled one of those vast bag-nets into the mouths of which the fishermen of Sicily and Sardinia, pushing in with a line of boats, herd the swarming tunny of the Mediterranean.
_{Elliot's plans.}

On July 28th Elliot set his flotilla in motion.* Advancing his Headquarters first to Koedoesdraai, and then to Walkraal, he sent Broadwood forward by a night march upon Bothaville, whilst de Lisle, crossing the Vaal below that town, blocked all the drifts of the Valsch behind it. Bothaville was found deserted, but a party of 300 Australians under Major J. S. Shea whom de Lisle had sent along the left bank of the Valsch, detected the lights of a Boer laager on the opposite bank before dawn on July 30th, and Shea immediately laid plans to take it.
_{Elliot marches on the Modder, July 28th, 1901.}

* See Chapter XI., page 196.

Discovering a convenient drift, he held it with fifty of his men, and with the rest galloped across the stream, past the encampment, and on to some high ground beyond, thus cleverly shutting in his quarry. Some of the Boers rushed for the drift, there to be captured by the detached party, and after a brief interchange of shots the whole laager was taken without a single casualty to the Australians. Shea rejoined de Lisle with twenty prisoners, twelve vehicles and a herd of ponies and stock. Next day, July 31st, when Elliot crossed the Vaal to Witkrans, Lowe scouting further up the Valsch towards Rhenoster Kop, surprised by night-marching two more small laagers, and halted with eleven prisoners and ten captured wagons at Besterskraal. Here he was joined by Western, on whose left rear Sir H. Rawlinson advanced from Vredefort to Van Stades Drift on the Honing Spruit. Only Garratt remained behind near Reitzburg with orders to bring up the rear. On the last day of July, then, all Elliot's forces were within the Orange River Colony, his general front from right to left curving from Witkrans (Headquarters and de Lisle), through Bothaville (Broadwood), Besterskraal (Lowe and Western) back to Van Stades Drift (Rawlinson).

On August 1st de Lisle followed the Vaal down to Leeuwkrantz, Broadwood (with Owen) crossed the Zand Spruit to Kruidfontein, Lowe and Western the Otter Spruit to De Rust and Leeuwpan, Sir H. Rawlinson the Honing Spruit to Rhenoster Kop, Garratt following to Witkop, west of Van Stades Drift. Henry, coming from the opposite direction, entered Hoopstad, capturing a few wagons, and driving more towards the advancing line. Next day, when the array pushed on towards the Vet river, the screens of both the right-hand columns gained touch with the wandering population whom the wide movement had set astir. At Graspan, close to Wonderfontein, which was to be Broadwood's bivouac for the night, two squadrons of Owen's King's Dragoon Guards, under Captain F. C. Quicke, captured a laager of sixty-five wagons and 4,000 cattle with little trouble. The South Australians from de Lisle's column which was nearing the Vet had even better fortune. Led as before by Shea, they crossed the river by night above Grootvallei,

EVENTS IN THE ORANGE RIVER COLONY. 257

and swinging down stream for Rooiwal discovered a commando in laager at Grootvallei. After a stealthy and undetected reconnaissance Shea galloped in from three sides, and his men were about to ride over the camp when they were checked by a barbed wire fencing. This accident aroused the Boers and gave them time to scatter into the bush, and the Australians, charging home on foot with the bayonet, were too late for their full reward. Some score of burghers were killed and wounded, however, and eleven, including two officers, captured; Shea's losses being two troopers wounded, and one killed, this last his orderly, a sowar of the 15th Bengal Lancers, who, rather than forego the adventures of a campaign in which his colour forbade him to draw sabre, had voluntarily ridden unarmed behind his officer.

On the evening of August 2nd de Lisle was at Grootvallei, Broadwood at Wonderfontein, Lowe at Zoete Inval, Sir H. Rawlinson at Valsch River Drift. Garratt took the road towards Kroonstad, where he was to obtain supplies, thus dropping out of the general movement for a few days. On the 3rd Henry joined in the advance by moving out of Hoopstad down to Langkuil, in line with de Lisle as he crossed the Vet river. Broadwood remained about Wonderfontein, his patrols capturing a further seven wagons and 2,000 stock. Lowe, pushing past his left, marched at 1 a.m. for Rietpan. Dawn brought him upon a large laager, which he attacked and captured entire, bringing in thirteen prisoners, eighty-six vehicles and 2,000 horses and cattle. On his left again came Western to Leeuwpan, beyond which Sir H. Rawlinson lined up at Kopje Alleen, whence he in his turn gained touch with Pine-Coffin's railroad column stretching a hand from Kroonstad, as Barker was preparing to do from Vet River station. On August 4th Henry on the right was thrown forward to Scheerpan, discovering a hidden magazine containing 12,000 rounds of ammunition and a quantity of dynamite at Aaronslaagte on his way. The rest of the army took up the line of the Vet river, prolonged by that of its northern fork, the Zand river. It was now time for Plumer to play his part. Leaving Modder

River station, he struck north-eastward to Kraal Kop, to be in readiness to close the angle between the Kimberley railway and the Modder river on the west, as Barker, again, was to do from the Bloemfontein line on the east. Paris, too, moved out into the arena with his convoy from Windsorton, awaiting the approach of Henry, to whom he was to hand over his supplies. On the 5th Henry halted at Scheerpan, feeling for de Lisle, with whom he had lost touch. Broadwood and all to his left likewise remained on the Vet at Bultfontein Drift and beyond, whilst the captures of the past few days were escorted in to the railway. Of the fighting front only de Lisle made a move forward, carrying out an advance to Karreepan, in the course of which he successfully entrapped a laager of fifty wagons and 1,500 stock. The chief activity on this day was on the part of the outlying "stops." In advance of the right front Plumer, still moving north-eastward, disposed Colvin and Sir J. Jervis in line from Biesjesbult, on the right, to Katdoornbult on the left. At the opposite angle of the enclosure Barker patrolled between Vet River station and Eensgevonden, beating back several attempted crossings by parties of Boers who were in full flight from Elliot's slowly encircling net. Finally, on the left rear, Garratt now came out of Kroonstad and followed the army as far as Goliathskraal.

On the 6th, whilst Garratt pushed on to Kaalvley, and Plumer edged his left up to Koppiesfontein, the whole line advanced, Henry to Boschput, de Lisle to Inktpan, Broadwood to Biessiepan, Lowe to Zandheuvel, Western and Sir H. Rawlinson keeping in close touch on the left along the Vet river. On the 7th Henry, taking nine wagons whilst seeking for Paris and his convoy, went forward to Elandsfontein, Plumer approaching him to Trekpoort and Kanonfontein. The rest of the force closed in somewhat towards its right, Broadwood and Lowe, with Western and Sir H. Rawlinson conforming, inclining to Holfontein, Harmsfontein and Waterbron towards de Lisle, who made a short march to Boschrandspan. After coming into bivouac de Lisle received intelligence that a Boer laager lay ten miles to the south-east. At 11 p.m.

EVENTS IN THE ORANGE RIVER COLONY. 259

he took out 300 mounted men, and at dawn on the 8th found himself in the midst of a bevy of small Boer convoys moving about in all directions. At the sight of him some 200 horsemen, who formed the various escorts, abandoned their charges and fled, and when de Lisle drew up at Palmietfontein in the evening he had taken forty prisoners, and drove into camp 102 carts and wagons and over 3,000 horses and cattle.

The enemy was now darting at the meshes on all sides, and in such small bodies that it was impossible to stop them all. There was scarcely a blockhouse from Winburg southward but had to repel parties which suddenly appeared upon the railway. At 1.30 a.m. on this day, the 8th, one such band, escorting ten wagons, courageously opened a way by hurling themselves against a blockhouse between Eensgevonden, where Pine-Coffin was, and Brandfort, compelling a surrender by bursting open the door and overpowering the inmates; and in several other parts there were partially successful attempts at breaking out. August 8th was a profitable day for nearly all the columns. Henry, mid-way on his march to join hands with Plumer at Quaggapan, captured twenty-five prisoners, thirty-eight vehicles, and 1,800 horses and stock; Broadwood took eight wagons about Sterkfontein; Lowe, marching for Zamerfontein before light, surprised and secured a laager of sixty-six carts and wagons, with twenty-seven prisoners. With less fortune Western advanced to Karoolaagte. Throughout the march he had seen but few of the enemy, and on his arrival in camp a patrol of twenty mounted infantry went forward confidently towards some Boer wagons which had been sighted three miles to the south-west. These proved to belong to a small laager, guarded apparently by some thirty men. The patrol instantly charged, captured the nearest wagons, and was making for the rest, when suddenly a body of more than 200 Boers appeared over a rise within twenty yards. The tables were at once turned. The patrol was forced to retreat, and lost nine men taken prisoners; but a more serious sequel to the affair was that the commando, which numbered in all some 400 men, all finely mounted and with many led horses, pushed on northward, broke through the line between Western's and Lowe's columns, and was soon at large behind them. On this day Sir H. Rawlinson, on the left of Western, reached Kaalpan, still touching Pine-Coffin, who moved to Brandfort, Barker going down beyond Alleman's Dam. On the left rear Garratt had moved by Du Preez Lager Drift, the scene of French's cavalry action of May 9th, 1900,* to Kalkfontein. On the evening of the next day, August 9th, the line was :—Henry and Plumer at Poplar Grove; Broadwood at Kopjes Kraal; Lowe, who captured a further twenty-one prisoners, twenty vehicles and 1,700 stock, at Twyfelkopspan. Western, on Lowe's left, all but touched the Modder at Kruitfontein after taking in the day's march nine prisoners, fifty-two carts and wagons, and a small herd of cattle; Sir H. Rawlinson was close on his outer flank at Zoutspruit. On August 10th every column was upon the banks of the Modder, and the operation was concluded.

Elliot at the Modder, Aug. 10th, 1901.

Thus, in summary fashion, has been described a manœuvre the scope of which can only be realised by a reference to the map and to the scale upon it. From the Vaal to the Modder, and from Kimberley to Kroonstad, a tract of some 120 miles in length by 100 in breadth, no corner had been left unsearched.

In some respects the elaborate scheme had failed of its purpose. The area had divulged far fewer fighting men than it actually contained. Elliot reported that he had seen only some 500 in all, and that those he had been unable to capture need not be reckoned with for the future, so little spirit remained in them.† It will appear later how greatly he undervalued, not only the numbers, but the quality of the game which had escaped him. He had, it is true, taken a large number of prisoners, 259 in all; but they produced between them but eighty-seven rifles, and though threats induced many to reveal where their weapons had been hidden on the veld, a large proportion of these men were undoubtedly non-combatants. Such, indeed, was invariably the case with "drives" of this cumbersome

Results of Elliot's march.

---

* See Volume III., page 52.

† Report by Lieut.-General E. L. Elliot, dated from Glen, August, 1901.

EVENTS IN THE ORANGE RIVER COLONY.

nature, manœuvres prone to entrap those who from age or youth were slower of foot and less resourceful than the full-fledged fighting burgher. But if the operation had not seriously reduced the enemy's strength in the field it had dealt a heavy blow to a pastoral people whose wealth and munitions went largely on wheels and hoof. Elliot, whose own casualties had been but eleven (two killed, nine wounded), sent into the line, or left destroyed upon the veld, 748 wagons and carts, 202,500 cattle and sheep. He also brought in 14,450 rounds of rifle ammunition, and 640 families, who, no longer able to exist in a province rendered uninhabitable, had now to be supported, like many thousand similar unfortunates, by the commissariat of their conquerors. At this time vast and growing numbers of surrendered Boers with their families were being cared for, fed, attended and even entertained in protected encampments at the expense of the British Government. There was scarcely a base town, or even any considerable post on the lines of communication which had not in close and often dangerous proximity to its defences a camp of refugees living under the protection of British rifles and upon British rations. That nation is fortunate which, doomed to defeat, suffers it at the hands of an opponent who has wealth proportionate to his humanity, and looking beyond the military needs of the moment, deliberately adopts means which are dissonant with every principle of warfare in order to preserve his victims.

Its task completed, the great combination dispersed at once. On August 13th Elliot himself took de Lisle, Broadwood and Lowe of his own division, together with Sir H. Rawlinson, to Glen. He immediately made ready for a fresh excursion, this time to the eastward, in which direction Barker and Pine-Coffin had already hurried from Karee Siding (11th) in pursuit of the Boer bands which had broken across the railway on the 8th. Garratt, turning northward past Kroonstad, made for the Transvaal again. Paris departed into Griqualand. Western, entraining at Bloemfontein, was conveyed to Aliwal North to strengthen the line of the Orange river against sundry pressing eventualities which will be shortly referred to. Plumer received

Dispersal of Elliot's columns.

orders to clear the country between the Modder and Orange rivers in conjunction with the troops of Bruce Hamilton, and with Henry. Most of these must now be followed separately.

Garratt may be briefly dismissed, for he was soon out of the arena. He scored a point before quitting it, however, which must be recorded. When on the march for Wonderwater Drift, on the Vaal, he was informed of a commando laagered at the junction of the Rhenoster river and Honing Spruit, and on August 17th he detached Lieut.-Colonel the Hon. H. F. White with 300 men of the 7th New Zealand regiment and New South Wales Bushmen to attempt a capture. On the 18th White attacked successfully, killed two of the band, and rejoined Garratt with twenty-five prisoners. Garratt then pursued his way to the Vaal, which he crossed at Wonderwater Drift on the 21st, his object being a second visit to the Los Berg, where he had encountered Smuts exactly a month before. How he fared there has been described.*

<small>Various operations.</small> Dealing still with the western side of the Bloemfontein railway, Plumer, having concentrated at Modder River station, marched on August 15th for Jacobsdal. Hence, Colvin on right flank and Sir J. Jervis on left, he moved by Doornhoek—Koffyfontein (17th)—Roodepan—Vaalpan (19th) to Stanhouders Kraal on the 20th, seeing no enemy and very little stock. Plumer was then ordered to sweep eastward upon the railway between Springfontein and Norval's Pont. On the 25th, when eight miles west of Luckhoff, he fell in with Henry, who, sent to work in the same area, had come south by Paardeberg Drift and Koffyfontein to Luckhoff on the 23rd. On the 26th and 27th Plumer marched to Berg river and Karreepoort, getting touch with three of Bruce Hamilton's columns which were found at Platberg, Somersfontein and Karreepoort. At Groen Kloof four prisoners were taken by Colvin as he moved to Klein Waaihoek on the 28th, when Jervis passed through Philippolis. Next day a report was received that a British post had been driven in on the left bank of the Orange, fifteen miles

---

* See Chapter XI., page 196.

west of Colesberg, and Plumer, who had already sent a party to Colesberg Bridge, joined with du Moulin from Philippolis and Crabbe from Colesberg in an attempt to round up the raiders. The combination was brought to nothing, however, by the band boldly plunging towards and past it in the night, and on the last day of August Plumer, leaving Henry about Luckhoff, went in to the line at Priors Siding with eight prisoners, ten vehicles and a small quantity of stock. Throughout this march nothing had been seen of Sir C. Knox, most of that commander's troops having been withdrawn from the line of the Riet river to act east of the railway on the same day as Plumer had left Modder River station.

Bruce Hamilton, as has been seen, remained to work with Plumer's column. A week before its appearance he had parcelled out the district amongst his columns, which he had now sub-divided into eight, namely, those of W. H. Williams, Rochfort, du Moulin, Byng, Damant, Dawkins, Lowry-Cole and S. B. Smith. All these had been busily engaged in raiding since early in August, co-operating first with Sir C. Knox's columns in the Jagersfontein hills, and when Plumer entered the area, confining themselves to that part east of the line Paardeberg—Koffyfontein—Luckhoff, beyond which the country was left to Plumer and Henry. Constantly employed, their joint captures amounted to some 135 prisoners by the end of August, when they were still out in their various allotments. Only Damant had been withdrawn from the group for a special object, the same that had drawn Sir C. Knox eastward from the Riet and Western down to the drifts of the Orange. This purpose, as it had become the central point of all the tactics in the Orange River Colony, must now be made clear.

It has been stated that when Elliot reported the presence of but few fighting Boers within the great net which he had cast over the western half of the Orange River Colony he was unaware that the real object of this and all other warfare, the enemy's main force, had slipped from his grasp. The best of the fighting men had escaped, some backward through the narrow gaps in the way, some through all the obstacles on the railway and the Modder. Amongst them was one who for the rest of the campaign was to cause well-nigh the keenest anxiety that could beset the British Headquarters. Rumours of this man's presence had indeed reached Elliot's ears from the outset. Certain of the prisoners taken by de Lisle in his brilliant little affair at Grootvallei on the night of August 2nd, had let slip the intelligence that they formed part of a force of some 450 men whom Assistant-Commandant-General J. C. Smuts, the State Attorney of the Transvaal, was leading through the Orange River Colony to the invasion of Cape Colony. Later, however, Elliot received information that this body had turned back into the Transvaal,* and he dismissed it from his mind. At that time Smuts, though he had already shown something of his quality, had little more reputation than that of being the most eloquent of the Boer patriots. Elliot's information concerning him was only partially correct. Smuts himself, with about one-fourth of his followers, had indeed retraced his steps, only, however, for the purpose of getting behind instead of in front of Elliot, the direction of whose "drive" was evident. The other three divisions of his force had already gone forward under Commandants Van der Venter, Bouwers, names to be heard of again, and Kirsten, all of whom contrived to land their commands, considerably damaged, on the safe side of the Bloemfontein railway between August 8th and 12th, for the most part between Brandfort and Eensgevonden. On the 15th Smuts himself arrived at the Modder river, to find that Elliot had withdrawn to one side, leaving only the Constabulary blockhouses to oppose him. Making the passage near Abrahams Kraal, he inclined south-eastward up the Kaal Spruit, over the Riet, which Sir C. Knox had by this time almost relinquished, and skirted the railway seeking for a crossing place. This he found near Jagersfontein Road about August 18th, whereupon he set his face for Smithfield and Zastron. Meanwhile his detachments, having broken through the Bloemfontein—Thabanchu line of blockhouses at Ramahutshe on the night

Smuts' evasion of Elliot.

---

* Report of Lieut.-General E. L. Elliot.

of the 12th, were making all haste southward towards the appointed rendezvous near Zastron. Smuts, hurrying thither to join them, found unexpected company in the shape of Kritzinger, breathless from the "desperate close" of French's columns in Cape Colony, which he had just, when near the last gasp, thrown off.* Suddenly, therefore, the country east of the railway between Bloemfontein and Norval's Pont, lately the least troublesome area of the Orange River Colony, became the focus of the enemy, and all the British strategy had to conform. *Smuts and Kritzinger meet on the Orange.*

This was an example of the salient disability of a regular army in contest with a horde of guerrillas manœuvring about their own country. Seldom in the course of the whole campaign in South Africa was it possible for the British Commander-in-Chief, or any of his lieutenants, to select their own sites for battle or ground for manœuvre. Well-nigh invariably these spots were dictated by the enemy, insignificant numbers of whom led great armies whither they would, so essential was it to keep in touch with them, so impossible to confine them. One result is that the larger force, even when most successful, always labours under an appearance of humiliation as it is thus bandied about at the will of handfuls of evasive freebooters. It is not easy for the troops to bear in mind that it is only an appearance of inferiority, that no seeds of victory lie in soil which is ever in motion, and that the more rapid the enemy's evolutions, the more desperate is in reality his case, the fate of one who can survive only so long as he can gallop being certain.

Now, therefore, every column received an impetus in a fresh direction. Elliot's division was to strike across the path of Smuts' descending detachments for the Brandwater basin, where B. Campbell, from Sir L. Rundle's command, was at this moment in command of the district. Sir H. Rawlinson, who had parted from Elliot at Glen, was directed on Dewetsdorp; Thorneycroft was sent to Pompey Siding; Pilcher a week later to Bethulie; Lord Basing was railed from the Western Transvaal to *Plans to enclose them.*

---

* See Chapter XIII., page 238.

Springfontein ;* Damant was withdrawn from Bruce Hamilton's Philippolis and Fauresmith operations, and Hart's troops co-operated from both sides of Aliwal North whither Western had already come by train. All these combined to deal with Smuts and Kritzinger, and especially to forestall the former at the drifts of the Orange. There was every prospect of success, and the preliminary movements of the various columns were well designed to convert the enemy's rendezvous into a veritable *cul de sac*. By August 25th Western and Pilcher, the latter with two columns under Lieut.-Colonel H. d'A. P. Taylor and Major K. E. Lean, covered the Orange river from Bethulie to Aliwal North, Hart carrying on the line eastward. Thorneycroft was at Commissie Bridge with orders to cross the Caledon and sweep up the left bank towards Runnymede, and towards Sir H. Rawlinson, who had taken over the chase from Barker and Pine-Coffin, and was to come from Dewetsdorp by Jammersberg Drift down the same side of the stream. Damant and Lord Basing were about Boesmans Kop and Carmel, north-west and south-west of Smithfield.

The whole success of the manœuvre depended upon the eastern columns keeping out towards the Basuto border so as to be always outside the commandos, which were known to be concentrating about Zastron. These tactics the Commander-in-Chief, with a clearer eye for the situation than his subordinates on the spot, repeatedly enjoined from Pretoria. But the natural difficulty of organising quickly combined action for a special purpose amongst a number of separated units, always one of the nicest problems of the military art, was here doubled first by the neglect to appoint a single and supreme commander on the scene of action, next by the clouds of vagrant Boers who floated around Smuts' place of concentration and utterly obscured the main issue. Meeting the enemy everywhere, unable either to count them or discover any general aim to their movements, and lacking central control themselves, the column commanders could never be certain whether they had Smuts,

---

* See Chapter XI., page 195.

EVENTS IN THE ORANGE RIVER COLONY. 267

Kritzinger, or a mere field-cornetcy in front of them. That the Boer leaders had been marked down in a certain spot on a certain day was of very little assistance; for this was warfare in which a report only a night old might be nearly a hundred miles wide of its reckoning. As a consequence, most of the columns so exhausted themselves with skirmishing that at a critical moment they had to put in to the railway to refit, Sir H. Rawlinson to Edenburg, Thorneycroft to Aliwal North, Damant and Lord Basing to Springfontein, leaving Kritzinger to recruit and Smuts to collect his men and reconnoitre the Orange for a crossing place in peace. Still there was time to effect the purpose. Smuts, misliking the preparedness of the troops along the Orange, made no movement. On September 2nd he was still north of the river, with Sir H. Rawlinson coming down upon him by Sweetwater, and Thorneycroft well placed to cut him off at Willemsfontein, south-east of Rouxville, where he had been since the day before, with Lord Basing on his left at Jurys Baken. But Thorneycroft came no further, and Smuts saw that he must seize his opportunity. Bidding adieu to Kritzinger, who promised to follow him as soon as possible, he crept towards the river, and on the night of September 3rd crossed with nearly 500 men at a weak spot which he had discovered, namely, Kiba Drift, hard by the Basuto border. In timing his crossing his skill or fortune attained its climax. At that moment Hart, in accordance with instructions received on September 1st to keep the enemy well to the north of the Orange, was loosening his watch over the river in order to throw troops across in the direction of Zastron.* Most of his mobile units, namely, Western, Lieut.-Colonels the Hon. A. Murray (Lord Lovat's Scouts), and M. G. Moore (Connaught Rangers M.I.) were no further eastward than the drift at Driefontein, on the northern side of which they were deploying prior to an advance, and to cover the tardy passage of their transport over the bad drifts behind. This

_{Smuts crosses the Orange river, Sept. 3rd, 1901.}

---

* For further reference to Major-General Hart's part in these events, see also Chapter XV., page 287. As has been the case with other portions of this work, the affairs there described so closely overlap those under review in the present chapter that some repetition is unavoidable.

was nearly completed when a second order was sent to Hart (September 3rd) forbidding him to leave the river; but it was then too late. His right flank was already turned, and Smuts, appearing from a country which Thorneycroft had on that very day reconnoitred and found clear as far as Elandskloof, *i.e.*, twenty miles east of Rouxville, was over the river before Hart could recall and once more extend his troops. Now the invader had burned his boats. Leaving the bevy of columns at a loss behind him, he penetrated into Cape Colony, braving one peril after another, and for many months after provided for the British province that most unhappy chapter in its history which has been written in another place.*

<small>Smuts invades Cape Colony.</small>

Thus vanished an opportunity as fair as had ever been offered of demolishing one of the main props of the Boer campaign. The British combination had signally, almost unaccountably failed. Allowing for all the difficulties of intelligence, communication, and for the bewilderment of Boer diversions, the task had been far more simple than many which had been carried to success by these very columns. Throughout his subsequent long career of adventure Smuts was never to be in more danger than he had been at its outset, and his cautious tactics of the next few days showed how thoroughly he was impressed by the narrowness of his escape. Yet it was not to be called escape. If the Boer leader had shown his heels, it was not to avoid a superior opponent, but rather to invade his enemy's own territory. Throughout the campaign in South Africa there was scarcely a more striking feat of perseverance, daring and good fortune than Smuts' ride of 300 miles, through one British army after another from the Gatsrand up to and over the banks of the Orange.

* See Chapter XV., and subsequent chapters on Cape Colony.

EVENTS IN THE ORANGE RIVER COLONY.

APPROXIMATE STRENGTH STATES OF COLUMNS REFERRED TO IN FOREGOING CHAPTER.

COLUMN.	Mounted Troops.	Infantry.	Guns, including Vickers-Maxims.	Machine Guns.	
July—August, 1901.					
Lt.-Col. W. H. Williams	449	—	2	1	Part of Major-General Bruce Hamilton's command.
Lt.-Col. the Hon. J. H. G. Byng	1,014	—	3	—	
Lt.-Col. T. D. Pilcher	1,182	—	5	1	Major-General Sir C. E. Knox in command.
Col. A. W. Thorneycroft	1,345	—	5	2	
Lt.-Col. C. St. G. Henry	542	260	3	1	
Major A. Paris	273	94	3	1	
Col. A. N. Rochfort	441	—	3	—	Part of Major-General Bruce Hamilton's command.
Lt.-Col. L. E. du Moulin	—	600	3	—	
Lt.-Col. W. L. White	500	—	2	—	
Lt.-Col. J. W. G. Dawkins	659	—	3	—	
Brig.-Gen. R. G. Broadwood	815	—	5	3	
Col. E. C. Bethune (later Col. Lowe)	1,618	—	5	2	Lieut.-General E. L. Elliot in command.
Lt.-Col. H. de B. de Lisle	1,005	—	3	2	
Maj.-Gen. B. B. R. Campbell	357	1,204	5	2	Lieut.-General Sir L. Rundle in command.
Col. G. E. Harley	275	610	3	2	
Lt.-Col. C. T. Reay	254	605	3	2	
Col. F. S. Garratt	900	269	5	1	
Brig.-Gen. G. M. Bullock	—	1,200	2	2	
Lt.-Col. M. F. Rimington	1,530	262	5	—	
Major J. H. Damant	571	99	3	1	
Major S. B. Smith	478	—	2	2	Lieut.-Colonel W. H. Williams in command.
Major G. N. Going	500	—	2	—	
Col. A. W. G. Lowry-Cole	505	—	2	—	
Lt.-Col. H. d'A. P. Taylor	726	—	2	1	
Lt.-Col. F. C. Minchin	695	—	3	2	
Major K. E. Lean	477	—	3	1	
Major F. C. Lloyd	210	—	—	—	
Major H. C. Copeman	457	—	2	—	
Lt.-Col. W. G. B. Western	641	211	3	—	
Col. Sir H. Rawlinson	1,095	185	4	—	
Major J. E. Pine-Coffin (later Holmes)	834	50	3	1	
Lt.-Col. J. S. S. Barker	500	—	3	—	
Col. Sir J. Jervis-White-Jervis	360	—	—	—	Brig.-General H. C. O. Plumer in command.
Major F. C. Lloyd	210	—	—	—	
Lt.-Col. F. F. Colvin	410	—	5	—	
Lt.-Col. H. M. Owen	350	—	2	1	
Lt.-Col. Lord Basing	500	—	3	1	
Lt.-Col. the Hon. A. Murray	250	—	2	1	Major-General A. FitzR. Hart in command.
Lt.-Col. M. G. Moore	250	250	—	1	

CHAPTER XV.

EVENTS IN CAPE COLONY*

(*Continued from Chapter XIII.*).

SEPTEMBER—OCTOBER, 1901.

Smuts in Cape Colony.
THAT Smuts had been so long redeeming the pledges given to De Wet in January† and February bore witness to the extreme difficulty under which the Boers were now waging war, for there was not to be found amongst the commandos a leader more sanguine and ardent than he. His promise of co-operation had been ratified four months later at the historic meeting on the Waterval.‡ Of the several plans of campaign born of that conference the participation of the Transvaalers in the invasion of Cape Colony was one of the most definite. De la Rey, the upholder of the cause in the Western Transvaal, was originally charged with the mission, and he left the council revolving schemes of shepherding the manifold but scattered sympathies of the British colony. Smuts was only to precede him with a small force for reconnoitring purposes, and to discover the hiding-places of disloyalty. But De la Rey found elsewhere full scope for his tremendous activity, and in the multitude of adventures in his own districts had neither need nor time to seek others beyond the frontier. To Smuts alone of the Transvaal Generals fell the duty of keeping compact with the Free Staters across the Orange, and, as has been seen, they waited long for his appearance.

* See map No. 63. † See Chapter IV., page 75.
‡ See Chapter XII., page 206.

Unlike De Wet, six months earlier, he had kept the secret of his plan of campaign. His start from the Gatsrand and his difficult passage through the Orange River Colony* had not attracted undue interest, at any rate from his opponents, for neither his plans nor his striking personality were as yet revealed. Yet both were dangerous. With many of his fellows Smuts shared the patriotism, the keen observation, the tactical opportunism, the mingled daring and caution which kept the cause of the Republics alive long after the States themselves were dead. But his observation was enlarged by a certain statesmanship and prescience which marked him out from those whose vision was bounded by the line of kopjes within artillery range. His patriotism was remarkable chiefly for the tinge of romance and enthusiasm which made it glow amidst the somewhat sombre prepossession of the majority of his fellow-countrymen. Sharing to the full their inextinguishable hope and bitterness, his hope rose to a higher and brighter flame, and his animosity against his country's enemies was ennobled by a species of soldiership or chivalry to which all but a few of his compatriots were contemptuous, or strangers. Such was the man who, already much exhausted, arrived on the left bank of the Orange river at dawn on September 4th, 1901. With him returned Fouché with a band of about 100 men; another party of the same strength had preceded them two days earlier and joined Myburg, who was facing Monro, east of Rhodes. Kritzinger, left at Zastron, was to follow shortly. Character of Smuts.

Smuts found affairs in Cape Colony in the position described in Chapter XIII. In the south, Scheepers and Theron maintained the cause almost within sight of the sea, and with good hopes of success, for they were ransacking the most fruitful fields of disloyalty in all the colony. The north-west was still harried by roving bands, to whom Maritz had not yet succeeded in giving a definite aim. Elsewhere, the capture of Lotter and the northward retreat of most of the other commandos had Situation in Cape Colony.

* See Chapter XIV.

practically demolished the Boer campaign. Of the difficulties which had arisen between the British Commander-in-Chief and the Cape Government, Smuts may have had no knowledge. The question was, as before, on the subject of martial law, especially at the ports, and it is sufficient to say that whilst doubling Lord Kitchener's difficulties in dealing with his anomalous and complicated campaign in Cape Colony, it exasperated those who might have done much to remove them. The Commander-in-Chief, with his thousand pre-occupations at Headquarters, French with all his energy in the field, and at the capital the Governor, Sir Walter Hely-Hutchinson, striving with tact and industry to keep the equipoise between the insistent demands of the military and the dread of suspended animation on the part of the Legislature, all these thus found themselves confused and weakened at a moment when in the absence of such obstacles Cape Colony might have been swept clear.

Smuts hesitates. Smuts plunged at once into difficulties. Though his designs on the colony had not long been known, the warning was enough. The three days following on his passage of the river, days which he spent in unnecessarily cautious fencing with the few local troops who stood in his way, saw the convergence of six bodies of troops towards his line of march. On September 6th Sir J. French ordered the column of Lieut.-Colonel B. Doran from Cradock and the 17th Lancers from Steynsburg both to Molteno, Gorringe from Venterstad to Stormberg. Pilcher's column, composed of two forces under Lieut.-Colonel H. d'A. P. Taylor and Major K. E. Lean, which had followed Smuts from the Orange River Colony, was detrained at Burghersdorp on the 7th. Monro, who was at Dordrecht, hurried out to cover Barkly East. Whilst these movements took place Smuts, leaving Fouché and Myburg behind in the Rhodes district, came southward, still skirmishing with levies of which he greatly exaggerated the strength and importance. On the 8th he was east of Dordrecht, and here, rather than attempt the Storm Bergen, which he imagined to be full of troops, he decided to break westward across the railway into the interior of the colony.

EVENTS IN CAPE COLONY.

Up to this point Smuts had evinced nothing either of his wonted fire or tactical ability. Ill-informed, and not yet acquainted with the country, chastened by his experiences in the Orange River Colony, and over-heedful, perhaps, of tales of hair-breadth escapes told by the recent invaders whom he had met rejoicing at their safety on the right bank of the Orange, he saw British troops everywhere, and confessed himself to be "completely hemmed in" and "practically hopeless"* of a situation which would have daunted not at all one of the seasoned marauders of the colony. Although he was in reality by no means surrounded, the place and moment adopted by Smuts for his turn westward might well have carried him straight into a cluster of columns. At Allemans Poort was Gorringe, with Taylor in line with him at Stryd Poort, on one side, and Monro at Vogel Vlei on the other, whilst Pilcher at Burghersdorp and B. Doran at Molteno formed a strong second line. Nevertheless, on September 10th Smuts made an attempt on the very centre of this combination, was repulsed by Gorringe and Taylor, and next day was caught in retreat by Monro, who attacked him with five squadrons and a gun. This force the Boers were able to hold in check until dark, when they retired northward, leaving Monro, who had lost ten killed and wounded, to bivouac on the Holle Spruit. Now Smuts exhibited one of those sudden miracles of judgment and endurance which had so often set at nought the closest meshes woven by surrounding columns. Monro in the course of his pursuit had opened a narrow interval between his left flank and the railway, to fill which B. Doran was marching eastward from Molteno. In a few hours the Sterkstroom—Dordrecht railway would be barred; but before the gap closed Smuts, though he had already fought continually for twelve hours, led his force at full speed between Monro and Doran, crossed the branch railway near Halseston, then rushing south-westward through a storm of rain, broke over the main line at Putters Kraal station and did not draw rein until, at daylight on September 11th, he stood on the heights of the

Smuts dashes southward.

---

* Report to the Boer Headquarters by Assistant-Commandant-General J. C. Smuts.

Wildschuts Berg, more than forty miles from his starting-point. A party of twelve of his burghers who lost their way during the march were no more seen; but like those fragments which are cast off by certain organisms, they began a separate existence, and even gathered around themselves a small fresh commando. Their loss was more than counter-balanced by the arrival in Smuts' laager of a band of local rebels, and these men, with their intimate knowledge of the country, made possible the certainty and celerity of movement to which Smuts was shortly to owe his safety.

Lieut.-General Sir J. French, who had been at Dordrecht, returned to Stormberg on finding his net empty, and made fresh dispositions. He had now to deal with a double problem. In the north Fouché and Myburg were too dangerous a threat to the river guards to be ignored, and French ordered both Monro and Pilcher with his twin command to operate against them from Dordrecht. The pursuit of Smuts was committed to Haig, who was given the columns of Gorringe and B. Doran, and the 17th Lancers, which had been railed to Tarkastad, Scobell also being ordered from Graaff Reinet to Cradock to block the west.

Pursuit of Smuts.

On September 15th Smuts made a short westerly movement to a neighbouring height, Bamboes Hoek. There he was engaged on the 16th by Gorringe, who with B. Doran had hurried after him from Putters Kraal. Smuts fell back slightly southward, intending to make for Maraisburg. The 17th Lancers, relieved by Doran at Tarkastad, had been posted in squadrons along the Elands river, less with the object of denying the drifts which were now unfordable from the incessant rain, than of blocking the southern exits of the mountains at Elands Poort and the adjacent passes. But Smuts was determined to gain his freedom. The numerical weakness of each particular detachment on the Elands river practically assured him of victory in an attack on any one of them, and when on the morning of the 17th he heard that the stream had fallen slightly, he sent his men forward against the nearest post. This was at Modderfontein, where "C." squadron 17th Lancers, under Captain

V. S. Sandeman, 130 strong, with a 9-pr. gun and a Maxim, was disposed on a long double-topped kopje which lay in the angle formed by the left bank of the Elands and a small tributary spruit which joined it from the east. The kopje faced northward, looking across a gentle slope to where, about 2,000 yards distant, the river made a short bend eastward parallel to the face of the position. Another thousand yards across this bend, that is, about 3,000 from his position, Sandeman had placed a post in observation of the mouth of Elands Poort. In rear of the kopje he had pitched his camp, behind which again, almost on the margin of the tributary streamlet, stood Modderfontein farmhouse. Four miles to the southward was the camp of another squadron, "A.," of the 17th Lancers. The chief defect of Sandeman's position consisted in the proximity to its left flank of a commanding hill, which rose some 800 yards distant on the other side of the river. Until mid-day on the morning of the 17th a fog obscured the encircling hills, and taking advantage of this, Smuts first surrounded Modderfontein at a distance too great for discovery by the cavalry patrols, who at noon reported "all clear." The earliest warning of the enemy's approach came from the observation post on the right bank of the river about 12.30 p.m., and Sandeman at once sent forward a troop to reconnoitre. The patrol duly gained touch with a mounted band to the northward, but the strange horsemen were seen to be wearing khaki clothing, and were accepted at once as the forerunners of Gorringe's column, which was known to be marching from that direction. A volley from the saddle which killed two troopers and a few horses revealed the truth, and both the patrol and the observation post were quickly borne back into camp. The Boers then crowded along the bank of the Elands river, where, as described, it curved to face Sandeman's position, and opening a hot fire from the bushes, extended southwards, and occupied also the above-mentioned hill on the right bank, thus gaining a dominating fire position within medium range of the kopje. The cavalry replied with vigour, and though the Maxim soon jammed and the fire was too severe for the service of the 9-pr., the Boers were effectually held, not only in

Attack on Modderfontein, Sept. 17th, 1901.

front, but on the right flank, where the narrow eastern end of the kopje fell directly to the bush-covered plain. All seemed to be going well with the squadron when a misfortune occurred against which no care or courage could have guarded.

About 1 p.m., when the action in front was at its height, a party of horsemen were seen approaching the farm on the southern foot of the kopje. These, like the surprisers of the patrol an hour before, wore tunics and breeches of khaki, and as they were riding straight from the direction of the camp of " A." squadron so near to the southward, there was no man on the position but imagined them to be comrades who had been brought to the scene by the sound of the firing. They were, in fact, a strong body whom Smuts had sent round under cover of his diversions on the opposite side, and their unimpeded approach sealed the fate of the already fully occupied squadron on the hill. Gaining the cover of the farm enclosures the burghers first poured an annihilating fire into the backs of the defence, then rushed in to close quarters. A handful of men whom Sandeman led in person to check the attack were all shot down, the officer himself being wounded. The rest fixed bayonets and defended themselves stubbornly until overcome by the superior numbers which fell upon them from all sides. When the kopje passed into the enemy's hands four officers and twenty-eight men had been killed and two officers and fifty-one men wounded, or three-quarters of the number actually on the position, for some of the patrols sent out in the early morning had not returned. The Boers, who had lost about thirty killed and wounded, then proceeded to destroy the camp and wagons. At that moment " A." squadron, whose commander, Captain N. T. Nickalls, had only been informed about 1 p.m. of Sandeman's situation, came in sight moving at full speed from the south. Making straight for the key of the position, Nickalls crossed the river, which was now just passable, and attacked and took the hill on the right bank. The effect was immediate. The Boers hurriedly made off towards Elands Poort, leaving the guns untouched, but driving before them three wagons containing dead and wounded, and all the surviving horses of the squadron, of which half had been already killed before the enemy closed upon the kopje.

Thus turned back, and finding himself still more effectually barred from the south by a westerly extension by B. Doran from Tarkastad, Smuts, with Gorringe in pursuit, strove to gain Maraisburg. But the local fencibles from that town denied all approach to the Bamboes mountains, and when on September 18th Doran closed up to Vlakpoort, the 17th Lancers to Kriegars Kraal, and Gorringe from Wildschuts Berg up to the head of the Elands river, Smuts appeared to be in a quandary. But by a manœuvre as bold and prompt as his recent feat at Dordrecht he quickly led his commando into the open. Espying the narrowing gaps between the columns, he wriggled between Gorringe and Doran on the night of the 19th, and raced southward without a halt for the Winter Berg, which he attempted to traverse on the 21st. But again the local forces turned him back, this time with loss, and doubling westward Smuts retired into the hills about Elands Drift on the Cradock—Tarkastad road. Scobell immediately sallied out from Cradock against him, the pursuing columns approached, and once more Smuts saw himself being surrounded. Once more, however, he achieved salvation by his resolution and the skill of his guides. On the night of September 23rd, when all but hemmed in, his rebel allies led him over the Winter Berg by an almost unknown bridle-path east of Quaggas Nek. A hundred horses succumbed by the way, but the commando, which had amply horsed itself by the success at Modderfontein, moved at incredible speed upon Adelaide. Then was resumed a chase such as had seldom awakened even the scoured counties of Cape Colony. Beaten back by the skilfully disposed local forces, first from Adelaide, next from Seymour, then from Carlisle Bridge on the Great Fish river, Smuts ran fast up the left bank of that stream and burst across the railway at Sheldon. Gorringe, now with both his own column and the 17th Lancers, followed hard, and on the last day of September came up with the band, which had swung southward, at Driefontein in the Zuurberg. A sharp skirmish resulted in Smuts again disappearing southward into the

Pursuit of Smuts.

Uitenhage district, Gorringe following on October 1st. Meanwhile B. Doran and Scobell, entrained by French's orders at Sheldon and Cookhouse respectively, steamed past the Zuurberg for Mount Stewart and Klipplaat on the Graaff Reinet line, in order to throw themselves between Smuts and the west, a notable use of the railway. Smuts, however, clung to the Zuurberg, his movements being for some hours crippled from a curious circumstance. Some wild trees, bearing attractive but deadly fruit, lured him and his men to eat, whereupon Smuts and half his commando were attacked by illness, from which they had barely recovered when Gorringe's appearance necessitated a hasty move. With some of his suffering burghers tied to their horses, Smuts then fled northward, to be overtaken and driven on with loss on the morning of October 3rd at Brakfontein, where a dismounted rush by the 17th Lancers destroyed one of his piquets. Next day Gorringe moved into Darlington, whence, in conjunction with the other columns, he so harassed the commando that on the 6th Smuts, who endeavoured for reasons which will appear later to gain an opening towards Port Elizabeth, divided his force, sending half under Commandant Van der Venter towards Somerset East, whilst he himself with Commandant Bouwers and the rest made for the Graaff Reinet railway, which he reached and crossed near Marais Siding on October 8th. Scobell, who had been detached in pursuit of Smuts with the 17th Lancers from Barroe on the 6th, passed through Marais a few hours behind him, hearing that the quarry had run by the north of Aberdeen. On the 10th and 11th Smuts was traced through Zeekoe Gat and Camdeboo to Sneeuw; but Scobell, though he travelled almost without a rest by day or night, was still behind the Boer, who was now reported to be on the Murraysburg border to the north-west. Another night march on the 12th, the third in four days, brought the column upon a deserted laager. Smuts had now turned southward, and was flying down the Kariega River valley. For four days the hunt drove on, a number of foundered horses and a few stragglers falling into Scobell's hands. On October 16th Smuts doubled westward near the junction of the Kariega and Salt rivers, and

Smuts divides his forces.

EVENTS IN CAPE COLONY.

striking across towards Prince Albert, fell in with a certain Com- Smuts joined by Pypers.
mandant S. Pypers, who was at the head of the force lately
commanded by Scheepers, that leader having vanished from the
scene in a manner soon to be described. Pypers was at this
moment occupied in evading Crabbe, who was seeking him from
Beaufort West, and as Scobell was now compelled to put into
Prince Albert (October 20th) for supplies, Crabbe undertook
the pursuit of the combined commandos of Smuts and Pypers,
following them down the Kouka river, then through Kandos
Poort and over the Groote Zwarte Bergen into the valley of the
Olifants. The Boers then turned westward, and Crabbe, moving
on Oudtshoorn, combined with Kavanagh from Ladismith and
the local troops extended from Willowmore to Prince Albert
in an attempt to surround them. Incessant exertions along
the Groote and Olifants rivers during the last week of October
were brought to nothing by the commandos breaking out west-
ward. On October 31st Smuts, with Pypers, after being chased Smuts enters the west of Cape Colony.
up to Constable by Kavanagh, crossed the Cape railway at that
place, and striking northward made for Sutherland and Calvinia.
There he became absorbed in a fresh scheme of aggression
which, slowly maturing under a strong and able leader, had
influenced for weeks past the movements of every Boer leader
in the midlands and south. But before describing the resulting
events, it is necessary to pick up several threads which, having
their origin in other parts, will be found to form part of the fabric
of the new campaign in the west.

First, then, to trace Van der Venter after his parting with Pursuit of other Boer leaders.
Smuts on October 8th. To all appearances this commandant
had been abandoned to a certain fate. The terrible marching
had all but exhausted his horses, and for the first four days of
his isolation he circled desperately about Jansenville, pursued
by B. Doran and by Lukin of the Cape Mounted Riflemen, who
had succeeded Gorringe on the transference of the latter to a
command in Egypt. MacAndrew, with a body of Cape Colonists,
lay at Pearston, ready to turn the commando back into the
arms of the columns; and when on the 10th the local force from
Somerset East joined hands with MacAndrew by extending upon

strong positions along the mountains between Pearston and their own town, Van der Venter's fate looked to be sealed. But the Boer, bearing with the unerring tactical instinct of his race upon the line of least resistance, staggered up the valley of the Vogel river, and on the 12th suddenly presented himself before the Somerset East contingent, who with scarcely a show of resistance surrendered not only the passes in their charge, but their persons, horses, arms and equipment to the delighted commandant. Replenishing bandoliers, and mounted on fresh horses, the commando sped on across the mountains, and on the 15th reached Garstlands Kloof, west of Cradock, whilst behind it MacAndrew, his *rôle* reversed, faced about; Lukin was hurried ahead by train to Letskraal Siding between Graaff Reinet and Middleburg, and B. Doran on the other flank pursued directly by way of Cradock. But Van der Venter had no intention of losing his so unexpectedly bestowed freedom. Drawing Lukin farther northward by advancing through Var Kens Kop and Spitz Kop to a position threatening the railway at Roode Hoogte, he suddenly (October 18th) doubled back and dashed westward across the line at the very spot just quitted by Lukin. Doran was then ordered to stand on guard at Letskraal Siding, and Lukin, pressing on in pursuit, overtook the enemy, and by a night march on the 20th surprised him in laager seven miles south-west of New Bethesda. The commando barely escaped destruction, and flying in confusion, left fourteen prisoners and many horses in the hands of Lukin. Continuing the chase, Lukin came in sight of Van der Venter again on October 24th at Elands Poort, south-west of Richmond. Three days before this, it will be remembered, Scobell had come in from his hunting of Smuts to Prince Albert, whence on October 21st he was pushed up to Beaufort West by Sir J. French, who foresaw Van der Venter's probable course. On receiving Lukin's report, French ordered Scobell still farther north to Victoria West Road, where he concentrated on the 25th facing Van der Venter, who was now moving cautiously upon the railway. During the day Scobell was informed that the Boers were making for Biesjes Poort. A night march to that place brought him to close quarters at 5 a.m. on the 26th, when an attack, somewhat prematurely delivered, turned Van der Venter back to the southeast. False information now misled Scobell, who took a line of pursuit too much to the west, whereupon Van der Venter, clinging obstinately to his determination to cross the line, dashed northward again and made for Victoria West. Lukin had meanwhile marched into Biesjes Poort, his horses and supplies alike exhausted. Not until the 29th could he recover mobility enough to follow with 350 men; then Van der Venter, easily avoiding him, made good his point and his crossing at Victoria West, and like Smuts steered his course with fresh hopes towards the bestirring west. *Van der Venter breaks into the west.*

As he struck the line a small band under Commandant Malan and Judge Hugo, which had joined him during the flight from New Bethesda, parted company again and made for Willowmore. This party had been led by Hugo into the colony on September 11th and, after being reinforced by Malan with the remnants of his veterans left from the adventures of the four previous months, had fought and stalked its way southward, surviving a host of narrow escapes at the hands of the cavalry from De Aar, the troops of Lund's column, and the garrisons of the blockhouses upon the railways. At one time not a burgher of the party remained horsed; at another all were in hiding in kloofs and caves; indeed, did space permit, how much might be written of the romantic adventures and the extraordinary tenacity of the score or so of weather-beaten riflemen who greeted Van der Venter's worn band, to vanish as suddenly as they had appeared. Nor is such an account willingly foregone, for it would depict in unmistakable colours the character of a race of fighting men of whom it is safe to say that their primitive peculiarities will soon be forgotten. Not alone of the soldier peoples of the world will the Boers, absorbed in the deep, calm waters of the *pax britannica*, invoke memory alone for the violent currents which gave to them character, and to their opponents a task of such enormous difficulty that rival nations, which began by gibing at a bungled task, ended by thanking fortune that it was not theirs to accomplish. The amazing *Pursuit of Malan.*

commingling of qualities which marked the burgher on commando, all guided by eyes keen as those of eagles to discern everything but foredoomed failure, nowhere is this more to be kept in mind than in studying the necessarily inanimate category of operations which must serve to compose the history of the campaign in Cape Colony, for only thus is the magnitude of the task, and the devotion of those who laboured at it, to be grasped.

Malan's characteristics. There were few Boer leaders whose liberty might become more dangerous than Malan. Possessing an intimate knowledge of the country, a knowledge gained in innumerable adventures, not one-half of which can be referred to, in well-nigh every county of Cape Colony, Malan had in addition the peculiar faculty of appearing after every disaster with a fresh following many leagues distant from where he had seemed to have been crushed out of existence. He was besides a notorious wrecker of trains, little less dreaded than Hindon in the Northern Transvaal. French accordingly determined not to lose sight of him, and observing him separate from Van der Venter at the railway, ordered B. Doran from Willowmore to keep touch with the band, which numbered no more than twenty-five men. At dawn on November 6th Doran closed with it, forty miles to the west of Willowmore. Malan had now been strengthened by a junction with Lategan, another wandering marauder of the same type as himself, and the forces of both were securely ensconced in the bed of a spruit. They soon made off, however, though not before B. Doran, who rode at the head of his men, had been wounded by their first volley, his horse being killed. Lieut.-Colonel W. Doran, the President of the Military Court at Graaff Reinet, was then summoned to replace his namesake in command of the column, which pressed after Malan, Hugo and Lategan in a north-westerly direction. Like the rest of their comrades, these parties now hastened their steps towards the west. Passing through Prince Albert, W. Doran vainly pursuing, on November 13th they crossed the Cape Town railway above Fraserburg Road station, and ten days later were deep in Sutherland, where for the moment they must be left.

Malan breaks into the west.

EVENTS IN CAPE COLONY. 283

To retrace Scheepers and Theron, the harriers of the south, it is necessary to revert to the early days of September, when the Ladismith and Oudtshoorn districts were crossed and recrossed by their tracks and those of Beatson's leash of columns in pursuit.

Theron may be briefly accounted for. It will be remembered how, on September 2nd, his descent upon Oudtshoorn had brought Kavanagh to Willowmore whilst the rest of Beatson's columns devoted themselves to Scheepers. On the 4th Kavanagh moved upon Oudtshoorn, whereupon Theron, forcing the passage of the Attaquas mountains by Robinson Pass, drew on towards Mossel Bay. But he was not destined to appear in a British port, though the report that he had achieved this crowning feat delighted for a moment the Boer Headquarters. Caught by Kavanagh at Brandwacht on the 9th, Theron was driven westward over the Gouritz river at Otters Hoek, running in such haste that he dropped fifty-two horses and much of his equipment on the road, besides losing several killed and wounded. On the 12th Kavanagh struck him again, and Theron sped on through Riversdale. On the night of the 12th a despatch for Kavanagh from Lieut.-Colonel Burke, the officer in command of the local troops in this district, fell into the hands of Theron, who gleaned from it that Heidelberg, which stood in his way, was but weakly held. Accordingly on the evening of September 13th he delivered a sharp attack on the township, which was defended by only twenty-eight men of the 4th West Yorkshire regiment, under Major Sir W. H. Mahon. Burke himself, who had already shown much promptitude and resource in the handling of his troops against Scheepers, was also present, and stoutly supported by his men, kept off Theron, and held his own until, on Kavanagh coming up from the east, the commando beat a hasty retreat, leaving several dead and wounded. Kavanagh pursued through Barrydale until the 17th, when he was forced to go into Swellendam to replenish supplies exhausted by a fortnight's incessant marching. Alexander from Laingsburg took up the chase, but was unable to head Theron. Wyndham, too, at Prince Albert, received orders

Pursuit of Theron.

to follow Theron; but his participation was prevented by an incident which illustrates the difficulties of campaigning in these regions. It was necessary to traverse a ravine eleven miles long, through which ran a road and a river, the former crossing the stream no fewer than twenty-three times within the defile. Soon after the column had entered, heavy rain fell, causing the water to rise so quickly that for twenty-four hours the troops were not only imprisoned but in considerable danger. On September 22nd Theron, drawn by the magnet in the west, crossed the Cape Town railway near Touws River, and disappeared into Sutherland.

Theron breaks into the west.

On September 9th Scheepers, headed from the Cape Town railway, turned inwards to the Klein Zwart Berg, and there showed the Boer's certain signal of distress by dividing his forces. He himself, followed by Atherton, moved with 150 men towards Swellendam; his detachment, 120 strong under Van der Merwe, went northward and was promptly encountered by Crabbe from Laingsburg, who on the 10th fell upon the commando at Seven Weeks Poort, east of the Buffels river, and destroyed it. Van der Merwe himself and two others were killed and thirty-seven burghers captured at a loss to Crabbe of two officers and three men killed and wounded.

Pursuit of Scheepers.

On September 12th Crabbe was at Ladismith, whence he joined in the pursuit of Scheepers down the Groote river and across the Gouritz (18th), whilst Atherton marched around by Oudtshoorn to bar the line of flight. In the entangled country lying on both sides of the Olifants river Scheepers turned and doubled for days. Theron, flying in the opposite direction, at this moment intensified Scheepers' predicament by his successful evasion of Alexander, who, with Kavanagh, was thus set free to turn upon Scheepers. It should be mentioned that the five columns in this area, namely, those of Crabbe, Alexander, Atherton, Wyndham and Kavanagh, now came under the single control of Major-General T. E. Stephenson, who had arrived at Matjesfontein on October 1st. Scheepers strove like an imprisoned panther to break through the cage of troops and precipices which held him in. Displaying infinite skill he succeeded in avoiding contact with the columns until October 5th, when Atherton, who was little less exhausted than his opponent, drove him between Barrydale and the Touws river into the arms of Kavanagh. With the loss of sixteen men and forty horses Scheepers ran for the Witte Berg, south of Matjesfontein, dropping stragglers and 150 more horses in his flight. On the 8th he lost a further sixty horses to Kavanagh, who allowed him not a moment's respite. By the time he gained the mountains the commando was on the verge of collapse. Most of the burghers had been dismounted on the way and had disappeared into hiding. Only some fifty or sixty remained horsed, and rallying these, Scheepers, rather than remain in the dangerous vicinity of Matjesfontein, struggled across the Buffels river, hoping to get clear into Prince Albert. His prospects were not entirely desperate. Of the pursuing columns three, those of Wyndham, Kavanagh and Atherton, had now to refit, the two first at Touws River, the last-named at Montagu, preparatory to taking the field in the rapidly embroiling west. Only Alexander and Crabbe remained, and whilst the former followed behind Scheepers, Crabbe took train to Beaufort West, intending to come down upon him from the north. But now fortune dealt to Scheepers a blow more unkind than any to be feared from his foes. On the banks of the Dwyka river he fell ill with fever, and unable to ride further, was laid in Wolve Hoek farm, whilst the commando, led by Pypers, went on towards the Gamka river. On October 11th the 10th Hussars, coming up to Wolve Hoek, found the long-sought guerrilla leader delivered into their hands by a common enemy. How great a disaster to his side was this sudden termination to Scheepers' career was confessed by President Steyn when he pronounced over the Commandant's departed leadership the following epitaph :—" From my heart I hope that it is not true, because he is nearly indispensable to our cause. If true, we will always with gratitude think of the good and inestimable service that he has done us, and honour his name."*

Capture of Scheepers.

---

* President Steyn to Commandant Hugo, October 27th, 1901.

Pursuit of Pypers.

Meanwhile Pypers fled on, and was soon free of all his pursuers but Crabbe, for Alexander was withdrawn into Prince Albert to refit, and being granted leave of absence, was replaced in command by Kavanagh, who in his turn handed over his own column to Lieut.-Colonel C. E. Callwell, R.A. At the same time Atherton was relieved in command of his column, prior to its being broken up, by Major the Hon. H. G. Heneage (12th Lancers). Eventually, in the manner already related, Pypers attached himself to Smuts, and with him penetrated into the north-west, when Callwell took up the pursuit of both commandos in the Sutherland district.

Operations in the north-east against Myburg and Fouché.

There remain unrecorded only the operations in the north-east of Cape Colony, where Hart from Aliwal North watched the Orange river, and Pilcher, recently arrived with his two columns from the Orange River Colony, and Monro dealt with Myburg and Fouché after the departure of Smuts for the south.

On September 14th Pilcher reached Dordrecht, and was immediately strengthened by the arrival of another force, Lieut.-Colonel W. G. B. Western's, from the Orange River Colony. The commandos were still to the east of Jamestown, and Sir J. French desired that they should be pushed north-eastward, and prevented from moving across the Drakensberg into the interior of the colony. On the 17th Myburg of his own accord forwarded this plan by moving towards Barkly East and Rhodes. Pilcher then drew a line of guards over the passes from Rhodes down to Dordrecht; but before this was complete Fouché placed himself outside the barrier by crossing the mountains into Elliot county, passing within artillery range across the front of Monro, who was marching on Barkly East. On September 23rd Monro heard that Myburg had destroyed a post of local troops, killing and wounding six and taking twenty-one prisoners at Lauriston. He accordingly moved thither, and in a running fight inflicted nine casualties on Myburg, drove him east of Rhodes, and occupied that place himself on September 27th. Two days later Pilcher was recalled to the Orange River Colony. Monro, thus left alone, was ordered to draw in his detachments, in order to cover the completion of the line of blockhouses from Stormberg to Queenstown. Leaving 250 local troops facing the frontier at Barkly East, Monro fell back on Dordrecht on October 4th.

Meanwhile Major-General Hart had received (September 1st) from Lord Kitchener orders to fend off from the north (right) bank of the Orange river the bands which roved about the Orange River Colony watching for an opportunity to cross and add to the turmoil within Cape Colony. A modification of these instructions, sent on the 3rd, did not reach Hart in time to be acted upon. Accordingly on September 3rd and 4th Hart threw across the stream troops drawn from Western's column, Moore's mounted Connaught Rangers and a detachment of Lord Lovat's Scouts under Lieut.-Colonel the Hon. A. Murray, which he disposed at Beestkraal, Willemsfontein, Zandfontein and Quaggafontein in a series of mobile and extended drift-heads from Aliwal North round to the north of Herschel. With these he patrolled constantly towards the north, co-operating with the columns of Sir H. Rawlinson, Plumer and Thorneycroft, which were engaged in that part of the Orange River Colony. He was just too late, it will be seen, to prevent the crossing both of Smuts, who, as related, contrived to pass around his right flank between Herschel and the Basuto border on the 3rd and 4th, and of smaller bodies who circumvented the opposite flank and entered Cape Colony between Aliwal North and Bethulie. Smuts, indeed, either by skill or fortune, made his dash at the precise moment when Hart, in the act of passing his troops and transport across the difficult drifts, was powerless to turn upon him.* In front of Hart there remained Kritzinger, who was about Zastron, awaiting a chance to follow Smuts, with whom he had recently arranged a plan of campaign. Hart had by this time left no passage unguarded, and Kritzinger saw that if he were to keep his pledge to Smuts he would have to force an entrance. Accordingly he reconnoitred the river line on September 19th from Vecht Kop, a height north-east of Zastron, approaching within sight of the outposts of Lovat's Scouts, who

* See also Chapter XIV., and footnote on page 267.

held the drift-head opposite Quaggafontein. Murray, whose strength had been in any case insufficient for the proper guardianship of his allotted length of river, which included several drifts, happened at this time to be weaker than usual owing to the absence of one of his two squadrons, with a gun, which had been despatched under Major Lord Lovat to the relief of Lady Grey, that place being reported to be in danger from Smuts' descending commando. Lord Lovat had departed on the 11th, and should have rejoined about the 16th; but the rising of the river enforced a long *détour* to regain Quaggafontein, and on the evening of the 19th he was still on the left bank near Elands Kloof Drift, with a difficult crossing before him and his draught animals exhausted by four days' hard marching. Arranging with Lord Lovat to join forces next morning, Murray, who had visited the detachment and inspected the drift in person, returned to his camp across the river at 8 p.m., hearing from his outposts that the Boer patrols seen during the day had returned to Vecht Kop.

Murray's force on the right bank of the Orange river now consisted of one gun and 106 men. Of these more than one-third were on night duty, a party of sixteen being on guard at a drift three miles from his camp, twenty-one more on piquet and horse-guard at the camp. Ordering reveillé to be sounded at 3 a.m., Murray retired to rest with small anticipation of being attacked, for the moon would shine brightly until midnight, and the Boers, having retired to their distant haunt at Vecht Kop, had very few hours of darkness in which to be dangerous.

<small>Kritzinger attacks the post at Quaggafontein, Sept. 19th— 20th, 1901.</small>

But immediately night had fallen Kritzinger led out his burghers to attack the enfeebled post at Quaggafontein. Marching by the rays of the moon he was within striking distance just as the light failed; he then ordered his men to dismount and advance in a crescent on foot. Murray's outposts were completely surprised. Not until the Boers had penetrated to the horse-lines was a shot fired, and then a semi-circle of musketry from 400 rifles at short range called the sleepers in camp to arms and many of them to instant death. Murray and Captain the Hon. J. Forbes-Sempill (The Black Watch) did their utmost to retrieve the already complete disaster. The colonel rallied a few men around the machine gun, which maintained a hot discharge until a bullet, striking the muzzle, rendered it useless. The enemy then closed upon it, and Murray, refusing to surrender, was shot by a rifle held close to his breast. Forbes-Sempill, who was severely wounded, called some rifles together under cover of the wagons, and offered a stout resistance until, seeing the whole camp in the enemy's hands, he withdrew his party and led them in safety back to Lord Lovat's camp. The Boers then took entire possession of the camp. Their stay was brief, and they made no attempt to push on across the Orange river, the main object of the expedition. About 1.30 a.m. they hastily abandoned their capture and retired towards Rouxville with many of Murray's horses and the gun, which was retaken by Thorneycroft next day.* *Seizes the camp but turns back.*

Kritzinger's unaccountable hesitation removed all danger of his co-operation with Smuts, and it was followed by months of inactivity which drew bitter complaints from his exasperated superior. When at last he made a brief and fateful reappearance he found himself alone in the scenes of his old adventures, for the campaign in Cape Colony had completely shifted its axis in a manner soon to be described.

* See Chapter XVIII., page 318.

APPROXIMATE STRENGTH STATES OF COLUMNS REFERRED TO IN FOREGOING CHAPTER.

COLUMN.	Mounted Troops.	Infantry.	Guns, including Vickers-Maxims.	Machine Guns.	
September—October, 1901.					
Lt.-Col. G. F. Gorringe	550	—	3	—	
Officer Commanding 17th Lancers	440	—	—	3	
Lt.-Col. S. C. H. Monro	600	—	3	2	
Lt.-Col. E. M. S. Crabbe	445	68	2	—	
Lt.-Col. H. J. Scobell	652	—	3	1	
Lt.-Col. B. Doran (later W. Doran)	443	—	2	—	
Lt.-Col. P. G. Wyndham	400	—	—	—	
Capt. F. T. Lund	580	—	2	—	
Lt.-Col. C. P. Crewe	350	—	2	2	
Lt.-Col. J. R. MacAndrew	495	—	—	—	Lieut.-Gen. Sir J. French in command.
Officer Commanding at Conway	150	—	1	—	
Lt.-Col. A. G. Hunter-Weston	700	—	4	6	
Lt.-Col. C. T. McM. Kavanagh (later C. E. Callwell, R.A.)	400	—	1	—	
Lt.-Col. H. Alexander	400	—	1	—	
Lt.-Col. T. J. Atherton (later the Hon. H. G. Heneage)	500	—	2	1	
Lt.-Col. H. T. Lukin	690	—	3	1	
Lt.-Col. the Hon. A. Murray	250	—	2	1	Major-Gen. A. FitzR. Hart directing.
Lt.-Col. M. G. Moore	250	250	—	1	
Lt.-Col. H. d'A. P. Taylor	538	—	2	1	Col. T. D. Pilcher in command.
Maj. K. E. Lean	505	—	3	1	
Lt.-Col. W. G. B. Western	506	89	3	—	

NOTE.—The columns of Lieut.-Colonels Crabbe, Alexander, Atherton, Wyndham and Kavanagh were controlled by Major-General T. E. Stephenson from October 1st.

CHAPTER XVI.

EVENTS IN THE WESTERN TRANSVAAL*

(Continued from Chapter XI.).

SEPTEMBER—NOVEMBER, 1901.

SEPTEMBER, 1901, opened with the manœuvre for which most of the columns referred to in Chapter XI. had suspended all other operations. This was a comprehensive attempt to surround Kemp, who since his eruption at Vlakfontein had remained quiescent in the eastern arm of the Zwart Ruggens mountains, a threat alike to the communications of Rustenburg, Klerksdorp, Ventersdorp, and all the western posts. By September 1st a cordon was drawn partially around him through south and east by seven columns which were posted as follows from left to right :—Lord Methuen at Brakfontein, Hickie at Bankdrift, Fetherstonhaugh at Leeuwfontein, E. C. Ingouville Williams at Rietfontein, G. Hamilton at Zandfontein, Kekewich at Magato Nek, Allenby at Boschhoek, all facing inwards towards a central point about Blokkloof. But the enclosure, close as it was around two sides, was open on the others, and an attempt by Lord Methuen to prolong his watch to the unguarded western exits resulted in the uncovering of those nearer at hand. Kemp was quick to utilise his chance. Seeing Lord Methuen's troops extending thinly northward, he dashed into the interval opening between them and Hickie's column, and made good his escape across the Elands river and out to the west. Lord Methuen's movement, however, which had been made in consequence of a report that the enemy was breaking out by Lindleys Poort, was

Operations to enclose Kemp.

Kemp escapes.

* See map No. 59.

not unproductive. An evading party was duly discovered and brought to book, being turned back with the loss of several killed and wounded and twenty-two prisoners. Kemp had left many more such bands behind him whilst he escaped. Three days' search by the columns produced more than 150 prisoners and a large amount of transport and supplies with which the Boer General had been unwilling to hamper himself. Nevertheless, the main object of the manœuvre had failed, and on September 4th the columns dispersed, Lord Methuen making for Zeerust, Allenby for Commando Nek, G. Hamilton for Olifants Nek; a few days later Fetherstonhaugh with Hickie and E. C. I. Williams marched for Ventersdorp, and Kekewich for Naauwpoort. Not without fighting did some of the columns make good their points. On September 5th Lord Methuen, skirting the Schurve Bergen near Wonderfontein, was waylaid by a commando in a most difficult valley, from which a long day's close fighting extricated him with the loss of eleven killed and twenty-six wounded, the enemy losing somewhat more in killed and wounded, and eleven prisoners besides. On the 9th Lord Methuen was in Zeerust, with twenty-three prisoners and some eighty wagons captured by himself and by von Donop, who had marched slightly detached to the southward, his own casualties during that time having been one officer and twelve men killed, two officers and twenty-eight men wounded. He then marched to Mafeking (September 11th) where he refitted, and was for some time thereafter busied in filling Zeerust and Lichtenburg with supplies. Of the other column commanders Allenby, when on his way to Commando Nek, received information of a laager situated at Schaapkraal, on the Sterkstroom river. On September 7th he surrounded it at dawn with 400 cavalry and two guns, and though the bulk of the commando had already escaped the net, twenty-two prisoners and all the camp equipment fell into his hands. On the 11th Allenby reached Pretoria, whence he was moved into the Eastern Transvaal. G. Hamilton, after a brief stay at Olifants Nek, went to Ventersdorp on the 9th and Klerksdorp a week later, taking twenty-nine prisoners on the way; soon after he was entrained

The columns disperse.

EVENTS IN THE WESTERN TRANSVAAL. 293

for Natal. Fetherstonhaugh's columns, after having thoroughly searched the Zwart Ruggens, went into Ventersdorp on September 13th with more than 100 prisoners captured during and since the movement against Kemp. At Ventersdorp Fetherstonhaugh remained until the 21st, when he again set out northward in search of Kemp, who was reported about Tafel Kop. The height, however, was found unoccupied on September 22nd, though touch was made with a party of some 300 Boers next day beyond the Elands river, and again on the 25th at Winkelhaak, north of the Zeerust road, sharp fighting resulting at both places. Until the end of September Fetherstonhaugh continued to raid in this neighbourhood. On the last day of the month he received orders to reinforce Kekewich, who had had a critical adventure close to the north-east.

After dropping out of the combination in the Zwart Ruggens Kekewich had remained a week at Naauwpoort, when orders to clear the northern slopes of the Magaliesberg about the Sterkstroom river sent him again into the field. Marching through Olifants Nek, he had gone some way on the other side of the mountains when fresh orders were received (September 17th) to desist from his north-easterly movement, and to remain instead within touch of Olifants Nek, so as to be at hand to co-operate with Fetherstonhaugh against the hostile bodies whom that General had found to the west of Naauwpoort. Accordingly Kekewich remained some days at Rhenosterfontein, moved into Rustenburg on the 22nd, and thence through Magato Nek to Moedwil on the Selous river, to the west of which his cavalry surprised and captured a laager of thirty-five Boers on the 24th. Kekewich then made a circuit northward along the Elands river to Lindleys Poort, and finding little to do, returned on September 29th to Moedwil, not a Boer being sighted on the march, which concluded at noon. On the evening of arrival Kekewich despatched his supply column by Magato Nek and Rustenburg towards Naauwpoort where it was to refill. With the wagons as escort went one and a half companies of the 1st Derbyshire regiment, and one and a half squadrons of the Scottish Horse. There remained with Kekewich at Moedwil four companies of the 1st

Kekewich at Moedwil.

Derbyshire regiment, four and a half squadrons of the Scottish Horse, and two companies of Imperial Yeomanry, some 800 men in all, with three guns of the 28th battery R.F.A., and a Vickers-Maxim. These were in a camp about 600 yards from the east (right) bank of the Selous river. The operations of the past week had apparently fixed the enemy in the neighbourhood at such insignificant strength that Kekewich, feeling safe from molestation, had chosen his camp with more regard to convenience than to tactical efficiency. It was pitched on the sky-line of a rise and faced west, towards the Selous river which bounded the entire front, the Zeerust—Magato Nek road roughly marking the left (southern) flank. The drift which carried the track across the river was thus at the left (south-west) corner of the front of the encampment; it was held by one and a half companies of the 1st Derbyshire regiment, the remainder of whom were distributed in piquets over the road along the left flank and around to the left rear, where the line of outposts was taken up by the mounted troops through right rear and right to front again, the circle being completed by their junction with the infantry at the drift. Although he had little expectation of being attacked, Kekewich had faced his men in the direction from which attack was most likely, namely, the west. Here the Selous river, as is common with such obstacles, provided a problem not easily to be decided. Beyond it lay broken and scrub-grown ground which required watching, though to do so properly would have demanded the assumption of the left (western) bank as a line of observation, and possibly of resistance. With so few troops at his disposal Kekewich considered this inadvisable. With the exception of a single infantry piquet posted in some native huts about 500 yards across the drift, he confined himself to his own bank of the river, which—though it lay dangerously near the camp, that is to say, both camp and outposts might be surprised together—was so steep and high that it seemed adapted to defence to the last against attack from across the river, and absolutely to forbid any lodgment by the enemy in the river bed itself. It appeared, in short, to do away with the necessity for surveillance of the

Position of his camp.

EVENTS IN THE WESTERN TRANSVAAL. 295

cover on the opposite side of the stream, other than such as could be carried on by small patrols, which Kekewich ordered to go out from every piquet an hour before dawn, and by two stronger mounted reconnoitring parties which were to start to search north-west and south-west at 4.30 a.m. The repeated failure of precautions of this particular nature during the campaign may well throw doubt on their utility. Should the enemy be gathering for an assault, he will usually do so earlier in the night than the hour of starting of such patrols, which, necessarily slow of movement and restricted in observation, are likely to precipitate rather than anticipate the onslaught, and that close to the outposts from which they issue. Further, in such an event the patrols themselves, moving in the open, must almost certainly be lost, and had far better be within the outposts, which they can usually in any case do little to warn. Thus it happened that about 4.30 a.m. on September 30th a patrol of the Imperial Yeomanry, going out from the north-westerly piquet of the mounted troops on the western front, ran into a strong body of Boers, who swept them aside at once, and in a few seconds were upon the piquet behind, which they destroyed to the last man. As little virtue remains in a broken outpost line as in a ruptured dam. Rapidly the breach widens on either side as the neighbouring piquets are rolled away by the outflanking fire from the place of the lost link. Both up and down the river the enemy pushed his men, covering them with a fusilade which annihilated first the Yeomanry piquet next to the northward, then the infantry guard at the drift in the opposite direction, both detachments withstanding resolutely to the last. By a curious chance the piquet across the drift passed unnoticed, and thus escaped destruction. In a brief space the line of the river bed, the sole defence of the camp, was lost, just as Clements' front on the Magaliesberg heights had been lost at Nooitgedacht. The Boers then poured so dense a fire upon the tents that it seemed as though the camp must fall within a few moments without an answering shot. Amongst the lines inevitable confusion arose. It was still half dark. As usual the tethered horses, the largest and most helpless targets, added to

De la Rey attacks Kekewich, Sept. 30th, 1901.

the riot by their wild stampeding, very many being killed, and scarcely one escaping unstruck as they blundered about the lines. The soldiers, roused by the rush of lead through their canvas walls, hurried into the open, fixing their bayonets as they ran, and seeking the orders which at such a time it is the hardest task to issue. But soon from the chaos was evolved a steady drift of men, and it was all toward the front. In a few moments the open space between the river and the boundary of the camp was barred by a mixed but solid firing line, which replied vigorously to the fire pouring from the river bed. As the light grew, and with it the certainty of the Boer positions, Kekewich's guns opened one by one, and the shooting of the troops became more and more powerful and accurate, until it equalled that of the enemy, who attempted in vain to push in to close quarters and overwhelm the camp. Advance after advance was shattered ere well begun, and the effect of the resistance was shown by the galloping off of small parties of daunted burghers. The majority remained, however, and whilst this fierce fire-fight was waged along the western front, a rumour arose that a strong body of Boers was riding round to surround the camp by the east or rear. At this moment Kekewich, having just been disabled by a wound, the second he had received, was in the act of delegating command to the Colonel of the Derbyshire regiment, H. C. Wylly. This officer immediately ordered Major C. N. Watts, of his own regiment, and Major R. A. Browne, of the Border regiment, to collect all the men they could and move in that direction, for had the report been true there was little hope of safety for the camp. But the east was found to be clear, and Watts, with a rapid grasp of the situation, at once swung his men northward, and sent them with fixed bayonets straight at the enemy in the bushes upon the river bank to the north-west of the camp. As the infantry charged they were joined by many of the Scottish Horse and Imperial Yeomanry, until a strong and resolute body bore down upon the flank of the enemy's position in the river bed. The effect was instantaneous. The Boers directly in the face of the onset broke and fled; those higher up the river bed, seeing themselves outflanked,

<small>Defeat of De la Rey.</small>

EVENTS IN THE WESTERN TRANSVAAL. 297

and already much disheartened by the inflexibility of the defence, began to disappear group by group. By 6.15 a.m. the whole were in full flight, the cup dashed from their lips, as that at Vlakfontein had been, by the effect of a counter-attack upon a soldiery unequal to a prolonged or redoubled effort to complete what they had brilliantly begun. Such indeed seemed the distinguishing trait of the commandos under De la Rey and Kemp, for they it was who, concentrating with extraordinary secrecy, had fallen upon Kekewich and so nearly ruined him. They could scarcely have failed to do so had their plan been carried out as designed. De la Rey had with him some 1,500 men, nearly all the local commandos in his jurisdiction. The report which had first misled and then guided Watts into the movement which decided victory for the British contained the essence of his scheme of attack. The camp was indeed to have been surrounded, by Kemp and Van Heerden from the east, by Steenkamp and Oosthuizen from the north, by De la Rey himself from west and south with the 900 men he kept under his hand along the Selous river. But every attack except his own miscarried; only a few burghers found their way to the British flanks and rear, where they acted too feebly to be worth repelling. The frontal attack alone was made in full power, and how nearly it came to success gave no uncertain hint of the fate of the camp had the plan been carried out in its entirety. Kekewich's losses were heavy; in an hour the fight had cost him about twenty-five per cent. of his force,* and so many of his horses that his order to pursue, which he gave immediately the enemy loosened, could not be obeyed. He himself had been twice wounded during the affray, towards the success of which his fine and cool leadership had greatly contributed.† De la Rey admitted forty-eight casualties; but that brilliant commander was prone to make as little of his defeats as of his successes in his reports to the Boer Headquarters, and the accuracy of his casualty list may be

Miscarriage of his plans.

---

* Casualties—Killed, officers five, men fifty-six; wounded, officers twenty-one, men 110; total, 192. No fewer than 512 animals, horses and mules, were killed

† For gallantry in this action Private W. Bees, 1st Derbyshire regiment, was awarded the Victoria Cross.

estimated from the fact that even a month later he included Kekewich amongst the British dead at Moedwil.*

<small>Fetherstonhaugh reinforces Kekewich.</small>

On the day after the action Fetherstonhaugh was on the spot with two of his columns, those of Hickie and E. C. I. Williams. Williams, bivouacking at Kosterfontein on the previous evening after a successful raid (sixteen prisoners), had actually been in signalling communication with Kekewich towards the close of the fight at Moedwil, learning that his assistance was not required. For a week Fetherstonhaugh searched in vain for Kekewich's aggressors, and on October 9th turned southward toward Ventersdorp, coming in to the line at Klerksdorp to refit on the 16th. Fetherstonhaugh was then removed from the district to take command of the Eastern (Delagoa Bay) line of communications, leaving his columns, of which that of E. C. I. Williams was entrained for Pretoria, whilst Hickie's was retained to cover the construction of a line of blockhouses to be built along the Schoon Spruit from Ventersdorp to the Vaal river. The necessity for protection here had been shown by an attack on the 8th, when Wolmarans, with a section of the Potchefstroom commando, killed and captured twenty-two men who had been engaged in fuel cutting on the proposed line, taking also a dozen wagons. Meanwhile Kekewich's column, temporarily commanded by Lieut.-Colonel H. C. Wylly, was refitting at Magato Nek, 320 horses and 200 mules for its use being ready within twenty-four hours of the engagement at Moedwil. The majority of the troops who had fought in that exhausting affair were now relieved by fresh units, the 2nd Norfolk regiment replacing the 1st Derbyshire. On October 13th Kekewich, sufficiently recovered from his wounds to resume command, took his column to Bashoek, where for a week he awaited the approach of Lord Methuen, who was coming from Mafeking to co-operate in a further search for De la Rey's vanished combination. Lord

<small>Lord Methuen marches east from Mafeking.</small>

Methuen had left Mafeking on October 2nd, and after a leisurely march, chiefly employed in the destruction of crops and stock, reached Zeerust on the 14th, and a week later Lindleys Poort,

---

* General De la Rey to Commandant-General Botha, October 28th, 1901.

EVENTS IN THE WESTERN TRANSVAAL. 299

where Kekewich, who had moved up to Rietfontein, gained touch with him. But the conjunction was brief and quite unprofitable. Lord Methuen, who had seen nothing of De la Rey, turned again almost immediately westward, and Kekewich in the opposite direction, the latter being back at Bashoek on the 25th. Lord Methuen's two columns, retracing the route to Zeerust, marched, according to their usual custom, by parallel but separate routes. Some miles from Lord Methuen's own left flank was Lieut.-Colonel S. B. von Donop's force, consisting of the 5th Imperial Yeomanry (680 men), 1st Northumberland Fusiliers (140 men), 1st Loyal North Lancashire regiment (190 men), four guns 4th battery R.F.A., a 5-in. howitzer of the 37th battery R.F.A., and two Vickers-Maxims. One hundred and two ox and mule wagons accompanied the detachment. It fell to von Donop to discover at last the whereabouts of De la Rey and his contingent, and in a manner as surprising as it was costly. At 7.30 a.m. on October 24th he was between Wilgeboomsspruit and Kleinfontein, south of the Zeerust road, Lord Methuen being at that moment about Rickertsdam, some twelve miles to the north-east. Von Donop was in the act of turning northward to reduce the distance between himself and his chief, whom he had arranged to meet next day, when some firing from a group of kopjes in front caused him to pause and open with his artillery in reply. The hostile demonstration was weak, and not at all unexpected, for these kopjes had been invariably occupied by Boer piquets and patrols. On this occasion, however, they formed part of a carefully laid trap to enclose Lord Methuen's detached column. Concealed by a belt of timber which ran parallel to von Donop's left flank, De la Rey with Kemp and Steenkamp lay in hiding with 600 men. Immediately the sound of the guns gave the signal that the British were engaged in front, De la Rey's force emerged from the recesses of the wood in three divisions, each two or three lines deep, and rode like a regiment of European cavalry straight for the centre of the convoy. The flanking parties with which von Donop had surrounded himself were obliterated almost in silence, and the train, laid open to the impact, was in a moment broken in three places.

His detachment under von Donop.

De la Rey attacks von Donop, Oct. 24th, 1901.

One body of the enemy, cutting the mule convoy in two, separated both it and the rearguard from the rest; another dashed straight for Lieutenant H. N. Hill's section of guns at the rear of the convoy; the third, galloping clean through the line of march, wheeled on the other side, and enveloped the same two guns from the north. Hill swung his pieces facing rearwards and came into action with case shot, but he had only time to fire three rounds before he and all but two of his gunners fell. But the escort, F. company of the Northumberland Fusiliers under Captain A. C. Girdwood, fought so valiantly, losing half its personnel, that though the Boers were amongst and on every side of the guns they never succeeded in capturing them, though a burgher, or, as some say, a man of the defence, fired one of the limbers. Lieutenant R. F. A. Hobbs (Royal Engineers), proceeding to the spot to ascertain what had occurred, found the pieces surrounded by disabled artillerymen, and with the aid of the only two unwounded men actually fired some rounds of shrapnel, and remained in possession, hoping for rescue. Owing to the thickness of the bush on either side of the column it was as difficult for von Donop to obtain information as to give orders. The Boers were in every part of the convoy. Many of the wagons of the rear of the convoy were being driven off; twelve had already disappeared; twenty more had been upset; nearly all the native drivers of the rest were shot, many incurring death by their devotion in refusing to drive away the booty for the enemies of their employers. Fearing from the silence of the field pieces with the rearguard that both were lost, von Donop sent a party of mounted troops to attempt to withdraw them. He next set himself to saving the bulk of his wagons, which he effected by collecting all the available mounted men and posting the other pair of guns and the howitzer in a commanding position. He then heard that his guns had not yet passed into the enemy's hands, and he immediately sent another mounted party and a Vickers-Maxim to extricate them. In all this he was successful. Once more the heat of De la Rey's attack cooled suddenly at the first show of resolute and organised opposition. It seemed as though his burghers were incapable of success unless

EVENTS IN THE WESTERN TRANSVAAL. 301

they achieved it at the first onset. At the very moment of victory they drew off; the fire of the artillery, now swelled by that of the two rescued guns—even of that which had been set on fire, so quickly had it been supplied with fresh fittings—sent them still further, and in half an hour the column was clear on every side and free to re-establish its broken array. The casualties amongst the troops numbered ninety;* forty-nine natives were killed, wounded or missing; twelve wagons had vanished altogether, many others were damaged or deprived of their teams. But the enemy's failure had cost him dear. Some fifty burghers were found dead on or near the field; many wounded had been carried away. Nevertheless, von Donop had had a narrow escape, and his experience cast doubts on the wisdom of allowing a detached force, heavily burdened with transport, to march alone so far from its parent column through "the worst portion of a most difficult route."† On October 28th both portions of Lord Methuen's command reached Zeerust, with nine prisoners and forty-eight wagons and carts, leaving behind them a broad belt of ravished country which accounted for some three-quarters of the entire harvest of the fertile Marico district, the enemy's most trusted granary.

De la Rey retreats.

Turning back now to Kekewich, that officer, last seen at Bashoek, was soon in possession of information which caused him to set his column again in motion. Within the confluences of the Hex, Elands and Crocodile rivers to the east considerable hostile assemblages were reported, and on October 28th Kekewich sallied out to come to terms with them. Marching by night and with great secrecy he reached Hartebeestspruit before dawn. Here his excellent Intelligence Service gave him notice of several bodies of Boers in the neighbourhood. He became aware, too, that his movements were being keenly watched by the enemy, and increased caution became necessary if good results were to accrue. At Beestekraal, twenty-five miles due

Kekewich operates eastward from Bashoek.

---

* Casualties—Killed, two officers, twenty-eight men; wounded, five officers, forty-nine men; missing, six men.

† Lord Methuen's report to the Adjutant-General.

eastward, lay the largest of the reported laagers. At 8 p.m. on the 29th Kekewich despatched Lieut.-Colonel C. E. Duff with all his mounted men with orders to surprise Beestekraal at dawn, he himself following shortly after with the infantry and baggage. Duff was at first delayed by missing the road in the darkness, but thereafter he marched rapidly, and daylight of the 30th found him across the Hex river, and within sight of Beestekraal, which was seen to be occupied. Duff was himself almost immediately discovered by the enemy, who began to fire from an outpost on a kopje opposite his left. Sending a squadron against these, Duff at once dashed for the drifts over the Crocodile, of which he captured two, one above, the other below the laager, which lay on the right bank of the Crocodile. Having thus gained an ingress, his men poured in from both sides and won the farmstead with little opposition. Meanwhile his squadron on the left had surrounded the kopje, where a commando of seventy men, in spite of the vigilance of its piquet, was completely surprised in the act of cooking breakfast, and captured. Altogether Duff took seventy-eight prisoners, with the loss of only two of his own men wounded, burned the farms and their contents, and on that afternoon was again in touch with Kekewich who had come on to Klipplaat, on the Elands river. The rain, which had fallen heavily throughout these operations, then brought the rivers down in flood, and after halting, Kekewich on the Elands river and Duff on the Hex, both returned to Rustenburg on November 2nd, thus concluding an expedition in which the value of good information and of decision in following it up had been well exemplified.

EVENTS IN THE WESTERN TRANSVAAL.

APPROXIMATE STRENGTH STATES OF COLUMNS REFERRED TO IN FOREGOING CHAPTER.

COLUMN.	Mounted Troops.	Infantry.	Guns, including Vickers-Maxims.	Machine Guns.	
September—November, 1901.					
Lt.-Gen. Lord Methuen ..	1,325	600	13	2	
Lt.-Col. S. B. von Donop ..	680	330	7	—	
Lt.-Col. W. B. Hickie ..	673	193	6	1	Maj.-Gen. R. S. R. Fetherstonhaugh in command.
Lt.-Col. E. C. Ingouville Williams	785	198	5	—	
Brig.-Gen. G. Hamilton ..	822	345	5	3	
Col. R. G. Kekewich ..	853	1,020	5	2	
Col. E. H. H. Allenby ..	1,104	—	5	4	

CHAPTER XVII.

EVENTS IN THE EASTERN TRANSVAAL*

(Continued from Chapter XII.).

THE ACTION AT BAKENLAAGTE,† OCTOBER 30TH, 1901.

Benson's operations in Sept. 1901. THE dangerous, but, as it proved, abortive attempt against Natal, had by no means put a stop to the offensive in the northern sections of the Eastern Transvaal. Sir B. Blood, though deprived of most of his strength by the urgent needs of the threatened colony, had nevertheless kept his remaining columns in full activity. On September 10th Lieut.-Colonel G. E. Benson, raiding from Carolina towards Middelburg, surprised numerous bodies of the enemy, from whom he took nearly fifty prisoners and a quantity of stock, marching on one occasion fifty-two miles in twenty-four hours to effect his purpose. On the 22nd he was back at Carolina, set out afresh on the 26th, and after activities too various to be related, by the end of the month had accounted for 117 Boers. Park during the same period had been circulating about Lydenburg, where he was on September 30th, whilst Bewicke-Copley from Springs covered the construction of a series of blockhouses from that place towards the Delagoa Bay railway. This line was intended for occupation by the men of the South African Constabulary, a corps recently formed, somewhat on the lines of the Cape Mounted Riflemen, by Major-General R. S. S. Baden Powell and Colonel J. S. Nicholson at Johannesburg. In this task a small column under Lieut.-Colonel F. Hacket-Thompson (Cameron Highlanders) also co-operated from

* See map No 95. † See map No. 57.

EVENTS IN THE EASTERN TRANSVAAL. 305

Bronkhorstspruit station, command of this unit being eventually transferred to Lieut.-Colonel the Hon. C. G. Fortescue (Rifle Brigade).

In October Benson continued the harrying tactics which had made his a name of terror to every body of Boers compelled to laager in his vicinity. From the 1st to the 13th he ranged the district between the Oliphant and Komati rivers, without great profit it is true, for his very reputation now scattered his quarry in every direction before he had time to close; but when he marched into Middelburg to refit, his train was swelled by many captives, wagons and cattle. After a week's rest Benson set out again, struck rapidly south-west across the Oliphant, and on the third day out surrounded and captured a laager midway between the Wilge and Oliphant rivers, and eighteen miles south of Brugspruit, taking thirty-seven prisoners, in spite of a hot attack upon his rear by a strong outlying commando. On October 25th he was close to Bethel, sparring with a force which, warned of his approach, was under arms when he appeared. Benson's losses here were seventeen officers and men, those of the Boers about the same, besides three burghers taken prisoners by the column. The resistance encountered by Benson in this affair and that of the 22nd was not without omen. These were no local bands, concerned more with escape than fighting. It was plain that the small column was in the way of the commandos retiring in angry mood from the borders of Natal, their exasperation heightening as the tale of damage reached their ears at every spot where Benson's lightning strokes had fallen.

[sidenote: Benson's operations in Oct. 1901.]

Commandant-General Botha, pausing gloomily at Ermelo with the officials of the Transvaal Government whom he did not dare to move, sent peremptory orders to General D. Opperman to keep his commandos together and "attack with all their force whenever possible."* The veld must be rid of Benson's "restless column"* which was rapidly demoralising the very centre of resistance. Benson himself, admirably informed as he had been

[sidenote: Botha orders an attack on Benson.]

* Letter from Commandant-General L. Botha to General C. Botha, October 23rd, 1901.

throughout by his Intelligence Officer, Colonel A. Wools-Sampson, was fully aware both of the increasing numbers and the changing temper of the enemy in his vicinity. His column was absolutely alone in the district. It was composed of unseasoned soldiers; for during the rest at Middelburg Benson had unwillingly seen many of his well-tried horse and foot exchanged for infantry which had been for a year and a half immured in blockhouses, and mounted infantry which for many months had ridden no further than around the outskirts of Middelburg.* On October 29th he informed Headquarters from Syferfontein, north-west of Bethel, that he was about to make for Brugspruit down the line of the Steenkool (or Steenbok) Spruit. He reported that he was being closely watched by strong hostile patrols, coming chiefly from the south and east. His convoy and forty-two prisoners might be expected at Brugspruit on November 2nd.

Benson at Syferfontein, Oct. 29th, 1901.

At 5 a.m. on October 30th the column left its camp on Syferfontein and began its north-westerly march, pointing on Bakenlaagte, where Benson intended to make a halt. The previous evening Wools-Sampson's scouts and spies had reported the presence of about 500 enemy in the immediate neighbourhood. Under cover of mist and storms of rain these Boers attacked early in the day, but not seriously enough to check the march. They were, in fact, less bent on fighting than on outstripping the column, and when after sundry delays, caused by the wagons at the drifts over the branching headstreams of the Steenkool (or Steenbok) Spruit, Benson's advance-guard approached the farm of Bakenlaagte about 9 a.m., it found the enemy already there. But to the surprise of all the Boers vanished at once, and seemed to be returning the way they had come outside the flanks of the column. Wools-Sampson, who was guiding the van, was now thoroughly suspicious. For days past he had viewed with apprehension the gathering numbers and mysterious tactics of an enemy whom none in South Africa

The events of Oct. 30th, 1901.

---

* Composition of Benson's column, October 30th, 1901—3rd mounted infantry (501), 25th mounted infantry (462), 2nd Scottish Horse (434), 84th battery R.F.A. (eighty-two), (four guns), CC and R sections of Vickers-Maxims (thirty-six), 1st Field troop R.E. (fourteen), 2nd battalion The Buffs (650).

EVENTS IN THE EASTERN TRANSVAAL.

knew better than he. Personally acquainted with numbers of his adversaries, knowing many more by sight and name, he had in addition that natural but rare instinct for feeling the pulse of his opponents which stamps the born intelligence officer, an agent whose guesses must be little less valuable than his actual information if he is to be of signal service to his side. He now scented grave danger, and urging Benson to look immediately to his rear, he himself led the convoy forward to the so strangely evacuated farmstead. But Benson had little need of warning. The failure of L. Botha's invasion of Natal, followed by the mustering of the commandos in the neighbourhood of his lonely column, had hinted plainly in whose path he stood, and much he regretted that owing to his weakness he had to move northward to avoid the stroke of Botha's forces instead of southward to challenge it. On this particular day the very quickness of eye which had so often delivered his enemy into his hand showed him his own danger. His troops had entered the very type of country where they were least effective. The veld, rolling in great but gentle curves, offered nowhere shelter or positions of defence, but everywhere covered approaches and hiding places for the gathering of an assault. In such ground a small force, especially if encumbered with wagons, is at the mercy of a swifter enemy; it can neither scout with safety on front or flanks, nor effectually guard its rear, for detached parties become immediately invisible to the rest, and may be lost without a sign; nor, when they quit the top of one broad saddle and descend the slope to make for the next, are they unlikely to be annihilated in the low ground between by opponents who have come up unseen from the other side. Thus, in whatever formation, a weak column is in momentary peril in the presence of the enemy; marching united, one valley may be the grave of all, or if in detachments, it may easily perish in detail. All this Benson, looking over the grassy ground-swell, knew well, and in a few moments the Boers were to show him that they too were not neglectful of the aid of their hereditary ally, the veld.

It happened that at about 1.45 p.m. one of the rearmost

wagons, lagging behind the rest, had become embedded in the mud of a drift. The rearguard consisted of two companies 3rd M.I., one company The Buffs (East Kent regiment), with a Vickers-Maxim gun. Brevet Major F. G. Anley (Essex regiment), who commanded these units, made every effort to extricate the wagon and bring it on. But the Boers, with whom he had been closely engaged since leaving camp, were increasing momentarily, and they pressed so hard that Anley, fearing to be cut off, ordered the wagon to be abandoned, and fell back towards Bakenlaagte. At this moment the order of march of the whole column was as follows :—Nearing the proposed camp at Bakenlaagte Farm was the supply column, guarded by the advance-guard of two companies of The Buffs, two guns 84th battery R.F.A., and two companies of the 25th (King's Royal Rifles) M.I., all under Major C. L. E. Eustace, the commanding officer of the 25th M.I. These troops were both escort to the convoy and formed the advance-guard, and had left camp an hour before the main body. The delays at the drifts, however, had brought the two portions of the column together, and close upon the van were now two more companies of the 25th M.I., three of The Buffs, a Vickers-Maxim gun, the remaining two guns of the 84th battery R.F.A., and the Scottish Horse. The six companies of The Buffs (the seventh being with Anley and the rearguard) closely surrounded the wagons, having two companies in front, and two on either flank, the exposed side of the latter being watched by a half company of Anley's 3rd M.I.

Benson, who had just posted the guns of the advance-guard on a ridge one and a half miles behind the reversed rearguard, letting the other two go on into camp, strongly disapproved of Anley's action, for he had never lost a wagon to the enemy, and as yet he knew nothing of the real straits of the outnumbered rearguard. Two companies of The Buffs, which the firing in rear had caused to linger behind some time earlier, had been ordered by Benson to march on to the camping ground, which they had now nearly reached. Sending word to these to come back to reinforce, and to Anley to hold on until they arrived, Benson himself took two squadrons (seventy-five men)

EVENTS IN THE EASTERN TRANSVAAL.

of the Scottish Horse, and hastened to the rear to help reclaim the derelict wagon. But Anley had been already forced back, and Benson, expecting the two companies of The Buffs to be up shortly, and fearing for the flanks of his distant convoy, ordered Anley to move to a position covering the north-east of the camp whilst the whole rearguard fell back. Anley's orders were clear, and he left at once, too promptly in truth for the safety of the rest.

Commandant-General Botha, pressing keenly, his force well in hand, espied the opening as soon as it was given. Instantly he launched upon the retiring troops a double crescent of twelve hundred horsemen. The few remaining mounted men of the rearguard had to gallop for it, and dashed through the extended company of The Buffs which, much disarrayed by this rush of their own friends, was in a few seconds over-ridden and dashed to pieces by the pursuing horde. Brandishing their rifles and firing from the saddle as they stormed yelling over the veld, the burghers, in their eagerness to catch the Scottish Horse, scarce noticed the scattered groups of foot soldiers who staggered amongst them like men overtaken by a flood. A little further on half of another company of the same regiment was similarly obliterated. This party had been acting as escort to the two guns posted by Benson, and when on the approach of danger these pieces had been removed at the trot to the next ridge, the infantrymen were left behind. As they toiled after they too were overtaken by the charging commandos. Seldom have troops found themselves in a more hopeless predicament than this group. The first press of Boers, hot on the track of higher game, having caught up the half-company, passed over it as if it had no existence, and surged on before without firing a shot, so that The Buffs looked into the backs of their receding adversaries as a swimmer in deep water sees a billow roll from him towards the shore. Behind these another rank of burghers came on fast; but they, more careful of the little band, instead of charging, dismounted and began to shoot them down, the noise of their firing calling many of those who had ridden on back upon the melting handful, which lost eighteen of its thirty-three men before it disappeared. Meanwhile Benson and most of the Scottish Horse had gained the second gun position, and turned to face the onset. On the ridge were the two guns of the 84th battery R.F.A., with Major E. Guinness in command; a section (twenty men) 25th (King's Royal Rifles) M.I., under Sergeant W. Ashfield; the King's Own Yorkshire Light Infantry company of the 3rd M.I., under Captain F. T. Thorold and Second Lieutenant L. H. Marten; a section (twenty men) of the 2nd Scottish Horse under Lieutenant J. B. Kelly, in addition to the seventy men or so of the same regiment from the rear-guard who were commanded by Major F. D. Murray, with Captains M. W. Lindsay and S. W. Inglis and Lieutenants E. O. Straker and C. Woodman, names then not famous, but now not to be left unrecorded by any historian howsoever pledged to brevity. A mile to the west, where the same great roll of the veld rose to a cup-topped knob overlooking a farm, were two sections of the King's Royal Rifles mounted infantry, under Captain F. M. Crum and Lieutenant R. H. Seymour. Another half-company of the King's Royal Rifles M.I., under Lieutenants W. P. Lynes and H. H. R. White, with a few of the Royal Dublin Fusiliers M.I., were on a detached rise 2,000 yards north-west of Crum, and here Eustace had posted a third gun of the 84th battery, having sent the fourth back into camp at Bakenlaagte. On came the federal regiments, their outriders swarming about the heels of the hindmost men of the Scottish Horse. As they galloped their numbers swelled. From every dip appeared mounted men; from behind the farm below Crum's post a strong body, emerging suddenly at full speed, joined in the charge, whilst others, scattering to the flanks, hotly engaged with fire both Crum's and Lynes' detached parties on the west and Anley's on the east. Two thousand horsemen raced down upon Benson and the men with him around the guns. So grand and terrible a spectacle had not been seen nor had the earth so shaken on any battlefield in South Africa. But the ancient splendour of the scene was not all with the furious squadrons of the Boers. Alone on the gigantic bosom of the veld the little knot with Benson calmly faced the approaching catastrophe.

Flight was still possible; the horses were at hand, and the undulations between the ridge and the camp offered good and sheltered galloping ground. But no man stirred from his place. Two lessons the band had vowed to teach, one to the enemy that not for him was the crowning glory of a charge home into British troops and guns; the other the last and greatest lesson of soldiers to all the soldiers in the world. So fast and steadily shot the men that the Boers, recalling the instinct which their rage had momentarily banished, winced, and drawing rein, flung themselves from the saddle into a dip some two hundred yards from the ridge. From its invisible recesses arose a chorus of the voices of leaders, threatening and exhorting. For a few moments the fortunes of the attack trembled in the balance, for a charge is a flame easily quenched, and then difficult indeed to relight. But here were fighting men who, in throwing themselves from the saddle to the ground, did but exchange one long-practised art for another. Extending rapidly they began to close on foot, each man knowing perfectly where his quarry lay and how best to approach it, each bent on shooting and on not being shot, none thinking of deeds of daring but all that victory must be won—troops more formidable than these marksmen who could crawl like Highland stalkers after a two-mile gallop have seldom made war. In a few moments a tempest of lead burst at point-blank range upon Benson's soldiers. Nothing now could avert their doom or diminish their glory. The two companies of infantry summoned by Benson, the last hope of saving the ridge, had not appeared, nor were they to be seen upon the hill and dale towards the camp. The foremost Boers gained ground rapidly, covered by a fire which laid low all the British gunners and mowed half the defenders from the ridge. Guinness still lived, and when after two last shots of case the guns were silent, he ordered up the horses to attempt to drag the pieces away. The teams were shattered as soon as they appeared on the rise, and not one of their riders rose from the heap. Soon after a third team arrived, sent to the rescue by Lieutenant N. H. C. Sherbrooke from his gun at Lynes' post on the west; it dropped beside the others, and Guinness himself, his duty ended, fell dead amidst his men and horses. The Boers, a line of riflemen 1,200 yards wide, now fastened upon the scene of ruin. Many were within twenty yards of the guns, using their Mausers like pistols but still crouching before the rifles and revolvers of the survivors on the ridge, who lay as immovable as their dead, only stirring to throw ammunition one to the other. Still no help came from camp. Yet if valour alone be reinforcement the defence grew stronger as it died. A few men of the King's Own Yorkshire Light Infantry, who had escorted the Vickers-Maxim into safety, were led back at full speed into the fight by Lieutenant R. E. Shepherd, who perished at their head. Out from camp, too, galloped Captain T. H. E. Lloyd (Coldstream Guards), Benson's Assistant Staff Officer. As he arrived on the summit his horse, and the man to whom he had thrown the reins to hold it, fell dead beside him. He walked towards the front. The Boers were in the act of closing upon the few remaining troops; the guns stood deserted but for the dead who covered their trails and blocked the wheels; on all sides were slain and wounded, foremost amongst the latter Benson himself, grievously injured. A whirlwind of bullets tore across the bloody grass, one of which struck Lloyd on the wrist and broke it. The officer saw that he had but one brief part to play in the tragedy so nearly ended. Thrusting his bleeding wrist into his coat, he sauntered, upright and smiling, through the dead and dying towards his commander, in full view of a thousand enemies not twenty paces away, and many who perished next moment rejoiced that they had seen his act before they died. In a few seconds he too was down. Space forbids the due relation of every deed like this, though to soldiers they represent military history as much as the movements of a brigade, aye, and may mean as much to the fortunes of a fight. What should be said of Murray of the Scottish Horse, who as he fought at close quarters with his pistol, never ceased to shout encouragement to all around him until his voice was silenced; of Squadron-Quartermaster-Sergeant Warnock, of the same regiment, an old grey-headed soldier, who, though his proper place was in camp and safety, dragged boxes of ammunition into the very front, together with two comrades, Trooper A. Cunningham and Corporal J. M'Carthy, and when his companions fell, went on himself and plied his rifle right and left in the very thick of the Boer lines, until three bullets threw him down amidst his admiring foes; of Trooper N. H. Grierson (Scottish Horse), who, hearing his wounded commander call for a messenger, leapt to his feet to obey, and was struck by the very shot which gave to Benson his second and mortal hurt; of Lance-Corporal J. Bell (Scottish Horse), who, when he, the only unwounded man by the guns, was summoned to surrender by the crowd of Boers upon him, answered only with his rifle and died for his reply; of Captain C. W. Collins (Cheshire regiment), who, until he was wounded near the guns, signalled continually for assistance; of Lieutenant T. D. Jackson (King's Own Royal Lancaster), who brought out ammunition from camp and distributed it to the vanishing firing line; of every officer and man of the King's Own Yorkshire Light Infantry mounted infantry, who were killed where they lay, each in his proper place in the firing line? Such soldiers have earned more than a line, unless, indeed, it be one as immortal as that brief ancient legend graven over the bones of men of like valour with them—"*Stranger, go tell the Lacedæmonians that we died in obedience to their laws.*"*

The final scene came soon. When silence told the Boers that resistance was extinguished they rose, and in five dense rows of foot poured over the ridge and swarmed about their handiwork, some still firing furiously, some stripping the corpses, some, with unusual ferocity, robbing and even shooting the wounded;† others hurrying forward to the reverse slope to seize the led horses, which, stampeding madly, added the thunder of their hoofs to the uproar. At that moment Benson, nearing

---

* Epitaph of the Spartans at Thermopylæ.

† The evidence of seventy-five officers, non-commissioned officers and men who suffered and witnessed ill-treatment on this occasion renders too certain outrages on the part of a usually chivalrous enemy mention of which would otherwise be omitted. In the words of the officer ordered to inquire into the case: "There seems no doubt that though the Boer Commandants have the will they no longer have the power to repress outrage and murder on the part of their subordinates."

death as he was, showed himself the bravest of all the brave who lay around him. Beckoning a soldier to him, a man stripped to his shirt by the looters, he bade him speed into camp, and order the guns to shell the ridge and clear it of the enemy. Rome boasted of such orders, and few legions but hers have heard them. The messenger, contriving to escape notice, performed his mission, and soon both shrapnel and Vickers-Maxim shells burst fiercely over the spot, sent from guns pushed out of camp by Major A. Young, R.H.A., Benson's Staff Officer, who had gone on earlier in the day to mark out the site of the intended camp. Benson and his wounded comrades, welcoming this final peril, exulted as they saw the Boers give back before the projectiles until the hill was nearly clear. But ambulances coming out of camp in spite of all efforts to detain them, masked the fire, and when it stopped about 5.30 p.m. the enemy crowded once more on to the ridge and dragged away the guns, to keep their hands from which had been Benson's last wish. Prisoners there were few to take. Of the approximately 280 officers and men on the ridge, sixty-six lay dead and 165 wounded.

In other parts of the field it had gone less badly, yet hardly enough, and more than once the little detachments seemed as likely as they were prepared to share the fate of the lost company on the gun ridge. Especially was Crum's party sore put to it to maintain itself in the elevated depression to the west of the guns. All day strong bodies, detached from the main Boer assault, hemmed in the group with fire, and though eight of the thirteen officers and men were hit, the rest, burrowing for cover with their bayonets and using several rifles apiece, were not to be shaken from their post, which they only quitted by order at the fall of evening. North and east of Crum, Lynes and Anley were heavily engaged until dusk in keeping the enemy from the camp, around which Wools-Sampson had disposed the infantry for a last defence. After their success on the gun ridge, however, the Boers came no further; they were both satisfied and exhausted by their triumph, to attain which many of them had ridden sixty miles in the preceding twenty-four hours. Thus the camp, which was almost at their mercy, was unmolested, and next morning the British scouts could find no trace of the horde which had wrought such mischief.

Within two hours of receipt of orders at Standerton, G. Hamilton was on the march to the rescue with his own, Allenby's and de Lisle's columns. A small column under Lieut.-Colonel C. St. L. Barter (successor to Bewicke-Copley), from the direction of Springs, set out with the same intent, and covering thirty miles between dusk and dawn, was the first to reach Bakenlaagte. A resolute march of fifty-two miles in sixteen and a half hours brought G. Hamilton with the rest of the relievers to the spot early on November 1st, whereupon Wools-Sampson, having sent his wounded into Springs, marched northward along the blockhoused (South African Constabulary) banks of the Wilge river, and regained the Delagoa Bay railway line at Brugspruit.

Approximate Strength States of Columns Referred to in Foregoing Chapter.

COLUMN.	Mounted Troops.	Infantry.	Guns, including Vickers-Maxims.	Machine Guns.
October, 1901.				
Lt.-Col. F. Hacket-Thompson (later the Hon. C. G. Fortescue)	538	126	3	4
Lt.-Col. G. E. Benson, R.A.	1,529	650	6	—
Brig.-Gen. G. Hamilton	897	272	5	3
Col. E. H. H. Allenby	1,288	—	5	4
Lt.-Col. H. de B. de Lisle	1,001	—	5	2
Lt.-Col. C. St. L. Barter	551	784	5	3

CHAPTER XVIII.

EVENTS IN THE ORANGE RIVER COLONY*

(*Continued from Chapter XIV.*).

AUGUST—NOVEMBER, 1901.

<small>After Smuts' disappearance.</small> THOUGH the columns devoted to the pursuit of Smuts had let slip the main prize, their work of the past fortnight had not been entirely fruitless. All had made captures, Damant being especially successful in this respect. On August 16th, when on the march from the railway to Smithfield, Damant had turned aside to clear the Klein Marsfontein hills, to the north of the road. A converging movement on the group of kopjes by four detachments resulted in the capture of nine Boers, and, scouting forward, Damant was soon on the trail of a convoy which was trekking between him and Boesmans Kop. This was well enveloped by his squadrons, which took eighty-seven prisoners and twenty-two carts.

Smuts was barely through the closing door before it was shut and bolted behind him. On September 4th Thorneycroft was sent to Zonneschyn with orders to block the river as far east as Inhoek, Murray and Moore prolonging his left to Willemsfontein. The day before both Plumer and Pilcher had moved to contract the circle. The former, marching from Priors Siding on a broad front from Helvetia down to Smithfield, was drawing near to close the line of the Caledon. Pilcher filled the gap on Plumer's right by striking up the Caledon towards Smithfield ; Sir H. Rawlinson was fast coming down the Basuto

* See map No. 64.

EVENTS IN THE ORANGE RIVER COLONY. 317

border by Runnymede and Oudenaarde. In short, the enclosure was now so complete, yet by a narrow margin of time so ineffectual, that both sides may well have learned anew the old military lesson of the value of hours. When it was seen that the main object of the concentration had fallen through, Damant was withdrawn to rejoin Bruce Hamilton at Fauresmith, whilst Pilcher, entraining for Burghersdorp, took up with Lieut.-General Sir J. French and the troops in Cape Colony the pursuit of the commandos which had so effectually outwitted the columns on the other side of the Orange.

There yet remained a chance of partially redeeming the failure. Kritzinger was still within the fence, and in his broken state was likely to prove an easier prey than his departed colleague. On September 8th Thorneycroft and Sir H. Rawlinson were in touch along the Orange river. The latter, however, was soon called away by more pressing needs elsewhere. At this time Commandant-General Botha was in the act of launching his commandos upon the frontier of Natal, drawing after him British columns from every quarter. Entraining at Burghersdorp Sir H. Rawlinson was at Heidelberg on September 26th, arriving there in time to take an active part in the pursuit of the discomfited Boer Headquarters in the Eastern Transvaal,* whither Bruce Hamilton had preceded him a fortnight before. _{Sir H. Rawlinson leaves for the Eastern Transvaal.}

Kritzinger seemed strangely difficult to find. Sir H. Rawlinson had arrived at Aliwal North, reporting all the country to the east of the Caledon to be absolutely clear, whilst between the 15th and 20th Thorneycroft retraversed the same route up to Wiesbaden without coming across anything more than patrols. With similar lack of success Plumer, crossing the Caledon at Arcadia and Commissie Bridge, swept up to Wepener and beyond, then south again to Rouxville, which he entered on September 22nd. The only sign of Kritzinger's presence was revealed by the Boer himself, when in an attempt to keep his pledge to Smuts on the night of September 19th, he delivered that fierce and successful attack on one of Hart's main camps _{Search for Kritzinger.}

* See Chapter XII.

318   THE WAR IN SOUTH AFRICA.

at Quaggafontein which has been narrated in a former chapter.* Declining the advantage of his victory, he remained in the Rouxville area, electing rather to endure in his own district the unknown, and so far not too pressing, ills which might beset him, than to brave those of which he had had full experience in Cape Colony. Immediately after his encounter on the Orange Kritzinger found himself at the same moment unexpectedly assisted in one quarter and all but annihilated in another. As he rode with his captured gun and horses back from the river, re-seeking his hitherto undetected sanctuary north of Vecht Kop, he was discovered on the evening of the 20th by Thorneycroft, who all unknown had come down from Lincelles to Bismarck. Thorneycroft immediately attacked with vigour and suddenness, and the commando was broken up, part flying back towards Vecht Kop, part towards Zastron. The latter party was hotly pursued, and though many got away in the gathering darkness, one band of forty were so hard pressed that, abandoning the gun by the wayside, they turned to bay in a donga at Florence. A determined charge by two companies of Thorneycroft's M.I., led by Captains R. Barrett and T. Thompson, promptly cleared out the shelter, Barrett and a sergeant being killed, and three others wounded in the attack. Thirteen Boers were taken here, eight in other parts; the gun was recovered, and the rest of Kritzinger's men, scattered all over the countryside, seemed likely to fare badly between Thorneycroft on one side and on the other Plumer, who was nearing Rouxville from Commissie Bridge. But at this moment Plumer was unfortunately called from the scene by an event which had recently occurred in another place.

Defeat of Kritzinger.

Affair near Sannah's Post, Sept. 19th, 1901.

It had happened that on September 18th a Boer laager had been discovered at Vlakfontein, south of Sannah's Post. On the next day two detachments of mounted infantry, some 160 in all, taken from the Sannah's Post—Thabanchu line, moved out to raid the camp, taking with them two guns of U. battery R.H.A., which had recently reinforced the line of

* See Chapter XV.

defences. The expedition, of which those in authority knew nothing, was incautious in the extreme ; the country was full of Boers who were watching for an opportunity to escape from the uneasy districts to the south, and the result showed the dangers of playing even one false card against opponents so alert. The paltry British force was itself quickly surrounded by superior numbers, and though it fought creditably for four hours, had to capitulate with the loss of both guns, an officer and five men killed, seventeen men wounded, and six officers and ninety-four men taken prisoners. At this stage of the campaign the loss of artillery was a moral gain to the enemy out of all proportion to the actual value of the capture, and the Commander-in-Chief urged every effort to retake the pieces. Plumer was ordered to hurry northward just as he was on the point of regaining contact with Kritzinger's broken commando ; from the western side of the railway Rochfort, who had succeeded Bruce Hamilton on the latter's departure for the Eastern Transvaal, transferred towards the scene of the disaster six columns under W. H. Williams, Damant, Lowry-Cole, Bogle Smith, A. C. Hamilton and du Moulin. On September 26th Plumer at Wepener got in touch with du Moulin at Droogfontein and Lowry-Cole at Jammersberg Drift, learning that the Boers were hastening southward in front of Damant and W. H. Williams, who were chasing them down from Vlakfontein. Damant was at that moment actually south of Plumer at Vaalspruit, watching the area between Helvetia and the Caledon ; W. H. Williams was at Buls Kop, in line with du Moulin ; Lowry-Cole held the Caledon drifts from Jammersberg down to Deep Dene. A. C. Hamilton and Bogle Smith were attending to the supplies from Springfontein and Edenburg. None had encountered the Vlakfontein commandos, though on the 24th du Moulin, passing the scene of the disaster, had recovered fifty-seven rifles and a quantity of the equipment which had been lost by the mounted infantry.

Falling in with the scheme of pursuit, and satisfied that no formed body remained north of Rochfort's columns, on September 27th Plumer turned southward again to sweep down the Caledon on the left bank in conjunction with du Moulin on the other. At Mokari Drift Plumer had a sharp skirmish with a commando on a strong position on the opposite side of the river, his advance-guard boldly crossing the stream to attack whilst Plumer signalled to du Moulin to co-operate. But du Moulin had wandered westward to Vermaakfontein, looking out for a convoy from Springfontein, and an opportunity for a combined attack was lost. With the loss of eighteen casualties, including two officers killed, Plumer's men cleared the kopjes, the enemy scattering westward; then, hearing nothing of du Moulin, Plumer crossed the river in chase to Lichtenstein on the 28th. Du Moulin had then joined W. H. Williams, and the two, taking up the tracks of Plumer's quarry, followed them, du Moulin towards Boesmans Kop, Williams down to Commissie Bridge, where Lord Basing was found on the 29th. Plumer, passing Commissie Bridge on the same day, reached Rouxville on October 1st, and Springfontein soon after. Thence, Plumer's force was conveyed by train to Volksrust, soon to find itself once more in its old hunting ground, the wooded gorges of the Pongola bush, sweeping up the fragments of Botha's dismembered " invasion." *

Plumer leaves for the Eastern Transvaal.

Meanwhile one Boer band under Commandant Dreyer, circling northward again, had once more gained the hilly country between Wepener and Dewetsdorp. Lowry-Cole got information of this at Jammersberg, and pushing out along the Dewetsdorp road, attacked at dawn with much success, capturing both Dreyer and his Field-Cornet, and inflicting ten other casualties.

The situation in the south-eastern corner of the Orange River Colony at the end of September, 1901, was, then, as follows: The double failure of the combination against Smuts and Kritzinger had left all the columns in the district busily and not fruitlessly engaged, it is true, but without any real object. It was not long before the operations here took a fresh shape, consideration of which must be deferred until the work of the forces in other parts has been traced up to the same point.

* See Chapter XII.

EVENTS IN THE ORANGE RIVER COLONY. 321

On August 18th Elliot, having dispersed the units of his great combination north of the Modder, marched eastward from Glen with his own division, to take up a line through Sannah's Post to Ladybrand, Barker and Pine-Coffin linking him to the railway. His intention was to sweep north-eastward, in the hope of driving the enemy into an enclosure which had been already partially formed by troops from other commands. In the Brandwater basin was B. Campbell, whom Sir L. Rundle had recently placed in command there, with orders to fortify himself and deny the whole of this magazine and stronghold to the Boers. Campbell was now the weaker by a battalion, the 2nd Scots Guards, which had been removed to Natal a fortnight earlier. Rimington and Spens, reinforced by Kitchener's Fighting Scouts under Lieut.-Colonel A. E. Wilson, were between Kroonstad and Lindley, raiding with so much success and over so wide a stretch of country that it seemed improbable that any considerable bodies would slip past them to the north. With Bethune, de Lisle, Lowe and Broadwood in line in this order from left to right, Elliot moved northward, pausing from August 22nd—26th to clear the Koranna Berg, and to take in supplies which were provided on the left by Winburg, on the right by Warringham. Though much was heard of the enemy —a commando 1,000 strong being reported near Wonderkop— nothing was seen of any formed body. The only affair of note was to the credit of the Boers themselves, who on August 22nd surprised and captured at Evening Star a party of sixty-five mounted infantry, detached from the garrison of Ladybrand, which incautiously went into the open hoping to drive some of the enemy's patrols into Elliot's arms. Broadwood rode hard to the rescue, but was too late. Then, whilst Barker and Pine-Coffin held Retief's and Slabberts Neks, Elliot continued his march eastward to the Witte Bergen, Bethune moving by Leyden, Braamboschfontein and Kaffirkraal to Rietvlei; de Lisle by Governors Kop and Groenfontein; Lowe and Broadwood through Ficksburg. The results were small, and communication with the outside columns so defective that a message sent to B. Campbell on the 31st requesting him to co-operate did

Elliot's operations.

not reach him until late on September 1st, whilst to the north Rimington, Spens and Wilson were at this moment busy upon a separate scheme which had no bearing on Elliot's operation. For three days Elliot remained near the Brandwater basin, clearing as much stock and produce as the difficulty of the country permitted, but unable to come to close quarters with the human population, who could be seen "climbing up the slopes of the mountains on their hands and feet to get away."*

The division then marched back to Winburg, into which on September 6th were taken nine prisoners, 100,000 stock and 140 vehicles, 850 tons of wheat having been destroyed on the way. This was so little profit from the richest and least harried district of the Orange River Colony that Elliot was almost immediately ordered to repeat his raid. On the night of September 8th he again marched eastward, practically by his former route and to his former stations, but with better results. First, on the 11th, de Lisle came in sight of a Boer convoy on the move near Governors Kop. A gallop of twelve miles delivered the whole into his hands, the capture consisting of seventeen prisoners, sixty-nine vehicles, a wheeled flour mill and some stock. On the 12th and 13th Bethune had small successes at Wonderkop and Rietvlei. The clearance of the western slopes of the Witte Bergen during the next five days not only yielded considerable booty, but had the effect of driving parties of Boers across to B. Campbell, who was still in his original position about Brindisi Drift in co-operation with Brigadier-General Sir J. G. Dartnell, who had recently brought the Imperial Light Horse brigade (1st and 2nd regiments) from Harrismith to Bethlehem and thence to Retief's and Slabberts Neks. On September 17th B. Campbell took seventeen prisoners near Steynsberg: his and Dartnell's captures of stock had already been immense, and the general clearance bade fair to become thorough, when affairs elsewhere somewhat interrupted it. Botha's threat at Natal was at this time fast developing, and the Commander-in-Chief was manœuvering all available troops within hail. Sir L. Rundle

<small>Effect of Botha's manœuvres in the Eastern Transvaal.</small>

* Report by Lieut.-General E. L. Elliot, September 8th, 1901.

EVENTS IN THE ORANGE RIVER COLONY. 323

had already been ordered to block every pass of the Drakensberg between Van Reenen's Pass and Witzies Hoek. On September 19th Elliot received orders to march on Bethlehem for Harrismith. On the same date Spens, from the northern trio of columns, and a few days later Dartnell with one of his regiments, were withdrawn for entrainment to Natal. His other unit Dartnell left in Bethlehem under Lieut.-Colonel C. J. Briggs, who displayed the greatest activity, capturing twenty prisoners before the end of the month. Elliot, his line of march harassed by sharpshooters throughout, reached Bethlehem on the 22nd, and Harrismith four days later, his total gains since September 10th having been thirty-six prisoners, 60,000 head of stock, 228 wagons and carts, and a mass of agricultural stuff. On September 30th Bethune followed Sir J. Dartnell to Natal.

Meanwhile Rimington, Spens and Wilson had made sundry successful raids from Kroonstad in combination. On September 2nd Wilson accounted for ten Boers near Zuurfontein, southeast of Kroonstad. On the next day Rimington ran down a Boer convoy at the head of the Bloem Spruit, taking twenty prisoners and seventy-four vehicles. Rimington then received information that De Wet and Steyn were between Heilbron and Frankfort. He accordingly moved thither, and although the Free State leaders remained invisible, long and rapid marches were rewarded by continual small captures. On September 23rd Rimington scoured the space between the Wilge and Klip rivers,* and after a ride of forty-eight miles brought into camp thirty prisoners and thirty-six vehicles. There was still news of De Wet, the most definite being a circumstantial report that the prize of the campaign was lying ill at a farm near Uitenhage, south-east of Serfontein station. On the evening of the 24th Rimington took 300 men, and riding all night a distance of fifty-seven miles, surrounded the building at dawn. But the information, as indeed all that had concerned De Wet, was false. Five Boers found asleep in the garden were the only

Rimington's, Spens' and Wilson's operations.

---

* The stream between Heilbron and Frankfort; not to be confused with that which joins the Vaal on the west of Standerton.

reward. Rimington then returned to Heilbron after a succession of forays such as the Boers themselves could scarcely have equalled in speed and distance, and, above all, in preservation of horseflesh; for it was no uncommon thing for the troopers to be called upon for a bout of the severest galloping as the termination of a march which would itself have brought in less skilfully managed men and horses exhausted and only fit for camp.

<small>Byng's and Dawkins' operations.</small>
There only remained to be accounted for in September two columns from Bruce Hamilton's late command. When that General's forces were dissevered early in September Byng and Dawkins, instead of following the rest across the railway, were detached on a special mission. At this time there was in process of construction a line of blockhouses from Potchefstroom through Scandinavia to Kopjes station, the work being carried out simultaneously by the 2nd Scots Guards from the western end and the Oxfordshire Light Infantry (recently come from Heilbron) from the eastern. The presence of some 600 Boers in the vicinity seemed likely to interfere, and Byng and Dawkins were ordered northward to drive them clear by working from east to west. On September 10th both columns reached Vredefort Road by train, and on the next day marched upon the Vaal. Brigadier-General G. G. Cunningham had previously occupied Lindequee, and beyond him Lieut.-Colonel A. H. M. Edwards, with 800 South African Constabulary, held the Los Berg; the Scots Guards were at Scandinavia Drift. On the night of September 12th Byng raided Parys and Vredefort, securing thirteen prisoners. Holding Reitzburg, Byng then scoured the lower Rhenoster river, having several smart skirmishes with local bands which were chiefly engaged in the guardianship of the large magazines of grain and the numerous women's laagers which had collected in this district. On the night of the 19th twenty prisoners were taken at Rensburgs Drift. Next day Dawkins secured nine more, and by September 24th sixty fighting men and more than 500 families had been gathered in. At every march the country seemed to become richer and more infested, and Byng reported that it would occupy at least three weeks

EVENTS IN THE ORANGE RIVER COLONY.

properly to deal with the Boers and the innumerable storehouses which he had met at every turn. Here may be noted another formidable difficulty of this singular campaign, namely, the extraordinary rapidity with which the enemy contrived to re-occupy districts which had been apparently denuded of every living and growing thing. This district but a month before had been the path of Elliot's line of columns on their way to the Modder; but its speedy replenishment was only an instance of many such feats performed in every quarter of the theatre of war. Thus Elliot, again, had lately found the very farms of the Witte Bergen which he had ransacked in the first week of September to be as full as ever of grain when he revisited them ten days later on his second excursion from Winburg. No resources are so difficult to dry up as those of an agricultural people. Manufacture, commerce, finance, war may kill at one blow; but the army which makes war upon the sons and stores of the soil has a long and tedious task.

About September 16th the last blockhouse of the new system was completed, its value being shown by the continual attempts to pierce it which occurred from this time forward. The Boers were gradually pressed towards Bothaville, Byng taking in all eighty-one prisoners before he moved up the Valsch towards Kroonstad, which he reached on October 3rd. His own losses had been small, the heaviest in one day having been one killed and ten taken prisoners in an attack made by a commando under Liebenberg upon a party of South African Light Horse which was returning from a patrol to Klerksdorp. Of the other columns in the west Henry had all this time been operating in the Ramah—Luckhoff district, and W. H. Williams between Fauresmith and Edenburg, accounting between them for 145 Boers in raids too frequent to be given in detail.

Within less than a week from his return to Kroonstad, Byng, now in command both of his own column and that of Dawkins (who departed to take up a command in the Northern Transvaal*), was once more in the Bothaville—

* See Chapter XXV.

Reitzburg area. Here he remained throughout October, operating with uniform success against his former opponents. On the 12th and 13th he took twenty-eight prisoners northeast of Bothaville. He then combined with Hickie, who pushed the enemy towards him from Dood's Drift whilst Byng himself came south from a visit to Klerksdorp. The result was that on the 26th Byng was able to surround a laager at Kameelfontein, and take a whole field-cornetcy of twenty-two men, including two officers. Making for Vredefort Road towards the end of the month, a sudden *volte-face* surprised the enemy's scouts as they tracked the line of march, and a further sixteen prisoners brought Byng's total captures for October to sixty-six. These and the prisoners of the previous month were especially valuable because all the Boers in this district were under orders to reinforce the invaders of Cape Colony, and Byng had not only considerably weakened the contingent, but thoroughly disorganised its preparations for the march southward. On November 1st Byng was in Vredefort Road. The only other columns working on the western side of the railway during October were those of Henry and W. H. Williams, who combined in a search for Hertzog between Fauresmith and the defended Riet river. Williams met with success on the 12th at Schraalfontein, one day's march from Edenburg, taking ten prisoners, including three officers. At the end of the month he was back at Edenburg, Henry going in the opposite direction to Modder River station. On the east of the railway there was more activity. The continually disturbed state of the area bounded by the Orange river, the railway, the Basuto border, and the Bloemfontein—Thabanchu—Ladybrand blockhouses, that is, the south-eastern quarter of the Orange River Colony, now caused the Commander-in-Chief to inaugurate fresh measures for its subjugation. Combinations of troops, " drives " and raids had all alike failed to free this district, a part the more important because it gave access to the main passages into Cape Colony. Abandoning the principle of moving columns, therefore, Lord Kitchener now ordered the assignment of fixed areas to the several columns within the zone,

New system in the south-east of the Orange River Colony.

EVENTS IN THE ORANGE RIVER COLONY.

each column to be made responsible for the complete clearance of " the enemy, as well as of every living creature "* from the country within its allotted section. In compliance with this scheme a number of columns drawn from Sir C. Knox and Rochfort (late Bruce Hamilton) were at once centred as follows : Du Moulin at Ventershoek ; Lowry-Cole at Jammersberg Bridge ; Bogle Smith at Schanskopjes on the Kaffir river ; Major A. C. Hamilton at Kransfontein ; Lord Basing at Humans Rust ; Minchin and Copeman, Thorneycroft's two wing commanders, at Elands Berg and Vecht Kop ; Western at Zandfontein, north of Aliwal North ; Taylor and Lean, the leaders of Pilcher's units (which returned from Cape Colony on October 5th), at Wolve Kop and Pampasfontein respectively. All were placed under the general command of Lieut.-General Sir C. Tucker, who controlled also the South African Constabulary posts along the line Kaffir River—Dewetsdorp—Wepener. Space fails to deal in detail with the doings of each and all of this assembly during the ensuing two months. There was never a moment's cessation of activity, never a day without fighting. In this district, scoured a hundred times as it had been, every column found an enemy, and sometimes alone, sometimes in combination with a neighbour, carried out schemes so numerous and varied, evolved with so much care and productive of so much labour that here, as in too many other portions of this history, a paragraph must do scant justice to what would adequately fill a volume. That the enemy survived at all in the narrow interstices between the revolving bodies of troops was striking evidence of his extraordinary military qualities. But he did more ; he was as ready as ever to take the offensive, and to deal prompt justice upon the most momentary lapse on the part of a column commander. As late as October 26th, when scarcely a yard of the region had been left unswept, a detachment of 200 men wandering too far afield at Klein Zevenfontein, north-west of Smithfield, found itself in extreme danger from a commando double its strength, which

Tenacity of the enemy.

---

* Telegram from Commander-in-Chief, September 28th, 1901.

charged in to within fifty paces of camp, killing an officer, wounding ten men, and destroying most of the horses. By a stout defence, aided by the approach of Lean from Pampasfontein, the Boers were driven off with loss. A few days earlier a patrol had been surrounded and destroyed near the same spot. Again, on the 27th a reconnoitring party sent out by A. C. Hamilton north of Bethulie was attacked by some 200 Boers near Grootfontein. On November 5th Bogle Smith and Lowry-Cole were in contact with a band of 200 near Daspoort; a week later a strong patrol was attacked at Rietput; on the 17th one of Lowry-Cole's patrols of 100 men had to fight for six hours at Roodepoort against a commando which all but succeeded in rushing the position, an officer and eleven men falling in the encounter; on the 19th A. C. Hamilton discovered a laager of 200 on the Slik Spruit; on the 27th a commando of 300 was reported at Commissie Hoek. These repeated apparitions were largely the work of the same roving bands, a fact which only exemplified the difficulty of clearing, even by the closest quartering, a single small area of the theatre of war. Nevertheless, the final balance was heavily against the enemy. By the end of November two-thirds of their armed strength had been removed by death or capture; their most secret storehouses had been ransacked, "sufficient wheat being found concealed in false ceilings and by false walls to feed the Boer forces in the district for years;"* scarcely a head of stock remained alive between Dewetsdorp and Aliwal North. The system, in short, proved more successful than any which had been yet attempted; and if its profits appear trifling in comparison with its enormous expenditure, such must always be the case when a nation of armed nomads, for such the Boers had now become, challenges its opponent to a war of extermination.

Elliot on the Natal border. Throughout October affairs on the Natal borders and the subsequent pursuit of Botha's defeated forces confined Elliot to the neighbourhood of Harrismith, where he held himself in readiness to reinforce the eastern troops should need arise.

* Colonel A. N. Rochfort's report, December 11th, 1901.

EVENTS IN THE ORANGE RIVER COLONY.

Nevertheless, he kept his columns continually employed, and his stay was more fruitful than many of his more comprehensive manœuvres had been. De Lisle, supported by Broadwood, and based on Verkykers Kop, scoured first the Witkoppies, then the valley of the Wilge river, in which on October 15th a laager of thirty-four vehicles was captured with fifteen prisoners. A movement upon the Botha's Berg, to be made in conjunction with Rimington from Standerton, fell through owing to rain and mist. The columns then separated, Broadwood's moving southward to Witzies Hoek in combination with a force despatched by Sir L. Rundle, whilst de Lisle, pushing on northward, skirmished his way by Pram Kop and De Lange's Drift (26th) to Standerton at the end of the month. Thirty-three Boers killed, wounded and taken prisoner, eighty-five vehicles and 26,000 head of stock were the gains of these operations. Rimington, it has been mentioned, was at Standerton at the time of de Lisle's northward marches from Verkykers Kop. He had been led thither partly in the hope of co-operating with Sir H. Rawlinson who, in the course of his operations in the Transvaal, was nearing the Vaal. As it was probable that bands would avoid him by crossing this frontier, Rimington had skirted the left bank of the river by Villiersdorp and Cornelia, and fording Roberts Drift on October 3rd, camped near Standerton until the 7th. He then made for the Botha's Berg, expecting to combine with de Lisle and Broadwood. But for the reasons given above Elliot's columns were not to be found, and Rimington circled northward in chase of several small convoys, some of which he captured. On October 14th he took twelve prisoners near Villiersdorp, and returning thence to Standerton with thirty-seven prisoners and eighty-two vehicles to his credit, was drawn into the pursuit of Botha's levies in the Eastern Transvaal. He returned to Standerton early in November.

Rimington leaves for the Eastern Transvaal.

In the first week of October Lord Kitchener ordered the construction of a fresh blockhouse line, to run in the first instance from Heilbron to Frankfort. In order that the work might be begun from both ends simultaneously, which was now the usual practice, Damant, last seen at Edenburg, was railed northward with orders to march to Frankfort, and Wilson was despatched to Heilbron with his regiment of Kitchener's Fighting Scouts. Wilson was strongly opposed on his march from Kroonstad. Rimington had now been absent for five days, Damant had only just reached Heilbron, and in the interval a strong body of Boers had gathered to the south of the town. On the 6th, after passing the Rhenoster, Wilson became hotly engaged. One of his parties was lured into an ambush and almost surrounded, thirteen men being captured; but the rest, holding out firmly, kept off superior numbers at thirty yards' range, and the force got through to Heilbron with the loss of four killed, and fourteen, including five officers, wounded. Damant, delayed by weather and the difficulty of equipping, did not leave Heilbron until the 12th, and employed the time in driving off Wilson's attackers, whom he ascertained to be part of a numerous body assembled by De Wet himself. On the 13th Damant was at Frankfort, and at once came in touch with a commando 500 strong which was on the march for the interior of the Orange River Colony from out of the Transvaal. From this time until the end of October strong hostile bodies were reported and observed in every direction. On the 21st there were some 1,500 Boers within reach of Heilbron, and Damant decided to strike. On the night of October 24th he marched against a laager discovered on the Vaal at Rietfontein, which he attacked at dawn. The majority of the Boers, who were some 300 strong, escaped, but nineteen were taken with thirteen wagons. Damant then (27th) pursued another commando along the Libenbergs Vlei river, capturing five, and thereafter continued to raid around Frankfort until, in the first week of November, he received orders concerning a manœuvre which must now be considered in some detail.

The experiences of Damant and Wilson revealed the presence of an unusually strong hostile concentration between Heilbron, Lindley, Reitz and Frankfort, collected, it was continually reported, by the long invisible De Wet. At this period no news was more gladly received by the British Headquarters than that of a tangible enemy, especially in the Orange River Colony,

EVENTS IN THE ORANGE RIVER COLONY. 331

where De Wet's tactics of dispersion had practically demoralised the campaign. But De Wet himself had now begun to suspect the ultimate futility of such methods against an opponent who was to be worn out neither by tedium nor expense. His multitudinous bands had in reality achieved little or nothing, and, gradually whittled as they were by incessant contact with superior forces, it was they, not the British columns, who were feeling the strain. Towards the end of September, therefore, De Wet had summoned the commandos of Bethlehem, Vrede, Heilbron, Ladybrand, Kroonstad and others to assemble on the Libenbergs Vlei river, and it was the gradual convergence of these forces that had caused the columns in the district daily to report the appearance of fresh bodies. *De Wet concentrates.*

Lord Kitchener at once prepared elaborate measures for taking advantage of so welcome an occurrence. The enemy's rendezvous appeared to be a farm, called Paardehoek, on the Libenbergs Vlei river, some forty miles south-east of Heilbron and twenty south of Frankfort. On all sides of this, but at a great distance from it, the Commander-in-Chief disposed a cordon of columns. The spot was in a measure already surrounded. At Harrismith were Sir L. Rundle and Elliot, the latter strengthened by McKenzie's 2nd Imperial Light Horse (of Brigadier-General Sir J. Dartnell's brigade) in place of de Lisle, who was at Standerton in company with Rimington; Damant was at Frankfort; Wilson with Kitchener's Fighting Scouts at Heilbron; the 1st Imperial Light Horse under Briggs (of Brigadier-General Sir J. Dartnell's brigade) at Bethlehem; Barker, W. H. Williams and Holmes (successor to Pine-Coffin) at Winburg. Completing the ring by bringing Spens to Botha's Pass and sending Byng to join Wilson in Heilbron, Lord Kitchener issued orders for a general movement on Paardehoek by all the columns with the exception of Sir L. Rundle's and those from Winburg, which were instructed to take up an impassable line from Lindley through Bethlehem to Harrismith, blocking all egress to the south. Unlimited ingenuity and thought were lavished on the scheme. It was to be carried out in six marches. Whilst the daily destinations of each *Plan to surround De Wet* column were strictly appointed, and carefully adjusted to equalise the pressure and allay the suspicions of the enemy, each commander was allowed to select his own route, and was enjoined above all to conceal his ultimate aim from the enemy. Deception, it was hoped, would be further assisted by Damant remaining motionless at Frankfort until the rest of the cordon had contracted by four days' marching. On November 6th the operation began, and the columns advanced from the circumference of a circle of a diameter of more than 150 miles in length. Six days later they drew up face to face at the appointed spot, having neither seen nor heard of any large hostile body, and with less than 100 prisoners amongst them all. Yet the plan and its execution, if they had failed to command success, had well deserved it. In spite of a hundred unforeseen difficulties the orders had been carried out as accurately as they had been drawn. Swollen rivers had baulked the arrangements of the commanders, heavy mists had blinded their scouts. In the obscured atmosphere the labour of deceiving the enemy was almost useless, yet it was faithfully borne. "No column marched straight upon its objective; some at times were actually moving away from it; and the marches of all were circuitous and misleading to a degree: yet none were late, and all reached their allotted points fresh and ready for the work which they hoped would ensue. . . . The results were less than the excellence of the work performed by officers and men deserved, and this was in a great measure due to accident."* Twenty-two Boers killed, ninety-eight captured, 200 wagons and 14,000 head of stock formed the total acquisitions of the thirteen columns. The Boers, in fact, had been so much more scattered than had been reported that many had drifted through the meshes without even being aware that a net had been thrown around them.

De Wet disperses. Every accident conspired to assist them. De Wet, finding supplies, and especially grass, insufficient to maintain a concentrated levy, had ordered another partial dispersal, and his detachments were now riding in all directions seeking pasture. By

---

* Lord Kitchener's despatch, December 8th, 1901.

EVENTS IN THE ORANGE RIVER COLONY.

pure good fortune their marches had led them out through the columns during the first three days of marching, when the gaps in the circle were still wide. Only one force of any strength had been sighted, when on the evening of November 9th some 400 men had passed between Elliot and Sir J. Dartnell moving south-eastward, to be quickly lost in the fog.

This effort concluded, all the units returned to the original points of departure except those of Rimington and Spens, who made for Frankfort and Standerton respectively. Even on the return marches only one column encountered a formed hostile body. On the morning of November 16th Byng and Wilson were boldly attacked in rear as they left bivouac at Jagersrust for the last day's march into Heilbron, and, hampered by an unwieldy mass of cattle and vehicles, had some difficulty in beating off their assailants. Eventually they handsomely repulsed the Boers, who left eight on the field and carried off many more, the casualties in the columns being an officer and man killed, three officers and nine men wounded, all of Kitchener's Fighting Scouts, which were ably handled by Wilson. Having arrived in Heilbron, Wilson resumed his task of guarding the construction of the blockhouse line, whilst Byng, going on to Vredefort Road, raided the Vaal basin about Lindequee, then came back to the railway at Kroonstad on November 24th.

Rimington and Damant entered Frankfort together on the 16th, only to quit it again still in company three days later for a joint foray down the valley of the Wilge in search of Commandant Buys, a noted leader who was reported from Headquarters to be in the neighbourhood. A party of South African Constabulary and Railway Pioneer regiment were detached to hold the drifts of the Vaal across the front. Buys was not on the Wilge, and Damant, whose special duty tied him to Frankfort, returned on the 19th. Rimington had a roving commission, and keeping out east of the Wilge, moved by Bendigo to Villiersdorp. Crossing the Vaal there on the 20th he then swung westward, and immediately came in touch with the enemy. On that morning a post of the Railway Pioneer regiment stationed at a drift at Bothaskraal had been rushed, and Rimington, sighting

Rimington's and Damant's operations.

a force on the march, found it to be the successful commando making off with its captives, some fifty in number, towards the Hex Rivier hills. At Rimington's approach the Boers scattered and fled, the prisoners were recovered, and shortly after the object of the operation, Buys himself, who had been wounded in the attack on the Railway Pioneer regiment, was discovered and captured as he was attempting to reach a hospital. Drawing supplies from Greylingstad, Rimington now for a short time covered the building of a line of blockhouses which was in progress from Greylingstad to Villiersdorp, taking eleven prisoners on the 22nd. Once more a combined operation was arranged with Damant, who, on the 23rd, drove northward from Frankfort towards Rimington, who lined the Vaal from Platkop to Villiersdorp. Few of the enemy were seen north of the Vaal, but Damant discovered several bands lurking beyond Perth, and accounted for sixteen Boers and eleven wagons before reaching Villiersdorp. Regaining Frankfort on the 24th, Damant was immediately despatched southward to follow a reported trail of De Wet. Six prisoners were the result of a night march to Houbaan and back to Frankfort on the 27th. Both Damant and Rimington, together with Wilson from Heilbron, were then ordered to conceal themselves near the Krom Spruit, in order to be able to descend suddenly southward, Rimington having news that De Wet was about to hold a Council of War in the midst of his forces half-way between Lindley and Reitz. This movement would also enable the columns to act effectively outside the right flank of Elliot in a manœuvre which must now be followed.

At the conclusion of the abortive convergence upon Paardehoek Elliot had returned to Harrismith on November 16th. Three days later he set out westward again, with orders to sweep back to Kroonstad by Bethlehem and Lindley, in conjunction with Sir J. Dartnell's and Sir L. Rundle's troops, who would hold the mountainous ground on both flanks for the first few stages of the march. Accordingly Sir J. Dartnell took the Imperial Light Horse brigade to Elands River Bridge; Reay moved to Witzies Hoek; Firman, with the 11th Imperial Yeo-

Elliot marches westward.

EVENTS IN THE ORANGE RIVER COLONY. 335

manry, to Oliviers Hoek Pass, and B. Campbell collected his long scattered troops at Fouriesburg to post them at Naauwpoort Nek, all on November 19th. On the same day Elliot pushed out Broadwood and de Lisle, both lightly equipped, towards the Brandwater basin, following himself two days later with Lowe and the transport of the whole division by the direct road to Bethlehem. Constant skirmishing attended the march, especially on the left where Broadwood, riding under the shadow of the mountains from Elands River Drift to the Roode Bergen, found himself almost beneath the rifles of sharpshooters perched upon the walls of every defile. He lost in this manner eight men on the 22nd. On the 23rd the three columns of Elliot's division concentrated east of Bethlehem, and Sir J. Dartnell's and Sir L. Rundle's troops turned to leave them and regain Harrismith; not, however, before the value of their assistance had been shown, for Dartnell was able not only to divert but to defeat an attack on the rear of Lowe's column as it drew on towards the others. Refilling their light wagons, Broadwood and de Lisle then pushed on through Bethlehem, Rimington, Wilson and Damant on the north, Byng in front, and Barker's and the other Winburg columns on the south-west all receiving orders to be on the alert both for fugitives and to cover Elliot's now open flanks.

After a night raid to Rexford by Broadwood, which just failed to secure Prinsloo's laager, Elliot's columns turned northward, Broadwood to Bankfontein, Lowe, now in the centre, to Rietpoort, de Lisle on the right to Middel Water. North-east of Lindley both flanks were engaged, and reports of several commandos were current. Nothing more was seen, however, than a few small laagers, several of which were taken, and on November 30th Elliot entered Kroonstad with eleven prisoners, 200 vehicles, 42,000 stock; heaps of destroyed farm stuff and implements marked his track across the veld. Towards the termination of his march, Rimington and Damant, as has been seen, came southward to Jagersrust, joining Wilson who had got touch with Elliot on November 27th. Rimington decided to test the truth of the report of De Wet's concentration by a

Rimington searches for De Wet.

surprise. On the 30th he pressed on to Spytfontein, ordering his convoy to follow on the Lindley—Heilbron road escorted by 250 mounted troops, 300 infantry and a gun under Major A. J. Bennett (New South Wales Mounted Rifles).

The accuracy of the information concerning De Wet was quickly proved. At the moment when Rimington ranged ahead across the Lindley—Reitz road, chasing groups of Boer scouts, De Wet was encamped close on his left front at Blydschap, with the commandos of General M. Prinsloo (Bethlehem), General Hattingh (Kroonstad) and Commandant H. Botha (Vrede) and others lying around him in scattered laagers. Hattingh was the first to espy the advancing troops, and sending word to De Wet, he circled round behind Rimington and attacked his wagons from right and rear. Soon after Prinsloo hurried up, and fell upon the left of the convoy, which was thus almost surrounded. The escort fought well, a troop of the 6th (Inniskilling) Dragoons especially distinguishing itself by a charge the leader of which, Second Lieutenant L. M. Oliver, was killed; but it must have gone hard with the convoy, which was now some seven miles behind the main body, had not a messenger despatched by Bennett safely reached Rimington with the news. The course of Rimington's pursuit had fortunately brought him at this moment back to the Lindley—Heilbron road about Groenvlei. The whole column immediately galloped back, and outflanking the attack, drove it off just as De Wet himself arrived on the field with the Vrede and Heilbron men. The Free State leader was now in superior strength, and he quickly restored order amongst his disconnected units. Expecting Rimington to make for Lindley, he disposed his commandos so as to envelop the road, and looked for another of those captures such as had marked this district as lucky ground for his arms. As his arrangements progressed, and Rimington appeared to be furthering his plans by advancing southward to Victoriaspruit, a torrential fall of rain brought both sides to a halt. The downpour continued until dark, and De Wet, whose extension had been interfered with by the storm, decided to postpone his attack until next day. He saw the British going into bivouac, and had so little doubt of their intention to march on Lindley, from which they were only five miles distant, that he placed no special outposts to keep watch on them. But Rimington had more than a suspicion of the dangers lying in wait for him. From a Boer scout captured at dusk he had learned the strength and composition of his opponents. Benson's fate exactly a month before had taught the risks attending isolated columns in the presence of a sudden concentration, and Rimington decided that for once he would adopt the only portion of his enemy's tactics in which he had not already excelled, that of evasion. Parading his column at 11.30 p.m. he marched all night, not to Lindley but northward towards Heilbron, leaving De Wet to marvel at his disappearance at dawn of December 1st. Rimington withdraws to Heilbron.

Approximate Strength States of Columns referred to in Foregoing Chapter.

COLUMN.	Mounted Troops.	Infantry.	Guns, including Vickers-Maxims.	Machine Guns.	
August—November, 1901.					
Lt.-Col. T. D. Pilcher (two columns)	1,182	—	5	1	} Major-General Sir C. Knox in command.
Lt.-Col. A. W. Thorneycroft	1,345	—	5	2	
Lt.-Col. C. St. G. Henry	542	260	3	1	
Lt.-Col. W. G. B. Western	641	211	3	—	
Major A. Paris	273	94	3	1	
Col. A. N. Rochfort	441	—	3	—	} Major-General Bruce Hamilton in command (later Col. Rochfort).
Lt.-Col. W. H. Williams	449	—	2	1	
Lt.-Col. the Hon. J. Byng	1,014	—	3	—	
Lt.-Col. L. E. du Moulin	—	600	3	—	
Lt.-Col. W. L. White	500	—	2	—	
Lt.-Col. A. Lowry-Cole	505	—	2	—	
Major A. C. Hamilton	504	—	3	—	
Major J. H. Damant	571	99	3	1	
Lt.-Col. J. G. W. Dawkins	659	—	3	—	
Major S. Bogle Smith	478	—	2	2	
Major G. N. Going	500	—	2	—	
Brig.-Gen. R. G. Broadwood	815	—	5	3	} Lieut.-General E. L. Elliot in command.
Col. E. C. Bethune (later Col. Lowe)	1,618	—	5	2	
Lt.-Col. H. de B. de Lisle	1,005	—	3	2	
Maj.-Gen. B. B. R. Campbell	357	1,204	5	2	} Lieut.-General Sir L. Rundle in command.
Col. G. E. Harley	275	610	3	2	
Lt.-Col. C. T. Reay	254	605	3	2	
Col. F. S. Garratt	900	269	5	1	
Brig.-Gen. G. M. Bullock	—	1,200	2	2	
Lt.-Col. M. F. Rimington	1,530	262	5	—	
Major H. d'A. P. Taylor	726	—	2	1	
Major C. F. Minchin	695	—	3	2	
Major K. E. Lean	477	—	3	1	
Major F. C. Lloyd	210	—	—	—	
Lt.-Col. H. C. Copeman	457	—	2	—	
Major J. E. Pine-Coffin (later Holmes)	834	50	3	1	
Lt.-Col. J. S. S. Barker	500	—	3	—	
Col. Sir J. Jervis-White-Jervis	360	—	—	—	} Brig.-General H. C. O. Plumer in command.
Major F. C. Lloyd	210	—	—	—	
Lt.-Col. F. F. Colvin	410	—	5	—	
Col. Sir H. Rawlinson	1,095	185	4	—	
Lt.-Col. Lord Basing	500	—	3	1	
Lt.-Col. the Hon. A. Murray	250	—	2	1	} Major-General A. FitzR. Hart directing.
Lt.-Col. M. G. Moore	250	250	—	1	
Brig.-Gen. J. Spens	1,119	—	8	—	
Lt.-Col. A. E. Wilson	600	—	—	2	
Lt.-Col. C. J. Briggs	635	—	3	—	} Brig.-General Sir J. Dartnell in command.
Lt.-Col. D. McKenzie	677	—	—	1	
Lt.-Col. A. H. M. Edwards	800†	—	—	—	
Lt.-Col. W. B. Hickie	642	152	5	1	

† South African Constabulary.

CHAPTER XIX.

EVENTS IN THE WESTERN TRANSVAAL*

(Continued from Chapter XVI.).

NOVEMBER, 1901—JANUARY, 1902.

EARLY in November, 1901, Lord Methuen and Kekewich were once more on the move towards each other by the now familiar routes. Withdrawn from an area in which he had made so excellent a start, and where there was still much left to do, Kekewich passed through Olifants Nek on the 4th, was at Naauwpoort on the 5th and 6th, and spent the next few days searching for Lord Methuen along the Zeerust road. Not until the 10th was indirect signalling communication by Magato Nek (or Hoek) gained with Lord Methuen, who, having left Zeerust on November 5th, had marched in pursuit of bands of freebooters and small convoys (nine prisoners) by the Zwart Ruggens to Lindleys Poort (November 10th). On the next day the two commanders joined forces at Brakfontein, to find that all combined work against De la Rey in the north was to be suspended in favour of a movement into the Klerksdorp area, whence Hickie, then engaged in covering the blockhouse building on the Schoon Spruit, had signalled that large bodies of the enemy were massing to the west and north-west of him. Accordingly both columns turned southward, Kekewich by Vlakfontein and Rietfontein to Ventersdorp which he reached on the 15th, on which day Lord Methuen, who travelled by Zuurfontein and Rietpan, had a sharp affair of patrols at Sterkfontein. Three days later both columns marched into Klerksdorp. Meanwhile Hickie, on the

_{Lord Methuen and Kekewich in combination.}

* See map No. 59.

13th, had sustained a serious loss at Brakspruit by the destruction of two squadrons of Imperial Yeomanry whom he had sent to reconnoitre northward, seven men being killed, twelve wounded and sixty-four officers and men captured. Both Lord Methuen and Kekewich remained at Klerksdorp until November 26th. Then, with Kekewich and Hickie on his right flank, Lord Methuen moved out westward through Hartebeestfontein. A number of Boers made off from that prolific hive as he approached, some of whom were overtaken next day (27th) at Kliprif, where seven Boers with eleven carts of their convoy were taken. That the enemy was in greater strength close by was proved when the convoy, taking a different route from that of the main column, was greeted with a hot fusilade as it approached some kopjes on Leeuwfontein. A general stampede of the draught animals ensued, seventy-seven horses were lost, two men wounded and eleven others injured by the unmanageable wagons.

On the 28th, still heading westward and marching by night, Lord Methuen had another minor success. Once more the rear of the Boer convoy, lingering at Kleinplaats, was caught up after a smart gallop and captured by Lord Methuen's scouting corps and the 19th Imperial Yeomanry, who brought back to Headquarters eight prisoners, eleven carts and wagons, and some horses, mules and stock cattle. From Kleinplaats Lord Methuen bent south-westward through Klipdrift to Tweepannen, where he checked his westward march and turned back towards Klerksdorp. Nearing Rooipoort, on the Makwasi Spruit, on December 1st further small convoys were sighted by one part or another of Lord Methuen's front, which covered nearly ten miles of the veld; nearly all those seen were portions of Liebenberg's transport, and were duly ridden down, the results of the day being nineteen prisoners, four carts and wagons, 9,000 head of stock, and nearly 150 horses, mules and donkeys. On December 4th Lord Methuen was again in Klerksdorp, bringing with him thirty-six prisoners, sixty-six wagons and carts, 14,000 head of stock, 200 draught animals, and much farm produce, many more tons having been destroyed on the way.

EVENTS IN THE WESTERN TRANSVAAL. 341

Meanwhile Kekewich, in occasional touch with Lord Methuen, had also been operating westward, circling chiefly about Hartebeestfontein from Geduld down to Rhenosterspruit and Yzerspruit. The sighting of a number of Boer patrols and rearguards proved the presence of a considerable force in the neighbourhood; but it always eluded approach, and on December 3rd Kekewich returned to Klerksdorp with three prisoners and a mass of booty. A week's rest at Klerksdorp refitted both Lord Methuen's and Kekewich's columns for the field, and on December 11th they once more moved out westward in combination. This time Lord Methuen's aim was the Makwasie Berg, north-east of Wolmaranstad, a range some twelve miles long by one mile broad, and difficult to search from its rugged and woody nature. In its recesses lurked the Wolmaranstad commando, led by Potgieter, under whose protection a great number of refugees and cattle were reported to be in hiding. On December 12th Kekewich, moving wide on Lord Methuen's right, reached Korannafontein, assisting Lord Methuen's movements by keeping from his flank a band of 300 Boers under Vermaas who were coming down through Witpoort. On the 13th a brisk affair, which cost Kekewich two officers and eight men wounded, was necessary to drive these away. Lord Methuen was at Palmietfontein on the 12th on the northern flank of the Makwasie. No enemy were encountered here, but the mounted troops, pushing on westward the same night, discovered a convoy on the move well to the west of Wolmaranstad. Lord Methuen immediately pursued, and after a seven-mile gallop on the 13th ran down and captured near Kareepan twenty-two wagons and carts, 3,000 head of stock, 130 draught animals, together with fourteen Boers who had been guarding them. These were a portion of Potgieter's transport. On the 15th, Kekewich having advanced to Klipdrift and Rooipoort, Lord Methuen swung southward to Kareepoort, in which direction it was reported that Potgieter's column had gone. He was not there, however, and had evidently doubled back into the Makwasie Berg, which the column had so far only skirted. Lord Methuen, having beaten up the outskirts, now decided to draw through the main covert.

Sending his divisional scouting corps to Leeuwfontein (southwest of Wolmaranstad), to block escape from the south, he requested Kekewich to come in nearer from the north, whilst he himself entered the range. Kekewich failed to receive these instructions, as did Lord Methuen likewise a despatch from him ; nevertheless, his movement on Palmietfontein on the 16th exactly coincided with the requirements of Lord Methuen's tactics, more especially as Kekewich, rightly appreciating the situation, demonstrated widely athwart the northern arm of the range, from Uitkyk on the west to his camp at Palmietfontein, effectually anticipating any northerly break-away. Lord Methuen's Leeuwfontein detachment scored the first success. Their retrograde march in the direction of Wolmaranstad had taken Potgieter by surprise, for tracking Lord Methuen as far as Kareepan, he had imagined him to be travelling westward. He had, therefore, as Lord Methuen soon discovered, turned back to his stronghold in the Makwasie Berg, and, being now in no haste, had allowed the rear of his transport to remain near Leeuwfontein. There on December 10th it was discovered by Major B. W. Cowan and the divisional scouting corps, who secured the whole, namely, ten prisoners, 5,000 sheep, and a number of vehicles. The southerly and westerly exits thus barred, on the 17th Lord Methuen made sure of the east with von Donop's and the mounted troops, and with 300 infantry advanced into the Makwasie. He found success unexpectedly easy. So close had his sudden turn northward brought him on to the heels of the Boers, that they had neither time nor courage to organise opposition along the formidable faces of the hills. A good track admitted the column into the innermost recesses of their stronghold. Soon the whole range was alive with stampeding burghers and cattle, and by evening Lord Methuen halted at Klippan with sixteen prisoners, 26,000 head of stock, 130 wagons, and 289 spare draught animals, the captures including the family of Potgieter himself. On the 18th Lord Methuen started to return to Klerksdorp, captured four more Boers on the 19th, and on the 20th re-entered Klerksdorp with thirty-six prisoners, 161

EVENTS IN THE WESTERN TRANSVAAL. 343

vehicles, 36,000 stock, 480 spare draught animals, and more than a quarter of a million pounds of grain. Kekewich, after his comparatively uneventful but most useful manœuvres more to the north, came into Klerksdorp on the same day with only one prisoner but a considerable quantity of stock and stuffs in his train. Lord Methuen and Kekewich in Klerksdorp Dec. 20th – 28th, 1901.

It cannot fail to have been remarked what hosts of cattle and sheep, masses of grain, farm implements, grinding mills, etc., the various columns brought in or destroyed upon the veld from time to time. Lord Methuen's short raid described above was but one of hundreds which had been and still were in progress all over the theatre of war, sometimes with less results, often with greater. In view of the vast quantities of provender thus accounted for, the statement that South Africa was a sparsely supplied and inhospitable country may be held to be belied. Nevertheless, for regular troops, moving, as they must, slowly and in compact bodies, it must be repeated that few countries could have been worse provided than South Africa. Only guerrillas, speedy, able to carry much on the saddle, and with an intimate knowledge of the country, could have subsisted, as did the Boers, on the widely disseminated resources of the veld farms. Yet the aggregate of such sustenance was of course incalculable; a tally merely of that burned by the columns would provide melancholy evidence of the destructive powers of war. The attempt to despoil the whole sub-continent—and the campaign had for some time resolved itself into nothing less than this—revealed both the charity of Nature to men who aided her so feebly as the Boer farmers, and the ruinous industry of the British columns; for enormous as were the stores of foodstuffs scattered over the veld, they were being surely whittled down. The time was drawing nigh when the whole Boer nation was to lie exhausted, not in spirit but in body. The task was long, and was not yet ended: the General who is compelled to grind the mill of destruction upon the provisions of an enemy whom he can rarely reach with the sword has taken a slow weapon into his hands. Nevertheless, it is a sure one; and every long train of captured stock and wagons brought into The supplies of the veld.

camp by the columns, and every wheat-field left burnt and black upon the veld was a drop indenting the stone which had so often turned, and sometimes shivered, the steel.

For the third time Lord Methuen and Kekewich sallied in company westward from Klerksdorp on December 28th, and once more the target was the Makwasie Berg and Wolmaranstad. A repetition of the tactics which had been successful ten days before found the hills nearly empty. Only Potgieter himself with a few followers broke away northward. Reconnaissance, however, disclosed the tracks of a much larger body which had disappeared in the opposite direction, and following these up, Lord Methuen withdrew out of all touch with Kekewich, passed through Schweizer Reneke on January 1st, 1902, and on the 6th entered Vryburg on the western line, having picked up nine prisoners, 8,000 head of sheep and cattle, and six wagons and carts.

<small>Lord Methuen at Vryburg, Jan. 6th, 1902.</small>

Kekewich, blocking, as before, the northern exits of the Makwasie Berg, on the 29th had vainly endeavoured to intercept Potgieter as he ran from the other column, which came in sight on the south. Thereafter communication with Lord Methuen ceased as the latter hurried westward, and Kekewich, completely at a loss as to his whereabouts, was obliged to forego the prearranged combination. He found, however, plenty to do in dealing with the bands which roved around his column and infested his camping grounds as soon as he had quitted them. One of these he outwitted on January 2nd by leaving a party concealed on the deserted ground, seven Boers being wounded and captured a few moments later. Still hoping to be of assistance to Lord Methuen, who should have been now at Doornbult, Kekewich moved to Holfontein on the 2nd. During the march the enemy avenged his mischance of the morning by setting an ambush for the scouts. Of an officer and the thirteen foremost troopers who rode into the midst of 250 Boers, six were wounded in the course of a hard fight, which ended in the capture of all. Kekewich now received warning that De la Rey and Kemp were close to the northward, and with Moedwil in his mind he doubly guarded his bivouacs. He

<small>Kekewich loses touch with Lord Methuen,</small>

EVENTS IN THE WESTERN TRANSVAAL. 345

still moved forward however, keeping to the north of the route which was to have been taken by the vanished column of Lord Methuen, until, wearying of the chase, and hearing that De la Rey was no nearer than between Tafel Kop and Lichtenburg, he turned on January 4th back for Ventersdorp, which he reached and enters on January 9th, having taken twenty-six prisoners, 7,000 beasts, twelve carts and wagons since starting out on December 27th.

Ten days earlier Tafel Kop had at last been denied to the enemy by the establishment upon it of a fortified post of the Suffolk regiment from Naauwpoort. The work of construction had been covered by Hickie's force. After seeing the Tafel Kop garrison securely seated, Hickie then protected the building of a line of blockhouses from the Kop down to Ventersdorp. The whole district was at this time busy in the erection of these chains of fortifications, Lieut.-Colonel Sir R. Colleton (Royal Welsh Fusiliers) being thus employed upon the line of the Vaal to Bothaville; Lieut.-Colonel G. N. Mayne (King's Own Scottish Borderers) from Ventersdorp to the Mooi river; Lieut.-Colonel G. F. C. Mackenzie (Suffolk regiment) upon the previously mentioned line from Ventersdorp to Tafel Kop. Space only permits of the briefest reference to the work of several small columns circulating in various parts of the Western Transvaal during the last quarter of 1901. On the Kimberley side a force under Colonel St. G. C. Henry had accounted for seventy prisoners in many forays since September. In the previous month a creditable action had been fought by the escort to a convoy under Major J. F. Humby which, proceeding with supplies towards Griquatown, had been determinedly attacked on August 24th in very much the same manner as von Donop in October.* Only Humby's promptness in laagering his wagons, and the good conduct of his troops (Imperial Yeomanry and Northumberland Fusiliers), who fought through an entire night, saved the whole from capture. The convoy was safely brought into Griquatown with the loss of ten killed and twenty-four wounded. In September a force from Vryburg, under Lieut.-Colonel W. H. E. Murray, captured twenty-three prisoners in a dashing attack on

marginal notes: and enters Ventersdorp. Blockhouse building. Minor columns in the west.

* See Chapter XVI.

superior numbers entrenched at Devondale, which cost him exactly the same number of casualties as the enemy.

Another praiseworthy affair in this part was that conducted by Lieut.-Colonel R. L. Milne towards the end of November. Ordered to proceed with a provision column to Schweizer Reneke on the 20th with 129 mounted men, 330 infantry and two guns, Milne found his progress opposed from the first, being finally intercepted by a strong body when a day's march from his objective. Eluding these by a flank march, he entered Schweizer Reneke on November 25th. Two days later he started to return, and though by disseminating false information he kept off the enemy's largest bodies, he had to fight sharply at O'Reilly's Pan to get back into Vryburg, which he reached on the 30th. The repulse of a band of 150 Boers two days earlier by a small blockhouse near Pitsani commanded by Sergeant H. Waring (1st Loyal North Lancashire regiment) also deserves mention in connection with the western line.

Nearer the centre of operations about the middle of September a small column was formed at Bank, under Lieut.-Colonel H. T. Hicks (Royal Dublin Fusiliers), with the object of supplying and covering the South African Constabulary in the Gatsrand and Los Berg. Hicks was out until October 11th, during which time he cleared the Venterskroon and Parys districts, and took a 7-pr. gun and some score of prisoners, amongst them a commandant, before returning to resume command of the garrison at Krugersdorp. He was also instrumental in procuring the surrender of twenty-seven burghers. Co-operating with Hicks, parties under Lieut.-Colonel J. E. Capper and Major C. Howard, both officers of the Railway Pioneer regiment, had been working about Lindequee blockhousing the drifts over the Vaal from October 1st onwards. This district continued to be disturbed throughout the rest of the year. Early in December an alarm that the Schoeman's Drift post was cut off drew Hickie from Klerksdorp and McMicking from Vereeniging to its assistance, and although they found the post surrounded more by water than by the enemy, the Vaal being in high flood and impassable, there were undoubtedly strong bands in its vicinity,

EVENTS IN THE WESTERN TRANSVAAL.

and constant skirmishes occurred. On December 19th G. G. Cunningham, who was commanding the Irene—Wolvehoek section of communications, organised a force of 400 officers and men* which he took into the angle between the Vaal, the Rhenoster and the central railway. On December 21st he attacked the hills south of Lindequee from two directions, and cleared them with the loss of fourteen officers and men. The enemy was then heard of in greater force near Reitzburg, and on the 23rd Cunningham reconnoitred in this direction, finding a strong position in front of him at Leeuwdoorns. The brisk skirmishing entailed by a successful movement against the foothills entailed seven casualties. Cunningham's wagons were now empty, and he paused to await the arrival of co-operating forces from Witkoppies and Kerr's Drift on the Rhenoster river. These arrived under command of Lieut.-Colonel the Hon. A. E. Dalzell (Oxfordshire Light Infantry) on Christmas Day, and on the 26th the Leeuwdoorn hills were cleared after a long day's close but inexpensive fighting. At Witbank on the Vaal next day the commando narrowly escaped being surrounded, but, escaping with the loss of four burghers, it broke up into two bands, one of which ran southward past Reitzburg, the other up the Vaal towards Parys. Whilst Dalzell pursued the first, Cunningham followed the latter, and both so hustled the fugitives that by the end of December Cunningham was able to report the district clear. His casualties during the operations had been three men killed, two officers and nine men wounded. Dalzell's assistance had been as energetic as it was timely. Both on December 27th and 28th he sharply engaged the enemy, driving them in succession from Rensburgs Drift and through Bothaville, which he thoroughly cleared. These, though many minor and often profitable affairs and expeditions must be omitted, are all that can be here recorded. To describe the skirmishes of every patrol, the attack on every blockhouse, the fighting at every drift, would fill many pages with tales of adventure which must be left to oblivion.

* McMicking's M.I., Royal Irish Rifles M.I., Reynolds' and Richardson's South African Constabulary, 4th Railway Pioneer regiment M.I.

Situation in the west at the end of 1901.

The campaign in the Western Transvaal at the close of 1901 was somewhat in a state of suspension. The enemy, shouldered away by lines of blockhouses, harried out of the best tactical positions by the incessant traffic of the columns, was little to be heard of along the usual routes or within hail of the lines of communication. Nevertheless, it was felt rather than known that he was by no means mastered. Somewhere out on the western veld there still roved leaders whose names might yet sound the rally in every Boer laager and the alarm in every British camp. In spite of the lull the Commander-in-Chief was well aware that scarce one of his columns, garrisons or posts between Rustenburg, Klerksdorp, Vryburg and Mafeking but was in daily risk of extinction. Such, however, must always be the uneasy position of the opponent of guerrillas. Though the general situation be never so safe, at any moment the wire, the telephone, the heliograph may bring him disagreeable surprises; but he is unfortunate indeed if they convey what would be the greatest surprise of all—that the enemy had achieved a success great enough to affect the issue of the campaign.

APPROXIMATE STRENGTH STATES OF COLUMNS REFERRED TO IN FOREGOING CHAPTER.

COLUMN.	Mounted Troops.	Infantry.	Guns, including Vickers-Maxims.	Machine Guns.
November, 1901—January, 1902.				
Lt.-Gen. Lord Methuen	1,325	600	13	2
Lt.-Col. S. B. von Donop	680	330	7	—
Col. W. B. Hickie	673	193	6	1
Col. R. G. Kekewich	853	1,020	5	2
Col. St. G. C. Henry	541	175	3	1
Lt.-Col. H. T. Hicks	250	560	3	1
Lt.-Col. R. L. Milne	129	330	2	—
Maj. H. McMicking	300	180	2	—
Brig.-Gen. G. G. Cunningham	400	—	2	1
Lt.-Col. the Hon. A. E. Dalzell	450	—	1	1

CHAPTER XX.

EVENTS IN THE NORTH-WEST AND WEST OF CAPE COLONY.*

APRIL—DECEMBER, 1901.

IT was characteristic of the limitations of the military talent of the Boers that the real joint in the strategic armour of Cape Colony remained undiscovered until the weapon which might have pierced it had been broken. In its midland and eastern parts the British province could never have been in extreme danger from such forces as the Boer States were able to bring against it from the end of 1900 onwards ; the country was too difficult, the barriers too numerous, the hostile communications, lengthy though they were, too well guarded, and the objectives too few. It was comparatively easy for the British commanders to cut up the terrain into so many enclosures, and so quickly to transfer the fencing, that the commandos, though they might long escape actual arrest, were always either in prison or flying from one *corral* to another. True, a more intelligent and coherent plan of campaign might have done much in the earlier days of the invasion ; but it must have eventually perished on one of the many ranges which barred the way to the sea. Moreover, even supposing that the Boer commandos should have pitched their laagers upon the coastline from Cape Agulhas to East London, Cape Colony, for all its rebellion, would still not have been theirs. The heart of the country beat elsewhere, and not only the British but the Boer heart. In Cape Town alone, and in the country immediately north of it, lay the true Republican forces, forces far more potent than the sentimental

<small>Strategical errors of the Boers in Cape Colony.</small>

---

* See map No. 63.

vapourings of Graaff Reinet—the forces of money, brains, organisation and a statesmanship only awaiting the proper hour to reveal itself, and astute enough not to emerge at all if that hour should never strike. If in Natal there had been no hope at all —for not the fall of Ladysmith, of Pietermaritzburg, or of Durban itself would have wrested that little community from the British flag—in Cape Colony there was but one hope, and one way to it. Only the capture, or even the investment, of Cape Town would have fired the sluggish but enormous explosive of rebellion lying dormant in Cape Colony; and the military road to Cape Town ran not within sight of the Indian but the Atlantic Ocean. Of all the many invaders, then, up to the time to which this narration has been brought, Hertzog alone had opened the Boer game aright. But weak, unsupported and timid as he had been, looking back to the Orange for De Wet rather than forward to his best reinforcements—the unawakened commandos of the western farmsteads—he had proved the least instead of the most dangerous of the disturbers of Cape Colony. Small rebellions, it is true, had followed, but they were equally aimless, and even less daring. Such were those of J. F. Froneman in Kenhardt and A. Van Niekerk in Calvinia. It was not until the middle of April that a leader appeared with an eye to see and an arm to wield the potentialities of a campaign in the west.

Maritz assumes command in the north-west; April, 1901.

This was the already referred to Commandant S. G. Maritz, an officer selected from the staff of Scheepers at the time when that leader was beginning his career of adventure upon the mountain staircases between the Cape Town and Port Elizabeth railways. Maritz, with four companions, made the long and hazardous journey to the north-west, some 300 miles, in safety, and in the middle of April appeared first in Brandvlei and next in Kakamas. He found the field not only untilled but actually impoverished by his predecessors. Hertzog had done no more than rob it of its most valuable military asset, its horseflesh; the others, by their high-handed conduct and incapacity, had disgusted hundreds who had been all for the cause. Maritz himself was a leader after the burghers' own heart. Physically of great strength, recklessly brave, a fine rider and shot, he had in addition those qualities of friendliness, patience and sympathy without which none could successfully command men who both in their own eyes and those of the law were his equals as much in the field as in the farm. His first act was to degrade the hated Froneman, who appealed in vain to the votes of the men whom he had mishandled. His next was to return to Brandvlei and take the offensive against the only British force in the district. This was the column of Major H. S. Jeudwine, R.A., which, as already related,* had moved from De Aar, in strength 420 men, of whom fifty were infantry, with two guns, on April 20th. On May 12th Jeudwine entered Brandvlei, having improvised his supply and transport in the face of great difficulties at Van Wyks Vlei. Moving upon Brandvlei from the south, in order to keep the Boer bands above him, Jeudwine encountered on the way only one of Maritz's patrols at Nelskop. The march from De Aar, indeed, had been no secret; from the moment he left the railway Jeudwine had been dogged by a party of Boer officers, under a Commandant E. Conroy, who were on their way to join Maritz at Brandvlei. Whilst Jeudwine was occupied at Van Wyks Vlei this band hovered on his communications in observation, but Conroy, as soon as he was certain that Jeudwine was marching upon Brandvlei, hurried thither, outriding the column. Maritz, who was unprepared to encounter an opponent of such strength, emptied the town of its inhabitants, goods and stock, and himself fell away twenty miles to the south of Nelskop, on which he left the afore-mentioned patrol to amuse Jeudwine. Soon after Maritz turned this enforced evasion both to his profit and prestige. Waylaying at Melkboschfontein two detachments of Calvinia district troops, he captured both, and though nearly all the prisoners subsequently contrived to escape, the, to the Boers, more valuable portion of the booty, consisting of several carts and wagons and 15,000 rounds of ammunition, remained in Maritz's hands. On the next day Jeudwine more than equalised matters by capturing on the Klaver Vlei road sixteen men of the Nelskop patrol, with

British troops in the north-west under Jeudwine; April, 1901.

* See Chapter XIII.

twenty vehicles and nearly 7,000 head of stock. Nevertheless, Maritz's easily earned success confirmed his ascendancy over his raw rebels. Especially did they admire the skill with which he had avoided the main British column, for, as with all men who fight as felons, the prospect of the penalties of unsuccessful fighting caused them to dread any encounter in which victory was uncertain. Unlike regular combatants, rebels, however numerous, are usually weakest in spirit at the opening of their campaign. Maritz knew this well. For weeks following this success he nursed both his followers and their friends by harmless but incessant marches over all the north-west, visiting as many farms as possible, and generally creating an impression of ubiquitous power in every homestead from Kenhardt down to Calvinia. Conroy he had early sent up to Kakamas to organise the numerous but vacillating rebels there, with what success will be referred to later.

<small>Maritz scours the country.</small>

Meanwhile Jeudwine moved to Tontelbosch Kolk on May 16th, and to Loeries Fontein a week later, hearing much but seeing little of the enemy. Thence his information took him first to Klaver Vlei, on to Katkop, then back to Klaver Vlei on June 1st, the troops and transport performing prodigies of marching over the almost impassable tracks. From Klaver Vlei he reconnoitred westward without result; then, on June 6th, converged once more on Brandvlei, which Maritz was reported to have re-entered two days before. The commando was not there, however, and Jeudwine, whose animals were now becoming exhausted, made for Tontelbosch Kolk, intending to rest them amid the good grazing ground. Arriving there on June 8th he was immediately drawn out again by news of Maritz at Loeries Fontein, but a forced march of fifty-four miles in twenty-four hours once more brought the troops upon an empty nest. A last effort against a reported laager fifteen miles further on proved equally fruitless, and Jeudwine then took his weary men and beasts into Calvinia to rest and refit, arriving there on June 16th. Once more his respite was brief. On the 18th the interruption of the telegraph to the post at Nieuwoudtville, forty-eight miles west of Calvinia, warned him of the enemy's

EVENTS IN N.-W. AND W. OF CAPE COLONY. 353

presence in that direction. Nieuwoudtville was held by but a dozen men, whose fate was certain without speedy relief. At 3 p.m. Jeudwine set out with all the troops he could mount, 200 in all, and marching all night through pouring rain and pitchy darkness, appeared before the place exactly twenty-four hours later. There at last he found the enemy, engaged in feebly beleaguering the handful of defenders. But still it was not the commando of Maritz, but that of a certain Commandant A. Louw, a rebel farmer of Calvinia, who had joined Maritz during his brief visit to Brandvlei in the first week of June, only to quarrel with and separate from him almost as soon as the two had met. Maritz himself was in the Bokkeveld mountains, south-west of Loeries Fontein, and thither Jeudwine, after driving off Louw, followed and found him with his patrols on June 21st. Thereafter he was constantly in touch, and on the 25th nearly forced the commando to an engagement at Gannenbosch. But Maritz was more bent on canvassing the district for recruits than on battle ; his fighting material was still untempered, his men had as yet learned little more than scouting, and the Commandant desired above all things not to alarm them and their families by losses in action. Though he was almost impregnably posted, he therefore declined a serious encounter, and instead led off his men on one of those extraordinary marches which had already taught them to respect him as one of their ideal leaders, one who conquered by speed and endurance rather than by the clumsy resort of battle. For 200 miles he rode without a halt, not for any fixed objective, but on a roaming, ringing course, first north-easterly through Tontelbosch Kolk, thence south-easterly to Williston, then west again past Calvinia, next into the valley of the Fish river, which he followed to the borders of Sutherland, finally, having thrown out the chase, settling into laager in a rich valley below the Roggeveld. He was now once more joined by Louw with a following of sixty-six burghers, and the two rested together for a few days.

Maritz refuses to fight.

Jeudwine had followed as fast as he was able. On July 2nd he reached Williston, where he captured a piquet which Maritz had apparently forgotten. On the 8th Jeudwine, after a sixty-eight-mile march, halted at Harde Heuvel. He was then called to Grahamstown on urgent civil business, and handing over command to Lieut.-Colonel T. Capper, temporarily bade adieu to the column which he had led for 1,150 miles in fifty-four days' marching, an average of over twenty-one miles a day, in the face of incredible difficulties of supply, transport and conditions of road. Capper was as unable as his predecessor to close with Maritz. Encumbered by guns and transport, his camps always overlooked from the precipices by which he was surrounded, he could do no more than obtain intermittent sight of the enemy, who fled, as active and as unhampered as goats, over the heights at the first appearance of danger. By devious ways Maritz approached within striking distance of Sutherland, around which he wove a network of small bands composed of local rebels, who watched every approach. Especially did he reconnoitre towards the Cape Town railway, the party-wall between himself and the midlands of Cape Colony; and this not so much in apprehension of his adversary as in expectation of his friends, for the time was drawing near when the sole strategically sound combination of all the Boer operations in Cape Colony was to be inaugurated. It was to this end that Maritz, denying himself the hazards of combat, had been industriously sowing tares of disloyalty amongst the sparse enough British wheat in the north-west. As yet, however, neither the crop nor the time were ripe; only half the road to Cape Town had been proved, and Attorney-General J. C. Smuts, the leader commissioned to reap the fruits of Maritz's industry as of that of all the other forerunners in Cape Colony, might well, as he perforce did,* delay his advent for a time. For the remainder of July Maritz remained in the vicinity of Sutherland, communicating freely with Scheepers, then gyrating in the Camdeboo† hills, whom he urged to come over to aid in the work of preparation. Less fortune attended his attempts to consult with De Wet, his despatch riders being captured on the road.

Early in August Maritz, having thoroughly investigated

---

* See Chapters XIV. and XV.   † See Chapter XIII.

EVENTS IN N.-W. AND W. OF CAPE COLONY.

Sutherland, made another of his wonderful marches, as long, as swift, as sinuous and as sudden as flashes of lightning, which marked him as one of the most able masters of man and horse who had yet appeared upon the veld. Rushing down the Tanqua Vallei, he swung northward at its junction with the Doorn river, and traversing half Calvinia, drew rein where the Bokkeveld mountains stand on the borders of Van Rhyns Dorp county. His recruiting had now outstepped his stores, and he was much in need of arms, ammunition, and supplies, and of the latter especially horseshoes, which wasted fast under such travelling as he imposed upon them. An attempt on a convoy making for the town of Van Rhyns Dorp miscarried, whereupon Maritz decided to possess the town itself. On August 7th he secured it, with all its contents and twenty-nine prisoners of the Western Province Mounted Rifles, retiring almost immediately to the Bokkeveld with forty rifles, six cases of ammunition, sixty-five horses, 300 carts, and three wagon loads of stores. Capper, following at his best pace, was in Van Rhyns Dorp four days after the Boers; but he was then drawn out to Clanwilliam by the necessity of guarding the approaches to Cape Town, a measure rendered advisable by the presence therein of the Heir to the British Throne, who had touched at the capital on his return voyage from India. Maritz, left untroubled in his mountains, made eastward at his leisure, and after a visit to the Hantam's Berg, went into laager at Brandwacht, near to his old hunting ground between Loeries Fontein and Tontelbosch Kolk.

Capture of Van Rhyns Dorp.

During the rest of August little was done on either side. Maritz had all to gain by delay, whilst Capper, even when released from Clanwilliam, was not only too numerically weak for active operations, but of the men he had, many had lost much of their efficiency from a strange cause. These were colonial troops, who, taking service originally for three months, found themselves still in the field after fifteen, and they did not scruple to assist towards the further prolongation of a campaign undertaken largely for their own salvation, some by active and some by that passive resistance to orders which can nullify the efforts of a commander as effectually as open mutiny. Jeudwine, it should be said, had returned to the west on August 8th, but there being an intention to fit out a second force for him, Capper remained in actual command. Jeudwine merely accompanied the column, serving of his own free will as Staff Officer to a force of which, but for an accident, he would still have retained the leadership. On the last day of the month Capper, after escorting a convoy into Calvinia, made a determined attempt to bring Maritz to book. Hiding by day and marching by night he actually surrounded the site of the laager at Brandwacht. But still the fortune of war was on the side of the enemy. A number of the burghers, led by Maritz himself, happened to be absent on a distant reconnaissance. They neither knew nor learned anything of Capper's approach until, on riding back towards their camp, they suddenly discovered that they were behind the British force. Maritz immediately despatched messengers by different roads to attempt to pass the column and warn the commando. Only one of these contrived to get in, but it was enough. Led by a Free State officer named Rudolph, the commando succeeded in galloping through a narrow and closing gap in the encircling troops, and thus escaped when on the very verge of being shut in. Only a few stragglers and fifty ponies remained to reward the skill and perseverance of the column and its leaders. Capper then received orders to march to Ceres, which was reached on September 15th. A fortnight later, after a vain attempt to intercept Theron's westerly movement, Capper was moved to Piquetberg Road station, and thence—Maritz's strategy becoming clearer—to Moorreesburg, where he lay until October 15th, barring the road to Cape Town to commandos reputed to number 1,200 strong. Meanwhile Maritz returned to the Bokkeveld, and thence to Van Rhyns Dorp. His reputation was higher than ever. Daily fresh bodies of recruits joined him from the districts under his control. The most considerable of these was a band of 120 collected in Sutherland by one of Maritz's staff officers, one Piet De Wet; another strong posse answered the call of Rudolph in Gries, a strategic post at the junction of the roads from Ookiep, Port Nolloth and Hondeklip Bay, which

Capper at close quarters with Maritz.

EVENTS IN N.-W. AND W. OF CAPE COLONY.

Maritz did not fail to occupy. This success was timely, for now was in sight the harvesting of the crop which he had sown and so long tended. Smuts was already in Cape Colony, and one by one the various Boer commanders might be expected to appear to the west of the Cape Town railway, to add their weight at last to a scientific blow at the British hold upon Cape Colony.

The Boer plan of campaign has already been referred to. It was drawn in broad and imposing lines. Whilst Smuts himself descended upon Port Elizabeth, Maritz, strengthened on his inner flank in Ceres by Scheepers, Theron and all the group of leaders who had embroiled the midland counties, would move upon Cape Town by Clanwilliam, Piquetberg and Malmesbury. Strategy of such a scope, more fitted to armies than to guerrilla bands, was indeed, with the materials now available, a *limbus fatuorum*. It presupposed much that was unlikely, or even impossible—that Smuts should fare triumphantly where De Wet and all others had failed; that the various units should enter upon it in fighting condition; that the scheme should materialise unobserved by the British, though it threatened the very vitals of their colony. It has been described how Smuts did in fact fare; how he and those of the lesser leaders who survived counted themselves fortunate when they reeled broken across the railway with a few exhausted followers, seeking safety at the side of Maritz rather than affording him support. Nevertheless, by the beginning of October, 1901, the storm-centre had definitely shifted from east to west, moving with a concentration of purpose which rendered it for the first time dangerous. It now lay over the vast plateau which is bounded on the north by the Orange river, on the east by the railway from the Orange down to Beaufort West, on the south by the line of the Doorn and Tanqua rivers, and their prolongation the Koms Berg and Nieuwveld ranges, on the west by the Kobe and Bokkeveld mountains, east of Van Rhyns Dorp. Over all this tract Maritz had hauled down the British and planted the Republican flag, and he held as his keep the noble and gigantic redan, whose parapets were 200 miles of mountains, having their

The Boer strategy.

salient in front of Sutherland and their gorge from Calvinia to Beaufort West.*

Maritz moves southward. But Maritz well knew that his conquest of the uplands provided him with little more than a base. Watching with dismay the appearance of one battered "supporter" after another, he saw, too, that now all depended on himself, and he determined to strike at once directly at the strategic point. In the first week of October he overran Clanwilliam and Piquetberg, masked the garrison of Piquetberg Town, and crossing the Great Berg river, entered Malmesbury. On October 11th he occupied Hopefield, less than three days' ride from Cape Town. In the stir which arose in the capital all varying interests were silenced. The proclamation of martial law two days earlier had at last given to the military the power so long begrudged, but which all hastened to invoke now that the enemy was so near the gates. At this moment Lieut.-General Sir J. French appeared on the scene at Piquetberg Road. The trend of the campaign had long been clear to him, and it was more than a month since he had assumed control of the operations in the west. During that time the General's chief aim had been, as it still was, to ruin the Boer combination by the wearing down of its units before they could come together. If he could not prevent Smuts, Scheepers, Theron and the others from joining Maritz, he was determined at least that they should carry across the railway but shreds of *Success of Sir J. French's tactics.* their fighting strength, and he saw his policy everywhere succeeding. Examining the situation in Piquetberg and Malmesbury from October 12th to 14th, he was, therefore, very little alarmed at Maritz's daring. To the 500 men or so whom the Boer had at his disposal, he could oppose at once the three mounted columns of Wyndham, who arrived at Piquetberg Road with him on the 12th; of T. Capper, who, with a reorganised and refitted force, was in Moorreesburg, in company with a recently formed column under Major F. Wormald (12th Lancers). When these were lined up from Hopefield through Klip Gat to Piquetberg Road

---

* The physical features of this part of Cape Colony are clearly shewn on the relief map to be found in the case of maps published with Volume I.

for a northward drive, Maritz himself saw the folly of pushing on further, and held to the line of the Great Berg river. Having placed all in order in the west Sir J. French returned to Middleburg, delegating command of the operations against Maritz to Major-General T. E. Stephenson.

Stephenson placed in command.

Before the columns moved against the Great Berg river, Maritz made a dash up the right bank, and hotly attacked a detachment of local troops at Halfmanshof on Twenty-Four river. The post was rescued on October 16th by a squadron of the 16th Lancers from Piquetberg Road, after a sharp affair which cost the squadron its commander (Captain R. W. D. Bellew) and three men killed and three men wounded, the Boers losing seven. On the 20th, the columns advanced, Wormald on the left, within touch of the coast, T. Capper in the centre, Wyndham on the right, and Maritz saw that he must fall back. The Great Berg river was yielded with little opposition, nor was a stand made upon any of the numerous ridges which traversed the counties of Piquetberg and Clanwilliam. Maritz drew his men northward in several bodies, which he reunited at Graaf Water and took into the Bokkeveld just as on October 24th the three columns halted on the line Clanwilliam—Lamberts Bay. But the Commandant's retreat was neither so aimless nor so precipitate as it appeared. Whilst Wyndham turned aside with a convoy for Calvinia, and Capper and Wormald laboured across the sandy wastes to Compagnies Drift on the Olifants river, several Boer leaders appeared to join Maritz, amongst them Theron, who, ever since his evasion of Wyndham and Alexander a month earlier, had been cautiously making his way about the borders of Ceres and Calvinia, looking for a chance to throw the remnants of his force into the western movement. On October 29th Maritz, his command much augmented, resumed his original plan and once more turned his face towards the south. On the 30th he crossed the Olifants between Compagnies Drift and the sea, and pushing on, captured and burned a convoy which was returning from Lamberts Bay to Clanwilliam on the 31st. Wormald, hurrying to save it, arrived too late, though he made a noteworthy forced march of sixty-five

Maritz falls back.

Again advances southward.

miles in seventeen hours, largely in the dark. With only 150 men he was himself in some danger below the Lange Berg until Capper hastened by night to support him. Maritz, having thus completely doubled on his former pursuers, now moved southward by way of the coast. On November 3rd he was at St. Helena Fontein, and turning the Piquetberg mountains, re-touched the line of the Great Berg river, up the right bank of which he marched as far as Zand Drift. Stephenson promptly called all his available units towards the spot. To T. Capper and Wormald orders were sent to face about and pursue southward; to Wyndham, who had safely deposited his convoy in Calvinia, to march on Clanwilliam. Kavanagh, arrived at Constable station on November 2nd, was directed to Moorreesburg. Crabbe was entrained at Laingsburg for Malmesbury. Nevertheless, for seven days Maritz marched unpursued, and almost unopposed. Not until November 8th did Capper and Wormald receive their instructions; Wyndham and Crabbe, at opposite ends of the sphere of operations, had far to come. Only Kavanagh, who arrived at Moorreesburg on the 5th, was within the zone, and until the others appeared he could do no more than cover in some measure Malmesbury and the approaches to the capital, though he was easily to be turned from the west. In short, the road to Cape Town was practically open, and a blow which, successful or not, might have roused all rebel Cape Colony, seemed about to fall. But at this critical moment

<small>Wastes time on a diversion.</small> Maritz, instead of rushing across Malmesbury, lingered on the Great Berg river to attend to a side issue. On the night of November 6th he sent Theron with half his force, some 300 men, to attack the neighbouring town of Piquetberg. The undertaking of a diversion so wasteful of time was forced upon him by his urgent need of arms and horses. His very success had now encumbered him with a large and growing band of unequipped rebel recruits; from Piquetberg county alone he had recently acquired more than one hundred, who made no secret of their chagrin and alarm at their helpless condition. Much depended, then, on Theron's mission, who, at 4.20 a.m. on the 8th, having surrounded Piquetberg, ordered his men to fall on.

EVENTS IN N.-W. AND W. OF CAPE COLONY. 361

But the burghers, deterred by the sharp reply of the garrison,* and kept at arm's length by the wire entanglements which surrounded the place, contented themselves with shooting almost harmlessly at the excellent defences. This fire they maintained for twenty-four hours, every moment of which was of value to Maritz's plans, after which Theron, fearing to delay longer, withdrew and fell back upon the main body at Zand Drift. His losses had been treble those of his opponents, whose casualties numbered three killed and four wounded.

On the 9th Maritz and Theron crossed the Great Berg river together, but separating soon after, pushed on rapidly through Malmesbury on divergent lines, Maritz pointing on Darling, and Theron, whose attack on Piquetberg had drawn Kavanagh northward, on Malmesbury. Next day Darling was in Maritz's hands, his patrols even appearing at Mamre, only thirty miles from the capital. But the stroke, daring as it was, even more daring than if it had been delivered, as it might have been, three days earlier, was too late. Stephenson had handled his only available unit with skill and rapidity. On the 10th, as Maritz rode into Darling, Crabbe's column detrained at Piquetberg Road station. It was immediately sent by road to Malmesbury, and entraining again at midnight for Kalabas Kraal, by daybreak on the 11th extended from the railway westward to the Little Salt river, barring all approach from the north. Nor was Crabbe confined to the defensive. At nightfall he was on the line of the Mooimook river. Pushing on next day he drove Maritz out of Darling, and halted in the evening on the line Groot Zwart Berg—Uilen Kraal—Vogelstruisfontein. Meanwhile Kavanagh, finding Piquetberg safe, had returned to Moorreesburg, near to which on November 13th he fell in with Theron, whom he chased southward past Riebeek Kasteel, then westward towards Kanon Berg. Crabbe on this day had pushed Maritz still further northward, back to the Great Berg river, across which he drove him on the 14th.

Maritz within thirty miles from Cape Town.

Maritz driven back.

---

* This consisted of eighty-six officers and men of the Town Guard, Western Province Mounted Rifles, District Mounted Police and other local troops, all under Major A. F. Pilson.

By this time T. Capper and Wormald had come into touch, and from Zuurefontein they manœuvred to intercept Maritz at the drifts of the Great Berg river. In this, however, they were unfortunate, and although Capper succeeded in engaging Maritz, the Boer got clear away towards Jan Boers Kraal, to the north-west.

Theron isolated.

Meanwhile Theron, vainly seeking his chief, had the worst of an encounter with an armoured train at Kanon Berg on the 13th, but pressed on westward, only to find himself actually far in rear of the very column engaged in hunting Maritz out of Malmesbury. Theron's position was now extremely critical. Crabbe, warned of his presence behind him, turned at Hopefield; Kavanagh was between that place and Moorreesburg; Capper and Wormald, now doubly alert, watched the Great Berg river from Piquetberg almost to its mouth, where a gunboat lay ready to deal with any evasion by way of the coast. Considerably bewildered by Maritz's disappearance, Theron made for Darling, and finding nothing there, laagered on the 16th at Elands Vallei, on the Zout river. He was discovered next day by Crabbe, who had come down to Schildpad Vallei on the other side of the river. Theron at once took to his heels. Never had he more need of speed, nor had he ever galloped with better fortune and skill. Dashing north-eastward, and evading both Crabbe and Kavanagh, he gained and crossed Vogelstruis Drift below Bridgetown, and disappeared on the other side of the river on November 18th. There was now a risk lest Theron should turn the whole combination by the east through Ceres, whilst Maritz did the same along the coast on the west. Keeping Capper at Klip Bank in reserve, Stephenson therefore directed Kavanagh through Porterville on Piekeniers Kloof for Elands Kloof and Clanwilliam, and Wormald by Ceres towards Sutherland, whilst Crabbe marched by Piquetberg, down Verloren Vallei, to Lamberts Bay, which Wyndham was at this time also approaching.

Theron escapes.

These dispositions were effective. The advance of Wormald to Wagen Drift, north of Ceres, turned Theron, who was, in fact, heading eastward, back through Kardouws Pass into the

Piquetberg mountains, whereupon Capper was moved up to Piquetberg Town in observation, whilst Wormald remained at Wagen Drift, and the other columns made their above-mentioned destinations. Little more was seen or heard of Maritz until in the last week of November it was reported that, in company with Malan, Bouwers, Pypers, Van der Venter and Van Reenan, he was closely investing the post at Tontelbosch Kolk, on the Zak river, fifty miles north-east of Calvinia. All these commandos were now under the orders of Smuts, who had assumed command of all the Boer forces in Cape Colony. The garrison at Tontelbosch Kolk consisted of only four officers and eighty-six men, of the Western Province Mounted Rifles and Bushmanland Borderers, under Captain R. M. Bertram, disposed in six small forts, and was of so little tactical importance that Wynne was in the act of withdrawing it when it was shut up. *Smuts assumes command of the Boer forces.*

To such futility, then, was reduced the long-talked-of combination of the commandos in the west. Sir J. French's policy of attrition in the midland areas had done its work. Maritz's six allies brought between them less than 400 men, and these bands were as spiritless as they were weak. A hot attack, which was gallantly repulsed, on November 28th, was the first and last bolt of the investment. Still further discouraged by losing Maritz, who received a severe wound, the Boers for seven days after relapsed into a respectful fusilade of the greatly outnumbered but indomitable garrison. On December 5th they departed after expending vastly more ammunition than they could spare, and four days later W. Doran, who had marched to the relief from Sutherland on the 6th with the greater portion of Callwell's column, withdrew the garrison, whose losses in a most creditable defence had numbered three killed and eight wounded. Doran's movement had been profitable in other ways. Covering the egregious siege of Tontelbosch Kolk was Louw, Maritz's former confederate, and Doran, surprising him on his last day's march towards the post, scattered the commando and took nine prisoners. Three weeks earlier Callwell himself, then taking up the pursuit of the various Boer bands entering Sutherland from across the Cape Town railway, had also *The "siege" of Tontelbosch Kolk.*

encountered Louw in the same neighbourhood; but on that occasion Van der Venter, Bouwers and Smit had come to Louw's assistance, and Callwell had to fall back with twenty-one casualties on Sutherland. There he was joined on November 17th by Doran, who had followed Malan up through Sutherland district. At the same period Lund's force had been detrained at Matjesfontein, and these three columns, W. Doran's, Callwell's and Lund's, were now placed under command of Colonel D. Haig, to be based on Sutherland.

Thus, by the beginning of December, 1901, the capital and the adjacent south-western portion of Cape Colony had been cleared, and Lord Kitchener determined on heroic measures to keep it inviolate for the future. On December 3rd his order was received for the construction of the most imposing line of blockhouses which had been yet attempted across the open veld. The line to be taken was from Victoria West, on the main railway, through Carnarvon, Williston, Calvinia and Clanwilliam, to Lamberts Bay, a distance of 320 miles. To cover the construction of the easterly section Wormald was sent to Victoria Road. The other columns remained in the west, for though their movements from December 1st to 4th had driven the commandos over the Doorn river, the cessation of the pursuit had been followed by a return of the enemy across the river, and there were signs of a strong concentration at Frederick's Dal, north of Clanwilliam. Theron was still actually behind the proposed blockhouse line until, on the 8th, T. Capper from Piquetberg engaged him at Witte Drift, and drove him northward to join the rest. It now became necessary to refill Calvinia with supplies, and Stephenson got ready a convoy of fifty wagons, which on December 19th left Clanwilliam under escort of the columns of Wyndham and Crabbe. It was fortunate that the guard selected was no weaker, for the preparation and destination of the wagons had been as little of a secret to Smuts as his own presence in force was to his opponents, and he had lined the route to Calvinia with his commandos. Three times the troops had to beat off determined attacks—on the 20th near Elizabethsfontein, two days later at Kordemoersfontein, when

Wyndham's fine handling of the rearguard foiled a bold bid for the convoy, and on the 23rd close outside Calvinia. On the last occasion the enemy, under Smuts himself, barred the road from strong entrenchments, but a determined rush full against the position by the 16th Lancers of Wyndham's column, this time in advance-guard, wrested the ridge from the burghers, who fled incontinently. In all these attempts the Boers suffered considerable losses. They left twenty burghers on the field at Kordemoersfontein alone, and gained not a rifle or an ounce of the munitions of which they were now in extreme need. The casualties among the escort had been some score in all, chiefly amongst the 16th Lancers, who bore the brunt of the fighting throughout the march with much honour. On December 23rd both columns entered Calvinia, whence they returned to Clanwilliam without further molestation, arriving on the 27th. Four days later the section of the blockhouse line from Clanwilliam to Lamberts Bay, which had been pushed on under protection of Kavanagh's column, was completed and fully manned, only a fortnight after its commencement. It effectually barred the true military road to the capital, and Smuts, who lay with the main body of the commandos about Van Rhyns Dorp, found himself without an object in an inhospitable and tactically unfavourable country.

For some time past he had anticipated some such anticlimax to Maritz's well-laid strategy. A month earlier the rapid concentration of the British columns and the damaged condition of his own adherents had convinced him of the impossibility of maintaining the war in the west with the forces available. He had insisted that the lack of men and material alone would prevent him from bringing the campaign to a successful conclusion in Cape Colony. "The future," he wrote, "is bright and promising. . . . Thousands are anxious to join us, but they have no horses, as the enemy have collected all animals in these districts, and I am convinced that if animals were not so scarce it would be quite possible to cause a general rising." Let but a thousand men be spared from the aimless operations in progress in the two Republics to lend weight to the blow which he knew how to strike at the centre of British rule in

Smuts' views on the situation.

South Africa. Especially he had urged the return of Kritzinger, whom he had long ago left idling in the Zastron district under promise of a speedy reappearance in Cape Colony. It was owing to his continued absence that the commandos in the midlands and east had fallen to pieces, thereby destroying the whole balance of the campaign in Cape Colony.* Smuts' sound and soldier-like appreciation of the situation contained a suggestion of the only possibility of success left to the republican arms.

The Boers' neglect of the strategical opportunity.

It had long been apparent to him how much might turn upon the enlargement of the invasion of Cape Colony from a mere diversion into the grand plan of campaign. But neither he nor his superiors perceived that the moment for such a transference of strategy was not approaching but passing away. Smuts himself actually deprecated the appearance of De la Rey, of which there was now fresh talk at the Boer Headquarters, on the ground that the operations were insufficiently advanced for such distinguished leadership. In the east of the main theatre of war Commandant-General Botha, in the west De la Rey, in the south De Wet, continued to expend in brilliant but fruitless feats of arms men whose presence in Cape Colony at this moment might have kindled a fresh struggle, the termination of which no man could have foreseen. In other respects Smuts' representations remained unanswered. No considerable reinforcements were despatched to him, nor, until his campaign in the west had evaporated, did even Kritzinger attempt to fulfil his part. Before he appeared only one insignificant band had come to recruit the Boer forces in Cape Colony. On November 22nd, a certain Commandant Naude led fifty men over the Orange river at Sand Drift. He was promptly intercepted by columns under Lieut.-Colonel A. G. Hunter-Weston and Captain Lord W. A. Cavendish-Bentinck, who had been posted between Colesberg and De Aar for such eventualities. Naude avoided them both, however, and on the night of the 29th broke westward across the railway between Hout Kraal and Potfontein, in spite of the blockhouses and armoured trains, and was lost to

* Summary of a report by Assistant-Commandant-General J. C. Smuts to the Boer Headquarters; undated, but written about November, 1901.

sight in the Prieska district. There he joined Conroy, who, ever since his parting from Maritz at Brandvlei in May, had been marauding, with many an adventure, between Griquatown, Katkop and Prieska. What success attended Kritzinger will now be seen.

On December 14th, nearly four months after his parting with Smuts in Zastron, Kritzinger dashed across Sand Drift and re-entered Cape Colony with 110 men. Before undertaking the expedition his burghers had been reviewed and addressed by Mr. Steyn, who urged them to fire their rebel brethren with tales of the havoc they had seen wrought by the hands of the British in the Orange River Colony. But the adventurers had little leisure for preaching a crusade. No sooner were they across the well-worn drift than they found themselves confronted by the columns of B. Doran from Bosch Duiven Kop and Lord W. A. Cavendish-Bentinck from Hamelfontein. Barely evading these by a turn southward, the commando was hunted down to the De Aar—Naauwpoort branch railway. On the night of December 16th, after a rearguard action at Boschvarkensfontein which cost him many horses, Kritzinger made an attempt to cross the intervening railway between Hanover Road and Franschmans Kop. But the Guards of Inigo Jones' brigade who held this portion of the line were on the alert, and gave the Boers a heavy reception. Kritzinger himself fell wounded and was taken prisoner; his adjutant, nine other burghers and eighty horses were also taken. Nothing, however, could arrest the rush of the rest through the severed wires. Led by L. Wessels, Kritzinger's second-in-command, who was also wounded, the commando sped on through Hanover and Richmond into Aberdeen, where, on December 20th, having clean outrun the chase, it disappeared into the tangle of the most famous covert of the Great Karroo, the Camdeboo mountains.

So much, then, for Smuts' most trusted ally and long-expected reinforcement in the centre of Cape Colony. In order to align his fortunes over all his sphere of operations up to the close of 1901, there remain to be traced from an earlier period the doings of his detachments in the north-east.

Marginalia: Kritzinger re-enters Cape Colony. Capture of Kritzinger.[1]

Events in the north-east of Cape Colony.

Whilst during November the incessant revolution of French's columns had cleared the midland and southern counties of Cape Colony, the north-east, with its all but inaccessible tangle of precipices, had resisted every effort to reclaim it. Fouché, Myburg and P. Wessels, still maintained themselves between Burghersdorp and Barkly East, observed, but unmolested, by Monro, whom the departure of Pilcher at the end of September had left alone and passive in his duty of covering the construction of the Stormberg—Lady Frere blockhouses. Not until November 14th, when Scobell's column, having been recruited after its exhausting chase of Van der Venter, became available, was it possible to resume the offensive in this quarter. At that time Fouché was in laager at Patriots Klip, Myburg and Wessels between Rhodes and Barkly East, their joint forces amounting to nearly 500 men. Sir J. French ordered a simultaneous movement by Scobell against Fouché, by Monro against the other two, whilst Hart from Aliwal North sent down Moore's Connaught Rangers mounted infantry and Lord Lovat's Scouts to co-operate. All three contingents were quickly in touch with their allotted opponents. Scobell, working with Lovat's Scouts, hunted Fouché uninterruptedly and always with success all over Jamestown, depriving him of twenty men and nearly 200 horses, and so harrying the commando that by the last day of the month it had broken up into the small bands which were the certain sign of exhaustion with Boer units. Scobell had then been led back to near Jamestown. Monro was equally successful with Myburg and Wessels. His movement from Dordrecht on Barkly East (14th to 20th) drove the Boers over the Drakensberg, on the other side of which, on the spur known as the Gatberg, they were encountered by a body of local defence troops under Captain H. W. D. Elliot. A sharp affair, in which Elliot was killed, resulted in the repulse of the enemy, who left eight killed and many wounded, as well as fifty horses, on the field as they made off northward. Basing himself on Barkly East Monro followed in three parties, and from November 22nd to 25th made further captures as far as Rhodes, though the main commando managed to escape him in the mists. At Barkly East,

EVENTS IN N.-W. AND W. OF CAPE COLONY.

on the 26th, Monro got news that the laager had been discovered in its old haunt at Drizzly Hill. Marching by night on the 28th he successfully surrounded the spot, broke up the camp, and in the running fight which ensued killed and wounded five of the enemy and captured eighteen with 100 horses, completely demoralising Myburg, who relinquished his independent command. On December 1st Monro was back at Barkly East, and a few days later made another attempt to catch Wessels towards Rhodes. It was attended by no success; but returning empty-handed to Barkly East on the 7th, Monro collided with Fouché, who was in the act of evading Scobell, and, attacking him near Cold Brook on the 8th, took two prisoners and more than 200 horses. On the 14th Scobell and Monro joined forces in Barkly East.

Meanwhile a fresh leader, Odendaal, had gathered together the fragments of Myburg's commando, and had established them in the old laager at Patriots Klip. The British columns had likewise received an addition. The Cape Colonial Government had recently formed a division which had been placed under Lieut.-Colonel H. T. Lukin, of the Cape Mounted Riflemen, and a detachment of this force had been sent, under Colonel R. H. Price, to assist the operations in the north-east. On December 14th Price's Kaffrarian Rifles resolutely attacked the laager at Patriots Klip, took five prisoners and some fifty horses and scattered the rest, after which Price took them back to Burghersdorp. Next, a movement by Scobell on Rhodes had the effect of driving Fouché and P. Wessels south-west. As they passed Barkly East Monro darted out upon them, and on the 15th, at Schilder Kranz, on the Dordrecht road, fell upon the rear and captured thirteen prisoners. The Boers then doubled north-westward towards Lady Grey, Monro pursuing until the 24th. Both he and Scobell then returned to Dordrecht, where the latter, whose incessant exertions now placed him on the sick list, was relieved in command of his column by Major S. W. Follett (9th Lancers). On December 27th Price, from Burghersdorp, made another successful sally upon a small laager discovered at Paarde Verlies, killing the rebel Field-Cornet, one Venter, and securing a prisoner and twenty-seven animals.

APPROXIMATE STRENGTH STATES OF COLUMNS REFERRED TO IN FOREGOING CHAPTER.

COLUMN.	Mounted Troops.	Infantry.	Guns, including Vickers-Maxims.	Machine Guns.	
April—December, 1901.					
Maj. H. S. Jeudwine (later T. Capper)	370	50	2	—	
Lt.-Col. G. F. Gorringe	680	—	3	—	
Officer Commanding 17th Lancers	316	—	—	2	
Lt.-Col. S. C. H. Monro	641	—	3	4	
Lt.-Col. E. M. S. Crabbe	449	70	2	1	
Lt.-Col. H. J. Scobell (later S. W. Follett)	625	—	3	1	
Lt.-Col. B. Doran	489	—	2	—	
Lt.-Col. P. G. Wyndham	550	—	2	—	
Maj. F. T. Lund	620	—	2	—	
Lt.-Col. C. P. Crewe	340	—	2	2	
Lt.-Col. J. R. MacAndrew	510	—	—	—	Lt.-Gen. Sir J. D. P. French in command.
Officer Commanding at Conway	210	40	1	1	
Lt.-Col. C. T. McM. Kavanagh	400	—	1	1	
Lt.-Col. A. G. Hunter-Weston	630	—	1	5	
Lt.-Col. H. Alexander	420	—	2	—	
Lt.-Col. T. J. Atherton	530	—	2	1	
Capt. Lord W. A. Cavendish-Bentinck	280	—	1	1	
Lt.-Col. H. T. Lukin	690	—	3	1	
Maj. F. Wormald	330	—	1	—	
Lt.-Col. C. E. Callwell	350	—	2	1	
Lt.-Col. W. Doran	420	—	2	—	
Lt.-Col. M. G. Moore	250	250	—	1	

NOTE.—Major-General T. E. Stephenson assumed command (under General Sir J. French) of operations in the west and south-west of Cape Colony in October, 1901.

CHAPTER XXI.

EVENTS IN THE EASTERN TRANSVAAL*

(*Continued from Chapter XVII.*).

NOVEMBER, 1901—JANUARY, 1902.

DURING the first half of November, 1901, there was a comparative lull over all the Eastern Transvaal whilst lines of blockhouses were pushed on along the Wilge river, and across the southern angle from Wakkerstroom to the Swazi border. Plumer, Colville, Sir H. Rawlinson, Garratt and Pulteney continued raiding in the south, whilst Bullock supervised the blockhouse building. Spens, returning by Botha's Pass into the Orange River Colony early in the month, came back into the Transvaal on the 17th, and remained for the next ten days at Standerton, into which town also came Allenby's and W. P. Campbell's forces. All these columns made small but constant profit in men and stock, the most considerable being the capture of a laager and fourteen Boers near Mahamba on November 8th, and a week later of another laager and twelve Boers at Plat Nek, both effected by Colville with his mounted troops; Major E. A. Wiggin, 13th Hussars, commanding the 26th battalion M.I., having a large share in the successes. A patrol of the 2nd West Yorkshire regiment under Second Lieutenant E. T. Welchman surprised and secured eight Boers in the Pongola Bosch on the 18th. Altogether about 100 of the enemy's fighting men were taken in operations too trifling for detailed narration. This was small gain, and it was plain that the main hostile bodies had now to be sought once more upon the High Veld, that vast tract which columns and armies had so often crossed and recrossed, leaving no traces more permanent than those of ships upon the ocean. On expanses like these the Boers could long fend off either defeat

The problem of the High Veld.

* See map No. 56.

or starvation, and though in truth they were being slowly filed down by isolated captures and surrenders, their numbers were still sufficient to render such a process well-nigh interminable, and enormously expensive in men, animals, and money to the British army, wasting itself in carrying it out. How, then, to master these giant meadows and their roving populations had become the main problem of the Eastern Transvaal. Lord Kitchener had long been occupied, and was now well advanced with schemes of which the map and measure alone can suggest the magnitude; nothing less, in short, than the fencing in of whole provinces with blockhouses and entrenched posts, which constantly contracting towards a common centre, would eventually choke each area in their grip as the ancient chambers of torture crushed their victims with converging walls. Something of this has already been referred to in these pages. Already in the Eastern Transvaal a line of blockhouses ran from Wakkerstroom to Piet Retief, a chain of posts from Greylingstad up to Wilge River station. Now (November 16th) whilst the South African Constabulary were ordered to advance their chain eastward from the line Wilge River station—Greylingstad to that of Brugspruit—Waterval station, Clements was to build blockhouses from Standerton across to Ermelo, to be extended later to Wonderfontein and Amsterdam, thus gridironing the High Veld into irregular rectangular figures enclosed by forts and the armoured railways which parcelled out its prairies into areas of manageable size. The immensity of labour and material entailed by these tasks must here be passed over in silence;* let it suffice to remember how far and in what quantities workmen, fabric and tools had to be transported, how often to be employed in remote spots, and in the presence of the enemy, and in how many different directions at once these fortified lines were being projected.

<small>Lines of blockhouses.</small>

To protect the advance of the Constabulary posts a strong covering force was necessary. Early in November Major-General Bruce Hamilton, having been placed in command of all operations in the Eastern Transvaal south of the Delagoa

<small>Bruce Hamilton placed in command.</small>

* See Appendix 2; and map No. 58.

EVENTS IN THE EASTERN TRANSVAAL. 373

Bay railway, led six columns into the field, and disposed them in various positions. These columns were gathered as follows: from Standerton, Colonels E. H. H. Allenby's and W. P. Campbell's (the last-named soon to be divided into two separate commands under Lieut.-Colonels F. D. V. Wing and G. G. Simpson); from near Springs, Colonel C. St. L. Barter's (lately Bewicke-Copley's); from Brugspruit, Colonel C. J. Mackenzie's (lately Benson's); from Wonderfontein, Lieut.-Colonel E. C. Ingouville Williams' with Lieut.-Colonel the Hon. C. G. Fortescue; from Volksrust, Colonel Sir H. Rawlinson with Lieut.-Colonel H. K. Stewart, whilst Brigadier-General J. Spens on his return to Standerton was sent to cover the construction of the Standerton —Ermelo chain of blockhouses, his column eventually forming a seventh under Bruce Hamilton's command. Behind these troops the work of building was rapidly pushed on. By November 22nd it was completed, and Bruce Hamilton, establishing his Headquarters in Bethel, prepared for more active operations.*

On the last day of November his troops faced eastward from the Delagoa Bay railway at Middelburg through Bethel down to the Vaal, with Mackenzie, Fortescue and Williams on the left; Barter, Wing and Simpson with the General in the centre; Sir H. Rawlinson next, and Spens on the right, standing on the bank of the Vaal. Allenby was posted in a supporting position behind the right centre. Still further to the south-east Plumer and Pulteney were at Brereton awaiting the subsiding of many flooded streams before marching northward to co-operate in the great movement which Bruce Hamilton was about to undertake. On December 1st, whilst Barter remained to hold Bethel, the line advanced, the trio on the left reaching Carolina on the 2nd, Bruce Hamilton and the centre halting between the source of the Vaal and Ermelo, Sir H. Rawlinson and Spens drawing near to that town from the south-west and south. On the 3rd Ermelo was entered by the centre and right, and the columns at once found themselves in the presence of the enemy. *Bruce Hamilton drives eastward.*

Bruce Hamilton at Ermelo.

The approach of so strong a line of British troops had put

---

* For gallantry on November 23rd, Lieutenant L. C. Maygar, 5th Victorian Mounted Rifles, was awarded the Victoria Cross.

the commandos in a ferment, which their admirable scouting only served to increase when from end to end of a hundred miles of front came only the word "the enemy!" Their position, in truth, would have spelt ruin to forces less mobile. They had been taken by surprise, and already there was but little space for manœuvring between the storm travelling from the west and the lee shore of the eastern frontiers of the Transvaal. Paardeberg and the Brandwater basin had intensified a hundredfold the Boers' natural terror of a *cul de sac*. With one accord they began to penetrate in small bodies the interstices of the line of columns, and Bruce Hamilton saw that unless he struck rapidly and on all sides he would have to turn and seek his quarry on the spaces behind him instead of in front. Such an emergency, one scarcely to be met with in any warfare but this, formed the strongest test of the acquired rapidity and elasticity of an army which, until this campaign, had not been remarkable for either because the need had so seldom arisen on a large scale. Nor could there have been on the spot any commander more able than Bruce Hamilton to snatch advantage from situations whose duration was to be measured in moments. Yet, surrounded as he was by dissolving hostile bodies, the most adroit General would have been helpless without good information. In war the power to strike is as widely dissociated from as it is dependent on the knowledge of where and when to strike: witness the spectacle, common in history, of strong armies wasting their vigour in purposeless blows, or so bewildered that they refrain from striking at all. Fortunately at this juncture Bruce Hamilton had the services of Colonel A. Wools-Sampson, the Intelligence Officer who had so often marked down the game for Benson. Tracking now the shifting units of the Boers, he was able to guide his commander to a series of successes which struck terror throughout the Eastern Transvaal.

The commandos break up.

On the very day of his entry into Ermelo Bruce Hamilton, informed that hostile bodies had filtered through his right wing, took all the available mounted men from the columns of Spens and Sir H. Rawlinson, and marching all night, fell upon a large laager at dawn on December 4th, capturing ninety-three prisoners,

Bruce Hamilton's successes.

EVENTS IN THE EASTERN TRANSVAAL.

116 horses, fifty-five carts and wagons, and a vast quantity of signalling and other gear. On the 9th he struck again, this time west of Bethel—so far had the enemy penetrated his lines—with results which make it doubtful which were the more amazing, the endurance or the valour of his men. By a march of thirty miles by night he brought the horsemen of Sir H. Rawlinson's, Wing's and Williams' columns upon the laager, which fell to an assault worthy of fresh troops. Nor did the discomfiture of the Boers end here; for six miles they fled before Hamilton's inexhaustible troopers, who by the end of the day had killed seven and secured 130 burghers and all the camp stuff, riding then over twenty miles more into Bethel with their booty. Retracing his steps towards Ermelo on the 12th, Bruce Hamilton received intimation of another laager twenty-five miles north-east of Bethel. For the third time he hurried through the night, with Sir H. Rawlinson's, Wing's and E. C. I. Williams' men, to burst at dawn upon the encampment and send its occupants flying over the veld. Once more a six-mile gallop in pursuit rewarded the soldiers, who garnered eighty-six of their foes and one of the guns lost at Bakenlaagte, before they were recalled to Ermelo, where they halted after a march of more than fifty miles. Nor had Bruce Hamilton's columns been idle in the intervals. On December 4th E. C. I. Williams, raiding along the Oliphant river, had accounted for seventeen Boers, and Allenby and Barter five; Sir H. Rawlinson had taken eight on the 7th, and Mackenzie six on the 13th, each securing much loot in cattle, wagons and crops.

After sundry minor operations Bruce Hamilton moved eastward from Ermelo with 2,150 mounted men from the columns of Sir H. Rawlinson, Williams and Wing, intending to push the remnants of Botha's forces against the Swazi border. Bad weather, drifts and guides delayed the first portion of the march until the Boers had warning and scattered. But Hamilton drove on, and assisted by Mackenzie from the north, ran down, killed or captured more than seventy burghers in the neighbourhood of Maryvale, taking nine more on his return march towards Ermelo on the 25th.

Altogether, up to the end of December, 508 Boers, 101 wagons and 10,000 cattle had fallen to Bruce Hamilton's troops. The effect of these misfortunes was great on an enemy who, until recently, had camped contemptuously close to British outposts ; who boasted that he had made the night and the veld tracks his own, and that he was not to be beaten at the game of surprise by the very impis of the Zulu. Realising on how formidable a successor the mantle of Benson had fallen, Botha's commandos became utterly demoralised, and nowhere was the end of the war more plainly in sight than in the Eastern Transvaal at the close of 1901.

<small>The enemy demoralised.</small>

During Bruce Hamilton's advance Spens, with his Headquarters on the Standerton—Bethel road, had forayed continuously with flying columns. He would have come out with profit but for a mischance to one of his strong patrols which, chasing a commando on the banks of the Vaal on December 19th, was led into an ambush from which it only emerged after desperate fighting, with the loss of about 140 killed, wounded and prisoners. Spens was then directed southward, and placed with Pulteney under command of Plumer for raiding west of Amersfoort, which was carried out with good results.

<small>Loss of a patrol, Dec. 19th, 1901.</small>

Barter and Allenby were likewise detached from Bruce Hamilton's forces in order to join a brigade of cavalry which had been sent down from Pretoria on the 15th under G. Hamilton, to deal with the broken bodies which had crept through Bruce Hamilton's lines, and were now wandering in some strength about the Constabulary blockhouse line east of Springs. Vigorous chasing resulted in the capture of thirty-four of these by Allenby's men, many more surrendering at the blockhouses ; a determined remnant under General Alberts, however, eluded capture, and remained to do much mischief in the future.*

<small>Events north of the Delagoa Bay railway.</small>

North of the Delagoa Bay line, Park from Lydenburg, and Urmston, with a roving base, but usually from Belfast, had patrolled the Dullstroom district, searching mainly for the Boer Government, and incidentally for the many small groups which, with constant loss, were attempting flight across the railway

* See Chapter XXIX.

EVENTS IN THE EASTERN TRANSVAAL. 377

from before Bruce Hamilton's advancing line of columns. The only formed body in the district was that of Viljoen, whose lieutenant, the daring Muller, fell hotly upon Park near Dullstroom on the night of the 19th, being repulsed with loss, but inflicting thirty-one casualties upon Park's command. Three days later Park responded with an onslaught on Muller's camp, the greater part of which fell into his hands, Muller abandoning also a Vickers-Maxim gun. Both columns returned to the line on the 26th, Park to Dalmanutha, Urmston to Belfast.

In Natal Bullock, covered by Garratt, continued to build blockhouses, now from Botha's Pass to Vrede, and this he continued to do with assiduity for a month to come. By the end of December the blockhouses along the Ermelo road were completed ; over those from Piet Retief to the Swazi border Colville remained on guard, whilst Chapman took out for a fortnight a raiding party 700 strong, which scoured the Zulu border from Nkandhla round to Nondweni. These were the doings in December, a month of great effort and results. *In Natal.*

The New Year (1902) found Bruce Hamilton busy amongst the demoralised knots of Boers who crept along the river beds seeking a way of escape from the narrowing space between the British columns and the Swazi border. On January 1st twenty-two of these were run down on the banks of the Umtali river, north of Amsterdam. Sixty-nine more, including Commandant Erasmus, fell victims on the 3rd, forty-nine of which were taken on the Compies river by Colonels A. B. Scott (temporarily commanding Sir H. Rawlinson's column), Stewart and Simpson, directed by Hamilton in person, the others falling on the Umtali to Wing, who next day added six more prisoners to his train on the Umpilusi north of Bell's Kop. On the 9th Bruce Hamilton, his task in the east reduced to the chasing of individuals, returned to Ermelo, around which he at once found fresh occupation amongst the bands who had broken through his lines at his first advance. These were now mere wanderers, ringed in by blockhouses, exhausted by incessant harrying, and so unnerved that they dared not approach the familiar farmhouses to seek for the provisions and fodder which they sorely lacked. Whether *1902 Further successes by Bruce Hamilton.*

or no, for men in such a case, capture were a relief from their unhappy lot, it duly befell many of them. On the night of January 10th Bruce Hamilton, leading out Wing and E. C. I. Williams, marched rapidly to Witbank, and surrounded a laager which yielded forty-two prisoners to the throw of the net at dawn, Major Wolmarans, the renowned State artillerist, being taken with two of his officers. A second raid by Hamilton with Scott, Stewart and Simpson in the same neighbourhood two days later, nearly miscarried, owing to the vigilance of a Boer piquet, and the troopers, who had ridden hard for thirty miles in the dark, had to gallop furiously for seven miles more before they were content to draw rein with thirty-six burghers to their credit. Sir H. Rawlinson's column now (January 14th) left the command for Standerton, and that of Simpson was broken up; but Spens had brought his force back to Ermelo on the 9th, and Allenby had returned to Bethel where also was Barter, so that there was no weakening of the chase. On the night of the 18th Bruce Hamilton once more cast his pack eastward, intending to draw the confluence of the Zand Spruit and Compies river, about Alkmaar. Twenty-seven prisoners had been brought to bag when the Vaal, coming down in flood, warned Hamilton to return, or be caught himself, and at midnight on the 19th Spens, Wing, E. C. I. Williams and Stewart, who had conjointly carried out the hunt, were back in Ermelo. On the 22nd a fresh series of blockhouses was begun from Ermelo to Carolina under cover of Fortescue's force, and the columns, prowling separately on both sides of the new line, secured a few more prisoners on the 24th and 29th. Next day Bruce Hamilton, receiving intelligence of a laager at Tafelkop, ten miles north-west of Ermelo, took Spens, Mackenzie and Stewart, with 850 men, and set out for another trophy, directing Allenby, who was midway between Bethel and Ermelo, towards the same spot. The columns, surrounding the lair at midnight, found it empty; but they followed hotly on the spoor which led southward from it. Near Springbokfontein they fairly ran down a marching commando which they instantly charged and shattered, hurling it against the Standerton—Ermelo blockhouses, ninety-four burghers,

EVENTS IN THE EASTERN TRANSVAAL. 379

including several officers, being accounted for. By the time the troops regained Ermelo they had covered sixty-five miles in twenty-four hours, in heavy rain, and without food or rest. So well had they learned from the enemy not how to endure, for that was as native in them as in the Boers, but that endurance was the hard road to success. The results achieved—338 prisoners during January, 850 during the two months' raid—showed that it was now for the enemy to learn something fresh, for his hereditary crafts had been mastered. Results of Bruce Hamilton's raids.

Meanwhile G. Hamilton's cavalry, strengthened up to January 14th by Barter's troops, and until the 21st by Allenby's, had continued to intercept to the east of Springs many of the fugitives from the zone which Bruce Hamilton had made uninhabitable. To the south Plumer, Pulteney (with Spens up to the 9th) and Colville had performed similarly, the first forming a roving stop between the Vaal and the fixed barrier of the Piet Retief—Wakkerstroom blockhouse line, whilst Colville patrolled the space between the terminus of that line at Piet Retief and the Swazi border. Operating first from Rotterdam, on the Mabusa Spruit, and subsequently from Wakkerstroom, Plumer had sundry encounters with bands whose strength and quality seemed to indicate that Bruce Hamilton had brushed southward the best of his opponents, perhaps Botha himself, in whose presence audacity and determination were ever to be expected. On the morning of January 3rd Plumer's New Zealanders pursuing too confidently a band seen retreating up the left bank of the Vaal, near Rotterdam, found themselves suddenly charged by 250 horsemen, who killed, wounded and captured thirty-one men, then drew off, and pursued their way. Next day Plumer pushed after across the Ermelo—Amsterdam road, north of which his advance-guard, under Major J. M. Vallentin (Somersetshire Light Infantry), having sighted no enemy all day, halted on the plateau of Onverwacht. Vallentin then descried a party moving north-east, and started in pursuit. No sooner was he well on the trail when a commando of 400 men, which had gathered during his halt, fell upon him in front and Plumer in the south. Affair at Onverwacht, Jan. 4th, 1902.

both flanks. A desperate *mêlée* followed, in which both combatants lost heavily. On the British side Vallentin himself and eighteen non-commissioned officers and men were killed, thirty-six officers and men wounded, and some fifty captured in the hand-to-hand fighting. The Boers lost Opperman, one of their bravest Generals, and many killed and wounded, but they were like to have annihilated Vallentin's party but for the opportune arrival of Pulteney's supporting troops, who drove the enemy from the field and far to the north. Soon after this event Plumer repaired to the neighbourhood of Wakkerstroom where the wooded gorges, peopled by lurking refugees, gave him full occupation for the next three weeks, and finally an opportunity of avenging his mischances earlier in the month. On the

Success by Plumer, Jan. 25th, 1902.

night of the 25th Plumer surrounded, with five bodies of troops, the kloofs between Spitz Kop and Castrol Nek, and at dawn next day sent his men through them. A number of Boers emerged, only to be driven against the blockhouse line where thirty-four prisoners were taken. Plumer then returned to Rotterdam, and, after some minor raids, went down with Pulteney to Volksrust to replenish supplies (February 4th).

Events north of the Delagoa Bay railway.

North of the Delagoa Bay line Park and Urmston manœuvred in the Roos Senekal area, but were much hampered by rain and fog. This was the more unfortunate because the Transvaal Acting-President and Government were at this time wandering near Dullstroom, in great straits, and virtually cut off from their main hope in this district, General B. Viljoen, who was now reduced to impotence at Pilgrim's Rest. Schalk Burger was anxious for more practical guardianship, and about the middle of the month summoned Viljoen to meet him at Windhoek in the Stenkamps Berg. In a few days Viljoen, accompanied by four adjutants, was beside his chief, and it was arranged that the official body should follow him back to Pilgrim's Rest, whither Viljoen himself set out on the 25th. It befell strangely that the Government had called their protector to his own destruction, for this ride proved to be the last of the Boer leader's many adventures. The British Intelligence Department was keenly watching the vagrant legislature; every outpost was alert, and ambuscades lay in many a likely spruit bed and rail and river crossing. Into one of these traps—laid by a party of the 1st Royal Irish regiment, sent out under Major A. S. Orr by Lieut.-Colonel H. Guinness—fell Viljoen as, having stolen past the outposts of Lydenburg, he made to ford the Spekboom river. Two of his adjutants were killed at once, three bullets brought down the General's horse, and soon one of the staunchest of the federal leaders was escorted into captivity.

<small>Capture of General B. Viljoen.</small>

APPROXIMATE STRENGTH STATES OF COLUMNS REFERRED TO IN FOREGOING CHAPTER.

COLUMN.	Mounted Troops.	Infantry.	Guns, including Vickers-Maxims.	Machine Guns.	
November, 1901—January, 1902.					
Lt.-Col. Sir J. H. Jervis-White-Jervis	520	—	—	—	⎫ Brig.-Gen. H. C. O.
Lt.-Col. F. F. Colvin	700	—	6	—	⎬ Plumer in command.
Lt.-Col. A. E. W. Colville	550	300	4	1	⎭
Col. Sir H. Rawlinson	1,100	182	6	1	
Lt.-Col. F. S. Garratt	450	290	5	1	
Col. W. P. Pulteney	800	261	3	2	
Brig.-Gen. J. Spens	1,550	267	7	—	
Col. E. H. H. Allenby	1,000	—	5	4	
Col. W. P. Campbell	1,300	1,130	8	4	⎫
Col. C. St. L. Barter	450	690	3	1	⎬ Maj. - Gen. Bruce Hamilton in command.
Col. C. J. Mackenzie	1,050	720	4	—	⎭
Lt.-Col. E. C. Ingouville Williams	550	—	3	—	
Lt.-Col. the Hon. C. G. Fortescue	520	473	3	5	
Lt.-Col. F. D. V. Wing ⎱ late Camp- ⎰ Lt.-Col. G. G. ⎱ bell's Simpson ⎰ column.	850 500	285 500	3 3	2 —	
Col. C. W. Park	440	639	5	1	
Lt.-Col. E. B. Urmston	500	467	2	2	
Lt.-Col. H. K. Stewart	700	—	3	2	
Brig.-Gen. G. Hamilton	750	259	5	3	

CHAPTER XXII.

EVENTS IN THE ORANGE RIVER COLONY*

(Continued from Chapter XVIII.).

DECEMBER, 1901—FEBRUARY, 1902.

<small>Effect of De Wet's concentration.</small>
WITH De Wet once more at the head of a force in being, the eastern part of the Orange River Colony became in December, 1901, the cynosure of all the theatre of war. This his presence would have ensured in any event, for now both sides had come to determine largely the chances, or rather the duration of the war, by the measure of the famous leader's forces and fortunes. It is true that not a British soldier doubted the issue of his prolonged exertions, but there were few who expected their cessation until De Wet was either killed or taken, for either event was expected promptly to terminate the fighting. The name of Jackson was not more celebrated in the camps of Pope, or of Rupert in those of Fairfax than that of De Wet in the numberless bivouacs which had dotted the veld of South Africa for two years. But, apart from his high reputation, there were other reasons why at this moment De Wet's return to activity should have absorbed the attention of the British Headquarters. In all other parts the Commander-in-Chief's patient, unrelenting methods seemed to be slowly doing their work.

<small>Improved situation in S. Africa.</small>
In the Eastern Transvaal Bruce Hamilton's six columns and the contracting rings of blockhouses were fastening upon the High Veld with a hold which Botha found it impossible to shake off.† Viljoen was practically isolated in Lydenberg. The Western Transvaal was less under control, but, after all, the

<small>* See map No. 64. † See Chapter XXI.</small>

EVENTS IN THE ORANGE RIVER COLONY.

chief difficulty of Lord Methuen and Kekewich was to discover De la Rey or any other tangible enemy.* In the Northern Transvaal Colenbrander was carrying all before him.† The Orange River Colony was seriously disturbed nowhere but in its eastern half. Cape Colony, the true foundation of the whole campaign, and one to be preserved from crumbling only by the most unremitting efforts, remained a keen anxiety, but even there things were brighter than they had been at any time during the past year. In the eastern part there was scarcely a Boer leader above the level of a bandit, and in the west Maritz's strategy, and with it the success of all Smuts' plans, had been confounded just as it had developed into a real danger.‡ De Wet, then, took the field at a moment when some striking performance was most needed by his own side and least desired by the other, and Lord Kitchener, knowing well what to expect, directed all his efforts towards anticipating the offensive on the part of the Free State levy.

The central point of De Wet's concentration seemed to lie about Elands Kop, between Lindley and Frankfort. Accordingly the following ingenious raid was instituted against the suspected locality. Whilst Elliot was to move out from Kroonstad, marching steadily up the Valsch, not widely extended, and keeping to the south of the real objective, Rimington, Damant and Wilson, coming from Frankfort would approach up the right or eastern bank of the Libenbergs Vlei river. These movements, it was hoped, would have the effect of deluding De Wet into the impression that a general easterly march was in progress which would leave him free behind the receding forces. When the Kroonstad and Frankfort forces should come into touch with the Libenbergs Vlei river, the whole would suddenly face about, and sweep over the country between the Lindley—Reitz and Heilbron—Frankfort roads. On December 8th Elliot, marching light, took out Broadwood, de Lisle and Byng (the latter in place of Lowe), and advanced up the Valsch, de Lisle on the left, Byng in centre and Broadwood on the right.

Operations against De Wet.

---

* See Chapter XIX.   † See Chapter XXV.   ‡ See Chapter XX.

384   THE WAR IN SOUTH AFRICA.

<small>De Wet discovered.</small>

Rimington and Wilson simultaneously started from Heilbron to join Damant at Frankfort. Elliot was in the midst of his first day's march when, about 11.30 a.m., De Wet was discovered by Broadwood to be sitting upon a strong position Klein Sedan—Quaggafontein, covering Lindley with 1,000 men. De Wet was at this moment meditating an attack on Barker, whose forays from Winburg had earned his special displeasure, and the appearance of the columns from Kroonstad, whilst it surprised him, only caused him to look with more certainty for a movement by Barker in his direction. Reserving himself, as usual, for the weaker opponent, he offered little resistance to Broadwood and Byng who lined up on his left, and after a skirmish of two hours, fell back rapidly on the Libenbergs Vlei. Elliot, who was on the extreme left with de Lisle, knew nothing of this important discovery, and it was not until five hours later that he heard from Broadwood, who had gone into camp at Quaggafontein at 3 p.m., how touch had been gained and lost. At

<small>Loss of contact.</small>

9 p.m. Broadwood endeavoured to recover contact by a long and difficult night march to Rietpoort; but De Wet, anticipating some such action, was also on the move, and circling southward, passed by the east of Broadwood and past Bethlehem, making for Kaffir Kop, north of Fouriesburg. Finding nothing at the end of a thirty-mile march in the dark Broadwood returned to resume his part in the set scheme. On the night of the 8th Elliot's front was Lindley—Mooifontein.

Nothing could have been more unfortunate than these events. The object of the whole manœuvre had now plainly vanished outside the right flank, and was to be sought rather at the head of the Valsch river than that of the Rhenoster. Only in an instant pursuit by every column towards Bethlehem was there any chance of regaining touch with De Wet, tactics in which the Frankfort troops might equally well have co-operated. But a plan had been formulated, and it was evidence of the inherent inelasticity of schemes laid down and controlled from Army Headquarters, that no attempt was made to depart from it. The march eastward was duly persisted in, Elliot actually feinting at Bethlehem, his proper target, with the object

EVENTS IN THE ORANGE RIVER COLONY.

of diverting attention from the now purposeless advance towards Reitz. On the 10th he was astride of the Libenbergs Vlei river on the line Bulhoek—Fanny's Home—Zwartfontein, whilst De Wet, still with an eye to Winburg, scouted secure from interruption from Kaffir Kop.

Meanwhile the Frankfort troops had joined hands with Elliot along the Libenbergs Vlei from Bordeaux and Zorgvleit. At 4 a.m. on December 11th all six columns turned and faced westward for the "drive" over Elands Kop. Broadwood, on the extreme left was thrown forward from Bulhoek so as to prevent a break-out by the south; escape by the north was barred by the line of blockhouses now standing between Wolvehoek and Frankfort. For the next four days the return march proceeded, the columns searching carefully and maintaining a line which it would have been difficult to penetrate. It was not surprising, however, that their discoveries were small. Every mile removed them further from De Wet's main gathering, which, even at the outset, had been forty miles to the southward. Some 300 Boers in all were sighted, and when on December 14th the operation concluded on the line Heilbron—Kaalfontein, only forty-three prisoners had been taken. Of convoys containing fugitive families there had been no lack, and 187 wagonsful were driven in. *Result of the operations.*

The whole of the eastern Orange River Colony, from Frankfort down to Thabanchu now became the scene of great activity on both sides. De Wet, whose strength increased daily, divided his forces, sending some 800 men under General W. J. Wessels northward to reconnoitre with a view to attacking any columns found outside Frankfort. There was good prospect of success here, because at this time Brigadier-General E. O. F. Hamilton was engaged in laying out a prolongation of the Heilbron—Frankfort blockhouse line to Tafel Kop, and the camp of his working parties was in the open at Dundas. De Wet himself returned from Kaffir Kop to his former ground between Bethlehem and Lindley. No sooner had he done so when, as if led by a malicious spirit, five columns converged on Kaffir Kop in search of him. From Kaalfontein came Elliot with his three *De Wet divides his forces.*

brigades, Barker issued from Winburg, and from the opposite direction Sir J. Dartnell came out of Harrismith by way of Elands River Bridge and Bethlehem. On December 17th all these should have met at Kaffir Kop; but even had the lair not been deserted, the mission might have miscarried from faulty communication. Although they duly arrived in the neighbourhood from opposite sides, Elliot and Dartnell failed to meet, whilst the latter, though he did get sight of Barker, was unable to establish signalling communication with him. Then, having seen so little of each other and nothing of the enemy, all five columns turned for the counter-march to their respective bases. De Wet, who had observed these manœuvres from above Bethlehem had actually hurried to attack Dartnell on his westward way, but was only in time to see the column disappear into Bethlehem, where B. Campbell had been recently installed with his wing of Sir L. Rundle's command. He therefore lay in wait some fifteen miles to the north-east of the town, and kept a watchful eye on the Harrismith road for the first sign of Dartnell's reappearance.

At 8 a.m. on the 18th Sir J. Dartnell cleared Bethlehem and set out on his return march to Harrismith. He had received double warning of De Wet's presence. First, a native captured the day before had stated that the Free State force had already placed itself between the column and its destination; next, just as Dartnell quitted Bethlehem a surrendering burgher rode up with the news that the Free State force was actually lying in wait only eight miles out upon the road. So certain did an attack appear that B. Campbell had agreed to send on his own mounted men in support of the march for a certain distance. Taking every precaution except that of attempting at all costs to discover and inform Elliot, Dartnell moved cautiously upon his way. As, about 11 a.m., the advance guard approached the drift which carried the road over the Tiger Kloof Spruit, a sudden and heavy volley from a hill close to the left front warned Dartnell that his informants had spoken truly. He instantly parked his wagons and pushed forward his artillery; but before the guns could unlimber for action, a fusilade broke upon him

EVENTS IN THE ORANGE RIVER COLONY. 387

from every side. De Wet's commandos had perfectly enveloped the road. Whilst a strong force of riflemen, aided by a Maxim-Nordenfeldt posted on the east of the Spruit, opened fire from the surrounding kopjes, smaller bodies galloped in and took cover at close quarters, and a united rush upon the column seemed imminent. For a few moments Dartnell's column was in danger of sharing the fate of others which had been waylaid in similar fashion by the arch highwayman of the veld ; but De Wet soon found that he had met his match. The Imperial Light Horse, the majority of whom were as experienced in such combats as himself, fought with determination, and utterly denied with their rapid shooting the 400 yards of open ground which separated them from the assaulting bodies. Moreover, the burghers by no means displayed their usual confidence in themselves or their leader. De Wet had ordered a general charge, but only half his men responded to the signal, and these, finding their comrades hanging back, declined to carry matters to a conclusion. De Wet was quick to see that an affair which had cooled at its first onset had miscarried ; and there were indications that he had not only failed, but would soon have to look to himself. As soon as the seriousness of the attack had become apparent, Dartnell had signalled to Campbell that the support of his mounted men, who had advanced to Vogelfontein, would be welcome, and Campbell had not only ordered them forward, but was coming on himself with his infantry. At 3 p.m. De Wet called his men from the field, and Dartnell, safe, but in no position to pursue, continued his march to Elands River Bridge and thence into Harrismith on December 23rd without further incident. His losses in the engagement were one man killed, four officers and ten men wounded; those of the enemy, five killed and nine wounded.* De Wet retired into the Lange Berg much chagrined by his discomfiture at the hands of a column which he had looked upon as a certain prey. In a few hours news reached him of a hot engagement in another quarter.

Repulse of De Wet.

* For gallantry on this occasion Surgeon-Captain T. J. Crean, 1st Imperial Light Horse, was awarded the Victoria Cross.

Rimington and Damant about Frankfort.

Within a week of their co-operation with Elliot's raid between the Libenbergs Vlei and Kroonstad, Rimington and Damant were again in combination in the Frankfort district, chiefly with the object of covering the contemplated extension of the blockhouse line from Frankfort to Tafel Kop. On the night of December 19th the two commanders set out on a pre-arranged enterprise, the general scheme of which was a circular sweep around Tafel Kop from the east, concluding with a drive down the valley of the Wilge back towards Frankfort. Soon after dawn on the 20th the columns, having encompassed Tafel Kop, were facing west, in line but not in touch, Rimington on the left at the head of the tributary Kalk Spruit, Damant at the head of the Riet Spruit some five miles to the north. From the start there had been reports of the presence of a considerable Boer force in the hills upon the right bank of the Wilge river, and both Rimington and Damant had captured more than one patrol and outpost. These were in reality the antennæ of Wessels, who, fearing to attack E. O. F. Hamilton's strongly fortified camp at Dundas, had lain between Tafel Kop and the Wilge observing the blockhouse building, and alert for any false step which would afford him a chance to sting. The advent of the two field-columns on the morning of the 20th came as a surprise to the Boer leader. Seeing Damant on one side of him and Rimington on the other, he imagined that he was being purposely surrounded,* whereas neither of the British commanders was in reality aware of his presence. This idea seemed to be confirmed when a third party—whether of his own men, or an advanced detachment of Damant's or Rimington's columns, or a reconnoitring patrol from Frankfort, cannot be ascertained—alarmed him by appearing to the west, and Wessels, certain that he was now shut in, thought that nothing could save him but a charge. Soon Damant's horsemen, galloping down the Riet Spruit in chase of a band which had been unearthed on the southern slope of Tafel Kop, arrived much scattered on the high ground overlooking the right bank. Damant himself, with eighty officers and men

* Report by Assistant-Head-Commandant W. J. Wessels to Chief Commandant C. De Wet.

EVENTS IN THE ORANGE RIVER COLONY. 389

and the three guns, drew rein about the centre of the line, taking post on a long straggling flat-topped kopje which fell steeply to the broad and shallow bowl of grass curving between the rise and the river. Five hundred yards on Damant's right a squadron of Damant's Horse had halted. Other portions of this regiment were on the opposite flank, that is, to the south, but so distant that Rimington, though completely out of touch with Damant himself, had picked them up on his way down the Kalk Spruit. The veld in front of Damant was covered with moving horsemen. Some were making up the river, others were crossing to the left bank. Five groups, each some 100 strong, could be distinguished from the rest, standing motionless under the shadow of the opposite slope. The men composing these were dismounted and holding their horses; they were clothed in khaki uniform, and were drawn up in so compact and orderly a fashion that Damant, who examined them closely, came to the conclusion that they were squadrons of Yeomanry from Heilbron or Dundas. This impression seemed confirmed beyond suspicion when the parties, turning their backs on Damant's position, took to firing at some invisible target in the opposite direction, certainly, so it seemed to Damant, the scattered Boers who were in retreat from his own advance. Next, portions of the groups broke up, and, collecting some cattle which were straying in the neighbourhood, drove them in the direction of Damant's position. Finally, all five groups mounted, and rode slowly in cavalry formation straight towards Damant. There was now no room for doubt; Damant's men allowed them to approach at leisure, and they were soon within hail of the position. Only when one of the knots rode within ten yards was the identity of the whole array suddenly revealed, and the troops became aware that they had admitted a strong Boer commando almost into their lines. Lieutenant W. Scott's squadron, that on Damant's right, was the first to discover the danger, and shot point-blank into the nearest band, putting it to flight with the loss of eight of its members. The rest of the intruders, throwing off all disguise, then galloped at full speed for the foot of Damant's kopje, which was so steep on that side that the ground at its foot was

Damant's action near Tafel Kop, Dec. 20th, 1901.

hidden from view. Realising the situation at last, Damant hurriedly collected a troop, and rushed forward to forestall the enemy on the edge of his crest-line; but he was too late. The Boers scrambled over the lip before he could reach it, and in one moment an overwhelming force poured in amongst the guns and covered the whole top of the kopje. Now ensued a combat as noble and as hopeless as that which had strewn Gun Hill at Bakenlaagte with dead seven weeks earlier.* The party with Damant was manifestly lost; the guns were already in the enemy's hands; but every man who had a rifle plied it where he lay, striving only how much he might cost the enemy before a bullet ended his own account. For an hour and a half the unequal contest was maintained, so long does it take men even so bold and skilful as Wessels' veterans to make an end of a resolute band six times smaller than itself.† At the end of that time, out of the eighty on the hill seventy-seven were killed or wounded, amongst the latter Damant himself.‡ When all resistance was quenched the Boers took possession of the kopje, sullying their triumph by permitting a few of their number to perpetrate those outrages on the wounded of which it seems impossible altogether to purify warfare, however humane the combatants. Their hold upon their capture was, however, but momentary. Whilst Wessels cast vainly around for means to remove the guns, every horse of which had long been shot, Scott came charging up from his detached position on the right with the squadron of Damant's Horse and the 30th and 31st companies Imperial Yeomanry, which with one united rush hurled the enemy from the hill almost as soon as he had won it. Soon after Rimington appeared from the south-west and completed the rout. Rimington had heard the first outburst of firing, and also its cessation; but he learned nothing of the

* See Chapter XVII., pages 310-13.

† For gallantry on this occasion Shoeing-Smith A. E. Ind, Royal Horse Artillery (XI. section pompoms) was awarded the Victoria Cross.

‡ Casualties, December 20th, 1901—Killed, two officers and twenty-nine men; wounded, six officers, forty men.

disaster until it was complete, when first a straggler from Damant and then a messenger from Scott informed him of the facts. He was then some miles distant, but, galloping for the scene, he arrived in time to chase the broken commando across the Wilge as far as the exhausted condition of his horses permitted. Thus ended an engagement remarkable for its startling changes of fortune and, it may be added, for the extraordinary report rendered of it by Wessels, whose undoubted daring with the sword was certainly equalled by that with the pen. De Wet, brooding over his late discomfiture in the Lange Berg, must have derived delusive solace from an account which informed him of charges delivered by only 130 burghers over a bare plain 6,000 yards broad against 2,000 Britons in position ; of incessant counter-charges incessantly repulsed ; of a hundred dead, and this but a third of the losses of the ill-fated column, being counted by himself in one spot.* Be this as it may, the Free State generalissimo could scarcely have learned the truth before he delivered a more than rival blow.

Since the middle of December the construction of the blockhouse line from Harrismith to Bethlehem had been steadily progressing. At this moment such work, in the absence of a strong and mobile covering force, was risky in the extreme. This was one of the rare occasions during the campaign on which information as to De Wet was absolutely reliable. The attack on Sir J. Dartnell on the 18th had disclosed both his strength and his anxiety to use it, and it was unlikely that such a leader would rest contented under the unaccustomed smart of the defeat of one of his favourite schemes. True, after the affair at Tiger Kloof Spruit, all touch with De Wet had immediately been lost, no special effort having been made to retain or regain it. Dartnell had moved on into Harrismith, taking with him the only mounted force in the district strong enough to beat for game so dangerous. Thereafter informatio was mainly dependent upon natives, who still reported the presence of the commandos in the Lange Berg. Both B. Campbell and Sir L. Rundle were

Weakness of the Bethlehem district.

* See footnote, page 388.

practically powerless for distant scouting. Their available forces were trifling, and would have been immobile even had they not been chained by protective and working purposes to the partially completed blockhouse line. The brigade of Imperial Light Horse had been broken up, Dartnell having resigned command on his return to Harrismith; and although the two regiments came out again on the 24th, they were not only under independent commanders, but were expressly excluded from Sir L. Rundle's jurisdiction, reporting instead directly to the Commander-in-Chief.* One (Briggs) was to be based on Bethlehem; the other (McKenzie) between that and Harrismith, Lord Kitchener intending, though he did not so inform Sir L. Rundle, that it should work from the blockhouse-head,† which it might effectually have protected. Finally, the Intelligence Department, lacking the only certain means of obtaining information, keen-eyed men on good horses, had to concern itself more with reports of distant British columns than of the nearer Boer commandos. Labouring under all these disabilities Sir L. Rundle remained as blind to De Wet's immediate presence as he was vulnerable to his attack, and it happened that Christmas Eve found him at his weakest. Blockhouse-head was then in the air at Tweefontein, nine miles to the west of Elands River Bridge, and was covered by some 500 men of the Imperial Yeomanry with a gun and a Vickers-Maxim, all under command of Major F. A. Williams (South Staffordshire regiment), who temporarily replaced Lieut.-Colonel R. B. Firman, whilst that officer was on leave of absence. This force lay some two miles to the west of the last completed blockhouse. Sir L. Rundle himself had gone into camp three miles behind Williams with 270 men of the Grenadier Guards (destined for B. Campbell) and sixty-six mounted men of the 1st South Staffordshire mounted infantry. These were all the troops at the front. The regiments of the Imperial Light Horse were not at blockhouse-head, but both together at Elands River Bridge, nine miles in rear of it, and

Situation on Dec. 24th, 1901.

---

* Telegram from Commander-in-Chief K. 9199, December 22nd, 1901.

† Telegram from Commander-in-Chief K. 9264, December 25th, 1901.

EVENTS IN THE ORANGE RIVER COLONY. 393

eleven miles from the force covering it. Beyond the undoubted fact of De Wet's presence there seemed, however, no special likelihood of an attack. The Intelligence summary on the evening of the 24th was entirely reassuring. The " situation to the south was quite clear. . . . Movement from north was unlikely." Only seventy-five Boers in all, posted as scouts and cattle guards, could be discovered anywhere.* Christmas Day had not dawned before De Wet, rushing out of this peaceful country, had disappeared into it again, dragging after him the relics of a British force.

F. A. Williams' position at Tweefontein much resembled that of Damant in the recently described encounter on the Wilge. His outposts lined the edge of the almost precipitous southern side of a kopje, the opposite slope of which, falling gently to the north, contained the camp and baggage. This northern side, being peculiarly vulnerable to attack, was strongly defended by entrenched outposts. The hill was the usual camping ground for all columns passing that way,† and was thus almost as well known to the enemy as to the troops. Nevertheless De Wet carefully reconnoitred it in person for two days, and having drawn the fire of the guns by means of his scouts, and ascertained the position of the various defences, he marked it as his victim. Remaining in observation himself, he ordered his burghers to meet him at a spot four miles distant from Tweefontein during the night of December 24th. This was duly carried out, and about midnight eight commandos, numbering some 1,200 men, advanced upon Tweefontein. It had long been an axiom with the Boers, and might by this time have well been conceded by their opponents, that the steepest side of a position is that most favourable to attack. The numberless proofs of this in history were probably unknown to men who studied warfare not from books but the face of nature ; but South Africa, from Majuba onwards, had provided lessons enough to both sides that difficulties of ground are nothing compared to the advantages of

Position of the force covering the blockhouse building.

De Wet reconnoitres the covering force.

---

* Intelligence summary, Harrismith District, December 24th, 1901.

† Sir L. Rundle's report, December 26th, 1901.

the cover from fire and view provided by the precipitous faces which at first sight seem impregnable. The force, therefore, which watches only the edge and neglects the foot of such a steep will always be in extreme danger from an active enemy by night. Wagon Hill and Spion Kop had taught the British, Elandslaagte and Driefontein the Boers, how much easier it is to lose than regain such a crest. At heavy cost F. A. Williams' Yeomanry were now to learn it again. De Wet steered straight for the southern face. At two o'clock on Christmas morning his men began to scale the height. Climbing in stockinged feet, they were undetected until the last moment, and then only a single sentry took the alarm. Five minutes later the whole outpost line was destroyed and the camp flooded from corner to corner with an overwhelming inrush of riflemen. Of defence there was none; every body of men on duty was instantly dashed to pieces; the troops in camp were of no more military value than any other collection of suddenly and so terribly awakened sleepers. But of battling with an inevitable fate, the peculiar quality of the British soldier, there was enough both to redeem the field to its losers and to increase the credit of the assault. Broken into groups, and lost in the darkness, the Yeomanry offered a fierce resistance, delivering time after time gallant but ineffectual charges, which were finely led wherever a leader could be found. The gunners stood and fell to a man by their pieces. De Wet himself, no unpractised judge of courage, bore witness to the gallantry of his victims. In less than an hour his work was done; 145 of the column were killed and wounded;* and as dawn broke he left the hill, taking with him the two guns and more than 200 prisoners of war.

The first shots fired in this disastrous affair were heard in Sir L. Rundle's little camp, and a quarter of an hour later the Staffordshire mounted infantry were led out by a Staff officer to ascertain the cause of the ensuing roar of musketry. As the scouts approached Tweefontein the faint light of a cloudy moon

---

* British casualties—Killed, six officers (including Major Williams) and fifty-one men; wounded, eight officers and eighty men. The Boer losses numbered about fifty, including three officers.

was sufficient to show them the state of affairs, and they themselves were so nearly discovered that the officer in command, who rode ahead to reconnoitre with two men, was summoned to surrender, his companions being actually captured. In an hour's time the patrol was back with Sir L. Rundle, who, on hearing their report, concentrated his small force and sent his aide-de-camp, Captain A. C. McLean, to summon the Imperial Light Horse from Elands River Bridge. His own position was extremely hazardous. Had De Wet turned upon him it is likely that he would have shared Williams' fate; but the Boer leader had allowed his men to scatter in search of the loot and as guards over the wagons, guns and prisoners, and he had only a small force with him when the rising sun revealed the adjacent camp. Even so, Rundle was in some jeopardy from the Boer stragglers. The Staffordshire mounted infantry, whom he sent at the gallop to seize a hill commanding his left and the road by which the reinforcements were expected, were all but forestalled by a hostile body of equal strength who raced for it from the other side; a stronger commando hovered on his right. Meanwhile McLean, riding at speed through the darkness, dashed into Elands River Bridge in less than an hour, and soon both regiments of Imperial Light Horse arrived at full gallop from the east. But the enemy had almost disappeared. A pursuit into the tangled spurs of the Lange Berg led the cavalry into country of such difficulty that it was unsafe to persist, and once more De Wet vanished. *De Wet disappears.*

It now fell to Elliot to take up the chase. On his return from the barren operation against Kaffir Kop, Elliot had reorganised his division into two columns under de Lisle and Major R. Fanshawe (Oxfordshire Light Infantry), Broadwood having proceeded on leave of absence. Since then these troops had been engaged in covering the construction of the Kroonstad—Lindley blockhouse line, based chiefly on Quaggafontein, with Byng behind at Kaalfontein. On the day of the occurrence at Tweefontein, Elliot received intelligence that De Wet was near Reitz. Calling Byng forward to guard the rapidly accumulating depôt at Quaggafontein, on the evening of December 26th, that *Elliot moves against De Wet.*

is, some forty-eight hours after the disaster, Elliot sent out de Lisle without guns or transport, with orders to conduct a wide-ranging reconnaissance, Fanshawe following at dawn on the 27th with the impedimenta. De Wet was reported with suspicious promptitude. On the 28th, when de Lisle was approaching the left bank of the Libenbergs Vlei by Fanny's Home, the heights on the opposite side were seen to be covered by an apparently strong force which made little effort to conceal its numbers or disposition. It appeared certain that De Wet was about to oppose the passage of the Vlei, and Elliot prepared for an encounter with the elusive marauder. But the General was doubly out in his reckoning. De Wet himself was far away, having ridden off to visit Steyn and the commandos of W. J. Wessels on the Wilge river. In the meantime he had entrusted the leadership to General M. Prinsloo, ordering him to lead the commandos west of Reitz, and it was this officer who now faced

Boer tactics on the Libenbergs Vlei.

Elliot across the Libenbergs Vlei. At the first news of the approach of the British column Prinsloo conceived a manœuvre worthy of De Wet himself. Sending the bulk of his men to cross the Vlei, an hour's ride down stream, he drew up a small but showy force opposite Fanny's Home, trusting that it would draw Elliot across the river and allow the undisturbed passage of his main body in the opposite direction. In this he was perfectly successful. By the time that Elliot, forced to deploy against unknown numbers, and further delayed by his transport at the damaged drift, had crossed the stream, nothing was to be seen but a few groups of scouts. Prinsloo's actual commandos were at that moment fording the river ten miles to the north, and were fast gathering upon the very bank which Elliot had just quitted with so much labour. Reitz was found deserted, and it was not until 5.30 p.m. that the news of a numerous body on the march west of Roodekraal, that is, almost behind him, showed Elliot how he had been outwitted.

Facing about, he at once sent five regiments and all his guns to gain contact, and hopes of a decisive engagement were renewed by the discovery of a strong rearguard embattled this time on the high ground on the left bank of the Libenbergs Vlei

EVENTS IN THE ORANGE RIVER COLONY. 397

river. The enemy was reported to number 2,000 men; it was known that they possessed guns, the trophies of Tweefontein, and ammunition for them. The situation of a commander in the presence of a hostile covering force of considerable but unknown strength has always been held to be one of the most difficult in warfare since the days when Ney shone in command of rearguards and Soult failed in attacking them. Elliot's problem on the Libenbergs Vlei, however differing in scale from the classic prototypes of the Peninsula and Russia, was even more difficult than they, for he was opposed to an enemy of unprecedented mobility, and in a campaign in which it were hard to say whether caution had proved the more profitless or dash the more dangerous. Where prudence gains the day it is useless to speculate on the possible gains or losses. Elliot, widely extending his troops, formally advanced against the position, duly disclosed the enemy's guns and firing lines, and accordingly missed his mark. Night fell upon his division still on the right bank of the Libenbergs Vlei river after a remarkable march of seventy miles; a few of his parties which had crossed to the other side were even recalled, and next morning the columns, extending once more on a front eight miles broad, marched over an empty position, and soon after completely lost touch even with the hoof and wheel marks of their quarry. On the last day of December Elliot returned to the blockhouse line to refill, bringing twelve prisoners and fifty-four carts and wagons. *Touch with the enemy lost.*

Thus the opening days of the year 1902 found the whole campaign almost come to a head in the eastern Orange River Colony and De Wet. The conflagration which elsewhere seemed to be flickering to its close here burned as fiercely as ever, for De Wet's renaissance was marked by an energy which recalled the earliest periods of the Boer campaign. From Ventersburg to Vrede and from Frankfort down to Fouriesburg there was not a convoy whose safe arrival could be counted on, not a garrison that did not stand continually to arms, not a column which even whilst it marched against the enemy had not to move with the strictest precautions of the defensive. The history of the next few months is one of continual effort to bring the guerrilla *The eastern Orange River Colony the centre of the campaign.*

chief to book. Columns from all parts drove and counter-drove from every base and every angle across his hunting ground; colossal lines of blockhouses daily cut up his sphere of action. Soon Heilbron was joined to Frankfort, Frankfort to Tafel Kop and Vrede, Vrede to Botha's Pass and Natal by these fortified buildings, of which an unbroken row stretched also from Harrismith through Bethlehem and Lindley to Kroonstad.* In bringing all this about De Wet had at once achieved his object and ended his occupation. He had roused a giant which might even by accident overpower him. To keep watch on the incessant gyrations of so many columns, the almost insensible tightening of the grip of the blockhouses on every horizon, demanded a hundred eyes. De Wet perceived that the moment had come for another disembodiment. Now, therefore, he again broke up the force which he had gathered for so short and adventurous a course, and in a few days there was scarcely a hill, hollow, hamlet or farm in all the countryside without its little population of armed men, whilst scarcely two hundred remained anywhere together to reward the powerful arrays which Lord Kitchener poured into the district. De Wet himself, with a moderate following, made for the Elands Kop district. With only a few hours' pause Elliot, knowing nothing of this, took the field again, and swept rapidly to Reitz, thence northward down the Libenbergs Vlei river and eastward to the Wilge river, gaining touch with Tafel Kop (January 4th), whither E. O. F. Hamilton had now successfully pushed his blockhouses. Nothing was to be seen and little heard of the enemy, and but for solitary scouts the country seemed deserted. A sudden dash back to the banks of the Libenbergs Vlei in the evening, often a profitable ruse against the Boers, resulted in the capture of eight prisoners; but the commandos had utterly vanished, and Elliot, whose men were now on reduced rations, gave the word for Lindley. On this day, January 4th, he covered sixty miles: the last five days' marching had totalled nearly 250 miles, a feat which the

---

* Fuller details of these and all other lines of blockhouse construction within the theatre of war will be found in Appendix 2.

EVENTS IN THE ORANGE RIVER COLONY.

most brilliant rewards have seldom been able to extract from troops, especially under service conditions of such rigour ; for it is never to be forgotten what incessant tension of mind and body added to the labours of columns surrounded by enemies who had time and again suddenly transformed themselves from a sprinkling of vedettes into a formidable offensive force.

No sooner was Elliot in Lindley (January 7th) than a rumour of De Wet's presence close to the north-east once more drew out his weary men and horses. The Boer leader was reported near Vecht Kop, moving west with the apparent intention of breaking across the railway about Roodewal. This proved true. On January 8th de Lisle and Fanshawe gained touch, and retaining it skilfully by another fifty-mile march, interposed between the railway and De Wet, who was already across the Rhenoster, and pushed him back beyond Vecht Kop, the Boer leader eventually drawing off out of reach towards Reitz again. Rest was now absolutely necessary for two out of Elliot's three columns. He remained based on Lindley, Fanshawe clearing the country around the place whilst de Lisle entrenched on Kaffir Kop to the south, so as to cover an extension of the Kroonstad—Lindley blockhouse line to that commanding hill. Whilst they were thus occupied Byng, who had remained in charge of Quaggafontein, took their place in the field, and endeavoured to pick up the slender threads which led to De Wet. He had therefore to make for Reitz, and moved in the first instance on Fanny's Home, where he expected to find two columns from Frankfort which had been placed under his command for the task. These were the forces of Garratt, and of Lieut.-Colonel J. W. Dunlop, R.A., the first of whom had recently been engaged in covering Bullock's blockhouse building from Botha's Pass to Vrede, whilst the latter had been performing similar service for E. O. F. Hamilton from Frankfort to Tafel Kop. Both were delayed one day on their southward march, but on January 20th all three columns united at Verkykers Kop, and for the rest of the month they drove and counter-drove between the Libenbergs Vlei and the Wilge rivers, returning to Fanny's Home with twenty-three prisoners on February 1st. By

Touch made with De Wet.

that date not only was Elliot again on the move, but three more columns had taken the field in the immediate neighbourhood to join in the unending search for De Wet, namely, those of Barker from Winburg, Dawkins (strengthened by the two regiments of Imperial Light Horse) from the Harrismith—Bethlehem blockhouse-head, and Sir H. Rawlinson who reappeared from Standerton. Rimington, too, came from Frankfort, on every side of which, from Villiersdorp to Heilbron and even down to Elands Kop, he had been raiding with his accustomed vigour since January 1st.

<small>A general scheme against De Wet.</small>

From the converging marches of all these units were evolved two grand tactical ideas, which were briefly as follows: First, to press De Wet south-eastward, either into the Drakensberg, or against the Harrismith—Bethlehem blockhouses; secondly, should this miscarry by De Wet breaking through the cordon in a westerly direction, to mass a line of columns behind him and drive him westward, either against a column to be dropped by Elliot during his advance or, failing that, into the strongly fortified angle between the Kroonstad railway and the Wolvehoek—Heilbron blockhouses. The columns did not come

<small>Incidents during the concentration of troops.</small>

together without sundry incidents on the way. In the last week of January when Elliot, keeping to the south of Reitz, was marching on a broad front towards Harrismith, Rimington was sweeping down the angle between the Libenbergs Vlei and the Wilge rivers, with Sir H. Rawlinson on his left, on the opposite

<small>Successes by Sir H. Rawlinson and Rimington.</small>

(right) bank of the Wilge. Rawlinson, who reached Cornelia on the 23rd, secured thirty prisoners by a skilfully managed round-up of the farms on the Venters Spruit on the next night. Four days later he was joined by Dawkins on the Hol Spruit, and continuing southward, drove before him a Boer convoy down to the junction of the Cornelis and Wilge rivers. This he surprised and rushed on the 30th, taking eleven prisoners and forty-five vehicles. Rimington, who had arrived and remained at Reitz January 26th—28th, was now abreast of Rawlinson, and resumed his march on Harrismith. On the night after Rawlinson's capture on the right bank of the Wilge, Rimington was equally successful within a few miles of the spot on the left bank.

EVENTS IN THE ORANGE RIVER COLONY. 401

He, too, had been pushing a Boer convoy southward, and on the evening of the 31st was so close to it that its capture on the next day would be almost certain. Rimington's keen observation of Boer tactics now prompted him to adopt a manœuvre after his opponent's own heart. Suspecting that the imperilled convoy would double past him in the dark, he himself made a night march backward, and at dawn on the 31st caught the whole convoy, with twenty-three prisoners and twenty-one wagons at Morgenzon, nine miles in rear of his bivouac of the evening before.

Lord Kitchener's expectation that De Wet would not be found in front of the foregathering columns was soon borne out. The troops made touch with Harrismith with no more serious encounters than those recorded, but Byng, whom Elliot had stopped at Fanny's Home, exactly fulfilled the purpose for which he had been left behind. On the night of February 2nd Byng, acting on intelligence that the enemy was on the move to the north, raided in that direction, and at once struck into the midst of a party under Commandants Mears and Wessels whom De Wet had ordered to extricate the captured guns from the closing cordon of troops. Byng at once attacked, and after a close combat in which his South African Light Horse and Garratt's New Zealanders and Queensland Bushmen much distinguished themselves, recaptured the three guns lost at Tweefontein, taking in addition twenty-seven prisoners, including three officers, and six carts. Besides these the Boers suffered the loss of some dozen killed and wounded, amongst the former being Wessels. Byng's casualties, in spite of, or perhaps because of the determined nature of his attack, numbered but three. *The army near Harrismith. Success by Byng.*

The quarry, though thus broken, was now out of the ring, and on February 4th the columns were turned and hurried into position for the westerly "drive." Could some aeronaut have poised high enough to enable him to survey the array in all its proportions, he would have beheld next day the veld of the Orange River Colony barred from Frankfort down to Kaffir Kop by an unbroken arc of horsemen, whose flanks were at the extremities of a chord more than eighty miles in length, closing, *The army faces westward.*

as they moved forward, the "gorge" of the vast open field-work into which the fortification of the railway and blockhouse lines had converted the whole of the eastern half of the province. The walls of this enclosure had been doubly strengthened for the event. Two additional battalions of infantry lined the defences between Kroonstad, Wolvehoek and Heilbron, which were patrolled incessantly by seven armoured trains. At Wolvehoek a battalion of mounted infantry lay in readiness to gallop to any quarter at a moment's notice. As for the disposition of the advancing semi-circle, on the left, from Lindley to near Fanny's Home, were Elliot's two columns, linking with Rimington, who reached to Stabbertswaag; next came Byng, extended as far as Marsala, north of which was Sir H. Rawlinson, whose right touched Frankfort and gave a hand to three columns under Damant, Wilson and Keir* drawn up in front of the Frankfort—Heilbron blockhouses. Barker remained in second line on Kaffir Kop behind Elliot. As this great horn, a colossal reproduction of the formation of the vanished Zulu impis, advanced, its embrace grew wider by the addition to Elliot's left of two columns under Majors W. R. Marshall and H. G. Holmes, from Sir C. Knox's southern district.

Progress of the operation. From February 6th—8th the unbroken curve rolled in upon the railway. Not an inch of the country was left unsearched by day. By night, when no officer or man in all the army was relieved from duty, all egress was denied by a continuous line of entrenched outposts, some distance in front of which fires were lighted both to increase the apparent depth of the formation and to disguise the real positions of the works. To attempt to break through such a barrier was a madman's venture; yet it was constantly attempted, especially against Rawlinson, who in three days took 129 prisoners, and at the northern blockhouses, which, dangerous as they were, seemed less fatal than the wakeful rank of troops out on the veld. In one of these encounters ten Boers were killed and many wounded; in all

* Lieut.-Colonel J. L. Keir, R.A., who, with a command of Royal Horse artillerymen serving as cavalry without guns, had been placed in charge of the operations covering the blockhouse building in the north.

EVENTS IN THE ORANGE RIVER COLONY. 403

of them the fugitives suffered losses by death and capture; but here and there parties and individuals, helped by fortune and their own valour, contrived to get through, in spite of every precaution. Amongst these evasions was one the bitter misfortune of which was well-nigh atoned for by the desperate daring of its carrying out. On February 6th De Wet himself, with a small following, was west of Elands Kop in the very centre of the circle. He was precisely informed of the converging forces by his heliographs which had begun to work from Blaauwkopje (between Bethlehem and Lindley) and Verkykers Kop as soon as the line of troops had passed them by. The dangers of the railway and the blockhouses radiating from it had long been known to him. At the first news of the army encompassing him he had ordered all his detachments to break out where they could, and he himself had now to determine quickly against which of the fences he should make his own rush for safety. For the blockhouses De Wet had invariably, both in conversation and his despatches, expressed such contempt that his decision was a foregone conclusion. Hiding himself near the Lindley—Kroonstad line late in the afternoon of February 6th, he waited for darkness to cover his salvation or ruin. His chances were small, but every moment's delay would make them less. Elliot was no further forward than Doornkloof; Holmes and Marshall had not yet come up into line from the south. When night was some hours old he gave the word to march, and at one o'clock on the morning of February 7th he found himself close against the wire entanglements which barricaded the narrow space between the blockhouses. In the intense darkness his approach had been quite undiscovered, and when the wires were cut De Wet himself and his foremost men effected the crossing in perfect silence. Close behind him, however, came a herd of driven cattle, the precious meat supply of the commando, and it was not until these began to blunder noisily amongst the wires that the garrisons in the blockhouses awoke to the situation and opened fire. Many of the beasts and a few burghers who were riding with them were shot; many were turned back, but the majority burst their way through and rejoined

Escape of De Wet.

De Wet when he gained the banks of the Valsch river and freedom at dawn.*

Close of the operation. Its results.

On the next day, February 8th, the great armament, its main object thus dissipated, checked its career at the railway and counted its gains. These were not inconsiderable, though there were few who would not have bartered the total yield for one prize which was not in the net. In killed, wounded and prisoners the manœuvre had deprived the enemy of some 285 men, perhaps one-sixth of those who had from time to time been reported, or had disclosed themselves during the past few weeks. The rest had disappeared, some with De Wet, the others as if they had been moles or bats, for the surface of the ground had been apparently utterly denied to them. Some, at least, had attempted to escape like fish, for Rimington actually made prisoners of men who had buried themselves all but their mouths under the waters of the Rhenoster, whilst many were raked from the mud and reeds of the adjacent banks! Such desperate devices to avoid a captor from whom no cruelty was to be feared may well arouse wonder, not at the length, but the shortness of the campaign which brought a nation of these stalwarts to its knees. Must not the Romans have encountered a like spirit when, under remarkably similar conditions of comparative discipline, organisation and resources, they found a period of nearly one hundred and fifty years all too short for the subjugation of Britain?

Desperate resources of the fugitives.

---

* There was much uncertainty on both sides with regard to this occurrence. It was believed by the British, and Lord Kitchener so reported in his despatch, that De Wet had driven the cattle as a ram against the wires, hiding himself and his men in the midst of the mob, a device of the credit of which the Boer leader would scarcely have deprived himself as he did in his own account of the affair ("Three Years' War," page 352). It is probable that, unknown to him as he rode ahead in the darkness, the majority of his followers did actually become involved in the stampede which carried the herd of 600 beasts through the line of defences.

EVENTS IN THE ORANGE RIVER COLONY.

APPROXIMATE STRENGTH STATES OF COLUMNS REFERRED TO IN FOREGOING CHAPTER.

COLUMN.	Mounted Troops.	Infantry.	Guns, including Vickers-Maxims.	Machine Guns.	
December, 1901—*February*, 1902.					
Brig.-Gen. R. G. Broadwood	1,030	—	5	—	⎫
Lt.-Col. H. de B. de Lisle	1,052	—	5	1	⎪ Lieut.-General E. L.
Lt.-Col. the Hon. J. Byng	1,284	171	5	1	⎬ Elliot in command.
Major R. Fanshawe	1,526	—	6	1	⎪
Lt.-Col. M. F. Rimington	1,620	365	5	—	
Lt.-Col. A. E. Wilson	569	180	1	2	
Major J. H. Damant	611	83	3	1	
Lt.-Col. J. S. S. Barker (two columns)	1,075	—	5	1	
Lt.-Col. C. J. Briggs *	583	—	2	—	⎫ Brig.-General Sir J.
Lt.-Col. D. McKenzie *	795	—	2	1	⎬ Dartnell in command.
Major-Gen. B. B. R. Campbell	393	1,486	7	2	⎫ Lieut.-General Sir L.
Major F. A. Williams	500	—	2	—	⎬ Rundle in command.
Col. F. S. Garratt	1,031	270	5	1	
Lt.-Col. J. W. Dunlop	721	—	1	2	
Lt.-Col. J. G. W. Dawkins	824	—	3	—	
Col. Sir H. Rawlinson	1,299	178	6	1	
Lt.-Col. J. L. Keir	884	—	3	—	
Major W. R. Marshall	571	25†	2	—	
Major H. G. Holmes	501	—	—	1	

* These two columns worked independently on Sir J. Dartnell relinquishing command.

† Scottish cyclists.

CHAPTER XXIII.

EVENTS IN THE WESTERN TRANSVAAL*

(Continued from Chapter XIX.).

JANUARY—MARCH, 1902.

Lord Methuen's movements.

LOST to sight, both of his colleague Kekewich and of Army Headquarters, Lord Methuen, in hot pursuit of a Boer convoy, had, as related, reached Vryburg on January 5th. His quarry, with two days' start, had disappeared, and Lord Methuen remained for a few days at Vryburg, employing the interval in scattering a laager discovered to the north-west (January 8th), from which his troops captured seven prisoners. On the 12th he struck eastward again, marching fast by way of O'Reilly's Pan and Mooiplaats across the Harts river to Rooiwal, beyond which, by hard galloping, he picked up a wandering Boer convoy of thirty-two vehicles and much stock on the 14th. Two days later, whilst heading for Boschpoort, at the head of the Little Harts river, Lord Methuen suddenly came upon the very convoy which had misled him across to Vryburg. Although it was strongly guarded it was quickly captured entire, forty-five vehicles, a herd of beasts and nineteen burghers falling into the hands of the mounted troops, who rode fifty horses to death in the pursuit. On January 19th the column entered Lichtenburg. Near this town the enemy, as he was so often fortunate enough to do, made amends for his losses on the 16th by inflicting a sharp blow on part of Lord Methuen's column. It happened that a party of some forty Boers had been reported at Treurfontein, some twenty miles to the south-east. On

---

* See map No. 59.

EVENTS IN THE WESTERN TRANSVAAL. 407

January 21st Lieut.-Colonel K. Chesney was despatched to engage them with 200 men. But the supposed small band proved to be a strong commando, under General Celliers, who, after demolishing Chesney's advance-guard squadron, proceeded to outflank and hustle the rest back towards Lichtenburg. Within six miles of the town the detachment, which had lost more than a third of its strength,* was fortunately met by Lord Methuen, who had heard of the affair and had sallied out to the rescue with 500 men and three guns. Rain and "rinderpest" kept Lord Methuen at Lichtenburg until the 26th, when he made for Klerksdorp by a circuitous route around Tafel Kop,† arriving on the railway on February 1st.

Kekewich, since his abortive combination with Lord Methuen, had been engaged during the previous month in covering the construction of a line of blockhouses along the Taaibosch Spruit to Vaalbank. This he effected chiefly from Rietfontein, employing his time in harrying any hostile parties within reach, from one of which, at Brakpan on January 16th, he took eleven prisoners and a small train of wagons. Altogether Kekewich took twenty-eight prisoners by these means during the month. On the 29th, the blockhouse line being completed to Vaalbank, it was decided to prolong it to Lichtenburg, and Hickie was called down from Tafel Kop to assist Kekewich in protecting the building operations. Hickie appeared on February 1st, and Kekewich immediately resumed his wonted activity. The northward extension of the blockhouses was carrying him daily into the heart of a region which had never failed to be infested with the enemy's most determined bands, such as had lately done damage to Chesney's party within a few miles. Not far to the north, at Roodepan, De la Rey himself was reported to be in laager, and there were other camps in the vicinity. All were known to Kekewich's Intelligence Officer, Mr. W. Carlisle, a man as subtle in the detective part of war as he was skilled

Kekewich's movements.

---

* Casualties—Killed, nine men; wounded, twenty-four men; captured, three officers and thirty-eight men; total, seventy-four.

† Not to be confused with the height of similar name in the Frankfort district of the Orange River Colony.

in fighting, to whom, as to Wools-Sampson in the Eastern Transvaal, well-nigh every burgher on this side was known by name and sight, and every camping ground and water-pan upon the vast tract a familiar haunt. On the night of February 4th Kekewich despatched Major H. P. Leader, of the 1st Scottish Horse, accompanied by Carlisle, to try their fortune with 634 mounted men and a Vickers-Maxim.

Success at Gruisfontein, Feb. 5th, 1902.

Leader, intent on the most important game, marched straight for De la Rey; but about 1 a.m. on the 5th, when on the way to Roodepan, a Boer piquet fell into his hands, from whom he learned that De la Rey had probably moved, but that another laager was certainly to be found at Gruisfontein, an intermediate farm. Leader decided to grasp at the substance rather than risk the shadow. With great skill he advanced on Gruisfontein, not from the south, which would have given the Boers a clear run in the direction most safe for them, but by a wide circling movement made in the dark from the north, which would both bewilder the enemy and drive him towards Kekewich, who was at Leeuwfontein, at the source of the Taaibosch Spruit. Before dawn on February 5th Leader arrived within charging distance of the laager. He disposed his men in three bodies, placing the scouts of the Scottish Horse in the centre, two squadrons (ninety-five men) of the same corps under Captain J. R. Mackenzie on the right, and the same (110 men) under Captain W. Jardine on the left. In this order the force rushed upon the laager during the last few moments of twilight, for Leader, fearing to be discovered, would not wait for day. The Boers were completely taken by surprise. Sleeping in various scattered kraals, each party in turn attempted resistance, and more than once by their rapid and resolute firing went near to checking the onset. But Leader had sent in his men with as much intelligence as determination. Pushing his flanks well in advance of his centre he had soon surrounded the whole group of kraals, from which, shoot as fiercely as they would, not a Boer could make his escape, whilst all were practically without cover from one side or the other. First, on the right, seventeen burghers were taken as they broke and fled; a moment later Jardine secured twenty-seven more from one of the huts on the left; finally, after hot fighting at close quarters, the centre had the satisfaction of receiving the surrender of Commandant Sarel Alberts, a noted commander, with seventeen of his officers and all his men, to the number of 131, of whom ten were wounded ; seven others were found dead. Leader's losses were comparatively trifling. Only eight officers and men were wounded, and twenty-eight horses killed, so completely had dismay ruined the aim of fine marksmen, though they had shot furiously at a few yards' range. Leader's march back, encumbered as he was by wounded and prisoners, was much facilitated by a movement by Kekewich westward, accompanied by an artillery demonstration, which effectually distracted attention from the returning detachment.

On February 8th Kekewich, still with Hickie, advanced on the Lichtenburg road to Rietvlei, and on the 15th to Rietgat, where he remained until the completion of the blockhouses on the 21st. He was then ordered back on Klerksdorp, Hickie handing over his command to Lieut.-Colonel H. M. Grenfell on the same date. On the 25th he reached Hartebeestfontein, and there he was met by the news that a convoy from von Donop's column had been lost to the south-west of Klerksdorp. There was not the faintest indication which way it had been removed, and Kekewich, feeling in all directions, entered Wolmaranstad on February 28th, determined to organise there a flying column for the rescue of the wagons. At Wolmaranstad he joined von Donop, whose presence here, and the circumstances of his loss must now be explained. *Kekewich joins von Donop in Wolmaranstad.*

Lord Methuen, it will be remembered, after his expedition to Lichtenburg had returned to Klerksdorp on February 1st. Here he remained for a week. On the 8th he was granted leave of absence prior to establishing his permanent Headquarters at Vryburg on the western railway ; for it was his intention to relinquish for a time the actual leadership of the column with which he had done such long and arduous work in the field. The command of the column then devolved upon Lieut.-Colonel S. B. von Donop, R.A., who had been Lord Methuen's lieutenant in all his expeditions. On the very day of his promotion von

Donop signally justified it. Hearing of a concentration of Boers under Potgieter—lately a fugitive from the Makwasie Berg—at Elandslaagte, eleven miles west of Klerksdorp, von Donop issued from Klerksdorp by night, and turning the laager from the north, fell upon it at dawn and completely overthrew it, capturing thirty-six prisoners. Potgieter himself again escaped, but so narrowly that he had to ride for it bareback, and clad only in his shirt. Von Donop then went into camp on a neighbouring farm. At 9 p.m. that night the enemy attempted to avenge their losses of the morning by a sharp attack on the baggage and supply columns, in which four men and twenty-six mules were shot, and some of the horses stampeded. Next day von Donop marched upon Wolmaranstad, which he had been ordered to make his base for clearing the district. There, making constant raids amongst the enemy's cattle, he remained during February until the occurrence of the incident which brought Kekewich to his side. On the 23rd it was necessary to send a convoy into Klerksdorp for supplies. The convoy, which consisted of 145 mule-wagons and six drawn by oxen, was escorted by 230 men of the 5th Imperial Yeomanry, 225 of the 1st Northumberland Fusiliers, twenty British South African Police, fifteen men of the 3rd South Wales Borderers with two guns of the 4th battery R.F.A., a Vickers-Maxim and two Maxims; the whole under Lieut.-Colonel W. C. Anderson, the commanding officer of the Imperial Yeomanry. Besides these there were seventy-eight men of Paget's Horse, who were proceeding on special duty to Klerksdorp, and therefore not properly to be considered as forming part of the escort. A similar convoy had travelled over and back by the same route a week previously. On the evening of the 23rd Anderson halted at Kareeboomskuil; on the following evening at Yzerspruit. The two days had been quite uneventful, nor did there seem any likelihood of danger attending the short march which would bring the column into Klerksdorp. Nevertheless every mile covered had brought the convoy into more imminent peril. A few days earlier General De la Rey had come down to the Wolmaranstad—Klerksdorp road in search of adventure, of supplies,

EVENTS IN THE WESTERN TRANSVAAL. 411

of revenge for many miscarried enterprises. He had come in full strength, with a following of 1,500 to 2,000 men under his most trusted subordinates, Kemp, Celliers and Liebenberg. His scouts, watching von Donop in Wolmaranstad, had immediately informed him of the departure of the convoy, and De la Rey, unaware that the wagons were empty, determined to take them. This with the force under his control he might have done at any spot upon the road, but with a true soldierly instinct, eager as he was, he wished to make his capture as little costly to his own troops as possible. He therefore deferred his stroke until there remained but one day's march to Klerksdorp, "for," said he, "seeing that in the vicinity of a fortified place the desire of the enemy to arrive there safely is more powerful, the English would offer less resistance in the neighbourhood of Klerksdorp, and more readily take to flight than out in the veld."* The added power of a military leader who knows human nature, and how to play upon it, has long been acknowledged: that such a one, that more than one, existed in the Boer forces may perhaps enlighten those who lavished scorn on the British army for being so long kept at bay "by a nation of farmers." As De la Rey lay watching Anderson on the 24th, he was nearly discovered by the posse of Paget's Horse, whom Anderson sent on ahead of the column into Klerksdorp, where they were urgently wanted for duty with another column. As these horsemen drew clear along the road, they passed close under De la Rey himself, who had taken post on a rise overhanging their road, and the Boer General confessed that it was with difficulty that he restrained himself from ordering their destruction.* But to open fire then might lose him the heavier booty behind, and the party, all innocent of its escape, disappeared towards Klerksdorp. At 4.30 a.m. on February 25th Anderson set his troops and wagons in motion towards Klerksdorp. The wagons moved four abreast, which reduced the length of road covered by them to 1,000 yards. In front went an advance-guard of forty-five men; twenty more extended as guards on either flank;

De la Rey attacks von Donop's convoy at Yzerspruit, Feb. 25th, 1902.

---

* Account of a Boer official present with General De la Rey.

sixty-two men with a Maxim acted as rearguard, all these riding from 1,000 yards to a mile wide of the column. The infantry marched in three bodies at equal intervals amongst the train, which was actually headed by 100 mounted men escorting the field guns and Vickers-Maxim. Long before the convoy had left its camping ground at Yzerspruit, De la Rey had laid his plans. Once more they were founded as much on the characteristics of his antagonists as on their strength and formation. The wagons, which he chiefly desired, he knew that the troops would naturally do their utmost to preserve, probably with all their none too great strength, at the very first threat at any part. To draw them away from the convoy he arranged first a frontal attack to be delivered at the head of the column by Liebenberg's Potchefstroom commando from a tree-covered ridge running athwart the road. When this should have brought the majority of the troops to the front, Celliers, who had already ridden off with the Lichtenburgers by a circuitous track, would push the column into disorder from the rear, whereupon Kemp with the Rustenburg commando would fall upon it in flank and complete the rout. The sequence of these orders should be noted. The relegation to the last of the blow at the side, the weakest point, is especially remarkable as an intelligent departure from precedent; for even had the other manœuvres failed, success here would be almost certain, so denuded must the flank of the convoy be by the efforts to repel the attacks on its front and rear. The column had marched about a mile and a half when a volley from the wooded crest close in front struck not only the advance-guard but the leading wagons, the mules of which promptly wheeled and raced in panic towards the rear. Anderson, reinforcing the front, lost no time in pushing his guns into action, and soon belaboured the wood with so heavy a shower of shot and shell that the riflemen therein, disagreeably surprised at the success of their *rôle*, began to break up and run for shelter to other parts. Anderson immediately ordered the leading infantry to rush the plantation, which was done with such success that the front was cleared, and it was possible to park the wagons under the crest of the high ground, where the guns also took post. But Anderson was not to be duped into premature confidence. He feared continually for his left flank, which he had already reinforced with a squadron. When the fighting in front had proceeded for a quarter of an hour he had seen a strong body of Boers circling in this direction, and it became almost a certainty that the real attack was to be made there. Anderson hastily sent thither every available man, cooks, servants, commissariat assistants, etc., and soon had his flank guarded by more than 150 rifles. This was done only just in time to ward off the summary annihilation of the column. Nine hundred horsemen appeared on the left. Having advanced in unbroken line to within 500 yards, firing from the saddle as they ambled forward, the whole body suddenly charged impetuously down upon the flank. A fire which was not to be faced met the stormers; three times they came on, wavered, and fled back out of range. Once under shelter they were steadied by their officers, and twenty minutes later advanced and charged again. For the fourth time they were hurled back by a terrible fusilade from the men of the flank guard who lay immovable, in the face of what were virtually repeated rushes of cavalry. Anderson seized this opportunity to send an officer at full speed to summon help from Klerksdorp. So far De la Rey's machinery had gone sadly out of gear; both his men and his tactics had signally failed. His frontal demonstration had been unexpectedly swept aside; Celliers had not yet appeared in rear to roll up the column for the finishing stroke of the flank attack, which had thus been delivered too soon. But De la Rey's strength was too great to penalise him fatally for his mischances. It was only a question of getting by patience what he had hoped to achieve by dash. Nor had he long to wait for the missing commando. Celliers, surprised by the early start of the column, had lingered in his hiding-place on the rear towards Jackalsfontein, but having discovered his mistake he rode hard to rectify it. Soon after the second repulse of Kemp from the flank he galloped on to the field with 500 men and immediately rode against the British rearguard. For a time it seemed as though this last throw, too, would fail. Like Kemp, Celliers met with a shattering reception; his men refused

Severe fighting.

to face the fire, and scattering backwards and outwards, contented themselves for the next two hours with bringing a cross fire to bear upon the rearguard, which suffered considerably but replied with vigour. The troops here were now in an unfortunate position. The very firmness of their resistance was momentarily robbing them of the chance of victory. Ammunition began to fail; the men were growing exhausted; the rest of the column had by this time closed up to the front and out of reach. Finally, when every round was spent, and to remain a moment longer meant massacre, the rearguard was ordered to fall back. It was of course the signal for its destruction. The enemy, rising from the bushes rode down in overpowering numbers upon the defenceless soldiers, and passing through them, as Botha's burghers had passed through the Buffs at Bakenlaagte,* moved straight up the wooded crest where stood the remnants of Anderson's convoy. At the same time, on the left, Kemp's beaten men took heart again, and began to extend on foot in skirmishing order, pouring in a hot fire. At the edge of the plantation Anderson did his utmost to stave off the end. The guns had been fought until they could be no longer served. The wagons were now both outflanked and totally exposed in rear. Ordering the officer in charge to get them on the move towards Klerksdorp, he sent his adjutant to urge the commander of the artillery to attempt to gallop his guns away to the town. The adjutant, however, was taken prisoner almost as soon as he had started, and the order never reached the guns. Anderson then endeavoured to collect men to form a fresh rearguard behind which guns and wagons might get clear. Descending the slope in search of the scattered soldiers, he suddenly found himself surrounded by men in khaki uniforms who, holding their rifles to his breast, demanded surrender. Other Boers, similarly disguised, were in a moment upon the guns, and soon the entire column passed into the enemy's hands after a resistance which had made its overthrow more creditable than many a victory. Of the 490 officers and men engaged 187 had been killed and wounded, the detachment of the Northumberland Fusiliers alone

<small>Capture of the convoy.</small>

* See Chapter XVII.

EVENTS IN THE WESTERN TRANSVAAL. 415

losing thirty-one killed and sixty-four wounded out of this number. Only one wounded officer and 108 men escaped and made their way into Klerksdorp.* The Boers owned to fifty-one killed and wounded, included amongst the former being one of their bravest officers, the young General Lemmer.

On the news of this disaster rescue parties were organised in all directions. Brigadier-General J. C. Barker, in command at Klerksdorp, had plainly heard the firing, and had indeed attempted to intervene with the few mounted troops at his disposal, but without success. He then collected some 300 Yeomanry, whom he ordered to proceed to join Kekewich who was hurrying towards Wolmaranstad. A small column which had been operating about Bothaville under Colonel Sir R. Colleton was called northward with orders to join von Donop, which it did at Wolvespruit on the evening of February 26th, von Donop having dashed across from Wolmaranstad, thirty miles distant, with 500 men the same morning. An anxious search to the northward revealed no sign of the enemy and his booty, and on the 27th von Donop turned back for Wolmaranstad, where, as already related, he was joined by Kekewich, who next morning entered the entrenched township. Kekewich at once prepared a mounted column for a last effort at retaking the convoy. On the evening of the 28th he placed Lieut.-Colonel H. M. Grenfell in command of a force of 1,654 officers and men and 1,823 horses, with four field pieces and a Vickers-Maxim. These he sent northward towards Rietfontein, on the Korannafontein—Klerksdorp road, on the trail of a convoy supposed to be that taken from Anderson. On March 2nd he himself evacuated Wolmaranstad, after destroying all the defences which had been thrown up by von Donop. The abandonment of a fortified place as the result of the loss of a convoy may be added to the list of curious tactical reagents. It was here, of course, chiefly entailed by the departure of all the garrison of the town for purposes of pursuit, but undoubtedly the retention of Wolmaranstad had become exceedingly precarious. Kekewich then

_{Search for De la Rey.}

_{Evacuation of Wolmaranstad.}

* Casualties—Killed, five officers, fifty-three other ranks; wounded, six officers, 123 other ranks; captured, one officer, 193 other ranks.

moved by Yzerspruit, where he found dead bodies still unburied, to Klerksdorp, which he entered on March 4th. Finally Lord Methuen, roused by the news at Vryburg, instantly took the field with one hurriedly formed column under Major A. Paris (Royal Marine Artillery) from his Headquarters, whilst he called Colonel A. N. Rochfort with another from across the Vaal. Lord Methuen communicated these movements to Kekewich, and requested him to send a force to meet him on March 7th about Rooirantjesfontein, due south of Lichtenburg, the intention being for Paris and Kekewich to stand between De la Rey and the Marico district whilst Rochfort, advancing from the south, should drive the as yet undiscovered Boer leader into their arms. For this Kekewich decided to employ Grenfell, who, on March 4th, had gone into camp at Rietkuil, outside Klerksdorp, after a vigorous search during which he had cast vainly around by the south of Lichtenburg, by Holfontein and Paardeplaats, at both of which he had slight engagements. Hearing from Lord Methuen that he was being delayed by bad roads, and would be late at the rendezvous, Grenfell only covered the first stage towards Rooirantjesfontein on March 6th, when he marched to Leeuwfontein. On the 8th he was at the appointed place; but there was no sign of the Vryburg column, and during the morning Grenfell learned why it would be vain to await its appearance.

Lord Methuen marches from Vryburg.

Lord Methuen, accompanying Paris's column,* had marched out of Vryburg on March 2nd, and following the meagre water supply of this parched district moved by Grootpan, Barberspan, and Leeuwspruit, at the junction of the two Harts rivers, to Tweebosch on the Little Harts river, which was reached on the evening of the 6th. Up to this stage his only trouble had been with the water supply, which had to be as carefully scouted for

---

* Composition—5th battalion I.Y., 184 men; 86th company I.Y., 110 men; Cape Police, 233 men; Cullinan's Horse, sixty-four men; B.S.A. Police, twenty-four men; Diamond Fields Horse, ninety-two men; Dennison's Scouts, fifty-eight men; Ashburner's Light Horse, 126 men; 4th battery R.F.A., two guns; 38th battery R.F.A., two guns; two Vickers-Maxims; 1st battalion Northumberland Fusiliers, 200 men; 1st battalion Loyal North Lancashire regiment, 100 men; about 1,200 men in all.

EVENTS IN THE WESTERN TRANSVAAL.

as the enemy. Not until this day, the 6th, had any considerable hostile body been met with, nor would the commando of 100 men or so which followed the troops through Leeuwspruit have attracted notice had it not been for the disquieting behaviour of the rearguard, a company of Imperial Yeomanry, who allowed the sniping of this paltry force so to disorganise their formations that Lord Methuen himself rode to the rear with two guns to steady them. The commando, which was under Van Zyl, retired under shell-fire towards Tweebosch, where, taking up a position in the bed of the Little Harts river, it remained in observation. Lord Methuen's intention had been to camp at Leeuwkuil. Learning that that place was waterless, he decided instead to follow the Boers to Tweebosch, which he reached in the forenoon, Van Zyl's men disappearing southward on their flanks being threatened by the mounted troops. Though it was still early in the day the heat of the weather, following upon the extreme hardships of the previous four days' marching, induced Lord Methuen to go into camp at Tweebosch. There was no cause for haste; his information ran that the guns and convoy captured from Anderson were still to the south of him;* he had warned Grenfell of one or possibly two days' postponement of their junction, the place appointed for which was but one march to the north-east. *[margin: Lord Methuen at Tweebosch.]*

At three o'clock next morning, March 7th, the column was set in motion, pointing northward towards Leeuwkuil. The enemy being to the south the rear was the vulnerable part, and Lord Methuen especially enjoined Major Paris to look to this quarter. For this reason also the transport travelled in front. It consisted of ox and mule wagons, the former preceding the latter, both escorted by a squadron of Cape Police, the 86th company Imperial Yeomanry, the detachments of Northumberland Fusiliers and Loyal North Lancashire, the two guns 4th battery R.F.A., and a Vickers-Maxim. Behind these, and leaving the bivouac an hour later, came the fighting portion of the column, disposed in three bodies, advance-guard, main body, and rearguard, *[margin: His order of march, March 7th, 1902.]*

---

* Lord Methuen to Commander-in-Chief, March 5th, 1902.

the last being composed of two detachments of irregular mounted levies. The country on either side was flat and open, unimpeded by either kopje or bush. Darkness, however, is better cover for an enemy than even these, and the head of the column had marched for two hours before the first streak of dawn. During that time the force was being shadowed, as a file of coolies is followed by the Indian tiger, by the most formidable depredator in all the theatre of war. Close behind the rearmost screen, invisible and noiseless, rode De la Rey and nearly 2,000 men, most of whom were fresh from the field of Yzerspruit, and under the same officers, Kemp, Celliers, the elder Lemmer, Vermaas and, finally, Van Zyl, the jackal who had "harboured" the game on the previous day. Enveloping the British rearguard under cover of the gloom, at break of day (5 a.m.) the commandos suddenly opened so terrible a fire from three sides that, with scarcely a pretence at resistance, the untrained, undisciplined irregulars broke and fled, before the guns of the 38th battery and the Vickers-Maxim, which were sent with other troops to their assistance, could come into action. The burghers were upon them at once, and, galloping forward amongst them in a confused mob, bore down upon the front and flanks of the mounted supports which had been moving with the guns to reinforce the now shattered screen in rear. For a short time these troops stood with some determination, but their resolution melted before the overwhelming numbers opposed to them, and soon the guns remained isolated in the midst of the enemy. Now, not for the first time, were training and tradition to illumine the blackness of disaster. Lieutenant T. P. W. Nesham and his artillerymen of the 38th battery were men of the same blood as they who had given way, but to them flight was not even a last resort, it was an impossibility. Until every man had fallen the guns were served with case, and even when the pieces were actually captured and lost to sight amidst the surging crowds of Boers, the young officer in command, the only unwounded member of the *personnel*, refused to surrender, and suffered death for his gallantry at the hands of some unchivalrous butcher amongst his enemies. This left the rest of

De la Rey attacks Lord Methuen at Tweebosch, 5 a.m., March 7th, 1902.

EVENTS IN THE WESTERN TRANSVAAL. 419

the column completely open to attack. The enemy's flanking parties had already outridden and assailed the slow moving convoy, and Lord Methuen, ordering the ox-wagons to halt, and the mule-drawn portion to close upon it, had disposed the troops of the escort for defence on both sides. Before the mule-wagons had drawn on far the bullets of the rear attack tore amongst them. Instantly appalling confusion ensued. Some of the teams wheeled round; the majority, maddened by fear, rushed on in a weltering mass past the ox convoy and far ahead, scattering northward over the veld pursued by the enemy, who was now close in upon three sides of the motionless ox-wagons. Lord Methuen strove as desperately as had Anderson at Yzerspruit to save what remained. His ox-wagons were immovable; no threats or entreaties could induce the native drivers, who lay panic-stricken beneath the wagons, to urge their teams forward. Espying a kraal on rising ground about a mile to the front towards Leeuwkuil, Lord Methuen then ordered Paris to rally there as many of the mounted men as he could collect, whilst he himself with the infantry and guns remained with the convoy. For two hours the devoted troops around him kept off their inevitable fate. Surrounded at point-blank range by a force of marksmen five times their number, their only prospect was to show how soldiers may perish. The two guns of the 4th battery were fought as nobly as those of the 38th had been. Even after Lieutenant G. R. Venning, their commander, was killed, the gunners remained at their work until all were down. The men of the Northumberland Fusiliers showed that even constant misfortune could not lower their spirit. This regiment had suffered in well-nigh every disaster in the Western Transvaal, and that through as little fault and after as stout fighting as on this occasion. The Loyal North Lancashire vied with the Fusiliers. Lord Methuen himself was the central figure of his forlorn hope until his horse was killed and he himself fell with a fractured thigh. Soon after the fighting here ceased, and he passed into the hands of General De la Rey who rode into the convoy. In this manner did Lord Methuen meet the Boer leader whom he and many others had long sought with intense assiduity. De la

Capture of Lord Methuen and his column.

VOL. IV. 27*

Rey, ever the most chivalrous of foemen, after treating his prisoner with the utmost kindness, with extraordinary generosity permitted him to be conveyed in his own wagon to Klerksdorp, and this in the face of considerable opposition by some of his colleagues, who objected to the liberation of so valuable a captive.

Meanwhile at the kraal there had been a short but sharp affray. Paris had been able to collect but forty men from the routed irregulars, and distributing these in the huts and around a patch of mealies, he strove to keep off Celliers, who turned upon him from chasing the panic-stricken mule train, and completely enclosed him. Celliers had with him three light guns, and when shells began to riddle the kraals and tumble them in, the defenders, who had fought stubbornly, were in a hopeless plight, and at 10 a.m. they surrendered. Thus, after five hours from its first surprise, Lord Methuen's column was completely destroyed. Three-quarters of the *personnel* were killed, wounded or taken prisoner.* The rest were scattered over the veld, making for Kraaipan, Maribogo and other places on the western railway line, which many reached before nightfall. It was long since so complete a catastrophe had befallen the British arms. Other disasters there had been of a similar kind during the campaign, but none involving the capture of an officer of high rank; moreover, not even much honour had been saved at Tweebosch, for the personal gallantry of Lord Methuen and the few who emulated him could not cloak the pusillanimity of those whose flight had sacrificed their comrades. Of the panic of the majority of the mounted troops lack of training, insufficiency and inexperience of officers, and above all, the heterogeneous nature of their composition were the main causes. But with many examples before them of fine defences offered by troops similarly handicapped, neither the soldier nor the historian can appeal too much to such apologies.

Effect of the action at Tweebosch.

Tweebosch sent the star of De la Rey, which after much wavering had for some time been in the ascendant, up to its zenith. The Western Transvaal was now in extreme danger, if

---

* Casualties—Killed, four officers, sixty-four other ranks; wounded, ten officers, 122 other ranks.

not of being reconquered by the Boers, at least of being rendered uninhabitable for the conquerors. One deliberately chosen depôt, Wolmaranstad, had been already evacuated ; all others wide of the main lines, especially Lichtenburg, were in danger either of attack or of isolation, for it was unsafe to move a convoy whilst such a hornet was on the wing. Yet, for the warning of those who base their hopes of defeating invasion on a last resort to guerrilla fighting, it cannot be too strongly pointed out that De la Rey, with all his brilliant successes, had scarcely so much as checked the sweep of the scythe which was mowing down his country. His feats, like those of Botha at Bakenlaagte, of De Wet at Roodewal and Korn Spruit, were nothing more than tactical and local annoyances, rockets which fell harmless almost as soon as they had dazzled. In them was none of the irresistible influence of some great but possibly noiseless strategic accomplishment, giving a momentum to a campaign which a hundred affairs such as those at Yzerspruit or Tweebosch could not stir either forward or backward. Recalling events not long past for a single instance, what had De Wet's sparkling capture at Waterval on February 15th, 1900, weighed against Field-Marshal Lord Roberts' intent herding of Cronje's commandos into the fatal bed of the Modder ?* It has not been the duty of the writer to point morals except by the narration of facts ; his space is limited, and the lessons of engagements, skirmishes, tactics and strategy in the war in South Africa are as innumerable as they are generally easily deduced. The greatest lesson of the campaign is, however, brief enough to be more than once insisted upon—that the nation which is robbed of or divests itself of broad military purposes, long conceived and long prepared, and leans instead upon the patriotism of irregulars and the delusive brilliance which so often illuminates their warfare, is about to vanish from its high place none the less surely because it sinks amid a cloud of falling stars.

Inutility of Boer successes.

* See Volume II., Chapter VI.

APPROXIMATE STRENGTH STATES OF COLUMNS REFERRED TO IN FOREGOING CHAPTER.

COLUMN.	Mounted Troops.	Infantry.	Guns, including Vickers-Maxims.	Machine Guns.	
January—March, 1902.					
Col. R. G. Kekewich	690	523	3	1	} Maj. - Gen. Mildmay
Col. W. B. Hickie	539	170	3	1	} Willson in command.
Lt.-Gen. Lord Methuen } Lt.-Col. S. B. von Donop }	1,687	409	5	3	
Maj. H. P. Leader	634	—	1	—	
Lt.-Col. H. M. Grenfell	1,654	—	5	—	
Lt.-Col. W. C. Anderson	250	240	3	2	
Col. Sir R. Colleton, Bart.	—	778	—	1	
Maj. A. Paris	891	300	6	—	} Lt.-Gen. Lord Methuen
Col. A. N. Rochfort	1,377	513	4	1	} in command.

CHAPTER XXIV.

EVENTS IN THE ORANGE RIVER COLONY*

(*Continued from Chapter XXII.*).

FEBRUARY, 1902.

WHILST the troops of the eastern part of the Orange River Colony rested on the railway, Lord Kitchener prepared plans for another expedition, which in dimensions and complexity far outstripped its predecessor. The scheme provided for convolutions by co-operating but separated bodies, which can best be rendered intelligible in parallel tabular form, as follows :— *A fresh scheme on the east of the railway.*

FIRST PHASE.

ELLIOT. (De Lisle, Fanshawe, Holmes, Marshall, Lawley,† Du Cane.†)	Rimington, Byng, Sir H. Rawlinson.
March east from line Kroonstad—Ventersburg—Doornberg to line Lindley—Bethlehem.	March east, right on Wolvehoek—Frankfort blockhouses, left on Heidelberg, to line Standerton—Tafel Kop.

SECOND PHASE.

Wheel eastward to line of Wilge river between Strijdpoort and Majoors Drift.	Wheel south, pivoting on Tafel Kop, on line between Wilge river and Standerton railway.

THIRD PHASE.

Hold above line on the Wilge, right prolonged to Harrismith by Sir L. Rundle.	March south to line of blockhouses Van Reenen's Pass—Elands River Bridge. Right flank blocked by Elliot on Wilge. Left flank (passes of Drakensberg) held by troops from Natal.

* See map No. 64.

† These fresh columns were provided as follows : Major J. P. Du Cane came from Colonel Rochfort's southern district ; Lieut.-Colonel the Hon. R. T. Lawley, with the 7th Hussars and 2nd Dragoon Guards, from Winburg.

The scope and intention of these operations will be understood by reference to the map better than by any written description. Briefly, their first aim was to herd the Boers of the eastern Orange River Colony into a closed funnel, formed by the Wilge river on the one side, the Klip river and the Drakensberg on the other, the Harrismith—Van Reenen's blockhouses completing the *cul de sac*. Down this lane the northern columns would then sweep from its entrance southward, pushing the enemy towards its blind end, just as the fowlers of past days used to drive the wild-fowl through the decoy " pipes " which ended in the fatal enclosure of the net.

Elliot was the first to move, quitting Kroonstad on February 12th and 13th, with his left (Fanshawe) on the Valsch, his right (Lawley and Du Cane) extending southward towards the Winburg—Senekal road. On the 14th his line from right to left was Senekal—Rienzi ; on the next day from Elands Spruit to the Molen Spruit. On the 16th he was between Lindley and Bethlehem, halting on that line until the distant factors of the operation should develop. A raid by his left flank against Elands Kop on the 17th resulted in the capture of ten prisoners and De Wet's invaluable heliograph.

Turning now to the north, where the driving force had been making ready : On February 16th Rimington's right was on the Heilbron—Frankfort blockhouses (the line of which, as before, had been stiffened by Damant, Wilson, and Keir), his left at Groenvlei, whence Byng carried the front across the Vaal at Grobler's Drift to join Sir H. Rawlinson, who was extended from Bierlaagte to Daspoort, south-east of Heidelberg. Rawlinson had already been busied in dealing with a Boer band which had attacked a Heidelberg detachment in the Zuikerbosch Rand ; this he did effectually on the 15th before taking up his line as above. With little incident the three columns now advanced on a solid front for three days, and on the 18th had arrived at the wheeling point, the line being then, from right to left, Tafel Kop—Zaam Dam—Lemoenskraal — Zamenkomst — Standerton. On the 19th there was a general halt for supplies, which were drawn from the opposite flanks—Tafel Kop and Standerton.

EVENTS IN THE ORANGE RIVER COLONY. 425

On the 20th, whilst Damant moved to connect Rimington's right with the Wilge river, an advance was made to the line Cyferpoort—Gruisplaats—Baviaanskraal—Paardekop, a front of nearly sixty miles. On the 21st Rimington, still pivoting on Tafel Kop, threw his left through Vrede to Paardenkop, Byng beyond, touching the Klip river at Eerstegeluk. Rawlinson, detaching his left from the Standerton railway, pushed down to Eerstegeluk—Zoetendalsvlei, the gap thus created between him and the railway being filled by a column from Paardekop station under Colonel J. E. Nixon, who cleared the Verzamel Berg on his way.

All was now set for the final act, and Elliot moved forward and seized the Wilge from Strijdpoort down to Majoors Drift, his left in touch with the Frankfort contingents, his right with those from Bethlehem. Facing him, and sixty miles distant, troops from Natal blocked every loophole of the Drakensberg; the men in the Harrismith—Van Reenen's defences stood to arms, and every side of the great alley was lined with guns and rifles. On February 22nd the line descending from the north reached Woodside—Botha's Berg—Poortje—Zeekoevlei. Except for a large capture of stock by Sir H. Rawlinson, on the left, as he passed over the Gemsbokhoek Berg, there had been so far little reward for so much marching and manœuvring. All depended upon the next few days, and before these had passed each side in turn had scored and suffered a grievous blow. *Elliot seizes the line of the Wilge.*

In order to comprehend ensuing events it is necessary to transfer the story to the Boer side, reverting first to De Wet, last seen emerging into safety on the left bank of the Valsch. Despite his adventures the Boer leader deliberately discarded the opportunity of escaping from the district to which his presence had drawn so many thousands of British troops. Instead, no sooner was he informed by his signallers on Elands Kop that the columns had come to rest upon the railway than with extraordinary temerity he turned back and once more made for the hilly country at the head of the Rhenoster river. In so doing it is hard to say whether he displayed even more than his customary daring or less of his strategical acumen, *De Wet returns into the area.*

for his mission was plainly ended in these districts, whereas there was now scarcely another in the Orange River Colony which was not thinly occupied and at the mercy of a sudden irruption by his commandos. Be this as it may, the first steps of his return all but led to his extinction. This time the Lindley—Kroonstad blockhouses were alert, and a hot reception greeted, but did not repel, his crossing. De Wet had not been many days in his old stronghold before he found himself once more in front of Elliot's line of columns coming out from Kroonstad for their above-described march to the Wilge. On the night of February 17th one of his signalling parties was captured, in the manner related, only four miles from his bivouac, de Lisle and Fanshawe little knowing how close they had been to the sleeping-place of the leader who had long robbed armies of their rest. De Wet then slowly fell back before Elliot across the Libenbergs Vlei, and happening upon the wandering Steyn at a farm north-east of Reitz, the two watched for a time the oncoming of the tide of troops which lapped without a break over every horizon. Soon they had to be gone, for Elliot was bearing down on the Wilge. On February 22nd they sidled away up the Cornelis river with eyes on every side, falling in continually with groups of burghers who were flying in all directions from one danger to another. Now W. Wessels, now H. Botha, Mentz, Ross and Beukes, all noted commandants, appeared and vanished, each with news of a fresh barrier on the north, east, south or west. De Wet had formed a plan of breaking through the blockhouse line between Vrede and Botha's Pass; but his own scouts brought him intelligence that Byng and Rawlinson were already in front of those despised obstacles. On the 23rd, as the columns still came on, De Wet, driven to definite action, determined to risk all upon a rush against whatever troops he might find immediately in front of him, and at set of sun he moved northward with four commandos, some 800 strong, for the decisive throw. On that evening Rimington lay behind the Hol Spruit from Pram Kop to Langverwacht, Byng thence to Strydplaats, Sir H. Rawlinson carrying on the line to the left bank of the Klip river. For the first time there

EVENTS IN THE ORANGE RIVER COLONY.

had been news of Boers within the cordon, the Vrede—Botha's Pass blockhouses reporting the passage two days earlier of a commando making southward. As De Wet approached the sleepless line of troops his scouts informed him that they had discovered a comparatively weak spot at Kalkrans, on the Hol Spruit, near the point of union between the columns of Rimington and Byng. Steering for this he crossed the Hol Spruit, and in the midst of a downpour of rain and thick darkness fell furiously upon the outposts of Garratt's New Zealanders, who were lined up before him. The onset was irresistible ; a section of the defence, standing firm to the last, was swept away, and the enemy poured in upon the flanks of the rest, who were partly rolled up from opposite sides. A desperate combat ensued. The New Zealanders yielded not an inch until they were dashed aside, and then the survivors fought on individually. Their resistance was of the greatest value, for it enabled Lieut.-Colonel F. Cox, the commanding officer, to swing some of his posts on to a new front, and endeavour to deny the passage by a flank fire. In this he was partly successful, his rifles doing such execution that many of the burghers refused to run the gauntlet and fled back. But nothing could stop De Wet's progress, which had itself acquired the momentum of a stampede. Many of the Boers, as they rushed through in the half light intermingled with vehicles, loose horses and cattle, confused the defence with friendly shouts, thereby considerably checking the shooting. For half an hour the intermittent onrush continued, and at the end of that time, when all who dared had passed, the New Zealanders closed up their broken front, and under the rising sun counted the cost of De Wet's escape. Eighty dead and wounded of both sides* lay mingled on the narrow field amidst the carcasses of the same number of Boer horses and a mob of carts and cattle, the whole of which De Wet had left behind him. For the moment neither the true gains nor the losses of the

De Wet charges the cordon at Kalkrans, Feb. 23rd, 1902.

De Wet breaks through with heavy loss.

---

* British casualties—Killed, two officers, eighteen men ; wounded, five officers, thirty-three men.

Boer casualties—Killed and wounded, twenty-one. De Wet ("Three Years' War") accounts for twelve more wounded, removed by himself, of whom two died.

event could be appraised. They were by no means unevenly balanced. On the debit side Steyn and some 500 men had burst the cordon with De Wet, and thus to some extent the whole combination had missed its aim. But De Wet had lost the whole of the moveable supplies on which he depended, and was still within an area intersected by lines of blockhouses, at any of which he might yet meet his fate. Moreover, a portion of his men, about 300 in number, had turned in fear from the dangerous breach in the New Zealanders' ranks, and these were still in front of the columns, doubtless spreading alarm amongst their comrades with the tale of the disastrous night's adventure.

On February 24th there was a partial halt whilst Sir H. Rawlinson somewhat advanced his outer flank and strengthened his union with Byng by transferring Nixon from the extreme left to about Boschfontein. On the next day all the columns made the line of the Cornelis river from its junction with the Wilge to the Drakensberg. Still so few of the enemy were met with that failure seemed to await the closing phase of the expedition. The 26th, however, put a more hopeful aspect on affairs.

Commandos still within the cordon.

Six or seven hundred Boers were sighted by the various columns, and in the skirmishing the Imperial Light Horse of Dawkins' column captured sixteen prisoners, and Byng's units twenty-eight. There was soon further evidence that De Wet had taken with him neither all the strength nor spirit of his forces. The line on the evening of the 26th was Majoors Drift—Pleasant Gift— the Dwaal Spruit to below Melani Kop, leaving but half a day's march to be accomplished on the morrow. The troops knew that within the narrow strip between this front and the Harri-smith—Van Reenen's blockhouses must be imprisoned all that was to reward the arduous beat of the last twelve days. Every man was alert, and only the vigilance of the troops saved them from being robbed of everything at the eleventh hour. At

Desperate attempts to escape.

midnight a body of nearly 700 desperate Boers suddenly rushed against the central groups of Nixon's outposts along the Dwaal Spruit. A few broke through; the rest were hurled back, ten remaining in the hands of the soldiers. An hour later the attempt was repeated on the left of the same section, with the same result. This was the final effort. Next morning, as Briggs took his Imperial Light Horse forward in advance of Sir H. Rawlinson, he was met by two envoys, who prayed for terms on behalf of the entrapped commandos. No conditions could be granted other than the retention of their personal belongings, and an hour was given them in which to consider. Before the expiration of that time 648 burghers came forward under the white flag and yielded themselves prisoners of war to Sir H. Rawlinson, together with 1,078 horses, forty-seven carts and wagons and 40,700 rounds of ammunition. Thus, for the third time, was signalised in fatal fashion for the enemy another anniversary of that victory of twenty-one years before, which had given to the Republics their brief summer and their final doom. Lord Kitchener, as he rode out from Albertina station to greet the troops on February 28th had no reason to be dissatisfied with the results of his vast calculations, even though the chief figures were missing from the account. The total captures numbered 778 prisoners, 25,000 head of stock, 2,000 horses, and 200 wagons. Thirty-nine prisoners had been picked up by Barker as he watched and raided on Elliot's right rear, and though for some time to come the eastern part of the Orange River Colony was to be still the scene of much activity, it was not because De Wet's power remained unbroken, but because he himself was still at large. *Surrender of 648 Boers, Feb. 27th, 1902.* *Total results of the operation.*

This is a suitable opportunity for tracing the movements in the Orange River Colony of other bodies of troops, the story of whom was interrupted by that of the great schemes which had their climax between the Wilge river and the Drakensberg. To do so it is necessary to make a retrospection of some three months, picking up first the ten columns under Sir C. Knox and Rochfort which were left at work in the basin of the upper Caledon. For the first half of December, 1901, there was little change in their occupation. Brand's scattered bands continued to haunt the district, and they to bandy him about from one to the other. About December 17th, however, there appeared signs that the country on the western side of the railway, so long quiet, was receiving the fugitives from other and more *Events in other parts of the Orange River Colony.*

Rochfort crosses to the west of the railway.

harried areas, and Rochfort was ordered to take his troops, now in five divisions under Lieut.-Colonels Western and du Moulin, Major D. P. Driscoll (Driscoll's Scouts), Major E. S. Bulfin (Yorkshire regiment) and Major P. A. Kenna (21st Lancers), across the line. A. C. Hamilton's column had already been sent to Philippolis at the first sign of renewed activity in the west. Sir C. Knox was left in the east with Lord Basing, Pilcher (two columns), and Thorneycroft (two columns).

Successes by both sides.

Rochfort found immediate occupation amongst the small commandos which had recently re-entered the district. At dawn on December 24th du Moulin surprised a laager near Jagersfontein Road and captured twenty-eight prisoners, including two officers. This success was promptly discounted. Christmas Day, so grimly celebrated by De Wet 250 miles to the north-east*, here also brought good fortune to the Boer arms. A. C. Hamilton, having discovered a commando at the head of the Berg river, attacked at dawn, scattered the laager, took sixteen prisoners and hotly pursued the rest into the Heen-en-Weers Kop, a stronghold north-west of Fauresmith. The chase took him far in advance of his baggage train, which was escorted only by some sixty men. Once more full payment was exacted for a momentary and not inexcusable mistake.

Capture of a convoy at Kokskraal, Dec. 25th, 1901.

When the wagons had reached Kokskraal they were suddenly surrounded by 250 Boers under Hertzog and Nieuwhoudt, the presiding genii of this part. Resistance was out of the question; the handful of guards were caught in the open and Hamilton was out of sight. Every wagon was quickly in the hands of the enemy, who having set fire to them all rode off with fifty-seven prisoners, the other casualties amongst the escort being four killed and five wounded. To what a level of brutality the long campaign had lowered a once honourable enemy was shown when the Boers, having shot three of the native drivers in cold blood, stripped some of the prisoners naked and compelled them, an officer amongst them, to walk in this plight more than thirty miles across the burning veld into Springfontein. Some amends was made for this mischance three days later when Driscoll,

* See Chapter XXII.

EVENTS IN THE ORANGE RIVER COLONY. 431

operating along the Riet river, accounted for twelve Boers in a chase of many miles; but when December closed it was plain that on the west of the railway there was full employment for Rochfort, whose task was not lightened by his having to send two of his columns, Kenna's and Bulfin's, to join Sir C. Knox at Ladybrand.

Since the first week of December Sir C. Knox had been disposing his forces for a general drive northward towards the Bloemfontein—Ladybrand blockhouses. On the 10th his left was north of Edenburg, his right near Bismarck on the Basuto border. A week later he drew up at the blockhouses, having met with scarcely a living thing on the way. During the halt here, Colonel T. P. B. Ternan succeeded to Thorneycroft's command, Major F. W. Heath to that of Taylor. At Christmas-time a move was made to the north of the blockhouses, and in conjunction with Barker from Winburg, and the two columns sent by Rochfort, all were now engaged in scouring the districts about Clocolan, Senekal, Governors Kop, the Koranna Berg and Mequatlings Nek. The country was by no means clear of the enemy, which was to be accounted for by the succession of sweeps in progress to the northward under Elliot and others, such operations invariably brushing a number of fugitives into the adjacent districts. There were several smart affairs, notably one on January 6th, when Lord Basing's outposts were hotly attacked near Ficksburg by 150 Boers under Van Niekirk. Later on Barker found considerable numbers about Rexford, and Ternan and Bulfin met with opposition in the Witte Bergen. Both sides of the railway below Kroonstad became thus once more the scene of a campaign which, though it had degenerated into the constant revolutions of strong patrols, might at any moment provide incidents such as compose the triumphs and disasters of guerrilla warfare. Rochfort had already experienced one such affair; he was soon to be the victim of another. His columns had continued to raid between Philippolis and the Modder with varying fortune. On January 26th Driscoll found Hertzog and Nieuwhoudt as far north as Makauws Drift on the Petrusburg road, and in a creditable attack took seventeen prisoners, including

Sir C. Knox on the east of the railway.

two officers. Subsequently he so harassed the Boer main body that its leaders endeavoured to shake him off by withdrawing southward. At this time du Moulin was north of the Riet river about Batsheba, and coming on the trail of the retreating commandos on the Emmaus road, he followed it southward, Western co-operating from Koffyfontein. On the night of January 27th du Moulin camped opposite Abrahamskraal* on the left bank of the Riet river, having pushed some of the enemy across the drift during the day. The night's dispositions consisted of a series of piquets posted on a semi-circle of kopjes overlooking the river; behind these, on either side of a small farmhouse, lay the horse lines and the parked transport wagons.

<small>Attack on du Moulin, Jan. 28th, 1902.</small>

At one o'clock on the morning of the 28th the sentries at the drift heard the sound of men fording the water. Before warning could be given, the whole piquet was overwhelmed by a rush of burghers who, seizing the point of vantage, kept the gap open whilst a strong body poured through into the camp. In a moment the horse lines and the outbuildings of the farmhouse were theirs, and every corner was searched by bullets. Du Moulin, who had passed the night in the house, emerged at the first shots, and calling a few men round him led a charge against the nearest Boers. He himself, with several others, fell dead immediately, but the kraals were cleared, and soon after another determined counter-stroke against the position of the piquet which had been first destroyed regained that also, and at 1.45 a.m. the enemy fell back. Brevet-Major A. R. Gilbert (Royal Sussex regiment), had now assumed command in place of du Moulin, and he quickly redistributed his men along the line of defence. His promptitude was fortunate, for in an hour's time a second attack was delivered against the outposts. This was smartly repulsed, and was not repeated. This affair cost the column its commander and ten men killed, six men wounded, and nearly 150 horses and mules lost or destroyed. The enemy left three on the field, and carried off some dozen wounded, for some of whom they next day begged an ambulance from Gilbert. When daylight came they were seen

<small>Du Moulin killed.</small>

<small>Boers repulsed.</small>

---

* Not to be confused with the place of similar name on the Modder river.

EVENTS IN THE ORANGE RIVER COLONY. 433

to be holding strong positions on both banks of the Riet, and Gilbert, cut off from both Western and Driscoll, prudently withdrew towards Jagersfontein.

During the first part of the month of February, whilst the country to the east of the line was being crossed and recrossed by the pack of columns there collected, Rochfort remained centred at Fauresmith, his columns circulating about him. On the 19th he moved northward to near Boshof, to co-operate with a column under Lieut.-Colonel W. H. Sitwell. The latter had come into the Orange River Colony after a month's raiding in Griqualand,* in the course of which he had had several sharp encounters with 400 Boers under De Villiers. On January 13th, when between Campbell and Griquatown, Sitwell had found this commando drawn up across his path, and after a close action had cleared the way by a dashing bayonet charge delivered by the Royal Munster Fusiliers. The column lost an officer and twenty-three men killed and wounded; the enemy was severely handled, and his losses numbered some forty. Two days later an officer and twelve men had been cut off and captured from Sitwell's rearguard. On February 5th Sitwell had returned to Kimberley, marching thence on the 9th towards Leeuwkop. On the 16th he found the local commandos strongly posted between Varkfontein and West Rietfontein. They remained immovable after an engagement of six hours' duration, followed on the next day by a searching bombardment of four hours, the column sustaining twenty-two casualties.† This affair was the cause of Rochfort's already referred to northward movement, the results of which must be narrated later. *Rochfort moves northward and combines with Sitwell.* *Sitwell's previous operations.*

Turning again to the east of the railway: early in February Sir C. Knox's columns were ordered to block the southern exits from the area about to be swept by Elliot's advance to the Wilge. This they did in connection with Barker, the whole line moving forward to the Senekal—Bethlehem road on the 16th. After Elliot had passed on his way Sir C. Knox resumed his *Sir C. Knox co-operates with Elliot.*

---

* See map No. 63.

† Casualties—Killed, one officer, four men; wounded, one officer, eight men; missing, eight men.

VOL. IV.

clearing operations, and soon after gave up command in the field to relieve Sir C. Tucker at Bloemfontein. About the same time Sir L. Rundle was similarly replaced at Harrismith by Major-General E. S. Brook.

APPROXIMATE STRENGTH STATES OF COLUMNS REFERRED TO IN FOREGOING CHAPTER.

COLUMN.	Mounted Troops.	Infantry.	Guns, including Vickers-Maxims.	Machine Guns.	
February, 1902.					
Lt.-Col. H. de B. de Lisle	1,913	—	7	—	
Lt.-Col. R. Fanshawe	1,626	—	6	1	
Major H. G. Holmes	501	—	—	1	Lieut.-General E. L. Elliot in command.
Major W. R. Marshall	571	25*	2	—	
Col. the Hon. R. T. Lawley	1,135	—	3	2	
Major J. P. Du Cane	413	—	3	—	
Lt.-Col. M. F. Rimington	1,513	470	5	—	
Lt.-Col. the Hon. J. Byng	1,242	155	5	1	
Col. Sir H. Rawlinson	1,113	200	3	—	
Major J. H. Damant	655	75	3	—	
Lt.-Col. A. E. Wilson	454	176	1	2	
Lt.-Col. J. L. Keir	893	—	2	—	
Lt.-Col. J. E. Nixon	1,102	—	3	2	
Col. F. S. Garratt	855	167	3	1	
Lt.-Col. J. W. G. Dawkins	716	—	3	—	
Lt.-Col. C. J. Briggs	570	—	2	—	
Lt.-Col. W. G. B. Western	327	—	3	—	
Lt.-Col. L. E. du Moulin (later Major A. R. Gilbert)	91	545†	3	—	Colonel A. N. Rochfort in command.
Major D. P. Driscoll	544	—	1	—	
Major E. S. Bulfin	458	—	2	—	
Major P. A. Kenna	602	—	2	—	
Major A. C. Hamilton	581	—	3	—	
Lt.-Col. T. D. Pilcher (two columns)	1,341	—	5	1	Major-General Sir C. Knox in command.
Col. A. W. Thorneycroft (two columns)(later Col.T.P.B.Ternan)	1,246	—	7	1	
Lt.-Col. Lord Basing	590	—	3	1	
Lt.-Col. J. S. S. Barker (two columns)	1,100	—	2	1	
Lt.-Col. W. H. Sitwell	552	236	3	1	
Major-Gen. B. B. R. Campbell	526	314	2	1	From Lieut.-General Sir L. Rundle's force.

* Cyclists. † Including sixty-four cyclists.

435

CHAPTER XXV.

EVENTS IN THE NORTHERN TRANSVAAL.*

APRIL, 1901—MAY, 1902.

THIS district, of which the town of Pietersburg formed the capital, had from the first played a rôle somewhat disconnected from that of the rest of the theatre of war, and this less from its remoteness, its unhealthiness for man and horse, and its paucity of inhabitants, than from its comparative strategical inutility. At Pietersburg the interests of both combatants seemed to end with the railway which found its terminus there. Beyond lay a waste so inhospitable that, as was pointed out in an earlier chapter, Rhodesia itself, even without a garrison, was almost safeguarded from Boer invasion, had it indeed been worth invading in a military sense, for it was more difficult to approach across the salty ridges which fell to the Limpopo than Cape Colony across the Karroos. True, in the earliest phases of the conflict the duels between Plumer and Grobelaar had seemed to point to mutual apprehension in this region;† but that campaign had died a natural death, and in a few weeks the Northern Transvaal had relapsed into its normal lethargy, the Boers only maintaining a weak and inactive garrison in the capital town itself. Not until the British army had swept up to the eastern frontier at Komati Poort did the interest revive at Pietersburg. Then Botha, escaping round Lord Roberts' left (northern) flank, made his way thither, followed in driblets by many of his men, and there, when he had collected a sufficient number, he ceased to be a fugitive and resumed his office of

<small>Remoteness of the district</small>

---

* See maps Nos. 56 and 59. † See Volume III., Chapter VII.

commander of the Transvaal army. In this he was quite undisturbed, and the respite he enjoyed undoubtedly enabled him to reconstitute a force which had been temporarily shattered in spirit and therefore—after the manner of the Boers—in numbers. Anent the omission to intercept or forestall the federal leader at Pietersburg contemporary criticism was as severe upon the British strategy as it was—as such criticism commonly is—unjust. Had Pietersburg been occupied in September, 1900, it was said, the enemy's last base, his last source of supplies, his last plotting place would have been denied to him, and the war consequently have been at an end. How little of this will bear scrutiny. Pietersburg might indeed have been seized and held with advantage, but only if such a measure had left sufficient troops for the eastern march of the British army, with its necessarily strong and remote flanking detachments, and its liability to heavy general engagements at any moment. Doornkop, Diamond Hill and Bergendal had warned the Commander-in-Chief that he must have strength at hand however fast fled the enemy. He had to deal with a hostile army which though seen to gallop away in disorder in the evening might be found lying embattled at the next dawn. Pietersburg might indeed have been taken, but both it and the long line of communication linking it with Pretoria must have been held in strength; it was quite in the air, the very mark for wandering commandos, for by no effort could Lord Roberts keep all the enemy before himself. The strong bands roving unaffected in the Waterberg district to the west could descend upon it at any moment. But even had it been occupied, Botha and his following would have been perfectly content to draw breath elsewhere. The Boers, unlike European forces, demanded no " place " in which to concentrate, to find sustenance, to plot or recuperate. Their bases were the numberless farms, their resting places the sheltered valleys of the veld ; their councils of war took place not in inns or mansions, but under the stars. Their warfare, which had survived the loss of Pretoria, was not likely to die at Pietersburg, nor did it die for many a long month after that town was securely in British hands. It is necessary to recount these

The neglect to occupy Pietersburg.

EVENTS IN THE NORTHERN TRANSVAAL. 437

facts less for the purpose of answering criticism than of anticipating it ; for the neglect of Pietersburg, if it did not prolong the general campaign, at least rendered portions of the British tactics more difficult, or even meaningless, especially the earlier operations north of the Delagoa Bay railway. When Pietersburg was eventually occupied in April, 1901, it became immediately useful. Thence Plumer, it will be remembered, based his blockade of the Oliphant river drifts, whilst F. W. Kitchener's and other columns scoured the area to the east. Thereafter, as Plumer returned no more to Pietersburg, the conduct of affairs devolved upon Lieut.-Colonel H. M. Grenfell, the commander of a corps called Kitchener's Fighting Scouts, which was composed of two regiments, commanded by Lieut.-Colonels J. W. Colenbrander and A. E. Wilson respectively. His are the operations now to be described.

Grenfell took with him to Pietersburg some 900 men of the 1st and 2nd Kitchener's Fighting Scouts, 400 of the 2nd Wiltshire regiment, ninety-six cyclists and three Vickers-Maxim guns. At Pietersburg already were parts of the 2nd Gordon Highlanders and 2nd Wiltshire regiment, three companies of the 12th M.I., two guns 18th battery R.F.A., and a 5-in. gun, these being under command of Colonel F. H. Hall, R.A., who was also in charge of the seventeen posts which held the line of communication down to Pretoria.* Information as to the enemy was meagre, as it could not fail to be in a district which the majority of the Boers therein had entered rather to escape observation as cattle guards, than with any idea of making active war. Certain fighting bodies there were, however, under the general command of Assistant-Commandant-General C. J. Beyers, a leader whose quality had been too well proved on the heights of the Magaliesberg† for his presence to be ignored. Towards the end of April Beyers, with a strong band, was reported to be at Klipdam, fifteen miles

_{Grenfell in command.}

---

* The 2nd Northamptonshire regiment, a company M.I., the 85th battery R.F.A., and portion of the 1st West Riding regiment, formed the remainder of Colonel Hall's command at this time.

† See Chapter I.

> Grenfell's operations against Beyers.

north of Pietersburg, and it became Grenfell's first task to find and engage him. Leaving Pietersburg on the evening of April 26th Grenfell marched northward in three divisions, of which the right was under Lieut.-Colonel J. W. Colenbrander, the centre under Major N. A. Thomson (12th M. I.), the left under Lieut.-Colonel A. E. Wilson. The laager was found at dawn on the 27th when Colenbrander, attacking from the east, drove the Boers into the arms of Wilson on the west. The whole laager, which proved to be under Commandant Van Rensburg, was secured with thirty-seven prisoners, seven Boers being killed. Next day four more prisoners and a *cache* of 76,000 rounds of ammunition fell into the hands of the patrols. Grenfell now got news of the Boer main body on the Haenertsburg mountain, due east of Pietersburg; with them was reported to be a 6-in. gun, rumours of which had long gone about the district. He immediately turned in that direction, and passing through Woodbush on the 29th, was greeted by the cannon from the high ground 10,000 yards to the south. The gun continued to shell his rapid advance; but the demonstration was only a plucky piece of bravado, for Lieutenant Du Toit (State Artillery), who was in charge of the piece, had been deserted by his proper escort, two commandants who were coquetting with surrender, and he was almost alone. Firing until the attack came within

> Destruction of a 6-in. gun.

3,000 yards, Du Toit then blew the weapon to fragments with dynamite cartridges and made his escape, ten of his men being taken by Grenfell in the pursuit. The troops then scoured the country in all directions, discovering enormous quantities of buried ammunition, whilst on May 4th, Thomson, with 100 men of his 12th M.I., surprised a Commandant Marais with forty men in laager, and captured the whole. Returning to Pietersburg Grenfell prepared another expedition, which set out on May 7th, 960 strong.* Louis Trichardt was occupied on the 9th, thirty-seven Boers being cut off and taken in the neighbourhood. Vigorous patrolling resulted in many surrenders, and on the 22nd in a considerable capture by Colenbrander, who,

* Kitchener's Fighting Scouts 350 men, 12th M.I. 150 men, 2nd Wiltshire regiment 360 men, two guns 83rd battery R.F.A., two Vickers-Maxims.

EVENTS IN THE NORTHERN TRANSVAAL. 439

with one casualty, took seventy-two prisoners in a surprise attack on a laager commanded by Field-Cornet Venter. On May 26th the column was back in Pietersburg. Grenfell's gains during the month's operations amounted to 265 Boers killed and captured, 1,766 voluntary surrenders, a Maxim gun, the destroyed 6-in. gun, nearly half a million rounds of ammunition, and farm and laager stuffs too numerous to detail. Results of Grenfell's operations in May, 1901.

Whilst Grenfell had been about Louis Trichardt, the reported approach of Beyers himself from the Waterberg district had caused two small columns to be concentrated for the protection of the railway, one* under Wilson at Naboomspruit, the other† under Major H. McMicking, who came up from Pretoria, at Nylstroom. These were intended to act in co-operation, but Wilson encountered Beyers alone at Boekenhoutskloof (twenty miles north-west of Nylstroom) on the 18th, and forced him back westward with the loss of a Field-Cornet and eighty burghers captured. Next day Wilson was in touch with McMicking, and the two, pushing Beyers back on to Zandrivierspoort, nearly surrounded him and took eighteen prisoners. The Boer leader fell back upon a strong main body laagered in the almost inaccessible fastness of Zandrivierspoort, where he had to be left until more strength could be brought against him. The Intelligence reports now gave information of other bands more to the south, abreast of Warm Bath, and Wilson, moving down to the Rooi Berg, made plans to round them up. But two squadrons which he despatched to turn the enemy in the desired direction fell in with commandos numbering 500 men under Commandants Uys and Pretorius on June 1st, and after a spirited fight were obliged to retire with the loss of thirteen killed and wounded. The Boers, who had suffered severely, made off also, only to come after all within reach of Wilson. He fell upon them heavily on the 2nd, and after a stubborn combat

---

* Strength—Four hundred Kitchener's Fighting Scouts, twenty-two Bushveld Carbineers, thirteen 12th M.I., 104 2nd Gordon Highlanders.

† Strength—Three hundred and ten 20th battalion M.I., 188 2nd Lincolnshire regiment, two guns 75th battery R.F.A.

which continued all day, utterly routed them, killing and wounding many and taking forty prisoners, with loss to his own force of only eleven. Wilson then went into Warm Bath, whence for the next three weeks he fended the enemy from the railway in conjunction with McMicking from Nylstroom.

Meanwhile Grenfell was preparing a force strong enough to deal with Beyers and his unexpectedly numerous following to the west of the line. On June 21st he marched from P. P. Rust with 1,300 men and three guns,* McMicking moving out of Nylstroom at the same time with 550† and two guns. Whilst the latter moved direct upon Zandrivierspoort, Grenfell, bent on getting well behind that stronghold, first trended north-west and gained the line of hills at Groethoek before he turned south-west towards his objective. Much delayed by his transport amongst the precipitous heights, he did not reach the Poort until the 28th, when he found McMicking already entrenched there and the Boer laagers in full retreat north-westward. Establishing a depôt, and leaving the infantry and convoy at the defile, he immediately set out in pursuit with his mounted men, and at dawn on July 1st overtook the fugitives at Hopewell, in the Rustenburg district. Beyers himself was not with them, and a few shots sufficed to bring to terms the Commandant, who was hampered by the presence of several hundred women and children. With a booty of 133 prisoners and seventy-seven wagons, Grenfell's men returned to Zandrivierspoort.

<small>Beyers driven from Zandrivierspoort.</small>

The captures of the past few months, considerable though they were, by no means disposed of the Boer strength in the Northern Transvaal; for Beyers was doing his utmost to maintain his numbers, even at the cost of constant flight and loss of material. The Boer General was fighting under the greatest difficulties. Sickness, especially amongst the horses, was never absent from his laagers, and its anxieties were doubled by the mobs of women and children whom his men insisted on carrying

<small>Beyers' difficulties.</small>

---

* Kitchener's Fighting Scouts, 12th M.I., 2nd Wiltshire regiment, two guns 85th battery R.F.A., one Vickers-Maxim.

† 20th battalion M.I., 2nd Lincolnshire regiment, two guns 75th battery R.F.A.

EVENTS IN THE NORTHERN TRANSVAAL.

about less from fear of the British than of the native tribes, who in this region were at open feud with the Transvaalers. The aloofness of the district with the consequent absence of news and its long neglect by the British invading columns had caused the burghers to relax in military ardour; many of them, hearing nothing of war, actually believed that peace had returned to the land, and were more intent on reaping their crops than guarding their camps. Here, too, far removed from the central spirit of resistance, there were many waverers and traitors. Important citizens, who had been fiery enough for the cause when at Headquarters, found their patriotism cooling rapidly in this outlying province, and daily Beyers discovered now one officer, now another, absent from his side, spirited away by the alluring terms of a Proclamation, or, worse, by the tempting voice of a comrade who had already sought shelter in the camp of his country's enemies. Against so many foes, visible and invisible, Beyers, strong as his character was, could do little. Determined, nevertheless, to preserve his men and their scarcely less valuable horses as long as possible, he gave strict orders that no laager on being attacked was to defend itself to the last; rather were the burghers to scatter from the spot, and abandoning all women, children and wagons, to make off with the food beasts. Thus Grenfell and his lieutenants, falling upon camp after camp, captured few but those who had obeyed their own solicitude for their families instead of the orders of their General, who travelled the lighter for their loss. Lighter also returned Grenfell from his many forays when he had abstracted all of these, the more clumsy or soft-hearted of his opponents. July and August were unproductive months. The most striking event of July was the destruction near Naboomspruit of a train from Pietersburg, an incident chiefly notable from the extreme gallantry of the escort, a party of the 2nd Gordon Highlanders, under Lieutenant A. A. Best. These held out until every man was out of action, the losses being the officer and thirteen men killed and ten wounded. On July 8th Grenfell, leaving McMicking at Zandrivierspoort, took a convoy into Nylstroom. Finding himself followed by Beyers he turned

Train-wrecking.

against him on the 12th, hoping to catch him between his own forces and those of McMicking* at the Poort. But six messages to that officer ordering co-operation all miscarried, and Grenfell, able to do no more than push the commandos far to the west, was back at Nylstroom on the 27th. During August, though constantly in touch with Beyers, Grenfell could by no effort or device come to grips with the elusive Boer, who lost less than a score of his men in the whole month's manœuvrings. Once more the most expensive operations were train-wrecking expeditions. Twice during the month these were perpetrated by a certain "Captain" J. Hindon, a ruthless expert in this class of damage, near Naboomspruit on August 10th, and Hamanskraal on the 31st. On the first of these occasions Hindon, having successfully derailed a mail train from Pretoria, was advancing on his prize when he found the scales suddenly turned against himself by the escort and by an armoured train behind, and he had to decamp, leaving six dead and seven wounded on the ground. His second venture was terribly successful. Having blown the train almost to fragments with a powerful charge, Hindon's men, who numbered 250, poured musketry upon it from all sides, though resistance was out of the question, so shattered were the trucks that held the stunned or maimed soldiers. An officer and thirteen men were killed, four officers and twenty men wounded, the other victims being a civilian passenger and two natives killed and a woman wounded. The Boers then looted the *débris* and made off eastward, to be pursued some days later by a small force under Lieut.-Colonel F. Hacket-Thompson (Cameron Highlanders), from the Hekpoort valley, who overtook the marauders at De Wagendrift on September 3rd, killing four and recovering a portion of the mails.

During the first half of September Grenfell continued to hunt Beyers west of Nylstroom, forcing him continually to change his ground, and always with some small loss in men and animals,

---

* Lieut.-Colonel Wilson had now left this district for recruiting duties at Cape Town, his column being absorbed by Grenfell. McMicking's force was shortly after absorbed in a similar manner.

EVENTS IN THE NORTHERN TRANSVAAL. 443

but never succeeding in bringing him to bay. On the 11th Grenfell himself left the district, handing over command to Colenbrander, who had never ceased to do useful work in a region intimately known to him for many years past. From September 15th—25th Kitchener's Fighting Scouts patrolled with success (fourteen prisoners) whilst Colenbrander collected at Warm Bath a column for a serious operation in the hitherto untraversed tract between the Pietersburg and Mafeking lines of railway. This, after an abortive expedition amongst the Klipdraai hills (September 27th), was begun on October 6th. Marching by Donkerpoort, Groethoek and Hopewell, Colenbrander covered the country with his patrols, scouting indeed so far and wide that on the 19th he found himself ten days' march from his base with only three days' provisions in his wagons. Magalipsi, on the Mafeking—Buluwayo railway, being just that distance ahead, he decided to continue his way, crossing the Crocodile river at Saasi's Drift, and arrived at that distant post on the 22nd with fifty-five prisoners and a great quantity of captured ammunition, wagons and stock. Behind him on the Pietersburg line a force had been left at Nylstroom under Lieut.-Colonel J. W. G. Dawkins, Byng's recent colleague in the Orange River Colony. This party worked with much success about Geelhout Kop, on one occasion feeling as far northward as Palala, where a laager and forty prisoners fell into Dawkins' hands, bringing his total captures to seventy-six. After this Dawkins was summoned south-eastward to keep watch outside the operations then in progress in the Lydenburg district. Thence, continually picking up prisoners as he roved, he worked across to Kameelfontein, the scene of French's critical share in the battle of Diamond Hill, eventually regaining the railway at Pienaars River station on November 13th with twenty-four more prisoners.

Colenbrander relieves Grenfell.

Colenbrander on the Mafeking railway. Dawkins at Nylstroom.

Meanwhile, since November 1st, Colenbrander had been marching back from Magalipsi, by way of Selika Drift and the Palala River valley to Palala. At the latter place he once more spread out his patrols, collecting them again on the Dwars river with thirty-seven prisoners in their hands. Further on, the Boers were once more encountered in strength, at their favourite haunt Zandriviersspoort, where Commandant C. Badenhorst, with three or four hundred, had taken the place of Beyers. Colenbrander attacked at once, drove the commando headlong, and after a chase of no less than forty miles, in which several Boers were killed, drew rein with eighteen prisoners at De Naauwte. Thence he went into Warm Bath, arriving there on November 19th with fifty-five prisoners of war and a mass of produce and stock. On November 23rd Colenbrander was out after Badenhorst again, in conjunction with Dawkins who left Nylstroom on the 21st. The two columns met at De Naauwte on the 27th, and when Badenhorst had been discovered in the hills near Hartebeestfontein, an enclosing movement was set on foot the next night which shut up the exits from four different directions. The commando fell to pieces at once, and breaking out at many points, was pursued piecemeal for five days by Colenbrander towards the west, and Dawkins to the south, with the result that there were 104 prisoners of war in the hands of both columns when the chase desisted on December 3rd. Sixty-two of these were cleverly taken in one band by an ambush laid by Thomson (12th M.I.). Badenhorst himself, with about sixty men, escaped; but his liberty was of short duration. It had happened that Dawkins had returned to Nylstroom for supplies, and Badenhorst, thinking that both his adversaries had left the field, camped with his remnant in fancied security at Sterkfontein. Here he was discovered on December 10th by Colenbrander, who had remained out at Zandriviersspoort, and Dawkins having by that time rejoined, the two once more enclosed Badenhorst's laager by a skilfully arranged night march. On the morning of the 11th, after a brief resistance, the Boer Commandant, hopelessly surrounded, gave himself up with five other officers and seventeen burghers. Two days earlier his chief, Beyers, had all but shared the same fate at Geelhout Kop. But a failure of combination between Colenbrander and Dawkins, caused by atrocious weather, had given him time to get so far clear to the north-west that a thirty-mile chase had failed to catch him.

On December 13th, leaving Dawkins in the Waterberg hills, Colenbrander once more pushed westward. He had information of laagers in the Rooi Berg hills, and on the banks of the Crocodile, the latter reported to be the moveable base of Kemp, De la Rey's lieutenant in the Western Transvaal. At Morgenzon, on the 16th, Colenbrander lightened himself of his infantry and wagons, which he sent back to Warm Bath, and taking on 300 of Kitchener's Fighting Scouts crossed the Aapies river, and on the evening of the 18th set out to surprise a Boer camp which his scouts had marked on the spot where he had expected to find it, Klipgat. But the camp had already been attacked and scattered by a party of South African Constabulary from Hamanskraal on that very morning, and Colenbrander had nothing to do but to beat up the district for the refugees, which he did by extending his troops in long lines. When on the evening of the 19th he called in his men at Jericho, they brought with them fifty-two prisoners gathered without loss from many spots in the dense bush. Further searching during the next two days produced only eight more, and Colenbrander, finding not enough to occupy him further, turned towards the line, and arrived with his captures at Hamanskraal on the 23rd. The season of horse-sickness was now due and active operations had to be suspended. Colenbrander was therefore removed into the Rustenburg district after three months of strenuous campaigning, during which he had lessened the enemy by twenty-two killed and wounded and 318 prisoners, including nineteen officers. Neither these results, nor his own trifling casualties, which numbered but four in all, were any gauge of the enormous exertions of his and Dawkins' troops in a region in some parts mountainous, in others densely clothed with bush, everywhere unhealthy, and at times so arid that more than once the men marched waterless for forty hours on end. In no part of the Transvaal had the work been more arduous, and its proportionately small rewards so hard to come by. Shortly after Colenbrander's departure Dawkins was also withdrawn, to entrain on December 27th for the Orange River Colony. For the same reasons Beyers, too, was forced to change his ground and seek

Horse-sickness stops operations.

the High Veld to the north ; but the departure of the columns encouraged him to attempt to deal a blow on his way. On January 21st, 1902, he was at Matala's Location, abreast of Pietersburg. His movements were fully known to the British, and some scouts from Pietersburg had even engaged and taken sixteen prisoners from his flanking parties. Nevertheless Beyers determined on a throw for the capital. Before dawn on the 23rd he actually succeeded in introducing forty of his men into the burgher refugee camp, from which they soon rode out with 148 perjured compatriots behind them. Beyers then blew up the line, crossed to the east of it, and from that side at 4 a.m. on January 24th assailed the town with hot musketry. Twenty minutes' sharp firing, during which the commando suffered several casualties, sufficed to drive off a hesitating attack, and Beyers, raiding cattle as he went, moved slowly away south-eastward to establish a laager in the sheltered, well watered, and well-nigh impenetrable valley between Malipspoort and Pylkop. The capture of nine wagon loads of grain on the 30th near Buffles went far to replenish his supplies. At Pylkop he remained throughout February, condemned like his opponents to idleness until the subsidence of the horse-sickness, which in this region drives troops to quarters as regularly as did winter in the campaigns of old. Beyers' stronghold was constantly reconnoitred by troops from Pietersburg under Major H. d'E. Vallancey (Pietersburg Light Horse), who hung as closely on the laager as his small force permitted, on one occasion (February 6th) dispersing and taking ten prisoners from a Boer patrol of 100 men which incautiously wandered too near him.

About the middle of March Beyers once more became active. Moving northward across the Spelonken mountains, about the head waters of the Klein Letaba river, he made for his old ground to the west of the railway, intending to reach it by circling round the extreme northern limit of the British communications. This—Louis Trichardt having been destroyed in the previous autumn—was at Fort Edward, a lonely little post held by but fifty men, with a limited and easily destroyed water supply. News of Beyers' march came at once to hand ; from

EVENTS IN THE NORTHERN TRANSVAAL.

its direction, it was certain that Fort Edward would be attacked, and on the 16th Vallancey moved up to Fort Dahl with 120 men of the Pietersburg Light Horse. On the 17th Beyers was at Ramagoep's Location, and three days later surrounded Fort Edward and cut off its water, Vallancey being too weak to interfere. A force of 550 of all arms* was thereupon despatched to relieve the place from Pietersburg under Lieut.-Colonel H. C. Denny (Northamptonshire regiment). Denny encountered the enemy at Vliegenpan, and at once attacked with his mounted troops. But the enemy was strongly posted, in number some 400, and Denny's men, a mixed band of surrendered Boers and other irregulars, who regarded each other with suspicion, fought badly. They were soon driven back, and Denny, despairing of doing anything against a strong position with such discordant material, abandoned his mission and fell back on the Dwars river. The fate of Fort Edward now seemed sealed. But Beyers, whose operations in the Northern Transvaal had lately seemed infected with the listlessness characteristic of the region, sat idly round the little post, and time was given for other measures. By good fortune Colenbrander, the scourge of the northern Boers, was at this moment within hail of Krugersdorp. Hurrying up by rail to Pietersburg with his column on March 27th, he marched the same evening for the Dwars river. On the next day he threw himself upon Beyers, dislodged him at once and chased him eastward, punishing him severely before he left his heels to take the weary troops back to Fort Edward on the last day of March. Thence Colenbrander moved down to Pietersburg to prepare to settle once for all his old antagonist.

Beyers surrounds Fort Edward, March 20th, 1902.

Colenbrander relieves Fort Edward, March 28th, 1902.

Strengthened by the arrival of 600 men of the 2nd Royal Inniskilling Fusiliers, on April 5th he was ready with about 2,000 men and four guns, one of the latter a 5-in. piece. Beyers, turned back from the north, was now again below Pylkop, and Colenbrander, who well knew the strength of that fastness, concerted careful measures to entrap him. On the evening

Beyers at Pylkop.

---

* Composition—One hundred Pietersburg Light Horse, 120 Beddy's Scouts, thirty National Scouts, 115 Steinacker's Horse, 100 2nd Northamptonshire regiment, 100 2nd Wiltshire regiment, two guns.

of his arrival in Pietersburg he made the first move by sending two parties, each of 400 men of Steinacker's Horse and the National Scouts, under Captain McQueen and an ex-Boer, Celliers, with orders to march by circuitous routes and close the south-eastern and south-western exits of Malipspoort. Both parties left at night, and circling round by Chunies Poort, arrived at their respective posts at the same hour before daybreak on April 8th. On the night of the 6th a third party of the same strength, under Captain J. C. V. Lyle (Kitchener's Fighting Scouts), moved out to block the western and nearer exits, whilst Colenbrander himself, twenty-four hours later, took the remaining mounted men and the infantry, intending to place himself across the tracks leading northward out of the Poort. All these movements, admirably planned and conducted, were carried out with such secrecy that Beyers, in spite of his hundred-eyed scouts, had caught not so much as a glimpse of the contracting toils.

Colenbrander attacks Pylkop, April 8th—10th, 1902.

At dawn on the 8th he was practically surrounded, and a few hours later his commando was fighting hard for its existence. Fixing their hopes on an escape northward, the Boers collected chiefly in the strong entrenchments which they had thrown up on that side, so that whilst McQueen and Celliers advanced towards Pylkop from the direction of Chunies Poort with little opposition, Colenbrander found his way disputed by numbers so formidably posted, that it was doubtful whether his infantry (2nd Royal Inniskilling Fusiliers) could seize the hills commanding Malipspoort and its exits. A long and anxious engagement ensued. The hills were steep and bushy, and the opposition more stubborn than had long been encountered from these northern Boers. The Inniskilling Fusiliers fought with valour; but the only party which succeeded in gaining the crest before nightfall was incontinently driven off again by superior numbers. Lyle, too, coming in from the west, was stoutly opposed, and could make but little inroad, and when darkness fell Colenbrander, seeing he was in for serious work, gave orders for all to entrench where they stood. Of the detachments from the south nothing had so far been seen, nor did they come in sight throughout the next day (9th), from dawn to

EVENTS IN THE NORTHERN TRANSVAAL. 449

dusk of which heavy interchanges of fire went on as Colenbrander and Lyle slowly gained ground southward and eastward into Malipspoort. During the night a mixed party of Inniskilling Fusiliers and Kitchener's Fighting Scouts clambered up a towering hill, seized the summit, and entrenching at once, found themselves at dawn in a position commanding the whole Poort from the west. The enemy ran forthwith, and Colenbrander, pushing on, swept away the laager, killing, wounding and capturing many of its defenders. The rest, amongst whom was Beyers himself, had already fled south-eastward during the night and should have fallen in with McQueen or Celliers, who had been posted for this precise contingency. But these detachments, arriving utterly exhausted after their long and rapid march from Pietersburg, had got no further northward than Pylkop, where they halted to rest on a mountain which indeed seemed to command the whole field. A gap to the south-east, however, was thus left open, and Beyers, with the Boer's unerring eye for a bolt-hole, dashed through it with the remnants of his commando, and made good his escape. By the time this was known to Colenbrander it was too late to follow, and he ordered a general sweep towards Lyle on the west who was still slowly fighting his way into Malipspoort. In its recesses remained many scattered parties of Boers, which, crushed between Lyle and the rest, surrendered as fast as they could be found. Colenbrander then went into bivouac at the northern end of the Poort, having killed and wounded twenty Boers and captured 108 in three days' fighting, during which his men had laboured incessantly without rest, and almost without food and water. Still he was unwilling to let Beyers go unharried. Scouting continually, he learned on April 14th that the General had fled north-east beyond Haenertsburg. Colenbrander pressed after with the mounted troops on the same day. On the 15th a trap was laid by long night marches, but in vain, for the enemy had warning and made towards Leydsdorp. Sending 230 men of Kitchener's Fighting Scouts under Captain Blaine with orders to follow them up, Colenbrander himself dashed with incredible speed by a roundabout route to intercept them, and on the 17th was on the lookout on the Groot Letaba river. But no enemy came into his arms, and Colenbrander, thinking he was too far north, hurried down through Oud Agatha to Burghersdorp, and once more lay in wait, this time along the Haenertsburg—Leydsdorp road. Two days passed here, with news neither of the enemy nor of their pursuer, Blaine. Of the latter Colenbrander had heard nothing since parting with him on the 15th, though two days later it had been reported to him that heavy firing had been heard from the direction which the chase had probably taken. Not until the 19th did he get any certain intelligence, and it accounted only too plainly for his own lack of success. Blaine had met with a reverse, and instead of pursuing was in retreat.

A detachment falls into an ambuscade, April 16th, 1902.

On the 16th Blaine had been so close to the retiring commando that he rode into a laager twelve miles south-east of Haenertsburg only a few moments after the Boers had abandoned it, finding therein all the indications of a hasty evacuation. Here he rested his travel-worn men, who breakfasted from the food left behind by the enemy. The appearance of a few Boer scouts drew several of the soldiers out to drive them off; more Boers appeared and were engaged by more of Blaine's men; and finally almost the whole detachment mounted and galloped against the enemy. The ground beyond the camp narrowed between low walls of rock, and no sooner had the troops passed the mouth of the defile when a heavy discharge from both sides warned them that they had ridden into an ambush. Now the enemy appeared in force on both flanks. Some 700 Boers were visible; many of the British groups became isolated and surrounded, and only the order for a *sauve qui peut* saved the rest from sharing their fate. Scattering singly the men made the best of their way out of the predicament and back to the infantry camp at Malipspoort, the detachment having lost in all twenty-three killed and wounded and thirty prisoners. On hearing of this Colenbrander ordered his infantry up to Haenertsburg and repaired thither himself on April 20th, intending to carry on the pursuit with all his force. But the intervention of an armistice to enable certain terms of peace

EVENTS IN THE NORTHERN TRANSVAAL.

then under discussion at Headquarters* to be conveyed to Beyers kept him idle until May 3rd, an interval spent in camp near Legalie's Location. By the time the truce had expired, Beyers himself had removed far out of reach to the north-east; but many of his burghers were known to have returned to Pylkop, and Colenbrander determined to endeavour to bring them to bay. He had never relaxed his hold on Malipspoort, the northern exit of the Pylkop gorges. On to the heights on each side of this, he sent two strong parties of infantry, with orders to move southward against Pylkop. The southern gateway, it will be remembered, was at Chunies Poort, and thither on the night of May 3rd Colenbrander took 900 men of Kitchener's Fighting Scouts, Pietersburg Light Horse, Steinacker's Horse, and Beddy's and the National Scouts. These were to advance northward on Pylkop. Whilst engaged in these manœuvres Colenbrander learned that nearly 450 of Beyers' commando had been traced elsewhere. Although this left but 150 or so to be accounted for at Pylkop, Colenbrander decided to devote himself to the task in hand before turning to seek the main hostile body. At daybreak on May 5th Colenbrander's detachment came suddenly upon the Boer laagers below the southern foot of Pylkop. The Boers scattered at once, climbing into such a confusion of precipices, gorges and thickets which lay behind that they may well have seemed lost for ever. But on their trail was an enemy whom they themselves, perhaps, had taught that where one man could run another could follow, though waterless, foodless and without rest. For three days and nights Colenbrander's men hunted foot by foot through the maze, taking here a single prisoner, there a worn-out batch of fugitives, and finally, on the afternoon of May 9th, the Commandant, Biermann himself, with thirty of his following. Then only did Colenbrander give the word to halt. Of the 150 Boers in the place he had secured 104. He soon discovered the hiding place of the remnant, and he had marked them for his own when Peace put an end to their danger and his own exertions.

Marginal notes: Colenbrander again attacks Pylkop, May 3rd—5th, 1902. Results of the attack.

* See Chapter XXX.

APPROXIMATE STRENGTH STATES OF COLUMNS REFERRED TO IN FOREGOING CHAPTER.

COLUMN.	Mounted Troops.	Infantry.	Guns, including Vickers-Maxims.	Machine Guns.
April, 1901—*May*, 1902.				
Lt.-Col. H. M. Grenfell	900	496*	3	—
Lt.-Col. A. E. Wilson	435	104	—	—
Maj. H. McMicking	310	188	2	—
Lt.-Col. J. W. Colenbrander	656	242	3	2
Lt.-Col. J. W. G. Dawkins	520	220	3	—
Lt.-Col. H. C. Denny	365	200	2	—

* Including ninety-six cyclists.

CHAPTER XXVI.

EVENTS IN CAPE COLONY*

(*Continued from Chapter XX.*).

JANUARY—MAY, 1902.

NOTWITHSTANDING the discouraging events recorded in Chapter XX. Smuts professed to welcome the dawn of 1902 with unabated confidence. Never was he more assured of Divine and hopeful of human assistance. Reviewing the whole campaign before his deposed President, in an epistle which glowed with love of his country and hatred of his enemies, he declared that all things pointed to a triumphant conclusion, and that in Cape Colony especially "the cause had made splendid progress."† Nor was the Boer leader's military vision entirely blinded. There were features in the apparently moribund invasion which by no means belied his asseverations. Smuts had now nearly 13,000 rebels in the field, a levy which, if largely powerless from lack of arms and horseflesh, was of a significance grave enough to have drawn from so cool-headed and stout-hearted an observer as the British High Commissioner the confession that "The condition of Cape Colony is deplorable, not so much for the material damage which is being done, as for the evidence it affords of the lawless and disaffected temper of the mass of the population."‡ Smuts was as well aware as Lord Milner that the overt revolters were but the scoria of treasonable forces which were as yet beneath the surface. He knew, even better

<small>Smuts' confidence.</small>

* See map No. 63.
† Report by J. C. Smuts to President Kruger; dated from Van Rhyns Dorp, January, 1902.
‡ Despatch by the High Commissioner, November 15th, 1901 (Colonial Office Letter, S.A. No. 43056).

perhaps than the High Commissioner, that at last the Boer army had put its hand, however timidly and however late, upon the only lever which bore upon the power of the British in South Africa. To him the unprofitable operations of the past months appeared as indications, not that the campaign in Cape Colony was about to be quenched, but that it was unquenchable. At the beginning of this, the third year of the struggle, his own forces and all but one of his most distant detachments still survived in an arena in which the mere existence of a commando was both a triumph and a recruiting agency for the republican cause. If these bands were too battered to wage effective war themselves, they were well placed to pass fresh fuel across the frontier to feed the enfeebled flame of invasion. From the Witte Bergen in the east to beyond the Kakamas uplands in the west his men held drift-heads upon the British side of the Orange river, and even of those passages which were not in Boer hands the British seemed unable to deny the use. Twice during the past six weeks one of the main thoroughfares into Cape Colony had been traversed without hindrance by his reinforcements. The mere territory under Smuts' control was enormous. It was a "plain fact," as Lord Milner, despising all foolish optimism, at this time reported, "that the rebels are still in undisturbed possession of about one-third of the Colony."[*] For all these reasons Smuts, whom the disappearance of Kritzinger had now formally installed as Commander-in-Chief of the Boer forces in Cape Colony, faced the new year with hope, and it was not long before he endeavoured to give a fresh turn to the campaign.

At this time all the energies of Sir J. French's columns in the west were devoted to keeping the enemy to the north of the partially completed blockhouse line,[†] the "Chinese Wall,"[*] which was to preserve the reclaimed portion of Cape Colony from a return of the tide of invasion, and in accumulating supplies for a general advance northward from that base. Smuts, seeing them thus engrossed, developed activity in two opposite directions at

[*] Lord Milner to Colonial Office ; Telegram No. 273/S.
[†] See Chapter XX.

once. Sending Maritz northward to overrun Namaqualand, he began to feel around the right flank of the columns by way of Williston. His primary object was to take Fraserburg, towards which Malan moved by circuitous routes, whilst, in order to divert suspicion, Hugo, Pyper and Van der Venter feinted strongly in the direction of Sutherland.* Malan, now promoted to General, was in charge of the manœuvre, Smuts himself proceeding into Calvinia, to a central position between his widely separated operations. As these tactics became declared, about January 15th, T. Capper and W. Doran were drawn out towards Sutherland, approaching Callwell, who was already at Ganstfontein, and Lund, who was escorting a convoy up from Matjesfontein. As it was uncertain how far eastward the Boer movement might extend Crabbe was railed from Piquetberg Road round to Beaufort West. At the same time Callwell was ordered to Prince Albert Road. This left Capper the foremost of the Sutherland columns, and failing to receive Callwell's intimation of his departure, on the 23rd he unexpectedly encountered the advance-guard of the Boer combination in the defile of Verlaten Kloof. Driving these back, Capper next day found the eastern exit of the Kloof at Jakals Vallei barred by entrenchments. But a prompt attack (five casualties) cleared the road, and on the 25th Capper entered Sutherland, where he was joined by Lund. As the enemy continued to collect between Sutherland and Fraserburg, a converging movement on the latter town was ordered to be carried out by Capper (with Lund) and Crabbe, from their opposite stations. Crabbe, who was escorting a train of donkey wagons carrying supplies for Fraserburg, was first in touch with the enemy. Passing Waterval on February 3rd he found himself in the presence of commandos nearly 800 strong, who so determinedly disputed the road to Fraserburg that, in view of their superior strength, Crabbe retired upon a defensive position. At the moment when Crabbe was checked, his convoy, which was marching twelve miles in rear of him, guarded by only 160 troops, had reached Uitspanfontein. A

Smuts' tactics in Jan., 1902.

Loss of a convoy, Feb. 5th, 1902.

* Instructions by Fighting General W. Malan to Commandant H. Hugo, January 9th, 1902; dated from Oude Muur.

message despatched to bring it forward miscarried, and throughout the 4th both Crabbe and his wagons remained separated, the former rendered immovable by the close investment of the enemy, who imagined that the much desired supplies were with him. Discovering their mistake, on the night of the 4th the Boers passed around the flanks of the column towards the convoy, which they easily captured at 4 a.m. on February 5th. Two hours later Crabbe, who had left his main body at Waterval, appeared, and with only 200 men made a daring attempt to recover his wagons. But, greatly outnumbered, he was fortunate to be able to fall back upon his column again. In the three days' fighting his losses had been fifty-three killed and wounded; those of the enemy more than seventy. By this time Capper and Lund had come up to Fraserburg, and by their union with Crabbe extricated him from an awkward predicament. Whilst the columns put in for re-fitting to Nels Poort and Rhenoster Kop the Boers withdrew to Lapfontein.

Pursuit of L. Wessels.

Meanwhile, not far to the east of the scene of these events, a totally distinct operation had been in progress. This was the chase of L. Wessels, Kritzinger's successor, last seen plunging for safety into the recesses of the Camdeboo mountains. Wessels was bent on breaking westward across the railway to join Malan, and quitted his hiding-place on January 2nd. For the next five weeks his history is one of twists and turns all over the Aberdeen, Murraysburg, Graaff Reinet, Cradock, and Somerset East districts in his efforts to accomplish his end. B. Doran and Lord W. A. Cavendish-Bentinck followed, first across Murraysburg to Leeuwfontein, thence to Rondavel, in Richmond, and round by the county town back to Niet Gedacht, where Doran caught up with him on the 15th and drove him on southward with the loss of eight burghers. A few days' further hunting in the west of Murraysburg took Doran into Nels Poort to refit on January 21st, Lord W. A. Cavendish-Bentinck having been previously withdrawn from the pursuit to take part in the operations against Malan on the other side of the railway. At Nels Poort Doran stayed three days, and, taking advantage of the respite, Wessels dashed eastward, burned the railway station at

Bethesda Road, and turned southward for the Tandjes Berg. Another column now appeared to replace Lord W. A. Cavendish-Bentinck's, namely, Wormald's, temporarily commanded by Major J. Vaughan. This force had been at Richmond Road on January 18th, and was thence directed against L. Wessels. On the 26th Vaughan crossed the Graaff Reinet railway at Letskraal, and getting in touch with Wessels, followed him southward to Water Kloof, where there was a skirmish (four casualties), which ended in Wessels disappearing down the Vogel river. Vaughan pursued to Pearston, where he was on the last day of January. Meanwhile, B. Doran had come forward by Houd Constant to Oudeberg on the same date. The pursuit was now strengthened by the arrival of Follett, Scobell's successor in the north-west, who had been withdrawn from that district after a series of operations which will be described later. Vaughan, Doran, and the newcomer tossed Wessels about between them in Murraysburg, until on February 12th the commando, reduced to under fifty men, at last succeeded in effecting its purpose by breaking through the blockhouses near Three Sisters station, not without further loss, and joining Malan north of the Nieuwveld. L. Wessels joins Malan.

When Follett quitted the north-east there had seemed little left to do in that part, for the disintegration of one commando and the temporary expulsion of the other left scarcely 200 Boers to carry on the war. A northerly movement by Follett from Dordrecht on December 28th had begun the clearance by turning P. Wessels in front of Lord Lovat, who in the first week of January was between Schilder Kranz and Jamestown, Monro remaining at Dordrecht. Pushing the Boers northward on the 4th, Lord Lovat drove them across the Holle Spruit, and on the 5th surprised the laager at Kings Crown, where he secured nine prisoners. Monro and Follett, concentrating at Clifford, then arranged a joint drive westward, that is, towards Lord Lovat, who returned to his former situation. This time Fouché came in the way of Major N. T. Nickalls with a squadron of the 17th Lancers and some Imperial Yeomanry at Mooi Hoek, west of Oorlogs Poort, on January 11th; but he was in considerable strength, and got away after inflicting fourteen casualties on the Operations in the north-east.

Lancers. P. Wessels, trending south-west before the advancing columns, found return impossible, and made for the railway below Molteno. He was intercepted by Price when sixteen miles from the line; but a dense fog on the morning of the 14th enabled him to avoid an action, and crossing near Cypher Gat, he made his escape into the Bamboes mountains, Price following. With one opponent thus outside the area, all the columns then turned upon Fouché, who had slipped back in the direction of Clifford. An elaborate " drive " eastward by five bodies on the line Schilder Kranz—Montagu Hill—Drizzly Hill—Lady Grey was unproductive, only Nickalls succeeding in engaging Fouché on the 22nd, and the end of January found the columns somewhat at a loss. Meanwhile Price, aided after January 25th by two squadrons from Follett's column under Nickalls, had been vainly endeavouring to come to terms with P. Wessels in the Bamboes mountains. Price's object was to drive him into the angle of the Steynsburg—Middleburg—Cradock blockhouse line. But Wessels, well aware of the trap, turned and doubled interminably, finally gaining an offing in precisely the opposite direction. From an attack by Price on January 30th he darted away north-eastward, recrossed the railway on February 4th, and hurrying back into his old district, eventually rejoined Fouché on February 17th, when that leader had himself cast back into Jamestown county. At that moment Monro's column, the only one in the vicinity, happened to be, for the first time, unready for concerted action. Fouché's commando had practically dissolved before the incessant harrying, and Monro had just dispersed his troops into separate posts for purposes of local raiding. Fouché and P. Wessels now seized the opportunity to escape together from a district where they had experienced so many adventures in company. Crossing the railway north of Molteno on the night of February 28th, they steered for the midlands, and their departure at last left the north-eastern counties free from trouble. Price, reinforced from Molteno by Monro's mounted troops under Colonel A. C. Baillie (Imperial Yeomanry), was ordered to follow. As this force moved westward Malan approached from the opposite direction in the act of

EVENTS IN CAPE COLONY. 459

evading a combination of columns which had completely broken up his own gathering in Beaufort West.

When the columns of Crabbe, Lund, Capper and B. Doran put in to the main railway in the middle of February, they were placed under command of Major-General T. E. Stephenson, who was ordered to act vigorously against the enemy in the district. He at once, on the 17th, launched a "drive" in a north-westerly direction, which took the following lines: Crabbe and Lund from Rhenosterfontein through Uitspanfontein, Lapfontein, Paarde Gras Vallei, and Spioen Berg to Gorras (February 20th); Capper, from Nels Poort through Dassiefontein, Bultfontein, Laken Vallei to Gans Vlei (February 23rd), and thence into Williston; B. Doran, from Three Sisters station through Doorn Kloof to Taaiboschfontein, where he was stopped in order to prevent the enemy breaking back eastward from his colleagues. This operation was successful in so far as it cleared the front of the Williston—Carnarvon—Victoria West section of the great blockhouse line; the Boers gave way everywhere, and in the small rearguard actions which ensued they suffered some losses, including Commandant Hugo, who was mortally wounded. But neither Smit nor Malan, who commanded the two bodies in which the enemy retreated, were brought to book, and they treated with contempt the fences by which they were surrounded. Smit, going northward, passed through the Carnarvon—Victoria West blockhouses on the 22nd, followed to Pampoen Poort by B. Doran, who then went into Richmond on the last day of February. Malan took a bolder line. Turning eastward across the face of the "drive," he crossed the railway below Victoria Road early on the morning of February 21st. The pursuit was immediately taken up by Wormald, now again in command of his column, who chased him by the south of Richmond down to Murraysburg, close to which, at Voet Pad, there was a skirmish. Malan, who was too weak to effect much, then dispersed and attempted to conceal his men until he could receive reinforcements from the west, whence he expected Smit eventually to follow him. But Wormald left him little peace, engaging him five times in one week.

Stephenson's operations from the main line.

The Boers disperse.

Operations in the west.

All this time Haig had been left in charge of affairs in the extreme west, having under him the columns of Wyndham and Kavanagh at Clanwilliam, Callwell about Sutherland, and W. Doran in the southern border of Calvinia. There were many signs that, though the danger to the western seaboard had been averted, strong bands still hovered within touch of the new blockhouses, and might at any time become the nucleus of a fresh descent upon the home counties of Cape Town. On February 6th a convoy proceeding to Calvinia in charge of part of Wyndham's column was hotly attacked by Theron's commando at Zoetwater. The return march, during which Kavanagh joined Wyndham at Zoetwater, was directed through Van Rhyns Dorp, where Bouwers, with a considerable force, was found and attacked. On this occasion Captain E. R. A. Shearman's squadron of the 10th Hussars charged superior numbers and accounted for some dozen of the enemy. Bouwers then dogged the march back to Clanwilliam, which was re-entered on the 11th, and Kavanagh was ordered northward again to drive him off. This he did with success, pushing the commando north of Clanwilliam, twenty miles beyond which, on February 14th, he surprised the laager and captured ten prisoners.

Earlier than this W. Doran, at Middel Post, had gained practical knowledge that the tide had not altogether receded. Having been informed that the Boers were making use of the farm De Hoop, situated at the foot of the Roggeveld not far to the west of him, on February 4th Doran took 100 men to attempt to surround it, leaving his baggage and guns entrenched at Middel Post in charge of 250 men. In the afternoon, during his absence, Van der Venter suddenly fell upon the encampment with nearly 400 men, and although he was beaten off with considerable loss on both sides,* he succeeded in setting fire to most of the wagons before he retreated, forcing Doran to go first into Ceres and then to Matjesfontein (24th) to refit. So numerous seemed the enemy in the west at this time that Haig became convinced that a fresh concentration was in progress about Van Rhyns

Fresh Boer concentration in the west.

---

* Doran's casualties—Killed, three officers, seven men ; wounded, seventeen.

Dorp, and on February 24th Sir J. French ordered Callwell from Sutherland to reinforce him.

If this renewed gathering was in military strength comparatively trifling, its origin rendered it more formidable than the British authorities could at that moment appreciate. Smuts had just received the strongest encouragement to maintain his hold on so much of the British colony as he possessed. At last his strategy had received the recognition of his leaders, and he saw the realisation of his dream approaching. Cape Colony, hitherto the scene of aimless marauding, the cockpit of insignificant forces, wherein no issue greater than the fate of a convoy or a Commandant had been or could be decided, was soon to become the main theatre of war. Both De Wet and De la Rey, undazzled by their own futile brilliance on the great Boer plateaux, had conceded, what Smuts had long contended, that "The question of complete independence for the people will be decided in the Cape Colony."* This forecast, it will be seen, was appended to the ratification of Smuts' appointment to be Commander-in-Chief in Cape Colony, with the significant proviso—" until such time as General De la Rey has arrived there." The added code of rules for regularising the fighting and administration in Cape Colony plainly showed that the guerrilla raiding was soon to be changed for warfare of a more legitimate and purposeful type. De la Rey's communication was even more practical. He promised troops, announcing his intention of detaching a strong force to descend upon the frontier by the west of the Mafeking railway about April. It had already been agreed that the Transvaal commandos should operate in the west of the Colony, leaving the east to Smuts.† Smuts, indeed, had less need of precepts than of reinforcements, from the lack of which the cause was now almost at a standstill. His governance of such parts of the territory as were within his

Reason of it.

Boers plan a general campaign in Cape Colony.

---

* Letter from Head Commandant De Wet to Mr. Advocate Smuts, dated from Winburg, February 8th, 1902. This document contains so much that is of interest in throwing light on the attitude of the Boer directorate during this, the final phase of the campaign, that it is inserted *in extenso* in Appendix 3.

† Report by Smuts to Botha; undated, but written early in February.

influence was regular enough ; he had already issued a proclamation announcing the supreme rule, and how it should be obeyed, of the Republics in "nearly all the Districts of the Colony north and west of the Cape Town railway line, and many other Districts and parts of Cape Colony . . . in which the enemy has only the chief villages in his possession and authority."*

Until the promised assistance should arrive Smuts could do little more on the offensive, and he contented himself with maintaining his positions from Van Rhyns Dorp to Tontelbosch Kolk, having especial care of Prieska, with its command over the drifts of the Orange river, and of Namaqualand, where still a single British column, that of W. L. White,† patrolled an area which Smuts had marked for his own, in view of its utility as a base for the next descent by the western seaboard. On the other side the British columns became little less inactive, being largely tied to the lines of blockhouses, both by the difficulty of supply over an area so enormous and so dangerous for convoys, and by the weakness of the lines themselves, which the enemy had proved that he could rupture almost at will without serious losses. It thus occurred that the month of March was almost the most uneventful period of the campaign. Only T. Capper, based on the almost inaccessible Williston, was severely engaged as he repeatedly thrust back Theron and L. Wessels from coming southward. One band alone eluded him, and this was unsuccessfully encountered on March 25th by a detachment of the 1st Colonial division from Sutherland, which had to fall back with loss. The strongest Boer concentration was in Prieska, where Smit, deprived of Malan, was reinforced instead by Van Reenan and two leaders named Pyper, the total force amounting to some 700 men. From his laager on Omdraai Vlei, Smit haunted the Prieska—De Aar road, lying in wait for convoys. But W. Doran and a column under Colonel G. J. Younghusband converging from Britstown and Strydenburg respectively upon Klip Drift, the passage which had defied De Wet a year before, cleared the

Both sides pause.

---

* Proclamation by Head Commandant J. C. Smuts, temporary Commander-in-Chief in Cape Colony; dated from Brandvlei, Calvinia, February 1st, 1902.

† See *post.* page 468.

EVENTS IN CAPE COLONY. 463

borders of the road between March 26th and 29th, and little further transpired in this quarter. The most active operations in progress were those against Malan's remnants about Richmond, and against Fouché after his above-described escape from the north-eastern area.

On March 1st B. Doran from Richmond Road joined Wormald in the pursuit of Malan. The commando soon broke up again under the pressure and, Wormald being withdrawn for service elsewhere, Doran kept touch with it alone. On the 10th a band was caught near Middle Mount, and worsted with the loss of four prisoners. Doran then chased Malan down to Murraysburg (13th), thence northward again towards Richmond. Doran's need of supplies now gave Malan a breathing space which he utilised by swinging down into the Camdeboo mountains, towards which he knew that a comrade was winding his way from a remote part of the country. This was Fouché from the north-east. Followed by Price and Baillie from Molteno from the last day of February, by March 8th Fouché had crossed the Cradock railway near Drennan. Price was before him however, and turned him back from the passes which led southward into Somerset East, whereupon Fouché avoided him by a wide cast to the north, appearing again on the 10th at Buffels Hoek, north-east of Pearston. An encounter here, in which the Boers lost five men, broke the commando into two, half, under Bezuidenhout, going into the Tandjes Berg by Petersburg, half, led by Fouché himself, persisting southward. Detailing Baillie to follow the first, Price pursued Fouché through Wheat Lands down to abreast of Jansenville. There Fouché swung westward, and on March 16th succeeded in crossing the Graaff Reinet railway between Saxony and Klipplaat. Next day Price overtook him near Vlak Laagte, on the borders of Aberdeen and Willowmore, capturing four prisoners. But Fouché was now sure of his mark. Nothing was now between him and the Camdeboo mountains, and darting northward he was soon in that stronghold by the side of Malan.

By this time B. Doran, having refitted at Graaff Reinet, had come to Houd Constant (March 24th), and was favourably

Pursuit of Malan.

Pursuit of Fouché.

Fouché joins Malan.

placed to co-operate with Price in a drive through the Camdeboo mountains. This was begun on the 26th. The Boers, hunted from the kloofs and recesses, scattered westward, and by the end of the month Doran put into Three Sisters station, and Price into Nels Poort, leaving the enemy scattered in groups too small to deal with all over the northern part of Murraysburg.

<small>Pursuit of Bezuidenhout.</small> Meanwhile Baillie, in pursuit of Bezuidenhout, had been drawn off rapidly in the opposite direction. The Boer first dashed across the western angle of Cradock to Spitz Kop, turned east there, crossed the railway north of Fish River station, and was soon after caught up for a moment by Baillie, who took four prisoners. Bezuidenhout then ran on through Doorn Nek and made for the Bamboes mountains, whilst Baillie, on March 24th, entered Maraisburg, and three days later out-manœuvred his opponent by skirting the Bamboes mountains and facing around at Sterkstroom. Bezuidenhout was now located at Spitz Kop, at the western end of the mountains; but Baillie traversed the range from east to west without result, and on March 31st was in Maraisburg again. Here he awaited the arrival of Major-General A. FitzR. Hart, who was expected to arrive at once from Aliwal North. Hart duly appeared, bringing with him the columns of Moore and Lord Lovat. But Bezuidenhout successfully evaded an elaborate attempt to enclose him, and on April 2nd crossed the railway north of Sterkstroom. He then made straight for the old quarters of the commando in the Jamestown district, whither he was followed by Lord Lovat and Moore, whilst Baillie was withdrawn to take part in the operations against Fouché. Alone as he was in the north-east Bezuidenhout had an uneasy time during the rest of April. Hunted from one corner to another, what little strength he had was whittled away, especially by Lord Lovat, who on the 15th, 16th and 25th attacked his laagers, securing a dozen prisoners, fifty horses, and nearly all his supplies and equipment, whilst on the 18th the local troops of Lady Grey took a further six prisoners. Under this rough treatment many of his remaining burghers surrendered, and by the end of April Bezuidenhout, though still uncaught, was practically harmless.

EVENTS IN CAPE COLONY.

Fouché and Malan, now in alliance, remained to be dealt with in Murraysburg. In the first week of April an easterly sweep by B. Doran and Price brought the columns to Oudeberg and Graaff Reinet respectively. On the 10th Price was entrained back to his proper sphere at Stormberg, in view of the reappearance of Bezuidenhout's commando. Baillie, on the other hand, who had as related been withdrawn from the pursuit of Bezuidenhout, now took a place in that of Fouché and Malan, coming to Graaff Reinet on April 18th. Three days later W. Doran joined him in Graaff Reinet, having marched across from Stephenson's sphere of operations in the Britstown district. There were thus present in the Graaff Reinet area B. Doran, W. Doran, and Baillie, and these made yet another effort to catch the enemy in the Camdeboo mountains. As before it was ineffectual, because practically impossible. By the end of April the Boers had scattered yet again into the north of Murraysburg; Baillie had gone to Nels Poort, W. Doran to Graaff Reinet, B. Doran to Schietkraal, east of Biesjes Poort station. Thrice again early in May the Camdeboo mountains were scoured, this time by Baillie and W. Doran alone, who crossed and recrossed the area from Oudeberg to Nels Poort, halting on the Zuurpoort pass of the Koudeveld on May 13th, when Baillie's column became absorbed in W. Doran's. B. Doran at the same time hunted Fouché, who had separated from the others, past Richmond through Middle Mount and Dassiefontein to Schietkraal, where he was on the 15th. B. Doran was soon after joined by another column from Stephenson's command, namely, that lately commanded by Younghusband, and now led by Colonel R. C. A. B. Bewicke-Copley (King's Royal Rifles). Other reinforcements were on the way, for Lord Kitchener had enjoined special efforts to make an end of Fouché and Malan, and Sir J. French had ordered both the Scots Greys and Lord Lovat's Scouts into the area. Before they arrived, and whilst the columns on the spot halted at Zuurpoort and Schietkraal, the enemy once more combined, and crossing the Koudeveld, moved upon Aberdeen. Accompanying Fouché and Malan was a certain rebel Commandant named Van Heerden, who at the head of a small

Pursuit of Fouché and Malan.

band had made an abortive raid on the outskirts of the town on April 7th, in which he had gained a knowledge of the disposition of the garrison. He now guided the rest in a second attack on Aberdeen on the night of May 18th. It was as unsuccessful as the first, for, though the enemy got into the town buildings, the blockhouses resisted every effort to rush them, and Van Heerden himself was killed.* Fouché and Malan then drew off eastward, crossed the Graaff Reinet railway, and turning southward, were marked on May 20th at Staple Ford, near the border of Jansenville. Meanwhile, Lord Lovat had reached Graaff Reinet, and Bewicke-Copley and B. Doran had marched into Aberdeen. Sir J. French now ordered all the columns to manœuvre so as to drive the Boers eastward across the Cradock line, and if possible into the Bamboes mountains, on two sides of which he had drawn an impenetrable wall of railway blockhouses, whilst on the other sides the Scots Greys at Maraisburg, and Colonel Lukin's Colonial troops at Tarkastad were to be placed to turn any attempt to avoid the trap. Then followed one of the most elaborate operations of all the complicated campaign in Cape Colony. As the pursuing column moved eastward, Lord Lovat surprised Fouché and Malan at Staple Ford and accounted for six Boers, nearly 100 horses and mules, and drove the commandos down the Sunday river towards Jansenville. Twelve miles above that town the Boers turned south-eastward, pointing on Slangfontein and the Cradock railway. The columns performed rapid evolutions to keep them enclosed. On May 25th Lord Lovat, who had followed closely, moved into Darlington to deny the Zuurberg; W. Doran hung upon the opposite flank at Pearston; Bewicke-Copley, who had entered Pearston the day before, pushed on for Cradock; B. Doran, who had been kept at Kendrew on the Graaff Reinet railway awaiting the trend of the chase, took train for Commadagga, which, though only to be gained by the circuitous route through Uitenhage to Alicedale, was reached on the 27th. On that day Fouché and Malan were at Allegrens Kraal, with Lord Lovat close behind them at Allemans Kraal, W. Doran

* Casualties—Killed, one; wounded, four.

EVENTS IN CAPE COLONY.

upon the left flank at Somerset East, B. Doran on the right at Commadagga. Despairing of crossing the alert and reinforced railway blockhouse line, which was constantly patrolled by armoured trains, the commandos turned desperately, and attempted to cut a way back. Somewhat in front of Lord Lovat was a party of district troops under Major Collet. These received the full force of the attack, and were at once surrounded. But fighting well, they kept the enemy at bay until Lord Lovat brought his men to the rescue, whereupon the Boers fled eastward again, leaving Malan severely wounded on the field. Fouché then at all costs made for the railway, which on the 28th he succeeded in crossing in the face of every obstacle. Flying through Bedford, and past Adelaide, on June 1st he was at Paling Kloof, blocked in front by Lukin at Tarkastad, by a force under Colonel A. E. Codrington at Baileyton, by the East London railway which was fortified round to Thebus, and reinforced by every infantry soldier whom Sir J. French had been able to muster. Behind, B. Doran and Lord Lovat near Elands Drift pressed closely, whilst a line of troops from Thebus down to Mortimer denied all return to the west. A column under Lieut.-Colonel J. A. G. Drummond-Hay was at Thebus, the Scots Greys lay at Maraisburg, Bewicke-Copley moved forward from Cradock, W. Doran from Mortimer. "In another forty-eight hours," declared Sir J. French, "Fouché must have been surrounded in the mountains." But the miracle which sometimes arrives to help those who have well helped themselves intervened to save the Boer leader. "The news arrived that peace had been signed and hostilities ceased."*

<small>Capture of Malan.</small>

<small>Fouché surrounded.</small>

All this time Smuts, awaiting the day of greater things, had been steadily prosecuting his campaign in the far north-west. The region, comprising Namaqualand and Kenhardt, now thus brought into the body of the campaign, had throughout the war been so remote from it that events therein have been barely alluded to in the course of this narration. Yet it had seldom been untraversed by either belligerent since the early days of the war. Fourteen months earlier than the events recorded

<small>Smuts' campaign in the north-west.</small>

* Lieut.-General Sir J. French's report.

Previous history of the north-west, 1901.

above, that is, in March, 1901, hostile bands had appeared at Pella, extending their depredations down to Ookiep; Kakamas had even raised a commando of its own, levied and led by Conroy, Maritz's assistant. The township garrisons at that time were commanded by Lieut.-Colonel W. Shelton, with Headquarters at Ookiep. Having no mobile troops or equipment he could do nothing in so vast, waterless and sparsely inhabited an area, and he had urged the introduction of a field column to deal with the bands, one of the worst effects of whose presence was that his own troops dared not leave their farms to go on duty with their corps.*

Not until August of that year, however, had it been possible to accede to his wish. Then a column was formed at Ookiep and placed under Lieut.-Colonel W. L. White, R.A., whose orders were, generally, to patrol the left bank of the Orange river, and clear the districts of Namaqualand and Kenhardt. His opponents consisted of roaming, thieving bands of rebels, grouped roughly under Conroy, Van Zyl and Jan Louw, parties with no aim but looting, and of small military effect except to subvert both British and Boer influence by their overbearing conduct to the settlers. They amounted, however, to the respectable total of some thousand men, and until White appeared were masters of all the tracts between the garrisoned posts. White quickly made his presence felt. Marching with great rapidity, in spite of the enormous difficulties of the country, to and fro from Ookiep eastward to Upington and southward to Van Rhyns Dorp, a desert area 117,000 square miles in extent, he established posts at the tactical centres, and obtained a hold on the country which, weak as it was, was never shaken off. His encounters were few, but some were more than skirmishes. In January, 1902, an attack which he delivered from Kenhardt on the commandos massed in superior numbers at Kakamas cost him two days' sharp fighting at Middel Post and Omkyk, and fifteen casualties. The incursion of Maritz into Namaqualand in February took him back to the south of Ookiep to cover that place and the railway to Port Nolloth. In the course of escorting

---

* Lieut.-Colonel Shelton's report, March 4th, 1901.

EVENTS IN CAPE COLONY. 469

a convoy to Garies he successfully surprised a laager on the road, but having arrived, he found himself unable to return to Ookiep, for Maritz, with his own and two other commandos, had appeared at Leliefontein, between him and his base. At Garies, however, White was secure with six weeks' supplies, and Lieut.-General Sir J. French, seeing that the campaign in this part might shortly become important, ordered White to hold on, and himself assumed the direction of affairs in Namaqualand, which had hitherto been controlled from Cape Town. French's forecast proved correct. Events in Namaqualand began to move rapidly. First Maritz overran Namaqualand with his patrols, carrying out the same process of thorough reconnaissance and recruiting as that which had long before swept together the rebels and supplies of Calvinia. This was but the prelude to the arrival of Smuts himself, who in the first week of April took command and prepared to open a fresh campaign. He came with a policy well adapted to, indeed, dictated by, the nature of the country. The occupation of the few scattered inhabitable spots would practically place him in possession of the country, and he at once set about reducing those within reach. Ookiep, the terminus of the railway to the coast was his prime objective, and it was quickly invested. Springbok and Concordia, both garrisoned places on opposite sides of the town, soon fell, the first with credit after a fight of sixteen hours, the latter by a disgraceful act of surrender on the part of the Town Guard without the interchange of a shot. The loss of this village was peculiarly unfortunate because it contained a large stock of arms and ammunition, and six tons of dynamite, which the enemy desired to possess for purposes of destruction upon the invaluable line of railway leading to the coast. On the last day of March Ookiep was surrounded, just as a train carrying a fresh supply of ammunition succeeded in making its way into the town. The enemy then took possession of the track as far as Steinkopf, where they took up a strong position, and prepared to move upon Port Nolloth. They got no further, however, towards the sea, their last hope of maintaining communication with the outer world. At Port Nolloth lay H.M.S. *Barracouta*, commanded

[margin: Smuts assumes command in the north-west. April, 1902.]

[margin: Capture of Springbok and Concordia.]

[margin: Ookiep surrounded.]

Prompt action by officers at Port Nolloth.

by Commander S. H. B. Ash, R.N. This officer at once grasped the situation, and landing a party of bluejackets with a gun, promptly occupied the light railway for some distance. The approaches to Ookiep were finally secured by Captain M. Macdonald (Namaqualand Border Scouts), who on his own initiative guarded Annenous and its adjacent viaducts with local troops. These were most valuable services, for the reconquest and reconstruction of the line would have indefinitely delayed the progress of a force for the relief of Ookiep, which was fast approaching by sea from Cape Town. Ookiep was separated from the coast by thirty miles of desert so impassable that a river of equal width would have been an easier obstacle than the sand. The bridge-heads, as it were, were at Annenous and Klipfontein, and fortunately Smuts had either overlooked or been forestalled in the seizure of posts which the destruction of the railway might well have rendered unapproachable. On April 11th and 12th a

Arrival of Ookiep relief column, April 11th—12th, 1902.

half-battalion of the 2nd East Surrey regiment landed at Port Nolloth, Colonel H. Cooper accompanying it to command the "Namaqualand Field Force," which was shortly completed by the arrival, also by sea, of Callwell's column. Whilst the disembarkation was in progress, Cooper himself hastened up the railway with local troops, and thanks to Ash's and Macdonald's foresight, and Smuts' lack of it, was able to occupy first Annenous, and next Klipfontein by April 17th, thus making good the huge obstacle of sand. The difficulties of the country convinced him of the inutility of mounted troops, and he asked for reinforcements of infantry. Accordingly the 2nd Royal Fusiliers were despatched from Cape Town, arriving at the front at the end of the month. Cooper's advent had the effect of causing Smuts to withdraw half his investing force to stand in the way of the column, which they did at Steinkopf, now strongly entrenched.

Siege of Ookiep, April 5th—May 1st, 1902.

Meanwhile, Ookiep was experiencing all the incidents of a regular siege. On April 5th Smuts demanded the surrender of the place. Shelton confidently refused the summons. In the short time at his disposal he had thoroughly organised his resources. The garrison, which consisted of some 700 officers and men of the 5th Royal Warwick regiment, Town Guard, Namaqualand Border

EVENTS IN CAPE COLONY. 471

Scouts and Imperial Bushmen, he strengthened by enrolling and arming at the last moment 275 volunteers drawn from the civilian population, which numbered 4,426 souls. These troops he disposed in two circles of defence about the town, the outer ring, five miles in perimeter, comprising thirteen blockhouses, a small fort, called "Fort Shelton," and four entrenched piquets; the inner line included four strongly entrenched posts at the angles of the town itself, these connected by a continuous series of sangars and loopholed walls. The enemy began active operations by occupying, on April 8th, the ridges to the north and east, from which they opened a rifle fire which seldom ceased from beginning to end of the siege. On the four following nights they made determined attempts to rush the northern defences. But in spite of the free use of dynamite bombs with which Concordia had supplied them, every attack was repulsed with loss, and only one outlying blockhouse fell into their hands on the 10th. The fourth and last attempt, on the night of the 12th, was more resolute than any. On that occasion the Boers, concentrating their fire power on two adjacent blockhouses, endeavoured to overwhelm both by sheer weight of lead. In this they were partially successful, the garrison of one of the houses being driven back to the inner zone after firing their last round. But as daylight drew on the enemy pressed the attack no further, nor did he again venture to close upon the town. For this the advance of the relief force was in the main responsible. On April 22nd Shelton was in heliographic communication with Cooper, then at Klipfontein. On that night part of the garrison made a sally, and drove the enemy from the blockhouse which had been lost on the 10th. Thereafter the defence was very little troubled, though the investment continued to be solid. About this time Smuts handed over control of the undertaking to Maritz, proceeding himself to attend the Peace Conference which had been inaugurated at Vereeniging. On April 29th, three days after a preliminary reconnaissance by Callwell, Cooper, not awaiting the arrival of the fresh battalion of infantry, delivered his attack on the covering position at Steinkopf. But the ground was so formidable and the enemy in such strength

Attacks on Ookiep.

Ookiep in communication with relief column, April 22nd, 1902.

Relief column repulsed, April 29th, 1902.

that he found the task more than he could accomplish, and fell back to Klipfontein. The Boers, however, suffered severely from his artillery fire, and appeared in no way encouraged to prosecute their enterprise at Ookiep. Nothing more active was undertaken by them than an attempt to blow up the place by a truck containing two tons of the dynamite obtained from Concordia, which was run along the line towards the outskirts at 4 a.m. on May 1st. But the truck, which was propelled by an engine under full steam, was derailed just outside the danger zone and, catching fire, its tremendous contents burned harmlessly away in sight of both belligerents. How great the danger thus averted might have proved was shown by the discovery of a force of some 800 Boers who lay under cover close behind the train, with the intention of rushing in at the height of the confusion to be caused by the explosion. During that day Cooper advanced for the second time against Steinkopf. But the enemy, abandoning the whole attempt against Ookiep, had

Relief of Ookiep, May 4th, 1902.

scattered in all directions, and three days later the column entered the town. Shelton's creditable defence of thirty days against a close and occasionally pressing investment had cost the well-sheltered garrison and inhabitants only seventy casualties, of which twenty-three were non-combatants. The enemy lost more than 100. Some 500 rounds of shrapnel were fired by the 9-pr. gun, which did excellent service, and 120,000 rounds of small-arm ammunition were expended.

Meanwhile White in Garies, though cut off from Ookiep, had not only preserved his communications with the south, but had operated with considerable success in the Kamies Berg. On April 29th his supplies were replenished by a convoy brought from Clanwilliam by Kavanagh, who returned to Van Rhyns Dorp. Soon afterwards White re-opened the road to Ookiep, and

Final operations in Cape Colony.

on May 20th joined Cooper there. Wyndham's column, now commanded by Major H. P. Kirkpatrick (16th Lancers), was then posted to the west of Van Rhyns Dorp as a connecting link between Namaqualand and the Clanwilliam defences. All other of Sir J. French's columns had been still occupied in covering the great line of blockhouses, a duty which absorbed all their

EVENTS IN CAPE COLONY. 473

strength and rendered them largely immobile. Those under Haig, in the extreme west, as has been seen, afforded aid both in the relief and to the communications of Ookiep. Further east, Stephenson's command of six columns had still sparred with Smit, Conroy and the two Pypers between De Aar and Williston, baulking every attempt to approach the blockhouse line. This produced a series of small encounters. Early in April L. Wessels and Theron, reconnoitring south-eastward from Tontelbosch Kolk, were driven back by T. Capper from Williston. The enemy's favourite bases for their investigations were the Pram Bergen and Storm Berg, west and north-west of Richmond Road, and twice during April expeditions had to be sent to drive them thence. On the 19th Bewicke-Copley, temporarily in command of Younghusband's column, threw Smit and the Pypers out of Varkfontein with loss. The latter retired to Dagga, Smit to Baznards Dam, where four days later he was again attacked, this time by Wormald from Richmond Road, who pushed him down the Ongers river back upon the Pypers at Dagga. Beyond this little occurred in this area either in April or May. The great cross-country blockhouse line had effectually paralysed the commandos between Tontelbosch Kolk and the main line of railway, and the failure at Ookiep promised to expose the right flank just as Fouché's abandonment of Barkly East and Jamestown had exposed the left. Smuts, when he quitted the siege of Ookiep to attend the Peace Conference at Vereeniging,* left his cause in Cape Colony in a condition of mingled promise and failure. His men kept the field in one vast diagonal line from Namaqualand down to Cradock. Though worn down, they were still unconquered; though scattered, they were well placed to resume the invasion, and to cover the passage of reinforcements from across the Orange river. In short, he had preserved the foundations of success, but nothing more; without powerful help the campaign had already failed upon the ground where he and his superiors had declared that it must be decided. His existing forces were so many dying embers; he, more than any Boer commander, must

Smuts leaves Cape Colony. His situation.

* See Chapter XXX

cast his vote at Vereeniging in accordance with the reports of leaders from other parts, for his own bolt was shot. Thus it transpired that at the very time when he had looked for the pouring in of fresh fuel, he was to invoke instead the extinguishing breath of Peace.

APPROXIMATE STRENGTH STATES OF COLUMNS REFERRED TO IN FOREGOING CHAPTER.

COLUMN.	Mounted Troops.	Infantry.	Guns, including Vickers-Maxims.	Machine Guns.	
January—May, 1902.					
Col. S. C. H. Monro	960	—	2	5	
Col. H. J. Scobell (Follett's)	1,010	—	6	2	
Capt. Lord W. A. Cavendish-Bentinck	150	—	1	1	
Lt.-Col. W. Doran	300	—	2	—	
Lt.-Col. B. Doran	385	—	2	3	
Maj. F. T. Lund (later Russell)	350	—	2	1	
Maj. F. Wormald	310	—	1	—	
Lt.-Col. E. M. S. Crabbe	500	80	2	1	
Lt.-Col. C. T. McM. Kavanagh	475	—	3	—	
Lt.-Col. P. G. Wyndham (later Kirkpatrick)	430	—	—	—	
Lt.-Col. T. Capper	530	18	2	1	Lt.-Gen. Sir J. D. P. French in command.
Lt.-Col. C. E. Callwell	350	—	2	3	
Maj. S. J. Lord Lovat	460	—	—	1	
Lt.-Col. W. L. White	280	54	1	—	
Lt.-Col. G. J. Younghusband (later Bewicke-Copley)	450	—	1	—	
Lt.-Col. M. G. Moore	200	160	—	1	
Lt.-Col. W. H. Hippisley	600	—	—	1	
Lt.-Col. H. T. Lukin	600	—	?	1	
Lt.-Col. the Hon. H. A. Lawrence	313	—	—	—	
Maj. R. Hoare	330	—	1	2	
Lt.-Col. A. C. Baillie	650	—	1	5	
Col. H. Cooper	60	1,040	2	2	
Col. E. C. Bethune	500	—	2	1	

CHAPTER XXVII.

EVENTS IN THE ORANGE RIVER COLONY*

(Continued from Chapter XXIV.).

MARCH—MAY, 1902.

THE minor issues in the Orange River Colony being accounted for as described in Chapter **XXIV.**, a return must be made to the arena which by common consent had become the cockpit of the whole campaign. By the end of February Botha in the Eastern Transvaal seemed to have done his worst; in the Western Transvaal De la Rey had scarcely awakened to his short but brilliant day of success upon the plains of Lichtenburg; Cape Colony, the real strategical touchstone of the campaign, remained, as it had begun, no more than a raiding ground in the plans of one belligerent, and an expensive nuisance in the eyes of the other. It could not yet be known how far the recent event on the Mill (Molen) river had robbed De Wet of his power to sting, and without delay Lord Kitchener inaugurated another enormous manœuvre for the purpose of discovering who still rode between Kroonstad and the Drakensberg, and between Bethlehem and the Vaal. As before, a parallel table will best show the various phases of the project. A fresh "drive" by twelve columns.

FIRST PHASE.

Elliot with de Lisle, Fanshawe, Lawley, Barker, Du Cane, Rimington, Keir, Wilson and Damant to move north from line Bethlehem—Majoors Drift up to the line Frankfort—Tafel Kop—Botha's Pass.	Garratt (replacing Byng), Sir H. Rawlinson and Nixon to sweep westward across Elliot's rear from line Majoors Drift—Mill (Molen) river confluence to line Lindley—Millerale, facing north-west.

* See map No. 64.

SECOND PHASE.

| Above columns to wheel about, pivoting on Frankfort, and form line upon the southern columns, right flank on Heilbron—Frankfort blockhouses. | Above columns await formation of line by the others, left flank on Bethlehem—Lindley blockhouses. |

THIRD PHASE.

A general advance in line westward to Kroonstad railway.

<small>The troops move on March 4th, 1902.</small>

On March 4th Elliot set out on his northward march with his columns on the appointed line in the following order from left to right: de Lisle, Fanshawe, Barker, Du Cane, Rimington, Keir, Damant, Wilson. By nightfall he had extended to the line Blydschap—Reitz—Newmarket. Colour was given to reports that De Wet was in front by three attempts to break back through Barker's outposts beyond Reitz during the night, all of which were easily repulsed. Very little more was seen or heard of the enemy during the following two days which brought the front through the line Aangaan—Bamboes Spruit to the turning point on March 6th. The chief event was the discovery by Major C. Ross, a Canadian officer skilled in scouting, of one of those hidden magazines which supplied the secret fuel of the Boer campaign. The site of the *trouvaille* was no less surprising than its amount. In a cave near Tafel Kop Ross unearthed 310,000 rounds of small-arm ammunition, several hundred shells for field artillery, thousands of fuzes, 600 Vickers-Maxim projectiles, a Maxim gun, three sets of field signalling and telegraph and one of telephone apparatus, all this from almost under the feet of a British garrison of long standing. The booty also included most of De Wet's personal effects.

Meanwhile the southern columns, marching on the 5th, passed athwart Elliot's receding rear by Dipka—Rust—Vinknest—Rondedraai to the line of the Libenbergs Vlei river on the 8th, meeting with even less opposition than Elliot had done. On

EVENTS IN THE ORANGE RIVER COLONY. 477

the 9th, Elliot having wheeled into his new front on the Libenbergs Vlei, all was ready for the final stage. The driving line had now been weakened by the falling out of four of the columns. Lawley, marching by Villiersdorp, made for the Eastern Transvaal by Heidelberg and Springs, his subsequent history being dealt with elsewhere.* The ill news from the Western Transvaal drew Keir, Wilson and Damant from the combination to entrain at Volksrust for Klerksdorp, where all was gloom after Lord Methuen's disaster on the Harts river.† On March 6th Sir C. Knox, suspending his clearing operations about Ficksburg, had concentrated at Senekal, moving thence to hold the line of the Valsch river from Kroonstad to Lindley. He thus formed, with the blockhouses, a double rail along the left flank of the general advance. *Four columns withdrawn.*

On March 10th the eight columns on the Libenbergs Vlei river moved westward. Hopes of another large capture did not run high. Several strong bands were known to have broken back around the open flanks of Elliot's columns as they drove northward; worst of all, it was certain that De Wet himself was outside the enclosure, he having safely crossed the railway near Wolvehoek as long before as the night of the 5th. The only remaining quarry seemed to be a commando of some 400 men under Commandant F. Mentz of Heilbron; nor were these long in danger. On the night of the 10th Mentz, with Rimington only an hour behind him, boldly charged the Heilbron branch railway close to Gottenburg, being so feebly received by the defensive posts on the line that he got across from south to north with all his men. He then doubled eastward in the direction of Villiersdorp. Another band had previously effected an even more daring escape through the double line of columns and blockhouses between Kroonstad and Lindley. As a consequence, on the conclusion of the "drive" on March 13th, it was found that the whole operation had yielded but eighty-two prisoners, forty-seven vehicles, and a small quantity of stock, poor return indeed for such an effort. *Operation concluded, March 13th, 1902.*

---

* See Chapter XXIX., page 518,   † See Chapter XXIII., page 418.

478   THE WAR IN SOUTH AFRICA.

The columns immediately separated and went in opposite directions on various missions. Sir H. Rawlinson's and Lord Basing's commands, and a small force under Major E. S. Bulfin (Yorkshire regiment), were deputed to pursue De Wet, and marched on Reitzburg. Elliot and the rest were ordered to undertake another sweep back over the ground by which they had come. The march was to be performed leisurely, with the object of effecting a thorough clearance of the supplies and hidden stores of the country, and would be conducted right up to the border of Natal.

Sir H. Rawlinson set out on March 13th, and after much delay caused by flooded rivers, manœuvred to hem De Wet in against the Vaal. But information was as scanty as the enemy, and on the 21st Rawlinson went into Klerksdorp, his arrival being welcome in the headquarters of a district which had fallen upon evil days. There, at the very moment when De Wet's power had been worn away by sheer attrition almost to vanishing point, Yzerspruit and Tweebosch had given his place in the forefront of the campaign to De la Rey and the Western Transvaal.*

De Wet takes refuge with De la Rey. Three days before Rawlinson's appearance De Wet himself, having led the ailing and half-blind Steyn safely past all the dangers of blockhouses and guarded drifts between Kroonstad and the Vaal, had been received in De la Rey's laager at Witpoort. He came almost in the guise of a refugee. He had faithfully played his part. His own commandos were ground and scattered like dust to the four winds; with equal envy of his brother commander and regret for his vanished stalwarts he found himself in the midst of a new force, strong, compact, daring, and inspired by a personality as masterful as his own. For a week he remained with the Transvaal General, then withdrew for the Boshof district, planning to muster what forces he could for a continuation of the struggle in the west of the Orange River Colony.

At this time Colonel Rochfort was also working slowly northward with four columns towards the confines of the Western

---

* For the situation see Chapter XXIII.

EVENTS IN THE ORANGE RIVER COLONY. 479

Transvaal. After clearing the country around Boshof during the early part of March (twenty-two prisoners), he subsequently absorbed Lord Basing's force and crossed the frontier to take part from time to time in the series of extensive operations which were to render the basin of the Harts river as familiar ground to British columns as the valleys of the Wilge and Libenbergs Vlei.*

On the sixth day after their return to the railway, Elliot, Barker, Nixon, Garratt and Rimington, in this order from right to left, struck out again over the well-trodden eastern veld on a line stretching from Doornkloof, on the Kroonstad—Lindley blockhouse line, to Heilbron on the left. Heavy rain by day and night marred the plans and prospects from the outset ; and when, after a march rendered miserable by the mud and the fatiguing delays at the Libenbergs Vlei and every other watercourse, the columns arrived at the Wilge river on the 27th, there was nothing for it but to halt on the bank and await the subsidence of the roaring flood. This was the more unfortunate because many Boer bands, amounting in the aggregate to 1,000 men, were reported so close in front, that their rearguards had barely time to swim the rising stream and avoid the oncoming line. For four days this enforced idleness continued, the hopes of good results falling faster than the water. Rimington, who had received orders to push ahead, and to act in advance of the rest, got across on the 31st by the bridge at Frankfort, losing twenty-four hours of his appointed precedence by the necessary *détour*. The others crossed on the next day, the majority by swimming, whilst almost all the transport had to be sent round to the few and widely-separated bridges, the water being still too deep for wheels.

"Drive" by seven columns to the Natal border begun March 19th, 1902.

On the night of April 2nd Elliot lay astride of the Cornelis river from Leeuwkop northward ; Barker joined Elliot at Middelkop, his other hand holding Nixon, who bivouacked on the scene of De Wet's recent deed of daring at Kalkrans. Next to Nixon Garratt was on both sides of Langverwacht, whilst

* See Chapter XXVIII.

Rimington, who had completely encircled the Botha's Berg during the day, rested on the Spruit Zonder Drift where it crossed the Tafel Kop—Botha's Pass blockhouse line.

<small>The enemy attempt to force the line.</small>
The chances of a profitable termination to the expedition had now somewhat improved. Whilst on the march Garratt had received information from some Boer women that the commandos had been ordered to concentrate on the night of the 2nd for a rush through the line of troops, and there was every evidence that the warning was well founded. From 9 p.m. onwards the sound of hoofs in front, now at one point, now another, drew a continuous fusilade from Garratt's outposts. The night was very dark, rain fell heavily, and all patrolling was impossible; but a wire fence, an effective entanglement against a night attack, ran parallel to the front of the piquets. Suddenly, at 1 a.m., two trumpets rang out close in front of the line, and immediately after a mob of mingled Boers and cattle burst against the wires and endeavoured to force a breach. The stout strands, and the heavy fire which poured through them, were too much for many of the Boers; but at one place in the fence the weight was irresistible. The wires snapped, the nearest piquet was swept away, and some hundreds of horsemen poured over the place and galloped westward into freedom. Next morning many of the cattle and eleven prisoners were taken in front of the line, but the last prospect of a great *coup* had vanished.

<small>Operation closes April 5th, 1902.</small>
On April 5th the "drive" terminated amongst the foothills of the Drakensberg from Melani Kop up to the Gansvlei Spruit. The results were ten Boers killed and wounded, seventy-six prisoners, 4,800 cattle and horses, 178 vehicles, and three 75 mm. Krupp field guns, the latter part of the original armament of the Orange Free State.* These pieces Nixon had discovered on March 22nd submerged in a deep pool of a tributary of the Libenbergs Vlei river.

<small>Other columns.</small>
It has been mentioned that Lord Basing, from Sir C. Knox's columns, had crossed the railway with Sir H. Rawlinson. When the latter made for Klerksdorp, Basing was left in the Bothaville

---

* See Volume I., page 85.

EVENTS IN THE ORANGE RIVER COLONY. 481

area in command of his own column and those of Bulfin, Driscoll and Sitwell, incorporating also the 9th M.I., under Major M. H. Tomlin. With these he operated for the latter half of March between Bothaville and Commando Drift, coming eventually under Rochfort. Sir C. Knox's other columns, namely, Pilcher's and Ternan's, soon followed across the railway. After searching the Doornberg (March 11th—14th), both columns were ordered westward to scour the Boschrand, and on the last day of March were at Hoopstad. Pilcher was then sent to Boshof and Ternan to Bultfontein, to raid from those bases with results which will be described later. Sir C. Knox's command was thus finally broken up. He himself, as already stated, had gone into Bloemfontein in relief of Sir C. Tucker, who had proceeded to England on leave of absence.

Early in April the great gathering of troops drawn up under the shadow of the Drakensberg after their miry march across the eastern part of the Orange River Colony was also partially dispersed. On April 11th, Colonels J. E. Nixon and F. S. Garratt, in this order from left to right, lined up facing northward between the Spruit Zonder Drift and Commando Spruit, south of Vrede, for a march across the Vaal and into the Transvaal. Two days later, as the front neared the Vaal, Nixon was sharply attacked by some 150 Boers who appeared not from the north, as might have been expected, but from behind him, the attack falling upon both flanks of his rearguard. The Boers, who were almost starving in the denuded country, were beaten off, and fled southward, leaving a wounded prisoner in the hands of Nixon, whose losses were one killed and six wounded. On April 14th these columns reached the Standerton railway near Greylingstad and were immediately absorbed by Bruce Hamilton, who was then engaged in that other great system of " drives " between the Delagoa Bay and the Standerton railways which ended his work in the east.* Soon, then, Nixon and Garratt found themselves acting as teeth in another vast harrow of troops, raking this time the veld of the Transvaal.

Nixon and Garratt depart for the Transvaal.

* See Chapter XXIX.

There remained in the east of the Orange River Colony, Elliot with de Lisle and Fanshawe, and Barker in charge of Marshall, Kenna, Holmes and F. C. Heath. All these repaired to Harrismith at the conclusion of the sweep to the Drakensberg, but they quickly parted. Elliot moved out westward on Bethlehem on April 11th; next day Barker struck down the right bank of the Wilge for Frankfort. At Harrismith de Lisle relinquished command of his brigade to take up that of the force recently led by Thorneycroft, which was now at Klerksdorp, Brigadier-General M. O. Little taking his place in Elliot's division. Elliot set out on the front Majoors Drift—Aberfeld, and swinging northward to the head of the Leeuw Spruit on April 13th, he passed between Reitz and Bethlehem. The enemy still haunted this often razed district. On the 14th Fanshawe's rearguard was attacked near Rietkuil by a band whose laager was discovered and scattered next day at Fanny's Home, Fanshawe taking four prisoners. A commando nearly 300 strong escaped him in a heavy mist, and for the rest of the week the columns pursued westward, entering Lindley on April 21st. The object of this march was to drive the enemy so as to be caught by a line of columns which were about to sweep southward from the Heilbron—Frankfort blockhouses; but its performance involved the neglect of a more insistent problem.

Elliot in Lindley, April 21st, 1902.

Before Elliot left Harrismith an emergency had arisen close at hand, and had his return march been made to the south instead of the north of the Bethlehem—Harrismith road much trouble might have been averted. From the beginning of April the Brandwater basin had shown itself to be re-occupied by hostile bands of a singularly daring and agressive nature, the collected *débris* of the incessant scourings of the valleys of the Valsch, the Libenbergs Vlei and the Wilge. These Boers were now well-nigh desperate, and their case was rendered worse by finding this, the last stronghold in the district, practically denied to them by the lines of blockhouses which were now complete from Bethlehem to Harrismith in one direction, and through Fouriesburg to Ficksburg in the other. They therefore applied themselves to what was nothing less than a systematic attempt

Disturbance in the Brandwater basin.

EVENTS IN THE ORANGE RIVER COLONY. 483

to wipe the blockhouses from the field, meeting with a measure of success which added a new item to the list of their military feats and a new anxiety to their opponents. The blockhouse lines, especially the section between Bethlehem and Fouriesburg, were nightly invested by detachments from a force of some 1,500 men, which was laagered about Snyman's Hoek. The customary tactics of these parties were those well known to campaigners in the hills of the Indian frontier. Every evening the sinking of the sun below the horizon was the signal for the first shot of a steady all-night rifle practice directed at the walls and especially the loopholes of the little buildings which usually held a non-commissioned officer and some half-dozen men. This procedure was at first sight aimless enough, but it struck so precisely at the weak point of the blockhouse system, that it did, in fact, practically eliminate them as a means of denying movement to the enemy at night. To reply to the fire was as useless as it was fatal, for the marksmen were scattered and well hidden, whereas the blockhouse, and even its loopholes, were marks by no means safe from a rifle in the hands of a Boer. To remain silent, on the other hand, was but to throw open the intervals between the blockhouses to any who wished to pass, for the intervening wires were never to be relied upon. Time after time they were cut to allow the passage of mounted bands; often a crossing was effected when but one of the strands had been severed. These adventures sometimes proved costly to the enemy, especially in horses, but they were more often carried out undetected, the only evidence being the broken wires and the marks of hoofs discovered by the troops next morning. Nor did the Boers confine themselves to mere annoyance. Before dawn on April 8th a fierce rush was made against the blockhouse on Stenekamps Kop and the three next to the south of it. The usual "sniping" had continued intermittently for the seven previous hours of darkness, and there was nothing to indicate any special effort on the part of the enemy until at 2 a.m. the two southernmost of the abovementioned blockhouses were suddenly surrounded at close quarters by 500 men, who poured such a crushing fire upon them

The enemy invest the blockhouses.

Destruction of two blockhouses, April 8th, 1902.

that the loopholes and even the walls crumbled under it in ten minutes, when there was nothing for the inmates but to surrender. The Boers then turned upon the next building with the same result, this house being actually set on fire. Finally, to complete the night's work, the blockhouse on Stenekamps Kop was similarly beset; but here the enemy met with an unexpected rebuff, being handsomely repulsed with the loss of some score men by the garrison under Captain B. J. Jones (Leinster regiment). They then returned to their laager with fifteen prisoners, the other casualties amongst the defence numbering three killed, five wounded. The deliberate nature of this enterprise was shown by the enemy's carrying off in a cart brought for the purpose 150 yards of the barbed wire used as obstacles.

The enemy's numbers increase.

For the next ten days there was no further attack, though the "sniping" continued unabated, and the wires between the blockhouses were constantly cut. But the enemy were seen to be increasing daily in the various laagers, and they practically dominated the district, as must always be the case when bodies of great mobility place themselves within reach of an opponent who, however superior his strength, cannot set it free to strike. On the night of April 19th a body of 200 Imperial Yeomanry and mounted infantry which had been sent to escort a convoy to Brindisi, instead of returning at once with the empty wagons, rashly undertook an expedition against a laager reported on the Moolmans Spruit. The party was promptly ambushed and severely handled, losing two officers and four men killed, three officers and twelve men wounded, and twenty-eight men taken prisoners. All these events, it will be seen, occurred before and during Elliot's unprofitable march to Lindley, when he might at any moment have wheeled southward and quelled the disturbance.

Elliot ordered into the Brandwater basin.

It was not until he entered Lindley on April 21st that he was ordered to return and make Bethlehem his base for a clearance of the Brandwater basin, and then two full days elapsed before he reached that town.

At this time, the preliminary negotiations for peace being in progress,* De Wet was riding from laager to laager to take

* See Chapter XXX.

EVENTS IN THE ORANGE RIVER COLONY. 485

the votes of his burghers, a safe-conduct carrying him unmolested across the scenes of a hundred adventures. On April 22nd he had visited the camp of the Vrede commandos about Pram Kop. Two days later he passed through Bethlehem on his way to meet the men of the Brandwater basin. But though the Free State leader was himself immune, there was no interruption to the campaign by either side. On the 26th Elliot marched to Retief's Nek, whence he scouted on every side, attempting to mark down the five different bands, amounting in all to 1,500 men, with information of which his Intelligence officers had furnished him. But the enemy remained quiet and invisible, and after a week of almost bloodless reconnaissance Elliot received orders which withdrew him once more from the infested district. *(Elliot at Retief's Nek, April 26th, 1902.)*

On May 2nd Bruce Hamilton, having exhausted all resistance in the Eastern Transvaal, threw seven columns across the Standerton railway to give the *coup de grâce* to the Orange River Colony.* The scheme was that in which Elliot's westerly march from Harrismith had been intended to co-operate. It included two phases, the first a "drive" from the line Vereeniging—Greylingstad across the Vaal on to the Kopjes station—Frankfort blockhouses, with Allenby (who had been at Villiersdorp since April 19th) closing the eastern flank from Villiersdorp down to Frankfort; the second an advance thence to the Kroonstad—Lindley line of blockhouses, which obstacle would be prolonged to the Libenbergs Vlei by Elliot's troops coming from Bethlehem. Barker, it will be remembered, had already gone towards Frankfort; his orders now were to block the eastern exits from the area covered by the second stage of the sweep by extending down the Libenbergs Vlei to the point of union with Elliot's right. By May 4th Bruce Hamilton's columns were on the following line: Rimington, Lawley, Nixon and Duff from Wonderheuvel on the Vereeniging railway to Gottenburg on the Heilbron branch line; Garratt from Gottenburg to Elandskop; Spens, Elandskop to Somerset; Colonel Colin Mackenzie, Somerset to the Krom Spruit; Wing thence *(Bruce Hamilton enters the Orange River Colony with seven columns, May 2nd, 1902. Bruce Hamilton "drives" southward towards Elliot.)*

---
* See Chapter XXIX.

to Frankfort, Allenby being aligned along the Frankfort—Villiersdorp road. There was little opposition, but in front of the line rode a number of desperate fugitives, some of whom broke southward through the blockhouses, and some eastward through Allenby's line. The rest, ninety in number, were taken prisoners, seventy-one falling to Mackenzie in one day within gunshot of the blockhouse line, which they dared not attempt. For the next two days the line drove steadily southward, whilst Elliot placed himself across the front from Lindley through Damplaats to Halfmaan on the Libenbergs Vlei river, and Allenby, his watch to the north over, fell in on the left and came down the left bank of the Libenbergs Vlei. The troops on the right flank found little to occupy them; but at the centre both "beaters" and "stops" had sport enough. On the last day, when the space between the advancing and stationary lines was fast narrowing to artillery range, two parties of Boers, some 400 in all, made heroic efforts to escape the closing jaws of the trap. At noon on the 6th one band, 270 strong, driven by Allenby through Deelfontein, flung itself against Elliot's right, burst through, and made good its escape with the loss of but one man and twenty-five horses. Two hours later the other commando, which was led by Mentz, also charged at Elliot, this time at the part of his line near Groenvlei. But the 7th Dragoon Guards who were posted there were impenetrable. The attack was roughly driven back, five Boers being killed, the same number taken and twenty-eight horses destroyed. Mentz then fell back and hid his force in the lands of the farm Grootdam. He was here directly in the path of Mackenzie, who was fast approaching, and there was nothing for it but a forlorn hope. As the Scottish Horse, marching at the right centre of the column, drew close, Mentz hurled a body of resolute men at them, and prepared, should a way be opened, to make a rush with the rest. For a few minutes he had a hope of success. The attack got into the flanks and rear of the supports of the Scottish Horse whose order was momentarily broken; but the reserves, galloping forward, turned the tables on the daring band, fell upon it in rear and took thirteen prisoners. This was the last

The enemy charges Elliot's line.

EVENTS IN THE ORANGE RIVER COLONY. 487

throw. Mackenzie's line was quickly re-formed, and pushing on to Grootdam, he came upon Mentz, who surrendered with 123 burghers. This event at once ended and doubled the gains of the operation, the net results of which were 311 Boers captured and ten killed. Mackenzie had had the good fortune to account for 155 of these. *The southward "drive" concludes, May 6th, 1902.*

On May 7th the whole line faced about for a return drive over precisely the same ground as that by which it had come, Elliot and Barker this time moving forward with the line, the former on the left bank of the Wilge, the latter on the right. Nor was the field as barren as might have been expected; indeed the gleanings might well have almost equalled the previous harvest. Once more some 300 Boers flitted before the advance, and once more it fell to Mackenzie to deal with them. In the forenoon of May 9th, when his column was marching down the Krom Spruit, its left in somewhat uncertain touch with Spens, a body of some 230 Boers who had concealed themselves in front suddenly charged the thinly filled point of union between the two columns, and successfully broke through, leaving only ten stragglers in the hands of Spens' and Mackenzie's flankers. Another party, about sixty in number, similarly doubled back through Elliot's line between Mowbray and Bezuidenhout's Drift on the Wilge. This accounted for well-nigh all the game left in the district, and when the "drive" terminated on the blockhouse line on the evening of the 9th, only twenty-two prisoners were brought in. *It is reversed next day, and finally closes on May 9th, 1902.*

With the close of this operation ends the long tale of fighting in the eastern half of the Orange River Colony. The survivors of the Boer nation had now chosen their representatives and charged them to obtain what terms they might at a conference soon to be held at Vereeniging under the protection of the British Commander-in-Chief.* Peace hovered in the air, and seemed so nearly about to alight that on May 10th Lord Kitchener forbade any further offensive action south of the Vaal. The whole gathering therefore dispersed, Spens and Lawley departing for Heidelberg; Mackenzie, Duff and Allenby for Greylingstad.

* See Chapter XXX.

The remainder, namely, Elliot, Barker, Garratt, Nixon and Rimington, spread themselves over the rectangle within the points Heilbron—Frankfort—Lindley—Majoors Drift, and omitting no precaution—for the enemy might yet reassert his boast of being inextinguishable—applied themselves to a systematic clearance of whatever crops or supplies still existed in this ravaged area. On May 15th even this was suspended, and all the troops returned to the railways to await the turn of the scale which wavered at Vereeniging.

Operations suspended, May 15th, 1902.

There still remain to be described the operations carried out by the troops on the west of the Bloemfontein railway from the first week in April, when Pilcher was traced to Boshof, and Ternan to Bultfontein. Rochfort, with his five columns, last seen at Commando Drift (Vaal river), now passes out of the area under review, his subsequent movements being accounted for in the chapter dealing with the final events in the Western Transvaal.* Pilcher, with Boshof as his base, raided the neighbourhood of that place until, on April 8th, he received orders to cross the railway and cover the placing of supplies in the various posts to the west of Kimberley. Skirmishing intermittently with the commando of De Villiers, Pilcher marched by Schmidt's Drift and Daniel's Kuil to Griquatown† (May 1st), returning on May 9th to Kimberley, where he relinquished command of the little force which he had led for eighteen months, during which time it had done and suffered much.

The work of other columns.

Meanwhile Ternan in the course of his clearance of the vicinity of Bultfontein had met with a reverse which for a time drove him off the veld. At 2.30 a.m. on April 8th he had despatched from Bultfontein a party of 200 men of the Burma M.I., Thorneycroft's M.I., and Imperial Yeomanry with orders to march westward on Hartenbosch and deal with any small bands which might be found. The day opened inauspiciously with the loss of a patrol which mistook the enemy for their own side. Having reached its destination the force turned to regain Bultfontein, eighteen miles distant. Scarcely two miles had been

A reverse near Bultfontein, April 8th, 1902.

---

* See Chapter XXVIII.   † See map No. 63.

EVENTS IN THE ORANGE RIVER COLONY.

covered when a body of some 300 Boers was sighted by the rearguard, coming rapidly from the west. Thereupon the officer in command ordered his men to trot for a good position which stood across the road about four miles further on ; but before this could be gained the enemy fell upon the rear and flanks and broke up all formation. A small party which attempted to make a stand to cover the retreat was quickly overpowered ; the rest scattered along the road, to be overtaken and captured group by group by the better mounted Boers, who in this way took 128 prisoners. The other losses were two officers and fifteen men killed and wounded, only one quarter of the force escaping. The affair practically crippled Ternan, who was ordered to Eensgevonden to refit. This was effected by April 15th when, after escorting a convoy to Hoopstad, Ternan marched to Bothaville on the 23rd. Thence he despatched Thorneycroft's M.I. to rejoin the officer from whom this veteran corps took its name, Thorneycroft being now at Klerksdorp in command of a new column of Australians and New Zealanders. Three days later Ternan took his force into Kroonstad, where it was broken up.

APPROXIMATE STRENGTH STATES OF COLUMNS REFERRED TO IN FOREGOING CHAPTER.

COLUMN.	Mounted Troops.	Infantry.	Guns, including Vickers-Maxims.	Machine Guns.	
March—May, 1902.					
Lt.-Col. H. de B. de Lisle (later Brig.-Gen. Little)	1,743	—	5	—	Lieut.-Gen. E. L. Elliot in command.
Lt.-Col. R. Fanshawe	1,226	—	6	—	
Lt.-Col. the Hon. R. T. Lawley	1,135	—	3	2	
Lt.-Col. J. S. S. Barker (four columns)	2,347	—	8	2	
Major J. P. Du Cane	731	—	3	—	
Lt.-Col. M. F. Rimington	1,921	196	5	—	
Lt.-Col. J. L. Keir	893	—	2	—	
Lt.-Col. A. E. Wilson	454	176	1	2	
Major J. H. Damant	654	—	3	—	
Col. F. S. Garratt	855	167	3	1	
Col. Sir H. Rawlinson (four columns)	2,800	—	10	1	Maj.-Gen. Sir C. Knox in command.
Lt.-Col. J. E. Nixon	1,474	—	3	2	
Lt.-Col. T. D. Pilcher (three columns)	1,903	—	8	2	
Col. T. P. B. Ternan (two columns)	1,615	—	4	—	
Lt.-Col. Lord Basing	670	—	3	1	Col. A. N. Rochfort in command.
Lt.-Col. W. H. Sitwell	755	174	3	—	
Major E. S. Bulfin	467	—	1	—	
Major D. P. Driscoll	536	—	—	—	
Lt.-Col. W. G. P. Western	501	—	1	—	
Major A. R. Gilbert	95	545*	3	—	
Major M. H. Tomlin	557	—	1	—	
Major P. A. Kenna	455	—	2	2	Lieut-Col. J. S. S. Barker in command.
Major W. R. Marshall	733	—	2	—	
Major H. G. Holmes	561	—	1	—	
Major F. C. Heath	598	—	3	1	
Brig.-Gen. J. Spens	1,159	—	5	2	Major-Gen. Bruce Hamilton in command.
Col. Colin Mackenzie	1,030	—	3	1	
Lt.-Col. C. E. Duff	800	—	2	—	
Lt.-Col. F. D. V. Wing	1,309	—	3	—	
Col. E. H. H. Allenby	957	—	3	1	

* Including sixty-two cyclists.

CHAPTER XXVIII.

EVENTS IN THE WESTERN TRANSVAAL*

(*Continued from Chapter XXIII.*).

MARCH—MAY, 1902.

IF the enemy could not be called supreme in the Western Transvaal, the hold of the British upon the district in the early part of March, 1902, was sufficiently loosened to cause extreme anxiety, not, indeed, for the result of the campaign, but for its duration. The troops on the spot were plainly unable to find De la Rey, and too few to defeat him if they found him. The Commander-in-Chief made haste to supply both deficiencies. Calling Wools-Sampson from his work in the Eastern Transvaal to act as Intelligence Officer in the west, he ordered F. W. Kitchener and Sir H. Rawlinson to bring their columns to Klerksdorp, the former by train from Standerton, the latter from out of the Orange River Colony by Schoeman's Drift and Potchefstroom. Rochfort's column, which it will be remembered had been intended to form a unit of Lord Methuen's last ill-fated scheme, was disposed along the line of the Vaal to the north of Hoopstad. Rochfort actually controlled seven small columns—those of Lieut.-Colonels W. H. Sitwell, Lord Basing and W. G. B. Western, and Majors D. P. Driscoll, E. S. Bulfin, C. D. Vaughan and P. G. Reynolds. These had been placed under his command for the purpose of keeping surveillance over the Vaal drifts in the Bloemhof district, which they did with much success. Under Kekewich, who was at Klerksdorp, were placed the recently organised flying columns of von Donop and Grenfell, the latter of whom was

_{More troops for the Western Transvaal.}

* See map No. 59.

recalled on March 9th from Rooirantjesfontein, where he still awaited co-operation with Lord Methuen, to Vaalbank. The garrison of Lichtenburg was rapidly reinforced by the 2nd Norfolk regiment, that of Klerksdorp by a Highland brigade. On March 19th Lord Kitchener himself hurried down to Klerksdorp to supervise preparations for a universal effort to extirpate De la Rey, which a few days later was put into operation.

Kekewich's operations. On the 22nd Kekewich concentrated his twin forces at Vaalbank, and on the next evening the whole of the troops above enumerated moved westward in light order, without guns or wheeled transport of any kind. The first object aimed at was to get unperceived outside Hartebeestfontein, where some of De la Rey's commandos were reported to have repaired after their recent triumphs. The columns, therefore, marched in close order throughout the night, and not until they had covered forty miles and were well to the westward did they turn about and shake themselves out for a wide sweep back towards the line of blockhouses along the Schoon Spruit, which had been strengthened by two battalions of Highlanders. This manœuvre, it will be seen, was to be in the Western Transvaal the first of the *The first great "drive."* greater " drives," such as in other parts had for some time constituted practically the whole offensive tactics of the campaign. As the columns faced round and extended they became aligned in the following order from left (north) to right. Kekewich, his left grazing the Lichtenburg—Vaalbank blockhouses, threw his right flank down to Geluk on the Little Harts river ; next to him came Sir H. Rawlinson, who covered the country to Gestopfontein, where F. W. Kitchener (who had a triple command of columns under Colonels W. H. M. Lowe and G. A. Cookson and Lieut.-Colonel J. L. Keir) took up the line to Zwartrand. The circuit should have been closed by Rochfort's forces moving up the Vaal, and with their right on the river filling the gap from Zwartrand to Klipspruit ; but Keir and Rochfort never gained touch. A glance at the map will indicate more than any description the vastness of this conception, and its primitive simplicity ; the extraordinary difficulty of carrying out even its preliminary formations in the dark and after an exhausting march

EVENTS IN THE WESTERN TRANSVAAL.

must be left to the knowledge of military and the imagination of other readers. Before the extension had well begun it became evident, first, that there were fish in the net; secondly, that the meshes must be knit closer than was possible with the forces available in order to prevent them escaping. Dawn had not broken before a band of 300 Boers, disguised in khaki clothing and shouting that they were a British corps, slipped between the rapidly closing flanks of Lowe and Keir, of F. W. Kitchener's contingent, and escaped to the west. Others evaded the line by skirting its extreme right flank. Space fails to recount the innumerable adventures of the several columns on the way back, how here a hostile band was turned and broken, there another missed and lost, another encountered and captured. Scarcely a unit but had fighting, none but endured labour and privations which would have been arduous had they come at the beginning instead of the midst of a march which was to total eighty miles, partly in drenching rain, before the troops regained their starting points. F. W. Kitchener took 102 prisoners, Kekewich thirty-eight, the last-named recovering also three field guns and two Vickers-Maxims which had been lost in the recent disasters. Every unit secured something, and those which had less fortune than others had not the less energy and toil. When the worn-out troops were stopped on the evening of the 24th, after twenty-six hours' incessant movement, they had accounted for 173 of the enemy, 103 wagons and carts and 1,671 horses and cattle. Kekewich put in again to Vaalbank, F. W. Kitchener and Sir H. Rawlinson to Klerksdorp, Rochfort's columns falling back to the Vaal near Commando Drift. The "drive" had not been vastly productive; too much, indeed, had been attempted; but the results of colossal sweeps such as this against a mobile enemy in an open country are not to be considered failures because the gains are small out of all proportion to the expense. They may be likened to safe investments, from which, with a minimum of risk, certain if limited increment is to be obtained. At any rate, they were now to be the set form of operations against an enemy upon whom experiment had exhausted itself in vain. The Commander-in-Chief, with such expedients

Results of the "drive."

forced upon him, knew that they must be often repeated to be profitable.

<small>A second "drive."</small>

Before the end of March the columns were again active, Kekewich making the first move of a fresh disposition by fortifying himself on March 29th on Middelbult, a strong place in the heart of De la Rey's country. It was henceforth held, and proved of great value. F. W. Kitchener, his right flank thus covered, moved out to Rietvlei, and on March 30th was in line with Kekewich at Driekuil, due south of Middelbult. Sir H. Rawlinson conformed to this westerly movement by advancing through Rhenosterspruit. Rumours of the enemy's presence now came thick, and on March 31st F. W. Kitchener despatched Cookson and Keir with about 1,800 men to search the junction of the Harts river and Brak Spruit about Doornbult, remaining himself in support at Driekuil. At the same time Kekewich, who had information of De la Rey's convoy to the westward, pushed a night expedition toward Leeuwpan, midway between Middelbult and the Mafeking railway. This proved abortive; but Cookson and Keir were more successful in discovering the enemy, though their good fortune nearly cost them their columns.

<small>The enemy met with in force.</small>

Working through Doornlaagte there was unmistakable evidence that a strong hostile force with guns was on the move down the Brak Spruit, and when, about 10 a.m., a body of 500 were discovered by the screen, Cookson halted his baggage and sent forward his mounted troops under Colonel J. H. Damant, supporting them with Keir's column. From Boschpan to Boschbult Damant's men pursued, their hope of a good capture rising to its height when at the latter place they nearly succeeded in riding round the enemy's left. But they were dealing with a band which had grown more accustomed to setting traps than falling into them. They had come into the presence of commandos trained by De la Rey and elated by victories. Suddenly

<small>De la Rey's attack at Boschbult, March 31st, 1902.</small>

at 10.30 a.m., on front and both flanks appeared large bodies of horsemen, and in a few moments Damant was well-nigh surrounded. The enemy, who appeared not to recognise his advantage, was successfully kept off by the 28th M.I., with the timely assistance of other mounted troops, who galloped

EVENTS IN THE WESTERN TRANSVAAL. 495

eight miles from the rear to reinforce the advance guard. But the situation was critical in one sense. The Boers had the advantage of position, and were in superior force. Recent events had shown how the fate of troops in such a case balanced on the razor edge of a moment's decision. Cookson had been completely and needlessly surprised, but if he was fortunate in being allowed a breathing space, he used it well. Retirement, even the shortest, would probably have been fatal, because impossible to check in the face of the avalanche which would surely have descended upon it. Instead, Cookson promptly advanced, disengaging himself from the bush which hampered him, and opened with his guns. This had the effect of causing the enemy to recoil slightly, whereupon Cookson ordered up his baggage and hastily entrenched himself on the Brak Spruit to await the arrival of the wagons. Keir's men were posted on the left facing Oshoek, Damant held the front and right, strengthening his defences on the flank by fortifying and holding with the R. H. A. Mounted Rifles (O., T. and P. batteries) with a Vickers-Maxim gun, a house and garden which stood detached some 800 yards distant. This was the key of the position, a miniature Bazeilles, the loss of which would jeopardise the whole camp. These measures speedily checked the Boers. About noon Cookson's wagons came up unmolested; they were speedily parked inside an entanglement of wire, and De la Rey found that, instead of a column scattered in the open, he had now to deal with a laager of considerable strength, which he had allowed to be formed under his very eyes. To a soldier of his methods the resort to artillery was somewhat of a confession of failure. At 1.20 p.m. he brought up four field guns and a Vickers-Maxim, and after bombarding heavily, sent a strong party with a rush against the two sides of the camp which were held by Damant and the 28th M.I. This was a critical moment for the defence. The shells, bursting over the transport, caused a stampede amongst the draught animals, many of which were still inspanned. Great confusion arose in the interior of the camp, whilst outside annihilation seemed to be fast approaching in the shape of a line of Boers spreading nearly four miles from flank to flank, who cantered against the front and right, many firing from the saddle. The screen of 28th M.I., and Damant's Horse, which had remained out in the bush in front to cover the formation of the camp, was forced back after determined fighting, during which each man fired 200 rounds. Many stirring incidents occurred during this retirement. The Boers pressed as closely as they dared, being only prevented from riding over the small force opposing them by the steady shooting of each successive front of the retreating échelon. A moment's weakness of one of these would have sacrificed the whole. But whilst all were admirably firm, perhaps the greatest devotion was shown by an officer (Lieutenant B. Carruthers) and twenty-one men of the Canadian Mounted Rifles, who, finding themselves cut off as they brought up the rear, fought on until eighteen of their number, including the officer, were down. But even this band had an especial hero in Private C. N. Evans, who after receiving a mortal wound, fired at the enemy two bandoliers full of cartridges, then with his dying hands broke his rifle in pieces lest the enemy should take it. Arrived at the fringe of the camp the mounted men, joining their fire to that of Cookson's main body, allowed no nearer approach. The imposing rank of Boers broke up into circling groups as the riders sought shelter from the tremendous discharges. They had even less success on the right, where the fire from the defended house and its enclosures, the occupation of which completely surprised them when they dashed heedlessly for it, caused heavy losses and effectually kept them from closing. Meanwhile Cookson had been collecting his scattered wagons and strengthening his defences. Sacks and the carcasses of dead horses were used to thicken the parapets, in front of which were strewn entanglements and trip wires. By the afternoon he was safely shut in, and though the Boers time after time attacked from all sides, they could make no impression and finally retired, pursued by shrapnel, but by nothing else, at 5.30 p.m.

Repulse of De la Rey.

The enemy's main tactical triumph in this affair at Boschbult was one too often conceded to them by British commanders, namely, the ease with which they had first made and then shaken

EVENTS IN THE WESTERN TRANSVAAL.

off at will contact with columns which should have been as mobile as themselves. On the other hand, they had lost considerably more than the 106 casualties* which it had cost Cookson to drive them off. They had lost, in addition, that reputation for infallibility which had been fast attaching to them. The resolute conduct of Cookson's troops had shown that small columns were not a certain prey, even when partially entrapped by the strongest and most brilliantly led force of Transvaalers in the field. Another lesson, of wider significance, was that a firmly-held rifle was still the match for a mounted charge in line, though it was strange that such a lesson should have been taught to riflemen *par excellence* by troops who had clung longer to the tradition of weight and the steel than any in christendom. Still more strange was it that the Boers themselves were to incur by their own act a repetition of the same lesson within a fortnight and within a few yards of this very spot.

About 2.30 p.m., when the fight was at its height, the sound of the firing became audible to F. W. Kitchener at Driekuil. He promptly marched westward with Lowe's column. Towards evening terrified natives were fallen in with, who announced the destruction of Cookson's expedition. The distant uproar had then ceased, arguing that for good or ill the combat had already been decided. Surrounded as he was by thick bush, with night coming on, and a possibly triumphant and superior enemy in the vicinity, Kitchener decided to return. His action, or lack of it, was undoubtedly the better part of valour, for, as it happened, De la Rey was aware of his approach, and had he persisted, fully intended to waylay him. Early on the next morning Kitchener took his whole force to the scene. On the way he was met by a driver of one of Cookson's batteries, who had been taken prisoner and stripped of his uniform, an ill omen of the fate of the rest. Not until noon was the unconquered camp discovered, surrounded by the bodies of 500 dead animals. The Boers had disappeared, but their ambulances still wandered amongst the bush seeking their dead and wounded. So many mules had been

F. W. Kitchener reaches Boschbult.

* Casualties—Killed, one officer, thirteen other ranks; wounded, eight officers, seventy-eight other ranks; missing, six other ranks; 364 horses and mules were shot.

shot that Kitchener, seeing it was impossible to get the wagons to Driekuil that day, halted in a clearing for the night. On April 2nd he withdrew the whole force to Driekuil, where he found Sir H. Rawlinson just come up from Rhenosterspruit.

Once more all energies were concentrated on finding De la Rey and bringing him to book, and once more that leader had disappeared as effectually as if the open veld had been shrouded in darkness, and his strong commandos a sergeant's patrol. A combined expedition to Makoiespan by the mounted troops of all the British columns in the neighbourhood, including those of Kekewich from his stronghold at Middelbult, though founded on apparently reliable information, proved profitless. It was evident that if De la Rey were to be mastered, or even discovered at all, and this now seemed vital to the retention of the Western Transvaal, the various columns must be directed by one mind. The Boer leader, if he had not actually reconquered the district, had completely transformed it from a playground for British columns into the scene of something very like a struggle for existence. The climax of his success was that he now forced his disconnected and heterogeneous opponents to turn themselves into an army, and compelled the Commander-in-Chief to deprive himself of his own Chief-of-the-Staff in order to provide a commander for it. For such a step Lord Kitchener had the precedent of his own intermittent delegation to command in the field when serving with Lord Roberts early in the campaign; but it was none the less a striking circumstance, the more so as it formed the most abrupt, indeed, almost the sole transition from the system of intense centralisation which had hitherto characterised Lord Kitchener's administration.

On April 8th Lieut.-General Sir I. S. M. Hamilton arrived at Middelbult from Pretoria to assume general command of the columns of Kekewich, F. W. Kitchener and Sir H. Rawlinson; a fourth column, under Colonel A. Thorneycroft, being prepared to join him from Klerksdorp. Hamilton immediately acted with his accustomed vigour. It was evident that De la Rey was still to the south of the Brak Spruit. Disposing his columns in a semi-circle around the right bank and head of that stream,

EVENTS IN THE WESTERN TRANSVAAL.

he ordered an extended movement southward to be carried out on April 11th. On the night of the 10th Kekewich on the right was entrenched at Rooiwal, near the confluence of the Brak Spruit and Harts river, Sir H. Rawlinson in the centre about Boschpan, F. W. Kitchener on the left at Klipdrift, all joining hands on their inner flanks. During the day's march which brought the troops into these positions there was some instructive finessing which showed the value of control under the clear eye of one commander. F. W. Kitchener, nearing Klipdrift, found a strong hostile force demonstrating boldly outside his left flank, that is, altogether outside the horns of the arc of columns. If this were the sought-for game, it had already escaped and was from its position a source of danger; but Sir I. Hamilton, knowing his enemy, became solicitous, not for his left flank, but instead for his centre and right. Ordering Kitchener on no account to pursue, but rather to close in towards Sir H. Rawlinson, he warned Kekewich, on the right, to move next day in battle formation, instead of the open "driving" order which had been intended, and to be more careful to reconnoitre far to his right across the Harts river than to keep his alignment with the other columns, which were to be inclined towards him on the morrow. Seldom has insight been of greater value. At 7.30 a.m. on April 11th, von Donop, who was in command of Kekewich's mounted screen, whilst moving westward down to Brak Spruit, sighted a strong force advancing towards his left front, a body so orderly and compact in appearance that von Donop, having at that very moment received warning from Headquarters that a co-operating column was approaching, inquired of Kekewich, who was at the front, whether the new comers were not the reinforcement in question, and actually ordered his signallers to open communication with the supposed advancing troops. When about a mile away the larger portion of the mass of horsemen, who were 1,700 strong in all, detached themselves from the rest and broke into a gentle trot which carried them onwards in a dense line, two, three and four files deep. As the array rolled forward its flanks began to protrude around the front and left of the column. At the same time a roar of musketry, breaking from

[margin notes: His operations. Kekewich's movements. The action at Rooiwal, April 11th, 1902.]

the advancing ranks, disclosed an imminent Boer attack. Part of the scattered British advance-guard, seeing itself about to be enveloped, and opposed by a superior fire, changed front to the right, and maintained a series of resolute but detached stands, which did much to keep back the enemy from this flank; some of the troops became actually mingled with the Boers. But their resistance did not prevent Grenfell's command, which was close behind von Donop's, from being much exposed. Grenfell knew nothing of the impending danger beyond what the bursts of firing in front, the ordinary noise of the progress of the van of a column on the veld, had told him. It was this shooting which had caused him to close up upon von Donop, who had just passed through the farmstead of Rooiwal. Grenfell was in low ground at this moment; the grass land on his front and left rising gently to an indefinite skyline some thousand yards away; but he had no fears, since von Donop's men were out in that direction, and their lines were actually to be seen defined upon the ridge which overlooked his left. But now an officer, galloping in at full speed from the south-west, informed Grenfell that the rows of riders in sight were not von Donop's soldiers, but Boers, that they were in great strength, that he himself had been actually amongst them. Behind him the enemy was fast descending the slope, and Grenfell, who at first had scarcely credited the news, saw that he had but a few seconds in which to prepare for the shock. With 460 men of the 1st and 2nd Scottish Horse, 420 Imperial Yeomanry, 290 South African Constabulary, two field guns and a Vickers-Maxim, he dashed to the front, and coming up to Kekewich carried out his orders as quickly as they were issued. Swinging the artillery into action at once to the west, the Constabulary remaining to guard it, Grenfell sent the Scottish Horse at the run on foot forward and to the left to seize a mealie-covered rise in the ground which faced the advancing enemy on the south-west, whilst the Yeomanry wheeled into line on their left. Lieut.-Colonel Leader smartly manœuvred the Scottish Horse in accordance with these instructions; the rest conformed, and in a trice a semi-circle of troops lay facing west, south-west and south, under a heavy

EVENTS IN THE WESTERN TRANSVAAL. 501

but ill-aimed fire, for the Boers, still advancing in line, were now shooting furiously from the saddle, a wild and imposing spectacle. By the time the last of Grenfell's men had rushed into his place the hostile van had come within 600 yards and was the target for 1,100 rifles. The Boers were still ambling slowly on, riding knee to knee, a ragged wall of horsemen, apparently as lost to all sense of tactics as of fear. In front cantered a few intrepid officers, Kemp, who was in command, in the absence of De la Rey (then discussing pourparlers of peace within the British lines), Van Zyl, von Tonder, and T. De Beer, and amongst the foremost a tall figure clad in blue, with long jack-boots, in whom the South African Colonials in Grenfell's ranks recognised Commandant Potgieter of Wolmaranstad. The volleys and rounds of case which burst upon the mass in no wise quickened its pace, nor turned it a hair's breadth from its calm and deliberate advance. A scene more strange had not been witnessed in this or any other campaign. The howling rush of the Dervish or Ghazi, the sonorous charge of European cavalry, the chanting onset of the Zulu impi were less impressive than the slow oncoming of this brigade of mounted riflemen. Minutes passed, during which most of von Donop's scattered troops, directed by Kekewich in person, rallied in line with the Scottish Horse, and their shooting swelled the volume of fire beating upon the Boer advance. The range shortened to 400 yards, to 300, then to 200; still the attack neither wavered nor charged, though some additional speed was imparted to its widely thrown wings. The Boer centre, in fact, was as if in leash, pausing for the flanks to swing forward and envelop the British line, just as the mass of Russian cavalry had checked its pace to open its arms to embrace the Heavy Brigade at Balaklava. The streams of bullets which poured from the magazines of Grenfell's riflemen had here to do the work of the sabres of Scarlett's troopers. To within 100 yards rode the intrepid burghers, Potgieter and a few more falling close by the Maxim gun of the Scottish Horse; then their plans and not their magnificent courage failed; it was madness to press further: not a man of the British column had run, not enough had fallen: by common impulse they themselves

The great Boer charge.

Defeat of the enemy.

turned and galloped away, and in that moment the spirit which had sustained them snapped under the irresistible influence of flight. A *sauve qui peut* set in. The veld was covered with falling and flying horsemen, and had a reserve of cavalry been available scarcely a burgher would have escaped. But many of Grenfell's horses had been shot, many more stampeded; the rest were some distance in rear, and nearly an hour elapsed before sufficient could be collected for the pursuit. During that time Sir I. Hamilton arrived on the scene, drawn thither by the tremendous din of the contest. Soon after, the Imperial Light Horse from Sir H. Rawlinson's column also galloped on to the field, striking in at a point which overlapped the left of the retiring Boers, who quickened their pace until, gaining the cover of a hollow, they faced about and were seen to form up in line once more. None could have been quicker than Sir I. Hamilton to recognise and deal with this, the psychological moment in the Boer ranks. The enemy were repulsed but not shattered; their action showed that a strong hand had gathered up the dangling reins. Hesitation on the part of Hamilton would either bring down the swarm of riflemen upon his ill-protected lines again, next time probably with more of their accustomed skill, or once more favour them with that loss of contact which had so often enabled them to recover. Taking the whole conduct of affairs into his own hands, Hamilton immediately ordered a counter-attack down the Harts River valley by all his available force, at the same time telegraphing to F. W. Kitchener to attempt to throw his column across the enemy's line of retreat, which pointed on Schweizer Reneke. Unfortunately Rochfort's columns, which were at Bloemhof, had not been included in Sir I. Hamilton's command on this occasion. As if foreseeing some such event as had actually happened, the General had requested that Rochfort might be at Schweizer Reneke on the 12th.* Had this been effected, Rochfort would have been exactly placed to intercept the exhausted commandos and great gain must have resulted.

* Telegram H 9, Sir Ian Hamilton to Commander-in-Chief, April 8th, 1902.

EVENTS IN THE WESTERN TRANSVAAL. 503

Now from Kekewich's lines some 2,000 troopers rode out through the fallen burghers, who lay where the highest tide of the attack had broken and turned. Spreading over the veld six miles from flank to flank, they cantered towards the crowded rise. For a few moments the enemy stood gazing at the advancing lines. But Sir I. Hamilton had felt their pulse; the offensive spirit had been blown away by the point-blank breath of the rifles, and the only magician who could have conjured it back was far away. De la Rey's "New Model" was broken, and another moment saw its fragments careering southward. For three hours the troops gave chase. But the bulk of the fugitives had too long a start along an open road; only stragglers whose horses had foundered were picked up. Grenfell, however, made an important capture in the shape of two 15-pr. guns and a Vickers-Maxim. At midday the force, its horses run to a standstill, drew rein at Kopjesvlei, midway to Schweizer Reneke, with twenty-three prisoners. All except Sir H. Rawlinson, who bivouacked at Nooitgedacht, then marched back to Rooiwal, which was reached at 9 p.m., fourteen hours from the beginning of the action. Considering the extraordinary nature of the day's fighting the losses on the British side had been large, on the other strangely few. A casualty list of eighty-seven killed and wounded* in Kekewich's two columns was greater than was to be expected in forces which had been mainly on the defensive against a reckless attack accompanied by a fire intended as much to intimidate as to do damage. Kekewich, moreover, lost some hundreds of horses. The counted Boer losses were fifty-one killed, forty taken prisoners wounded, and thirty-six captured unwounded, 127 in all. This was comparatively small injury, even allowing for the numerous wounded who had been carried off during the fight, a task for which with the burghers no fire was too hot or crisis too intense. The soldiers had been confronted by a target such as British troops had not seen since the battle of Omdurman. At that engagement the musketry of trained soldiers had piled the desert thick and high

Considerations on the losses.

---

* Casualties—Killed, two officers, ten other ranks; wounded, ten officers, sixty-five other ranks; horses, about 300.

with the riddled tribesmen of the Soudan. But in Kekewich's ranks at Rooiwal stood but a handful drilled in rifle practice. The majority of the troops were irregulars, and their failure to kill, which against many an opponent would have cost them the day, was but another tribute to the necessity of training to empower men to preserve their marksmanship, even in the face of so astounding a spectacle as " the transmigration of the soul of the Dervish into the heart of the Dutchman."*

Effect of the Boer defeat. This striking encounter, of which only the outlines have been given, broke the power of the enemy in the Western Transvaal. It was the culminating failure of that change in the Boer method of attack which had begun with success at Bakenlaagte, continued at Lake Chrissie, Vlakfontein and Moedwil, and had wavered at Doornbult ; and it supplied another assurance of a fact which may always be counted on in this description of warfare, that up to a point guerrillas grow more daring the nearer they approach exhaustion. The news of the repulse soon penetrated to the Council Chamber in Pretoria, where De la Rey and his brother leaders were entering upon the long struggle for terms which is recounted in another place.† Apart from its inevitable, if invisible, effect upon the negotiations, it is easy to imagine how deeply De la Rey himself was moved by the fate of the splendid force which he had levied, schooled and led to many triumphs, only to hear of its ruin in his absence by the impetuosity of his young lieutenant. Rupert's valorous folly at Naseby and Marston Moor had not wounded his cause so deeply as Kemp's rash onset at Rooiwal, where was gambled away the last striking force left to his side in the field. From this time until the end of the war De la Rey's commandos were driven like sheep over the country which they had once hunted like a pack of wolves. As for their gallant and humane old General, he was now to raise the voice which had urged them to victory in favour of their submission, for he knew that now that the weapon which he

---

* "A Military History of Perthshire—'The Scottish Horse at Rooiwal,'" by Captain L. Oppenheim, 2nd Dragoon Guards (Queen's Bays).

† See Chapter XXX.

EVENTS IN THE WESTERN TRANSVAAL.

had forged was shivered, there was nothing left in the armoury of his country.

Two days after this Sir I. Hamilton changed front eastward for a sweep back to Klerksdorp, with Kekewich on the left at Middelbult, Sir H. Rawlinson and F. W. Kitchener covering the ground through Doornlaagte to Driekuil on the south and right. Various small bands darted about in dismay before the columns, sixty-four burghers—of whom F. W. Kitchener took thirty-eight—being captured by the time the force entered Klerksdorp on the evening of the 15th, after a march of over forty miles during the day.

Rochfort, whose co-operation in the pursuit from Rooiwal had been so severely missed, had been nevertheless successfully employed elsewhere. After sundry minor manœuvres on the banks of the Vaal during the first week in April, Rochfort had concentrated his columns at Bloemhof, whence, on April 11th, he made a night march, capturing a small laager (five prisoners) at Kareeboschfontein to the north. The mounted troops, 1,200 strong, were then ordered to go on to Vuurfontein with the object of eventually co-operating with Sir I. Hamilton; but torrential rain, falling on the 12th, sent the troops back to Bloemhof, when a march of the same distance westward might have resulted in the interception of some of Kemp's defeated bands. Almost equal results were, however, attained a few days later, when Rochfort, having carefully laid his plans, surrounded the township of Schweizer Reneke before dawn on April 16th. Well-nigh every burgher refuging therein was taken, including Douthwaite, a well-known Commandant, also one of General C. De Wet's adjutants, and the brother of the renowned De la Rey. In all fifty-seven prisoners were captured. On the 18th Rochfort marched back to Bloemhof, his flankers discovering twelve Boers, part of the ungathered harvest of Rooiwal, lying wounded in farmhouses by the way, on that day, and five more on the next, when the force evacuated Schweizer Reneke, followed by a hot fire from a commando under T. De Beer, which entered the town as soon as the troops were clear. The Boers lost several more men, and were deterred from coming

Rochfort's operations.

to closer quarters. Rochfort next based himself on Hoopstad, in the Orange River Colony, whence he raided the farms of the intricate "pan" district towards Boshof. By means of good information a laager of twenty-five Boers was successfully surprised at Groot Gannapan on April 23rd. Rochfort then swept both banks of the Vaal between Christiana and Bloemhof, around which he continued to rove until called to take part in more important operations in the first week of May.

<small>Sir Ian Hamilton's great "drive" westward.</small>

Whilst Sir I. Hamilton's troops remained a week at Klerksdorp to rest and refit, that General prepared plans for another great excursion across the Western Transvaal. On April 25th he made the first moves of a scheme so elaborate, yet so direct in its purpose, that it must be studied in detail. The main object was to herd the widely-scattered enemy into the angle of Bechuanaland lying between Vryburg and the western boundary of the Transvaal. A commander could have set himself no more difficult, nay in its entirety, impossible task; for such a sweep, to be fully effective, must be flanked, or better still, intersected by obstacles to form the walls of the enclosures, such as mountain ranges, deep rivers, or the lines of blockhouses which Lord Kitchener had constructed to take the place of these natural barriers. But in this part of the Western Transvaal no such aids existed. The country was so open and featureless that the widest possible extension would still leave its flanks in the air, free to be circumvented by the enemy as soon as he had located them; it was so vast that double the number of troops available could scarcely have covered it all; finally it was so poorly supplied with water that the majority of the long array of men must be always from fifteen to twenty miles distant from the muddy pools which alone were to be found. A bluff advance would therefore be doomed to failure, and Sir I. Hamilton determined to trust largely to deceptive manœuvring. Everything depended upon his power to hold the enemy in front of him, and to keep them ignorant until too late of his uncovered flanks and the inevitable gaps in his line. For this purpose he seized upon the only condition in his favour, that of precedent. Every column, or line of columns, which had previously traversed

EVENTS IN THE WESTERN TRANSVAAL. 507

the Western Transvaal had, with the exception of a small incursion by Lord Methuen, faced about after marching some distance eastward, for the return drive towards the Klerksdorp railway. So often had this been done that the Boers had come to consider themselves safe so long as they could only keep to the westward of the British. Sir I. Hamilton made every effort to encourage them in this belief. Behind a veil of reports, busily spread by spies and natives, that he intended to halt and turn back when within three days' march of Vryburg, he moved his pieces for a drive to the very edge of the board, the fortified Vryburg railway, which had been rendered doubly impenetrable by the reinforcement of four battalions of infantry, and six armoured trains each provided with a powerful searchlight. Two additional columns were now at his disposal, Thorneycroft's, previously referred to, and that of Rochfort, who, on May 6th, was at Bloemhof. By the evening of that day Sir I. Hamilton had leisurely manœuvred his columns into the westward-facing line* Rooirantjesfontein (Kekewich)—Nooitverwacht (Thorneycroft, Sir H. Rawlinson)—Korannafontein (F. W. Kitchener). It will thus be seen that a great gap existed between F. W. Kitchener's left flank and Rochfort, and much depended on this being undetected before it could be closed. On May 8th Rochfort began to reduce it by moving inwards to the line Vuurfontein—Kareeboschfontein, athwart the road to Schweizer Reneke, whilst Sir I. Hamilton pushed his four columns forward through the line Biejesvallei—Schoonoord—Kareekuil—Witklip up to that of the Great Harts river. This was the critical moment of the operation. The enemy, who had sidled away westward, narrowly watching the advancing lines of troops, now expected to see them turn and make eastward. The continuation of the westward march could not fail to enlighten them as to the real intention, and there were still wide avenues of escape. On the morning of May 9th Rochfort was at Schweizer Reneke, whilst F. W. Kitchener, on his right, was still nearly twenty miles distant to the north at Schietfontein, forming there the left of a line which now curved through Bulpan and

Marginal notes: Position of the troops on May 6th, 1902. May 8th. May 9th.

* See map No. 60.

Geysdorp to the western railway at Maribogo, a secure barrier to any attempt at escape towards Lichtenburg. In addition to the interval between Kitchener and Rochfort, the latter in his march towards Schweizer Reneke had now opened another on his own left flank, by which the enemy could get out in the direction of Christiana. To deter them from these gateways Sir I. Hamilton adopted a ruse worthy of his resourceful antagonists themselves. Sending a few scouts at dusk to spread themselves thinly across the gaps, he instructed them to set fire to the veld, so that when the Boers, now thoroughly alarmed, looked out into the night for the dark gaps which should show the empty spaces between the bivouac fires of the columns, they beheld instead an unbroken line of light stretching from Maribogo down to the Vaal, and thought themselves shut in.

May 10th. On May 10th the line, picking up a few prisoners on the march, advanced to the Transvaal border, and, throwing forward its flanks, drew an uninterrupted arc from Doornbult Siding, where Kekewich rested his right flank, to Brussels Siding, which Rochfort, who was now in one line with F. W. Kitchener, touched with his left. By a curious and unpremeditated coincidence this alignment penned the Boers into the only tract of country in which on the morrow it would be lawful to attack them. At this time the Boer leaders were sitting in conference, discussing the desirability of continuing the war, and Lord Kitchener, in order to facilitate their meeting, had consented, as one of the terms of armistice, that all commandos whose officers were attending the conference should be free from molestation *within their own borders* from May 11th until the termination of the truce. On the night of the 10th Sir I. Hamilton himself lay along the frontier, and having pushed the enemy into British territory, presumed himself to be entitled to deal with him there. The point, however, was not uncasuistic, and might have given birth to a new and nice case of military jurisprudence, had not the Boers removed all cause of argument by throwing themselves in small bands against Hamilton's line in an endeavour to break back into their own country. In this only a single individual succeeded; the rest, despite numberless

EVENTS IN THE WESTERN TRANSVAAL.

devices, being turned back by the strong entrenchments which the columns had thrown up on this, as on each night of the movement. It was a strange scene. The troops were now within fifteen miles of the railway, and the armoured trains, steaming up and down, threw across the dark veld from their searchlights great beams of light against which the enemy's bands were plainly silhouetted to the eyes of Hamilton's soldiers, whose defences had been traced not on the crests of the undulations, but half-way down the reverse slopes, bringing the skylines into sharp relief. It was a grievous night for the Boers, and its effects were evident next day. No sooner had Thorneycroft's column moved off in its place between F. W. Kitchener's and Sir H. Rawlinson's for the last day's drive to the railway line, when Colonel H. de B. de Lisle was met by an emissary with a white flag who came from 200 burghers, the remnants of the now famous commandos of Van Zyl and T. De Beer, who desired to surrender. As the British troops moved onward, these men were met and disarmed, and in a few more hours the whole British line rolled up to the Kimberley railway, having captured 367 prisoners of war. Thus ended an operation which may be taken as a type of many of which space has forbidden so full a record. The difficulties entailed in its successful performance can only be outlined, though to ignore them altogether might be to inspire a delusive confidence in the future. Only by a trusted and trustful commander with a corps of troops of supreme excellence can such a scheme be carried out. Sir I. Hamilton had under him men who were able and willing to make no halt by day and take no rest by night, for each long day's march, often nearly foodless and waterless, was intended only to bring them to the place of vigil or of fighting. Their labours were almost incredible. Long and deep trenches, impervious wire entanglements, fortified laagers of wagons, redoubts to hold from seven to twenty men—not only bullet-proof, but proof against artillery—sprang up each night under the hands of men who had already performed the extremity of toil since dawn, and were to do the same on the morrow, and for days after. During the day every man was a scout; at night not one

May 11th.

Results of the "drive."

Difficulties of such an operation.

but had to become a sentry, with eyes, ears and rifle alert. Such efforts would cause more casualties amongst inferior troops than amongst their adversaries. For a like reward they have seldom been equalled by soldiers in the field, and indeed there have been few who could have sustained them. Finally, to achieve success in a manœuvre of this scope and nature, there must be a leader, who is able to issue the clearest orders, and to consider them once launched as irrefragable. To attempt to supervise or alter the details of so vast a line when once in motion would result in confusion. In the manœuvre above described, Sir I. Hamilton, having given to his subordinates their several lines of march, in itself a calculation of no small complexity, left everything else to their discretion.* Their modes of marching, scouting, piqueting and fortification were all their own, and differed widely, though all were uniformly successful.

On May 17th the columns began to return independently to their respective bases. On the 23rd Sir I. Hamilton was back in Pretoria, where a week later peace was signed.

* Sir I. Hamilton's complete orders for the operations will be found in Appendix 4, and it will be useful to study them in amplification of the above text.

EVENTS IN THE WESTERN TRANSVAAL.

APPROXIMATE STRENGTH STATES OF COLUMNS REFERRED TO IN FOREGOING CHAPTER.

COLUMN.	Mounted Troops.	Infantry.	Guns, including Vickers-Maxims.	Machine Guns.	
March—May, 1902.					
Lt.-Col. A. B. Scott	600	—	3	—	Col. Sir H. Rawlinson in command.
Lt.-Col. J. W. G. Dawkins	700	—	3	—	
Col. C. J. Briggs	650	—	3	—	
Lt.-Col. W. H. Sitwell	422	174	3	—	
Col. Lord Basing	380	—	3	1	Col. A. N. Rochfort in command.
Lt.-Col. W. G. B. Western	762	363	2	1	
Maj. D. P. Driscoll	500	—	—	—	
Maj. E. S. Bulfin	400	—	1	—	
Maj. C. D. Vaughan	200	—	—	1	
Maj. P. G. Reynolds	200	—	—	1	
Lt.-Col. W. H. M. Lowe	1,320	—	3	—	Maj.-Gen. F. W. Kitchener in command.
Lt.-Col. G. A. Cookson	1,134	—	4	1	
Lt.-Col. J. L. Keir	626	—	4	1	
Col. R. G. Kekewich:—					
Lt.-Col. H. M. Grenfell	1,471	—	4	1	
Lt.-Col. S. B. von Donop	1,346	—	3	1	
Maj.-Gen. F. W. Kitchener:—					
Lt.-Col. G. A. Cookson	1,050	—	4	1	Lt.-Gen. Sir I. S. M. Hamilton in command.
Lt.-Col. J. L. Keir	626	—	4	1	
Lt.-Col. A. Wilson	375	775	1	1	
Lt.-Col. W. H. M. Lowe	1,200	—	3	—	
Col. Sir H. Rawlinson:—					
Lt.-Col. A. B. Scott	584	—	3	—	
Lt.-Col. J. W. G. Dawkins	690	—	3	—	
Col. C. J. Briggs	637	500	3	—	
Col. R. G. Kekewich	Two columns as above.				
Col. Sir H. Rawlinson	Three columns as above.				
Col. A. W. Thorneycroft:—					
Lt.-Col. R. H. Davies	1,100	—	3	—	
Lt.-Col. H. de B. de Lisle	1,447	—	3	1	Lt.-Gen. Sir I. S. M. Hamilton in command.
Maj.-Gen. F. W. Kitchener	Three columns (Cookson, Keir and Lowe).				
Col. A. N. Rochfort:—					
Lt.-Col. W. G. B. Western	756	414	1	—	
Maj. E. S. Bulfin	354	—	3	—	
Col. Lord Basing	569	—	3	1	
Lt.-Col. D. P. Driscoll	596	—	—	—	
Lt.-Col. W. H. Sitwell	651	160	3	1	

CHAPTER XXIX.

EVENTS IN THE EASTERN TRANSVAAL*

(Continued from Chapter XXI.).

FEBRUARY—MAY, 1902.

IN that part of the Eastern Transvaal controlled by Bruce Hamilton little of importance was undertaken during the greater part of February 1902, except the commencement by Barter of another blockhouse line along the Amsterdam road from Ermelo to the Vaal. It seemed to be impossible to find hostile bodies considerable enough to be worth pursuit. Yet though the columns had apparently exhausted their occupation, the very thoroughness of their work had, as usual, cast out to the fringe of the zone of operations many vagrant bands of fugitives, and soon one of these somewhat rudely broke the pause.

On February 4th the Commander-in-Chief, believing the country to be completely swept, ordered Major J. Fair, the commanding officer of the South African Constabulary around Heidelberg, to push his line of posts farther out into the veld. Fair prepared to comply, but before moving his main body despatched a party from Val to reconnoitre the ground east of the Waterval river, which his information led him to suspect was occupied by the enemy in some strength. The reconnaissance was carried out on the 8th by 130 picked men of the South African Constabulary under Captain A. Essex-Capell, and it immediately justified Fair's precaution. Fifteen miles north of Vlaklaagte station a commando more than 400 strong, with a large convoy, was discovered. The Boers replied to a

<small>Affair near Vlaklaagte, Feb. 8th, 1902.</small>

* See map No. 56.

EVENTS IN THE EASTERN TRANSVAAL. 513

somewhat over-bold attack on their laager by a vigorous counter-stroke which immediately threw the Constabulary on the defensive and would have done worse but for the tenacity of Capell's men and his skill in drawing them off. After an exciting contest, during which many brave deeds were performed,* the reconnoitring party disengaged with the loss of two officers and four men killed, an officer and eight men wounded and five men missing. The enemy lost more heavily, the majority of their casualties being incurred in repeated attacks on a party of twenty-four men under Lieutenant Swinburne, who refused either to retire or surrender, even after the main body had left the field, eventually so intimidating their assailants that they declined to renew the attack.

For G. Hamilton, patrolling east of Springs, February was a month which produced very varying fortunes. Assisted intermittently during the first half of the month by Wing's column, from Bruce Hamilton's command, G. Hamilton was in constant motion, accounting on February 3rd for thirty-four Boers by a converging movement on the Upper Wilge river, followed by a long gallop by the 5th Dragoon Guards of his own force and the 18th and 19th Hussars of Wing's; a few more captures were made on the 10th. On the 16th, in consequence of information from good sources that an exhausted commando of about 200 men was moving east of Heidelberg, G. Hamilton headed in that direction with about 400 men of the Royal Scots Greys and 5th Dragoon Guards, all that the lack of remounts and Wing's departure on the 14th had left to him. On the 18th two squadrons, which he had detached to circumvent a small commando falling back before him, ran into the enemy, to find him not, as reported, a weary two hundred, but a watchful and aggressive force, nearly 700 strong, which first destroyed the detachment, then proceeded to attack the main body itself, of the weakness of which they were fortunately ignorant. G. Hamilton withdrew to Springs in safety, and though the affair had cost him more than sixty casualties, forty-seven of

Affair near Springs, Feb. 18th, 1902.

* For gallantry on this occasion Surgeon-Captain A. Martin-Leake was awarded the Victoria Cross.

these were by capture and the prisoners were released the same evening.

These affairs accentuated the fact that although Bruce Hamilton had crushed the shell of the Boer resistance in the Eastern Transvaal, the kernel had escaped him. Commandant-General Botha was still at large, and surrounded by adherents whose numerical weakness was never to be despised so long as they were inspired by his presence. More than any troops are guerrillas, more than any guerrillas were the Boers, to be estimated rather by the quality of their leadership than by their own strength or military excellence. The campaign had abounded in instances of commandos which exchanged futility for heroism, or the reverse, with a change in the personality of the commander. To catch Botha, then, was still the most insistent problem in the east, and for the moment he seemed to have disappeared. Not until the end of February was his path discovered, and its direction was both a surprise and an alarm. For Botha, weary of being buffeted about the High Veld, had passed around the eastern extremity of Colville and his blockhouses, and was now heading straight for Vryheid, and presumably once again for Natal. Instantly, as if drawn by a powerful magnet, a bevy of columns were on the march southward. Taking with him Spens, Mackenzie, Allenby and Stewart, and calling on Plumer, Pulteney and Colville to co-operate, Bruce Hamilton was at Wakkerstroom on the 28th, and at Vryheid on March 5th, Wing meanwhile being left in Ermelo, and Barter on his partially constructed blockhouse line. Plumer and Pulteney, who had been raiding successfully in the Rand Berg, securing twenty-six prisoners, were now ordered to join Wing in a drive westward, for there was a rumour that Botha had escaped into the Orange River Colony. They departed on this mission, and concluded a fruitless search on March 8th at Standerton, where both columns were broken up. Amongst the units thus dispersed were the 5th Victorian Rifles, who by seven months' admirable service under Pulteney had fully retrieved their misfortune of the previous June. Meanwhile Bruce Hamilton scoured the south-eastern angle of the Transvaal throughout March, not without

Effect of Botha's freedom.

Botha discovered on the borders of Natal.

EVENTS IN THE EASTERN TRANSVAAL. 515

success, though that most desired, the capture of Botha, was still missed, once only by a hair's breadth. Twenty-seven Boers, including General C. Emmett, were taken on the 15th in a night raid in the Ngotsi hills, about the head waters of the Mkusi river near Broedersrust, where Bruce Hamilton, outpaced by a band of fugitives, resorted to the ruse of a feigned retirement, which had the effect of luring the enemy back to him to their ultimate confusion. Again on the 18th, in the tangled Ngomi forest, night operations resulted in the capture of six Boers, with whom Botha himself had been present the night before. A third night expedition, on April 1st, gathered seventeen prisoners from the Intombi river. Then Bruce Hamilton, having lost all trace of Botha, turned his face once more towards Ermelo, which he reached on April 5th. *Touch with Botha lost.*

Turning to the zone of operations north of the Delagoa Bay railway—The certainty of the Transvaal Government's presence in the Roos Senekal area had induced the Commander-in-Chief to resume active operations in that quarter. Appointing Major-General R. S. R. Fetherstonhaugh to command from Middelburg, he ordered energetic operations with three columns —those of Colonel C. W. Park and Lieut.-Colonels E. B. Urmston and E. C. Ingouville Williams—which by the middle of February were concentrated on the railway at Pan. Another column under Lieut.-Colonel the Hon. C. G. Fortescue patrolled the line and kept communication. The exact situation of the Boer officials was uncertain, but Muller, Viljoen's successor, was known to be near Roos Senekal, and Trichardt in the Botha's Berg, and Fetherstonhaugh, watching the comings and goings between these two, ordered the first dash to be made against the hills. At 7 p.m. on the 19th Park led the mounted men of all three columns, followed an hour later by the infantry, north-eastward up the line of the Steelpoort river, and by a swift night march turned the Botha's Berg by the east before dawn on the 20th. Opposite the eastern flank of the range Urmston was dropped to attack the southern slopes whilst Park went on to near Blinkwater to command the northern. The expedition then turned eastward against the Botha's Berg, and was soon absorbed in a *Events north of the Delagoa Bay railway, Feb. 1902.*

series of successes. First two small laagers were suddenly come upon by the 4th mounted infantry and Williams' Australians. The latter attacked brilliantly and took thirty-nine prisoners by one rush. Next Trichardt's own encampment was discovered, eight burghers were captured, and the rest with their leader driven into the kloofs, the southern exits of which Urmston was in the act of blocking. A hue and cry followed. Trichardt himself escaped, but for hours his followers were hunted from their hiding places until 164 prisoners were marshalled, the victims as much of their own negligence as of their enemy's dash, for though Trichardt had been warned of Park's approach by Muller from east of the Steelpoort, the British had been undetected by so much as a single scout or sentry. Leaving E. C. I. Williams on the Botha's Berg, Park and Urmston then turned towards the base. Further searching of the kloofs next day resulted in another twenty-eight captures by Williams, who on the 23rd took five more, and then received orders to come in.

On February 24th Fetherstonhaugh's command was back on the line, along which he moved his units by train to Bronkhorstspruit station for a descent on Langkloof, where the Acting-President of the Transvaal was reported to be sheltering. Railway delay marred a promising plan; a thirty miles' march by E. C. I. Williams ended in the surrounding of an empty farm; but Park, finding he could not be up in time, searched the ground about Rhenoster Kop and returned with seventeen prisoners, including an officer of the State artillery. These captures, together with over 100 voluntary surrenders at the railway posts, brought the yield in this quarter for the month of February to the total of some 470 fighting men. In March the raiding continued, chiefly to the west of the Wilge and Oliphant rivers. On the 11th Park, moving at night from Wilge River station, fell upon a group of small laagers a few miles north-west of the junction of the Wilge and the Oliphant, and took fifteen prisoners. The same night E. C. I. Williams, from Bronkhorstspruit station, captured five Boers near Rhenoster Kop, where Park joined him at dusk on the 12th, having marched seventy miles in the previous twenty-four hours. Next day both columns crossed the Wilge, having first detached a party westward to the head of the Moos river, where eleven Boers were surprised and taken. After reaching Balmoral on the 16th further raids, involving night marches of great length, were undertaken to the south of the railway which Fortescue remained to guard, with Urmston, who was short of horses, near him. Finding little to gain, the columns continued southward, and marched up to near the head of the Steenkool (or Steenbok) Spruit, where orders were received for a combined sweep to be made on the 23rd in conjunction with Wing's column, which had returned to Bethel the previous day with a convoy from Paardekop.

The drive was to be based on the line Driefontein—Elands- fontein—Bethel, and to be directed against the railway between Standerton and Val stations. By the evening of the appointed day the troops were in position, Wing on the left keeping touch with the Ermelo—Standerton blockhouses. But the line, advancing at dawn on the 24th, encountered very few of the enemy, and pulled up on the Standerton railway with only seven prisoners, results very disappointing to men many of whom had marched seventy-six miles in sixty hours to attain them. There was, however, no pause. On the 29th Park, E. C. I. Williams and Wing were out again, bent on an eastward drive to Ermelo, based on a line of which Bethel was the centre, Schurvekop and Roodekrans the left and right extremities. Ermelo was entered on April 4th with only three prisoners taken, and thereafter Park and Wing manœuvred towards Lake Chrissie, whilst Williams went into Carolina. Altogether during the month of March the four columns, namely, Park's, E. C. I. Williams', Urmston's and Fortescue's, had accounted for forty-six of the enemy in field operations and 118 by voluntary surrender. Meanwhile, as already narrated, Bruce Hamilton came up to Ermelo on the 5th after his expedition into the southern angle of the Transvaal. With him, or close behind, were Spens, Mackenzie, Allenby and Stewart, and Hamilton now assumed command also of Park, Williams and Wing. Continuing his northward way Hamilton was about to make for Carolina on the 9th when he received orders to employ all his seven columns

"Drive" to the Standerton railway.

Results in the north.

Bruce Hamilton in command of seven columns

in a great south-westerly " drive " against the Standerton railway, starting with his right at Groot Oliphants station, the termination of the Constabulary blockhouse line, his left at Carolina, where ended the blockhouses from Ermelo. On April 11th he was in position and ready to march, but before describing the operation it is necessary to refer briefly to an incident which had occurred a few days previously near Springs.

There G. Hamilton having been invalided after two years' command in the field, his brigade of cavalry had been broken up and Colonel the Hon. R. T. Lawley had taken over the surveillance of a district which no effort seemed to be able to clear. Lawley brought with him from the Orange River Colony the 7th Hussars and the 2nd Dragoon Guards (Queen's Bays). He at once inherited from his predecessor the task of dealing with the numbers and aggressiveness of the bands which refuged here from the scoured and enclosed areas further east. On the last day of March Lawley was at Boschmanskop, eighteen miles southeast of Springs, whence on the morning of April 1st he despatched three squadrons (295 officers and men) of the 2nd Dragoon Guards, under Lieut.-Colonel H. D. Fanshawe, to endeavour to surprise some Boer piquets which were visible about twelve miles toward the east. The enterprise opened well, several Boers, including a Commandant Pretorius, being captured before daylight; but the squadrons, pushing on, found themselves in the presence of a commando over 800 strong which, after a heavy fusilade, charged in at full speed to close quarters, shooting from the saddle, whilst many drew out around the flanks of the outnumbered cavalry. Fanshawe, seeing that he must fall back or be surrounded, then disposed his men for a rearguard fight towards Boschmanskop. His backward march was attended with extreme difficulty. Day had not yet broken, and the Boers, galloping where they pleased in the semi-darkness, not only threw themselves repeatedly against the rear, but occupied the flanking points of vantage on the line of retreat, so that the force was shouldered away from the direct line and in momentary danger of being cut off. Yet though deprived of six of their eleven officers, the troopers, fighting with unimpaired discipline,

Affair at Boschmanskop, March 31st, 1902.

EVENTS IN THE EASTERN TRANSVAAL.

were manœuvred with great skill from position to position, and kept the enemy at bay until, nearing Boschmanskop, they were met by the 7th Hussars and covered by Lawley's guns. They then withdrew to camp with the loss of two officers and eighteen men killed, four officers and fifty-seven men wounded and three men missing. The Boers lost at least as heavily; they had exposed themselves courageously, and the Bays had time after time struck down the foremost groups of their pursuers.

Thus closed an affair as creditable as it was costly to the troops engaged, but of minor importance in itself were it not an illustration of the singular difficulties encountered in this campaign. How closely and continually must an enemy be watched who can, when near exhaustion, glean suddenly nearly a thousand well mounted men with transport and ambulances complete (for Fanshawe's adversaries had both) from a field swept by marching armies and intersected by fortifications, who can secretly place such a force within a day's march of its opponent's depôts and lines of communication, and within two hours' ride of one of his most mobile and vigilant columns. Against such an adversary the provision of suitable checks everywhere is an impossibility. To attack him, or to await his attack, must remain a speculation up to the last shot, for the strength of a posse or a brigade may lie in ambush, gathered in the last few hours unseen by the keenest of scouts or spies. In such a case for small columns every throw is a gamble. Only the most certain information is safe to act on, and as that is rarely obtainable, operations, especially at night, are so dangerous that the punitive force will usually find itself marching and operating as if on the defensive. The attack, then, would seem to be in the more need of consolidation the more the enemy disintegrates, and to do this over a theatre so vast as South Africa demanded forces which were apt to seem disproportionately large to the results attained, or indeed attainable. The General confronted with widespread guerrilla warfare may well send for more troops rather than dismiss any of those he has.

The enemy's power of recuperation.

To Lord Kitchener's recognition of this was due the initiation first of the blockhouse lines and next of those extensive sweeps, or "drives" as they were called by an army which drew much of its phraseology as of its spirit from the field of sport. To thresh out large areas of country with immense and uninterrupted lines of troops may seem a primitive device only to those who consider nothing of the enormous difficulty of collecting, aligning, supplying and ordering large bodies of men to move with coherence and with a common object on a front whose flanks were often three days' march apart. Of such a nature had been most of the larger manœuvres in 1902, and yet another was that about to be set on foot by Bruce Hamilton when the narrative was interrupted for the inclusion of Fanshawe's significant little action at Boschmanskop.

Difficulties attending the "drives."

Groot Oliphants station and Carolina are more than sixty miles apart. Near the former stood Park, with E. C. I. Williams, Wing, Spens, Mackenzie and Allenby between him and Stewart by Carolina. On April 12th this line advanced to the front Welstand—Klipstapel. The enemy stirred like game indeed before it. The majority scurried away, of whom many were taken; but some, of sterner stuff, turned and charged the beaters, and sweeping over every obstacle, literally smashed a way through the solid rank and gained their freedom to the north. On the 14th Bruce Hamilton's men drew up with 136 prisoners on the Standerton line, where they were joined on the 16th by columns under Rimington, Nixon, Lawley and Garratt, fresh from Elliot's great foray in the Orange River Colony.* The country east of the line of South African Constabulary blockhouses having been thus swept, on the 17th eight of the columns turned their faces northward for a return drive northward west of that line. The enemy here was now desperate, but his skill and cunning grew with his peril. Detecting a small leak on the extreme left of the British line, the majority of the Boers poured back through it on the night of the 19th, and the troops, on their arrival on the Delagoa Bay railway next day, had only three prisoners to show for their exertions. Three days later Rimington, Nixon and Lawley left in company to clear the angle of country which had been omitted between Springs,

Bruce Hamilton's great "drive," April 12th—20th, 1902.

* See Chapter XXVII.

EVENTS IN THE EASTERN TRANSVAAL.

Pretoria and Brugspruit, whilst the rest, facing about once more, prepared to sweep the veld down to Heidelberg and Val. This was completed on the 27th, and the meagreness of its results—four prisoners taken—seemed to prove that at last this covert was bare. It must again be recorded what labour such operations entailed on the troops. Each day, in rain or wind or under tropical sun, they marched from dawn to dusk, each night they dug entrenchments, and strung up leagues of barbed-wire entanglements before they lay down in the open, to the brief rest which many, from the necessity of finding innumerable outposts, never obtained at all. In short, here, as over all the theatre of war, the British soldier was at this time registering his capacity to endure the extremity of fatigue, his willingness to display the extremity of fortitude and discipline. As for his enemy, mounted, knowing how to subsist and find shelter easily upon his native veld, the Boer suffered physically far less than his opponent. His was the keener suffering of the patriot soldier who knows himself, his tactics, and his country to be mastered beyond all hope of recovery, and that he remains alive in the dying days of his national cause. *[margin: Endurance of the troops.]*

The beginning of May, 1902, saw the war at a low ebb indeed in the Eastern Transvaal. Seven of Bruce Hamilton's columns quitting the district, entered the Orange River Colony to sweep up the country below Vereeniging.* Only to the north of the Delagoa Bay line, in the never-to-be-pacified Roos Senekal area, was there work still to be done, and here Park and Urmston operated briskly until the 12th, taking in all thirty prisoners and about sixty wagons. The opposition encountered from Muller's men was, however, occasionally considerable, and though Park incurred but five casualties, the enemy more than once took stand upon positions and in numbers to attack which with the forces available involved great risk. Park clung closely to him, and was in a fair way to stamp out this last flicker in the Eastern Transvaal when Peace, dropping " as the gentle rain from Heaven," put out with merciful shower the whole conflagration which had so long tormented South Africa.

* See Chapter XXVII.

Approximate Strength States of Columns referred to in foregoing Chapter.

COLUMN.	Mounted Troops.	Infantry.	Guns, including Vickers-Maxims.	Machine Guns.	
February—May, 1902.					
Lt.-Col. Sir J. H. Jervis-White-Jervis	520	—	—	—	⎫ Brig.-Gen. H. C. O.
Maj. F. F. Colvin	700	—	6	—	⎬ Plumer in command.
Lt.-Col. A. E. W. Colville	550	300	4	1	
Col. W. P. Pulteney	800	261	3	2	
Col. C. St. L. Barter	450	690	3	1	
Brig.-Gen. G. Hamilton	750	259	5	3	
Col. C. W. Park	400	547	3	1	⎫
Lt.-Col. E. B. Urmston	500	271	2	2	⎬ Maj. Gen. R. S. R
Lt.-Col. E. C. Ingouville Williams	700	112	3	1	⎬ Fetherstonhaugh in command.
Lt.-Col. the Hon. C. G. Fortescue	200	153	—	—	⎭
Lt.-Col. F. D. V. Wing	775	—	3	—	⎫
Brig.-Gen. J. Spens	500	—	4	—	⎬ Maj.-Gen. Bruce
Lt.-Col. C. J. Mackenzie	600	—	3	1	⎬ Hamilton in command.
Col. E. H. H. Allenby	700	—	3	4	
Lt.-Col. H. K. Stewart	600	—	1	1	⎭
Col. M. F. Rimington	1,300	102	5	—	
Lt.-Col. J. E. Nixon	1,000	—	3	2	
Col. the Hon. R. T. Lawley (late G. Hamilton's)	1,000	—	3	2	
Col. F. S. Garratt	700	178	3	1	

CHAPTER XXX.

THE CONCLUSION OF PEACE.

FOR more than a year before the stage to which events have been brought in the preceding chapters, the Boers had cognisance of the terms of peace which the British Government was prepared to offer to their nation.

Only passing reference has been made to a meeting between Lord Kitchener and Commandant-General L. Botha at Middelburg on February 28th, 1901.* At that meeting, which as it proved ineffectual was not entered upon in detail in the course of the narration, the Boer leader had declared himself to be doubtful of bringing about a cessation of hostilities unless national independence, the soul of his country's aspirations, should be conceded as a fundamental condition. The interview was therefore abortive from the outset, for Lord Kitchener declined even to discuss what was now virtually the whole *casus belli;* but it was not entirely unprofitable.

<small>First reference to terms of peace, Feb. 28th, 1901.</small>

For the first time the British Government obtained an insight into other questions which in the minds of its opponents stood prominent as conditions of submission. These were (i.) the speedy inauguration of representative government; (ii.) equal rights for the Dutch language; (iii.) the postponement of the franchise of Kaffirs; (iv.) the integrity of Dutch Church property; (v.) the assumption by Great Britain of all the debts of the Republics, especially of notes, requisitions and other liabilities incurred during the war; (vi.) that no war tax should be imposed on farmers; (vii.) the early return of prisoners of war; (viii.) financial assistance to ruined farmers; (ix.) amnesty to all at

---

* See Chapter VI., pages 119 and 120.

the conclusion of war ; (x.) the retention of rifles by those liable to danger from the natives.

The Boers, on the other hand, learned definitely the price of peace. A week after the Middelburg interview Lord Kitchener, having in the meantime communicated with London, supplemented his provisional and verbal replies to Commandant-General Botha's queries by the despatch of the following letter :—

<blockquote>

"Pretoria,

"March 7th, 1901.

"YOUR HONOUR,

"With reference to our conversation at Middelburg on the 28th February, I have the honour to inform you that, in the event of a general and complete cessation of hostilities, and the surrender of all rifles, ammunition, cannon and other munitions of war in the hands of the burghers, or in Government depôts, or elsewhere, His Majesty's Government is prepared to adopt the following measures.

"His Majesty's Government will at once grant an amnesty in the Transvaal and Orange River Colony for all *bond fide* acts of war committed during the recent hostilities. British subjects belonging to Natal and Cape Colony, while they will not be compelled to return to those Colonies, will, if they do so, be liable to be dealt with by the laws of those Colonies specially passed to meet the circumstances arising out of the present war. As you are doubtless aware the special law in the Cape Colony has greatly mitigated the ordinary penalties for High Treason in the present case.

"All prisoners of war, now in St. Helena, Ceylon, or elsewhere, being burghers or Colonists, will, on the completion of the surrender, be brought back to their country as quickly as arrangements can be made for their transport.
</blockquote>

The terms offered in 1901.

THE CONCLUSION OF PEACE.

"At the earliest practicable date military administration will cease, and will be replaced by civil administration in the form of Crown Colony Government. There will, therefore, be, in the first instance, in each of the new Colonies, a Governor and an Executive Council, composed of the principal officials, with a Legislative Council consisting of a certain number of official members to whom a nominated unofficial element will be added. But it is the desire of His Majesty's Government, as soon as circumstances permit, to introduce a representative element, and ultimately to concede to the new Colonies the privilege of self-government. Moreover, on the cessation of hostilities a High Court will be established in each of the new Colonies to administer the laws of the land and this Court will be independent of the Executive.

"Church property, public trusts, and orphan funds will be respected.

"Both the English and Dutch languages will be used and taught in Public schools when the parents of the children desire it, and allowed in Courts of Law.

"As regards the debts of the late Republican Governments, His Majesty's Government cannot undertake any liability. It is however prepared, as an act of grace, to set aside a sum not exceeding one million pounds sterling to repay inhabitants of the Transvaal and Orange River Colony for goods requisitioned from them by the late Republican Governments, or subsequent to annexation, by Commandants in the field being in a position to enforce such requisitions. But such claims will have to be established to the satisfaction of a Judge or Judicial Commission, appointed by the Government, to investigate and assess them, and, if exceeding in the aggregate one million pounds, they will be liable to reduction *pro rata*.

"I also beg to inform Your Honour that the new Government will take into immediate consideration the possibility of assisting by loan the occupants of farms, who will take the oath of allegiance, to repair any injuries sustained by destruction of buildings or loss of stock during the war, and that no special war tax will be imposed upon farms to defray the expense of the war.

"When burghers require the protection of fire-arms, such will be allowed to them by licence, and on due registration, provided they take the oath of allegiance. Licences will also be issued for sporting rifles, guns, etc., but military fire-arms will only be allowed for purposes of protection.

"As regards the extension of the franchise to Kaffirs in the Transvaal and Orange River Colony, it is not the intention of His Majesty's Government to give such franchise before representative Government is granted to those Colonies, and if then given it will be so limited as to secure the just predominance of the white race. The legal position of coloured persons will, however, be similar to that which they hold in the Cape Colony.

"In conclusion I must inform Your Honour that, if the terms now offered are not accepted after a reasonable delay for consideration they must be regarded as cancelled.

"I have, etc.,

"KITCHENER, General,

"Commander-in-Chief, British Forces, South Africa.

"To His Honour COMMANDANT-GENERAL LOUIS BOTHA."

Terms of 1901 refused. It is unnecessary to insist on the liberality of these terms, which embodied concessions the mere asking of which by the beaten side the conquerors of no long past era would have heard with derision. They were, however, promptly refused by the Boers, or rather by the Boer leaders: for, as it had ever been in the Boer States, the pretended free-will of the people was largely submerged in that of the oligarchy which ruled them. In only one spirit could the British terms have been read in the laagers, if indeed they were read at all, when submitted with such recommendation as that to be derived from the accompanying letter from General Botha:—

THE CONCLUSION OF PEACE.

ADDRESS OF LOUIS BOTHA TO BURGHERS.

(*Translation.*)

"DEAR BROTHERS,

"The spirit of Lord Kitchener's letter makes it very plain to you all that the British Government desires nothing else but the destruction of our Afrikander people, and acceptance of the terms contained therein is absolutely out of the question. Virtually, the letter contains nothing more, but rather less, than what the British Government will be obliged to do should our cause go wrong. Notice that they will give us a Legislative Council consisting of their own officials and members nominated by themselves. The voice of the people is thus totally unrecognised. It is also proposed, and this as a favour, to place only one million pounds disposable for covering our State Debts, whereas, according to general legal advice, should the cause unexpectedly go wrong with us, the British Government must bear the responsibility of all State Debts, and not simply walk away with the State's assets.

[Botha's address to the burghers, March 15th, 1901.]

"Our burghers have fought heavily, but how can it be otherwise, when the existence of our nation is unlawfully threatened? The blood and tears that this war has cost has been hard, but giving up our country will be doubly hard.

"I feel from the bottom of my heart for those burghers whose families have been removed. Do not let this make anyone desperate, because he who becomes desperate and gives up the struggle, does not only an injustice to his people, but also loses all trust in himself.

"The more we are aggrieved by the enemy the more steadfastly we ought to stand for our goods and lawful rights.

"Let us, as Daniel in the lions' den, place our trust in God alone, for in His time and in His way He will certainly give us deliverance.

"LOUIS BOTHA,
"Commandant-General.

"Ermelo, March 15th, 1901."

528   THE WAR IN SOUTH AFRICA.

Some reasons for the Boers' refusal of terms in 1901.   The time, indeed, was not ripe for peace. It has been shown elsewhere how at this moment the Boer forces were actually becoming more compact by the stripping off of the impedimenta, the traitors, the weaklings, the pseudo-regular organisations which had hampered their earlier campaign. The day of strategy, which they so little understood, had ended with Lord Roberts' occupation of every line of communication in South Africa. The day of elemental tactics, in which they excelled their opponents, was at hand. Their armies had been greatly reduced, but the reduction had laid bare a core of stalwarts who tacitly accepted a war of extermination, and were by no means inconsiderable in numbers. There were still nearly 50,000 burghers in the field. De Wet had refilled the Orange River Colony with his scattered but easily collected bands; De la Rey was in the act of organising the strong " flying commando,"* which was long to dominate the veld of the Western Transvaal; French's greatest efforts had been unable to clear the Eastern Transvaal; Kritzinger, Fouché, Scheepers and Malan still embroiled Cape Colony, and undeterred by De Wet's expulsion, kept the British province open for the next invasion. Under these circumstances it was not surprising that it was long before there was any further mention of peace, and when it came again it emanated not from the enemy in the field, but from those who wished them well in Europe.

The Netherland Government reopens the question of peace, Jan. 1902.   Towards the end of January, 1902, the Marquess of Lansdowne, Secretary of State for Foreign Affairs, received from Baron Gericke, the Netherland Ambassador in London, a communication proposing the good offices of the Government of the Queen of Holland in the cause of peace. The document, which was in the form of an *Aide-Mémoire*, was in the following terms :—

---

* Letter from General De la Rey to Commandant-General Botha, March 18th, 1901.

THE CONCLUSION OF PEACE.

CORRESPONDENCE WITH THE NETHERLAND GOVERNMENT REGARDING THE WAR IN SOUTH AFRICA.

Aide-Mémoire communicated by Baron Gericke.

January 25th, 1902.

(*Translation.*)

"1. In the opinion of the Government of Her Majesty the Queen, the exceptional circumstances in which one of the belligerent parties in South Africa is placed, and which prevent it from communicating directly with the other belligerent, constitute one of the reasons for the prolongation of the war, which is still raging without pause or end in that country, and which is the cause of so much misery. Proposals by the Netherland Ambassador.

"2. It is, in fact, an exceptional circumstance that one of the belligerent parties is completely shut in and separated from the rest of the world, and that the Boer representatives in Europe are deprived of all means of communicating with the Generals commanding their forces. The difficulty thus arises that the authorities who ought to negotiate on the Boer side are divided into two sections, which are deprived of all means of deliberating together. It is evident that the Boer Delegates in Europe can do nothing, because they do not know the state of affairs in Africa, and that the Boers in the field are obliged to abstain from taking any steps, because they are not cognizant of the state of affairs in Europe.

"3. Moreover, the Delegates in Europe are bound by their letters of credence, which were drawn up in March, 1900, and which bind them so strictly to the independence of the Republics that they would not even be permitted to accept the re-establishment of the *status quo ante bellum* if the mode of settling disputes which might arise were not laid down at the same time.

"4. These circumstances give rise to the question whether an offer of good offices could not usefully be made by a neutral Power, in order to render at least possible negotiations which could not otherwise be opened.

" 5. For this reason, it would be important to ascertain whether it would be agreeable to His Britannic Majesty's Government to make use of the good offices of a neutral Power if such good offices were confined to the task of placing in communication the negotiators to be appointed by the two parties.

" 6. The Government of Her Majesty the Queen might perhaps be considered as indicated for the performance of this task, seeing that the Boer Delegates are in Netherland territory and are accredited to that Government alone.

" 7. If His Britannic Majesty's Government should agree in this view, the Government of Her Majesty the Queen would have to inquire of the Boer Delegates whether they would be willing to proceed to Africa to deliberate with the Boer leaders on the spot, returning to Europe after a stay of fixed length (say a fortnight), armed with adequate full powers, providing for all eventualities, and authorising them to conclude a Treaty of Peace which should bind absolutely both the Boers in Europe and the Boers in Africa.

" 8. In the event of an affirmative reply, it would be for His Britannic Majesty's Government to hand to the Netherland Government three safe-conducts permitting the Boer Delegates to proceed freely to Africa, to remain there freely for the time agreed upon, and to return freely to Europe. It would further be necessary for the British Government to allow the use of a telegraph code with a view to appointing the place where the said Delegates could meet the Boer leaders.

" 9. On their return, the Government of Her Majesty the Queen could place them in communication with the Plenipotentiaries appointed for the purpose by His Britannic Majesty's Government, and would willingly undertake to place at the disposal of these gentlemen the accommodation necessary for their meetings.

THE CONCLUSION OF PEACE.

" 10. The Government of Her Majesty the Queen would then consider their task as at an end.

" 11. It is quite evident that, in spite of everything, the negotiations thus begun might lead to no result ; but the possibility of the contrary is also not excluded, and in this condition of affairs it appears desirable to endeavour to open negotiations in the hope that they may be successful. And in face of the difficulty which exists for all belligerent parties of taking the first step in this direction, it might be useful that a third party should undertake the matter and serve as an intermediary."

These proposals, for all their good intentions, involved obvious difficulties which Lord Lansdowne was quick to point out in the following reply :—

THE MARQUESS OF LANSDOWNE TO BARON GERICKE.

" Foreign Office,

" January 29th, 1902.

" SIR,

" You were good enough to lay before me on the 25th instant a communication from the Netherland Government, in which it was proposed that, with the object of bringing the war to an end, His Majesty's Government might grant a safe-conduct to the Boer Delegates now in Holland for the purpose of enabling them to confer with the Boer leaders in South Africa. It is suggested that after the conference the Delegates might return to Europe with power to conclude a Treaty of Peace with this country, and the Netherland Government intimate that, in this event, they might at a later stage be instrumental in placing the Boer Plenipotentiaries in relation with the Plenipotentiaries who might be appointed by His Majesty's Government.

" The Netherland Government intimate that if this project commends itself to His Majesty's Government, they

Lord Lansdowne's reply.

will inquire of the Delegates whether they are prepared to make the suggested visit to South Africa.

"It may therefore be inferred that the communication which I received from you was made on the responsibility of the Netherland Government alone, and without authority from the Boer Delegates or leaders.

"His Majesty's Government have given it their best consideration, and, whilst they entirely appreciate the motives of humanity which have led the Netherland Government to make this proposal, they feel that they must adhere to the decision, adopted and publicly announced by them some months after the commencement of hostilities by the Boers, that it is not their intention to accept the intervention of any foreign Power in the South African War.

"Should the Boer Delegates themselves desire to lay a request for safe conduct before His Majesty's Government, there is no reason why they should not do so. But His Majesty's Government are obviously not in a position to express an opinion on any such application until they have received it and are aware of its precise nature, and the grounds on which the request is made.

"I may, however, point out that it is not at present clear to His Majesty's Government that the Delegates retain any influence over the Representatives of the Boers in South Africa, or have any voice in their councils. They are stated by the Netherland Government to have no letters of credence or instructions later in date than March, 1900. His Majesty's Government had, on the other hand, understood that all powers of government, including those of negotiation, were now completely vested in Mr. Steyn for the Boers of the Orange River Colony, and in Mr. Schalk Burger for those of the Transvaal.

"If this be so, it is evident that the quickest and most satisfactory means of arranging a settlement would be by direct communication between the leaders of the Boer forces in South Africa and the Commander-in-Chief of His Majesty's forces, who has already been instructed to forward immediately any offers he may receive for the consideration of His Majesty's Government.

"In these circumstances His Majesty's Government have decided that if the Boer leaders should desire to enter into negotiations for the purpose of bringing the war to an end, those negotiations must take place, not in Europe, but in South Africa.

"It should, moreover, be borne in mind that if the Boer Delegates are to occupy time in visiting South Africa, in consulting with the Boer leaders in the field, and in returning to Europe for the purpose of making known the results of their errand, a period of at least three months would elapse, during which hostilities would be prolonged, and much human suffering, perhaps needlessly, occasioned.

"I have, etc.

"(Signed) LANSDOWNE."

The *Aide-Mémoire* was, however, immediately forwarded to Lord Kitchener for distribution to Mr. S. W. Burger, the Acting President of the Transvaal, and his colleagues, with the result that Mr. Burger expressed himself as "desirous and prepared to make peace proposals,"* when he should have consulted with Mr. Steyn as to the terms thereof. After some delay caused by the difficulty of ascertaining the whereabouts of the deposed head of the Orange Free State, who was then under medical care in De la Rey's laager,† Messrs. Burger and Steyn were eventually brought together, on April 9th, at Klerksdorp, the following leaders also coming in to the conference, Generals C. R. De Wet and De la Rey, with the State Secretaries of both Republican Governments, and some others. The next two days were spent in discussion amongst these officials; the state of the campaign in every district was reviewed, and a decision to make proposals to the British Government being arrived at,

The Boer leaders meet to consider the proposals,

---

* From Acting State President S. W. Burger, to Lord Kitchener, March 10th, 1902.
† See Chapter XXVII., page 478.

the following request for a meeting with Lord Kitchener was despatched to Pretoria :—

(*Translation.*)

"Klerksdorp,
"April 10th, 1902.

"EXCELLENCY,

"We have the honour to herewith send Your Excellency the following decision, taken here to-day.

"The Government of the S. A. R. and that of the O. F. S. having met in connection with the sending in by His Excellency Lord Kitchener, of the correspondence, exchanged in Europe between the Government of His Majesty the King of England and the Government of Her Majesty the Queen of the Netherlands, regarding the desirability of procuring the Governments of these Republics occasion to come into communication with their Plenipotentiaries in Europe, who are still enjoying the confidence of both Governments;

"Considering the spirit of reconciliation which thereby appears to exist on the side of His Britannic Majesty's Government, and the desire therein expressed by Lord Lansdowne, on behalf of his Government, to cause an end to be put to this struggle.

"Are of opinion that it is now a suitable moment to once more show their willingness to do everything possible to put a stop to this war, and

"Therefore decide to make certain propositions to His Excellency Lord Kitchener, as representative of His Britannic Majesty's Government, which may serve as a base for further negotiations in order to bring about the desired peace;

"Further decide: That it is the opinion of both these Republics that, in order to accelerate the achievement of the desired object, and to avoid misunderstanding as much as possible:

THE CONCLUSION OF PEACE. 535

"His Excellency Lord Kitchener be requested to meet these Governments personally, time and place to be appointed by him, in order to directly lay before him peace proposals which we are prepared to make, by which we shall be enabled to settle all questions which may arise, at once by direct conversation and parley with him, thereby making certain that this meeting will have the desired effect (bear the desired fruit).

"We shall be glad to have Your Excellency's decision about this as soon as possible.

"We have the honour to be

"Your Excellency's obedient servants,

"S. W. BURGER,
"Acting State President S. A. R.

"M. T. STEYN,
"State President O. F. S.

"To His Excellency LORD KITCHENER,
"Commander-in-Chief of H. M. Troops in South Africa."

In the forenoon of April 12th Lord Kitchener received the Delegates in a saloon of his official residence at Pretoria. As the proceedings were to be confined to hearing what the Boers had to propose, the Commander-in-Chief was unaccompanied by any political officer. The meeting, in short, was purely a discussion between the military heads of both sides, and as such its termination was far from promising. Once more the question of independence barred the way. Neither party could even discuss it, Lord Kitchener because he knew it to be the *sine quâ non* of his Government's requirements, the Boers because they were constitutionally precluded from treating on the subject without the authorisation of the full vote of the Boer peoples.

Nothing remained, therefore, but for the deputation to frame its proposals, omitting all mention of the only item of vital importance, and this was done in the terms set forth in a

_{Lord Kitchener meets the Boer leaders at Pretoria, April 12th, 1902.}

telegram transmitted to London by Lord Kitchener in the evening :—

FROM LORD KITCHENER TO THE SECRETARY OF STATE FOR WAR.

"Pretoria, April 12th, 1902.

"9.22 p.m.

The Boer demands submitted to the Secretary of State for War.

"At meeting of all Boer representatives to-day they wished the following telegram sent :—

"'The Boer representatives wish to lay before His Majesty's Government that they have an earnest desire for peace, and that they consequently decided to ask the British Government to end hostilities, and to enter into an agreement by which, in their opinion, all future war between them and the British Government in South Africa will be prevented. They consider this object may be attained by providing for the following points :—

"'(1) Franchise.
"'(2) Equal rights for Dutch and English languages in education matters.
"'(3) Customs Union.
"'(4) Dismantling of all forts in Transvaal and Orange River Colony.
"'(5) Post, telegraph and railways union.
"'(6) Arbitration in case of future differences, and only subjects of the parties to be the arbitrators.
"'(7) Mutual amnesty.'

"But if these terms are not satisfactory, they desire to know what terms the British Government would give them in order to secure the end they all desire. . . .''

Such requirements, presuming independence and equality in every phrase, could meet, as Lord Kitchener plainly warned the meeting, with but one reception. The inevitable reply was in his hands before dawn.

THE CONCLUSION OF PEACE.

(*Extract.*)

FROM THE SECRETARY OF STATE FOR WAR TO LORD KITCHENER.

" War Office,
" April 13th, 1902.
" 2.30 a.m.

" His Majesty's Government sincerely share the earnest desire of the Boer representatives for peace, and hope that the present negotiations may lead to that result ; but they have already stated in the clearest terms, and must now repeat, that they cannot entertain any proposals which are based upon the continued independence of the former Republics which have been formally annexed to the British Crown. . . ." Reply of the Secretary of State for War.

The Right Honourable St. John Brodrick, the Secretary of State for War, further enjoined that the Commander-in-Chief and Lord Milner should jointly interview the Boer representatives, and encourage them to put forward fresh proposals, to be based on the assumption of the relinquishment of independence.

On the resumption of the conference on the morning of April 16th the Delegates received this reply with well-simulated dismay. Further discussion, then, they said, was impossible, for it must be based on a foundation which they were impotent to accept. The Constitutions of the Boer Republics empowered the Governments to make peace, but not to surrender the independence of the people. They were doubtful, indeed, whether they had not already discussed questions which were beyond their authority. In view of the resulting deadlock, they proposed first an armistice, secondly the summoning of one of their Delegates from Europe who might bring them the views of the banished statesmen. Both these procrastinating resorts were promptly discountenanced by Lords Kitchener and Milner, the first on military grounds, the second not only because of Conference at Pretoria resumed April 16th, 1902.

the inevitable delay, but because, in the opinion of the British Government, the deputation wandering over Europe had certainly resigned all power as an Executive, and probably much of its influence over the burghers. Moreover the counsel of men who had borne little of the burden and heat of the war, was not such as could be safely invited by parties who were all desirous of peace. Too long already the deputation had shown itself to be of the ancient fraternity of him who, having removed himself into safety, " bade the rest keep fighting."

With the agreement of all the meeting was adjourned whilst the dilemma was referred to the British Government by means of the following telegram :—

From Lord Kitchener to the Secretary of State for War.

Points referred to the Secretary of State for War.

"A difficulty has arisen in getting on with proceedings. The representatives state that constitutionally they have no power to discuss terms based on surrender of independence, inasmuch as only the burghers can agree to such a basis; therefore, if they were to propose terms it would put them in a false position as regards the people. If, however, His Majesty's Government would state the terms that, subsequent to a surrender of independence, they would be prepared to grant, the representatives, after asking for the necessary explanations, without any expression of approval or disapproval, would submit such conditions to the people."

This, it will be seen, was a step forward in so far as the principle of the surrender of independence was by implication not discarded. By such painful gradations does Peace regain her throne!

Two days elapsed before a reply to the above was received, and the Boer leaders, who had themselves argued so earnestly in favour of every means of procrastination, now expressed impatience at the delay. Not until the morning of April 17th did the conference reassemble to hear the proposals this time of the British Government :—

THE CONCLUSION OF PEACE. 539

"London, April 16th, 1902.

"1.55 p.m.

"We have received with considerable surprise the message from the Boer leaders as contained in your telegram No. 976. The meeting has been arranged at their request, and they must have been aware of our repeated declarations that we could not entertain any proposals based on the renewed independence of the two South African States. We were, therefore, entitled to assume that the Boer representatives had relinquished the idea of independence and would propose terms of surrender for the forces still in the field. They now state they are constitutionally incompetent to discuss terms which do not include a restoration of independence, but ask us to inform them what conditions would be granted if, after submitting the matter to their followers, they were to relinquish the demand for independence. *[Reply of the Secretary of State for War.]*

"This does not seem to us a satisfactory method of proceeding or one best adapted to secure at the earliest moment a cessation of the hostilities which have involved the loss of so much life and treasure. We are, however, as we have from the first been, anxious to spare the effusion of further blood and to hasten the restoration of peace and prosperity to the countries afflicted by the war; and you and Lord Milner are authorised to refer the Boer leaders to the offer made by you to General Botha more than twelve months ago, and to inform them that although subsequent great reduction in the forces opposed to us and the additional sacrifices thrown upon us by the refusal of that offer would justify us in imposing far more onerous terms, we are still prepared, in the hope of a permanent peace and reconciliation, to accept a general surrender on the lines of that offer, but with such modifications in detail as may be mutually agreed upon.

"You are also authorised to discuss such modifications with them, and to submit the result for our approval. Communicate this to Lord Milner."

The whole prospect of peace, therefore, stood once more on the basis on which Lord Kitchener had placed it at Middelburg in the letter quoted on page 524. A copy of that letter was immediately supplied to the delegates, at the request of Botha, who must have pondered on the probable effect of his former hostile presentation of it to the burghers. The proposals were the same; the change must be in the attitude of the Commandant-General towards them if the desired results were to be obtained. For the third time the Boer representatives, professing their powerlessness to reply to the terms without reference to the people, repeated their desire for an armistice and the attendance of one of the European delegates; for the third time both were refused by Lord Kitchener. Of what value, said the Commander-in-Chief, was the presence of men who had not fought, and who knew nothing of the situation on which it was proposed to invite their views? As for an armistice, his duty to his own army forbade any such concession. The conference had so far revealed nothing tangible, he had no evidence that the Boer representatives seriously intended to make peace. A profitless truce would operate to his own military disadvantage, and his refusal to grant both requests had already been sustained by his Government. He was prepared, however, without suspending hostilities, to grant every facility to the Delegates for trying the temper of the burghers on the terms submitted. Let them meet the commandos, each on a day appointed, and protected by a local armistice, take their votes and return with those full powers to treat, the absence of which had so far rendered every conference nugatory. After much discussion this was accepted. Before the meeting broke up, it was addressed by Lord Milner. The High Commissioner deplored the slowness of the methods adopted, anticipating the interminable discussions which would ensue in the Boer laagers whilst the bloodshed and destruction continued on every side. He urged a clear presentment of the definite and immutable terms offered by the conquerors, deprecating especially any alterations or additions which would only result in the return of the representatives time after time with fresh and unacceptable

Lord Kitchener suggests a referendum to the commandos.

THE CONCLUSION OF PEACE. 541

proposals. Before separating, Lord Kitchener and the Boer Generals arranged the details of the forthcoming meetings of the commandos. Sixty representatives, thirty for each Republic, would be elected by ballot to carry the wishes of the community to a general assembly to be held at Vereeniging on May 15th. A local suspension of hostilities would ensure the security of the voters at each centre of election. Lord Kitchener had to name but two stipulations, the exclusion from the voting both of foreigners and of any commandos operating in Cape Colony.

On the evening of April 18th the Boer officials quitted Pretoria. Mr. Steyn, whose illness grew worse daily, repaired to Wolmaranstad, and from this time forward took no active part in the negotiations. The rest, provided with safe-conducts, began the long ride which was to carry the terms of peace from one laager to another throughout the theatre of war. They took with them, for the information of the people, a paraphrase of the whole negotiations up to this point. Day after day, until May 13th the voting proceeded. At the meetings two questions were submitted to the burghers : (1) that of the adherence to independence ; (2) the selection of representatives for the Vereeniging conference. *The Delegates leave Pretoria April 18th, 1902.*

The resolution taken on the main point seemed to bode ill for peace. The majority, especially in the Orange Free State, stood firm for independence at all costs ; but this attitude represented the wish rather than the hope of the conquered. No other decision was to be expected from an army of brave men still in the field ; but with this truly national militia an overmastering yearning for peace was as inevitable as the vote for continued resistance. A sore conflict rent the bosom of every burgher at the moment of voting. He approached the ballot-box divided against himself, the soldier within him warring with the citizen, the father, the husband, the landowner, as to which should doom to destruction his dearest prize. The very clearness of the issue increased the bitterness of the trial. Peace on these terms meant political and military annihilation ; to fight on led but to extermination, along a path strewn the thicker with such *Results of the referendum to the commandos.*

miseries as were already scarcely to be borne. If then, to the lasting honour of the Boer army, the shout still went up for war, the cry, for all its unanimity had so wavering a note that one of the boldest leaders of the commandos was to confront the gathered representatives at the final conference with the exclamation : " You may say what you will, resolve what you will ; but whatever you do here in this meeting is the end of the war ! "

<small>The elected representatives of the commandos meet at Vereeniging, May 15th, 1902.</small>

Certainly, when at 11 a.m. on the appointed day, May 15th, the elected Delegates entered the Council tent at Vereeniging, they took with them varying commissions from their constituents. Some were pledged irrevocably to the maintenance of independence ; some had plenary powers, with discretion to decide according to circumstances ; in fact the conflicting nature of the mandates bade fair to wreck the conference at the outset, until the legal advisers of the Republics gave it as their opinion that Delegates so appointed must be bound by their convictions rather than by any immutable injunction laid upon them by their electors. Nothing indicated so favourably the pacific temper of the assembly than its ready reception of this ruling, a decision undeniable for parliaments or other civil bodies, but somewhat vulnerable in the light of the specific purposes of the conference. This initial difficulty thus happily removed, the meeting, with General C. F. Beyers in the chair, proceeded to hear from the various commanders the state of the country and the campaign in their several districts. For two days the Delegates listened to speech after speech, continued until far into the night. Many were the melancholy tales of destruction, exhaustion and suffering, but it soon became apparent that the desire for peace on the part of each speaker was in exact ratio with the damage sustained by his command. The conference thus resolved itself into two opposing parties, the delimitation of which closely followed that of the Boer States concerned.

<small>Views of the Transvaal.</small>

The Transvaal confessed herself to be ruined. Food was so scarce that in some parts the commandos were dependent on the natives for supplies, a condition even more humiliating to a Boer than asking succour of his enemy. One-third of the

THE CONCLUSION OF PEACE. 543

burghers in the field were without horses; the remainder were being daily dismounted by the ravages of horse-sickness. Cattle, grain and all forms of supply were so scarce that the country stood at the threshold of a famine. The condition of the women, many of whom still remained on the blasted veld, was indescribable. Only in the extreme west and north was there any hope of survival, Beyers and De la Rey both announcing their capacity to hold out for a year to come. All but six of the Transvaal representatives, including many who had come to the meeting pledged to resistance, were for ending the struggle as the only means of escaping utter destruction.

This decision was largely influenced by the noble attitude of the Transvaal chiefs. Acting-President Burger, Commandant-General Botha and General De la Rey in turn urged the representatives to think of their country and not their personal feelings. They had sworn indeed to fight to the bitter end; but had that end not come, or was the last hour only to strike when the last burgher lay in his grave or in prison across the seas?

Smuts, fresh from the failure at Ookiep,* held out no hopes of success in Cape Colony. He had laid the foundation of an effective campaign in the British province, but even this was crumbling, and it was plain that his leaders were in no position to supply fresh material, much less a superstructure.

General C. R. De Wet, on the other hand, spoke as earnestly for continued resistance. They had listened to the recital of many melancholy facts, but this, he declared, was a war of faith and not of facts. Should it not be carried through in the same faith as that in which it had been begun? Evil days had been tided over in the past too often for despair to have a place now. The representatives of the Orange Free State stood solidly by their leader. Their country had indeed suffered far less than the Transvaal, food being still comparatively plentiful, but their inflexibility sprang not only from material reasons. It was partly the expression of a sense of grievance against the ally for whose sake the Orange Free State had entered upon this

Views of the Orange Free State.

* See Chapter XXVI.

544   THE WAR IN SOUTH AFRICA.

disastrous war, only to be now counselled to accept the conqueror's domination. They resolved to decline negotiation on any basis which excluded independence.

With the meeting thus divided, and the prospect of a unanimous vote apparently hopeless, Mr. F. W. Reitz, the State Secretary of the Transvaal, came forward with a proposition for a middle course. A beaten people must yield something both in territory and in liberty; he suggested for the consideration of the British Government fresh terms to be based on the retention of only so much independence as would be left after the surrender of the following concessions :—

A proposal to the British Government, May 17th, 1902.

1. The relinquishment of foreign relations and embassies.
2. The acceptance of the protectorate of Great Britain.
3. The surrender of a portion of territory of the Republics.
4. The conclusion of a defensive treaty with Great Britain with regard to South Africa.

With some reluctance this resolution was adopted on May 17th, the third day of the conference, and a Commission was promptly elected to carry the terms to the British Headquarters. The Commission was further empowered to negotiate on any basis likely to lead to peace, subject to the ratification of its resolutions by the assembly of representatives. The Commission left for Pretoria the same evening and at 11.30 a.m. on May 19th Generals Botha, C. De Wet, De la Rey and Smuts, with Judge Hertzog, met Lords Kitchener and Milner, and handed them the following minute :—

A Commission carries the proposal to Pretoria. Meeting with Lords Kitchener and Milner, May 19th, 1902.

" YOUR EXCELLENCIES,

" With a view of finally ending the present hostilities, we have the honour, in accordance with authority from the Governments of both Republics, to propose, in addition to the points already offered in the negotiations of April last, the following points as a basis for negotiations :—

" (*a*) We are prepared to surrender our independence as regards foreign relations.
" (*b*) We wish to retain internal self-government under British supervision.

"(c) We are prepared to surrender a part of our territory.

"If your Excellencies are prepared to negotiate on this basis, the above-mentioned points can be further worked out.

(Signed) "LOUIS BOTHA.
"C. R. DE WET.
"J. H. DE LA REY.
"J. B. M. HERTZOG.
"J. C. SMUTS."

It would be tedious to follow in detail the long arguments which ensued. The Boer proposals were manifestly so widely divergent from those which the British Government had declared to be final, that Lords Kitchener and Milner plainly expressed their disinclination even to telegraph them for consideration. The Boer Commissioners, on the other hand, stoutly maintained that they were practically identical with the Middelburg terms until Lord Milner, suddenly accepting the premise, overthrew it at the same instant by urging that if there were indeed no inconsistency between the two it would be better to base the discussion on the older and indubitably clearer and more detailed document. With this description of thrust and parry the discussion continued for three hours, to be adjourned at 2.30 p.m. without result.

Debate on the proposal.

On reassembling at 4 p.m. Lord Milner read to the Commissioners the following article which he and the Commander-in-Chief had drafted as a necessary preamble to the terms of peace set forth in the Middelburg document :—

"General Lord Kitchener of Khartoum, Commanding-in-Chief, and His Excellency Lord Milner, High Commissioner on behalf of the British Government, and   , acting as the Government of the South African Republic, and   , acting as the Government of the Orange Free State on behalf of their respective burghers, desirous

Lords Kitchener and Milner reply with a final preamble.

to terminate the present hostilities, agree on the following articles :—

"1. The burgher forces in the field will forthwith lay down their arms, handing over all guns, rifles, and munitions of war in their possession or under their control, and desist from any further resistance to the authority of His Majesty King Edward VII., whom they recognize as their lawful Sovereign.

"The manner and details of this surrender will be arranged between Lord Kitchener and Commandant-General Botha, Assistant Commandant-General De la Rey, and Chief-Commandant De Wet."

These words sounded the knell of their proposals of the morning to every member of the Commission. Receiving in answer to a direct question a definite reply to this effect, Commandant-General Botha made a passionate appeal for better terms. But the Middelburg document was immovable, and Lord Milner could hold out no more hopes than that of some alleviation of its details, as distinct from its main principles, which might render it more acceptable to the Boer peoples. It was finally arranged that a Sub-Committee, consisting of Lord Milner, Hon. Sir Richard Solomon, and Generals Smuts and Hertzog should meet on the morrow to endeavour to draw up such a modification. The whole of May 20th was thus spent by the Sub-Committee, and at noon on the 21st the results of its labours were brought to the conference in the form of a document of twelve articles which followed the previously quoted preamble as under :—

Provisional terms drawn up, May 21st, 1902.

"General Lord Kitchener of Khartoum, Commanding-in-Chief, and his Excellency Lord Milner, High Commissioner, on behalf of the British Government, and Messrs. S. W. Burger, F. W. Reitz, Louis Botha, J. H. De la Rey, L. J. Meyer, and J. C. Krogh, acting as the Government of the South African Republic, and Messrs. M. T. Steyn, J. Brebner, C. R. De Wet, J. B. M. Hertzog, and C. Olivier, acting as the Government of the Orange Free State, on behalf of their respective burghers, desirous to terminate the present hostilities, agree on the following articles :—

"1. The burgher forces in the field will forthwith lay down their arms, handing over all guns, rifles, and munitions of war in their possession or under their control, and desist from any further resistance to the authority of His Majesty King Edward VII., whom they recognize as their lawful Sovereign.

"The manner and details of this surrender will be arranged between Lord Kitchener and Commandant-General Botha, Assistant Commandant-General De la Rey, and Chief-Commandant De Wet.

"2. Burghers in the field outside the limits of the Transvaal or Orange River Colony, on surrendering, will be brought back to their homes.

"3. All prisoners of war at present outside of South Africa, who are burghers, will, on their declaring their acceptance of the position of subjects of His Majesty King Edward VII., be brought back to the places where they were domiciled before the war.

"4. The burghers so surrendering, or returning, will not be deprived of their personal liberty, or their property.

"5. No proceedings, civil or criminal, will be taken against any of the burghers so surrendering, or returning, for any acts in connection with the prosecution of the war.

"6. The Dutch language will be taught in public schools in the Transvaal and the Orange River Colony where the parents of the children desire it, and will be allowed in Courts of Law when necessary for the better and more effectual administration of justice.

"7. The possession of rifles will be allowed in the Transvaal and Orange River Colony to persons requiring them for their protection, on taking out a licence according to law.

"8. Military administration in the Transvaal and Orange River Colony will, at the earliest possible date, be succeeded by civil government and, as soon as circumstances permit, representative institutions leading up to self-government will be introduced.

"9. The question of granting the franchise to natives will not be decided until after the introduction of self-government.

"10. No special tax will be imposed on landed property in the Transvaal and Orange River Colony to defray the expenses of the war.

"11. A judicial commission will be appointed to which Government notes issued under Law No. 1 of 1900 of the South African Republic may be presented within six months.

"All such notes as are found to have been duly issued in the terms of that Law, and for which the persons presenting them have given valuable consideration, will be paid, but without interest.

"12. As soon as conditions permit, a Commission, on which the local inhabitants will be represented, will be appointed in each district of the Transvaal and Orange River Colony, under the presidency of a magistrate or other official, for the purpose of assisting the restoration of the people to their homes and supplying those who, owing to war losses, are unable to provide for themselves, with food, shelter, and the necessary amount of seed, stock, implements, etc., indispensable to the resumption of their normal occupations. Funds for this purpose will be advanced by Government free of interest and repayable over a period of years."

Debate on the provisional terms. It was, in the suddenness of its change of ground, somewhat characteristic of Boer tactics that in the long day's discussion

THE CONCLUSION OF PEACE. 549

which followed the reading of this document the Commissioners unanimously directed their criticism against but a single clause, namely, No. 11, that dealing with the liquidation of Government money notes issued during the war. The matter was by no means simple, for besides the legally issued Government notes, there were in flotation a multitude of receipts for goods commandeered in the field, some by authorised, others by unauthorised, officers. The whole of these the Boer Commissioners urged should be accepted by the British Government, on the plea that a conqueror acquiring the assets of his victims should equally undertake their debts. A further complication was introduced by the difference of the laws governing such transactions in the two Republics. In the Transvaal the issue of notes had been by law limited to face value of £1,000,000, though vast numbers of receipts over and above the authorised issue were in circulation, having been signed by officers unprovided with the legal currency.

The question of liabilities incurred in the field.

In the Orange Free State there had been no such restriction, and the army and Government had depended solely on impromptu receipts issued as required. The result was that an unknown liability hung over the heads of both legislatures, and this they wished to transfer to the British Government, for, said they, the honour of every signatory to a receipt was bound up in its eventual acceptance by the ruling Power.

So bent were they on the point that one and all the Commissioners declined to recommend to the representatives at Vereeniging the acceptance of the terms of peace unless some such proviso were inserted. Yet it was impossible to consider the request in its entirety. Should the British Government accede to it even partially, it would to that extent, as Lord Milner pointed out, be paying the expenses of the enemy for his efforts against itself. This the Government had already pledged itself to do to the extent of £1,000,000 in the Middelburg proposals, and Lords Kitchener and Milner, with considerable reluctance, intimated their willingness to recommend a further grant if only a definite sum could be named by the Commissioners. In order to arrive at an approximate calculation the Boers withdrew from the meeting for a time. On their return they announced an estimate of £3,000,000, the recommendation for which they suggested might be appended to Clause 11 of the preceding terms as the following addendum :—

"ADDENDUM TO CLAUSE 11.

Proposed addendum with reference to liabilities incurred in the field.

"All receipts given by the officers in the field of the late Republics, or under their orders, may likewise be presented to the said Commission within six months, and if found to have been given *bonâ fide* for goods used by the burgher forces in the field, will be paid out to the persons to whom they were originally given. The sum payable in respect of the said Government notes and receipts shall not exceed £3,000,000 sterling, and if the total amount of such notes and receipts approved by the Commission is more than that sum, there shall be a *pro rata* diminution. Facilities will be afforded the prisoners of war to present their Government notes and receipts within the six months aforesaid."

This was done, and after some further discussion as to the rights of debtors and kindred matters, the document was redrafted as a whole, and at 4.50 p.m. telegraphed to London for the approval of the Cabinet.

The British Government objects to the proposed addendum.

It was now the turn of the British Government to object. Voicing, as they had throughout the war, the sentiments of the vast majority of the nation, the Ministers took exception not to the amount but the allocation of the sum proposed to be paid under Clause 11, and its addendum. Under those conditions a large proportion of the grant might conceivably be absorbed by foreigners who had supplied munitions of war to the Republican forces. In substitution of the proposal submitted, the Cabinet suggested on May 23rd the amalgamation of the proposals under Clauses 11 and 12 as a means of achieving the desired end without wounding the susceptibilities of either party. Two days later an amended form of the clauses in question, assented to by both sides, was telegraphed to London for sanction. In a covering telegram Lord Kitchener begged for a speedy decision on the part of His Majesty's Government. The suspense of the protracted negotiations was having anything but a reassuring effect on the Delegates assembled at Vereeniging, some of whom were even suspected of contemplating escape. But the Ministers in London were not to be charged with tardiness. At 10.30 a.m. on May 28th Lord Milner was able to hand to the Delegates at Pretoria the final reply of the British Government.

It contained the following alterations to the document of May 21st and its subsequent modifications :—

Clauses 2 and 3 should be put together and will run as follows :—

Modification of the proposed addendum received from the British Government, May 28th, 1902.

"Burghers in field outside limits of the Transvaal or Orange River Colony, and all prisoners of war at present outside of South Africa, who are burghers, will, on duly declaring their acceptance of the position of subjects of His Majesty King Edward VII., be gradually brought back to their homes as soon as transport can be provided and their means of subsistence ensured."

Clause 5.—Add at the end of clause the words :—

"The benefit of this clause will not extend to certain acts contrary to usages of war which have been notified by Commander-in-Chief to the Boer Generals, and which shall be tried by Court-Martial immediately after the close of hostilities."

Clauses 11 and 12 must be omitted, and following clause substituted :—

"As soon as conditions permit, a Commission, on which the local inhabitants will be represented, will be appointed in each district of the Transvaal and Orange River Colony, under the presidency of a magistrate or other official, for the purpose of assisting the restoration of the people to their homes and supplying those who, owing to war losses, are unable to provide for themselves with food, shelter, and the necessary amount of seed, stock, implements, etc., indispensable to the resumption of their normal occupations.

"His Majesty's Government will place at the disposal of these Commissions a sum of £3,000,000 sterling, for the above purposes, and will allow all notes, issued under Law No. 1 of 1900 of the Government of the South African Republic, and all receipts, given by officers in the field of the late Republics or under their orders, to be presented to a judicial Commission which will be appointed by the Government, and if such notes and receipts are found by this Commission to have been duly issued in return for valuable consideration, they will be received by the first-named Commissions as evidence of war losses suffered by the persons to whom they were originally given. In addition to the above-named free grant of £3,000,000, His Majesty's Government will be prepared to make advances as loans for the same purposes, free of interest for two years, and afterwards repayable over a period of years with three per cent. interest. No foreigner or rebel will be entitled to the benefit of this clause."

It probably came as a relief to all parties that the proposals thus composed were absolutely final. They admitted of no possible answer other than "Yes" or "No" from the Vereeniging assembly. Furthermore, the British negotiators were instructed to add that if this opportunity of an honourable termination of hostilities were not accepted within a time to be fixed by themselves, the Conference and the proposals would be alike annulled, and the Government would consider itself absolved for the future from any reference to its present offer.

With the maze of ten days' tortuous argument ending at last in a blank wall, the morning's discussion was significantly brief. There was indeed a last attempt on the part of the Boer Commissioners to lessen the rigidity of the provisos, but it only elicited from Lord Milner the unmistakeable pronouncement that "This is an absolutely final document, and the answer must

THE CONCLUSION OF PEACE. 553

be 'Yes' or 'No.'" The burghers might, if they chose, reject the document as a whole, but its separate provisions were unalterable. He would only communicate to the Commissioners the decision of his Government upon a point outside the proposals which had often been referred to in the discussions of the past days, namely, the treatment to be meted out to rebels in Natal and Cape Colony.

Much had been informally made of this subject by the Commissioners, who, as in the case of the receipts and notes, not unnaturally held that a point of honour was bound up in the question. They could not fail to see that the British Government would be within its rights in refusing even to discuss its intention with regard to men who had placed themselves outside the pale of all negotiations. Nevertheless the Boer leaders were unwilling to leave to an unknown fate thousands who had become felons in aid of the lost cause, and the British Government, which had been in communication on the subject with the Colonial legislatures, had seen fit to indulge them by forwarding the following declaration which was now read by Lord Milner to the Commissioners:— *The question of the treatment of rebels.*

"His Majesty's Government must place it on record that the treatment of Cape and Natal colonials who have been in rebellion and who now surrender will, if they return to their Colonies, be determined by the Colonial Government and in accordance with the laws of the Colonies, and that any British subjects who have joined the enemy will be liable to trial under the law of that part of the British Empire to which they belong. *British Government's decision of the question of the treatment of rebels.*

"His Majesty's Government are informed by the Cape Government that the following are their views as to the terms which should be granted to British subjects of the Cape Colony who are now in the field or who have surrendered or have been captured since the 12th April, 1901. With regard to the rank and file, they should all, upon surrender, after giving up their arms, sign a document before the resident magistrate of the district in which surrender takes place acknowledging themselves guilty of high treason, and the punishment to be awarded to them, provided they shall not have been guilty of murder or other acts contrary to the usages of civilized warfare, should be that they shall not be entitled for life to be registered as voters or to vote at any Parliamentary, Divisional Council, or Municipal election.

"With reference to Justices of the Peace and Field-Cornets of the Cape Colony, and all other persons holding official positions under the Government of the Cape Colony, or who may occupy the position of Commandant of rebel or burgher forces, they should be tried for high treason before the ordinary Court of the country, or such special Court as may hereafter be constituted by law, the punishment for their offence to be left to the discretion of the Court, with this proviso, that in no case shall penalty of death be inflicted.

"The Natal Government are of opinion that rebels should be dealt with according to the law of the Colony."

It only remained to set the limit of time within which the Vereeniging assembly should be required to return its answer. This was eventually arranged to be by the evening of May 31st, at latest. At seven o'clock on the evening of May 28th the Boer Commissioners, their task accomplished, took train for Vereeniging, carrying with them a number of copies of the document, the nature of the reception of which by the representatives would decide the fate of the Boer peoples.

The Boer Commissioners leave Pretoria, May 28th, 1902.

In the presence of the grievous calamity which had overtaken their nation it was not easy for either the Commissioners or the general body of the Delegates to realise how much had been spared them, and how much was now offered them. They were fast in the grip of a power incalculably stronger and even more determined than themselves, a power, moreover, which might well be exasperated at the cost in blood and treasure entailed by a resistance which from the point of view of western warfare had almost ceased to be admirable because it had become so

THE CONCLUSION OF PEACE. 555

hopeless. The Boer States were now represented solely by the quarter of their manhood—the population of a British township—which remained in the field, a body without a government, without towns, possessions or power of any description. Every inch of their territory, except that actually within the outposts of their laagers, was in the hands of hostile troops. If ever a people can lose its entity by war, the Boers had done so now, yet to this vagrant, dispossessed tribe came the Commissioners from Pretoria bearing a message from the conqueror couched in terms as formal as and less severe than might be addressed by one sovereign Power to another at the crisis of a first-class campaign. The very form of the British proposals was an honour paid to the vanquished; their purport was a triumph for his nationality, and it must be remembered that to a Boer his nationality was a thing more precious even than his home, more precious even than victory. He and his fathers had often viewed with equanimity the destruction of their domestic life, nay, had even uprooted it themselves in order to preserve the national life, the hunger for which had originally driven them out into the veld. And here, on the very verge of the utter annihilation of the national body and soul, the hand put forth to save both, was that to whose profit it was to give the last push over the brink.

<small>Lenience of the Terms of Peace.</small>

The assembled representatives might well have read with amazement from the document which was placed in their hands on the morning of May 29th that the national language, the preserving amber of all social existence, was to be taught in the schools; that British gold would first rebuild and then repopulate the ruined homes of the veld; that for the first time in history the conquered, instead of paying indemnity for his downfall, would receive it; finally, and most unprecedented pledge of all, that representative government, and eventually actual autonomy, was promised to a people who had not yet wrung the last of nearly three hundred millions of pounds and thousands of lives as the price of the elimination of the device "independence" from their standard. Truly the Delegates might now have retorted upon their opponents the charge which had been often

<small>The assembly of representatives at Vereeniging receive the final Terms of Peace, May 29th, 1902.</small>

levelled against themselves—of fighting for a mere idea. Under the terms submitted to them only the Republics would perish; the Boer States would live on, governed as before by men of their own choosing, the heart, it might still well be, of the South African federation which had been the dream of every Boer leader since the Great Trek. But the Boers would perceive in the proffered terms none of these things. Steyn, to whom the proposals were read before submission to the meeting in the tent wherein he lay ill, denounced them *in toto*, and overcome by illness and the misery of a capitulation which he probably foresaw to be inevitable, resigned his Presidency on the spot and was driven into the British lines for medical treatment. As for the Delegates, blind to everything but the loss of their independence, the whole document appeared to them so distasteful that within a few moments of its first presentment they were within an ace of voting for its rejection. Fortunately an appeal for a fuller consideration prevailed, and for three days the Council tent rang with impassioned argument; but it was plain that at any moment the voice of the soldier might drown that of the patriot, when the assembled leaders would rush back to arms and to destruction. It would serve no purpose to describe at length the ebb and flow of that momentous and unhappy debate. Once more reason, still largely represented by the Transvaal Delegates, warred with the obsession of the Free State irreconcilables, the grave eloquence of Burger, Botha, De la Rey and Smuts contending with the splendid folly of such speeches as those in which De Wet, Froneman and other advocates for war threw all reason to the winds and urged the burghers to seek independence in death rather than resign it living.

On one point there was a noble unanimity. There was not in all the assembly an individual who personally wished to surrender, whose spirit was broken or his endurance exhausted. The line of demarcation ran solely between those who could not disregard the inexorable logic of facts, and those who, like a hero of their enemy's race, turned a blind eye to the unmistakeable signal to withdraw from the battle. Up to the last the contest continued, but as the decisive hour of voting drew on, it became

THE CONCLUSION OF PEACE. 557

clear that one by one the adherents of the war party were being influenced by the recital of miseries of which many had known nothing, or had thought to be peculiarly their own. The tension, too, of the bitter mental struggle was doing its work. By the morning of the final day, Saturday, May 31st, the meeting had swayed sensibly towards peace. Nevertheless the result was far from certain and became still more doubtful when the wavering Delegates had to stand the strain first of a trumpet-toned Motion by two fiery Free State Generals sounding the instant resumption of hostilities, next of a declaration by one of the most trusted officials of the Transvaal that he, for one, would never consent to be one of the signatories of any terms of peace involving the surrender of independence. *[The terms again near rejection.]*

Had the Motion been pressed to a division or the official's avowal have had its designed effect, the Delegates would have streamed from the Conference rifles in hand. But now, in the words of the only chronicler* of these pregnant days, "something great occurred." No less a personage than De Wet, effacing every personal consideration in the desire to save his country, intervened to quench the fire which he himself had kept alight. Calling his burghers from the Council tent to his own, he there in private confessed the truth. The struggle must end; but let it end with dignity, with union amongst the fallen, and for their *apologia* the following Motion which at De Wet's suggestion was drawn up for submission to the Conference by the State Attorneys of the two Republics :— *[De Wet decides for peace; his Motion of May 31st, 1902.]*

"We, the national representatives of both the South African Republic and the Orange Free State, at the meeting held at Vereeniging, from the 15th of May till the 31st of May, 1902, have with grief considered the proposal made by His Majesty's Government in connection with the conclusion of the existing hostilities, and their communication that this proposal had to be accepted, or rejected, unaltered. We are sorry that His Majesty's Government has absolutely declined to negotiate with the Government of the Republics

* The Rev. J. D. Kestell, chaplain to President Steyn and General C. De Wet.

on the basis of their independence, or to allow our Government to enter into communication with our deputation. Our people, however, have always been under the impression that not only on the grounds of justice, but also taking into consideration the great material and personal sacrifices made for their independence, that it had a well-founded claim for that independence.

"We have seriously considered the future of our country, and have specially observed the following facts :—

"*First*, that the military policy pursued by the British military authorities has led to the general devastation of the territory of both Republics by the burning down of farms and towns, by the destruction of all means of existence, and by the exhausting of all resources required for the maintenance of our families, the existence of our armies, and the continuation of the war.

"*Secondly*, that the placing of our families in the concentration camps has brought on an unheard-of condition of suffering and sickness, so that in a comparatively short time about twenty thousand of our beloved ones have died there, and that the horrid probability has arisen that, by continuing the war, our whole nation may die out in this way.

"*Thirdly*, that the Kaffir tribes, within and without the frontiers of the territory of the two Republics, are mostly armed and are taking part in the war against us, and through the committing of murders and all sorts of cruelties have caused an unbearable condition of affairs in many districts of both Republics. An instance of this happened not long ago in the district of Vrijheid, where fifty-six burghers on one occasion were murdered and mutilated in a fearful manner.

"*Fourthly*, that by the proclamations of the enemy the burghers still fighting are threatened with the loss of all their moveable and landed property—and thus with utter ruin—which proclamations have already been enforced.

"*Fifthly*, that it has already, through the circumstances of the war, become quite impossible for us to keep the many thousands prisoners of war taken by our forces, and that we have thus been unable to inflict much damage on the British forces (whereas the burghers who are taken prisoners by the British armies are sent out of the country), and that, after war has raged for nearly three years, there only remains an insignificant part of the fighting forces with which we began.

"*Sixthly*, that this fighting remainder, which is only a small minority of our whole nation, has to fight against an overpowering force of the enemy, and besides is reduced to a condition of starvation, and is destitute of all necessaries, and that notwithstanding our utmost efforts, and the sacrifice of everything that is dear to us, we cannot foresee an eventual victory.

"We are therefore of opinion that there is no justifiable ground for expecting that by continuing the war the nation will retain its independence, and that, under these circumstances, the nation is not justified in continuing the war, because this can only lead to social and material ruin, not for us alone, but also for our posterity. Compelled by the above-named circumstances and motives, we commission both Governments to accept the proposal of His Majesty's Government, and to sign it in the name of the people of both Republics.

"We, the representative Delegates, express our confidence that the present circumstances will, by accepting the proposal of His Majesty's Government, be speedily ameliorated in such a way that our nation will be placed in a position to enjoy the privileges to which they think they have a just claim, on the ground not only of their past sacrifices, but also of those made in this war.

"We have with great satisfaction taken note of the decision of His Majesty's Government to grant a large measure of amnesty to the British subjects who have taken up arms on our behalf, and to whom we are united by bonds of love and honour; and express our wish that it may please His Majesty to still further extend this amnesty."

560   THE WAR IN SOUTH AFRICA.

The representatives accept the Motion and the Terms of Peace.

After a short adjournment the Delegates reassembled, and the voting on this, the supreme Motion, began. Before 3 p.m. the Boer peoples, by fifty-four votes to six, had accepted their doom and their salvation. The decision was communicated to the British Headquarters in the following terms :—

"FROM BOTH STATE PRESIDENTS TO LORDS MILNER AND KITCHENER.

"Vereeniging,
"May 31st, 1902.
"3.55 p.m.

"Both Governments are prepared, being authorised thereto by a resolution of the people's Delegates, and which resolution they will submit to Your Excellencies, to accept and sign the proposals of His Majesty's Government. They are ready to proceed to Pretoria for this purpose at any time which Your Excellencies may fix."

Signing of the Terms of Peace, May 31st, 1902.

The appointed signatories lost no time in hastening to Pretoria. At 10.30 p.m. they were in the presence of the representatives of the British Government in the now well-known room in the Commander-in-Chief's house. A few moments later the following Terms of Peace were duly signed and sealed :—

Text of the Terms of Peace.

"Army Headquarters, South Africa.

"General Lord Kitchener of Khartoum, Commanding-in-Chief, and his Excellency Lord Milner, High Commissioner, on behalf of the British Government, and Messrs. S. W. Burger, F. W. Reitz, Louis Botha, J. H. De la Rey, L. J. Meyer, and J. C. Krogh, acting as the Government of the South African Republic, and Messrs. C. R. De Wet, W. J. C. Brebner, J. B. M. Hertzog, and C. H. Olivier, acting as the Government of the Orange Free State, on behalf of their respective burghers, desirous to terminate the present hostilities, agree on the following Articles :—

"1. The burgher forces in the field will forthwith

THE CONCLUSION OF PEACE. 561

lay down their arms, handing over all guns, rifles, and munitions of war in their possession or under their control, and desist from any further resistance to the authority of His Majesty King Edward VII., whom they recognize as their lawful Sovereign.

"The manner and details of this surrender will be arranged between Lord Kitchener and Commandant-General Botha, Assistant Commandant-General De la Rey, and Chief-Commandant De Wet.

"2. Burghers in the field outside the limits of the Transvaal and Orange River Colony, and all prisoners of war at present outside South Africa, who are burghers will, on duly declaring their acceptance of the position of subjects of His Majesty King Edward VII., be gradually brought back to their homes as soon as transport can be provided and their means of subsistence ensured.

"3. The burghers so surrendering or so returning will not be deprived of their personal liberty or their property.

"4. No proceedings, civil or criminal, will be taken against any of the burghers so surrendering or so returning for any acts in connection with the prosecution of the war. The benefit of this clause will not extend to certain acts contrary to the usage of war which have been notified by the Commander-in-Chief to the Boer Generals, and which shall be tried by Court-Martial immediately after the close of hostilities.

"5. The Dutch language will be taught in public schools in the Transvaal and the Orange River Colony where the parents of the children desire it, and will be allowed in Courts of Law when necessary for the better and more effectual administration of justice.

"6. The possession of rifles will be allowed in the Transvaal and Orange River Colony to persons requiring them for their protection, on taking out a licence according to law.

"7. Military administration in the Transvaal and Orange River Colony will at the earliest possible date be succeeded by civil government, and, as soon as circumstances permit, representative institutions, leading up to self-government, will be introduced.

"8. The question of granting the franchise to natives will not be decided until after the introduction of self-government.

"9. No special tax will be imposed on landed property in the Transvaal and Orange River Colony to defray the expenses of the war.

"10. As soon as conditions permit, a Commission on which the local inhabitants will be represented, will be appointed in each district of the Transvaal and Orange River Colony, under the presidency of a magistrate or other official, for the purpose of assisting the restoration of the people to their homes and supplying those who, owing to war losses, are unable to provide for themselves, with food, shelter, and the necessary amount of seed, stock, implements, etc., indispensable to the resumption of their normal occupations.

"His Majesty's Government will place at the disposal of these Commissions a sum of three million pounds sterling for the above purposes, and will allow all notes, issued under Law No. 1 of 1900, of the Government of the South African Republic, and all receipts given by the officers in the field of the late Republics or under their orders, to be presented to a Judicial Commission which will be appointed by the Government, and if such notes and receipts are found by this Commission to have been duly issued in return for valuable consideration, they will be received by the first-named Commissions as evidences of war losses suffered by the persons to whom they were originally given. In addition to the above-named free grant of three million pounds, His Majesty's Government will

THE CONCLUSION OF PEACE.

be prepared to make advances as loans for the same purpose, free of interest for two years, and afterwards repayable over a period of years with three per cent. interest. No foreigner or rebel will be entitled to the benefit of this clause.

" Signed at Pretoria this thirty-first day of May, in the year of Our Lord one thousand nine hundred and two.

" (Signed)   " (Signed)
  " S. W. BURGER.   " KITCHENER OF KHARTOUM.
  " F. W. REITZ.   " MILNER."
  " LOUIS BOTHA.
  " J. H. DE LA REY.
  " L. J. MEYER.
  " J. C. KROGH.
  " C. R. DE WET.
  " J. B. M. HERTZOG.
  " W. J. C. BREBNER.
  " C. H. OLIVIER.

THE END.

APPENDICES

APPENDIX I

(CHAPTER VI.).

SUMMARY OF SUPPLIES SENT BY THE NATAL DISTRICT FOR GENERAL FRENCH'S FORCE, GARRISONS, &C., DESPATCHED FROM NEWCASTLE AND VOLKSRUST FOR PIET RETIEF AND FROM DE JAGER'S DRIFT FOR VRYHEID.

Date.	From	To	Europeans (No Meat).	Indians.	Biscuits.	Groceries.	Maconochie.	Medical Comforts.	Oats.	Wagons.
			b Rations.	Rations.	a lb.	a Rations.	Rations.	Diets.	lb.	
February 1901 12th and 13th	Newcastle	Lüneberg	60,000	120	—	—	30,000	4,000	674,000	155
15th*	,,	,,	42,400	—	—	—	—	4,000	2,488,000	68
17th*	,,	,,	100,000	2,000	—	—	—	4,000	—	49
20th	* ,,	,,	80,000	2,000	—	—	—	—	—	} 56
†	,,	,,	42,400	—	—	—	—	—	—	
23rd	,,	,,	... ... Rum and Sundries to complete foregoing rations ...							11
‡	,,	,,	—	—	—	—	—	—	158,800	34
	,,	Utrecht	—	Supplies for Utrecht and L. of C. ...					... ...	31
24th	Umbana	,,	—	,,	,,	,,	,,	...	... ...	11
		Total	324,800	4,120	—	—	30,000	12,000	3,320,800	415
28th	Volksrust	Piet Retief	100,000	—	—	100,000	—	4,000	—	71
27th March	De Jager's Drift	} Vryheid	96,000	1,600	—	—	—	—	85,680	60
		Total	196,000	1,600	—	100,000	—	4,000	85,680	131
7th March	De Jager's Drift	} Vryheid	—	1,000	—	—	—	—	267,000	57

* a included in Rations (Europeans) complete at b.
† Unloaded at Utrecht and taken on by 58 wagons from ‡.
‡ 58 wagons loaded up with † unloading 16 wagon loads of oats.

APPENDIX 2.

THE EVOLUTION OF THE BLOCKHOUSE SYSTEM IN SOUTH AFRICA.*

WHEN the army first reached Pretoria it was clear that its long lines of communication lay undefended, and orders were issued that all posts along the railways were to be fortified. By July 1st, 1900, defences consisting of trenches and stone-sangars had been prepared at most points, and their numbers and strength increased as the attacks of the Boers grew more frequent. The wrecking of the railroads reached its climax at the end of 1900, and it was obvious that a more elaborate form of defence work was required. At some important points near large bridges masonry blockhouses were erected. These were usually of two stories, and from the roof a machine-gun could fire. Entrance was by ladder: parapets supported by brackets projected from the upper angles, and loopholes in the lower part enabled the garrison to fire on the ground below. But the cost of such a blockhouse amounted to from £800 to £1,000; the time required for its erection was almost three months, and a garrison of about thirty men was needed. Some type of work more economical of time and material was imperatively demanded by the situation.

The first corrugated-iron blockhouses were erected by a Lourenço Marques contractor at Nelspruit, Kaapmuiden, and Komati Poort in January, 1901. They were of an oblong form, measuring ten by fifteen feet, and consisted of two rows of posts (three by three inches), two inches apart, with a "skin" of corrugated iron fixed to each. Stony sand filled the space between the "skins." The loopholes measured three by four inches and were in steel plates, two feet wide and nine inches deep, and were fixed in wooden casings placed in openings cut in the corrugated iron walls. A corrugated iron roof completed the structure.

* See maps Nos. 58, 61 and 62.

NOTE.—For names mentioned in the text but not shown on the blockhouse maps, see maps Nos. 56, 59, 63 and 64.

APPENDIX 2.   569

The result of this first attempt at a novel form of blockhouse was a strong work; yet the elaboration of a network of blockhouses intersecting the whole sub-continent, which was now Lord Kitchener's purpose, required the evolution of some type of work still less cumbrous and less costly of time and material.

Major S. R. Rice, R.E., commanding the 23rd (Field) company, was the parent of the necessary invention. In February, 1901, he evolved a type of blockhouse which fell within the requisite limitations.

The material and design were, of course, chosen on the assumption that cover against artillery fire would rarely be required. Advantage was taken of the disruptive effect of shingle on rifle-bullets, and a blockhouse was designed, the walls of which were composed of an inner and an outer " skin " of corrugated iron. The " skins " were some six inches apart, and the intervening space was filled with hard shingle. For each blockhouse some five cubic yards of shingle were required, small enough to pass through a one and a half inch mesh; flint shingle was preferred. The original plan was an octagon fifteen feet in diameter. To uphold the walls, the iron " skins " were fixed to wooden uprights placed at each angle of the octagon, care being taken that at all points the prescribed thickness of shingle was observed. Each wall was ingeniously pierced with cross-shaped loopholes measuring six by three inches, and splayed inside and outside. The roof was not bullet-proof, being made only of one corrugated iron sheet, and was in the form of a square gable.

Major Rice's company of Royal Engineers, then at Middelburg in the Transvaal, soon became a blockhouse-factory. The manufacture of each separate part was placed in the hands of the same workmen, and so well were they constructed, that the members of all the blockhouses were practically standardised. Experience proved that under heavy rifle-fire the " skins " of these octagonal blockhouses bulged, and a subsidence of the enclosed shingle ensued. A greatly improved modification of the octagonal form was therefore evolved, which, as a rule, took the following approximate shape :

A circular " skin " of iron, thirteen feet six inches diameter and four feet high, acted as an interior revetment against which a parapet of earth was thrown, or a wall, two feet thick, of rough stone was built. Upon this base a circular shield was arranged, formed of iron " skins " disposed in concentric circles, the outer " skins " being in tension, the inner in compression. Between the two " skins " was a filling of shingle some six inches thick. In this type of blockhouse the " skins " were in the best position for resisting the strain caused by the impact of the bullets when broken up upon the shingle, and the subsidence of the shingle consequently ceased. Moreover, in the circular blockhouse all woodwork was eliminated from the walls, the portability of the blockhouse was greater, and the cost, time and labour of erecting it less.

The loopholes were still usually cross-shaped, and the roof was gabled as before. Another form of roof, however, was found to be less penetrable and conspicuous, and more economical of time and material, namely, a low, circular design, known as the " pepper-pot." This was a variation of the " Rice " pattern.

The door was but two feet square and closed by a bullet-proof shield. It led into a fire-trench some four feet six inches deep, which surrounded the blockhouse and served as a protection to the sentry. At a distance of from ten to twenty yards from the trench a high wire entanglement completely encircled the blockhouse. This was usually constructed of parallel fences with criss-cross wires between. The total cost of this blockhouse was ultimately reduced to some £16, and for a working party composed of five Sappers, aided by ten natives, only four to five hours were required for its erection.*

---

* (A) COMPARATIVE COST OF BLOCKHOUSES BY CONTRACT :—

(1) By Contracts made at Cape Town by C. R. E., Cape Colony.

	£	s.	d.
Circular blockhouse with gable roof ...	30	0	0
Erection, including freight	14	0	0
	£44	0	0

(2) By Contracts made at Pretoria by C. R. E., Pretoria.
Circular blockhouse, including materials,
labour and railway freight £37 4 0

(B) "RICE" PATTERN BLOCKHOUSE :—
Circular blockhouse (gable roof) with
R.E. labour £16 0 0

N.B.—The average cost of an entanglement between blockhouses (at "coast" price) erected by the troops was about £50 per mile.

The system finally included over 8,000 blockhouses, covering a total distance of about 3,700 miles. The total cost, with entanglements, was under £1,000,000.

APPENDIX 2.

Drawings and descriptions of this circular blockhouse were at once forwarded to all officers commanding Royal Engineers, and the type became the general pattern. The Commander-in-Chief wishing to hasten the construction of this type, factories were started at the Headquarters of every R.E. company, and at all coast ports, and soon these circular blockhouses arose along all the railway lines, the work being in full progress by the end of March, 1901, when parties of Sappers from every R.E. company in South Africa were building blockhouses along all the lines of railway.

The blockhouses were at first erected at intervals of some one and a half miles. Even then they largely prevented the destruction of the railway lines and trains; but with so wide a separation, it was impossible to stop parties of the enemy from crossing the line at night. The interval was therefore decreased and was ultimately from a half to three-quarters of a mile. There was no advantage to be gained by reducing it still further, for the centre of the intervening space was now within the range of " fixed sights " from the rifles of the occupants of any two adjacent blockhouses.

Between the blockhouses ran at first only a slight barbed-wire fence. This was gradually strengthened by adding "aprons" on each side, by twisting several strands of wire into a thick rope, and by using thick unannealed steel wire, which was unseverable. The fence was stayed, the stays being anchored to buried stones and sandbags.

The fences splayed outwards, so that the blockhouses should not fire into each other; a trench was dug between the blockhouses, in order to prevent wagons from crossing, should the fence be cut or overturned. Along the fences automatic alarms and flares were placed, also fixed rifle-batteries of four or six rifles, which could be fired by one man. Each blockhouse was connected with its neighbours by telephone, and contained its own water supply and reserves of food and ammunition; and to each native scouts were attached for the purpose of patrolling by night. The usual garrison was one non-commissioned officer and five or six men.

Up to June, 1901, the blockhouses had been erected solely along the railroads to secure the lines of communication. In that month the idea was developed further by the commencement of a cross-country blockhouse line from Groot Oliphants River station on the Komati Poort line to Val station on the Natal line. A battalion of infantry was detailed as escort and to assist in the work of erection.

The work was rapidly executed, and the Royal Engineer parties were ready with fresh blockhouses and transport, when in July Lord Kitchener ordered them to go west to Frederikstad and run a line up the Mooi river to its source, and thence across to Naauwpoort. This line was finished in August, 1901.

The next cross-country line was begun at both ends from the junction of the Mooi and Vaal rivers to Kopjes station on the Orange River Colony railway. The 1st Oxfordshire Light Infantry, with Royal Engineer parties, worked from Kopjes, and the 2nd Grenadier Guards, with a detachment of Sappers, from the Mooi river end. This line had not long been completed when Lord Kitchener ordered that it should be moved forward, for the area of country which it enclosed was soon cleared of the enemy. Blockhouses were therefore erected along the Rhenoster river from its junction with the Vaal, to Witkop, and thence to the Lace Diamond Mines, whither a line had already been run from Kroonstad. The Rhenoster river—Witkop section of this line was eventually demolished, and a line was run from the Lace Mines along the Valsch river to Bothaville. This was begun on December 6th, 1901, and completed on February 19th, 1902. Meanwhile Heilbron and Frankfort had been connected by a line of blockhouses, which was extended to Tafel Kop on December 29th, 1901; and another line of blockhouses from Inketeni (near Majuba) had reached Botha's Pass on December 30th. Botha's Pass and Tafel Kop were then connected by a line of blockhouses, which was completed by the end of January, 1902. In the eighty-seven miles which intervened between Frankfort and Tafel Kop were 187 blockhouses, garrisoned by 2,558 men, or thirty men to a mile.

Other lines of cross-country blockhouses were :—

(1) Kroonstad—Lindley: fifty miles, with 108 blockhouses and four posts. Commenced November 18th, 1901; finished January 9th, 1902, with a branch from Kaalfontein to Valsch River bridge; eight blockhouses.

(2) Lindley—Bethlehem, *via* Kaffir Kop and Naude's Kop: eighty miles; ninety-four blockhouses, with a garrison of 1,934 men, or twenty men to the mile.

(3) Harrismith—Bethlehem: fifty miles, 134 blockhouses and two posts. Bethlehem bridge—Bethlehem: four miles, seventeen blockhouses; garrison, 1,894 men, *i.e.*, in the fifty miles, Harrismith—Bethlehem, thirty-eight men to the mile.

APPENDIX 2.

(4) Elands River—Elands River bridge: ten miles, twenty blockhouses.

(5) Van Reenen's—De Beer's—Plat Berg: twenty miles, thirty-one blockhouses.

(6) Harrismith—Oliver's Hoek: twenty-three miles, sixteen blockhouses.

(7) Bethlehem—Brindisi: forty miles, forty-seven blockhouses.

(8) Volksrust—Wakkerstroom: eighteen miles, twenty-one blockhouses.

(9) Wakkerstroom—Derby: seventy miles, 100 blockhouses, with posts at Castrol Nek, Mabola, and two other points; garrison, 1,524 men, or twenty-one men to the mile.

(10) Standerton—Ermelo: commenced November 11th, 1901; finished January 20th, 1902; fifty-six miles, 131 blockhouses and six posts.

(11) Ermelo—Carolina: commenced (from each end) January 21st, 1902; finished February 9th, 1902; thirty-four miles, eighty-five blockhouses; on one section of this line, comprising seventy-three miles, there were 2,232 men, or thirty men to the mile.

(12) Wonderfontein—Carolina: commenced December 30th, 1901; finished January 17th, 1902; twenty-five miles, fifty-five blockhouses and posts.

(13) Eerstefabrieken—Groot Oliphants River station: fifty-five miles, with 1,700 men, or thirty to the mile.

(14) Ermelo—Bank Kop—Amsterdam: finished to Bank Kop at armistice on March 29th, 1902.

(15) Frederikstad—Naauwpoort: commenced July, 1901; finished August, 1901; forty-four miles, thirty-seven blockhouses.

(16) Wonderfontein—Komati Poort: along the railway, 175 miles, with 3,200 men, or eighteen men to the mile.

(17) Rooidraai (Mooi river)—Ventersdorp: nineteen miles, twenty-one blockhouses; commenced December 19th, 1901; finished January 5th, 1902; demolished February 12th, 1902.

(18) Vaal River—Ventersdorp: fifty miles, fifty-six blockhouses and three posts; completed December 9th, 1901, with 491 men, or ten men to the mile.

(19) Ventersdorp—Tafel Kop: twenty-seven miles, fifty-nine blockhouses and three posts; commenced December 19th, 1901;

finished January 31st, 1902; garrisoned by 689 men, or twenty-five men to the mile.

(20) Tafel Kop—Naauwpoort: commenced February 12th, 1902; finished March 4th, 1902; forty-five miles, garrisoned by 566 men, or twelve men to the mile.

(21) Buffelsvlei—Lichtenburg: commenced January 19th, 1902; finished February 20th, 1902; forty miles, seventy-nine blockhouses and two large posts, garrisoned by 1,011 men, or twenty-five men to the mile, including Lichtenburg garrison.

(22) Mafeking—Lichtenburg *viâ* Polfontein.

(23) Polfontein—Maretsani.

(24) Machadodorp—Lydenburg: line of posts from three to nine blockhouses each, forty-five miles, fifty-five blockhouses.

(25) Vaal River (Koedoesdraai—Bothaville): nine posts.

(26) Dundee—Vryheid: forty miles, seventy-three blockhouses.

(27) Victoria Road—Carnarvon: eighty miles, 112 blockhouses and three posts; commenced December 12th, 1901; finished January 24th, 1902.

(28) Carnarvon—Williston: commenced January 25th, 1902; finished April 20th, 1902.

(29) Williston—Calvinia: commenced May 3rd, 1902; finished May 31st, 1902.

(30) Calvinia—Clanwilliam: commenced January 15th, 1902; finished May 28th, 1902.

(31) Clanwilliam—Lambert's Bay: thirty-four miles, fifty-three blockhouses; commenced December 14th, 1901; finished January 15th, 1902.

(32) Bethulie—Herschel: eighty miles, six posts and Aliwal North.

(33) Bloemfontein—Maseru: eighty-two miles, seventy-nine blockhouses (including posts), divided into three sections:—(i.) Bloemfontein—Sannah's Post: twenty miles, seventeen blockhouses, 288 men; (ii.) Sannah's Post—Thabanchu: twenty miles, twenty-five blockhouses, 467 men; (iii.) Thabanchu—Maseru: forty-two miles, thirty-seven blockhouses. In (ii.) there were also four posts on the adjacent hills and six round Thabanchu. In (iii.) Springhaan Nek and four other posts were occupied.

(34) Lines of posts radiated from and connected Dundee with other near outlying strategical positions.

Mention must also be made of the lines of moveable posts erected by the South African Constabulary. These were, as a rule, in the form of rough redoubts. Often, however, a simple fire-trench was dug and roofed overhead by " skins " of corrugated iron, the latter being covered with any material affording protective colouration. Sometimes the trench would be deep, but a rough lying-down trench of the following dimensions was often found to be adequate :—

A trench seven feet wide and one foot deep was dug, and a low notched parapet was arranged on either side. Upon this " skins " of corrugated iron were laid so as to form overhead cover, and upon the " skins " the excavated earth was piled. If the trench was merely required to face in one direction a lean-to roof was made resting on the parapet. In all cases the loopholes were wide and low.

The strategy which underlay the evolution of the blockhouse system in South Africa was both defensive and offensive. The blockhouses upon the railway secured the vulnerable lines of communication, upon the integrity of which the existence of the Field Army depended; and having fulfilled that defensive duty, required no further justification. Advantage was taken of the power of the modern rifle; as many men as possible were relieved of the duty of guarding the railway, and the force available for offensive action was proportionately increased.

The strategy which governed the erection of the cross-country blockhouse lines was of a different character. The earliest use of such barriers in guerrilla warfare is lost in the darkness of antiquity. That the undue multiplication of such works may lead to ineffectual dispersion, thereby condemning the strategy of their employer to a passive defensive, was proved by the Spanish War in Cuba of 1898. But the South African blockhouse line cannot be considered without its complement, the " drive." As the tentacles of the blockhouse lines closed upon the theatre of war, the area of manœuvre contracted, the bases of the raiding British columns multiplying as those of the Boers diminished. Without the " drives " the blockhouse line would have been as barren as the Spanish " trocha "; without the cross-country blockhouse lines the " drives " would have beaten the air. It need only be noted that the combination of " drives " and blockhouses imply an *assured* superiority in strength and capacity for supply. Without these it would be exceedingly dangerous to undertake them.

The only apparent alternative to such a system is one sanctioned by history—the "decentralised vigour" of Marshal Bugeaud in Algeria. The immediate and daily control of the several movements of individual commanders then passes from the hands of the Commander-in-Chief into those of his lieutenants, who, with adequate mobile forces, acting from fixed centres and upon local intelligence, are made severally answerable for the pacification of their particular districts.

APPENDIX 3

(CHAPTER XXVI.).

LETTER FROM GENERAL C. R. DE WET TO GENERAL J. C. SMUTS, APPOINTING HIM SUCCESSOR TO KRITZINGER, AND GIVING INSTRUCTIONS AS TO THE CONDUCT OF THE CAMPAIGN IN CAPE COLONY.

Dist. Winburg,
In the Field,
February 8th, 1902.

THE MOST HONOURABLE ADVOCATE SMUTS,
    Asst. Commandant-General
  of the S.A.R. Fighting Forces in the C.C.

MOST HONOURABLE SIR,
    Having heard that Asst. Hoofd. Commandant Kritzinger was severely wounded and captured in the C.C., I have thought it advisable to appoint you Head of all the Fighting Forces in the C.C., formerly under Asst. Hoofd. Comdt. Kritzinger, until such time as General De La Rey shall have arrived.

Your appointment is enclosed herein.

I wish to bring the following to your notice, not that I, nor the Government have any doubt that you will make war in a civilized manner, but I only consider it my duty to bring one thing and another to your notice, more especially as the enemy continues in his uncivilized deeds.

I am convinced that we are of the same opinion, viz., that the (key) question of the absolute Independence of the people will be decided in the Cape Colony.

It is my duty to draw your attention to the following points which have repeatedly been impressed by me and are anew impressed upon all (N.C.O.'s) under Officers.

1. To continue the War (wage War) in the civilized manner, in which we commenced it and have now carried it on for twenty-eight months.

Though we have to deal with a barbarous Government and Commanding Officers, judging them by the uncivilized actions they have committed, the which it is not necessary for me to specify (enumerate). It is well known to you and everyone what England has done in the line of civilized actions since the commencement of the war, to which Government and People (the noble excluded) we never shall nor can bend.

I suppose you deplore as much as I do, and every civilized person, as also, if not the majority, then at least a large portion of the British Race does, the deeds of the British Government and its Chief Leaders in S.A. and abhor it.

We hear from time to time that the Noble Classes of the British increase daily, and that they strongly condemn the actions of their Government and leaders in South Africa. This information (report) we have from several reliable sources.

By strictly adhering to the course we have chosen, we will ultimately win, if not the universal sympathy, at least the sympathy of the majority of the British People, not to say anything of the sympathy of the whole of the Civilized World.

The sympathy of the British people, as that of her Civilized Colonies, for us, would have been great, were it not that for years before the war already, and during the war they had been deceived by England's War Office and leaders in S.A. who, with an evil object, had distorted matters and painted untrue pictures of the same.

The tension experienced by the British people and by almost the whole (of the) World, distinctly (shows) proves that they have had a fair insight into matters (seen what is behind the screen). Should the British Parliament vote a further amount for the war, we have the firm belief and conviction, when looking upon the past, that the result will only be the loss to England of the whole of South Africa.

We do acknowledge that it is a bitter pill for England to swallow, but by continuing (the War) the pill will become the more bitter and the larger.

Just compare England's credit to-day to what it was just before the war, and in what disrespect she is held (and how she is falling from time to time in the estimation) of every Nation of the World, which disrespect will increase day by day, should the War continue longer, or at all events, if it be waged in the uncivilized manner they are doing it now.

APPENDIX 3.

2. Do not permit any Native under us to carry arms against Britain, neither in the Republics, nor in the Cape Colony, nor are any Natives to be used (for the purpose of scouting) as Scouts, in spite of the fact (though) that Natives are (used) employed by the enemy, not only as scouts but thousands are armed against us.

3. Strict attention is to be paid to the fact that no Colonial is to be forced to take up arms against England, they are to join voluntarily until such time as the Colonials shall proclaim their own independence and shall have formed a temporary Government.

4. Reprisals as far as the burning of houses are concerned, are not to be permitted, although some time back a circular was circulated there, issued by His Honour our State President and myself, wherein we threatened to take reprisals, we do not consider that the time to take reprisals generally upon persons in the C.C. who are evilly (unkindly) disposed towards us, which time I hope shall never come, has arrived yet.

At that time we meant and we are still of the firm intention, to, should it unexpectedly (come to it) be necessary, use such steps, before and rather than sacrifice our Independence. In a few instances reprisals have been taken, for which the Officers concerned had reasons and the owners were strongly against us.

No reprisals are therefore to be taken upon persons (the properties) so generally as heretofore, who may be unkindly disposed towards us, before receiving further instructions, for the more the enemy continues his barbarous and uncivilized dealings, the plainer (more clearly) it is to be observed that God is with us as only a few days ago, when the enemy with an overwhelming force tried to corner us between the railway line and his B.H. Lines, God opened a safe way for us and we crossed the so-called famous B.H. Lines. I have experienced what I have always said and thought of the, by the enemy so-called famous, blockhouse lines, viz., that it is merely a White Elephant; not only did we cross safely, but we brought a large number of cattle through too. At another spot where cattle were being brought across, the burghers were fired upon from the blockhouses, the only result being that some of the horses and cattle were hit.

The question in short is, when has, or will the enemy be able (to stop us from) keep us away from his lines of communication. Was he able to do so at the Orange River, at the Ladybrand—Bloemfontein line of fortifications ?—where our vanguard, in the morning before dawn, chased the enemy, who had thought to stop us, away. How many times when we had to cross (when it was necessary to cross) the line, have we crossed it by force, which still occurs daily. He was, is not, and never will be, able to stop us nor the cattle, crossing the railway or B.H. Lines, not that I wish to speak disrespectfully of the enemy's tactics, but the blockhouses is one of the most ridiculous of tactics that I have ever seen since the commencement of the War. Suppose that we are ultimately obliged to leave the Republics owing to want of food, our people are now already determined that we shall then go to the Cape Colony and Natal. Want of food (scarcity of food) was, is, and never shall be the cause or reason of surrender with us, for so long as the enemy remains in S.A. he has to live and eat and we will also do the same, even as we are now continuing the war almost exclusively with the rifles and ammunition of the enemy even so will we be provided with his food.

5. Do not allow anything such as Horses, Eatables, Clothing, etc., etc., to be taken without giving receipts, not even from those persons who are unkindly disposed towards us, should it afterwards appear that they were not kindly disposed towards us, and deserve not to be paid out, it will be a matter for the Government to decide.

Wishing you and your Officers and Burghers fortune (prosperity) and a blessing,

I have the honour to be,
Your Most Honourable's
Obedient Servant,
(Sd.), C. R. DE WET,
Hoofd. Commandant of the O.F.S.

APPOINTMENT.

Herewith the Most Honourable Gentleman Advocate Jan Smuts is appointed Head (Chief) of all the Fighting Forces in the Cape Colony, formerly under Asst. Hoofd. Commandant Kritzinger, whom, the enemy assert, is captured.

Given by me this 8th day of February, 1902.

(Sd.), C. R. DE WET,
Hoofd. Commandant O.F.S.

APPENDIX 4

(CHAPTER XXVIII.).

ORDERS BY LIEUTENANT-GENERAL SIR I. S. M. HAMILTON, K.C.B., D.S.O., COMMANDING COLUMNS OPERATING IN WESTERN TRANSVAAL.

Palmietfontein,
May 6th, 1902.

The itinerary of the marches of the various columns is set forth in the attached table, and in default of further orders it must be strictly adhered to. Itinerary.

Column commanders should detail an officer on each flank, who should be held responsible that the flanks join up at the places laid down. Flanks.

After leaving Rooirantjesfontein, Nooitverwacht, Korannafontein, columns will line out at night, and hold a continuous cordon, which should be strongly entrenched during the afternoon and evening, and strengthened with wire as much as possible. Lining out.

Columns will march daily at 7.30 a.m. Hours of march.

Columns will not outspan until reaching the line that they are going to hold in the evening. Outspans.

Signals may be made on the Pom-pom,* as follows, but should not be employed without the direct order of the officer commanding a group of columns. Signals.

The "Friendly Signal," which will merely be used to indicate the position of friendly troops will be :— Friendly signal.

   Pom-Pom Pom-Pom Pom-Pom.

  *I.e., Vickers-Maxim automatic quick-firing gun.

Signal for help.

The "Signal for Help," which should only be used if a large force of more than 500 Boers is visible and threatening to break through :—

    Pom-Pom-Pom   Pom-Pom-Pom   Pom-Pom-Pom,

followed by a belt fired as rapidly as possible.

Breaking of line.

The line must on no account be broken by small bodies of troops chasing Boers in front of it. Should it be considered desirable to break the line at all, it must be by the direct order of the officer commanding a group of columns, who must judge whether the situation warrants such action.

Directing flank.

In lining out, each column commander will be responsible that his Left is in touch with the column on his Left.

(Sd.), IAN HAMILTON,
Lieut.-General.

APPENDIX 4.

See Map No. 60.

Date.	Colonel Rochfort.	General F. W. Kitchener.	Colonel Sir H. Rawlinson and Colonel Thorneycroft.	Colonel Kekewich.
May 6th.		Korannafontein.	Nooitverwacht.	Rooirantjesfontein.
May 7th.	Witklip.	South corner of Kareekuil.	North-east corner of Schoonoord.	If the enemy does not seem numerous, let right sweep round to Biejesvallei.
May 8th.	Left to your discretion.	South-east corner of Jouberts Rust.	As near as possible to figure* of Zandvallei.	*Centre.* Leeuwpan.
May 9th.	Schweizer Reneke. / Left to your discretion.	North end of Boesmans Pan.	Pan of Bulpan.	*Centre.* Geysdorp.
May 10th.	South corner of Mooifontein.	West corner of Kaalplaats.	Drift on Donkerspoort.	*Centre.* Doornbult Siding.
May 11th.	*Centre.* Honing Spruit. / Brussels.	Vryburg.	Devondale.	Come down line if possible to Kinderdam, or neighbourhood.

Columns will march at 7.30 a.m. daily. No midday outspan.

(Sd.), Ian Hamilton, Lieut.-General.

* Refers to Jeppe's map.

APPENDIX 5.

NOTES ON THE SUPPLY SYSTEM IN SOUTH AFRICA, 1901—2.

In order that a general reserve of 120 days' supplies for men and animals should be as nearly as possible maintained, each Staff Officer for Supplies in South Africa reported weekly by telegraph to the Director of Supplies in that country, stating the number of mouths in his particular district and the supplies on hand. The Director of Supplies in South Africa was thus enabled to strike a balance of his total requirements, which he communicated in a fortnightly cablegram to the War Office. As far as possible all demands for supplies were made three months in advance, so as to afford time for collection.

This fortnightly statement by the Director of Supplies was the first cause of all demands, and formed the root of the system of supply of the army in the field. It was first examined in the Quarter-Master-General's department at the War Office; next, an indent based thereon was forwarded to the "Supply Reserve Depôt" at Woolwich, which then fulfilled demands either from its own stock, or under "running contract," or by application through the Quarter-Master-General to the Director of Army Contracts. In the last case the quantity, quality and description of supplies required were defined by the Quarter-Master-General's department, and it became the duty of the Director of Contracts to comply with the specifications. In order to fulfil such requisitions, the Director of Contracts issued tenders, or made private purchases, or dealt through brokers.* The trade is reported to have met all requirements well; but, naturally, to obtain large quantities of certain commodities not in common demand (*e.g.*, 1-lb. tins of preserved meat, tents, saddles) time was required, and at first substitutes had to be provided.

Delivery of goods was made either at the Reserve Depôt at Woolwich, or from the factory direct to the ship's side (whether in London

* Flour, tea, sugar, rum, hay, oxen, were not supplied by contract, but either by brokers, or by the Colonial Governments themselves by direct shipments.

APPENDIX 5.

or the provinces); or supplies were shipped from the Colonies to South Africa, under arrangements made by the Colonial Governments upon behalf of the Director of Contracts. In all cases a prolonged examination by "Staff Officers for supply inspection" took place upon delivery: supplies were weighed and marked with the date of receipt; samples were tested by the Government Analyst, Somerset House, and in special cases examined by the Professor of Hygiene at Netley; whilst supplies forwarded direct from the Colonies to South Africa were inspected by the officials of the Colonial Governments.

Shipment was made under the auspices of the Admiralty. As soon as the Quarter-Master-General knew what his requirements would be, he informed the Admiralty, whose duty it became to obtain sea transport, and to advise the Quarter-Master-General when it would be available. The transport department of the Admiralty made requisition upon shipping agents, at the same time defining what class of ship was to be engaged, the agents being paid either at a rate per ton or in a lump sum. Large ships of fair speed were used. The War Office notified the Director of Supplies in South Africa by letter on the fourth day of each month what supplies had been ordered for shipment during that month, as well as cabled to him the contents of the ships which had actually sailed.* The Director of Supplies in

* Specimen "Return of Ships with Supplies on Board to Arrive."

Name of Vessel.	Cargo.	Date of Sailing.	Expected arrival.	Remarks.
Manhattan ...	Miscellaneous	1.10.00	21.10.00	Cape Town for orders.
Windsor	Alfalfa	2.10.00	19.10.00	Cape Town for orders.
Gulf of Ancud.	Oats and preserved meat	3.10.00	21.10.00	Durban for orders.
Galeka	Compressed forage .	3.10.00	24.10.00	For Port Elizabeth.
Blackheath ...	Hay and oats	4.10.00	22.10.00	Durban for orders.
Gaul	Compressed forage .	10.10.00	3.11.00	For East London.
Lake Erie	Miscellaneous	10.10.00	3.11.00	Optional South African ports.
Riverton	Hay	11.10.00	29.10.00	Call at Cape Town for orders.
Greek	Hospital supplies ..	11.10.00	2.11.00	For Port Elizabeth.
Umvoti	Miscellaneous	11.10.00	8.11.00	For Natal.
Klondyke.....	Oats.............	11.10.00	29.10.00	Durban for orders.
Falls of Keltie.	Hay and oats	11.10.00	29.10.00	Durban for orders.
Umbilo	Hospital supplies ..	15.10.00	12.11.00	Natal.

South Africa was thus enabled to decide, before they arrived, at what point the ships were to discharge their cargoes. The time occupied in unloading the ships depended, not alone upon the capacities of the South African ports, but also upon the storage room near the docks and upon the carrying powers of the railroads up-country; for the congestion of the single lines of railway often prevented the evacuation of the sheds at the docks, and this in turn obstructed the discharge of cargoes and caused heavy demurrage. The Naval Transport authorities were responsible for delivery of supplies to the Army Service Corps in South Africa at high-water mark. Cargoes were discharged at Cape Town alongside the quays, elsewhere for the most part in lighters, and were handed over by the harbour authorities, under payment of their dues, to the Army Service Corps sheds.

Subject to the approval of the Director of Contracts, the Deputy-Adjutant-General for Supply and Transport for South Africa had, in October, 1899, contracted with the Cold Storage Company in Cape Town for the supply of fresh meat to the army in the field. This contract was extended from time to time at diminishing rates.* The meat thus purchased by contract was destined solely for troops on, or within three miles of the lines of railway. The mobile columns carried, as a reserve, a store of preserved meat sufficient for at least four days; but except under the stress of an emergency, they lived on captured stock, which was slaughtered either by the column itself, or by the contractors, who at a fixed rate purchased the animals alive from the supply officer to the column, slaughtered them, and sold the meat to him again by the pound.

Upon the Director of Supplies in South Africa devolved the task of maintaining not only his general reserve of 120 days' supplies in that country, but also such local reserves in various stations as (subject to the maintenance of minimum reserves at certain points specially ordered by the Commander-in-Chief) were demanded by the officers commanding districts or columns.

The country was divided into supply districts, and local supply officers reported weekly to the Staff Officers for Supply of their district the state of supplies and numbers in their stations, or columns. About the end of 1901 there were twenty-one such districts in the

* During the early part of the war 9d. per lb. was paid for frozen and 11d. for fresh meat. This was reduced in February, 1901, to 7d. and 10d. respectively, and in the February of 1902 to 5½d. and 9d.

APPENDIX 5.

theatre of war. Within these districts a local reserve of at least thirty days' supplies had to be maintained in over 100 depôts. The following list will show :—

The Number of "Rations" fixed early in 1902 as the prescribed Supply Reserves at the Stations named.

Supply District.	Station.	Number of Rations.			
		Men's.	Medical Comforts.	Grain.	Hay.
Pretoria	Pretoria (Supply Depôt)	1,500,000	150,000	2,000,000	2,500,000
	Irene	15,000	1,500	5,000	5,000
	Rietfontein W.	90,000	9,000	90,000	60,000
Northern L. of C., north of Pretoria.	Pietersburg	150,000	15,000	150,000	170,000
	Nylstroom	25,000	2,500	2,000	2,500
	Warm Bath	20,000	2,000	6,000	6,000
	Pienaars River	10,000	1,000	1,500	2,000
Germiston	Vereeniging	25,000	2,500	25,000	25,000
	Zuurfontein	10,000	1,000	2,000	2,000
	Springs	50,000	5,000	50,000	80,000
	Elandsfontein	2,000,000	200,000	2,000,000	2,500,000
	Johannesburg	100,000	10,000	100,000	120,000
L. of C. west of Johannesburg	Krugersdorp	100,000	10,000	100,000	150,000
	Naauwpoort W.	50,000	5,000	50,000	50,000
	Rustenburg	50,000	5,000	50,000	25,000
	Coal Mine Drift	50,000	5,000	50,000	50,000
	Potchefstroom	60,000	6,000	60,000	100,000
	Ventersdorp	35,000	3,500	35,000	20,000
	Klerksdorp	300,000	30,000	300,000	350,000
Heilbron	Heilbron	120,000	12,000	120,000	150,000
	Frankfort	50,000	5,000	50,000	25,000
	Tafel Kop	50,000	5,000	50,000	25,000
Kroonstad	Brandfort	20,000	2,000	20,000	25,000
	Smaldeel	3,000	300	3,000	4,000
	Winburg	35,000	3,500	35,000	40,000
	Kroonstad	300,000	30,000	300,000	400,000
	Lindley	50,000	5,000	50,000	50,000
	Wolvehoek	3,000	300	3,000	4,000
	Doornkloof	25,000	2,500	10,000	10,000
	Kaffir Kop	50,000	5,000	50,000	25,000
Bloemfontein	Norval's Pont	35,000	3,500	35,000	40,000
	Bethulie Bridge	50,000	5,000	50,000	50,000
	Bethulie	25,000	2,500	25,000	30,000
	Springfontein	60,000	6,000	60,000	70,000
	Edenburg	30,000	3,000	30,000	30,000
	Bloemfontein	500,000	50,000	500,000	600,000
	Thabanchu	30,000	3,000	30,000	35,000
	Ladybrand	100,000	10,000	100,000	100,000
	Ficksburg	100,000	10,000	100,000	50,000

THE NUMBER OF "RATIONS" FIXED EARLY IN 1902 AS THE PRESCRIBED SUPPLY RESERVES AT THE STATIONS NAMED (*continued*).

Supply District.	Station.	Number of Rations.			
		Men's.	Medical Comforts.	Grain.	Hay.
CAPE COLONY:					
Cape Town..	Cape Town Green Point Wynberg Durban Road Simon's Town	40,000	4,000	40,000	40,000
Southern ...	Oudtshoorn	5,000	500	5,000	5,000
	Swellendam	5,000	500	5,000	5,000
	Mossel Bay	5,000	500	5,000	5,000
Eastern	East London	5,000	500	10,000	10,000
	King William's Town	5,000	500	5,000	5,000
	Queenstown	30,000	10,000	40,000	50,000
	Dordrecht	30,000	3,000	20,000	30,000
	Stormberg	30,000	3,000	20,000	30,000
	Burghersdorp	40,000	4,000	30,000	40,000
	Aliwal North	60,000	6,000	60,000	60,000
North-Wstrn.	Prieska	60,000	6,000	60,000	70,000
	Kenhardt	40,000	4,000	40,000	50,000
	Upington	30,000	3,000	30,000	40,000
South-Wstrn.	Clanwilliam	120,000	12,000	120,000	150,000
	Endekuil	100,000	10,000	100,000	120,000
	Lambert's Bay	30,000	3,000	30,000	40,000
	Calvinia	40,000	4,000	50,000	60,000
Western	Stellenbosch	15,000	1,500	30,000	30,000
	Worcester	20,000	2,000	60,000	60,000
	Matjesfontein	30,000	3,000	20,000	20,000
	Beaufort West	40,000	10,000	30,000	40,000
	Victoria West Road	100,000	10,000	100,000	150,000
	Carnarvon	100,000	10,000	100,000	150,000
	Richmond Road	5,000	1,000	10,000	10,000
	Richmond	15,000	1,500	15,000	15,000
	De Aar	300,000	30,000	300,000	300,000
	Britstown	20,000	2,000	20,000	20,000
	Phillipstown	20,000	2,000	20,000	20,000
	Deelfontein	50,000	50,000	1,000	1,000
	Williston	50,000	5,000	75,000	80,000
Midland	Colesberg	20,000	2,000	20,000	30,000
	Cradock	10,000	1,000	10,000	10,000
	Graaff Reinet	20,000	2,000	20,000	20,000
	Grahamstown	5,000	500	5,000	5,000
	Hanover Road	20,000	3,000	10,000	10,000
	Naauwpoort	150,000	15,000	150,000	150,000
	Rosmead	20,000	1,000	20,000	20,000
	Port Elizabeth	5,000	500	15,000	15,000
	Steynsburg	30,000	2,000	20,000	20,000
	Middleburg	10,000	1,000	10,000	10,000
Namaqualand	O'Okiep	180,000	10,000	100,000	100,000

APPENDIX 5.

THE NUMBER OF "RATIONS" FIXED EARLY IN 1902 AS THE PRESCRIBED SUPPLY RESERVES AT THE STATIONS NAMED *(continued).*

Supply District.	Station.	Number of Rations.			
		Men's.	Medical Comforts.	Grain.	Hay.
Kimberley	Orange River	100,000	10,000	100,000	100,000
	Modder River	20,000	2,000	20,000	25,000
	Jacobsdal	6,000	600	3,000	2,000
	Douglas	10,000	1,000	4,000	3,000
	Campbell	6,000	600	3,000	2,000
	Griquatown	15,000	1,500	5,000	5,000
	Koffyfontein	10,000	1,000	4,000	2,000
	Kimberley	300,000	30,000	300,000	350,000
	Barkly West	10,000	1,000	4,000	2,000
	Daniel's Kuil	6,000	600	3,000	2,000
	Boshof	35,000	3,500	35,000	15,000
	Warrenton / Fourteen Streams	35,000	3,500	35,000	40,000
	Christiana	50,000	5,000	50,000	20,000
Western (Vryburg)	Vryburg	50,000	5,000	50,000	60,000
	Mafeking	300,000	30,000	300,000	350,000
	Zeerust	30,000	3,000	30,000	20,000
	Lichtenburg	35,000	3,500	35,000	20,000
	Buluwayo	5,000	500	5,000	5,000
Standerton	Standerton	300,000	30,000	300,000	350,000
	Heidelberg	60,000	6,000	60,000	60,000
Natal	Eshowe	35,000	3,500	35,000	35,000
	Melmoth	25,000	2,500	25,000	25,000
	Maritzburg	10,000	1,000	10,000	10,000
	Howick	15,000	1,500	2,000	2,000
	Mooi River	50,000	20,000	150,000	150,000
	Ladysmith	10,000	1,000	10,000	10,000
	Dundee	100,000	10,000	100,000	100,000
	De Jager's Drift	50,000	5,000	50,000	50,000
	Vryheid	100,000	10,000	100,000	50,000
	Newcastle	100,000	10,000	100,000	120,000
	Utrecht	50,000	5,000	50,000	50,000
	Botha's Pass	100,000	10,000	100,000	100,000
	Volksrust	120,000	12,000	120,000	150,000
	Wakkerstroom	50,000	5,000	50,000	50,000
Harrismith	Harrismith	300,000	30,000	300,000	350,000
	Elands River	50,000	5,000	50,000	50,000
	Tiger Kloof	50,000	5,000	50,000	50,000
	Bethlehem	35,000	3,500	35,000	10,000
	Brindisi	20,000	2,000	15,000	15,000
Eastern Transvaal	Komati Poort	20,000	2,000	20,000	20,000
	Barberton	100,000	10,000	100,000	100,000
	Machadodorp	100,000	10,000	100,000	120,000
	Schoeman's Kloof	5,000	500	5,000	5,000
	Lydenburg	100,000	10,000	100,000	50,000
	Wonderfontein	50,000	5,000	50,000	50,000
	Middelburg	500,000	50,000	500,000	600,000
	Witbank	25,000	2,500	15,000	15,000
	Balmoral	50,000	5,000	50,000	50,000

The standing orders of the Director of Supplies in South Africa—which dealt with routine matters, and with the normal requirements of the Field Force—were elastic, and encouraged decentralisation. As described, supply stations (upon which minor posts and blockhouse lines drew) and columns reported their wants to the Staff Officer for Supplies of the district in which they were, whereupon the latter, without reference to Headquarters, made his requisitions direct upon the Base Reserve Depôt at the nearest port of entry. He refilled the convoys of columns in his district as opportunity served, and from the nearest convenient point. The amount of reserves in the hands of columns or stations was left to the discretion of the officer commanding the district or the column.

The Director of Supplies confined himself to supervision, to maintaining his general reserve of 120 days' supplies, and to meeting abnormal demands. The reports of Staff Officers of districts were merely intended to give the Director of Supplies the necessary information on which to base his requisitions upon England, so as to maintain his general reserve.*

At Army Headquarters, the Director of Supplies reported himself in person to the Commander-in-Chief each day at 8.30 a.m. Copies of all telegrams received and despatched lay upon a table in the Commander-in-Chief's quarters. With these all the officers of the Headquarters Staff made themselves conversant, so that the Director of Supplies was informed of all impending movements before his daily visit to Lord Kitchener. His own familiarity with the geography of the country, and with the fact that movements of troops repeated themselves—columns being drawn time after time towards certain points as to a magnet—rendered it unnecessary for him to demand specific orders. If, for example, columns were likely to approach the neighbourhood of the Natal line, he promptly filled Heidelberg or Standerton with supplies; or in the case of a " drive," convoys were passed out from some point upon the line along the rear of the " drive."

On each day the Army in Africa consumed some 3,000 tons of supplies. Three hundred ten-ton railway trucks were therefore required daily to keep pace with the consumption of the troops. As

---

* For a specimen state of supplies from a single district, see Table at end of this Appendix.

APPENDIX 5. 591

many trucks as possible were daily allotted solely to the service of supply by the Director of Railways. The provision of the necessary railway transport from the coast ports was the principal difficulty which confronted both the Directors of Supplies and of Railways. For this transport a charge was entered to the credit of the Railway Department and to the debit of the Army of 7d. per mile for each ten-ton truck, and of 1s. 2d. for each twenty-ton truck.

THE FIELD FORCE CANTEEN.

Brief mention must here be made of the work of the "Field Force Canteen," which was initiated in Natal in the early days of the war. Permission was granted to Lieut.-Colonel H. G. Morgan, the officer in charge of supplies, to purchase all goods required by the troops in the field; to hire his own transport for these commodities, and to sell them at a slight profit—the increment being distributed amongst the next-of-kin of the men who died in Natal. Subsequently the system was extended to the whole army in Africa, and everything in current demand amongst the troops was sold. The Field Force Canteen eventually purchased transport for its own use. Although profits were small, the turnover was large and rapid. Ultimately the entire capital of the Field Force Canteen was actually turned over five times in one month. During the latter period of the war the turnover exceeded £4,000,000 per annum. Soldiers' necessaries were sold at a fraction under, officers' necessaries and luxuries at a fraction over, cost price. At the close of the war, after distributing some £88,000 of the profits in grants to the wounded, to the next-of-kin of those who died, and to regimental institutes, the accounts of the Field Force Canteen Fund still showed a balance credit of £470,000. The major part of this was allotted to the South African Garrison Institutes as capital with which to inaugurate a civilian establishment, and to erect buildings at places where troops were stationed. It would be difficult to exaggerate the comfort and consequent increased efficiency afforded to the army in South Africa during the two last years of the war by this novel department, which in every sense strikingly justified its existence.

Owing to the great length of the Lines of Communications, to the exigencies of war, which caused trucks or convoys to be incessantly diverted from their intended destinations to meet sudden wants elsewhere, and to the inexperienced personnel, it was often impossible for

Supply Officers to trace goods which had been consigned to them, but had never reached them. Consequently they were frequently unable to balance their accounts. The arrival of goods by rail or road was never to be counted on. Trucks or wagons were constantly intercepted on their journey; loads were lightened or abandoned, and often none, or merely a fraction, of the original load reached its destination. Trucks passed over several lines of railroad, and no one would or could take responsibility for their passage. A train of ten trucks, starting from Durban, for example, would be broken up repeatedly to enable it to surmount the steep gradients; if not thereafter diverted or intercepted the trucks composing it would arrive at their destination at intervals of days or weeks. Alarms would occur on the line and supplies would be hurriedly unloaded at, or loaded and despatched to, any safe place. It sometimes happened that convoys destined for one point were hastily off-loaded in the dark at another, when the heaps of supplies might be largely depleted by passing columns, or perhaps partly scattered over the veld. Again, a convoy would be delayed on its way, and the escort, falling consequently short of rations, would supply themselves from its contents, with the result that on reaching its destination there were deficiencies which no one could account for. Even in peace, with a well-trained staff of accountants enjoying ample leisure, much time would have been occupied in tracing a fraction of the discrepancies which arose in any one week of the war. With an inadequate and inexperienced staff, working at high pressure to keep the army fed, with accountants in arrear and oppressed by the labour of attempting to explain discrepancies, it was impossible for the individual supply officer to attempt to close his accounts.

In order to deal with such miscarriages a central "Clearing House" account was created, to which supply officers forwarded the way-bills of goods which had been despatched to but had never reached them. Discrepancies were enquired into, and accounts balanced at Headquarters, which was in closer touch with the field columns than the latter were with one another.

APPENDIX 5.

THE DEPARTMENT OF CIVIL SUPPLIES.

This department was called into existence by the necessities of the civil populations of the captured South African towns. Its functions were as follows :—

1. To control the importation of goods of every description.
2. To control the transportation of all goods from place to place within the sphere of its operations, whether by rail or road.
3. To regulate and provide for the food supplies of the population.
4. To allot to each Civil Government Department a share of the railway truckage so that Government work of all descriptions could be carried on. The principal departments to which truckage had to be allotted were the Railways (first as Imperial Military Railways and subsequently as Central South African Railways), the Public Works, Repatriation, Land Settlement, Burgher Camps, Native Refugee Camps.
5. To secure, through its purchasing depôts, supplies of grain for Native Refugee Camps, Burgher Concentration Camps, Civil Government Departments, the Army Service Corps, etc., etc.
6. To provide for the preservation of cattle during a portion of the war with a view to aiding in the re-stocking of the country. (This was done by the Cattle Preservation Branch of the Department of Civil Supplies. It was abolished about April, 1902.)
7. To direct the operations of the Cold Storage Companies as touching frozen and fresh meat supplies for the population.
8. To regulate the selling price of foodstuffs and liquors.
9. To control the consumption of liquors, wines, spirits, etc., for which purpose " Permits " to purchase rigidly limited quantities were issued to persons of good repute.

A limited proportion of the available truckage was set apart for Civil requirements, and under the High Commissioner a department was created to control issues, to re-establish a produce market, and to regulate " Trading Licences," first in Johannesburg, and later at Pretoria and in the Transvaal generally. For this purpose certain bases were chosen as centres of distribution ; and as a larger amount of truckage was gradually allotted to this department a greater variety of articles could be imported.

The elaboration of the blockhouse lines tended to facilitate the work of the department, for the carrying power of the congested railways was supplemented by wagon transport passing along the blockhouse lines. Simultaneously the scope of the work of the department broadened as the areas under effective control extended. When the mining industry began to raise its head, stamps were being dropped, and the population of Johannesburg was returning, the pressure upon the Director of Civil Supplies became heavy, and great discrimination had to be exercised in the task of granting transport and " Trading Licences."

It is recorded that an aggregate of goods weighing 6,000,000 tons was transported by the Department of Civil Supplies. Of this the importations during 1901 provided merely foodstuffs and clothing, whilst those during 1902 included also large quantities of building material, and live stock for re-stocking the country.

With the cessation of hostilities the pressure was at once relieved: The military requirements, which had been paramount, diminished, and more transport and personnel could be placed at the service of the department.

Soon the Civil authorities resumed control of the railways, making provision for the wants of the Army of Occupation; and gradually the control of the issue of supplies and of " Trading Licences " was abandoned. Four months after the signing of peace the work of this department came to an end.

APPENDIX 5.

Specimen State of Supplies (Dated 27.10.'00).

from western line of communications (Kimberley to Buluwayo).

Estimated number fed :—Men, 21,000 ; Animals, 13,000.

Supplies.		At Kimberley.	At Out-stations between Kimberley and Mafeking.	At Mafeking and Out-stations between Mafeking and Buluwayo.	On Rail from coast.	Total.	In thousands of rations.	Number of days' supply for Troops and Animals fed.
Biscuits	lbs.	520,403	495,000	632,257	110,280	1,757,000	—	—
Flour	,,	500,070	1,275,000	69,786	—	1,844,000	3,941	188
Meal	,,	324,657	13,000	2,604	—	340,000	—	—
Preserved meat	,,	376,410	827,700	459,438	45,472	1,709,000	—	—
Meat and vegetable ration	,,	240,000	256,000	22,318	—	294,000	2,288	109
Rabbit	,,	6,285	—	—	—	—	—	—
Cheese	,,	21,442	53,300	603	—	75,000	—	—
Bacon and ham	,,	69,107	65,000	733	—	135,000	—	—
Soup	tins	—	—	—	—	—	—	—
Coffee	lbs.	17,920	24,800	7,369	2,000	52,000	2,736	130
Tea	,,	6,617	14,000	6,325	2,000	28,000	—	—
Chocolate	,,	7,220	1,100	795	—	9,000	—	—
Pepper	,,	1,057	2,200	1,052	384	4,000	2,304	109
Salt	,,	27,378	60,000	10,751	10,107	108,000	3,456	164
Sugar	,,	86,160	264,000	117,928	40,033	508,000	2,709	129
Soups, portable	tins	20,762	25,000	21,292	—	67,000	—	—
Compressed vegetables	lbs.	44,798	63,000	27,309	—	135,000	—	—
Fresh vegetables	,,	—	—	—	—	—	—	—
,, potatoes	,,	—	3,600	3,269	—	6,000	2,451	117
Preserved potatoes	,,	—	—	—	—	—	—	—
Fresh onions	,,	—	—	1,448	—	1,000	—	—
Preserved onions	,,	—	—	—	—	—	—	—
Rice	,,	26,680	1,840	280	—	28,000	2,004	95
Jam	,,	133,666	285,000	63,277	20,016	501,000	1,280	61
Lime-juice	gallons	2,479	982	999	—	4,000	1,088	61
Rum	,,	5,497	10,500	1,542	—	17,000	—	—
Wood	lbs.	12,960	612,000	512,375	—	1,137,000	—	—
Coal	,,	—	17,000	1,324	—	18,000	—	—
Matches	dozen	—	1,400	86	—	1,000	—	—
Candles, stearine	,,	17,604	10,700	1,119	5,000	34,000	—	—
,, magazine	,,	—	—	—	—	—	—	—
Colza	gallons	120	270	5	—	395	—	—

THE WAR IN SOUTH AFRICA.

SPECIMEN STATE OF SUPPLIES (Dated 27.10.'00) (*continued*).

FROM WESTERN LINE OF COMMUNICATIONS (KIMBERLEY TO BULUWAYO).

Estimated number fed:—Men, 21,000; Animals, 13,000.

SUPPLIES.		At Kimberley.	At Out-stations between Kimberley and Mafeking.	At Mafeking and Out-stations between Mafeking and Buluwayo.	On Rail from coast.	Total.	In thousands of rations.	Number of days' supply for Troops and Animals fed.
		Remains as per Telegrams.						
Paraffin	gallons	1,483	700	36	—	2,000	—	—
Tar	lbs.	6	—	—	—	6	—	—
Wick	yards	—	—	5	—	5	—	—
Chaff	lbs.	—	—	—	—	—	—	—
Oat hay	,,	12,161	—	548	—	12,000	—	—
Hay	,,	1,696,756	954,000	470,460	364,140	3,485,000	349	27
Alfalfa	,,	—	—	—	—	—	—	—
Bran	,,	514,677	400,500	215,191	109,300	1,239,000	—	—
Oats	,,	1,326,782	6,820,000	2,487,355	780,533	11,410,000	1,265	97
Mealies	,,	—	—	—	—	—	—	—
Forage, cake	,,	17,760	—	16,000	—	33,000	—	—
,, bundles		—	—	—	—	—	—	—
Oil cake	,,	4,800	—	—	—	4,000	—	—
Horse food	,,	22,000	—	—	15,000	37,000	—	—
Compressed fodder	,,	33,524	—	—	—	33,000	—	—
Linseed	,,	3,546	1,840	—	—	5,000	—	—
Coarse salt	,,	33,862	—	6,287	—	40,000	1,280	99
Vinegar	gallons	—	—	—	—	—	—	—
Emergency rations	lbs.	102,004	14,600	4,898	—	121,000	—	—
Tobacco	,,	11,457	23,000	6,057	—	40,000	—	—
Hops	,,	—	25	18	—	43	—	—
Baking powder	,,	1,124	600	435	—	2,159	—	—
Yeast	cakes	—	—	—	—	—	—	—
,, cakes	,,	65,640	31,300	8,560	—	105,500	—	60
Arrowroot	,,	872	320	263	—	1,455	—	173
Barley	,,	2,105	1,370	—	—	3,475	—	No scale.
Butter	,,	1,848	—	—	—	1,848	—	—
Calf's-foot jelly	bottles	2,160	1,050	72	504	3,786	—	76
Cinnamon	lbs.	—	—	4	—	4	—	No scale.
Cocoa paste	tins	7,434	3,500	85	—	11,019	—	275
Condensed milk	,,	19,721	60,000	2,085	4,032	85,838	—	143
Cornflour	lbs.	1,210	891	112	—	2,213	—	184
Egg powder	,,	2,224	24	89	—	2,337	—	No scale.

APPENDIX 5.

Item	Unit							
Meat extract	lbs.	—	—	—	—	—	—	—
" (Brand's essence)	"	1,392	976	208	—	2,576	—	174
" (Bovril)	"	488	475	2	—	965	—	No scale.
" essence or extract	"	1,590	1,560	81	49	3,231	—	71
" Extractum Carnis	"	180	142	—	1,008	371	—	105
Mustard	"	1,380	520	82	—	2,990	—	166
Oatmeal	"	374	976	964	—	2,314	—	—
Sago or tapioca	"	3,756	180	—	—	3,936	—	—
Soup, Brand's	"	1,092	264	660	—	2,016	—	—
" Maggis'	packets	432	—	—	—	432	—	—
Sugar	lbs.	—	—	—	—	—	—	—
Spirits of wine	gallons	—	—	10	—	10	—	No scale.
Roast fowl	lbs.	2,339	561	100	—	3,000	—	61
Chicken	"	1,896	—	—	—	1,896	—	—
Mutton broth	"	200	300	—	—	200	—	—
Benger's food	tins	432	—	—	512	432	—	—
Oxtail soup	"	42	—	—	1,000	342	—	—
Tapioca	lbs.	4,201	945	184	—	512	—	66
Brandy	bottles	2,736	228	36	—	6,330	—	75
Champagne	"	—	—	—	—	3,000	—	—
Gin	"	4,529	1,874	175	1,000	7,578	—	135
Port	"	868	442	207	—	1,517	—	76
Whisky	"	2,292	590	—	—	2,978	—	60
Claret	"	216	—	46	96	216	—	40
Ale	"	11,820	93	—	—	11,959	—	—
Stout	"	18	4	6	—	28	—	—
Soda water	"	10,296	24,200	864	—	35,360	—	No scale.
Sparklets	"	30,528	864	144	—	31,536	—	—
" charges	"	—	1,350	—	—	1,350	—	—
" powder	"	—	1,000	487	—	—	—	—
Tabloids, soda	"	—	3,400	3,115	—	26,485	—	32
Alum	lbs.	24,998	196	172	—	6,515	—	—
Lime	"	—	—	—	—	1,352	—	—
Chloride of lime	"	984	875	13	—	—	—	—
Disinfecting powder	"	—	2,100	—	—	—	—	—
Izal	gallons	1,305	—	—	2,040	2,193	—	200
Carbolic powder	lbs.	5,678	10	—	—	7,778	—	1,110
Ghi	"	1,307	—	—	—	3,347	—	—
Atta	"	12,380	—	—	—	12,380	—	—
Goor	"	360	—	—	—	360	—	—
Powa	"	5,900	—	—	—	5,900	—	—
Amchur	"	1,760	—	—	—	1,760	—	—
Dhall	"	9,680	—	—	—	9,680	—	—
Tin openers		50	—	—	—	60	—	—
Mustard oil		420	—	110	—	420	—	—
Per. potash		—	—	220	—	110	—	—
Gypsum		—	10	—	—	220	—	—
Sail covers		280	293	—	—	573	—	No scale.

APPENDIX 6.

NOTES ON THE TRANSPORT SYSTEM IN SOUTH AFRICA, 1901—2.

THE change in the character of the operations which occurred towards the end of 1900, and the numbers of flying columns produced by it, necessitated a reorganisation of the Transport Service of the Army in South Africa. Divisions and brigades had vanished, and in their place a swarm of forces were in the field of varying numbers and composition, and known only by their commanders' names. Attached to these were detachments of Transport Companies; but at a time which essentially demanded the presence of many transport depôts such organisations were practically non-existent.

It was the duty of the Ordnance Department to supply transport stores; of the Remount Department to supply transport animals. Units demanded whatever they required direct from the remount depôt or the ordnance stores; but there was little means of checking or controlling their requisitions, and in the absence of any intermediary transport depôts animals and stores were being wasted "like water poured through a sieve";* the small reserves of transport were being squandered, and a system adapted to the changes which had occurred in the organisation of the troops in the field was urgently needed. The importance of mobility was now more than ever dominant; nothing but mule transport was of much service to the columns. Efficient mules were, however, scarce, owing to the facts that the supply from overseas could not always be relied on, that imported animals needed rest after a long sea-voyage before they could leave the remount depôts, and that even after being posted to the Army Service Corps, they required for a time special supervision. Ox transport was still in use for Supply Columns and for local work on the lines of communication, and casualties in oxen were large owing to the prevalent diseases of the country. Moreover, a large proportion of the second-line transport consisted of hired oxen and wagons.

* Report of a Staff Officer for Transport, South Africa.

APPENDIX 6.

The system of hired transport—suitable in a brief campaign—is costly in a protracted war; and the time had come when State-owned transport would be more economical of public funds.* The purchase of the hired transport added greatly to the amount of Government property, and proportionately to the onus of responsibility resting upon the Army Service Corps. It was clear that the number of accounting units was insufficient to cope with the increased amount of Government transport, and that the depôts were unable either to equip the numerous columns with transport or to maintain it in a state of efficiency.

Yet a system productive of economy in animals and vehicles was a prime necessity to the new Commander-in-Chief; for upon the mobility of his columns depended the duration of the war. A reorganisation of the service of transport was therefore initiated in November, 1900, and eventually developed upon the following lines :—

Individual officers were relieved of the double responsibility for supply as well as transport. With regard to the Transport Service, a grave difficulty at once presented itself in the paucity of officers of the Army Service Corps, who were at once trained in and available for the work. This was partially overcome by the employment of attached officers from various branches of the Service. These underwent a preliminary training at the transport depôts, and after a few months' experience, often developed into valuable transport officers.

An Assistant-Adjutant-General for Transport, with an adequate Staff, was appointed at the Headquarters of the Army in Pretoria. By means of a system of weekly, fortnightly and quarterly returns from all officers commanding columns, districts or Transport Companies, as well as from all other transport officers, this official could estimate the amount of Government transport in the four colonies. Staff Officers for Transport were appointed to all the large commands; under them, companies were posted as transport depôts at important centres of distribution. At such points they carried out local transport duties, met the requirements of columns, established grazing farms and repairing workshops; formed a reserve of transport, and offshot similar but smaller affiliated depôts at the minor stations in their districts.

* The discharges of hired wagons began to take effect about August, 1900; by the end of that year little except State-owned transport was in use.

At Bloemfontein, for example, when the new system was initiated, a repairing depôt was established with a large staff of civilian workmen; gradually radiating from this, smaller depôts were formed at Kroonstad, Springfontein, Edenburg, Brandfort, Winburg and Heilbron. Thus, whenever a column touched the railway, a transport depôt was accessible from which vehicles, equipment or animals could be repaired or replaced. The direct demands hitherto made on the Ordnance or Remount Departments were now submitted to the Staff Officer for Transport (Orange River Colony), who met them from his own depôts, which the Ordnance and Remount Departments supplied with reserves of stores and animals sufficient to meet possible requirements. Columns therefore drew what they required from transport depôts upon instructions from the Assistant-Adjutant-General for Transport (Orange River Colony). An example of the working of the system may be given. In April, 1901, Major-General E. L. Elliot's five columns, on reaching Glen after prolonged operations, telegraphed to the Staff Officer for Transport at Bloemfontein that their transport required overhauling and repairing. Within forty-eight hours the columns were refitted by the Assistant-Adjutant-General for Transport and his repairing staff; ninety-six unserviceable vehicles were exchanged; 124 were repaired; over 500 unserviceable wheels were replaced; all harness was repaired or exchanged; 300 mules were issued to replace casualties; and 200 mules were exchanged. In the earlier days of the war such demands for transport stores would have been met directly by the Ordnance Department by means of convoys sent to the columns. This was productive of much waste. It was frequently found that many of these demands had been unnecessary, and that the columns had no means of carrying the stores so issued. For example, a column commander would wire urgently for spare wheels. In response a convoy might meet the column and deliver the wheels; but if the column was just about to march, it had then no time to effect the exchanges, nor could it carry a large number of spare wheels, which therefore would be burned on the veld. There were cases in which large amounts of costly goods were thus wasted. Often, again, when a column received new vehicles or harness in a remote spot it burned the discarded articles, which, perhaps, only a moderate expense would have sufficed to repair and render available for re-issue.

Now, to obviate such useless destruction, column commanders

APPENDIX 6.

were required to shepherd into the local depôts any abandoned vehicle or animal which they had collected on the veld, and the officer in charge of each depôt reported weekly by telegram to the Staff Officer for Transport what reserves of transport he thus acquired or had in hand. He was then authorised to make small issues, or to replace transport on demand whenever he considered this necessary. If, however, the demand was abnormal, he referred to the Assistant-Adjutant-General for Transport, who kept careful count of the general reserve in his command, and applied for more to the Remount or Ordnance Departments as occasion arose.

The depôts kept their workmen busy in repairing all unserviceable vehicles and harness, thus greatly relieving the pressure upon the Ordnance Department. No wagon was now considered utterly unserviceable; it was always immediately put in hand for repair. Local depôts had little difficulty in meeting normal wants: the mules, oxen and vehicles captured on the veld and driven into the depôts by the columns were usually enough to keep pace with the losses caused by wear and tear. For oxen, in particular, no indent was ever made. Depôts were supplied with oxen by the columns, who swept them in from the surrounding country, in numbers more than sufficient to satisfy ordinary requirements.*

Abnormal demands for stores were met by the Staff Officer of the district, who drew first upon his scattered general reserve. For example, when in February, 1901, Lieut.-General French's force approached the Swazi border, an immense convoy was required at short notice, to fill Lüneberg with supplies. In order to muster such a convoy, the Assistant-Adjutant-General for Transport in Natal first concentrated and exhausted the whole of his reserves, then commandeered transport wherever he could find it. Again, when at a later date Brigadier-General Plumer's force arrived in the Orange River Colony from the Transvaal without any transport animals, and was ordered to march again as soon as possible, the Assistant-Adjutant-General for Transport in the Orange River Colony called upon his general reserve and soon found 1,300 mules fit for work.

---

* Captures of oxen were sometimes large; but lung sickness and rinderpest, as well as Boer raids on grazing farms, often invaded the reserves at the transport depôts. Inoculation, which rendered the oxen immune to lung sickness, necessitated throwing them out of work for six weeks, and this, of course, was not always possible.

APPENDIX 7.

NOTES ON THE ROYAL ARMY MEDICAL DEPARTMENT IN SOUTH AFRICA, 1901—2.

THE Medical Department of the Army was less affected than others by the change which at the end of 1900 was occurring in the character of the war. Up to then the maintenance in efficiency of the medical field units and the establishment of hospitals behind the central force advancing towards Pretoria had been of equal importance. With the occupation of Johannesburg and Pretoria, and the establishment of large hospitals in those places, the further advance to the east and the irregular movements which took place both in the Transvaal and the Orange River Colony had little effect on the hospital arrangements. The main centres were already established, and the changes which took place in them were a mere development of their resources.

But inasmuch as the number of columns was now increased while their individual strength was reduced, so additional but smaller medical field units were required. Moreover, as it was impossible to say when and where concentrations of troops might take place, all the hospitals in the Colonies had to be maintained almost at their maximum accommodation, so as to provide for sudden demands for beds consequent on the arrival of a large body of troops. This resulted in local excesses of permanent accommodation, and a dispersion of personnel, where, had the circumstances been different, a concentration both of beds and staff would have been economical.

As the campaign continued, certain districts became quieter, and it was possible to reduce some hospitals in order to enable others to be opened at a distance from the trunk lines, so that the latter might be in touch with the troops as these gradually pushed further into the field and came less frequently to the railway; and finally the development of the system of lines of blockhouses enabled hospitals to be maintained and relieved of their sick by convoy.

The subjoined tables will show the places at which hospitals existed, and the dates on which they were opened and closed.

APPENDIX 7.

General Hospitals.

Name of Hospital.	Station.	No. of Hospital Beds.*	Date of First Return.	Date of Last Return.	Remarks.
1 General Hospital	Wynberg	773	20.10.99	31. 5.02	
2 ,, ,,	{ Wynberg	—	8.12.99	1. 6.00	
	{ Pretoria	672	20. 7.00	31. 5.02	
3 ,, ,,	{ Rondebosch	—	22.12.99	1. 6.00	
	{ Kroonstadt	592	1. 6.00	31. 5.02	
4 ,, ,,	Mooi River	520	12. 1.00	31. 5.02	
5 ,, ,,	Cape Town	940	30. 3.00	31. 5.02	Preceded by Base Hospital, Cape Town, from 13.10.99.
6 ,, ,,	{ Naauwpoort	—	2. 3.00	13. 7.00	
	{ Johannesburg	822	27. 7.00	1.10.01	
7 ,, ,,	{ Estcourt	—	13. 4.00	26.10.00	
	{ Pretoria	692	9.11.00	31. 5.02	
8 ,, ,,	Bloemfontein	814	27. 4.00	31. 5.02	
9 ,, ,,	Bloemfontein	553	20. 4.00	31. 5.02	
10 ,, ,,	{ Bloemfontein	—	4. 5.00	7. 1.01	
	{ Norval's Pont	520	18. 1.01	31. 5.02	
11 ,, ,,	Kimberley	600	18. 5.00	31. 5.02	Preceded by Town Hospital from 20.10.99.
12 ,, ,,	Springfontein	500	11. 5.00	31. 5.02	Formerly Section No. 3 General Hospital.
13 ,, ,,	{ Wynberg	—	20. 7.00	1. 2.01	
	{ Johannesburg	520	3. 5.01	31. 5.02	
14 ,, ,,	Newcastle	520	10. 8.00	31. 5.02	Took over from No. 4 Stationary Hospital.
15 ,, ,,	Howick	536	20. 7.00	31. 5.02	
16 ,, ,,	Elandsfontein	536	1. 2.01	31. 5.02	Formerly No. 2 Statnry. Hosp.
17 ,, ,,	Standerton	520	1. 2.01	31. 5.02	Formerly No. 4 Statnry. Hosp.
18 ,, ,,	Charlestown	520	8. 2.01	31. 5.02	Formerly No. 1 Statnry. Hosp.
19 ,, ,,	Pretoria	201	15. 6.00	31. 5.02	
20 ,, ,,	Elandsfontein	600	1. 3.01	31. 5.02	
21 ,, ,,	Deelfontein	800	5. 4.01	31. 5.02	Formerly Imperial Yeo. Hosp.
22 ,, ,,	Pretoria	520	20. 9.01	31. 5.02	Formerly Imperial Yeomanry Branch Hosp.

Notes.

No. 10 General Hospital took over the town hospitals in Bloemfontein on arrival on 11th April, 1900, and rendered its first return as a general hospital on the date shown.

Nos. 1 to 11, Nos. 13 and 14, were sent out from England; six were formed in South Africa as shown in the column of remarks; the remaining three were entirely formed in South Africa.

* The actual accommodation varied considerably from time to time. The number of beds shown is that available on November 2nd, 1901, in the case of the hospitals that were open on that date. In the case of the hospitals that had been closed before that date, the number shows the accommodation that had previously been available in them.

STATIONARY HOSPITALS.

Name of Hospital.	Station.	No. of Hospital Beds.*	Date of First Return.	Date of Last Return.	Remarks.
1 Stationary Hospital	Frere and Modder Spruit ..	—	12. 1.00	13. 7.00	
	Charlestown ..	—	27. 7.00	1. 2.01	See No. 18 General Hospital.
2 ,, ,,	East London ..	—	22.12.99	8. 6.00	
	Johannesburg .	—	20. 7.00	24. 9.00	
	Elandsfontein..	—	28. 9.00	25. 1.01	See No. 16 General Hospital.
3 ,, ,,	De Aar	370	1.12.99	31. 5.02	
4 ,, ,,	Frere & Chieveley	—	5.12.99	8. 6.00	
	Newcastle	—	15. 6.00	10. 8.00	
	Standerton ...	—	31. 8.00	25. 1.01	See No. 17 General Hospital.
5 ,, ,,	Bloemfontein .	219	6. 4.00	31. 5.02	
6 ,, ,,	Greenpoint ...	6	10.11.99	31. 5.02	
7 ,, ,,	East London ..	250	1.12.99	31. 5.02	No. 2 Stationary Hospital from 22.12.99 to 8.6.00.
8 ,, ,,	Port Elizabeth.	200	1.12.99	31. 5.02	
9 ,, ,,	Queenstown ...	60	23. 3.00	31. 5.02	
10 ,, ,,	Naauwpoort ..	377	13. 7.00	31. 5.02	From Section No. 6 General Hosp.
11 ,, ,,	Winburg	150	1. 6.00	31. 5.02	
12 ,, ,,	Wakkerstroom .	150	7. 9.00	31. 5.02	
13 ,, ,,	Pinetown Bridge	250	20. 4.00	31. 5.02	Formerly Princess Christian Hospital.
14 ,, ,,	Pietermaritzburg	150	13.10.99	31. 5.02	Formerly General Hospital, no number.
15 ,, ,,	Heidelberg	150	13. 7.00	31. 5.02	
16 ,, ,,	Mafeking......	150	10. 8.00	31. 5.02	
17 ,, ,,	Middelburg (Transvaal)..	400	17. 8.00	31. 5.02	
18 ,, ,,	Krugersdorp...	250	27. 7.00	31. 5.02	
19 ,, ,,	Harrismith ...	350	24. 8.00	31. 5.02	
20 ,, ,,	Waterval Onder	120	7. 9.00	31. 5.02	
21 ,, ,,	Machadodorp ..	125	12. 9.00	31. 5.02	
22 ,, ,,	Pietersburg....	100	19. 4.01	31. 5.02	
23 ,, ,,	Warm Bath ...	75	5. 4.01	31. 5.02	
24 ,, ,,	Aliwal North ..	225	30.11.00	31. 5.02	
25 ,, ,,	Johannesburg..	100	4.10.01	4. 4.02	On closing of No. 6 General Hosp.
26 ,, ,,	Beaufort West.	100	3. 5.01	31. 5.02	
27 ,, ,,	Burghersdorp .	90	28.12.00	31. 5.02	
28 ,, ,,	Worcester	60	31. 5.01	2. 5.02	
29 ,, ,,	Heilbron	120	15. 6.00	31. 5.02	
30 ,, ,,	Lindley	180	17. 1.02	31. 5.02	
31 ,, ,,	Ermelo	86	20.12.01	31. 5.02	
32 ,, ,,	Klerksdorp ...	100	22. 6.00	31. 5.02	
33 ,, ,,	Zeerust	100	2.11.00	31. 5.02	
34 ,, ,,	Ladybrand ...	40	29. 6.00	31. 5.02	
35 ,, ,,	Potchefstroom .	100	2.11.00	31. 5.02	
36 ,, ,,	Barberton	200	5.10.00	31. 5.02	

* See previous footnote.

APPENDIX 7.

STATIONARY HOSPITALS (*continued*).

Name of Hospital.	Station.	No. of Hospital Beds.*	Date of First Return.	Date of Last Return.	Remarks.
37 Stationary Hospital	Lydenburg	125	5.10.00	31. 5.02	
38 ,, ,,	Rustenburg ...	100	12.10.00	31. 5.02	
39 ,, ,,	Rietfontein ...	100	19.10.00	31. 5.02	
40 ,, ,,	Dundee	100	12.10.00	31. 5.02	
41 ,, ,,	Ficksburg	143	8. 2.01	31. 5.02	

NOTES.

No. 10, Naauwpoort. Left behind when No. 6 General Hospital was moved to Johannesburg.

No. 14, Pietermaritzburg. The original Station Hospital, Pietermaritzburg, was increased to form a general hospital, which was not numbered, and which was reduced again when the pressure ceased in Natal.

The first five Stationary Hospitals were sent out from England; the remainder were formed in South Africa. Many had been in existence for some time before being given a number, hence the sequence of numbers is not according to dates of opening.

TEMPORARY HOSPITALS.

Name of Hospital.	Station.	No. of Hospital Beds.*	Date of First Return.	Date of Last Return.	Remarks.
Field Hospital	Eshowe	16	13.10.99	31. 5.02	
Palace ,,	Simon's Town .	67	20.10.99	31. 5.02	
Temporary Hospital ..	Naauwpoort ..	20	20.10.99	3.11.99	
Convent ,, ..	Estcourt	100	10.11.99	15. 6.00	
Temporary ,, ..	Nottingham Rd.	12	1.12.99	8.12.99	
,, ,, ..	Putters Kraal..	30	1.12.99	8.12.99	
,, ,, ..	Brynvilla Camp	5	15.12.99	29.12.99	
,, ,, ..	Stellenbosch ..	9	19. 1.00	31. 5.02	
,, ,, ..	Sterkstroom ..	107	16. 2.00	6. 4.00	
,, ,, ..	Klip Drift	16	23. 2.00	16. 3.00	
,, ,, ..	Modder River..	50	23. 3.00	1. 6.00	
,, ,, ..	Orange River .	40	23. 2.00	31. 5.02	
,, ,, ..	Prieska	22	30. 3.00	31. 5.02	
Sanatorium	Claremont.....	50	30. 3.00	7. 6.01	Originally opened December, 1899.
Temporary Hospital ..	Thabanchu ...	20	11. 5.00	31. 5.02	
,, ,, ..	Boshof........	40	18. 5.00	31. 5.02	
,, ,, ..	Norval's Pont..	75	25. 5.00	15.10.00	
,, ,, ..	Smithfield	25	1. 6.00	3. 8.00	
Race Course ,, ..	Pretoria	60	15. 6.00	31. 5.02	
St. Andrew's College Hospital	Bloemfontein ..	61	15. 6.00	4. 1.01	
Temporary Hospital ..	Rouxville	5	15. 6.00	14. 9.00	
,, ,, ..	Dewetsdorp ...	60	29. 6.00	29.11.00	
,, ,, ..	Wepener	26	29. 6.00	25. 1.01	
,, ,, ..	Kroonstadt Hotel	14	29. 6.00	13. 7.00	
,, ,, ..	Lindley	120	6. 7.00	27. 7.00	
,, ,, ..	Viljoen's Drift .	20	20. 7.00	14.10.00	
,, ,, ..	Senekal	80	20. 7.00	24. 8.00	
,, ,, ..	Vereeniging ...	40	20. 7.00	12.10.00	

* See footnote. page 603.

TEMPORARY HOSPITALS (continued).

Name of Hospital.	Station.	No. of Hospital Beds.*	Date of First Return.	Date of Last Return.	Remarks.
Temporary Hospital ,,	Pienaar's Poort	16	24. 8.00	13. 8.01	
,, ,, ,,	Edenburg	25	24. 8.00	31. 5.02	
,, ,, ,,	Vrede	100	19.10.00	15. 3.01	
Railway Rest ,, ,,	Pretoria	—	3. 8.00	17. 1.02	No further returns rendered. Hospital remained open till end of war.
Temporary ,, ,,	Otto's Hoop	4	26.10.00	28.12.00	
,, ,, ,,	Lichtenburg	50	7.12.00	31. 5.02	
,, ,, ,,	Ventersdorp	50	4. 1.01	31. 5.02	
,, ,, ,,	Rouxville	5	21.12.00	4. 1.01	
,, ,, ,,	Vryburg	27	11. 1.01	31. 5.02	
,, ,, ,,	Buluwayo	45	18. 1.01	31. 5.02	
,, ,, ,,	Carnarvon	32	4. 1.01	31. 5.02	
,, ,, ,,	Graaff Reinet	61	4. 1.01	31. 5.02	
,, ,, ,,	Griquatown	5	4. 1.01	31. 5.02	
,, ,, ,,	Frankfort	100	12.10.00	1. 2.01	
,, ,, ,,	Komati Poort	60	22. 2.01	31. 5.02	
,, ,, ,,	Eerstefabrieken	10	17. 8.00	3. 5.01	
,, ,, ,,	Daniel's Kuil	11	26. 4.01	31. 5.02	
,, ,, ,,	Aberdeen	17	21. 6.01	7. 3.02	
,, ,, ,,	Kuruman	14	7. 6.01	31. 5.02	
,, ,, ,,	Cradock	50	12. 7.01	31. 5.02	
,, ,, ,,	Koffyfontein	18	2. 8.01	31. 5.02	
,, ,, ,,	Calvinia	37	21. 6.01	31. 5.02	
,, ,, ,,	Tarkastad	25	31. 5.01	10. 1.02	
,, ,, ,,	Christiana	18	22.11.01	31. 5.02	
,, ,, ,,	Schmidt's Drift	5	23. 8.01	31. 5.02	
,, ,, ,,	Douglas	5	13. 9.01	31. 5.02	
,, ,, ,,	Ladysmith	16	4.10.01	14. 3.02	
,, ,, ,,	Matjesfontein	25	17. 1.02	31. 5.02	
,, ,, ,,	Greytown	24	4.10.01	1.11.01	
,, ,, ,,	Vryheid	50	25.10.01	31. 5.02	
,, ,, ,,	Krantz Kop	18	8.11.01	3. 1.02	
,, ,, ,,	Pienaars River	81	20. 9.01	24. 1.02	
,, ,, ,,	Tiger Kloof	40	24. 1.02	31. 5.02	
,, ,, ,,	Port Nolloth	50	18. 4.02	31. 5.02	
,, ,, ,,	Ladysmith	30	13.10.99	31. 5.02	

NOTES.

This list includes only those temporary hospitals which maintained an independent existence. Those which afterwards became numbered stationary hospitals, or which were merged in other hospitals, have not been included, as, for example, the second hospital at Naauwpoort, which was merged in No. 6 General Hospital on its arrival in Naauwpoort.

On the other hand, several of these temporary hospitals were in existence before the dates shown, but they were then staffed by certain field hospitals and the patients in them were accounted for in the returns from these field hospitals. For example, Modder River Hospital was first opened about the end of December, 1899, but only rendered separate returns from the date shown, when the field hospitals which had staffed it moved into Kimberley and it was furnished with a separate staff. The hospital at Orange River was actually opened in September, 1899, by a detachment from a Cape field hospital, but only entered on an independent existence with a fresh staff after the advance into the Orange Free State, when all the field units were required.

* See footnote, page 603.

APPENDIX 7.

CIVIL HOSPITALS.

Name of Hospital.	Station.	No. of Hospital Beds.*	Date of First Return.	Date of Last Return.	Remarks.
Edinburgh Hospital ...	Norval's Pont..	150	18. 5.00	18. 1.01	
	Deelfontein....	1,000	23. 3.00	29. 3.01	
Imperial Yeomanry Hospitals	Pretoria	530	24. 8.00	13. 9.01	
	McKenzie's Farm	—	24. 8.00	29. 3.01	
	Elandsfontein .	138	19. 7.01	20.12.01	
Irish Hospital	Bloemfontein ..	100	20. 4.00	29. 6.00	
,, ,,	Pretoria	—	15. 6.00	9.11.00	
Langman Hospital	Bloemfontein ..	180	13. 4.00	20. 7.00	
,, ,,	Pretoria	—	3. 8.00	26.10.00	
Portland ,,	Rondebosch ...	160	—	—	No returns. Sick included in No. 3 General Hospital.
,, ,,	Bloemfontein ..	—	27. 4.00	21. 7.00	
Princess Christian Hospital	Pinetown Bridge	200	20. 4.00	—	
Scottish National Hospital	Kroonstadt....	300	8. 6.00	12.10.00	
Welsh Hospital	Springfontein .	200	8. 6.00	3. 8.00	
,, ,,	Pretoria	—	17. 8.00	24. 9.00	

LIST OF HOSPITALS OPENED AFTER NOVEMBER 1ST, 1901.

Unit.	Station.	No. of Hospital Beds.	Date of First Return.	Date of Last Return.	Remarks.
	General Hospitals.—Nil.				
	Stationary Hospitals.				
No. 30 Stationary Hospital	Lindley	180	17. 1.02	31. 5.02	
No. 31 ,, ,,	Ermelo	86	20.12.01	31. 5.02	
	Temporary Hospitals.				
Temporary Hospital	Christiana.....	18	22.11.01	31. 5.02	
,, ,,	Krantz Kop ...	18	8.11.01	3. 1.02	
,, ,,	Matjesfontein .	25	17. 1.02	31. 5.02	
,, ,,	Tiger Kloof....	40	24. 1.02	31. 5.02	
,, ,,	Port Nolloth ..	50	18. 4.02	31. 5.02	

* See footnote, page 603.

Plague.

In November, 1900, cases of plague occurred among natives near King Williams Town, and the Principal Medical Officers of the lines of communication and the base were warned to watch for suspicious cases, and to take precautions. In January, 1901, plague appeared at Cape Town at the docks, and thence spread to the native, and later to the European, population of the city. This was a serious complication, for Cape Town was the principal port for disembarkation of troops and for the discharge of foodstuffs. The preventive measures put in force were the following : (1) Cape Town, as far as possible, ceased to be a port of discharge for supplies. A complete stoppage could not be effected owing to the needs of the western line, and of the troops in Cape Colony itself, but every precaution was taken in the supply depôts to limit the possibility of infection being conveyed by foodstuffs, forage, etc. (2) Cape Town was evacuated as far as possible, particularly Greenpoint Camp, which was close to the docks, and provided the largest number of cases. (3) Movements of troops from Cape Town could not entirely cease, but arrangements were made for the inspection of troops passing up country at the various stations at which the trains halted. In April a conference was held at Cape Town to arrange for common action upon the above lines by the military and civil authorities, and a special plague hospital was established at Maitland, with a bacteriological laboratory. The precautions taken against the conveyance of plague by the moving troops were successful. Of some 900 cases of plague which occurred, only twenty-four belonged to the Imperial forces. One only occurred outside Cape Colony, at Mafeking; there was one near Wellington, another at Port Elizabeth, both of which places were in frequent communication with Cape Town. One case also occurred on board ship, between Cape Town and Durban. Of the remaining twenty cases, eleven occurred at Greenpoint, five in Cape Town itself, and four at Maitland.

Reorganisation of field units.

Owing to the multiplication of small columns, the medical field units were reorganised. It was no longer possible to maintain the field hospitals as distinct from the bearer companies. A unit to fulfil both functions was therefore formed by adding ambulance transport to the field hospitals, or by sending additional equipment to the bearer companies. The total strength and equipment of the combined unit was thus reduced, resulting in greater mobility.

Tongas were found to be useful, or, in their place, Cape carts or the four-wheeled " spiders."

In the operations in Cape Colony the nature of the country made it impossible for wheeled ambulance transport to keep in touch with the troops, and in these conditions, as formerly in Natal and the Eastern Transvaal, the Indian bearers, with dhoolies from the Indian field hospitals, were of service. These men were collected from the various hospitals, and a number of dhoolies were sent down to the colony.

The use of small medical units was only rendered possible by the fact that a column was never long away from its advanced base, and that casualties were limited, while the actual distance to some point on the line of communications was never great. At first columns came to the line to refit ; later they obtained supplies from advanced bases pushed forward into the veld, and here the advanced hospitals were posted, from which the sick left by the columns were conveyed to the hospitals on the line of communications.

When " drives " took place, the hospitals on the line of communications where the " drive " was destined to end, were evacuated so as to make room for the incoming sick, and hospital trains were moved to convenient points so as to meet the columns on their arrival.

Local emergencies in various districts often necessitated the sudden formation and despatch, at short notice, of fresh columns, so that at any time an unforeseen demand for a medical unit might arise. One or two units were generally available to meet such demands. Columns were being constantly broken up, leaving a medical unit unattached. An opportunity would thus arise of bringing it into some central position whence it could be railed to the latest point of concentration. It was not, however, always possible to obtain such early intimation of impending movements as would enable medical units to be sent to join new columns. Such personnel, equipment, and transport as were available in the neighbourhood were in these cases hastily concentrated, and an improvised field unit would be formed from them.

Continuous movements pressed heavily on the personnel of the medical field units. Many were incessantly in the field during the whole period, except for short delays whilst the columns to which they were attached were refitting. The wastage in personnel was therefore large, and it was often difficult to keep units up to strength. Wastage of personnel.

The nucleus was formed of Royal Army Medical Corps N. C. Officers and men, but the rest of the personnel was made up principally of the specially enlisted men of the Royal Army Medical Corps, Cape Medical Staff Corps, and a similar body enlisted under the general term of South African Irregulars, with, for a time, some of the Imperial Hospital and the Imperial Bearer Corps.

Natal Hospitals.

The part played by the Natal hospitals should be mentioned. From the end of 1900 to the close of the war the medical arrangements in Natal remained unchanged. These hospitals were of much importance, for, as already noted, they received the overflow from the hospitals in the Transvaal. A regular system of evacuation was maintained through Natal, *viâ* Durban, to England. Invalids, collected in the hospitals in Pretoria, Johannesburg, and Elandsfontein, from the eastern, northern, and western lines, were transferred by hospital train to the Natal hospitals at Newcastle, Charlestown, Howick, Pietermaritzburg and Pinetown. There, many of the cases recovered, and the rest were sent home by hospital ship or sick transport. From the time when traffic on the line between Elandsfontein and Charlestown had become regular, all the invalids from the Transvaal passed through the Natal hospitals, while all the invalids south of the Vaal passed through Cape Town. The invalids from Harrismith were also sent through Natal, and the hospitals in that colony were thus steadily employed till the end of the war. Both in Natal and Cape Colony hospital camps were established for the reception of officers and men needing rest and change during convalescence, or in the state of exhaustion which induces disease. The chief of these were at Mooi River in Natal, at Wynberg in Cape Colony. The benefits derived were most marked. Many potential invalids were re-equipped for the field, both physically and mentally, by the interlude of quiet thus afforded, whilst many extraordinary recoveries from actual disease were recorded. It is probable that in the future, campaigns of long duration will inevitably demand the institution of such rest camps for the reinvigoration of those whose organisation has temporarily succumbed to the exhausting tension of modern warfare.

The insufficiency of Medical Officers.

It had been foreseen that the establishment of officers of the Royal Army Medical Corps would not be sufficient for the needs of the field force, and from the first civil surgeons formed a large proportion of the staff of the general hospitals despatched from England.

APPENDIX 7.

Later, civil surgeons sent by the War Office, or engaged locally, were employed in every capacity—in medical charge of regiments, with field medical units, in ambulance trains, in the smaller hospitals, and in charge of posts on the line, as well as in the general and stationary hospitals.

Up to the end of 1901, of the total number of medical officers employed, about forty-two per cent. only, were officers of the Royal Army Medical Corps. Of the remainder, about four per cent. were Militia, Volunteer, and Colonial officers, while the remaining fifty-four per cent. were civil surgeons, of whom about forty per cent. were engaged by the War Office. In 1902 the officers of the Royal Army Medical Corps numbered about forty per cent., the War Office civil surgeons about forty-six per cent., and those locally engaged about ten per cent.

Before the outbreak of the war there were a number of medical men, who had been in practice in the Transvaal, in the larger towns of the English colonies, especially in Cape Town and Pietermaritzburg. Many of these, being without employment, at once offered themselves for service as civil surgeons, and were engaged. As the war continued more medical men became available. Some were driven from their practices as the result of the war, others arrived in the country in the hope of obtaining employment. With certain exceptions, practically every medical man who offered himself locally was engaged. In addition to the civil surgeons engaged locally for general service it was always convenient to utilise the services of medical men in practice in many of the smaller towns (especially in the Orange River Colony and Cape Colony), to look after the smaller bodies of troops stationed there, or parties of sick and wounded dropped by the columns in improvised hospitals. Many of these did good work and set free the general service personnel for more urgent duties. The senior medical officer of a column was thus enabled to arrange for the care and custody of the patients whom he left behind. Most of these civil surgeons had considerable local influence among the Boers, and so ensured better treatment for isolated parties of sick than could have been obtained for them by a stranger to the district. The Principal Medical Officer in South Africa recorded his opinion that the civil surgeons sent out from England at the beginning of the war were, on the whole, more efficient than the majority of those who came out later, the latter being for the most part young men, fresh from the hospitals ; and that, of the civil surgeons engaged in Africa, some were exceptionally good men, whose local knowledge, and practical experience of the country, were particularly valuable. In addition to the civil surgeons, a certain small proportion of colonial medical officers were employed during the war. Most of these belonged to certain units, *e.g.*, the Canadian Field Hospital, the New South Wales Ambulance, and the Cape Medical Staff Corps.

Nursing Sisters. Brief mention must also be made of the work of the Nursing Sisters.

The authorised establishment of Sisters for a general hospital was one lady superintendent and eight sisters. This number was found to be insufficient, owing to the paucity of trained orderlies of the Royal Army Medical Corps, and the staff of Sisters was increased to an average of five for every hundred beds. This proportion was prescribed as the standard to be maintained. The Nursing Sisters were obtained from four sources—the Army Nursing Service, the Army Nursing Service Reserve, the Colonial Sisters, and those locally engaged in South Africa. The following tabular statement shows the approximate composition per cent. of the Nursing Service in South Africa in the months given :—

	Army Nursing Service.	Army Nursing Service Reserve.	Colonial.	Locally Engaged.
June, 1900....	9	57	1	32
May, 1901	6	71	4	19
May, 1902	8	74	4	14

In addition to the nurses employed in the hospitals in South Africa, a large number were employed on the sick transports and hospital ships..

During the war 337 nurses were engaged at Cape Town, of whom 216 were for duty in the homeward-bound transports, the remainder for duty in the hospitals on shore. Mention must also be made of the Nursing Sisters from the oversea colonies. They came from Queensland, Victoria, New South Wales, South Australia, Western Australia, Tasmania, and New Zealand, while Canada also sent others in November, 1899, and February, 1900, and again in 1901. Most of these Sisters were originally sent free of expense to the

APPENDIX 7.

Imperial Government, their services having been engaged either by their respective Governments or by private societies. Others came with recommendations from their colonies, and were engaged immediately on their arrival in South Africa. The Principal Medical Officer in South Africa placed on record his opinion that by far the most efficient of the nurses obtained from all outside sources were those who came from the staffs of the large hospitals in the British Islands.

"Invaliding" was carried out in the army in South Africa much more freely than has been usually considered necessary on foreign service. At first the probable duration of the war was underestimated, and many were invalided home in the belief that they would not again be fit for duty before the end of the campaign. Later it became probable that a man might be sent home and return in time to take part in the war for a second time. In fact, many such invalids rejoined their units long before the cessation of hostilities. A rapid rate of invaliding diminished the pressure on the hospitals in South Africa, where the accommodation was often strained. The hospital ships and sick transports provided early accommodation for all who were fit to travel. It was unnecessary (as is the case in ordinary peace conditions) that an invalid should wait a considerable time for a transport. A sick man was therefore often sent home for recovery, when, under peace conditions, he would have recovered and returned to duty before an opportunity of embarking him occurred. It was actually more economical to provide for cases on a returning transport than to accommodate them in Africa. There were, however, certain conditions inherent in the Army in South Africa (not shared by other British expeditionary forces) which tended to raise unduly the percentage of invalids in its ranks; and these conditions should severally be recorded. In addition to the Regulars, the Army was composed of Militia, Volunteers and Yeomanry, as well as of various corps of over-sea Colonials. The physique of the first Regular troops (including a large proportion of the Reserves) was excellent. Afterwards, the quality deteriorated, and reached its lowest level when the last drafts arrived containing many immature lads of poor physique. The Militia were, in general, physically inferior to the Regulars: a large proportion were only eighteen years of age, whereas in the Regulars, Volunteers, and Imperial Yeomanry the average was twenty years. The Volunteers

"Invaliding."

were, generally, of good physique, as were the first contingent of Imperial Yeomanry. The succeeding contingents of Yeomanry were less satisfactory, while the last contained many men and some officers who should never have been sent from England.

The rate of invaliding in a composite army must always be greater than among an equal number of men regularly enlisted. In the latter case, even after the primary and stringent medical test, a process of elimination has developed, causing the weaker to drop out during the early period of their service, and leaving the fittest to survive. Amongst the auxiliary units in the South African War this normal elimination was in process during the whole campaign, and at an accelerated rate, owing to the conditions of campaigning. The rate of invaliding in such an army is therefore not comparable with that obtaining in one composed solely of regular troops.

Other causes contributed to increase the percentage of invalids. It has been stated that as the campaign proceeded, the quality of the recruits deteriorated. There was no doubt that much of this deterioration was due to want of care in the medical examination of men for active service. At the beginning of the war the examination was in the hands of the officers of the Royal Army Medical Corps, who have a practical knowledge of what is required of soldiers on service. But when the home stations were denuded of officers of the Royal Army Medical Corps, the examinations were made by those who did not possess this special knowledge—and were often not conducted with the necessary care. The Militia showed a larger proportion of men who should not have been sent out than either the Regular troops or the Volunteers, but the last contingent of Imperial Yeomanry was by far the worst in this respect.

The over-sea Colonials were of good physique, as were the earlier regiments of South African Colonials; but as the campaign continued the proportion of unsuitable men enlisted in the South African irregular forces increased till it became a serious question. They blocked the hospitals, and were a source of needless expense. Recruiting for these corps was little under control. Each had its own surgeon (locally engaged by the officer commanding the corps), who examined the recruits obtained at the headquarters of the corps, while other recruits were sent up from their base depôts. No other arrangement was possible, for officers of the Royal Army Medical Corps could not be spared from their important duties.

APPENDIX 7.

Officers in the Transvaal were invalided by Boards in Pretoria and Elandsfontein, under the Principal Medical Officer of the district. Similar Boards officiated in Natal; in Cape Town a standing Medical Board was early established for this purpose.

The hospital train service, as used during the campaign, may be classified as follows :— *Hospital trains.*

(1) *Hospital trains*, specially fitted, equipped, and staffed as such, for "lying-down cases." They were usually composed of seven coaches, and carried ninety-two patients and a staff averaging twenty-two.

(2) *Improvised Hospital Trains.*—These were, as a rule, first-class corridor-carriage trains, with a kitchen-car attached, for the conveyance of less severe cases and of convalescents. A medical officer accompanied each convoy of sick, but there was no permanent staff.

(3) *Ambulance Coaches.*—These were specially fitted carriages placed at convenient intervals on the railways. They were used to pick up small parties of sick from the various posts along the lines, and were attached to passing trains for conveyance to the nearest hospital. Many had a regular service, usually twice a week up and down their own stretch of line. As a rule one N.C. Officer and one orderly were attached for duty to these carriages, and the medical officers along the lines of communication attended to the wants of the sick as the carriages passed the various posts.

During the period of the war 3,116 officers and 72,314 warrant and N. C. Officers and men were shipped to England as invalids from South Africa. *Hospital ships.*

Their transport by sea was carried out by hospital ships and sick transports; smaller parties were despatched by the mail and "intermediate" steamships from Cape Town and Durban.

The hospital ships were of two classes :—

(1) Those fitted and equipped in England.

(2) Those prepared in South Africa.

(1) Of those fitted and equipped in England, the *Spartan*, with accommodation for 132 sick, and the *Trojan*, for 144 sick, were fitted out by the Admiralty for the War Office.

In addition to these, the Red Cross Society fitted out and equipped the *Princess of Wales* (accommodating 184 sick). The *Maine*, with accommodation for 163 sick, was provided by a group of American ladies. The above ships ceased to be employed a considerable time before the end of the war.

(2) The hospital ships prepared in South Africa were selected and converted at Durban by the Naval Transport Department on requisition from the Principal Medical Officer.

The ships were : *Nubia* (284 sick), *Lismore Castle* (214 sick), *Orcana* (209 sick), *Simla* (278 sick), *Avoca* (302 sick), and *Dunera* (284 sick). A regular service was maintained by these vessels between Durban (and Cape Town) and England, and was carried on to the end of the campaign.

Even this fleet was insufficient to cope with the number of sick and wounded sent home, and full use was made of the large passenger ships which arrived with troops and would have returned empty to England. These required no structural alteration; the accommodation for invalids was ample and good; and a suitable medical staff was placed on each vessel, with the necessary stores and equipment.

NOTE.—For numbers wounded, deaths from wounds and disease, invalided, etc., see Appendix 16.

APPENDIX 8.

NOTES ON THE ARMY ORDNANCE DEPARTMENT IN SOUTH AFRICA.

Ordnance Stores were obtained principally upon orders originating at Woolwich Arsenal and the Royal Army Clothing Department; but large quantities of articles were drawn from India,* and local purchases were also made in order to supplement supplies from home.† These sources of supply were further augmented by the establishment of workshops, which were mainly engaged in repairing equipment, but also executed manufactures when necessary. Under the Inspectors of Ordnance-Machinery, some excellent emergency work was done, such as the mounting of the 9.2-in., 6-in. and 5-in. B.L. guns on railway and travelling carriages, and the retubing of the 12-pr. B.L. guns.

In addition to providing for all the wants of the Army,‡ the camp followers, the native drivers, etc., and the labour depôts—the Ordnance Department equipped the various burgher and refugee camps with tents, furniture, utensils and clothing; received and stored all articles of equipment or of store which were not required by the troops, the arms and equipment of the dead, and of the captured, and carried out periodical technical inspections of guns, vehicles and ammunition in the hands of the troops. The largest number of persons employed upon these multifarious duties in South Africa under this Department (including natives) numbered 2,060. The prime difficulty in the supply of ordnance stores to so great a force for so long a period and at such a distance from its bases, lay in the obstacles to distribution caused by the congestion of the single

* Notably : Boots, helmets, tentage, " British warm " coats and frocks.

† Principally of transport stores and equipment. The cost of such local purchases of ordnance stores throughout the war averaged some £25,000 per mensem. These purchases were made as far as possible by tender.

‡ Except food, forage and fuel.

lines of railway; but from 300 to 500 trucks a month were usually allotted to the Ordnance Department for the carriage of their stores from the four Base Ports* to the Depôts up-country.

The system on which Ordnance Depôts were formed was briefly as follows :—

An Issuing and Receiving Depôt was established when the number of troops at any place justified its existence, and the required stores were pushed up to it from the Base Depôts. As the troops worked forward, Transit and Repair Depôts were opened at suitable places. When necessary, the Transit Depôt was expanded into an Issuing and Receiving Depôt, and this in its turn threw out further Transit Depôts as required. On each Line, or where necessary, portions of Lines, a Chief Ordnance Officer was placed in charge, with Headquarters at the Central Depôt of the area which he controlled. He arranged for the forwarding of stores from the Base, moved personnel and stores from one Depôt to another to meet fresh concentrations of troops, opening and closing Transit Depôts when necessary. Owing to the fact that there were no Ordnance Officers with the troops in the field—the Department being represented only on the Lines of Communication—there was frequently delay and confusion, on the one side in ascertaining the actual wants of the troops, on the other as to the spots whence ordnance stores could be drawn. The lack of Ordnance Officers in the Field was, in fact, so greatly felt, that an organisation has since been approved whereby an Ordnance Officer is henceforward to be attached to each Division in the field. In addition to the Chief Ordnance Officers of Lines and Areas, and the officers at the different Depôts, there was a Principal Ordnance Officer of the Army, and a Chief Ordnance Officer of the Lines of Communication on the Western Line and also in Natal. The Headquarters of the Army Ordnance Department in Cape Town and Natal worked practically on independent lines up to July, 1901. The Principal Ordnance Officer and his Staff then moved to Pretoria, and the Department was reorganised in five areas, each under a Chief Ordnance Officer directly responsible to the Principal Ordnance Officer. These areas were as follows :—

    1. Cape Colony south of De Aar.
    2. Western Line from De Aar to Buluwayo and Western Transvaal.

* See Table at end of this Appendix.

APPENDIX 8.

3. Orange River Colony (excluding Harrismith area).
4. Transvaal (except Standerton area and New Republic).
5. Natal, including Zululand, Standerton and Harrismith areas, and the New Republic.

The provision of stores was entrusted, under the authority of the Principal Ordnance Officer, to a Chief Ordnance Officer of the Base Ports with Headquarters at Cape Town.

The following is a list in detail of the distribution of the Ordnance Depôts formed throughout the war :—

WESTERN LINE.

Cape Town............Opened as a Grand Base Depôt October 11th, 1899. Large Base Workshops were eventually formed in which some 400 men were employed. A Transit Depôt was formed at the Dock for reception of stores landed from vessels.

Stellenbosch........... Opened October 4th, 1899, in connection with a scheme for mobilisation of units after landing; closed December 9th, 1899.

De Aar................The First Advanced Depôt opened October 10th, 1899, to meet the wants of the 1st Division and eventually to supply the Army under Lord Roberts prior to its march on Bloemfontein. It remained a large Issuing and Receiving Depôt throughout the war.

Orange River ....Transit and Repair and small Issuing Depôt to facilitate supply of the Army concentrating in the vicinity, opened November 16th, 1899; closed April 1st, 1900.

Modder River..........Transit Depôt, opened December, 1899, for distribution of stores for the Army; closed March 11th, 1900.

Kimberley ....Opened February 25th, 1900, as a Transit Depôt for forwarding stores after the Army *en route* for Bloemfontein. Eventually formed into large Issuing and Receiving Depôt and remained so throughout.

Vryburg ....Small Transit Depôt, opened May 20th, 1900, and closed shortly afterwards.

Mafeking..............Opened June 11th, 1900, as a Transit Depôt ; extended to a Receiving and Issuing Depôt. It took up the supply of the Rhodesian Field Force on its arrival from the North.

Buluwayo (Rhodesia) ...Opened January 8th, 1901, for troops operating in the vicinity.

Piquetberg Road.......Transit Depôt, opened January 11th, 1901 ; closed April 8th, 1901; reopened March 5th, 1902, and closed a few weeks later.

Victoria Road..........Transit Depôt, opened April 7th, 1902 ; closed shortly afterwards.

Port Nolloth...........For supply of Namaqualand Field Force; opened May 11th, 1902.

Eastern Line.

East London...........Base Depôt, opened October 26th, 1899, to meet wants of 3rd Division, and later to facilitate landing of stores to Army in South Africa at large.

Queenstown ....Opened November 8th, 1899, as an Issuing and Receiving Depôt to meet wants of 3rd Division ; moved December 18th, 1899.

Sterkstroom ....Closed May 12th, 1900.

Aliwal North ....Opened December 1st, 1900.

Midland Line.

Port Elizabeth ....Base Depôt, opened November 1st, 1899, for supply of units on Midland Line and to facilitate landing of stores for the Army in South Africa at large. This formed the main Clothing Depôt throughout the war.

Naauwpoort ....Issuing and Receiving Depôt, opened November 28th, 1899, for supply of Cavalry Division and troops working in operations near Colesberg.

APPENDIX 8.

Rensburg ....Repair and Transit Depôt, including supply of ammunition, opened end of December, 1899; evacuated at midnight February 13th, 1900, and moved to Arundel on retirement of the Force.

Bloemfontein ....Opened as a small Depôt March 18th, 1900, to take over captured arms and ammunition; extended to a large Issuing and Receiving Depôt with extensive workshops, and remained one of the principal Depôts throughout the War. Up to June, 1901, Bloemfontein acted as a base for the Transvaal.

Springfontein ....Opened April 22nd, 1900, as a Transit Depôt chiefly; closed August 18th, 1900; re-opened May 14th, 1901, and closed November 25th, 1901.

Johannesburg..........Opened June 12th, 1900, for taking over captured arms and ammunition; extended to a Receiving and Issuing Depôt; closed April 20th, 1902.

Pretoria...............Opened as a Receiving and Issuing Depôt June 19th, 1900; extensive workshops formed. It remained one of the principal Depôts throughout the war.

Kroonstad ....Opened for Transit work June 24th, 1900; extended to a Receiving and Issuing Depôt, and remained open until near the close of the war.

Graaff Reinet..........Opened January 10th, 1901, as a Receiving and Issuing Depôt; closed February 20th, 1902.

Middelburg (Transvaal)..Opened as a Receiving and Issuing Depôt April 2nd, 1901.

Winburg (O.R.C.).......Opened November 27th, 1901; closed June 17th, 1902. Issuing and Receiving Depôt.

Klerksdorp............Opened as an Issuing and Receiving Depôt March 25th, 1902.

NATAL.

Durban ....Base Transit Depôt for stores landed from vessels ; remained open throughout the war.

Pietermaritzburg ....Grand Base Depôt ; remained one of the principal Ordnance Depôts throughout the war.

Mooi River ....Small Advanced Depôt ; closed after relief of Ladysmith.

Estcourt ....Small Advanced Depôt ; closed after relief of Ladysmith.

Frere ....Small Advanced Depôt ; closed after relief of Ladysmith.

Colenso ....Formed when Tugela Heights had been secured ; closed shortly before the move from Ladysmith.

Ladysmith ....Opened when hostilities appeared imminent. Supplied troops throughout the siege in conjunction with an Indian Ordnance Park. The stores of the latter were taken over by A.O.D. after the relief. Closed November, 1901.

Harrismith ....Issuing and Receiving Depôt formed after occupation of the place, and remained open until close of war.

Dundee ....Small Depôt and Magazine, chiefly for Transit work ; closed in November, 1901.

Newcastle ....Issuing and Receiving Depôt with workshop formed on occupation of the town after advance from Ladysmith ; remained open throughout the war.

Volksrust..............Opened as Advanced Depôt when Sir R. Buller crossed the border into the Transvaal ; closed later.

APPENDIX 8. 623

Standerton ....Issuing and Receiving Depôt opened for troops operating in Eastern Transvaal; remained open throughout the war.

RHODESIAN FIELD FORCE.

The Rhodesian Field Force was equipped with stores purchased by the British South Africa Company, chiefly from private firms, and were not as a rule of service patterns. These were eventually taken over by the A.O.D.

The following Depôts were established :—

Marandellas ....Base Depôt for Rhodesian Field Force, opened April 28th, 1900 ; closed October 26th, 1900.

Buluwayo (R.F.F.)......Opened June 8th, 1900 ; closed January 7th, 1901.

Victoria..............Opened August 21st, 1900 ; closed December 18th, 1900.

Mafeking (R.F.F.). .....Opened August 1st, 1900 ; closed as a R.F.F. Depôt October 15th, 1900.

Tuli ....Opened November 5th, 1900 ; closed December 10th, 1900.

When the Imperial Yeomanry arrived in South Africa they at first formed Ordnance Depôts of their own at Maitland, Bloemfontein, Kimberley, Mafeking and Pretoria; but, since the Yeomanry had of necessity to be equipped from Army Ordnance Depôts, confusion was caused and the remaining stocks at the Yeomanry Store Depôts were eventually taken over by the Army Ordnance Department about the end of 1900. The Yeomanry Depôts were then closed.

There were, in addition, in Cape Colony and Natal, Ordnance Depôts under the Cape and Natal Colonial Forces ; also, during the early part of the war, yet another group under the Indian Ordnance Department—a multiplication of sources of supply which often caused complications when the time came for final adjustment.

Appended is a list of some items which were sent out from England during the war, *over and above the complete equipments taken out by all the troops:* it must be borne in mind that they were, in many cases, largely supplemented from other sources as above described :—

Small-arm and machine-gun ammunition..	137,000,000 rounds.
12-pr. and 15-pr. gun ammunition	456,000 ,,
12-pr. and 15-pr. guns	422
Machine guns	315
Rifles	117,700
Saddlery, sets	76,000
Blankets	1,246,600
Tents	93,000
Transport wagons and carts..	3,800
Ambulance wagons	350
Stretchers (hospital)	7,300
Sets of mule harness	119,000
Horse and mule shoes	3,772,400
Head-dresses	1,336,400
Garments	7,556,000
Shirts	1,700,000
Boots and shoes	2,820,000 pairs.
Socks	2,750,000 ,,

There were also equipped and shipped from Woolwich Arsenal five complete Stationary Hospitals, sixteen General Hospitals (of 520 beds each), and two Ship Hospitals; six spare Batteries of Field Artillery and two Batteries of Horse Artillery.

APPENDIX 9.

NOTES ON THE ARMY POST OFFICE CORPS IN SOUTH AFRICA.

AT the beginning of the campaign the strength of this corps was three officers, eighty-nine other ranks, composing one company of the 24th Middlesex (Post Office) Volunteers. These men, like all the 24th Middlesex, were drawn from the London Post Offices, and were those who had been specially enlisted for a period of six years in the Army Reserve to render them available for foreign service. This original force, which proceeded to the seat of war in October, 1899, soon became totally inadequate to the growing needs of the Army. Reinforcing drafts followed rapidly, drawn at first from the 24th Middlesex, but later from the postal services of all the provinces of Great Britain, and even to a small extent from those of Canada, Australia, Cape Colony and India. The greatest strength attained at the height of the campaign was ten officers, a warrant officer, and 396 other ranks, with, in addition, twenty civilian clerks and 100 soldiers attached for orderly duties.

ORGANISATION.

The system was founded upon a Base Office at Cape Town (a base office for Natal at Pietermaritzburg was employed in the earlier part of the campaign, but discontinued later). From this radiated a number of forwarding offices, which served for intermediate despatch of mail matter, and for the reception and forwarding of cross-post letters. Next, the fixed camp and station post offices, seventy-one in number, dealt directly with the receipt and delivery of mails to the troops at and around normal centres of operation. Finally, there was a system of travelling post offices, which, traversing the railways in box trucks and sorting carriages specially fitted up by the

Imperial Military Railways, delivered and received mail matter, cashed and sold postal orders at any spot upon the lines where their services were required.

The bulk of the work which fell to the Army Post Office Corps was naturally that of the distribution of the inward mails and the exporting of the mails for oversea. The former presented extraordinary difficulties. The railway service, being completely beyond the control of the Post Office Department, could not be relied on for automatic delivery of the mails. Trains were apt to be delayed for military purposes, or by the enemy who frequently destroyed them. In the latter case the Post Office men on the train would be called upon to take rifle in hand and defend their charge. Thus at Roodewaal,* June 7th, 1900, an officer and nineteen men of the A.P.O.C. fought with the troops, and lost five killed and wounded, and fifteen taken prisoners. On that occasion 2,000 bags of mails were destroyed by the enemy, and postal stock (stamps, postal orders, etc.) lost to the value of £4,284. On two other occasions travelling post offices were captured by the enemy. Another complication was that units and individuals were in incessant movement and flux. Forces were broken up or transported rapidly from one end of the theatre of war to the other, or were perhaps unapproachable, or even not to be traced at the required moment. Individual officers and men constantly, and several times in a short period, left their units for duty in other parts, for hospital, for leave of absence, or for home. Their letters and parcels were frequently insufficiently addressed. "Private Smith, Field Force, S. Africa," was an actual conundrum which regularly confronted the Post Office officials. Many correspondents, too, instead of quoting the corps of the intended receiver of their missive, would merely inscribe his last address, possibly that of a place at which he had only halted for a few hours or minutes. Finally, very many men—*e.g.*, the batches of Imperial Yeomanry—arrived in South Africa without regimental numbers, posted to no unit, and generally almost unidentifiable as soon as they had disappeared into the enormous whirlpool of the campaign. In short, there was no difficulty with regard to the actual identification of packages which did not present itself in full measure at every arrival of a mail.

* See Volume III., page 130

APPENDIX 9.

With all these, and many other formidable difficulties, the A.P.O.C. coped with, in general, extraordinary ingenuity and success. The greatest obstacle in the early part of the campaign, that of getting timely information of the multitudinous movements of detached units and men, was surmounted by the institution of a system of rolls, which were sent weekly from all hospitals, depôts, departmental corps, casualty offices, etc., into the Base Office at Cape Town. Alphabetical lists of names were carefully compiled from these. So elaborate became the system of listing, that the A.P.O.C. was often able to furnish other military departments with the whereabouts of an individual who had got out of ken.

The mode adopted of distributing an incoming mail was briefly as follows : Since mobile units instead of fixed stations had to be dealt with, the sorting, instead of being divided into " roads," was divided according to military units. It was next sub-sorted into twenty-four alphabetical divisions, which on comparison with the above-mentioned alphabetical lists, furnished at once information regarding any detached addressee. The " redirections " were divided into two classes : (i.) " ordinary," *i.e.*, individuals who were constantly absent from their proper units on detached duty ; (ii.) " casual," such as patients in hospital, persons on leave of absence etc. An A.P.O.C. officer was allocated a certain batch of units as his peculiar charge, and these he catered for, irrespective of their geographical position at the moment. To economise time, labour and expense in telegraphing, etc., each unit was given a code number, which it bore throughout the campaign in all the offices of the A.P.O.C. Latterly, when the troops became almost exclusively embodied in mobile columns, columns superseded corps as Post Office units. The mails for the several columns were then made up separately, so that even if consigned to an abandoned address, they could be redirected *en bloc*, diverted to any point, and, if necessary, follow the columns about until caught up.

The following figures relative to the extent of the dealings of the A.P.O.C. may prove of interest :—

(i.) Greatest number of Army Post Offices at work, 71.

(ii.) Average number of articles received each week at Cape Town
- Letters 190,000
- Newspapers and packets 300,000
- Parcels 8,400

(iii.) Heaviest mail received (December 24th, 1901).. { Letters 303,000
Newspapers, etc. 368,000
Parcels.............. 31,858

(iv.) Value of Postal Orders sold in the field............ } More than £1,000,000.

(v.) Casualties of A.P.O.C..... { Killed, 2; wounded, 3; died of disease, 45.

(vi.) Average weekly account rendered to the Comptroller and Accountant-General, London................ £400,000

APPENDIX 10.

NOTES ON THE MILITARY RAILWAY SYSTEM IN SOUTH AFRICA.

THE main duties of a Director of Military Railways and his staff may be briefly summarised as follows :—

(1.) To be the intermediaries between the Army and the technical working administration of the railway.

(2.) To see that the ordinary working of the railway is carried on in such a manner as to ensure the greatest military efficiency.

(3.) To satisfy the demands of the Army on the railway without disorganising the working of the railway system as a whole.

In war these services are essential, for the officers of a *civil* railway administration cannot discriminate between the demands of the various branches and departments of the Army, or class them in order of urgency.

The question of organisation in South Africa had been deliberated by Brevet-Major E. P. C. Girouard, R.E., the officer appointed to be Director of Railways (D.R.) during his voyage to the seat of war. It was tentatively decided that

(i.) As regards those lines of railway under efficient civil control in friendly parts of the country, the Director would act only as intermediary between the Headquarters Staff of the Army and the Civil Administration.

(ii.) In disaffected country the Director would assume full control of the lines, naming them "Communication Sections" for military purposes. To enable him to carry out his duties he was to be in close communication with the Governing Power, the Railway Boards and the General Managers of the Railways.

(iii.) It was necessary to appoint a staff of R.E. officers acquainted with technical railway working, whose duty it would be to co-operate with the civilian staff of the railways in meeting military demands.

(iv.) "Communication Sections" were to be controlled by officers styled Assistant Directors of Railways (A.D.R.). They were to be under the orders of the General of Communications within whose district their line ran, and under the D.R., and were to co-operate with the General Managers of lines within the district.

(v.) Deputy A.D.R.'s were to be stationed at Divisional Traffic points. These officers were to be under the A.D.R.'s and were to co-operate with the civil officials.

(vi.) Under the orders of D.A.D.R.'s were to be Railway Staff Officers (R.S.O.), who were to superintend the movement and transport of troops at railway stations.

(vii.) An A.D.R. "Communications" was to act for the Director in details of civil railway policy; it would be his duty also, in consultation with the officers already named, to formulate and to submit for the approval of the G.O.C. and of the Director all orders and proposals relating to movements of troops and stores, diversions of rolling stock, interruptions to ordinary traffic, and the protection of trains and railway property.

The principle underlying these proposals was the creation of a Military Staff corresponding grade by grade with the civil organisation. A lack of properly trained officers was at once felt. For the Cape lines three D.A.D.R.'s were required, as well as an A.D.R. and an R.S.O. at Cape Town; whereas only two officers in all were available. Accordingly, the Eastern and Midland Sections were not provided for.

Nor had there as yet been laid down any clear rules regarding the relative duties of the General Staff of the Lines of Communication and the Staff of the Director of Railways. Consequently, Commandants on the Lines of Communication were ignorant of the position and duty of the Military Controlling Staff under the D.R. A step towards regulating matters was therefore made by the publication of the following order:—

LINES OF COMMUNICATION ORDERS.

No. 687, DATED DECEMBER 27TH, 1899.

Duties of Staff Officers, Lines of Communication Railways :—

(1.) The working of the railways is carried out by the civil staff of the Cape Government Railways with a staff of military officers to assist and direct the military traffic. This staff forms part of the staff of the L. of C., and is the only means of communication authorised between the military authorities and the civil railway officials.

(2.) The Military Railway Staff will consist of :—

(i.) One A.D.R., on the staff of the Inspector-General Lines of Communication (head office, Cape Town), in charge of all communications.

(ii.) One D.A.D.R., on the staff of the Assistant I.G. L. of C., Western Section (head office, De Aar), in charge of Western Section, Cape Town to Modder River.

(iii.) One D.A.D.R., on the staff of the A.I.G. L. of C., Midland Section (head office, Naauwpoort), in charge of Port Elizabeth to Naauwpoort, Naauwpoort to De Aar, and Rosmead to Stormberg.

(iv.) One D.A.D.R., on the staff of the A.I.G. L. of C., Eastern Section (head office, Queenstown), in charge of East London to Stormberg.

(v.) One D.A.D.R., on the staff of the Base Commandant and as S.O. to A.D.R. (head office, Cape Town), in charge Cape Town only.

(vi.) R.S.O.'s on the staffs of the Station Commandants, at stations as required.

(3.) The duties of the various Staff Officers on the railway are as follows :—

The Assistant Director of Railways is responsible for the whole working of Railway L. of C., and is the channel through which should pass all communications on Railway (Communications) matters from the I.G. L. of C. and the D.R. He should keep up a complete account of the state of traffic and position of rolling stock on the railway, and should keep in touch with the General Traffic Manager of the system. He should keep himself informed, through the D.I.G. and A.I.G. L. of C., of the work carried out by D.A.D.R.'s, and see that proper control is exercised over the districts in their charge.

(4.) *Deputy Assistant Directors of Railways*, under the orders of the D.I.G. and A.I.G. L. of C., should keep themselves completely informed of the state of traffic in their sections. They should, through the Station Commandants, exercise a general supervision over the work of the railway staff in their districts. They should keep careful watch on the distribution of rolling stock on their sections, and are responsible that it is utilised in the best way. They should keep in touch with the Traffic Manager of their sections of the Railway. No work of any nature will be undertaken by the Civil Railway Department for the Military, unless the approval of the D.A.D.R. has previously been obtained. The D.A.D.R. is responsible that any irregularity on his section, which he cannot rectify himself, is reported to the A.I.G. L. of C. The office of the D.A.D.R. should be located at the same station as that of the District Traffic Manager, and he is responsible that either himself or his Staff Officer is present at that station.

(5.) *Railway Staff Officers*, under the orders of the Station Commandants, are responsible for the traffic at the stations where they are located. They are responsible that no train is delayed for military requirements, except in extremely urgent cases on the authority of the Station Commandant. They are especially responsible for seeing that trucks loaded with military stores are released as quickly as possible. They should report immediately to their D.A.D.R. any deficiency or irregularity of traffic in their stations. They should similarly address their D.A.D.R. on any questions concerning railway matters on which they require information or orders. They are responsible for all detraining and entraining operations at their stations, and the comfort of all troops passing

APPENDIX 10.

through. They will furnish such returns on railway matters as may be required to their D.A.D.R. direct. All communications from R.S.O.'s must be sent through Station Commandants.

It was thus sought to modify the original organisation by allotting to the A.D.R.'s and D.A.D.R.'s definite positions on the L. of C. staff; and, though R.S.O.'s remained on the staffs of Station Commandants, the circumstances under which they were to refer to D.A.D.R.'s were specified.

A similar system to that adopted upon the Cape Government Railways was put in force when Lord Roberts advanced into the Orange Free State and the Transvaal. The *Imperial Military Railways* (I.M.R.) were then created. The obstacles to smooth handling of traffic in the Orange Free State were at first serious; the bridges at Norval's Pont and Bethulie (giving access to the railways of Cape Colony) were broken, all rolling-stock on the north bank of the Orange river had been withdrawn by the retreating enemy, and no staffs remained at the stations (*see* Appendix 3, vol. iii.).

It now became a matter of paramount importance to centralise into the hands of the D.R. the control of the railway; with this object in view instructions were issued by Army Headquarters, dated April 23rd, 1900.

As the Orange Free State and Transvaal fell into British hands, so the mileage under the control of the Imperial Military Railways increased. New A.D.R.'s were appointed at Bloemfontein and Johannesburg, with deputies at Kroonstad, Johannesburg and Pretoria.

In the absence of a railway working staff it became necessary to create one; though many of the members were military officers, the technical and controlling staffs were kept distinct.

After the occupation of Pretoria, when further experience had been gained, all applications for the use of the railways were sent to the Chief of the Staff, who, after consulting the D.R., issued the necessary permits. At the same time the A.D.R. was informed and he communicated with all railway officials concerned. At this time the lack of rolling-stock, and especially of engines, greatly handicapped the controlling staff.

The strain resulting from lack of these necessaries was relieved after the occupation of Komati Poort, in September, 1900. By October, 1900, not only had temporary repairs been completed upon every line of railway in the country, but the makeshifts were being gradually replaced by repairs of a semi-permanent and permanent type, executed by the Works Department of the Imperial Military Railways; but the activity of the enemy made it impossible to run trains by night, and consequently the full carrying capacity of the line was not available. In order to cope with the attacks on the lines of railway which occurred at the end of 1900, the D.R. selected stations throughout the theatre of war where there was siding accommodation for construction trains, and there a permanent-way inspector and his gang were quartered, with an R.E. Section whose duty it became to take charge of the construction train, if necessary.

Every effort was made to ensure rapid transmission to the construction train of news of any break in the line. Gangers patrolled the line at dawn, and all military posts reported alarms to the nearest telegraph station, which in turn informed the Deputy Superintendent of Works, who telegraphed his orders to the construction train situated nearest to the break. Officers in charge of construction trains had orders to proceed with all speed to any reported break, whether or not the report had been confirmed. It is recorded that in the Orange River Colony alone, during eight months of the war, seventy-eight destructive raids were made on the railway. Yet the system of intelligence and the scheme for executing repairs were equal to every call. For example, on January 1st, 1901, at 2.30 a.m., information reached the Deputy Superintendent of Works at Bloemfontein that the line had been broken at Wolvehoek. The break, which was sixty-three miles distant, was repaired by 8 a.m. The gradual extension of the blockhouse system ultimately procured more immunity for the railways, and by April, 1901, the worst of the actual train-wrecking was over.

Examples of Troop-Moves.

The success of the Imperial Military Railways in dealing with the transmission of troops will be gathered from the following instances:—

(i.) From December 18th to 27th, fifty-two trains of 1,305 trucks were transmitted from various points in the Transvaal and Orange River Colony to Norval's Pont.

APPENDIX 10.

(ii.) During the period January 31st to February 8th, 1901 (nine days), eighty-nine troop-trains were despatched from Bloemfontein to Cape Colony, containing 315 officers, 8,980 men, 7,632 horses, 6,810 mules, 47 guns and 373 trucks of oxen and wagons.

(iii.) Major-General Bruce Hamilton's and other troops—of 6,391 personnel, 27 guns, and 605 truck-loads of animals, wagons, etc. (in all, twenty-seven trains)—were, meanwhile entrained at Smalldeel and Winburg in two days, and detrained at Bloemfontein January 30th to February 3rd. Whilst their trains were being off-loaded at Bloemfontein, the above troops for Cape Colony passed simultaneously through to the south, with no retardation of the normal supply traffic from south to north.

(iv.) MOVEMENT OF TROOPS BETWEEN 5.9.01 AND 11.10.01 TO REPEL INVASION OF NATAL.

Col. Garratt's Column.	Total number of trains—12.
80 officers. 1,373 other ranks. 1,191 horses. 750 mules. 600 oxen. 117 trucks of wagons.	1st train left Vereeniging 12.20 p.m., 5th Sept. 12th ,, ,, ,, 1.0 a.m., 8th ,, 1st train arrived Paardekop 8.45 a.m., 6th Sept. 12th ,, ,, ,, 7.45 p.m., 8th ,,
Major-General Bruce Hamilton's Column.	Total number of trains—14.
85 officers. 1,901 other ranks. 1,934 horses. 1,100 mules. 7 guns. 36 oxen. 64 wagons.	1st train left Springfontein 11.30 a.m., 8th Sept. 14th ,, ,, ,, 1.20 p.m., 12th ,, N.B.—1st, 2nd and 14th trains detained at Heilbron, remainder at Vredefort Road. 1st train arrived Heilbron 8.0 p.m., 9th Sept. 14th ,, ,, ,, 1.30 a.m., 15th ,,
Colonel Pulteney's Column.	Total number of trains—8.
38 officers. 793 other ranks. 948 horses. 214 mules. 20 carts. 20 trucks of wagons.	1st train left Newcastle 12.30 a.m., 9th Sept. 8th ,, ,, ,, 3.45 p.m., 9th ,, 1st train arrived Volksrust 5.40 a.m., 9th Sept. 8th ,, ,, ,, 4.10 a.m., 10th ,,

(iv.) Movement of Troops between 5.9.01 and 11.10.01 to Repel Invasion of Natal (*continued*).

Lieut.-Colonel Gough's Mounted Infantry. 14 officers. 524 other ranks. 644 horses. 242 mules. 62 oxen. 16 trucks of wagons.	Total number of trains—4. 1st train left Kroonstad 5.0 p.m., 10th Sept. 4th ,, ,, ,, 3.0 a.m., 11th ,, 1st train arrived Dundee 5.45 p.m., 12th Sept. 4th ,, ,, ,, 10.30 p.m., 12th ,,
Colonel Allenby's Column. 44 officers. 1,474 other ranks. 1,280 horses. 630 mules. 8 guns. 18 trucks of wagons.	Total number of trains—16. 1st train left Pretoria 5.50 p.m., 16th Sept. 16th ,, ,, ,, 7.5 a.m., 18th ,, 1st train arrived Newcastle 12.45 a.m., 18th Sept. 16th ,, ,, ,, 8.25 a.m., 19th ,,
53rd battery Field Artillery. 4 officers. 158 other ranks. 6 guns.	Total number of trains—2. 1st train left Pretoria 2.30 p.m., 16th Sept. 2nd ,, ,, ,, 12.50 p.m., 17th ,, 1st train arrived Volksrust 7.40 p.m., 17th Sept. 2nd ,, ,, ,, 7.30 a.m., 18th ,,
2nd battalion Scottish Rifles. 27 officers. 880 other ranks. 135 horses and mules. 16 wagons.	Total number of trains—2. 1st train left Springs 4.30 p.m., 18th Sept. 2nd ,, ,, ,, 8.30 p.m., 18th ,, 1st train arrived Newcastle 6.30 p.m., 19th Sept. 2nd ,, ,, ,, 11.50 p.m., 19th ,,
1st Yorkshire Regiment. 16 officers. 434 other ranks. 4 horses. 47 mules.	Total number of trains—2. 1st train left Pretoria 8.50 p.m., 18th Sept. 2nd ,, ,, ,, 9.10 p.m., 18th ,, 1st train arrived Ladysmith 11.0 a.m., 20th Sept. 2nd ,, ,, ,, 12 noon, 20th ,,

APPENDIX 10.

(iv.) MOVEMENT OF TROOPS BETWEEN 5.9.01 AND 11.10.01 TO REPEL INVASION OF NATAL (*continued*).

Colonel Garratt's Column. 25 officers. 650 other ranks. 355 horses. 130 mules. 12 wagons.	Total number of trains—5. 1st train left Volksrust 8.40 a.m., 19th Sept. 5th ,, ,, ,, 4.25 p.m., 19th ,, 5 trains arrived Newcastle and detrained by 12 noon, 20th September.
Brigadier-General Spens' Column. 62 officers. 1,298 other ranks. 1,191 horses. 950 mules. 6 guns. 78 trucks of wagons.	Total number of trains—10. 1st train left Kroonstad 8.55 a.m., 19th Sept. 10th ,, ,, ,, 9.45 a.m., 20th ,, 1st train arrived Dundee 2.30 a.m., 21st Sept. 10th ,, ,, ,, 6.15 p.m., 22nd ,,
Natal Mounted Rifles. 7 officers. 118 other ranks. 130 horses. *Natal Field Artillery.* 3 officers. 67 other ranks. 60 horses. 2 guns.	Left Durban 19th Sept.; arrived Pietermaritzburg 9 p.m., 19th Sept.
Lieut.-Colonel Du Moulin's Column. 27 officers. 688 other ranks. 1,217 horses and mules. 3 guns.	Total number of trains—5. 1st train left Springfontein 12 noon, 20th Sept. 5th ,, ,, ,, 6.25 a.m., 21st ,, 5 trains arrived Bloemfontein by 12 noon, 21st Sept.
Brigadier-General G. Hamilton's Column. 47 officers. 1,650 other ranks. 1,100 horses. 650 mules. 54 wagons.	Total number of trains—12. 1st train left Klerksdorp 10.30 a.m., 20th Sept. 12th ,, ,, Potchefstroom 9.45 a.m., 23rd ,, 2nd and 3rd trains both broke down between Bank and Krugersdorp; delayed 2 hours. 2nd train derailed between Zandspruit and Paardekop; 22 hours' delay. 1 engine and 18 trucks derailed; 6 persons injured; 25 horses killed, 30 injured. 1st train arrived Dundee 12.45 a.m., 23rd Sept. 12th ,, ,, ,, 10.15 p.m., 24th ,,

(iv.) MOVEMENT OF TROOPS BETWEEN 5.9.01 AND 11.10.01 TO REPEL INVASION OF NATAL (*continued*).

1*st Cameron Highlanders.* 10 officers. 344 other ranks.	Left Pretoria 3.50 p.m., 20th Sept. Arrived Dundee 3.0 p.m., 22nd ,,
Colonel Sir H. Rawlinson's Column. 77 officers. 1,605 other ranks. 2,740 horses and mules.	Total number of trains—13. 1st train left Aliwal North 7.30 p.m., 21st Sept. 13th ,, ,, Burghersdorp 5.45 p.m., 23rd ,, 3 trains loaded at Aliwal North ; remainder at Burghersdorp. Last 3 trains detained at Heidelberg ; move delayed owing to suspension of night running north of Bloemfontein by order of General Knox. 1st train arrived Elandsfontein 3.0 p.m., 23rd Sept. 13th ,, ,, Heidelberg 1.0 a.m., 26th ,,
Black Watch. 6 officers. 290 other ranks.	Left Bloemfontein 2.25 p.m., 23rd Sept. Arrived Ladysmith 2.0 a.m., 26th ,,
Natal Mounted Rifles. *General Depôt, Composite battalion.* 9 officers. 166 other ranks. 156 horses and mules.	Total number of trains—3. 1st train left Pietermaritzburg 2.30 a.m. 3rd ,, ,, ,, 4.30 a.m. } 23rd Sept. 3 trains arrived Greytown
Major-General F. W. Kitchener's Details. *Lieut.-General Elliot's Details.* 26 officers. 745 other ranks.	1st portion left Middelburg 22nd Sept. Last portion arrived Volksrust 24th Sept.
Imperial Light Horse. 26 officers. 459 other ranks. 443 horses. 250 mules. 23 wagons.	Total number of trains—5. 1st train left Harrismith 7.0 a.m., 25th Sept. 5th ,, ,, ,, 11.0 p.m., 25th ,, 1st train arrived Dundee 9.0 p.m., 25th Sept. 5th ,, ,, ,, 3.10 a.m., 26th ,,

APPENDIX 10.

(iv.) MOVEMENT OF TROOPS BETWEEN 5.9.01 AND 11.10.01 TO REPEL INVASION OF NATAL (*continued*).

Natal Carbineers. 3 officers. 62 other ranks. 85 horses and mules.	Left Pietermaritzburg 9.30 a.m., 26th Sept. Arrived Greytown 5.30 p.m., 26th Sept.
Scots Guards. 22 officers. 825 other ranks. 121 horses and mules.	1st portion left Potchefstroom 9.30 a.m., 24th Sept. Last portion arrived Volksrust 9.20 a.m., 29th Sept.
Brigadier-General Plumer's Details. 5 officers. 328 other ranks. 16 horses.	Left Springfontein 4.30 a.m., 25th Sept. Arrived Bloemfontein 10.30 a.m. 25th Sept.
7 officers. 554 other ranks. 380 horses.	1st train left Kroonstad 12.30 p.m., 1st Oct. 2nd ,, ,, ,, 5.25 p.m., 1st ,, 1st train arrived Volksrust 10.0 p.m., 2nd Oct. 2nd ,, ,, ,, 11.50 p.m., 2nd ,,
2nd West Yorkshire Regiment. 21 officers. 717 other ranks. 216 horses and mules.	1st portion left Frederickstad 2.25 p.m., 26th Sept. Last portion arrived Volksrust 4.30 p.m., 29th Sept.
Imperial Light Horse. 3 train loads of men, horses, mules and wagons. 2 train loads do. do.	Left Glencoe Junction 27th Sept. Left Pietermaritzburg 27th Sept. Last train left Durban for Tugela 29th Sept.
Durham and Edinburgh Garrison Artillery Militia. 4 officers. 115 other ranks.	Left Ladysmith 5.50 a.m., 27th Sept. for Volkrust.

(iv.) MOVEMENT OF TROOPS BETWEEN 5.9.01 AND 11.10.01 TO REPEL INVASION OF NATAL (*continued*).

Ox Transport. 180 ox wagons. 2,880 oxen.	1st portion left Middelburg 7.15 a.m., 26th Sept. Last ,, ,, ,, 4.0 p.m., 30th ,, Last portion arrived Volksrust 4.30 p.m., 2nd Oct.
Composite Infantry battalion, Ammunition Column and Volunteer Medical Staff. 10 officers. 400 other ranks. 43 horses and mules.	Left Pietermaritzburg in 3 trains for Greytown on 28th Sept.
Drafts ex SS. "Lake Erie." 15 officers. 525 other ranks.	Left Durban at 4.20 p.m. and 6 p.m., 27th Sept. Arrived Pietermaritzburg at 12.30 a.m. and 1.30 a.m., 28th Sept.
Ammunition Column, Field Hospital and Border Mounted Rifles. 2 officers. 20 other ranks. 190 horses and mules.	Left Pietermaritzburg in 3 trains for Greytown on 28th Sept.
Black Watch. 4 officers. 183 other ranks. 22 horses and mules. 4 carts.	Left Ladysmith 8.50 p.m., 29th Sept. Left Durban 2.45 p.m., 30th Sept., for Tugela.
21st battery Royal Field Artillery. 1 officer. 38 other ranks. 70 horses and mules. 2 guns.	Left Pietermaritzburg in 3 trains, 30th Sept.—1st Oct. Left Durban 1st Oct., for Tugela.

APPENDIX 10. 641

(iv.) MOVEMENT OF TROOPS BETWEEN 5.9.01 AND 11.10.01 TO
REPEL INVASION OF NATAL (*continued*).

Royal Irish Fusiliers, "S" Pom-pom section, 83rd battery Royal Field Artillery and Royal Engineers. 16 officers. 406 other ranks. 208 horses and mules. 80 oxen. 24 wagons. 3 guns.	Total number of trains—2. 1st train left Newcastle 1.10 p.m., 30th Sept. 2nd ,, ,, ,, 3.35 p.m., 30th ,, 1st train arrived Dundee 5.30 p.m., 30th Sept. 2nd ,, ,, ,, 10.0 p.m., 30th ,,
Colonel Bethune's Column. 63 officers. 839 other ranks. 1,342 horses. 1,274 mules. 2 guns. wagons.	Total number of trains—9. 1st train left Harrismith 1.45 p.m., 30th Sept. 9th ,, ,, ,, 5.0 a.m., 2nd Oct. 1st train arrived Durban 8.0 p.m., 1st Oct. 9th ,, ,, ,, 3.25 p.m., 4th ,,
Black Watch. 11 officers. 319 other ranks. 6 trucks of horses and mules. 4 trucks of wagons.	Left Kroonstad 12.30 p.m., 1st Oct. Arrived Dundee 9.30 p.m., 2nd Oct.
Lieut.-Colonel Damant's Column. 15 officers. 400 other ranks. 970 horses and mules. 40 trucks of wagons.	Total number of trains—4. 1st train left Bloemfontein 1.50 p.m., 2nd Oct. 4th ,, ,, ,, 6.45 a.m., 3rd ,, 1st train arrived Heilbron 10.30 a.m., 3rd Oct. 4th ,, ,, ,, 8.0 a.m., 4th ,,
Drafts ex SS. "St. Andrew." 1 officer. 250 other ranks.	Left Durban 6.5 p.m., 2nd Oct. Arrived Dundee 9.15 a.m., 4th Oct.

VOL. IV.

THE WAR IN SOUTH AFRICA.

(iv.) MOVEMENT OF TROOPS BETWEEN 5.9.01 AND 11.10.01 TO REPEL INVASION OF NATAL (*continued*).

	Brigadier-General Plumer's Force.	
Details	4 officers. 260 other ranks.	Left Springfontein 12.40 p.m., 3rd Oct. Arrived Volksrust 10.30 p.m., 5th Oct.
Column	45 officers. 618 other ranks. 650 horses. 645 mules. 6 guns.	Total number of trains—7. 1st train left Springfontein 9.30 a.m., 8th Oct. 7th ,, ,, ,, 7.45 p.m., 8th ,, 1st train arrived Volksrust 1.0 p.m., 10th Oct. 7th ,, ,, ,, 7.10 a.m., 11th ,,
	Remounts. 4,798 horses. 168 horses. 70 mules.	Left Mooi River for north between 2nd Sept. and 8th Oct. Left Pietermaritzburg for Greytown, 23rd Sept.

GRAND TOTAL MOVED BY RAIL.

Officers...................... 882
Other ranks.................. 23,536
Animals...................... 32,836
Guns 45

APPENDIX 10.

(v.) Troop Moves on Eastern Line between April 5th and 12th, 1901, to form Columns under Lieut.-General Sir Bindon Blood.

Date.	Trucks.	Officers.	Men.	Trucks of Horses.	Trucks of Mules.	Trucks of Oxen.	Wagons.	Guns.
April 5th, 1901.								
12.25 p.m. {	90	2	265	26	18	2	12	—
	23	—	—	16 &	mules	—	4	—
1.15 p.m.	22	—	—	12	do.	—	6	—
1.35 p.m.	20	—	—	12	do.	—	6	—
2.10 p.m.	22	13	500	19	do.	—	—	—
Totals	177	15	765	85	18	2	28	—
April 6th, 1901.								
5.5 a.m.	5	—	—	—	—	—	—	—
6.15 a.m.	23	—	15	6	—	2	1	—
10.48 a.m.	23	1	139	—	6	—	14	—
11.15 a.m.	23	2	110	12	—	—	6	3
12.20 p.m.	28	4	80	5	5	7	6	—
1.15 p.m.	23	3	90	12	—	—	6	—
1.55 p.m.	24	4	70	10	3	—	4	—
Totals	149	14	504	45	14	9	37	3
April 7th, 1901.								
4.0 a.m.	26	—	28	20	—	—	—	—
4.25 a.m.	21	14	257	—	—	—	2	—
5.5 a.m.	11	1	50	3	—	—	—	—
5.50 a.m.	19	1	20	—	10	—	8	—
6.45 a.m.	22	4	80	3	5	2	6	—
7.40 a.m.	33	6	139	16	2	—	11	—
11.45 a.m.	24	2	106	5	13	—	4	—
2.0 p.m.	16	1	125	10	—	—	—	—
4.23 p.m.	28	3	120	16	8	—	—	—
Totals	200	32	925	73	38	2	31	—
April 8th, 1901.								
4.0 a.m.	32	8	248	1	5	—	15	—
4.35 a.m.	24	9	300	1	3	2	3	—
5.58 a.m.	30	3	136	20	—	—	1	—
6.0 a.m.	23	2	77	10	2	—	8	—
6.45 a.m.	23	2	20	2	1	9	10	—
4.35 p.m.	24	—	35	4	16	—	4	—
5.5 p.m.	31	—	14	8	—	—	10	—
Totals	187	24	830	46	27	11	51	—

(v.) Troop Moves on Eastern Line between April 5th and 12th, 1901, to form Columns under Lieut.-General Sir Bindon Blood (*continued*).

Date.	Trucks.	Officers.	Men.	Trucks of			Wagons.	Guns.
				Horses.	Mules.	Oxen.		
April 9th, 1901.								
4.30 a.m.	23	—	—	1	—	4	4	—
4.42 a.m.	22	—	—	2	—	—	—	—
5.40 a.m.	29	3	60	0	8	—	7	—
Totals	74	3	60	23	8	4	11	—
April 10th, 1901.								
4.20 a.m.	24	—	—	13	2	—	6	—
4.40 a.m.	31	—	—	20	—	—	5	—
5.20 a.m.	23	13	250	18	—	—	—	—
11.0 a.m.	20	—	38	1	2	2	4	—
2.10 p.m.	18	—	33	—	9	—	8	—
Totals	116	13	321	52	13	2	23	—
April 11th, 1901.								
4.5 a.m.	24	2	99	—	—	14	10	—
5.10 a.m.	25	5	49	14	—	1	8	—
5.20 a.m.	25	1	38	5	5	5	7	—
7.5 a.m.	22	3	108	9	3	—	4	—
10.25 a.m.	23	5	111	12	2	—	4	—
11.35 a.m.	26	1	27	1	1	17	6	—
1.25 p.m.	29	8	95	10	5	—	8	—
3.20 p.m.	—	—	—	—	—	—	—	—
9.25 p.m.	22	6	100	10	4	—	2	—
Totals	196	31	627	61	20	37	49	—
April 12th, 1901.								
12.25 a.m.	30	10	100	19	—	—	—	—
7.15 a.m.	25	2	69	11	4	—	7	—
10.50 a.m.	31	3	125	—	—	20	10	—
12.50 p.m.	32	3	130	—	13	2	14	—
1.35 p.m.	40	9	220	4	—	20	6	—
3.30 p.m.	16	1	66	—	—	7	9	—
5.0 p.m.	35	5	187	10	11	—	8	4
10.55 p.m.	32	3	130	7	4	—	11	2
Totals	241	36	1,027	51	32	49	65	6
Grand Totals..	1,340	168	5,059	436	170	116	295	9

APPENDIX 10. 645

(vi.) Move of Brigadier-General G. Hamilton's Column from Greylingstad to Krugersdorp, June 1st to 4th, 1901.

The Force, strength as under, was ordered on May 30th to march to Greylingstad and entrain on arrival :—

Troops.	Officers.	Men.	Horses.	Mules.	Wagons.	Guns.
13th Hussars	16	678	760	127	20	—
Q. battery R.H.A.	2	45	90	—	10	2
64th battery R.F.A.	1	41		—	—	2
East Lancashire regiment	13	360	10	80	8	—
3rd Field troop R.E.	1	39	90	—	12	—
Transport	—	—		130	16	—
5th Dragoon Guards	20	379	428	—	16	—
Bearer company	5	34	—	210	14	—
Totals	58	1,576	\multicolumn{2}{c}{1,925}	96	4

On the first intimation of this move the R.S.O. at Greylingstad was ordered to detach suitable "empties" from passing trains. Traffic officers were further ordered to collect all available empties at Elandsfontein and Heidelberg in readiness to be despatched to Greylingstad as soon as the hour of the column's arrival should be approximately known. It was not thought advisable to block Greylingstad with trucks in anticipation, for trains were running at short intervals on the line and a congestion of traffic might have resulted. G. Hamilton's force arrived at 10 a.m., June 1st, and the regular entrainment began at midday.

Trains left as under :—

```
1st —  4.30 p.m. .. June 1st     10th —  7.25 a.m. .. June 3rd
2nd —  5.25  ,,    ..  ,,   ,,    11th — 10.20  ,,   ..  ,,   ,,
3rd — 10.0   ,,    ..  ,,   ,,    12th — 12.40  ,,   ..  ,,   ,,
4th —  3.0   a.m.  ..  ,,  2nd    13th —  3.15 p.m. ..  ,,   ,,
5th — 11.25  ,,    ..  ,,   ,,    14th —  7.25  ,,   ..  ,,   ,,
6th —  1.30 p.m.   ..  ,,   ,,    15th —  8.35  ,,   ..  ,,   ,,
7th —  6.1   ,,    ..  ,,   ,,    16th — 11.35  ,,   ..  ,,   ,,
8th — 10.30  ,,    ..  ,,   ,,    17th —  2.50 a.m. ..  ,,  4th
9th —  1.10 a.m.   ..  ,,  3rd    18th —  1.10 p.m. ..  ,,   ,,
```

The up and down mail *and* supply trains ran as usual without interruption to or from this move, a note which applies generally to the greater part of the troop-moves here detailed.

(vii.) TROOP-MOVES IN ONE MONTH THROUGH PRETORIA STATION.
March 19th to April 19th, 1901.

	Trains.	Trucks.	Horses.	Mules.	Oxen.	Carts and Wagons.	Guns.	Men.
Arrivals from South.........	136	3,632	10,882	4,796	1,143	659	26	14,960
Departures East..	74	1,828	4,509	2,660	2,524	501	11	6,479
Departures North	64	1,272	2,350	580	972	185	8	4,224
Totals	274	6,732	17,741	8,036	4,639	1,345	45	25,663

THE LOCOMOTIVE DEPARTMENT.

Mention must be made of the work of this department, on which devolved primarily the duty of repairing engines, coaches and trucks. The department was also called upon to execute work for the Army, which, under other circumstances, might have been done by the Army Ordnance Department, *e.g.*, the mounting of Vickers-Maxim and 12-pr. Q.F. guns on armoured trucks. As an illustration of the work of this department, it may be recorded that between May and October, 1901, the following repairs were effected in their workshops at Pretoria, Johannesburg and Bloemfontein :—

Locomotives 141
Coaches 558
Trucks 1,955

The need of additional engine-power and truckage was early realised, and during 1901 the rolling stock was increased by 106 locomotives and 1,740 thirty-ton cars.

RAILWAY STAFF DEPÔT; EMPLOYMENT OFFICE; NATIVE LABOUR DEPÔT.

As already noticed (Appendix 3, Vol. III.), the supply of men required to operate the railways had to be supplemented from outside the ranks of the R.E. companies. A *Railway Staff Depôt* was therefore formed at Johannesburg in June, 1900, in order to deal with volunteers from the ranks of the Army who applied for special employment upon the railways. A *Railway Employment Office* was simultaneously opened in Cape Town; it was freely advertised in the South African newspapers, and applications poured in fast from the civilian population. Applications were examined, enquiry was made with regard to the character of the applicants, and a regular system of registration was instituted, so as to ensure the admission of none but desirable men to the ranks of the Railway Staff. This office, to which all departments of the Imperial Military Railways might apply when in want of additional labour, abundantly justified its institution. It received 7,500 applications for work during the succeeding nine months, and engaged some 800 employés.

Mention must also be made of the *Native Labour Depôts*, established at De Aar, Bloemfontein and Johannesburg. Upon these all departments of the Army were entitled to make requisition. Large batches of natives were employed in reconstructing the railway, and in loading and off-loading supplies from trucks. At the end of 1900 some 4,500 native boys were upon the books of the Johannesburg Labour Depôt alone.

Armoured Trains.

Soon after Lord Kitchener assumed command he decided regularly to organise the armoured trains as fighting units. He therefore appointed to his Staff an officer termed the Assistant Director of Railways for Armoured Trains. This officer was also on the Staff of the Director of Railways, and was placed in charge of all the armoured trains in South Africa—some twenty in number.

The principal duties of these trains may be said to have been the following :—

(1.) In conjunction with columns in the field, to intercept the enemy whom the columns were driving on to the line.
(2.) To act on the flank of a column or line of columns, the train being well advanced so as to prevent the enemy breaking to that flank.
(3.) To reinforce stations and camps on the railway which were threatened by the enemy.
(4.) To escort ordinary traffic trains.
(5.) To reconnoitre.
(6.) To patrol by day and night.
(7.) The general protection of traffic routes.

The A.D.R. for Armoured Trains was held responsible for the efficiency of the garrisons, armaments and equipments of all his trains. It was his duty to see that the armoured train rolling stock was in good working condition, and that the officers commanding were instructed in the manner of fighting their trains, and conversant with ordinary traffic working. Like other officers of the Headquarters Staff, he had access to all telegrams sent and received by the Chief; this privilege, and that of seeing the Commander-in-Chief daily, enabled him to foresee events and to dispose his trains accordingly. It was his duty also, whenever a concentration of trains was decided upon, to attach himself to one of them and take charge of the concerted action of the whole.

The garrison of an armoured train was composite. In addition to the infantry escort, it contained R.A. and R.E. detachments. The latter consisted of one N.C.O. and six Sappers, skilled in railway repairing work and in re-setting derailed engines and trucks; two telegraph linesmen, one telegraph clerk, two engine drivers and two firemen. All the men of this detachment were counted as effective rifles when the train was engaged, with the exception of the driver and fireman on the footplate; even the latter carried rifles in the engine cab to drive off an enemy endeavouring to gain possession of their engine.

It was important that the officer commanding the train should be a man of judgment and strong nerve. He was often called upon to act on his own responsibility. His strong armament and defences enabled him to attack superior forces. Yet his vulnerable points were many. He had ever to be alert that the enemy did not cut the line behind him. In addition to his visible foes and the constant risks of traffic in war time, he had to contend with skilfully used automatic and observation mines, and had to keep his head even amid the roar which followed the passage of his leading truck over a charge of dynamite, and then to deal with the attack which almost certainly ensued. Officers, therefore, had to be chosen from men of no common stamp. The danger from contact mines was to a certain extent obviated by a standing order that each train should propel a heavily-loaded bogie truck. Such trucks had low sides and ends; they in no way obstructed the view, or fire, from the train; and they performed the double purpose of exploding contact mines and carrying the railway and telegraph materials. The necessity for this propelled unoccupied bogie was exemplified on several occasions,

APPENDIX 10.

For example, No. 6 Armoured Train exploded a mine near Kroonstad, when, through some unfortunate oversight, it was not propelling its material truck; the Officer Commanding was killed instantly, the leading fighting truck was overturned, and several men in it were injured. This would undoubtedly have been avoided if a loaded bogie had been in front. A few days later this same train, having again been put in commission, ran over a contact mine near Heilbron. On this occasion the propelled bogie fired the mine, and a length of three feet of rail was blown out; but as the mine was laid on a straight portion of the line, the whole train bumped across the break and kept the rails. Three minutes after the explosion it was engaging the enemy with the 12-pr. Q.F. gun. There were no casualties on the train.

No. 5 Armoured Train was similarly blown up west of Middelburg, Transvaal, when running to reinforce Uitkyk, which the Boers had attacked by night. Again the propelled bogie fired the mine; but in this case two box trucks in rear of the engine were thrown off by the broken rail; the officer commanding promptly disconnected these, and steamed forward with the front portion of his train to assist in the defence of Uitkyk.

All trains carried a special gun-truck, on which was a pedestal-mounted Q.F. gun. They carried also a machine gun at each end, arranged with a lateral sweep, to allow the fires to cross at either side of the train at a distance of from fifty to eighty yards.

Armoured trains were officially recognised as moving telegraph offices, and equipped with field sounders, vibrators, phonophores and telephones; and whenever trains stopped away from a regular office, which they did nearly every night, they were never out of communication with the neighbouring stations and blockhouses.

When several trains patrolled one section, it was found advisable, especially at night, that they should all halt at fixed intervals and connect up with the telegraph wires to receive instructions and news. Such a train carried out the whole of Brigadier-General Plumer's telegraph work when he crossed the railway near Houtkraal in Cape Colony in pursuit of De Wet.

One of the later improvements made to armoured trains was the addition of a strong electric light. The steam for the engine and turbines working the dynamos was supplied by a flexible pipe from the engine dome, the pipe being fairly protected by steel plates,

APPENDIX II.

NOTES ON THE ARMY REMOUNT DEPARTMENT.

It has been remarked that in the Crimean war the wastage of horseflesh amounted to some forty per cent. annually less than in the South African war. Whilst the comparison is scarcely fair—inasmuch as the first named campaign was largely a war of infantry, and infantry engaged in the least mobile of operations, the prosecution of a siege—nevertheless, the South African statistics show heavy figures. Of the numbers of horses and mules upon the ration list, ten per cent. were usually sick, and some thousand animals were, as a rule, each week destroyed as incurable; these irrespective of the numbers killed in action or dead of disease.

The extent of the demands for horses and mules made upon the Remount Department, and the manner in which they were met, may be judged from the following table showing the numbers of remounts supplied to the Army in Africa up to the end of January, 1902 :—

Quarter ending.	Demanded.		Supplied.	
	Horses.	Mules.	Horses.	Mules.
31st December, 1899	4,272	12,900	5,901	18,095
31st March, 1900	13,930	18,000	14,155	15,092
30th June, 1900	19,830	20,600	34,104	18,749
30th September, 1900	18,530	6,000	19,751	9,988
31st December, 1900	10,072	5,000	10,090	6,055
31st March, 1901	35,394	6,000	25,118	4,467
30th June, 1901	30,716	7,000	23,468	5,971
30th September, 1901	31,716	6,000	30,855	7,500
31st December, 1901 and for	30,816	6,000	40,365	5,113
31st January, 1902	9,972	2,000	13,056	3,000
	205,248	89,500	211,863	94,030

SYSTEM OF PURCHASE AT HOME.

The purchase of horses at home was carried out as in peace time, except that the enormous requirements necessitated the employment of additional purchasing officers. Attempts were made to buy from horse owners, at fairs, and by advertisement, but the results were not commensurate with the cost involved.

The horse registration system was also brought into operation. As a means of supplying horses to meet artillery requirements this reserve proved a success; the class of horse registered by the omnibus companies and large owners of van transport was suitable; but as regards the lighter class of horse required for riding, the results were not so successful. Of the 14,105 horses on the registered reserve list, 3,682 were taken in 1899, and 1,679 in 1900. It was then found that horses could be bought cheaper in the open market, and the number thus obtained (amounting at the end of 1901 to 73,000), was greatly in excess of the expectations founded on previous experience. The increase in the number of horses available in the open market was attributed both to the improved means of transport by railway and sea, bringing the breeding grounds nearer to the sale-yards, and also to the advancing substitution of mechanical for horse traction.

It is to be observed that whereas the estimated cost in October, 1899, for horses purchased in the United Kingdom was £55 a head, the actual cost proved little over £43. The total number bought in three years, 1899 to 1901 inclusive, was 60,980 horses and 12,083 cobs, costing £2,711,279 and £351,732 respectively. Of these, 5,361 horses from the horse reserve were purchased in 1899 and 1900, costing £300,860, *i.e.*, an average of a little over £56 each; and the remaining 55,619 horses purchased in 1899, 1900, and 1901 cost an average of £43 6s. each. The cobs purchased during the same years cost an average of £29 each.

SYSTEM OF PURCHASE ABROAD.

(i.) *Of Mules.*

The consular reports from mule-producing countries—giving full information with regard to animals in those countries—having been examined by the purchasing officers—on September 23rd, 1899, an order was given to begin buying mules in Spain, Italy and at

New Orleans. Purchases of mules were thereupon effected at the following approximate prices, and in numbers as given below :—

	Approximate price at port of embarkation.	Approximate total numbers of mules bought.
Spain	£20	18,500
Italy	£20 to £22	8,000
United States	£12 to £15	75,000

(ii.) *Of Horses.*

Argentina. Anent the foreign horse-markets little information was recorded in the Inspector-General's office, except with reference to Argentina. When it had become clear that more horses would be required than the home market could supply, the Inspector-General of Remounts, encouraged by the favourable reports received in 1897 from South Africa upon 2,000 Argentine horses which had then been sent thither, first turned to Argentina, whence at a price of some £8 per head (delivered at the port of embarkation) some 26,000 horses and cobs

Australia. were ultimately obtained. Soon after, recourse was also had to Australia, where suitable animals were purchased " f.o.b."* at a price of from £10 to £12 for cobs, and £14 for horses. Some numbers were also purchased in Australia " c.i.f."† Under the latter terms the losses occurring on the voyage fell upon the seller, and the horses safely delivered in South Africa cost the Government from £31 to £33 each. From Australia a total of some 25,000 horses and cobs was eventually obtained.

United States. Early in 1900 the mule-purchasing commission of officers in the United States were ordered to buy horses also, and here, at prices ranging from £17 to £25 on delivery, some 97,000 horses in all were purchased.

Canada. Simultaneously some 14,000 horses and cobs were purchased in Canada, at prices ranging from £25 to £30 as delivered on the wharves at Montreal.

Austria-Hungary. In order that the horse-markets of Australia, Argentina and America should be left to the Inspector-General of Remounts, the Yeomanry Committee, charged with the duty of mounting the Imperial Yeomanry, drew upon Austria-Hungary for its requirements. Some

* Free-on-board.

† Cost, insurance, freight—*i.e.*, cost of the article, its insurance while on the voyage, and freight.

three months later the task of finding horses for the Imperial Yeomanry devolved upon the Inspector-General of Remounts, but the same system was continued.

Here the prices varied from £35 for artillery to £30 for cavalry horses, and £20 for Croatian cobs. These were later supplemented by large shipments of Russian cobs purchased in Hungary. In all some 45,000 of these horses and cobs were bought " f.o.b." at Fiume.

The experience of the war led the Assistant-Inspector of Remounts to record his opinion that the horses, cobs and mules from the various countries ranked in the following order of merit for the purposes of this particular campaign.

Horses.	Cobs.	Mules.
1. South African.	1. South African.	1. American (U.S.).
2. British.	2. British.	2. South African.
3. American (U.S.).	3. Australian.	3. Spanish.
4. Australian.	4. American and Canadian.	4. Italian.
5. Canadian.	5. Hungarian.	
6. Hungarian.	6. Argentine.	
7. Indian (country-bred: Arabs and walers).		
8. Argentine.		

Supply of Veterinary Surgeons.

There was great difficulty in obtaining veterinary surgeons. The supply afforded by the Army Veterinary Department was soon exhausted, and the number of civil veterinary surgeons who were obtained at home was insufficient to meet the demands of the Army in South Africa as well as of the Army Remount Department.

For the important duty of conducting the veterinary examination of animals purchased in foreign countries, competent veterinary surgeons were with difficulty procured. For service on board horse-ships they could not always be obtained at all. The purchasing officers in America and Australia were authorised to engage local veterinary surgeons; some of these did good service, but the incompetence of others was in some instances the cause of serious loss to the public. Owing to the difficulties experienced in obtaining veterinary surgeons locally, a few ships from foreign ports sailed without them, but no ships conveying remount horses left home ports without a veterinary surgeon in charge. The reason given for the difficulty in obtaining qualified veterinary surgeons was simply the excess of demand over supply. Those in military employment in April, 1902, amounted to ten per cent. of the whole profession in the United Kingdom.

Transport of Remounts by Sea.

In time of peace the transport by sea of horses and mules is a service rarely required ; in war this duty is performed by the Transport Department of the Admiralty. In the case of mounted troops, provision has to be made for carrying in the same ship, not only horses, but also men, saddlery, and equipment. Ships employed on this duty are taken up on time charter, and are specially fitted for the service, according to plans prepared beforehand by the Admiralty in communication with the War Office.

The already large export trade of horses and cattle from Argentina was carried on under a well-established system which was adopted for the despatch of remount animals from that country to South Africa. The shipowners fitted the ship according to specification, and undertook to provide forage and attendants for the voyage, the service being paid for by a capitation rate for the number of animals embarked. The ships chartered by the Admiralty for the transport of mules from foreign ports to South Africa were engaged on similar terms. The ships chartered to take remount horses from England were all engaged on the same conditions, viz., a capitation rate which covered all expenses of the voyage. The amounts paid for capitation rates varied greatly, being governed by the differing conditions of the length and nature of the voyage, and the general cost of freight which obtained at different times. The rate was at first calculated on the number of animals embarked ; but after a short experience it was deemed advisable to divide the capitation rate into two parts, one being paid for each animal embarked, and the other, by way of bonus, for each animal landed. It thus became the interest of the shipowner that the animals should be carried safely to their destination. Each ship called at Cape Town for orders, and might be required to proceed thence to any other port in South Africa for disembarkation, without extra charge.

In the charter of every ship a condition was made that accommodation should be provided for a conducting officer and a veterinary surgeon ; it was soon proved that the condition in which animals landed in South Africa largely depended upon the efficiency of these officers.

Cases occurred in which ships put to sea short of the proper proportion of attendants, and the animals suffered accordingly. The proportion laid down was that of one man to twenty mules, and one man to fifteen horses; this, in the opinion of the Quarter-Master-General, was sufficient, provided the conducting officer and the veterinary officer did their duty. But neither conducting officer nor veterinary officer was always available, and the master of the ship could not invariably concern himself with the way in which the attendants carried out their duties. The provision of a sufficient number of competent attendants to take charge of horses and mules on board ship was, in fact, a matter of much difficulty, both in British and in other ports. The attendants were drawn from all classes, and, being engaged and paid by the owners, it was difficult to keep them under discipline, and they frequently deserted the ship as soon as it arrived in port. In several cases it was reported that ships were overcrowded, owing to the desire of the owner to carry as much freight as possible. It was usually a condition of the charter that five per cent. of the stalls should be vacant, so as to allow of horses being shifted in case of necessity, and also to get at the stalls and horses for cleaning purposes. This condition was not always observed.

Att ndants.

REMOUNT DEPÔTS IN SOUTH AFRICA.

In the Tables of War Establishments, which had been prepared at the War Office, provision was made for (i.) a base depôt for 1,000 horses, personnel of seven officers and 274 N.C.O.'s and men; and (ii.) an advanced remount depôt for 300 horses, personnel of three officers and fifty-six N.C.O.'s and men. These depôts were to form part of the line-of-communication troops and in accordance with the regulations were to be under the Director of Transport. It was intended that Army Service Corps companies should form the nucleus of all remount depôts, their personnel being expanded by transport conductors and natives:

Before the war, remount depôts had been established at Stellenbosch, in Cape Colony, and at Nottingham Road (Natal), the personnel of which was furnished from the troops serving in the command, aided by native establishments. When war appeared imminent, a number of Army Service Corps companies were sent out for the lines of communication. Five of these were allotted to remount work, depôts being formed at De Aar, Naauwpoort, Queenstown, Port Elizabeth, in addition to that at Stellenbosch. On the arrival of Lord Roberts in January, 1900, the needs of the transport service necessitated the withdrawal of the whole of the Army Service Corps personnel, European and native, from remount work. A new staff had then to be improvised, with civilian and native labour, aided by Indian N.C.O.'s and syces, who were arriving with horses from India.

About the end of March, 1900, seven base remount depôts arrived from England. Of these, two only brought men; the other five, of which two were sent to Natal, were cadres comprising officers and N.C.O.'s only. During the next three months, the soldiers belonging to the two complete depôts were withdrawn to join the ranks of the Field Army. In July, 1900, the personnel of the base and advanced depôts, nine in number (excluding Natal), consisted of 4,425 of all ranks, which included 2,303 Cape boys and Kaffirs, 1,475 Indians and only 337 British N.C.O.'s and men. The whole of these were under the charge of Lieut.-Colonel W. H. Birkbeck, Assistant-Inspector of Remounts.

Subsequent additions made to the remount depôts in South Africa brought the total on March 1st, 1902, to twenty-four remount depôts, ten of which were composed entirely of civilians and natives.

TABLE SHOWING NUMBER OF HORSES SHIPPED, COUNTRY OF EMBARKATION, AND PERCENTAGE OF LOSS INCURRED ON THE VOYAGE, FROM SEPTEMBER 1ST, 1899, TO DECEMBER 31ST, 1901.

HORSES (Remounts only).

	Shipped.	Loss.	Percentage of Loss.
United Kingdom.			
1899............................	2,308	172	7.45
1900............................	16,871	886	5.25
1901............................	26,859	1,865	7.95
Totals	46,038	2,923	6.34

APPENDIX II.

Horses (Remounts only) (*continued*).

	Shipped.	Loss.	Percentage of Loss.
India.			
1899	245	2	0.81
1900	2,805	58	2.06
Totals	3,050	60	1.96
Australia.			
1899	706	10	1.41
1900	7,196	297	4.12
1901	11,828	318	2.60
Totals	19,730	625	3.16
United States.			
1900	20,086	843	4.19
1901	56,045	1,605	2.14
Totals	76,131	2,448	3.21
Argentina.			
1899	2,981	6	0.20
1900	22,891	186	0.81
Totals	25,872	192	0.74
Austria.			
1900	6,999	212	3.02
1901	16,939	285	1.68
Totals	23,938	497	2.07
Canada.			
1900	3,738	196	5.27
1901	7,566	262	3.46
Totals	11,304	458	4.05
Grand Totals	206,063	7,203	3.49

TABLE SHOWING NUMBER OF MULES SHIPPED, COUNTRY OF EMBARKATION, AND PERCENTAGE OF LOSS INCURRED ON THE VOYAGE, FROM SEPTEMBER 23RD, 1899, TO DECEMBER 31ST, 1901.

MULES (Remounts only).

	Shipped.	Loss.	Percentage of Loss.
Spain.			
1899	3,919	16	0.40
1900	14,600	488	3.34
1901	24	—	—
Totals	18,543	504	2.71
Italy.			
1899	5,102	28	0.54
India.			
1899	500	1	0.2
United States.			
1899	9,074	373	4.11
1900	35,499	1,079	3.03
1901	23,051	361	1.56
Totals	67,624	1,813	2.68
GRAND TOTALS	91,769	2,346	2.55

APPENDIX 12.

NOTES ON REFUGEE CONCENTRATION CAMPS IN SOUTH AFRICA.

THE subjoined telegrams account for the initiation of these camps at the end of 1900 :—

From Lord Kitchener to the Secretary of State for War.
(Telegram.)
  (No. 117, cipher.)   " Pretoria,
          " December 27th, 1900, 8.20 a.m.
  " As I consider some steps are necessary to induce Boers in field to surrender voluntarily, I am issuing instructions that all who do so will be allowed to live with their families, property, and live-stock in laagers, under our protection, near railway in their district. Those who took the oath of neutrality will also be allowed this privilege, unless it is proved that they went out on commando again without coercion.

  " At present, Boers who surrender are removed from their district, making others afraid to come in. Boer families will be brought into these laagers in their district, and notices posted up that burghers still out are free to join them until country is safe for them to return to their farms. I have formed a Burgher Peace Committee here, consisting of influential surrendered burghers ; they are sending delegates to each district to induce Boers in the field to come in and do away with present misrepresentations of Boer leaders."

From the Secretary of State for War to Lord Kitchener.
(Telegram.)
  (No. 322, cipher.)   " War Office,
          " December 28th, 1900.
  " Your No. 117, cipher. We fully agree with proposed policy. Is it not possible to extend it to 'undesirables' rather than send them into Cape Colony, where they produce similar result to Boers on parole ? "

In a circular despatched by the Commandant-General of the Boer Forces in the Transvaal to all his commandants, dated Roos Senekal, November 6th, 1900, the following extract occurred :—

> "Do everything in your power to prevent the burghers from laying down their arms. If they do not listen to this, I shall be forced to confiscate everything from them, movable or immovable, and to burn their houses."

At the meeting which subsequently took place at Middelburg between the rival Commanders-in-Chief,* this subject was raised by Lord Kitchener ; and General Botha then declared his views as follows :—

> "I am entitled to force every man to join me, and if they fail, to confiscate their property and leave their families on the veld. The only thing that you can do is to send them out of the country as if I catch them they must suffer."

To this expressed intention Lord Kitchener replied to General Botha in a letter dated Pretoria, April 16th, 1901, from which the following is an extract :—

> "As I informed your Honour at Middelburg, owing to the irregular manner in which you have conducted and are conducting hostilities by forcing unwilling and peaceful inhabitants to join your commandos . . . I have now no other course open to me except to take the unpleasant and repugnant step of bringing in the women and children."

In addition, therefore, to the burghers who voluntarily surrendered, and to the families of surrendered burghers who came into the British lines of their own accord, many such families were compulsorily brought in solely in order to save them from the reprisals of the enemy. There were, however, two other categories of refugees for whom the camps were intended :—
    (a) Families who had habitually engaged in passing intelligence to the enemy.

* See Chapter VI., pages 119 and 120, and Chapter XXX., page 523.

APPENDIX 12.

(b) Families from farms which had been constantly used by the enemy either as shelters from which to fire on the troops, or as commissariat depôts.

Refugees were therefore differentiated as follows :—

(1) Self-supporting refugees who had voluntarily sought the protection of camp for themselves and their stock.
(2) Refugees who were unable to support themselves, but who had sought the protection of the camps.
(3) Families of persons who had been brought into camp either for protection or for military reasons. This class were in a minority in most camps and formed usually the malcontent portion of the inhabitants of a camp.*

With the above objects in view, camps were initiated early in 1901 by the military authorities, and were taken over by the civil governments of the Transvaal and Orange River Colonies on March 1st, 1901, and of Natal on November 1st, 1901. The increase of the concentration camps during 1901 can be gauged by the table of expenditure attached to this Appendix.

Accommodation for the refugees was provided as far as possible in wood and iron buildings, but mainly in marquees and bell-tents. Overcrowding was in all cases prohibited. Persons who arrived in camp without bedding, plates, knives, etc., were supplied with these articles at Government expense ; clothing also was supplied free to destitute refugees. Dutch reformed ministers were encouraged to hold services in the various camps and received their usual stipends for so doing. Native servants were usually allowed to attend their employers. Refugees were permitted to correspond with their friends subject to censorship. Baths and wash-houses were provided, and as far as possible a continuous water supply was laid on.

The weekly ration per head varied, but was approximately as follows :—

For adults and children over twelve years :—7 lbs. of meal or flour ; 4 ozs. salt ; 6 or 7 ozs. coffee ; 12 or 14 ozs. sugar ; 3 to $3\frac{1}{2}$ lbs. meat ; $\frac{1}{2}$ to 1 lb. rice ; 14 lbs. fuel ; $3\frac{1}{2}$ lbs. potatoes.

Children under twelve years received the same ration, with the exception of meat, of which they were given usually one half the quantity allowed to adults. In many camps soap and candles also

* Reports on Working of Concentration Camps, November, 1901 (Cd. 819).

formed part of the weekly rations, and children under twelve received oatmeal and milk.

Provision of medical comforts was also made by the Colonial Administrations, at a total cost in the Transvaal and Orange River Colony camps alone of some £7,000 per mensem. It was on so liberal and comprehensive a scale that the Committee of Ladies appointed by the Secretary of State to report on the condition of the camps declared it "very difficult to discover any suitable channel into which they could direct the flow of private charity."*

The Colonial Administrations adopted the policy of offering paid employment to the inmates of the refugee camps for work done in the camps. In some cases families received as much as £20 a month for such work. The monthly bill for labour in the Transvaal camps alone amounted in August, 1901, to some £6,000—the whole of which sum was paid into the pockets of the refugees. Eventually labour for three hours daily for the good of the camp was usually made compulsory for all adult males in the camps. Whenever, as was usually the case, the camp was in the neighbourhood of a town, able-bodied men had the opportunity of earning wages at the usual Colonial rates of pay, still living on free rations in the camp. Ultimately, however, owing to the dissatisfaction this caused in the labour market, the free rationing of competitors for employment outside the camps was abandoned.

In each camp shops were established containing supplies of groceries, clothing, and a few luxuries—of which the price was regulated by martial law. In addition, large charitable gifts of clothing were distributed to the refugees free. Arrangements were also made by which such refugees as had cattle or other stock with them obtained grazing under their own guards, so as to protect them from the depredations of marauding parties of the enemy.

Soon after the refugee camps were initiated a systematic effort was made by the Education Department to provide the means of free education for the children in the camps. Tents, frame-houses or more solid structures were erected as school houses; furniture, books and other apparatus were provided, and a staff of teachers was employed at the expense of the Colonial Governments. An unique opportunity was thus seized for placing the means of education

* Report on Concentration Camps, by a Committee of Ladies appointed by the Secretary of State for War (Cd. 893, page 4).

APPENDIX 12.

within reach of many children who hitherto had lived in remote parts of the veld, many miles from any school. Early in 1901 " organising inspectors " were sent to open schools in the camps ; and soon, in spite of the difficulties caused by want of accommodation, of furniture and other requisites, and of teachers—in spite also of the sickness in the camps and of the hostile feelings of the refugees—in almost every camp in South Africa there was a flourishing school, and in many the number of children, who, without compulsion, at once attended school, was large.* Moreover, the schools were open to adults ; and many young men and women availed themselves of this their first opportunity of receiving an elementary education.† Ultimately, attendance at school was made compulsory for all children in the camps. By the end of 1901 there were more children receiving education in the refugee camps than had been known in the history of the State Schools. Much of the charitable funds at the disposal of an organisation called the "Victoria League" was employed in providing school teachers of cooking and of hygiene—and in forming lending-libraries of books for the benefit of the inmates of the camps.

The principal officials at each camp usually consisted of the following :—

> One superintendent,
> One storekeeper (with clerks),
> One medical officer,
> One dispenser,
> One matron with nurses and assistants as required ; the latter being drawn at first when procurable from the refugee women in the camp, who were encouraged to seek paid employment at work calculated to promote the benefit of the camp.

The successful organisation of each refugee camp depended primarily upon the superintendent. " Each camp bore the impress of the character of its superintendent."† Good water, drainage, and sanitation, an excellent hospital and teaching staff were important factors in the successful conduct of such a camp ; but the paramount

* Up to the end of September, 1901, that is to say, for some six months, the camp schools cost £7,250. This figure does not include the cost of the schools in Natal, nor of the refugee schools in the towns.

† See footnote page 662.

element was the capacity of the individual superintendent, and the extraordinary difficulty of his task may be imagined.

As the war continued, considerable experience was gained in the management of the refugee camps. Travelling inspectors of camps, with a staff of an inspecting medical officer, and an inspecting water engineer, were appointed, who practically standardised the best features of camp management throughout the country. Public boilers for boiling water and public ovens for baking were supplied by the Administration to all camps. Vegetables, lime juice, butter and jam were added to the rations of adults, and more milk to that of small children. More school teachers were applied for. The number of matrons* in the camp was increased, and the supply of foodstuffs on sale in the camp shops was supplemented. Additional doctors and nurses† were despatched to those camp hospitals which were particularly in need of their services; and as far as possible a reserve staff of doctors and nurses was formed.

The dispensaries were invariably well-stocked; the supply of invalid food was almost unlimited; and in spite of the insufficient number of medical officers and trained nurses, the work of the medical and nursing staff in most cases left little to be desired.

A certain amount of transport was allowed to all superintendents so that they might deal efficiently with the sanitation and water supply of their camps. Every effort was made to supply the refugees with beds, and the number of inmates of any individual camp was as far as possible limited; any sites found to be insanitary were moved; and the fencing-in of camps and restrictions upon free ingress and egress in the interest of health gradually became universal.

The death-rate, especially amongst the children, in the camps was naturally higher than normal; it was to be attributed:—(1) To the insanitary condition of the country engendered by the war. Small children were peculiarly susceptible to the tainted drinking water and atmosphere, and to the want of food suitable to their age; but these conditions would have been at least " as severely felt by the child population had they been left to live on their farms."‡

* See previous footnote.

† Hitherto the usual proportion of doctors had been one per thousand, and of nurses three per thousand inhabitants.

‡ Report on Concentration Camps by a Committee of Ladies appointed by the Secretary of State for War (Cd. 893, page 15).

APPENDIX 12.

(2) To causes within the control of the refugees themselves. Even under the best circumstances protracted existence in stationary camps has always been productive of disease, especially of enteric disorders. The massing together of large numbers of persons is, in itself, liable to cause the propagation of disease, owing to the resultant contact between them. In the concentration camps conditions were particularly unfavourable owing largely to the character and inexperience of their inhabitants. " The majority of the refugees were filthy in their habits,"* and did not realise that " what might be comparatively harmless when family was separated from family by miles of open veld was dangerous when thousands of people were gathered together in a small area." Moreover, the Dutch refugees had a rooted objection to sending their children into hospital, and did all in their power to conceal cases of disease among them. Thus infection was spread broadcast. The cubic space in the tents was small, and the infected patient came into intimate contact with every other occupant of the tent. The mothers had little idea of feeding and nursing a sick child—and their neglect in this respect, and their invariable objection to proper ventilation, rendered any check on infection a matter of extreme difficulty.

Europeans, hardened by the frequent recurrence of epidemics in Europe, enjoy a certain immunity from infection, which appears to have been lost by the South African Dutch, owing, perhaps, to their long sojourn in that country and to the complete isolation of their homes.* Whatever the cause, the susceptibility of the Africanders to infection of most kinds was markedly greater than that of Europeans. Such diseases as measles, pneumonia, whooping cough, chicken-pox, mumps —all of a malignant type—spread rapidly amongst the refugees, both children and adults, in a manner unheard of amongst a similar population of Europeans. The variation of temperature was also a potent factor in the production of disease. It was often as much as 60° Fahrenheit, and provided, especially for children and aged persons, the very conditions most conducive to the germination of disease.

Often, too, the refugees were admitted to camp in a low and destitute state, particularly in the case of women and children who had been following a commando. In one case at Kroonstad, a

* Papers relating to the Refugee Camps (Cd. 853, pages 113 and 114).

batch of refugees brought into camp eight moribund cases and three dead bodies. It was unquestioned that the epidemics were primarily caused by the sufferings of women and children previous to entering the camps, and no sooner did one species of disease germ die out in a camp than it was quickly re-introduced by fresh arrivals from the veld. Under similar circumstances in the future, some system of quarantine camps where suspected incomers could be kept under observation before being given free pratique to the permanent camp, would be advisable.

The subjoined Tables contain much statistical information with regard to the camps:—

APPENDIX 12. 667

TABLE SHOWING POPULATION OF CONCENTRATION REFUGEE CAMPS DURING THE LAST PHASE OF THE WAR.

TRANSVAAL, 1902.

Camp.	January.			February.			March.			April.			May.		
	Men.	Women and Children.	Total.	Men.	Women and Children.	Total.	Men.	Women and Children.	Total.	Men.	Women and Children.	Total.	Men.	Women and Children.	Total.
Barberton	248	1,329	1,577	241	1,292	1,533	233	1,275	1,508	236	1,319	1,555			
Balmoral	425	2,278	2,703	414	2,019	2,433	479	1,852	2,331	459	1,807	2,266			
Belfast	245	1,100	1,345	268	1,206	1,474	266	1,114	1,380	274	1,154	1,428			
Heidelberg	484	1,763	2,247	477	1,725	2,202	477	1,687	2,164	454	1,456	1,910			
Irene	935	3,132	4,067	946	3,116	4,062	957	3,197	4,154	1,216	4,236	5,452			
Johannesburg	502	2,055	2,557	483	1,728	2,211	400	1,332	1,732	337	1,247	1,584			
Klerksdorp	511	3,468	3,979	506	3,477	3,983	473	3,059	3,532	415	2,580	2,995			
Krugersdorp	991	3,638	4,629	903	2,945	3,848	930	3,013	3,943	914	3,008	3,922			
Meintjes-Kop	11	68	79	57	269	326	81	346	427	92	366	458			
Middelburg	1,026	4,032	5,058	1,132	4,039	5,171	1,083	3,913	4,996	951	3,381	4,332			
Mafeking	787	3,525	4,312	798	3,530	4,328	807	3,540	4,347	727	3,331	4,058			
Nylstroom	291	1,359	1,650	290	1,333	1,623	272	1,202	1,474						
Potchefstroom	1,129	5,997	7,126	1,023	4,763	5,786	919	4,344	5,263	910	4,248	5,158			
Standerton	628	2,826	3,454	774	2,655	3,429	762	2,633	3,395	726	2,708	3,434			
Vereeniging	167	770	937	187	768	955	183	761	944	184	770	954			
Volksrust	685	4,488	5,173	919	2,869	3,788	884	2,669	3,553	869	2,520	3,389			
Vryburg	282	1,318	1,600	357	1,419	1,776	361	1,517	1,878	350	1,499	1,849			
Lydenburg Military Post					95	95		95	95		95	95			
Pretoria Relief	102	1,120	1,222	107	1,123	1,230	110	1,140	1,250	87	812	899			
Johannesburg Relief	283	3,016	3,299	249	2,685	2,934	213	2,266	2,479	135	1,231	1,366			
Vryheid Military Post	11	150	161	11	97	108	13	151	164	13	149	162			
Vryburg (Town)	—	—	—	38	157	195	50	304	354	74	460	534			
Pietersburg	561	2,322	2,883	66	368	434	24	111	135	29	122	151			
Totals	10,304	49,847	60,151	10,246	43,478	53,724	9,977	41,521	51,498	9,452	38,499	47,951	9,279	37,871	47,150

TABLE SHOWING POPULATION OF CONCENTRATION REFUGEE CAMPS DURING THE LAST PHASE OF THE WAR (*continued*).

ORANGE RIVER COLONY AND CAPE COLONY, 1902.

Camp.	January.			February.			March.			April.			May.		
	Men.	Women and Children.	Total.	Men.	Women and Children.	Total.	Men.	Women and Children.	Total.	Men.	Women and Children.	Total.	Men.	Women and Children.	Total.
Aliwal North	827	3,687	4,514	815	3,657	4,472	813	3,671	4,484	799	3,684	4,483			
Bloemfontein	879	4,970	5,949	966	4,914	5,880	972	4,722	5,694	977	4,677	5,654			
Brandfort	629	3,514	4,143	624	3,466	4,090	572	3,329	3,902	581	3,547	4,128			
Bethulie	638	3,450	4,088	629	3,414	4,043	630	3,417	4,047	503	2,534	3,037			
Heilbron	545	2,333	2,878	544	2,315	2,859	174	747	921	173	783	956			
Harrismith	210	1,260	1,470	93	515	608	62	286	348	61	291	352			
Kroonstad	649	2,896	3,545	626	2,874	3,500	620	2,908	3,528	608	2,879	3,487			
Kimberley	641	2,828	3,469	639	2,864	3,503	628	2,257	2,885	649	2,794	3,443	7,734	37,412	45,146
Norval's Pont	672	2,513	3,185	703	2,776	3,479	713	2,763	3,476	716	2,772	3,488			
Springfontein	422	2,170	2,592	415	2,158	2,573	412	2,152	2,564	404	2,140	2,544			
Vredefort Road	310	1,577	1,887	303	1,568	1,871	290	1,576	1,866	114	637	751			
Winburg	484	2,494	2,978	423	2,138	2,561	419	2,118	2,537	374	2,044	2,418			
Orange River	226	1,480	1,706	226	1,473	1,699	223	1,465	1,688	222	1,446	1,668			
East London									1,850 (about)	353	1,594	1,947			
Uitenhage										290	1,694	1,984			
Totals	7,232	35,172	42,404	7,006	34,132	41,138	6,528	31,411	39,789	6,824	33,516	40,340	7,734	37,412	45,146

APPENDIX 12

TABLE showing Population of Concentration Refugee Camps during the last Phase of the War (*continued*).

NATAL, 1902.

Camp.	January.			February.			March.			April.			May.		
	Men.	Women and Children.	Total.	Men.	Women and Children.	Total.	Men.	Women and Children.	Total.	Men.	Women and Children.	Total.	Men.	Women and Children.	Total.
Ladysmith															
Colenso															
Howick															
Pietermaritzburg	1,386	10,820	12,206	Not shown separately.		19,175	3,010	17,711	20,721	3,362	20,659	24,021	3,418	20,858	24,276
Merebank															
Jacobs															
Wentworth															
Eshowe															
Totals	1,386	10,820	12,206			19,175	3,010	17,711	20,721	3,362	20,659	24,021	3,418	20,858	24,276

GRAND TOTAL POPULATION of Concentration Refugee Camps during the last Phase of the War.

Colony.	January.	February.	March.	April.	May.
Transvaal	60,151	53,724	51,498	47,951	47,150
Orange River and Cape Colonies	42,404	41,138	39,789	40,340	45,146
Natal	12,206	19,175	20,721	24,021	24,276
Totals	114,761	114,037	112,008	112,312	116,572

With regard to the expense of the system, in the absence of figures for the year 1902, an average may be estimated from the following Tables, which show the monthly expenditure, *in the Transvaal alone*, from January to November, 1901, the last four months in detail.

January.	February.	March.	April.	May.	June.	July.
£ s. d.	£ s. d.	£ s. d.	£ s. d.	£ s. d.	£ s. d.	£ s. d.
23,247 15 2	15,008 9 6	14,482 5 3	15,451 0 5	28,576 12 5	33,671 8 5	39,733 1 2

	August.	September.	October.	November.
	£ s. d.	£ s. d.	£ s. d.	£ s. d.
Rations issued..................	16,032 6 0	17,768 16 1	27,398 1 2	26,138 13 8
Medical comforts issued.........	2,688 4 0	2,942 16 9	3,643 8 1	4,070 3 1
Clothing distributed............	2,324 13 7	3,758 13 11	2,514 12 5	845 2 10
Wages to refugees and natives ..	5,291 16 11	5,443 7 8	6,693 12 0	7,232 9 5
Other charges...................	1,964 18 6	3,515 9 9	2,545 16 1	1,839 17 5
Staff pay	3,936 1 11	4,351 19 3	5,243 17 10	5,663 15 6*
Railage on stores	4,087 6 2	4,902 0 10	1,732 10 1*	1,046 2 0*
Railway fares	281 2 2	1,351 7 9	1,707 0 5	799 0 1
Travelling, refugees............			23 2 3	76 16 6
Stationery	91 18 10	23 5 0	135 12 1	3 5 6
Stores lost in transit	158 4 10	64 9 8	72 10 0	134 8 10
Depreciation and loss				
	36,856 12 11	44,122 6 8	51,712 7 7	47,849 14 10
Mafeking.......................	4,919 18 3	3,422 15 3	727 11 11	157 0 7
Other centres	1,249 13 3	535 8 10	54 10 0	
Medical attendance				
	43,026 4 5	48,080 10 9	52,494 9 6	48,006 15 5
Total number of rations issued	1,881,692	1,940,779	2,179,294	1,841,688
Cost per head per day	4.70d.	5.45d.	5.70d.	6.23d.

* Cape Government Railways railage account for October and November not included.

APPENDIX 13.

Strength of the Garrison in South Africa on August 1st, 1899, and Reinforcements, etc., from Home and Colonies during the War up to May 31st, 1902.

	Officers, exclusive of Staff.	Non-commissioned Officers and Men.					Total Officers and Men.
		Cavalry.	Artillery.	Infantry and Mounted Infantry.	Others.	Total.	
I. Garrison on 1st August, 1899	318	1,127	1,035	6,428	1,032	9,622	9,940
II. Reinforcements, 1st August, 1899, to 11th October, 1899 (outbreak of war)—							
(1.) From Home	280	—	743	5,620	—	6,363	6,643
(2.) From India (some of these did not reach South Africa until after the outbreak of hostilities)	259	1,564	653	3,427	—	5,644	5,903
	539	1,564	1,396	9,047	—	12,007	12,546
III. Further reinforcements from 11th October, 1899, to end of July, 1900—							
Regulars—							
(1.) From Home and Colonies	5,748	11,003	14,145	110,292	14,347	149,787	155,535
(2.) From India	132	713	376	670	—	1,759	1,891
	5,880	11,716	14,521	110,962	14,347	151,546	157,426
Colonials—							
(1.) From Colonies other than South Africa	550	287	692	9,788	267	11,034	11,584
(2.) Raised in South Africa	1,387	—	—	—	—	28,932	30,319
	1,937	—	—	—	—	39,966	41,903
Militia	831	—	617	19,753	256	20,626	21,457
Imperial Yeomanry	536	—	—	—	—	10,195	10,731
Volunteers from United Kingdom	342	—	358	9,995	434	10,787	11,129
Total all arms sent to, and raised in South Africa, up to 1st August, 1900, including garrison on 1st August, 1899	10,383	14,694	18,619	165,973	16,336	254,749	265,132

STRENGTH OF THE GARRISON IN SOUTH AFRICA ON AUGUST 1ST, 1899, AND REINFORCEMENTS, ETC., FROM HOME AND COLONIES DURING THE WAR UP TO MAY 31ST, 1902 (*continued*).

	Officers, exclusive of Staff.	Non-commissioned Officers and Men.					Total Officers and Men.
		Cavalry.	Artillery.	Infantry and Mounted Infantry.	Others.	Total.	
Brought forward ...	10,383	14,694	18,619	165,973	16,336	254,749	265,132
IV. Further reinforcements from 1st August, 1900, to 30th April, 1901—							
Regulars—							
From Home and Colonies ...	1,157	5,427	3,129	12,588	2,686	21,830	22,987
Colonials—							
(1.) From Colonies other than South Africa ...	265	—	—	—	—	5,525	5,790
(2.) Raised in South Africa ...	937	—	—	—	—	21,158	22,095
Militia from Home and Colonies ...	116	—	—	3,823	—	3,823	3,939
Imperial Yeomanry ...	429	—	—	—	—	16,304	16,733
Volunteers from United Kingdom ...	164	—	—	—	—	5,641	5,805
South African Constabulary from United Kingdom	2	—	—	—	—	5,178	5,180
	13,453					334,208	347,661
V. Further reinforcements from 1st May, 1901, to 31st December, 1901—							
Regulars—							
From Home and Colonies ...	1,244	3,871	1,115	14,286	2,230	21,502	22,746
,, India ...	108	1,206	—	2,540	3	3,749	3,857
Colonials—							
(1.) From Colonies other than South Africa ...	54	—	uncertain.	—	—	1,140	1,194
(2.) Raised in South Africa ...	numbers						

APPENDIX 13.

Militia	301	—	289	7,869	103	8,261	8,562
Imperial Yeomanry	44	—	—	—	—	877	921
Volunteers	14	—	—	—	—	393	407
Scottish Horse	7	—	—	—	—	447	454
South African Constabulary, from Home	13	—	—	—	—	1,696	1,709
,, ,, ,, Canada	29	—	—	—	—	1,209	1,238
Total sent to, and raised in South Africa, from 1st August, 1899, to 31st December, 1901, including garrison on 1st August, 1899	15,267	15,198	21,152	207,079	21,358	373,482	388,749
VI. Further reinforcements from 1st January, 1902, to 31st May, 1902:—							
Regulars—							
(1.) From Home and Colonies	777	2,047	1,294	13,502	2,640	19,483	20,260
(2.) From India	69	—	—	6,496	13	6,509	6,578
Colonials—							
(1.) From Colonies other than South Africa	538	numbers	uncertain.	—	—	10,289	10,827
(2.) Raised in South Africa							
Militia	443	—	—	11,165	—	11,165	11,608
Imperial Yeomanry	384	—	—	—	—	6,751	7,135
Volunteers	69	—	—	—	—	2,446	2,515
Scottish Horse	8	—	—	—	—	371	379
South African Constabulary from Home	4	—	—	—	—	380	384
Total sent to, and raised in South Africa, from 1st August, 1899, to 31st May, 1902, including garrison on 1st August, 1899	17,559	17,245	22,446	238,242	24,011	430,876	448,435

STRENGTH OF THE GARRISON IN SOUTH AFRICA ON AUGUST 1ST, 1899, AND REINFORCEMENTS, ETC., FROM HOME AND COLONIES DURING THE WAR UP TO MAY 31ST, 1902 (*continued*).

SUMMARY OF TABLES I.—VI.

	Officers, exclusive of Staff.	Non-commissioned Officers and Men.					Total Officers and Men.
		Cavalry.	Artillery.	Infantry and Mounted Infantry.	Others.	Total.	
VII. Garrison on 1st August, 1899—	318	1,127	1,035	6,428	1,032	9,622	9,940
From Home { Regulars	9,206	22,348	18,426	156,288	21,903	218,965	228,171
Militia	1,691		906	42,610	359	43,875	45,566
Yeomanry	1,393					34,127	35,520
Scottish Horse	15					818	833
Volunteers	589					19,267	19,856
South African Constabulary	19					7,254	7,273
Total from Home	12,913					324,306	337,219
From India { Regulars	568	3,483	1,029	13,133	16	17,661	18,229
Volunteers	16					289	305
Total from India	584					17,950	18,534
From Colonies { Colonial Contingents	1,391					27,699	29,090
South African Constabulary (Canada)	29					1,209	1,238
Total from Colonies	1,420					28,908	30,328
Raised in South Africa	2,324*					50,090*	52,414*
Totals	17,559					439,876	448,435

* These numbers are uncertain.

APPENDIX 14.

Drafts, etc., Despatched to South Africa during the War, 1899—1902.

	Regulars					City of London Imperial Volunteers.	Volunteer Service Companies.	Imperial Yeomanry.	Militia.	Total all Arms.
	Cavalry.	Artillery.	Infantry.	Others.	Total.					
From 1st August, 1899, to 31st January, 1900	993	411	9,661	1,545	12,610	—	—	—	6	12,616
During February, 1900	1,675	67	6,514	624	8,880	—	—	—	81	8,961
,, March, ,,	83	209	7,345	282	7,919	—	—	—	117	8,036
,, April, ,,	415	567	3,971	929	5,467	—	—	482	929	6,878
,, May, ,,	581	17	4,199	284	4,915	—	—	—	174	6,113
,, June, ,,	298	55	8,489	303	9,428	—	—	—	—	9,428
,, July, ,,	170	45	583	132	1,058	147	1,024	—	906	2,111
,, August, ,,	171	101	3,299	332	3,902	—	—	—	—	3,902
,, September, ,,	387	218	2,398	18	2,805	—	—	—	984	3,789
,, October, ,,	481	145	1,810	3	2,345	—	—	—	—	2,345
,, November, ,,	—	—	1,474	253	2,208	—	—	—	—	2,208
,, December, ,,	553	—	—	235	788	—	—	—	—	788
,, January, 1901	470	282	—	303	1,055	—	—	—	—	1,055
,, February, ,,	569	462	—	674	1,708	—	—	—	—	1,708
,, March, ,,	1,545	3	3	466	2,014	—	—	23	—	2,037
,, April, ,,	99	15	1	181	296	—	—	—	—	296
,, May, ,,	508	49	929	393	1,879	—	—	—	34	1,913
,, June, ,,	388	224	65	139	816	—	—	—	—	816
,, July, ,,	301	3	1,434	152	1,890	—	—	—	—	1,890
,, August, ,,	434	—	3,215	184	3,833	—	—	—	—	3,833
,, September, ,,	80	6	1,173	178	1,437	—	—	—	—	1,437
,, October, ,,	202	15	371	200	788	—	—	—	—	788
,, November, ,,	687	485	1,788	427	3,387	—	—	—	—	3,387
,, December, ,,	233	197	531	411	1,372	—	—	—	—	1,372

Drafts, etc., Despatched to South Africa during the War, 1899—1902 (continued).

		REGULARS.					City of London Imperial Volunteers.	Volunteer Service Companies.	Imperial Yeomanry.	Militia.	Total all Arms.
		Cavalry.	Artillery.	Infantry.	Others.	Total.					
During January, 1902:— From Home	...	138	21	3,852	391	4,402	—	—	—	1,100	5,502
,, India	...	—	—	—	1	1	—	—	—	—	1
,, February, 1902:— From Home	...	2	22	13	227	264	—	—	—	485	749
,, India	...	—	—	3,146	1	3,147	—	—	—	—	3,147
,, March, 1902:— From Home	...	200	14	862	527	2,198	—	—	—	—	2,198
,, India	...	595	—	2,392	11	2,403	—	—	—	—	2,403
,, April, 1902:— From Home	...	144	23	5,332	688	6,187	—	—	—	18	6,205
,, India	...	—	—	—	—	—	—	—	—	—	—
,, May, 1902:— From Home	...	968	1,214	2,487	807	5,476	—	—	—	—	5,476
,, India	...	—	—	—	—	—	—	—	—	—	—

APPENDIX 14.

SUMMARY.

STRENGTH OF UNITS AND DRAFTS DESPATCHED TO SOUTH AFRICA UP TO MAY 31ST, 1902, INCLUDING GARRISON ON AUGUST 1ST, 1899.

	Cavalry.	Imperial Yeomanry.	Horse and Field Artillery.	Mountain and Garrison Artillery.	Engineers, Army Service Corps, Army Ordnance Corps, Royal Army Medical Corps, Army Pay Corps, and Army Post Office Corps.	Infantry and Mounted Infantry.	City of London Imperial Volunteers.	Volunteer Service Companies.	Militia.	Contingents from Colonies and India.	South African Constabulary.	Scottish Horse.	Total.
Embarked with Units...	13,688	33,642	12,230	3,490	11,683	98,110	1,520	16,517*	39,018†	27,688	8,465	—	266,051
Embarked in Drafts ...	13,370	482	4,870		11,301	77,337	147	1,024	4,857	231	—	817	114,526
Totals	27,058	34,124	20,590		22,984	175,447	1,667	17,541*	43,875†	27,919	8,465	817	380,577

* Including Artillery, 235; Engineers, 1,157; and two Cyclist companies, 218.   † Including Artillery, 906; Engineers, 359.

APPENDIX 15.

STATEMENT SHEWING :—

A. COMPARATIVE RECRUITING FIGURES OF THE ARMY AND MILITIA PRIOR TO AND DURING THE WAR IN SOUTH AFRICA.

B. RECRUITING FIGURES DURING THE WAR OF THE IMPERIAL YEOMANRY, VOLUNTEERS, SOUTH AFRICAN CONSTABULARY, ETC.

A.

RECRUITING FIGURES PRIOR TO THE WAR IN SOUTH AFRICA.

The average take of Recruits was (7 years) :—
33,815 per year for the Army.
39,523 per year for the Militia.

DURING THE WAR THE FIGURES WERE AS FOLLOWS :—

Raised during	Army.	Militia.
Last Quarter of 1899	13,063	10,337
,, ,, ,, 1900	47,700	37,853
,, ,, ,, 1901	45,157	37,644
Five Months of 1902	20,229	20,010

The average number of Recruits per year amounted to :—
47,305 for the Army.
39,691 for the Militia.

The Nett yearly gain to Recruiting during the War, as compared with previous years, amounted roughly to 13,500 for the Army, while the Recruiting for the Militia remained at the same figure.

APPENDIX 15.

B.

RECRUITING FIGURES DURING THE WAR OF THE IMPERIAL YEOMANRY, VOLUNTEERS, SOUTH AFRICAN CONSTABULARY, ETC.

Detail.	1900.	1901.	1902.	Total.	
Imperial Yeomanry.					
First Contingent, Army Order 1 of 1900	10,242	—	—	10,242	
Drafts, Army Order 40 of 1901	—	16,597	—	16,597	34,715
Drafts, Re-enlisted Men, Army Order 208 of 1901	—	655	—	655	
Drafts, Army Order 8 of 1902	—	—	7,221	7,221	
Volunteers.					
Infantry, Army Order 29 of 1900	10,568	—	—	10,568	
City of London Rifle Volunteers, Army Order 31 of 1900	1,664	—	—	1,664	
Drafts, Infantry, Army Order 41 of 1901	—	4,530	—	4,530	19,393
Cyclists, Army Order 92 of 1901	—	218	—	218	
Drafts, Infantry, Army Order 29 of 1902	—	—	2,413	2,413	
Engineers:—					
Fortress, Army Order 30 of 1900					
Electrical, Army Order 30 of 1900	469	828	163	1,460	
Fortress, Army Order 66 of 1901					
Medical:—					
Volunteers for South Africa, Army Order 58 of 1900					
Volunteers for Home Duty, Army Order 58 of 1900	784	886	191	1,861	
Compounders (Circulars)					
Trained Men, Army Order 86 of 1901					
Artificers	722	75	69	866	
Army Post Office Corps	235	239	40	514	
Telegraphists	300	—	—	300	
Army Service Corps, Clerks, Army Order 118 of 1902	—	—	611	611	
Royal Reservists, Army Order 48 of 1900	24,130	—	—	24,130	
Time-expired Men in South Africa to extend for one year for £5	—	13	—	13	
Time-expired Men in India to extend for Bounty	—	16,612	—	16,612	
South African Constabulary	—	7,739	635	8,374	
Totals	49,114	48,392	11,343	108,849	

Period two years five months:—
    Enlistments 92,224
    Bounty extensions 16,625

        Total 108,849

APPENDIX 16.

CASUALTIES, WASTAGE, ETC., IN THE ARMY IN SOUTH AFRICA DURING THE WAR, UP TO MAY 31ST, 1902.

		Non-commissioned Officers and Men.					
	Officers, exclusive of Staff.	Cavalry.	Artillery.	Infantry and Mounted Infantry.	Others.	Total.	Total Officers and Men.
A. Numbers—							
(1.) Killed to 31st May, 1902	518	—	—	—	—	5,256	5,774
(2.) Wounded to 31st May, 1902	1,851	—	—	—	—	20,978	22,829
(3.) Died of wounds or disease, or accidentally killed in South Africa to 31st May, 1902	554*	—	—	—	—	15,614	16,168
(4.) Disbanded and discharged in South Africa	377*	—	—	—	—	6,308*	6,685*
(5.) In hospital in South Africa on completion of hostilities	291	—	—	—	—	9,422	9,713
B. Numbers left South Africa—							
(1.) For England, not invalids	4,075	—	—	—	—	64,456	68,531
(2.) For England, sick, wounded, and died on passage	3,116	—	—	—	—	72,314	75,430
(3.) For India direct from South Africa, including 2 Regiments of Cavalry, 6 Batteries Royal Field Artillery, and 3 Battalions of Infantry	275	—	—	—	—	9,859	10,134
(4.) For Colonies direct from South Africa—							
(a.) Regulars, including 2 Battalions of Infantry, to Ceylon and 1 Battalion to Bermuda, and 3 Companies Royal Garrison Artillery to Bermuda, 2 Companies to Mauritius, and 1 Company each to St. Helena and Gibraltar	169	—	—	—	—	3,409	3,578
(b.) 1 Battalion of Militia to St. Helena	10	—	—	—	—	379	389
(c.) Colonials	512	—	—	—	—	11,782	12,294
Total left South Africa	8,157	—	—	—	—	162,199	170,356

* These numbers are uncertain.

APPENDIX 17.

STATEMENT OF CASUALTIES, BY CORPS, DURING THE WAR IN SOUTH AFRICA, 1899—1902.

NATAL.

RETURN OF CASUALTIES which occurred in the above Colony during the War in South Africa.

Corps and Regiments	Killed or Died of Wounds.		Died of Disease.		Wounded.		Captured by the Enemy.		Missing.		Total.		Remarks.
	Officers.	Warrant, N.C.O.'s and Men.	Officers.	Warrant, N.C.O.'s and Men.	Officers.	Warrant, N.C.O.'s and Men.	Officers.	Warrant, N.C.O.'s and Men.	Officers.	Warrant, N.C.O.'s and Men.	Officers.	Warrant, N.C.O.'s and Men.	
Staff	5				10		1				16		
Royal Navy and Royal Marines	1	5		19	1	15		4			2	43	
Household Cavalry (Composite regiment)			1	1							1	1	
3rd Dragoon Guards				2								2	
5th „		7	2	38	3	15				2	5	62	
6th „				1								1	
1st Dragoons		4	2	37	1	7	1	8			4	56	
2nd „		1		1								2	
3rd Hussars				3		2						5	
4th „				3								3	
5th Lancers	1	3	1	15	8	22					10	40	
6th Dragoons				1								1	
7th Hussars					1						1		
8th „		1		12		2				2		17	
Carried forward	7	21	6	133	24	63	2	12		4	39	233	

NATAL. RETURN OF CASUALTIES (*continued*).

Corps and Regiments	Killed or Died of Wounds.		Died of Disease.		Wounded.		Captured by the Enemy.		Missing.		Total.		Remarks.
	Officers.	Warrant, N.C.O.'s and Men.	Officers.	Warrant, N.C.O.'s and Men.	Officers.	Warrant, N.C.O.'s and Men.	Officers.	Warrant, N.C.O.'s and Men.	Officers.	Warrant, N.C.O.'s and Men.	Officers.	Warrant, N.C.O.'s and Men.	
Brought forward	7	21	6	133	24	63	2	12	…	4	39	233	
9th Lancers	…	…	…	3	…	…	…	…	…	…	…	3	
10th Hussars	1	…	…	3	…	1	…	…	…	…	…	4	
11th ,,	…	…	…	3	…	…	…	…	…	…	…	…	
12th Lancers	…	5	…	5	2	…	…	…	…	…	3	5	
13th Hussars	…	4	1	36	2	6	…	…	…	2	3	49	
14th ,,	…	…	…	8	…	3	…	…	…	…	1	15	
16th Lancers	…	…	…	…	1	…	…	…	1	…	1	…	
17th ,,	…	…	…	2	…	…	…	…	…	…	…	2	
18th Hussars	…	8	…	11	4	39	4	85	…	…	8	143	
19th ,,	…	…	2	76	…	17	…	…	…	3	2	100	
20th ,,	…	4	…	5	…	…	…	…	…	…	…	5	
Royal Regiment of Artillery	3	22	2	205	16	212	5	84	…	52	26	575	
Royal Engineers	3	14	1	61	4	23	…	…	…	…	8	98	
2nd bn. Grenadier Guards	…	…	…	15	…	…	…	…	…	…	…	15	
1st ,, Scots Guards	…	…	…	11	…	…	…	…	…	…	…	11	
2nd ,, Royal Scots	…	…	…	…	1	…	…	…	…	…	1	…	
1st ,, Royal West Surrey	…	…	…	…	1	…	…	…	…	…	1	…	
2nd ,, East Kent	3	35	…	45	10	273	…	…	…	…	13	353	
2nd ,, Royal Lancaster	1	…	…	1	9	1	1	…	…	…	1	2	
1st ,, Royal Warwickshire	8	122	…	31	…	241	…	31	…	9	18	434	
2nd ,, Royal Fusiliers	1	…	…	…	3	76	…	…	…	…	1	…	
1st ,, Liverpool	1	7	2	17	…	10	…	…	…	…	4	100	
	…	12	…	66	3	…	…	…	…	…	2	88	

APPENDIX 17.

Battalion													
2nd bn. Norfolk	...	...	...	1	...	...	...	...	...	...	...	1
1st ,, Devonshire	4	25	...	39	9	69	...	...	...	...	13	133
2nd ,, Devonshire	...	30	...	33	7	189	3	31	...	...	10	283
1st ,, Suffolk	...	...	...	1	...	...	...	...	...	...	...	1
2nd ,, Suffolk	...	16	...	20	2	71	...	...	...	...	6	107
1st ,, Somersetshire Light Infantry	4	30	...	15	11	185	1	6	...	...	14	236
2nd ,, West Yorkshire	2	...	...	9	...	...	...	2	...	...	...	11
1st ,, East Yorkshire	...	...	...	2	...	...	...	...	...	...	...	2
2nd ,, Bedfordshire	...	...	...	1	...	...	...	...	...	...	1	1
1st ,, Leicestershire	1	6	1	70	1	35	...	...	...	...	3	111
2nd ,, Leicestershire	...	...	...	3	...	...	...	...	...	...	...	3
1st ,, Yorkshire	...	...	...	...	1	...	1	139	...	...	1	...
2nd ,, Yorkshire	...	...	...	22	14	248	6	40	...	...	20	502
1st ,, Lancashire Fusiliers	5	93	1	7	6	100	...	...	...	...	16	184
2nd ,, Lancashire Fusiliers	3	37	1	12	2	54	...	...	...	...	5	76
1st ,, Royal Scots Fusiliers	2	10	...	2	...	...	...	...	...	...	...	2
2nd ,, Royal Welsh Fusiliers	...	...	...	...	...	...	...	...	...	...	...	...
1st ,, South Wales Borderers	1	...	...	25	10	102	...	1	...	12	1	177
2nd ,, King's Own Scottish Borderers	6	49	1	22	16	222	1	5	...	3	17	349
1st ,, Scottish Rifles	6	88	3	37	8	108	17	307	...	...	26	517
2nd ,, Royal Inniskilling Fusiliers	1	62	...	...	...	...	...	...	...	...	26	...
1st ,, Gloucestershire	...	...	...	29	8	181	...	...	...	1	9	251
1st ,, Worcestershire	1	41	...	16	7	163	...	...	...	...	8	198
2nd ,, Worcestershire	1	18	...	...	...	...	...	...	...	...	...	4
1st ,, East Surrey	...	...	...	4	3	30	...	1	...	1	4	84
2nd ,, Border	...	4	1	48	4	130	...	11	...	4	9	237
1st ,, Hampshire	4	36	1	56	...	...	...	...	...	...	...	1
2nd ,, Dorsetshire	...	...	...	1	...	...	...	...	...	...	...	2
1st ,, South Lancashire	...	...	...	2	1	...	...	...	...	...	...	1
1st ,, Welsh	...	...	...	1	...	...	...	...	...	...	...	1
1st ,, Royal Highlanders	...	...	...	1	...	13	...	...	...	...	2	17
1st ,, Oxfordshire Light Infantry	1	4	...	...	...	3	...	...	...	...	...	3
1st ,, Essex	...	...	...	...	...	...	...	...	...	...	...	1
2nd ,, Nottinghamshire and Derbyshire	...	...	...	1	...	...	...	...	...	...	...	1
2nd ,, Northamptonshire	...	...	...	...	...	...	...	...	...	...	...	17
2nd ,, Royal West Kent	...	...	...	4	...	...	...	...	...	...	...	3
2nd ,, Yorkshire Light Infantry	...	1	...	...	...	...	...	...	...	...	...	5
Carried forward	**70**	**804**	**23**	**1,224**	**187**	**2,868**	**41**	**755**	**1**	**91**	**322**	**5,742**

NATAL.   RETURN OF CASUALTIES (continued).

Corps and Regiments.	Killed or Died of Wounds. Officers.	Killed or Died of Wounds. Warrant, N.C.O.'s and Men.	Died of Disease. Officers.	Died of Disease. Warrant, N.C.O.'s and Men.	Wounded. Officers.	Wounded. Warrant, N.C.O.'s and Men.	Captured by the Enemy. Officers.	Captured by the Enemy. Warrant, N.C.O.'s and Men.	Missing. Officers.	Missing. Warrant, N.C.O.'s and Men.	Total. Officers.	Total. Warrant, N.C.O.'s and Men.	Remarks.
Brought forward	70	804	23	1,224	187	2,868	41	755	1	91	322	5,742	
2nd bn. Middlesex	4	43	...	44	4	68	...	7	...	...	8	162	
1st ,, King's Royal Rifles	8	43	...	81	8	180	1	39	...	2	17	345	
2nd ,, ,,	3	26	...	107	...	75	...	1	...	20	3	229	
3rd ,, ,,	3	46	1	59	11	195	...	...	...	8	15	308	
4th ,, ,,	...	...	...	...	...	1	...	...	...	...	...	1	
1st ,, Manchester	...	52	...	56	11	91	...	...	...	...	12	199	
2nd ,, North Staffordshire	...	...	...	10	...	...	...	...	...	...	...	10	
1st ,, York and Lancaster	2	30	...	57	4	162	1	1	...	...	4	250	
1st ,, Durham Light Infantry	...	28	...	21	6	129	...	...	...	...	8	178	
2nd ,, Seaforth Highlanders	...	...	...	1	...	...	...	...	...	...	...	1	
1st ,, Gordon Highlanders	...	...	...	1	...	...	...	...	...	...	...	1	
2nd ,, ,,	8	54	...	26	11	107	1	...	...	...	20	187	
1st ,, Cameron Highlanders	...	...	...	2	...	...	...	...	...	...	...	2	
1st ,, Royal Irish Fusiliers	2	32	...	19	9	88	14	518	...	...	25	657	
2nd ,, ,,	1	16	...	8	8	95	...	...	...	19	9	138	
1st ,, Connaught Rangers	...	48	...	20	10	228	1	7	...	5	11	308	
1st ,, Argyll & Sutherland Highlanders	...	...	1	...	1	...	...	...	...	...	1	1	
2nd ,, Leinster	...	...	...	...	1	...	...	...	1	...	1	...	
1st ,, Royal Munster Fusiliers	...	2	...	4	...	3	...	...	...	...	...	9	
2nd ,, Royal Dublin Fusiliers	3	70	...	27	8	219	...	...	...	18	11	334	
1st ,, ,,	3	41	...	17	10	151	...	...	...	116	14	325	
2nd ,, Rifle Brigade	...	25	...	34	13	163	...	6	...	...	14	222	
1st ,, ,,	5	53	...	61	9	106	...	...	...	...	14	226	

APPENDIX 17.

3rd bn. Rifle Brigade	...	...	...	...	2	...	...	...	...	...	2	...
Other Units of the Regular Forces	5	1	13	131	7	5	...	1	...	1	25	139
Militia	...	10	3	44	2	28	...	...	...	2	5	84
Imperial Yeomanry	...	1	...	18	...	6	...	...	...	2	...	27
Volunteers	1	1	4	61	1	3	...	...	...	...	6	65
Australian Contingent	...	2	1	2	...	...	...	...	...	...	1	4
Canadian ,,	...	...	...	3	...	...	...	...	...	...	...	3
New Zealand ,,	...	...	...	4	...	2	...	...	...	...	...	6
South African ,,	21	127	10	162	37	311	...	43	3	123	71	766
Civil Surgeons, Civilians in Military employment, &c.	1	...	...	10	3	2	...	...	...	...	4	12
Totals	141	1,555	56	2,315	363	5,286	59	1,378	5	407	624	10,941

RETURN OF CASUALTIES which occurred in the CAPE, ORANGE RIVER and TRANSVAAL COLONIES during the War in South Africa.

Corps and Regiments.	Killed or Died of Wounds.		Died of Disease.		Wounded.		Captured by the Enemy.		Missing.		Total.		Remarks.
	Officers.	Warrant, N.C.O.'s and Men.	Officers.	Warrant, N.C.O.'s and Men.	Officers.	Warrant, N.C.O.'s and Men.	Officers.	Warrant, N.C.O.'s and Men.	Officers.	Warrant, N.C.O.'s and Men.	Officers.	Warrant, N.C.O.'s and Men.	
Staff ...	6	...	5	...	20	...	...	...	...	...	31	...	
Royal Navy and Royal Marines ...	4	13	3	19	4	92	...	...	...	...	11	124	
Household Cavalry (Composite regiment)	2	8	2	44	2	42	1	40	...	2	7	136	
1st Dragoon Guards ...	4	8	...	27	8	29	2	...	...	5	14	69	
2nd ,, ,,	3	22	1	18	5	51	...	...	...	...	9	91	
3rd ,, ,,	1	5	...	53	2	15	...	...	...	13	3	86	
4th ,, ,,	...	1	...	...	1	1	...	...	...	...	1	2	
5th ,, ,,	...	2	...	3	2	12	...	...	...	12	2	29	
6th ,, ,,	5	25	1	31	4	55	...	20	...	8	10	139	
7th ,, ,,	3	20	...	34	8	54	...	54	...	...	11	162	
1st Dragoons ...	2	6	...	10	1	20	...	43	...	...	3	79	
2nd ,,	6	28	1	33	4	95	1	88	...	...	12	244	
3rd Hussars ...	1	4	...	10	...	8	...	2	...	2	1	26	
4th ,,	1	1	...	7	1	1	...	...	...	...	2	9	
5th Lancers ...	...	16	...	12	1	52	...	44	...	2	1	126	
6th Dragoons ...	4	31	1	42	10	81	2	17	...	...	17	171	
7th Hussars ...	...	2	...	6	2	3	...	...	...	...	2	11	
8th ,,	3	12	...	19	8	40	...	2	...	...	11	73	
9th Lancers ...	5	38	1	22	14	119	1	11	...	16	21	206	
10th Hussars ...	4	61	1	46	8	57	2	22	...	10	15	196	
11th ,,	...	1	1	3	...	4	...	...	...	...	1	8	
12th Lancers ...	3	22	2	33	8	71	...	...	...	...	13	126	

APPENDIX 17.

Regiment													Total
13th Hussars	...	...	12	...	22	2	38	...	...	32	...	2	106
14th ,,	...	...	12	1	32	1	18	...	...	...	...	2	62
16th Lancers	7	...	20	1	20	10	86	...	1	...	19	2	146
17th ,,	5	...	55	...	26	9	67	...	...	1	...	14	149
18th Hussars	3	...	29	...	30	6	46	...	1	34	...	9	139
19th ,,	1	...	21	...	38	2	53	...	...	45	3	3	160
20th ,,	1	...	1	...	...	1	2	...	...	...	...	1	3
21st Lancers	...	...	...	...	3	...	...	...	...	...	...	...	3
Royal Regiment of Artillery	27	...	156	22	600	80	595	6	...	...	195	141	1,622
Royal Engineers	1	...	13	8	239	12	42	2	...	76	...	23	361
1st bn. Grenadier Guards	...	...	...	...	2	...	...	...	...	67	...	...	2
2nd ,, ,,	2	...	40	2	66	7	133	...	...	8	...	11	247
3rd ,, ,,	5	...	53	2	86	11	153	...	...	4	...	18	296
1st ,, Coldstream Guards	...	...	27	1	72	8	99	...	1	6	...	9	204
2nd ,, ,,	5	...	29	...	81	5	108	...	...	...	...	11	218
1st ,, Scots Guards	...	...	33	2	42	6	79	1	...	...	...	8	154
2nd ,, ,,	1	...	15	...	50	5	50	...	...	...	...	6	115
3rd ,, ,,	...	...	...	...	1	...	1	...	...	...	...	...	1
1st ,, Irish Guards	...	...	4	...	63	1	32	...	1	6	...	2	5
1st ,, Royal Scots	2	...	17	2	38	3	21	...	...	...	...	8	118
2nd ,, Royal West Surrey	...	...	3	1	81	1	183	...	4	76	4	2	62
2nd ,, East Kent	3	...	61	4	24	11	23	4	...	3	1	22	405
1st ,, Royal Lancaster	2	...	5	...	9	3	8	...	...	26	...	5	56
2nd ,, ,,	3	...	6	...	35	15	189	...	...	628	...	3	49
1st ,, Northumberland Fusiliers	9	...	85	...	28	6	103	...	9	...	...	24	309
2nd ,, ,,	3	...	37	...	44	...	...	...	...	...	...	18	796
3rd ,, ,,	1	...	...	1	...	5	44	...	...	7	3	1	...
2nd ,, Royal Warwickshire	1	...	11	...	9	2	25	...	...	1	7	7	109
3rd ,, ,,	...	...	10	...	4	...	6	...	...	...	...	2	52
4th ,, ,,	...	...	3	...	...	...	...	...	...	...	...	...	13
1st ,, Royal Fusiliers	1	...	...	...	...	1	16	...	...	...	...	2	...
2nd ,, ,,	...	...	9	1	41	1	...	...	...	...	1	1	67
3rd ,, ,,	...	...	...	...	...	...	...	...	...	...	...	1	...
4th ,, ,,	1	...	3	...	3	1	8	...	...	...	...	2	14
Carried forward	143	...	1,096	67	2,261	328	3,130	33	1,364	6	305	577	8,156

RETURN OF CASUALTIES which occurred in the Cape, Orange River and Transvaal Colonies (*continued*).

CORPS AND REGIMENTS.	Killed or Died of Wounds.		Died of Disease.		Wounded.		Captured by the Enemy.		Missing.		Total.		Remarks.
	Officers.	Warrant, N.C.O.'s and Men.	Officers.	Warrant, N.C.O.'s and Men.	Officers.	Warrant, N.C.O.'s and Men.	Officers.	Warrant, N.C.O.'s and Men.	Officers.	Warrant, N.C.O.'s and Men.	Officers.	Warrant, N.C.O.'s and Men.	
Brought forward	143	1,096	67	2,261	328	3,130	33	1,364	6	305	577	8,156	
1st bn. Liverpool	1	38	...	19	2	180	2	187	...	1	5	425	
2nd ,, Norfolk	4	11	...	55	5	39	2	15	...	2	11	122	
1st ,, Lincolnshire	...	...	...	...	1	...	...	...	...	...	1	...	
2nd ,, Devonshire	1	34	...	59	8	68	1	86	...	15	10	262	
1st ,, ,,	1	11	...	12	1	23	...	...	...	1	2	47	
2nd ,, Suffolk	...	6	1	38	2	14	...	9	...	...	3	67	
1st ,, Somersetshire Light Infantry	6	36	...	93	7	103	6	97	...	...	19	329	
2nd ,, West Yorkshire	4	5	1	64	2	...	1	22	...	...	7	76	
2nd ,, East ,,	3	44	...	37	4	66	1	...	...	4	8	169	
1st ,, Bedfordshire	2	9	4	59	3	55	...	...	...	...	9	127	
2nd ,, Leicestershire	5	20	...	73	4	65	1	20	...	...	10	178	
1st ,, ,,	1	9	...	41	3	36	...	...	...	...	4	86	
2nd ,, Royal Irish	...	...	1	2	...	...	1	...	...	...	1	2	
1st ,, Yorkshire	5	39	...	39	8	87	...	32	...	4	14	201	
1st ,, Lancashire Fusiliers	1	73	...	77	10	132	...	3	...	...	11	285	
2nd ,, ,, ,,	2	9	...	2	3	11	1	66	...	...	5	88	
3rd ,, ,, ,,	1	17	...	15	3	18	...	4	...	...	5	54	
4th ,, ,, ,,	1	...	...	1	1	3	1	...	...	...	2	4	
2nd ,, Royal Scots Fusiliers	...	...	...	2	...	3	...	...	...	...	...	5	
2nd ,, Cheshire	2	15	1	35	6	43	...	30	...	18	9	93	
1st ,, Royal Welsh Fusiliers	1	2	...	54	1	53	...	...	...	3	2	157	
2nd ,, South Wales Borderers	3	32	...	57	15	91	1	42	...	17	19	225	
1st ,, King's Own Scottish Borderers	2	32	1	81	4	94	2	148	...	14	9	372	
1st ,, ,,	4	27	4	52	5	90	...	4	...	...	13	187	

APPENDIX 17.

2nd bn. Scottish Rifles	4	7				28		3			5	68
1st ,, Royal Inniskilling Fusiliers	2	8	1	30		28		4			4	70
2nd ,, ,,	1		1	30	3	5					4	5
1st ,, Gloucestershire					1						1	13
2nd ,, ,,	1	27		13	3	91	5	209		3	10	402
1st ,, Worcestershire		12		75	1	33		1		15	4	96
2nd ,, ,,	4	37		47	3	74		2		1	9	195
3rd ,, ,,		1		67	4	4					1	11
4th ,, ,,		6		5	4					2	1	20
1st ,, East Lancashire	1	19	6	11		39	1	30		1	9	125
2nd ,, ,,		9		36	1	25					2	66
1st ,, East Surrey		32		32	2	49	1	14			12	149
2nd ,, Duke of Cornwall's Light Infantry	4	55	1	54	6	188	1	1			17	319
1st ,, West Riding	3			75	13	17	1	8			3	29
2nd ,, ,,	1	9		2	1	36					3	80
2nd ,, Border	1	33		35	2	79		3		4	10	181
1st ,, Royal Sussex	2	13		65	7	40	1			10	7	119
2nd ,, Hampshire	3	51		53	4	56	4			2	8	152
1st ,, South Staffordshire	4	16		78	4	62				1		99
2nd ,, Dorsetshire		20		15		7						9
1st ,, South Lancashire		2			12	187	1			2	22	348
1st ,, Welsh	5	67	4	92		2						6
1st ,, Royal Highlanders		3		1	17	347		85			29	600
2nd ,, Oxfordshire Light Infantry	12	119		49	8	88	1	1		14	12	200
1st ,, Essex	3	29	5	82	7	170	4	33			15	365
2nd ,, ,,	2	51		97		15		12			8	53
1st ,, Nottinghamshire and Derbyshire		3	1	23	4	137		2		2	16	242
2nd ,, ,,	2	57		44	13	20				1	2	39
1st ,, Loyal North Lancashire		8	3	10	2	107	2	110			17	301
2nd ,, ,,	4	27		57	8	9	2	1		3	6	32
2nd ,, Northamptonshire		7		12	4	29					6	115
1st ,, Royal Berkshire		8		78	6	2					1	4
1st ,, Royal West Kent	1	23	1	79	5	93		5		5	7	205
2nd ,, ,,	2	10	1	83	1	46		2		8	4	149
Carried forward	255	2,285	108	4,659	572	6,525	70	2,656	6	459	1,011	16,584

RETURN OF CASUALTIES which occurred in the Cape, Orange River and Transvaal Colonies (continued).

Corps and Regiments.	Killed or Died of Wounds.		Died of Disease.		Wounded.		Captured by the Enemy.		Missing.		Total.		Remarks.
	Officers.	Warrant, N.C.O.'s and Men.	Officers.	Warrant, N.C.O.'s and Men.	Officers.	Warrant, N.C.O.'s and Men.	Officers.	Warrant, N.C.O.'s and Men.	Officers.	Warrant, N.C.O.'s and Men.	Officers.	Warrant, N.C.O.'s and Men.	
Brought forward	255	2,285	108	4,659	572	6,525	70	2,656	6	459	1,011	16,584	
1st bn. Yorkshire Light Infantry	1	5	...	3	...	4	...	...	...	...	1	12	
2nd ,, ,, ,, ,,	6	55	2	47	11	151	1	2	...	20	20	275	
1st ,, Shropshire Light Infantry	1	...	...	...	...	...	...	...	...	...	1	...	
2nd ,, ,, ,, ,,	...	44	1	64	12	105	1	9	...	42	14	264	
2nd ,, Middlesex	...	4	...	7	2	8	1	8	...	...	4	27	
3rd ,, ,,	1	...	...	...	...	...	...	...	...	...	1	...	
1st ,, King's Royal Rifle Corps	3	29	1	14	3	54	...	...	...	...	7	97	
2nd ,, ,, ,, ,, ,,	...	3	...	9	1	3	...	...	...	...	1	15	
3rd ,, ,, ,, ,, ,,	3	13	2	31	3	20	...	3	...	27	8	94	
4th ,, ,, ,, ,, ,,	3	9	...	20	8	39	...	...	...	6	11	74	
2nd ,, Wiltshire	2	33	3	66	6	79	...	44	2	105	13	327	
1st ,, Manchester	4	18	...	22	5	26	...	4	...	1	9	71	
2nd ,, ,,	2	7	...	39	5	19	...	18	...	2	7	85	
3rd ,, ,,	...	2	...	2	...	...	...	...	...	...	...	4	
4th ,, ,,	...	...	1	...	1	1	...	...	...	...	1	2	
2nd ,, North Staffordshire	1	9	3	36	1	1	...	...	...	1	5	47	
1st ,, York and Lancaster	1	...	...	4	1	...	...	...	...	...	2	4	
1st ,, Durham Light Infantry	2	10	...	30	2	18	...	...	...	19	5	77	
2nd ,, ,, ,, ,,	1	6	1	6	2	8	2	8	...	...	3	28	
1st ,, Highland Light Infantry	4	30	...	44	9	161	2	138	1	1	15	374	
2nd ,, ,, ,, ,,	...	3	...	10	2	10	...	...	...	...	2	23	
2nd ,, Seaforth Highlanders	10	121	...	22	20	276	1	76	1	9	32	504	
1st ,, Gordon Highlanders	8	50	1	42	16	181	...	...	...	...	25	273	
2nd ,, ,, ,,	1	9	...	1	1	10	...	...	...	...	2	20	

APPENDIX 17.

Unit												Total
1st bn. Cameron Highlanders	3	22	…	31	8	65	1	5	…	…	12	123
2nd " Royal Irish Rifles	1	…	…	…	…	…	…	…	…	…	1	…
1st " Royal Irish Fusiliers	3	31	…	23	11	106	12	673	…	…	26	833
2nd " "	…	8	1	25	2	8	2	44	…	…	5	85
1st " Connaught Rangers	3	20	1	33	1	53	…	10	…	81	5	197
2nd " "	…	10	…	26	6	24	…	11	…	…	6	71
1st " Argyll & Sutherland Highlanders	4	85	…	52	14	208	…	…	…	3	19	348
1st " Leinster	1	3	4	64	…	31	…	21	…	1	5	120
2nd " "	…	…	…	6	1	9	…	…	…	…	1	15
1st " Royal Munster Fusiliers	5	13	…	43	4	70	…	2	…	…	9	128
2nd " "	…	…	…	1	…	…	…	…	…	…	…	1
1st " Royal Dublin Fusiliers	1	13	…	10	…	38	…	…	…	…	6	61
2nd " "	…	…	1	31	3	…	…	…	…	…	2	31
1st " Rifle Brigade	6	23	2	33	5	77	6	61	…	45	11	179
2nd " "	3	22	…	16	3	63	…	…	…	1	8	102
4th " "	…	…	…	15	5	30	…	…	…	1	2	51
Other Units of the Regular Forces	8	5	53	520	37	43	27	700	1	24	105	667
Militia	15	19	35	1,012	32	340	42	899	…	3	109	2,205
Imperial Yeomanry	67	150	25	821	131	1,230	42	6	8	52	273	3,471
City Imperial Volunteers	1	469	…	51	…	58	…	…	…	6	2	131
Volunteers	1	10	…	466	11	114	1	47	…	9	20	664
Australian Contingent	29	28	7	256	77	658	5	99	…	43	119	1,276
Canadian	7	220	8	73	23	255	1	20	…	35	34	470
New Zealand "	7	87	3	83	26	174	2	35	…	6	39	376
South African "	98	78	4	1,376	291	2,694	53	1,134	11	407	512	6,838
Other Contingents	2	1,227	59	5	…	14	1	8	…	…	3	33
Civil Surgeons, Civilians in Military employment, &c.	4	6	…	…	…	…	…	…	…	…	…	…
	4	14	23	166	20	53	2	15	2	1	51	249
Totals	578	5,308	350	10,418	1,395	14,113	231	6,757	31	1,410	2,585	38,006

RECAPITULATION OF CASUALTIES which occurred during the War in South Africa.

Corps and Regiments.	Killed or Died of Wounds.		Died of Disease.		Wounded.		Captured by the Enemy.		Missing.		Total.		Remarks.
	Officers.	Warrant, N.C.O.'s and Men.	Officers.	Warrant, N.C.O.'s and Men.	Officers.	Warrant, N.C.O.'s and Men.	Officers.	Warrant, N.C.O.'s and Men.	Officers.	Warrant, N.C.O.'s and Men.	Officers.	Warrant, N.C.O.'s and Men.	
Staff ...	11	...	...	...	30	...	1	...	...	...	47	...	
Royal Navy and Royal Marines	5	18	5	38	5	107	...	4	...	...	13	167	
Household Cavalry (Composite regiment)	2	8	3	45	2	42	...	40	...	2	8	137	
1st Dragoon Guards	4	8	3	27	8	29	2	...	...	5	14	71	
2nd " "	3	22	...	18	5	51	...	...	...	...	9	91	
3rd " "	1	5	1	55	1	15	...	...	...	13	3	88	
4th " "	...	1	...	...	1	1	...	...	...	...	1	2	
5th " "	5	9	2	41	5	27	...	20	...	14	7	91	
6th " "	3	25	1	32	4	55	1	54	...	8	10	140	
7th " "	2	20	...	34	8	54	1	51	...	...	11	162	
1st Dragoons	6	10	2	47	2	27	...	88	...	...	7	135	
2nd "	1	29	1	34	4	95	...	2	...	2	12	246	
3rd Hussars	1	4	...	13	...	10	...	...	...	...	1	31	
4th "	1	1	...	10	1	1	...	...	...	...	2	12	
5th Lancers	4	19	1	27	9	74	2	44	...	2	11	164	
6th Dragoons	...	31	1	43	10	81	...	17	...	...	17	172	
7th Hussars	3	2	...	6	3	3	...	...	...	2	3	11	
8th "	5	13	1	31	8	42	1	2	...	2	11	90	
9th Lancers	4	38	1	25	14	119	2	11	...	16	21	209	
10th Hussars	1	61	1	49	8	57	...	22	...	10	15	199	
11th "	1	1	1	6	2	5	...	...	...	...	4	12	
12th Lancers	3	22	2	38	8	71	...	...	...	...	13	131	

692

APPENDIX 17.

Regiment												Total
13th Hussars	...	17	...	58	4	44	...	32	...	4	5	155
14th "	...	16	...	40	...	21	...	...	...	...	3	77
16th Lancers	7	20	2	20	11	86	1	1	...	19	20	146
17th "	5	55	1	28	9	67	...	1	...	...	14	151
18th Hussars	3	37	...	41	10	85	...	119	...	...	17	282
19th "	1	25	2	114	2	70	4	45	...	6	5	260
20th "	1	1	...	5	1	2	...	...	...	...	2	8
21st Lancers	1	...	...	3	...	...	...	...	...	...	1	3
Royal Regiment of Artillery	30	178	24	805	96	807	11	160	6	247	167	2,197
Royal Engineers	4	27	9	300	16	65	2	67	...	...	31	459
1st bn. Grenadier Guards	...	...	...	2	...	...	...	...	...	...	...	2
2nd " "	2	40	2	81	7	133	...	8	...	...	11	262
3rd " "	5	53	2	86	11	153	...	4	...	...	18	296
1st " Coldstream Guards	...	27	1	72	8	99	...	6	...	...	9	204
2nd " "	5	29	...	81	5	108	1	...	...	...	11	218
1st " Scots Guards	...	33	2	43	6	79	...	...	...	...	8	155
2nd " "	1	15	...	61	5	50	...	...	...	...	6	126
3rd " "	...	4	...	1	...	1	...	...	...	...	...	1
1st " Irish Guards	1	17	...	63	1	32	1	6	...	...	9	118
1st " Royal Scots	2	...	2	...	4	...	...	...	...	...	9	...
1st " Royal West Surrey	...	...	...	...	1	...	...	...	...	...	1	...
2nd " "	3	38	1	83	11	294	...	76	...	4	15	415
2nd " East Kent	4	61	4	82	11	184	4	3	...	1	23	407
1st " Royal Lancaster	2	...	...	24	3	23	...	57	...	...	5	56
2nd " "	11	128	...	40	9	249	1	...	...	9	21	483
1st " Northumberland Fusiliers	9	85	...	35	15	189	9	628	...	...	24	309
2nd " "	3	37	...	28	6	103	...	...	...	...	18	796
3rd " "	1	...	...	1	...	...	...	...	...	...	1	...
1st " Royal Warwickshire	1	11	1	44	5	44	...	7	...	3	7	109
2nd " "	...	10	...	9	2	25	...	1	...	7	2	52
3rd " "	...	3	...	4	...	6	...	...	...	...	...	13
4th " "	1	...	...	...	1	...	...	...	...	...	2	...
1st " Royal Fusiliers	1	16	...	58	4	92	...	...	...	1	5	167
2nd " "												
Carried forward	170	1,335	78	2,930	404	4,097	45	1,576	7	375	704	10,293

RECAPITULATION OF CASUALTIES which occurred during the War in South Africa (continued).

Corps and Regiments	Killed or Died of Wounds Officers	Killed or Died of Wounds N.C.O.'s and Men	Died of Disease Officers	Died of Disease N.C.O.'s and Men	Wounded Officers	Wounded N.C.O.'s and Men	Captured by the Enemy Officers	Captured by the Enemy N.C.O.'s and Men	Missing Officers	Missing N.C.O.'s and Men	Total Officers	Total N.C.O.'s and Men	Remarks
Brought forward	170	1,335	78	2,930	404	4,097	45	1,576	7	375	704	10,293	
3rd bn. Royal Fusiliers	...	...	1	...	...	...	...	...	...	...	1	...	
4th ,, ,,	...	3	...	3	1	8	...	...	...	...	2	14	
1st ,, Liverpool	1	50	...	85	2	190	2	187	...	1	7	513	
2nd ,, Norfolk	1	11	2	56	5	39	2	15	...	2	11	123	
1st ,, Lincolnshire	4	...	...	...	1	...	...	...	...	...	...	...	
2nd ,, Devonshire	1	34	...	59	8	68	...	86	...	15	10	262	
1st ,, Suffolk	5	36	...	51	10	92	1	...	...	1	15	180	
2nd ,, ,,	...	36	1	71	9	203	3	40	...	...	13	350	
1st ,, Somersetshire Light Infantry	6	36	...	94	7	103	6	97	...	...	19	330	
2nd ,, West Yorkshire	8	21	1	84	4	78	...	...	...	...	13	183	
2nd ,, East Yorkshire	5	74	...	52	15	251	2	28	...	...	22	405	
1st ,, Bedfordshire	2	9	4	68	3	55	...	2	...	4	9	138	
2nd ,, ,,	...	...	...	2	...	...	...	...	...	...	...	2	
1st ,, Leicestershire	5	20	...	74	4	65	1	20	...	...	10	179	
2nd ,, ,,	2	15	1	111	4	71	...	...	...	...	7	197	
1st ,, Royal Irish	...	...	...	5	1	...	...	...	...	...	...	5	
2nd ,, Yorkshire	5	39	1	39	8	87	...	32	...	4	14	201	
1st ,, Lancashire Fusiliers	1	73	...	77	10	132	...	3	...	...	11	285	
2nd ,, ,,	...	...	...	...	...	...	...	...	...	...	...	...	
1st ,, ,,	2	9	...	2	3	11	...	66	...	...	5	88	
2nd ,, ,,	6	110	...	37	17	266	2	143	...	...	25	556	
3rd ,, ,,	1	...	...	1	1	3	...	...	...	...	2	4	
4th ,, ,,	...	...	...	2	...	3	...	...	...	...	...	5	
2nd ,, Royal Scots Fusiliers	5	52	2	42	12	143	6	40	...	...	25	277	

APPENDIX 17.

2nd bn. Cheshire	1	2		54	1	53		30		18	2	157
1st " Royal Welsh Fusiliers	5	42		69	17	145	1	42		3	24	301
2nd " South Wales Borderers	2	32	1	83	4	94	2	148		17	9	374
1st " King's Own Scottish Borderers	5	27	1	52	5	90		4		14	14	187
2nd " Scottish Rifles	10	56	4	55	10	130		4			22	245
1st " Royal Inniskilling Fusiliers	8	96	2	52	17	250	1	9		12	30	419
2nd " "	1					5					4	5
1st " Gloucestershire	1	62		50	3	108	17	307		3	27	530
2nd " "	1	27		75	9	91	5	209			10	402
1st " Worcestershire		12	1	49	3	33		1		3	4	98
2nd " "		37		67	4	74	1	2		15	9	195
3rd " "	4	1		5	4	4				1	1	11
4th " "		6		11		1					1	20
1st " East Lancashire		19	6	36	1	39	1	30		2	9	125
2nd " East Surrey	1	50		61	10	206				1	11	317
1st " Duke of Cornwall's Light Infantry	1	32	1	54	6	49	1	14			12	149
2nd " West Riding	4	55		75	13	188	1	1			17	319
1st " "	3	2		2	1	17		8			3	29
2nd " "	1	27	1	51	9	199				1	11	278
1st " Border	2	33		65	7	79		3		4	10	181
2nd " Royal Sussex	2	13		57	4	40				10	7	123
1st " Hampshire	3	16		78	4	56		2		2	8	152
2nd " South Staffordshire	4	24	1	63	3	92				2	4	183
1st " Dorsetshire		38	1	56	4	137	1	11		4	9	246
2nd " South Lancashire	4	67	4	93	12	187				2	22	349
1st " Welsh	5	3		3		2						8
1st " Royal Highlanders		119		49	17	347	1	85			29	600
2nd " "	12	29		83	8	88		1			12	201
1st " Oxfordshire Light Infantry	3	51	5	98	7	170	1	33		14	15	366
1st " Essex	2	3		23	4	15	4	12			8	53
2nd " "		57	1	44	13	137		2		2	16	242
1st " Nottinghamshire and Derbyshire	2	12		10	3	33				1	4	56
1st " Loyal North Lancashire	1	27	3	57	8	107	2	110			17	301
2nd " "	4	7		12	4	9	2	1		3	6	32
Carried forward	322	3,047	129	5,637	746	9,220	111	3,404	7	536	1,315	21,844

RECAPITULATION OF CASUALTIES which occurred during the War in South Africa (continued).

CORPS AND REGIMENTS.	Killed or Died of Wounds. Officers	Killed or Died of Wounds. N.C.O.'s and Men	Died of Disease. Officers	Died of Disease. N.C.O.'s and Men	Wounded. Officers	Wounded. N.C.O.'s and Men	Captured by the Enemy. Officers	Captured by the Enemy. N.C.O.'s and Men	Missing. Officers	Missing. N.C.O.'s and Men	Total. Officers	Total. N.C.O.'s and Men	Remarks.
Brought forward	322	3,047	129	5,637	746	9,220	111	3,404	7	536	1,315	21,844	
2nd bn. Northamptonshire	...	8	...	78	6	32	...	...	...	...	6	118	
1st ,, Royal Berkshire	...	...	...	1	1	2	...	...	...	...	1	4	
2nd ,, ,, ,,	1	23	1	79	5	93	...	5	...	5	7	205	
2nd ,, Royal West Kent	2	10	1	84	1	46	...	2	...	8	4	150	
1st ,, Yorkshire Light Infantry	1	5	...	3	...	4	...	...	...	...	1	12	
2nd ,, ,, ,, ,,	6	56	2	51	11	151	1	2	...	20	20	280	
1st ,, Shropshire Light Infantry	1	...	...	...	...	...	...	...	...	...	1	...	
2nd ,, ,, ,, ,,	...	44	1	64	12	105	1	9	...	42	14	264	
2nd ,, Middlesex	5	47	...	51	6	76	1	15	...	...	12	189	
3rd ,, ,,	...	...	...	...	1	...	...	...	...	...	1	...	
1st ,, King's Royal Rifle Corps	11	72	1	95	11	234	1	39	...	2	24	442	
2nd ,, ,, ,, ,, ,,	3	29	...	116	1	78	...	1	...	20	4	244	
3rd ,, ,, ,, ,, ,,	6	59	3	90	14	215	...	3	...	35	23	402	
4th ,, ,, ,, ,, ,,	3	9	...	20	8	40	...	...	...	6	11	75	
2nd ,, Wiltshire	3	33	3	66	6	79	...	44	...	105	13	327	
1st ,, Manchester	5	70	...	78	16	117	...	4	...	1	21	270	
2nd ,, ,,	2	7	...	39	5	19	...	18	...	2	7	85	
3rd ,, ,,	...	2	...	2	...	...	...	...	...	...	...	4	
4th ,, ,,	...	...	...	...	...	...	...	...	...	...	...	2	
1st ,, North Staffordshire	1	9	3	46	1	...	...	...	...	1	5	57	
1st ,, York and Lancaster	1	30	...	61	5	162	...	1	...	...	6	254	
1st ,, Durham Light Infantry	4	38	1	51	8	147	...	...	...	19	13	255	
2nd ,, ,, ,, ,,	1	6	...	6	2	8	...	8	...	...	3	28	
1st ,, Highland Light Infantry	4	30	...	44	9	161	2	138	...	1	15	374	

APPENDIX 17.

2nd bn. Highland Light Infantry	...	3	...	10	2	10	...	...	...	...	2	23
2nd ,, Seaforth Highlanders	10	121	...	23	20	276	1	76	1	9	32	505
1st ,, Gordon Highlanders	8	50	...	43	16	181	...	...	...	...	25	274
2nd ,, Gordon Highlanders	9	63	1	27	12	117	1	...	...	...	22	207
1st ,, Cameron Highlanders	3	22	...	33	8	65	1	5	...	...	12	125
2nd ,, ,, ,,	1	...	...	...	...	...	...	...	...	...	1	...
2nd ,, Royal Irish Rifles	3	31	...	23	11	106	12	673	...	...	26	833
1st ,, Royal Irish Fusiliers	2	40	1	44	11	96	16	562	...	...	30	742
2nd ,, Royal Irish Fusiliers	4	36	...	41	9	148	...	10	...	100	14	335
1st ,, Connaught Rangers	...	58	1	46	16	252	1	18	...	5	17	379
1st ,, Argyll & Sutherland Highlanders	4	85	2	52	14	208	...	...	...	3	20	348
2nd ,, ,, ,,	...	...	...	...	1	...	...	...	...	...	1	...
1st ,, Leinster	1	3	...	65	1	31	...	21	...	1	6	121
2nd ,, ,,	...	...	4	6	1	9	...	...	...	...	1	15
1st ,, Royal Munster Fusiliers	5	13	...	43	4	70	...	2	...	...	9	128
2nd ,, ,,	...	2	...	5	...	3	...	...	...	...	...	10
1st ,, Royal Dublin Fusiliers	4	83	...	37	13	257	...	...	...	18	17	395
2nd ,, ,,	3	41	1	48	11	151	...	...	...	116	16	356
1st ,, Rifle Brigade	6	48	2	67	16	240	1	1	...	45	25	401
2nd ,, ,,	8	75	...	77	14	169	...	6	1	1	22	328
3rd ,, ,,	...	...	...	...	2	...	...	...	...	...	2	...
4th ,, ,,	...	...	...	15	2	30	...	...	...	1	2	51
Other Units of the Regular Forces	13	5	66	651	44	48	6	62	1	25	130	806
Militia	15	20	38	1,056	34	368	27	700	...	5	114	2,289
Imperial Yeomanry	67	160	25	839	131	1,236	42	899	8	54	273	3,498
City Imperial Volunteers	...	470	...	51	...	58	...	6	...	6	2	131
Volunteers	2	10	11	527	12	117	1	47	...	9	26	729
Australian Contingent	29	29	9	258	77	658	5	99	...	43	120	1,280
Canadian ,,	7	222	3	76	23	255	5	20	...	35	34	473
New Zealand ,,	7	87	4	87	26	176	2	35	...	6	39	382
South African ,,	119	78	69	1,538	328	3,005	53	1,177	14	530	583	7,604
Other Contingents	2	1,354	...	5	...	14	1	8	...	...	3	33
Civil Surgeons, Civilians in Military employment, &c.	...	6	...	...	...	...	...	...	...	...	...	...
	5	14	23	176	23	55	2	15	2	1	55	261
Totals	719	6,863	406	12,733	1,758	19,399	290	8,135	36	1,817	3,209	48,947

APPENDIX 18.

EXPENDITURE INCURRED ON ARMY VOTES IN

	1899—1900.			1900—1901.		
	Extra Charges.*	Savings and Extra Receipts.	Net Extra Charge.*	Extra Charges.*	Savings and Extra Receipts.	Net Extra Charge.*
	£	£	£	£	£	£
1.—Pay, &c., of Army..	2,793,000	3,400	2,789,600	9,410,950	715,450	8,695,500
2.—Medical Establishment ..	149,000	—	149,000	795,000	5,000	790,000
3.—Militia, Pay, Bounty, &c.	283,500	1,500	282,000	1,690,100	103,700	1,586,400
5.—Transport and Remounts..	10,228,000	38,500	10,189,500	21,640,000	476,000	21,164,000
7.—Provisions, Forage, &c. ..	5,336,700	56,000	5,280,700	16,022,000	750,000	15,272,000
8.—Clothing ..	1,230,000	—	1,230,000	3,578,000	54,000	3,524,000
.—Warlike and other Stores	2,976,000	—	2,976,000	9,654,300	—	9,654,300
9.—Works, Buildings, and Repairs..	152,700	—	152,700	1,499,100	—	1,499,100
.—Educational Establishments	—	900	900†	2,000	4,600	2,600†
.—Miscellaneous	14,500	23,768	9,268†	178,450	342,850	164,400†
.—War Office ..	17,130	130	17,000	56,400	600	55,800
.—Non-effective Charges—Officers	29,627	63,359	33,732†	378,500	190,000	188,500
.—Non-effective Charges—Men	—	—	—	74,400	26,000	48,400
Totals £	23,210,157	187,557	23,022,600	64,979,200	2,668,200	62,311,000

* In excess of estimated peace expenditure.

CONSEQUENCE OF THE WAR IN SOUTH AFRICA.

1901—1902.			1902—1903.			1903—1904.			TOTAL.		
Extra Charges.*	Savings and Extra Receipts.	Net Extra Charge.*	Extra Charges.*	Savings and Extra Receipts.	Net Extra Charge.*	Extra Charges.*	Savings and Extra Receipts.	Net Extra Charge.*	Extra Charges.*	Savings and Extra Receipts.	Net Extra Charge.*
£	£	£	£	£	£	£	£	£	£	£	£
15,249,000	752,000	14,497,000	14,893,125	701,125	14,192,000	969,846	127,846	842,000	43,315,921	2,299,821	41,016,100
796,500	2,700	793,800	528,660	10,660	518,000	—	18,000	18,000†	2,269,160	36,360	2,232,80
1,216,300	73,200	1,143,100	1,006,255	9,755	996,500	—	—	—	4,196,155	188,155	4,008,00
18,562,500	310,000	18,252,500	10,692,115	3,287,515	7,404,600	1,537,438	790,438	747,000	62,660,053	4,902,453	57,757,60
19,106,600	1,670,300	17,436,300	12,588,050	2,341,050	10,247,000	2,676,773	1,340,773	1,336,000	55,730,123	6,158,123	49,572,00
2,944,200	—	2,944,200	1,769,470	107,270	1,662,200	47,000	23,000	24,000	9,568,670	184,270	9,384,40
6,000,000	200,000	5,800,000	3,081,000	573,000	2,508,000	74,494	361,494	287,000†	21,785,794	1,134,494	20,651,30
1,755,500	53,000	1,702,500	1,215,380	185,380	1,030,000	78,663	113,663	35,000†	4,701,343	352,043	4,349,30
—	—	—	—	—	—	—	—	—	2,000	5,500	3,50
195,600	423,900	228,300†	418,500	621,500	203,000†	27,229	18,229	9,000	834,279	1,430,247	595,96
78,500	—	78,500	71,200	—	71,200	—	—	—	223,230	730	222,50
522,000	177,500	344,500	583,700	112,000	471,700	213,000	—	213,000	1,786,827	542,859	1,183,96
246,000	18,000	228,000	448,300	39,500	408,800	438,000	39,000	399,000	1,206,700	122,500	1,084,20
66,672,700	3,680,600	62,992,100	47,295,755	7,988,755	39,307,000	6,062,443	2,832,443	3,230,000	208,220,255	17,357,555	190,862,70

† Net Savings and Extra Receipts.

APPENDIX 19.

A LIST OF RECIPIENTS OF THE VICTORIA CROSS DURING THE WAR IN SOUTH AFRICA, 1899—1902.

BATTLE.	DATE.	NAME AND RANK.
Mafeking (Action near)	14th Oct. 1899	Captain C. Fitzclarence, Royal Fusiliers, *Lond. Gaz.* 6th July, 1900.
Elandslaagte (Natal)	21st Oct. 1899	Captain M. F. M. Meiklejohn, Gordon Highlanders, *Lond. Gaz.* 20th July, 1900.
,, ,,	21st Oct. 1899	Sergeant-Major Wm. Robertson, Gordon Highlanders, *Lond. Gaz.* 20th July, 1900.
,, ,,	21st Oct. 1899	Captain R. Johnstone, Imperial Light Horse, *Lond. Gaz.* 12th Feb. 1901.
,, ,,	21st Oct. 1899	Captain C. H. Mullins, Imperial Light Horse, *Lond. Gaz.* 12th Feb. 1901.
Ladysmith (Action near)	30th Oct. 1899	Second Lieutenant J. Norwood, 5th Dragoon Guards, *Lond. Gaz.* 20th July, 1900.
Magersfontein	11th Dec. 1899	Corporal J. Shaul, Highland Light Infantry, *Lond. Gaz.* 28th Sept. 1900.
,,	11th Dec. 1899	Lieutenant H. E. M. Douglas, Royal Army Medical Corps, *Lond. Gaz.* 29th March, 1901.
,,	11th Dec. 1899	Captain E. B. Towse, Gordon Highlanders, *Lond. Gaz.* 6th July, 1900.
Colenso (Natal)	15th Dec. 1899	Captain W. N. Congreve, Rifle Brigade, *Lond. Gaz.* 2nd Feb. 1900.
,, ,,	15th Dec. 1899	Lieutenant Hon. F. S. Roberts, King's Royal Rifle Corps, *Lond. Gaz.* 2nd Feb. 1900. (Died of wounds.)
,, ,,	15th Dec. 1899	Corporal G. E. Nurse, 66th battery Royal Field artillery, *Lond. Gaz.* 2nd Feb. 1900.
,, ,,	15th Dec. 1899	Captain H. L. Reed, 7th battery Royal Field artillery, *Lond. Gaz.* 2nd Feb. 1900.
,,	15th Dec. 1899	Major W. Babtie, C.M.G., Royal Army Medical Corps, *Lond. Gaz.* 20th April, 1900.
,, ,,	15th Dec. 1899	Private C. Ravenhill, Royal Scots Fusiliers, *Lond. Gaz.* 4th June, 1901.
,, ,,	15th Dec. 1899	Captain H. N. Schofield, Royal Field artillery, *Lond. Gaz.* 30th Aug. 1901.
Game Tree (near Mafeking)	26th Dec. 1899	Trooper H. E. Ramsden, Protectorate regiment, *Lond. Gaz.* 6th July, 1900.
,, ,, ,, ,,	26th Dec. 1899	Sergeant H. R. Martineau, Protectorate regiment, *Lond. Gaz.* 6th July, 1900.

APPENDIX 19. 701

A List of Recipients of the Victoria Cross (*continued*).

BATTLE.	DATE.	NAME AND RANK.
Colesberg (Reconnaissance near)	5th Jan. 1900	Lieutenant Sir J. P. Milbanke, Bart. 10th Hussars, *Lond. Gaz.* 6th July, 1900.
Cæsar's Camp (Ladysmith)	6th Jan. 1900	Private J. Pitts, Manchester regiment, *Lond. Gaz.* 26th July, 1901.
,, ,, ,,	6th Jan. 1900	Private R. Scott, Manchester regiment, *Lond. Gaz.* 26th July, 1901.
Wagon Hill (Ladysmith)	6th Jan. 1900	Lieutenant J. E. I. Masterson, 1st battalion Devonshire regiment, *Lond. Gaz.* 4th June, 1901.
,, ,, ,,	6th Jan. 1900	Lieutenant R. J. T. Digby Jones, Royal Engineers, *Lond. Gaz.* 8th Aug. 1902. (Killed.)
,, ,, ,,	6th Jan. 1900	Trooper H. Albrecht, Imperial Light Horse, *Lond. Gaz.* 8th Aug. 1902. (Killed.)
Paardeberg	18th Feb. 1900	Lieutenant F. N. Parsons, Essex regiment, *Lond. Gaz.* 20th Nov. 1900. (Killed at Driefontein, 10th March, 1900.)
,,	18th Feb. 1900	Sergeant A. Atkinson, Yorkshire regiment, *Lond. Gaz.* 8th Aug. 1902. (Died of wounds.)
Tugela Heights (Natal)	23rd Feb. 1900	Private A. E. Curtis, 2nd battalion East Surrey regiment, *Lond. Gaz.* 15th Jan. 1901.
Arundel (Plewman's Farm, Cape Colony)	24th Feb. 1900	Sergeant J. Firth, 1st battalion West Riding regiment, *Lond. Gaz.* 11th June, 1901.
Hart's Hill (Natal)	24th Feb. 1900	Lieutenant E. T. Inkson, Royal Army Medical Corps, *Lond. Gaz.* 15th Jan. 1901.
Terrace Hill (Tugela, Natal)	27th Feb. 1900	Captain C. Mansel-Jones, West Yorkshire regiment, *Lond. Gaz.* 27th July, 1900.
Bloemfontein (Action near)	13th Mar. 1900	Sergeant H. Engleheart, 10th Hussars, *Lond. Gaz.* 5th Oct. 1900.
Korn Spruit	31st Mar. 1900	Major E. J. Phipps-Hornby, Q. battery Royal Horse artillery, *Lond. Gaz.* 26th June, 1900.
,, ,,	31st Mar. 1900	Sergeant C. Parker, Q. battery, Royal Horse artillery, *Lond. Gaz.* 26th June, 1900.
,, ,,	31st Mar. 1900	Gunner Isaac Lodge, Q. battery Royal Horse artillery, *Lond. Gaz.* 26th June, 1900.
,, ,,	31st Mar. 1900	Driver H. Glasock, Q. battery, Royal Horse artillery, *Lond. Gaz.* 26th June, 1900.
,, ,,	31st Mar. 1900	Lieutenant F. A. Maxwell, D.S.O., Indian Staff Corps, attached Roberts' Horse, *Lond. Gaz.* 8th March, 1901.
Wakkerstroom	20th Apr. 1900	Lieutenant W. H. S. Nickerson, Royal Army Medical Corps, *Lond. Gaz.* 12th Feb. 1901.

702   THE WAR IN SOUTH AFRICA.

A LIST OF RECIPIENTS OF THE VICTORIA CROSS (continued).

BATTLE.	DATE.	NAME AND RANK.
Wakkerstroom	22nd Apr. 1900	Corporal H. Beet, 1st battalion Derbyshire regiment, Lond. Gaz. 12th Feb. 1901.
Crows Nest Hill (near Johannesburg)	29th May, 1900	Corporal J. F. McKay, Gordon Highlanders, Lond. Gaz. 10th Aug. 1900.
Delagoa Bay Railway	2nd June, 1900	Corporal F. Kirby, Royal Engineers, Lond. Gaz. 5th Oct. 1900.
Lindley	26th June, 1900	Private C. Ward, 2nd battalion Yorkshire Light Infantry, Lond. Gaz. 28th Sept. 1900.
Wolve Spruit (near Standerton)	5th July, 1900	Sergeant A. H. L. Richardson, Lord Strathcona's Corps, Lond. Gaz. 14th Sept. 1900.
Krugersdorp (Action near)	11th July, 1900	Captain D. R. Younger, Gordon Highlanders, Lond. Gaz. 8th Aug. 1902. (Killed.)
Leehoek, or Doornbosch Fontein (near Krugersdorp)	11th July, 1900	Captain W. E. Gordon, Gordon Highlanders, Lond. Gaz. 28th Sept. 1900.
Vredefort	24th July, 1900	Captain N. R. Howse, New South Wales Medical Staff Corps, Lond. Gaz. 4th June, 1901.
Mosilikatse Nek	2nd Aug. 1900	Private W. House, 2nd battalion Royal Berkshire regiment, Lond. Gaz. 7th Oct. 1902.
Essenbosch Farm	7th Aug. 1900	Sergeant T. Lawrence, 17th Lancers, Lond. Gaz. 15th Jan. 1901.
Van Wyks Vlei (Transvaal)	21st Aug. 1900	Corporal H. J. Knight, 1st battalion Liverpool regiment, Lond. Gaz. 4th Jan. 1901.
,, ,, ,, ,,	21st Aug. 1900	Sergeant H. Hampton, 2nd battalion Liverpool regiment, Lond. Gaz. 18th Oct. 1901.
,, ,, ,, ,,	23rd Aug. 1900	Private W. Heaton, 1st battalion Liverpool regiment, Lond. Gaz. 18th Jan. 1901.
Bergendal (Transvaal)	27th Aug. 1900	Private E. Durrant, 2nd battalion Rifle Brigade, Lond. Gaz. 18th Oct. 1901.
Warm Bad (Transvaal)	1st Sept. 1900	Private J. H. Bisdee, Tasmanian Imperial Bushmen, Lond. Gaz. 13th Nov. 1900.
,, ,, ,,	1st Sept. 1900	Lieutenant G. G. E. Wylly, Tasmanian Imperial Bushmen, Lond. Gaz. 23rd Nov. 1900.
Geluk (Transvaal)	13th Oct. 1900	Major E. D. Brown, 14th Hussars, Lond. Gaz. 15th Jan. 1901.
Zeerust (Action near)	20th Oct. 1900	Lieutenant A. C. Doxat, 3rd battalion Imperial Yeomanry, Lond. Gaz. 15th Jan. 1901.
Komati River	7th Nov. 1900	Lieutenant H. Z. C. Cockburn, Royal Canadian Dragoons, Lond. Gaz. 23rd April, 1901.
,, ,,	7th Nov. 1900	Lieutenant R. E. W. Turner, Royal Canadian Dragoons, Lond. Gaz. 23rd April, 1901.
,, ,,	7th Nov. 1900	Sergeant E. Holland, Royal Canadian Dragoons, Lond. Gaz. 23rd April, 1901.

APPENDIX 19. 703

A LIST OF RECIPIENTS OF THE VICTORIA CROSS (*continued*).

BATTLE.	DATE.	NAME AND RANK.
Dewetsdorp	22nd Nov. 1900	Private C. Kennedy, 2nd battalion Highland Light Infantry, *Lond. Gaz.* 18th Oct. 1901.
Nooitgedacht	13th Dec. 1900	Sergeant D. Farmer, 1st battalion Cameron Highlanders, *Lond. Gaz.* 12th April, 1901.
Monument Hill (Belfast)	Night of 7th—8th Jan. 1901	Private J. Barry, Royal Irish regiment, *Lond. Gaz.* 18th Aug. 1902. (Killed.)
Naauwpoort (Action near)	28th Jan. 1901	Farrier-Major W. J. Hardham, 4th New Zealand contingent, *Lond. Gaz.* 4th Oct. 1901.
Bothwell Camp	6th Feb. 1901	Sergeant W. B. Traynor, 2nd battalion West Yorkshire regiment, *Lond. Gaz.* 17th Sept. 1901.
Strijdenburg	24th Feb. 1901	Corporal J. J. Clements, Rimington's Guides, *Lond. Gaz.* 4th June, 1901.
Derby	3rd Mar. 1901	Lieutenant F. B. Dugdale, 5th Lancers, *Lond. Gaz.* 17th Sept. 1901.
Brakpan	16th May, 1901	Lieutenant F. W. Bell, West Australian M. I., *Lond. Gaz.* 4th Oct. 1901.
Lambrecht Fontein	18th May, 1901	Lieutenant and Adjutant G. H. B. Coulson, King's Own Scottish Borderers 7th M.I., *Lond. Gaz.* 8th Aug. 1902. (Killed.)
Thabanchu	15th June, 1901	Sergeant Jas. Rogers, South African Constabulary, *Lond. Gaz.* 18th April, 1902.
Vlakfontein	3rd July, 1901	Lieutenant W. J. English, 2nd Scottish Horse, *Lond. Gaz.* 4th Oct. 1901.
Springbok Laagte	4th July, 1901	Private H. G. Crandon, 18th Hussars, *Lond. Gaz.* 18th Oct. 1901.
Ruiters' Kraal	13th Aug. 1901	Sergeant-Major A. Young, Cape Police, *Lond. Gaz.* 8th Nov. 1901.
Blood River Poort	17th Sept. 1901	Lieutenant L. A. E. Price-Davies, D.S.O., King's Royal Rifle Corps, *Lond. Gaz.* 29th Nov. 1901.
Itala (Zululand)	26th Sept. 1901	Driver F. G. Bradley, 69th battery Royal Field artillery, *Lond. Gaz.* 27th Dec. 1901.
Moedwil	30th Sept. 1901	Private W. Bees, 1st battalion Derbyshire regiment, *Lond. Gaz.* 17th Dec. 1901.
Geelhoutboom	23rd Nov. 1901	Lieutenant L. C. Maygar, 5th Victorian Mounted Rifles, *Lond. Gaz.* 11th Feb. 1902.
Tygerskloof	18th Dec. 1901	Surgeon-Captain T. J. Crean, 1st Imperial Light Horse, *Lond. Gaz.* 11th Feb. 1902.
Tafelkop (Orange River Colony)	20th Dec. 1901	Shoeing-Smith A. E. Ind, Royal Horse artillery, XI. section Pom-poms, *Lond Gaz.* 15th Aug. 1902.
Vlakfontein	8th Feb. 1902	Surgeon-Captain A. Martin-Leake, South African Constabulary, *Lond. Gaz.* 13th May, 1902.

APPENDIX 20.

STATEMENT OF BOER PRISONERS OF WAR, showing how disposed of— December 27th, 1900.

Cape Colony	Confined at Green Point (near Cape Town)	4,825
	„ „ Simon's Town	1,901
	„ in Hospital	81
	On parole at Cape Town	236
	„ in the Colony	310
	Total	7,353
Natal	Confined in	607
	On parole in	126
Ceylon	Confined in	4,335
	On voyage to	633
St. Helena		2,456
Dead		245
	Total prisoners	15,755

STATEMENT OF BOER PRISONERS OF WAR, showing how disposed of— June 1st, 1902.

In South Africa	1,733
„ India	9,125
„ Colonies	15,136
Total	25,994
Released on parole	789
Dead	812
Returned to refugee camps	3,194
Burghers on parole	2,552
Total	33,341

APPENDIX 20.

MONTHLY COMPARATIVE STATEMENT FOR 1901—2, showing approximately the Casualties in the Boer Forces during that period.

1901.	Killed.	Wounded.	Killed or wounded, not specified which.	Prisoners.	Surrenders.	Prisoners or surrenders, not specified which.	Total.
January	227	442	14	98	78	—	859
February	161	175	405	530	501	—	1,772
March	199	234	23	610	406	—	1,472
April	105	118	18	3	—	2,193	2,437
May	183	324	—	9	—	2,069	2,585
June	220	193	—	970	894	—	2,277
July	160	135	—	1,074	451	—	1,820
August	185	60	—	1,363	554	—	2,162
September	242	164	—	1,505	334	—	2,245
October	155	97	—	1,192	162	—	1,606
November	133	118	—	844	162	—	1,257
December	148	64	—	1,338	375	—	1,925
1902.							
January	124	70	—	1,013	256	—	1,463
February	150	146	—	1,921	344	—	2,561
March	70	85	—	599	261	—	1,015
April	128	121	—	736	164	—	1,149
May	29	6	—	924	28	—	987
Totals	2,619	2,552	460	14,729	4,970	4,262	29,592

SUMMARY, showing Decrease of Boer Forces at specified periods of the War.

Original Strength of Boer Forces (*Vide* Volume I., Appendix 4, page 459)		87,365
Prisoners of war, December 27th, 1900	15,755	
Casualties, 1899—1900	21,239	
		36,994
Forces in the Field, January 1st, 1901		50,371
Casualties, 1901—2		29,592
Total Forces in the Field on conclusion of peace, May 31st, 1902		20,779*
* Transvaal	11,232	
Orange Free State	5,833	
Rebels	3,574	
Renegades and foreigners	140	
Total	20,779	

INDEX

INDEX TO VOLUME IV

AANGAAN, 476.
Aapies river, 445.
Aaronslaagte, 254, 257.
Aasvogels Krans, 246.
Abandonment of Wolmaranstad, 415.
Aberdeen, and district, 72, 74, 173, 175-6, 226, 228-9, 367, 456, 463, 465; attack on the town, 466.
Aberdeen Road Station, 74, 173, 237, 278; attack on, 228.
Aberfeld, 482.
Abrahams Kraal (Modder river), 95, 264.
Abrahamskraal (east of Koffyfontein), 432.
Action of: Bakenlaagte, 304-15; Boschbult, 494-6; Boschmanskop, 518-19; Forts Itala and Prospect, 219-21; Graspan, 105; Gruisfontein, 408; Moedwil, 295-7; Nooitgedacht, 13-22; Onverdacht, 57; Onverwacht, 379-80; Quaggafontein, 287-8; Richmond, 226; Rooiwal, 499-503; Sannah's Post, 318-19; Scheepers Nek, 217-18; Springhaan Nek, 51; Tabaksberg, the, 76; Tafel Kop (Orange River Colony), 389-90; Tiger Kloof Spruit, 386-7; Treurfontein, 406-7; Tweebosch, 417-20; Tweefontein, 394; Vlakfontein, 186-8; Wilmansrust, 203; Yzerspruit, 411-14; Zuur Vlakte, 234-5.
Acting-President, South African Republic. *See* BURGER, S. W.

Address to burghers, by L. Botha, 527.
Adelaide, 174, 277, 467.
Adjutant-General, The, 301.
Administration of: Cape Colony, 176-8, 224, 230-1; the Orange River Colony and the Transvaal, on conclusion of peace, 525, 548, 560-3.
Aide-Memoire, from the Netherland Government (peace proposals), 529-31.
Akel, 164.
Albert, 60.
Albert Junction, 179.
Albertina station, 429.
Alberts, Commandant H., 210, 376.
Alberts, Commandant Sarel, 409.
Alderson, Brigadier-General E. A. H., C.B., A.D.C., 21-2, 111, 113, 115, 117, 119-22, 127.
Alettasdraai, 160-1.
Alexander, Lieut.-Colonel H., D.S.O., 237-8, 242, 244, 283-6, 290, 359, 370.
Alexanders Kraal, 229.
Alicedale, 466.
Aliwal North, 46, 60, 62-4, 78, 97, 163-5, 168, 176, 179, 234, 236, 253, 261, 266-7, 286-7, 317, 327-8, 368, 464.
Alkmaar (Delagoa Bay line), 208.
Alkmaar (or Spitzkop), 200, 378.
Allegrens Kraal, 466.
Alleman's Dam, 260.
Allemans Kraal, 466.

Allemans Poort, 273.
Allenby, Colonel E. H. H., 111, 113, 115–17, 119–21, 127, 142, 149–52, 155, 188–9, 192–4, 197, 216, 219, 222–3, 291–2, 303, 315, 371, 373, 375–6, 378–9, 381, 485–7, 490, 514, 517, 520, 522.
Ambuscades, 154, 191, 233, 330, 344, 376, 381, 444, 450, 484.
America (U.S.A.), 25.
America siding, 57.
Amersfoort, 116–17, 147, 154, 199–200, 376.
Ammunition, 81, 109 ; Boers, capture of, by, 351, 355, 469 ; expenditure of, 363 ; short of, 125, 355 ; British, capture of, by, 52, 135, 141, 146, 158, 208, 211, 241, 257, 261, 429, 438–9, 443, 476 ; exhaustion of, at Yzerspruit, 414 ; expenditure of, 221 ; at Bakenlaagte, 312–13 ; Boschbult, 496 ; Itala, 220 ; Ookiep, 472.
Amnesty, general, 532–4, 536, 560–3.
Amos Poort, 74.
Amsterdam, and district, 114, 117, 148, 199, 204–5, 216, 222, 377, 379 ; blockhouse line to, 372, 512.
Anderson, Lieut.-Colonel W. C., 410–15, 417, 419, 422.
Anley, Major F. G., 308–10, 314.
Annenous, 470.
Appendices, 567–705.
Arbitration, 536.
Arcadia, 317.
Argyll and Sutherland Highlanders. *See* REGULAR UNITS.
Arming of loyalists in Cape Colony, 69.
Armistice, proposals for, 107, 450 ; terms of, for peace, 508.
Armoured trains, 80–1, 209, 228, 238, 362, 366, 402, 442, 467, 507, 509.
Arms : Boers, short of, 355 ; capture of, by, 469 ; laying down of, by, 107 ; thrown away by, 202. *See also* PEACE CONDITIONS.

Army, British, strength of in South Africa. *See* STRENGTH ; *also* APPENDIX 13.
Army Medical Corps, Royal. *See* REGULAR UNITS ; *also* APPENDIX 7.
Army Ordnance Department. *See* APPENDIX 8.
Army Post Office Corps. *See* APPENDIX 9.
Army Remount Department. *See* APPENDIX 11.
Army Service Corps. *See* REGULAR UNITS ; *also* APPENDICES 5 and 6.
Articles of peace, 547–63.
Artillery, Royal. *See* REGULAR UNITS.
Arundel, 66.
Ash, Commander S. H. B., R.N., 470.
Ashburner's Light Horse. *See* COLONIAL UNITS.
Ashfield, Sergeant W., 310.
Assegai river, 119–21, 201.
Astan Drift, 246.
Atherton, Lieut.-Colonel T. J., C.B., 237, 242, 244, 284–6, 290, 370.
Atlantic Ocean, seaboard of, 65, 74, 350.
Attack, steepest side of position most favourable to, 393–4.
Attack on : Aberdeen, 466 ; Belfast, 37–40 ; blockhouses, 205, 208–9, 259, 346, 483–4 ; Dalmanutha, 36–7 ; Delagoa Bay railway, 35 ; Du Moulin's camp, 432 ; Helvetia, 26, 42 ; Lichtenburg, 134 ; Machadodorp, 36, 42 ; Modderfontein (Cape Colony), 274–6 ; Modderfontein (Gatsrand), 130 ; Nooitgedacht, 40 ; Pan, 41 ; Wildfontein, 40 ; Wonderfontein, 40 ; railways, 125 ; Smith-Dorrien's camp, 114 ; Vryheid, 30–2. *See also* CONVOYS.
Attaquas mountains, 283.
Attitude of Cape Colony, 60, 330–1.
Australia, 25.
Australian contingents. *See* COLONIAL UNITS.

INDEX.

Avontuur (Botha's Berg, Eastern Transvaal), 143.
Avontuur (Cape Colony), 73, 242.

BABANAGO, 153-4.
Babington, Major-General J. M., 128-30, 134-8, 148, 155, 181-2, 197, 204-5, 207-8, 210, 223.
Baden-Powell, Major-General R. S. S., C.B., 304.
Badenhorst, Commandant C., 12, 14, 16-17, 113, 123, 190, 444.
Bag-nets, 255.
Baileyton, 467.
Baillie, Colonel A. C., D.S.O., 458, 463-5, 474.
Bakenlaagte, 375, 390, 414, 421, 504; action of, 304-15.
Bakoven Pan, 87.
Balaklava, British and Russian cavalry at, 501.
Balmoral (Delagoa Bay line), 23, 77, 128, 145-6, 208, 517.
Balmoral (Mabusa Spruit), 200.
Bamboes Hoek, 274.
Bamboes mountains, 174, 179, 225-6, 236, 277, 458, 464, 466.
Bamboes Spruit, 476.
Bangor, 66.
Bank, 346.
Bankdrift, 291.
Bankfontein (south of Lindley), 335.
Bankfontein (north of Middelburg), 143.
Bankhoek, 151.
Bank-notes, South African Republic, 144.
Bankpan, 207.
Banon, Major F. L., 165, 171.
Bapsfontein (or Bapsfon.), 111, 113, 130.
Barbed wire, 33, 35, 40, 257, 403, 484.
Barberspan, 416.
Barberton, 23.
Barker, Captain F. C. C., 212.
Barker, Brigadier-General J. C., 23, 415.

Barker, Lieut.-Colonel J. S. S., 45, 53-6, 59, 110, 170, 254-5, 257-8, 260-1, 266, 269, 321, 331, 335, 338, 384, 386, 400, 402, 405, 429, 431, 433-4, 475-6, 479, 482, 485, 487-8, 490.
Barkly East, and district, 163, 225, 234, 272, 286-7, 368-9, 473.
Barkly West, 60.
Barracouta, H.M.S., 469.
Barrett, Captain R., 318.
Barroe, 278.
Barry, Private J. (awarded the Victoria Cross posthumously), 38.
Barrydale, 283, 285.
Barter, Lieut.-Colonel C. St. L., C.B., 315, 373, 375, 378-9, 381, 514, 522.
Barton, Major-General G., C.B., C.M.G., 1, 193-4, 197.
Bas Berg, 80-1, 89.
Basfontein, 184, 190, 194.
Bashoek, 190, 298-9, 301.
Basing, Colonel G. L., Lord, 194-5, 197, 265-7, 269, 320, 327, 338, 430-1, 434, 478-80, 490-1, 511.
Bassons Hoek, 74.
Bastards Nek, 90.
Basutoland, and border of, 97-8, 164, 253, 265-7, 287, 316, 326, 431.
Bath, the order of the, 170, 180, 217, 224.
Bathfontein, 141.
Batsheba, 432.
Baviaans Kloof mountains, 73.
Baviaanskraal, 425.
Bazeilles, in miniature at Boschbult, 495.
Baznards Dam, 473.
"Beaters," 486; definition of, 114.
Beatson, Major-General S. B., 139, 142-5, 150, 152, 155, 199, 203-5, 207, 211-12, 214, 223, 243, 283; arrives in Cape Colony, 242.
Beaufort West, 69-70, 72-4, 175, 237, 279-80, 285, 357-8, 455, 459.
Bechuanaland, 130, 506.
Beddy's Scouts. *See* COLONIAL UNITS.

Bedford (county in Cape Colony), 226, 467.
Bedfordshire regiment. *See* REGULAR UNITS.
Been Kraal, 74, 229.
Beer Vlei, 84, 87.
Bees, Private W. (awarded the Victoria Cross), 297.
Beestekraal, 301-2.
Beestkraal, 287.
Beginderlyn, 115-16, 146, 149, 202.
Belfast, and road, 23, 26, 34-5, 126, 143-4, 148, 376-7; attack on, 37-40; casualties at, 44.
Belgian monarchy, 24.
Bell, Lieutenant F. W. (awarded the Victoria Cross), 148.
Bell, Lance-Corporal J., 313.
Bell's Kop, 377.
Bellew, Captain R. W. D., 359.
Belmont, 251.
Bendigo, 333.
Bengal Lancers (15th), 257.
Bennett, Major A. J., 336.
Benson, Lieut.-Colonel G. E., 131, 133, 135-6, 138-9, 143-5, 148-9, 155, 199, 204, 207-8, 210-12, 214-15, 223, 337, 373-4, 376; at Bakenlaagte, 304-15.
Berkshire regiment, The Royal. *See* REGULAR UNITS.
Berg river, 262, 430.
Bergendal, 9, 436.
Bergfontein, 141.
Bergvleit, 203.
Berlin, 24.
Bertram, Captain R. M., 363.
Best, Lieutenant A. A., 441.
Bestershoek, 189.
Besterskraal, 256.
Bethanie, 161.
Bethel, and district, 42, 113, 150-2, 199, 203-4, 209, 215, 305-6, 373, 375-6, 378, 517.
Bethesda, 240.
Bethlehem, and road, 54, 57-8, 97, 101, 108, 157-8, 169, 322-3, 331, 334-6, 384-6, 403, 423-5, 433, 475, 482, 484-5; blockhouse line to, 391, 398, 400, 476, 483.
Bethlehem commando. *See* COMMANDOS.
Bethulie, 62, 77-9, 97, 163-4, 176, 253, 265-6, 269, 287, 328.
Bethulie commando. *See* COMMANDOS.
Bethune, Colonel E. C., 65, 67, 69-70, 72, 92, 94-7, 100, 102-4, 110, 165, 168-9, 171, 197, 246-7, 250, 321-3, 338, 474.
Bethune's Mounted Infantry. *See* COLONIAL UNITS.
Beukes, Commandant, 426.
Bewicke-Copley, Lieut.-Col. R. C. A. B., C.B., 215, 223, 304, 315, 373, 465-7, 473-4.
Beyers, General C. J., 10-13, 19, 21-2, 75, 113, 128-30, 437-42, 444-9, 451; chairman at peace conference, 542-3.
Bezuidenhout, Field-Cornet, 463-5.
Bezuidenhout's Drift, 487.
Bierlaagte, 424.
Biermann, Commandant, 451.
Biesjes Poort, 175, 280-1, 465.
Biesjesbult, 258.
Biesjesvallei, 507.
Biessiepan, 258.
Bismarck, 318, 431.
Blaauwbank, 213.
Blaauwkopje, 403.
Blackwoods Camp, 145.
Blaine, Captain, 449-50.
Blauw Kop, 147, 183, 206.
Blesbokspruit, 150.
Blink Kop, 84.
Blinkklip, 192.
Blinkwater, 143-6, 211, 515.
Blockhouses, lines of, etc., 46-7, 153, 194, 196, 222, 233, 237-8, 252, 264, 286, 298, 304, 324-6, 329, 333-4, 339, 344, 346, 348, 364-6, 368, 376-80, 382, 385, 388, 391-2, 395, 398-400, 402-3, 407, 409, 423-8,

INDEX. 713

431, 458-9, 462, 466-7, 471-3, 476-7, 480, 482, 486, 506, 512, 514, 517-20; attack on, 205, 208-9, 259, 346, 457; attack on, omission of, 347; evolution of system of—see APPENDIX 2; systematic attempt to destroy, 483-4; system in Eastern Transvaal, 371-3.
Bloed river, 145, 213-14.
Bloem Spruit, 323.
Bloemendal (south-east of Springs), 150.
Bloemendal (east of Vryheid,) 121.
Bloemfontein, and road, 53, 77, 93, 95-7, 170, 176, 202, 250, 252, 254, 261, 434, 481, 488; blockhouse line to, 264, 326, 431; railway of, 93, 167-8, 255, 258, 262, 264-5.
Bloemhof, and district, 133, 160, 191, 254, 491, 502, 505-7.
Blokkloof, 291.
Blomfield, Colonel C. J., 31-2, 216.
Blood, Lieut.-General Sir B., K.C.B., 139-40, 142-4, 146-8, 152, 199, 203-5, 207-12, 214, 216, 223, 249, 304.
Blood river, 122.
Blydschap, 336, 476.
Boekenhoutskloof, 439.
Boers: arms of, abandoned, 202; brutality of, towards British prisoners and natives, 430; capitulation of, rumours of, 123; characteristics of, 281; combination of, in the Magaliesberg, 11; concentration of, Western Transvaal, 184; council of war of, 206, 334; delegates of, to Europe, 24; demoralisation of, 376-7; depression among, 124, 216, 260; desertion of, 145; dismounted, 86; dispersion of, 96, 143, 332; effect of defeat of, 504; families of, 261; fearlessness of, at Rooiwal, 501; festival, annual, of, 21; free from molestation during peace negotiations, 508; Government of the—see GOVERNMENTS; in British territory, 508; independence of, to be decided in Cape Colony, 461; intelligence — see INTELLIGENCE, BOER; inutility of successes of, 421; irresolution of, at Forts Itala and Prospect, 221; magazine of, 104; military talent of, 349; mobility of, 68; plan of campaign—see CAMPAIGN; plans of, at Nooitgedacht, 9; recruits for (Cape rebels), 356; recuperative powers of, 519; reinforcements for, 226, 454; remount depôt of, 104; shooting, stripping and robbing the British dead and wounded at Bakenlaagte, 313; spies of, 68; spirit of, 404; States of, 21; statistics of—see APPENDIX 20; strategy of—see STRATEGY; strength of — see STRENGTHS OF BOER FORCES; strongholds of, 104, 183-4; supplies: need of, 3, 68, 355, 377; plenitude of, 199; tenacity of, 327; the veld, their "place" of concentration, 436.
Boesmans Kop, 266, 316, 320.
Bokkeveld mountains, 353, 355-7, 359.
Boksburg commando. See COMMANDOS.
Bonnefoi, 148.
Bordeaux, 385.
Border Horse. See COLONIAL UNITS.
Border regiment. See REGULAR UNITS.
Borderers, King's Own Scottish. See REGULAR UNITS.
Borderers, South Wales. See MILITIA and REGULAR UNITS.
Bosch Duiven Kop, 367.
Boschbult, 497; action at, 494-6.
Boschfontein (south of Breedts Nek), 10, 193.
Boschfontein (west of Lydenburg), 141.
Boschfontein (east of Olifants Nek), 193.

Boschfontein (south-east of Vrede), 428.
Boschhoek (south-west of Botha's Pass), 104.
Boschhoek (west of Lydenburg), 141, 143.
Boschhoek (north-west of Rustenburg), 189, 291.
Boschhoek (or Boschoek) (south of Waterval Onder), 148–9.
Boschmansfontein (west of Frankfort), 246.
Boschmansfontein (south of Pan), 203.
Boschmanskop (south of Middelburg), 113.
Boschmanskop (south-east of Springs), 153, 520; affair at, 518–19.
Boschpan, 494, 499.
Boschpoort, 406.
Boschput, 258.
Boschrand, 481.
Boschrandspan, 258.
Boschvarkensfontein, 367.
Boshof, and district, 99, 167, 433, 478–9, 481, 488, 506.
Bosjesman's Drift, 88.
Botha, Commandant C., 249.
Botha, Commandant C. J., 237–9.
Botha, General Chris., 34–5, 220, 305.
Botha, Commandant H., 336, 426.
Botha, Commandant-General L., 1, 9, 35, 37, 39, 42–4, 63, 112–17, 123–6, 129–30, 140, 146–7, 149, 205–6, 215, 217–20, 298, 307, 317, 320, 322, 328–9, 366, 375–6, 379, 382, 414, 421, 435–6, 461, 475, 514–15; address of, to burghers, 527; attacks Benson, 309; at the peace conference, 523–6, 533, 539–40, 543–7, 556, 560–1, 563; dismisses T. Smuts, 212; excuse for failure at Itala, 222; orders to Opperman, 305; plans of, 34, 42, for invasion of Natal, 216; refuses terms of peace, 119; visits De Wet, 123.
Botha, Assistant-Head-Commandant P., 54–6.

Botha's Berg (Eastern Transvaal), 23–4, 34, 143–4, 208, 213, 515–16.
Botha's Berg (Orange River Colony), 246, 251, 329, 425, 480.
Botha's Pass, 102–4, 153, 331, 371, 475; blockhouse line to, 377, 398–9, 426–7, 480.
Bothaskraal, 333.
Bothaville, 160–1, 196, 253, 255, 325–6, 347, 415, 480–1, 489; blockhouse line to, 345.
Bothwell, 114, 201.
Bottomley, Captain H. R., 154.
Bouwers, Commandant B. D., 264, 278, 363–4, 460.
Bowers, Captain J. *See* PREFACE.
Boyes, Major-General J. E., 54–9, 93, 97, 110, 171.
Braamboschfontein, 321.
Brabant's Horse. *See* COLONIAL UNITS.
Brabazon, Lieutenant J. H., 144.
Bradley, Driver F. G. (awarded the Victoria Cross), 220.
Brain T., private secretary to Ex-President Steyn, 248.
Brak river, 81–4, 86.
Brak Spruit, 494–5, 498–9.
Brakfontein (Elands river, Western Transvaal), 189, 291, 339.
Brakfontein (south of Pearston), 278.
Brakpan, 132, 138, 181, 407.
Brakspruit, 137, 183, 340.
Brand, Commandant G., 67, 89, 429.
Brand Kraal, 122.
Branddrift, meeting of Boer leaders at, 205–6.
Brandewyns Kuil, 67.
Brandewynskuil, 191.
Brandfort, 95, 97, 159, 161, 166–8, 245, 253, 259–60, 264.
Brands Drift, 52.
Brandvallei, 166, 252.
Brandvlei, 350–4, 367, 462.
Brandwacht (north of Calvinia), 355–6.
Brandwacht (north of Mossel Bay), 283.

INDEX. 715

Brandwater basin, 46, 112, 157, 169, 265, 321-2, 335, 374, 482, 484-5.
Brebner J., Treasurer, Orange Free State, 546, 560, 563.
Breda, 200.
Breedt (Cape rebel), 226.
Breedts Nek, 3, 10-11, 21, 129-30, 189, 192-4.
Bremersdorp, destruction of, by T. Smuts, 212.
Brereton, 200, 373.
Bridges, Captain G. T. M., 79.
Bridgetown, 362.
Bridging, the work of, 116-17.
Brigade of Guards, 367.
Brigades. See CAVALRY, COLUMNS and HIGHLAND.
Briggs, Lieut.-Colonel C. J., 135, 323, 331, 338, 392, 405, 429, 434, 511.
Brindisi, 484.
Brindisi Drift, 322.
Britain, subjugation of, by the Romans, 404.
British, the, ascendency of, in South Africa, 69; Government of, 119, 230, 261; peace negotiations by, 525-63; peace terms of, refused by Botha, 119; protection of Boer families by, 261; rule of, 60, 365-6; terms of peace offered by, 523-4; territory of, Boers in, during peace negotiations, 508.
British South Africa Police. See COLONIAL UNITS.
British Throne, Heir to, 355.
British troops, behaviour of, at Bakenlaagte, 310-14; Tweebosch, 419; Tweefontein, 394; difficulties of campaign for, 68, 198-9, 230-1, 265; endurance of, etc., 242, 379, 399, 449, 493, 521; stigma on arms of, 229; the shooting of, at Rooiwal, 503-4.
Brits Kraal, 81.
Britstown, and district, 65, 67, 90, 239, 462, 465.

Broadwood, Brigadier-General R. G., C.B., 1-3, 6-11, 14, 16, 21-2, 100, 102, 110, 128, 159, 168, 171, 193, 197, 246-51, 255-61, 269, 321, 329, 335, 338, 383-5, 405.
Brodrick, The Right Hon. St. John, M.P., Secretary of State for War, 537.
Broedersrust, 515.
Bronkhorst Spruit, 215.
Bronkhorstspruit station, 41, 211, 305, 516.
Bronsfontein, 57.
Brook, Major-General E. S., C.B., 434.
Browne, Major R. A., 296.
Brugspruit, 77, 146, 152, 203, 208-9, 305-6, 315, 373, 521; blockhouse line to, 372.
Brussels siding, 508.
Bryan, Mr., 25.
Buffalo, border of, 219.
Buffalo river, 42-3, 112, 217.
Buffels Hoek, 463.
Buffels river, 284-5.
Buffelsdoorns, 131.
Buffelshoek, 195.
Buffelspoort, 3-4, 7, 10.
Buffelsvlei (south of Frankfort), 102.
Buffelsvlei (north of Heilbron), 109.
Buffelsvlei (west of Roos Senekal), 144.
Buffles, 446.
Bufts, The (East Kent regiment). See REGULAR UNITS.
Bulfin, Major E. S., 430-1, 434, 478, 481, 490-1, 511.
Bulhoek, 385.
Bull river, 175.
Buller, General The Right Hon. Sir R. H., G.C.B., G.C.M.G., V.C., 25.
Bullock, Brigadier-General G. M., C.B., 118-19, 147, 149-50, 154-5, 199-200, 202-3, 222-3, 249, 269, 338, 371, 377, 399.
Bulpan, 507.
Buls Kop, 319.
Bultfontein (Cape Colony), 459.

Bultfontein (Orange River Colony), 97, 167, 481, 488.
Bultfontein Drift, 258.
Buluwayo, railway to, 443.
Burger, Acting-President of the South African Republic Schalk W., 123–6, 140, 205–6, 380, 516; at the peace conference, 533, 543, 546, 556, 560, 563; peace proposals of, 534–5.
Burghers, restoration to their homes, liberty and property of, 547–8; to vote on peace proposals, 540–1. *See also* BOERS.
Burghersdorp (Cape Colony), 60, 65, 174, 179, 225, 234, 236, 272–3, 317, 368–9.
Burghersdorp (west of Leydsdorp), 450.
Burke, Lieut.-Colonel, 283.
Burma Mounted Infantry. *See* INFANTRY, MOUNTED.
Burn-Murdoch, Brigadier-General J. F., C.B., 119.
Busby, 117.
Bushmanland Borderers. *See* COLONIAL UNITS.
Bushveld Carbineers. *See* COLONIAL UNITS.
Buys, Commandant S. B., 28, 209–10, 333–4.
Byng, Lieut.-Colonel The Hon. J. H. G., 46–51, 53, 59, 65–6, 71–2, 74, 89, 90, 92, 110, 161, 163–5, 167, 171, 245, 251–2, 263, 269, 324–6, 331, 333, 335, 338, 383–4, 395, 399, 401–2, 405, 423–8, 434, 443, 475.

CALEDON RIVER, and area, 1, 42, 45–7, 54, 62, 75, 97, 161, 163, 165–6, 316–17, 319, 429. *See also* LITTLE CALEDON.
Calitzdorp, 243.
Callwell, Lieut.-Colonel C. E., 286, 290, 363–4, 370, 455, 460–1, 470–1, 474.

Calvinia, and district, 70–1, 224, 279, 350, 352–3, 355–6, 358–60, 363–5, 455, 460, 462, 469; blockhouse line to, 364.
Calvinia District Troops. *See* COLONIAL UNITS.
Camdeboo mountains, and district, 74, 175, 178, 227–9, 231, 278, 354, 367, 456, 463–5.
Cameron, Lieutenant G. E., 107.
Cameron Highlanders. *See* REGULAR UNITS.
Campaign: Boer plan of, 68, 172, 349, 461; difficulties of, for British, 68, 198–9, 265; in Cape Colony, 230–1; lessons of, 421, 497, 504; prolongation of, by action of Colonial troops, 355; scheme of, in Orange River Colony, 423–4, 475–6.
Campbell, Major-General B. B. D., M.V.O., 58–9, 93, 99, 110, 156–8, 169, 171, 246, 265, 269, 321–2, 335, 338, 386–7, 391–2, 405, 434.
Campbell, Colonel W. P., 23, 111–13, 115, 118–21, 127, 204–5, 207, 210, 212–14, 216, 218, 222–3, 371, 373, 381.
Campbell (town), 433.
Canada, 25.
Canadian contingents. *See* COLONIAL UNITS.
Canadians, Royal (Leinster regiment). *See* REGULAR UNITS.
Cape Agulhas, 349.
Cape Colony, 25, 42, 45, 53, 93, 96, 98–100, 111, 123, 126, 161, 163–5, 195, 252, 265, 268, 317–18, 326–7, 435; attitude of inhabitants in, 60–3; blockhouse lines in, 454; commands in, 176, 224; correspondence with Government of, 230; cost of troops in, 230; descent upon, 1, 131; dual control in, 224; effect in, of De Wet's invasion, 172; Government of, 230, 272, 369; independence of, 75; legislature of, 177, 272; local

defence troops in, 225, control of, 230; physical features of, 358; ports of, martial law for, 178; proclamation, by Smuts, for governance of, 462; railways of, 279; rebellion in, 60–1, 68, 172, 224, 349–50, 360; reinforcements for, 465; re-invasion of, by De Wet, 42–3, 54, 58, 62, 108; renewed invasion of, warnings of, 231; situation in, 224, 230–1, 271, 349–50, 383, 453–4; situation of Boers in, 365–6, 461, 473; special efforts to deal with Fouché and Malan in, 465; Smuts' invasion of, 264, 268, 270; Smuts to command Boer forces in, 363; the main theatre of war, 461. *See also* EVENTS IN, *and* APPENDIX 3.

Cape Mounted Riflemen. *See* COLONIAL UNITS.

Cape Police. *See* COLONIAL UNITS.

Cape Town, 63–5, 69–70, 72, 123, 176, 227, 230, 242–3, 349–50, 354–8, 360, 460, 469–70; headquarters of treason and rebellion, 177; Maritz thirty miles from, 361; martial law for, 358; measures for safety of, 364; railway to, 242, 279, 282, 284, 354, 357, 363, 461.

Capitulation of Boers, rumours of, 123.

Capper, Lieut.-Colonel J. E., 346.

Capper, Lieut.-Colonel T., 354–6, 358–60, 362–4, 370, 455–6, 459, 462, 473–4.

Capricorn, Tropic of, 69.

Capron, Captain G., 154.

Captures: by Boers—20, 27, 29, 38, 41, 55, 73, 76, 95–6, 101, 167, 192, 204, 209, 218, 225, 233, 251, 280, 289, 298, 319, 321, 333, 340, 355, 450, 456, 469; by British—52, 85, 88, 94, 102–3, 105, 113, 121–2, 127, 132, 135, 137, 143–4, 179–82, 192, 195–6, 211, 213–15, 225, 229, 232, 241, 248–9, 252, 256, 292, 330, 400–1, 429, 476, 480, 493; of stock, etc., by British, 32, 96, 99, 101, 103, 107–9, 116, 118–19, 121–2, 133, 136, 141, 146, 149–50, 152–3, 158–9, 161, 163–5, 168–9, 182, 192, 200–3, 208, 211, 249, 251, 253, 255–61, 263, 304, 322–3, 329, 332, 335, 340–5, 352, 371, 376, 429, 443–4.

Carabiniers. *See* REGULAR UNITS.

Carleton, Lieut.-Colonel G. D., 23.

Carlisle, Mr. W., Intelligence officer, 407–8.

Carlisle Bridge, 277.

Carmel, 266.

Carnarvon, 67, 71; blockhouse line to, 364, 459.

Carolina, 34, 43, 113, 115, 148–9, 199, 201, 203–5, 207, 214–15, 254, 304, 373, 517, 520; blockhouse line to, 378, 518.

Carolina commando. *See* COMMANDOS.

Carruthers, Lieutenant B., 496.

Castrol Nek, 380.

Casualties: Boer—101, 108, 116–17, 132, 149, 154, 158, 164, 166–8, 189, 201, 211, 213–15, 225, 249, 283–5, 292, 301, 305, 318, 320, 332–6, 340–5, 361, 365, 374–81, 387, 401–4, 427, 429, 432, 438–40, 445, 449, 456–7, 480, 486–7, 509, 513, 519; at Aberdeen, 466; Avontuur, 73; Basfontein, 194; Belfast, 39; Blinkklip, 192; Boschbult, 497; Bothwell, 115; Brakpan, 137; Brakspruit, 137; Drizzly Hill, 369; Geduld, 135; Graspan, 107; Groen Kloof, 241; Grootvallei, 257; Gruisfontein, 409; Itala, 220–1; Lichtenburg, 134; Modderfontein (Cape Colony), 276; Ookiep, 472; Pan, 23; Platrand, 212; Rensburghoop, 152; Rietvlei, 209; Roodekranz, 144; Rooiwal, 503; Roos Senekal, 146; Steynsburg, 180; Uniondale, 72; Utrecht, 30; Victoria, 52 Vlakfontein, 188; Wildfontein Farm

Casualties: Boer—*continued*.
(Cape Colony), 179; Wolvepan, 254; Wonderfontein, 126; Yzerspruit, 415; in the Los Berg, 196; near Hopetown, 88; on L. of C. east of Pretoria, 44; on Taaibosch Spruit, 135; British—183, 298, 328, 345–6, 359, 361, 441–2, 450, 484, 513; at Belfast, 38, 40; Bothwell, 115; Brakspruit, 137; Buffelspoort, 6; Dalmanutha, 37; Graspan, 107; Helvetia, 27; Kromspruit, 55; Lauriston, 286; Lichtenburg, 134; Modderfontein (Western Transvaal), 130; Nels Poort (Cape Colony), 232; Nooitgedacht (Eastern Transvaal), 41; Nooitgedacht (Western Transvaal), 20; Ookiep, 472; Pan, 23; Richmond, 226; Rietvlei, 28; Roodewal, 29; Sannah's Post, 319; Utrecht, 30, 34; Ventersburg, 93; Vryheid, 31; Wildfontein, 40; near Barberton, 23; near Carolina, 43; on the Schurwe Berg, 32; on L. of C. east of Pretoria, 44; on the Tabaksberg, 76–7; Alexander's, 242; Allenby's, 194; Anderson's, 414–15; Babington's, 135; Beatson's, 152, 204; Benson's, 210, 305, 314; Blood's, 141; Byng's, 325, 333, 401; B. Campbell's, 157–8; Chapman's, 153, 221; Chesney's, 407; Cole's, 328; Cookson's, 497; Crabbe's, 284, 365, 456; Cunningham's, 130-1, 347; Damant's, 390; Dartnell's, 387; Dixon's, 188; W. Doran's, 460; du Moulin's, 432; Elliot's, 101, 249, 261; H. D. Fanshawe's, 519; French's, 122; Garratt's, 196, 427; Gough's, 218; Grey's, 209; A. Hamilton's, 430; B. Hamilton's, 168; E. Hamilton's, 154; G. Hamilton's, 192, 513–14; I. Hamilton's, 503, 509; Harley's, 249; Henniker's, 81; Hickie's, 340; Kekewich's, 297, 341, 344; F. W. Kitchener's, 214; Leader's, 409; Lund's, 227; Methuen's, 133, 192, 292, 340, 420; Monro's, 162–3; Moore's, 235; Nixon's, 481; Paris', 99; Park's, 377; Parsons', 175; Pilcher's, 96, 160–1, 167, 253; Plumer's, 79–80, 201, 320, 380; Rawlinson's, 137; Rundle's, 158, 249, 251; Sandeman's, 276; Scobell's, 175, 241–2; Shea's, 257; Sitwell's, 433; Spens', 376; Ternan's, 489; Thorneycroft's, 161, 168, 253, 318; Von Donop's, 292, 301, 410; White's, 468; E. C. I. Williams', 182, 190–1; F. A. Williams', 394; Wilson's, 330, 333; Wyndham's, 365. *See also* APPENDICES 16, 17 *and* 20.
Cattle driven against wire fences, 403–4.
Cavalry, British and Russian at Balaklava, 501; Royal Horse artillerymen as, 402.
Cavalry brigades, 148, 182, 188, 204, 376.
Cavendish-Bentinck, Captain Lord W. A., 238–9, 366–7, 370, 456–7, 474.
Celliers, General J., 134, 407, 411–13, 418, 420.
Celliers (National Scout), 448–9.
Ceres, 70, 231, 356–7, 359, 362, 460.
Cessation of hostilities in Boer territory during peace negotiations, 508.
Chance, Major H., 17; at Vlakfontein, 185–8.
Chapman, Major A. J., 33, 153–5, 219-20, 377.
Chesney, Lieut.-Colonel K., 407.
"Chinese Wall," blockhouse line in Cape Colony, 454.
Christiana, 167, 245, 253, 506, 508.
Chunies Poort, 448, 451.
Church property, Dutch, 523, 525.
Civil proceedings, not to be taken against burghers, 547.
Clanwilliam, 69–70, 355, 357–60, 362, 460, 472; blockhouse line to, 364–5.

INDEX. 719

Clearance of crops, stock, etc., 98, 139, 147, 157, 160, 163–4, 166, 193, 199, 201–4, 207–8, 245, 247, 298, 301, 322, 410, 434, 477–9, 488; measures for, in Orange River Colony, 326–7.
Clements, Major-General R. A. P., D.S.O., 1–3, 128–30, 138, 193, 209, 216, 221, 295, 372; at Nooitgedacht, 13–22; in the Magaliesberg, 6–12.
Clifford, 457–8.
Clocolan, 53, 157, 431.
Coal Drift, 253, 255.
Coal Mines, 195.
Codrington, Colonel A. E., 173–4, 176, 180, 467.
Coetzee, 39.
Coke, Major-General J. Talbot, 32.
Cold Brook, 369.
Coldstream Guards. *See* REGULAR UNITS.
Cole, Lieut.-Colonel A. W. G. Lowry, 252, 263, 269, 319–20, 327–8, 338.
Colenbrander, Lieut.-Colonel J. W., 70, 142, 173, 175, 180, 383, 437–8, 444–5, 447–52; relieves Grenfell in Northern Transvaal, 443.
Coles Kop, 89.
Colesberg, 60, 65–6, 78, 89, 94, 263, 366.
Colesberg Bridge, 90, 238, 263.
Collet, Major, 467.
Colleton, Lieut.-Colonel Sir R. A. W., Bart., C.B., 345, 415, 422.
Colliery, and hills (Belfast), 39.
Collins, Captain C. W., 313.
Colonial Defence Forces. *See* COLONIAL UNITS, *also* CAPE COLONY.
Colonial Division. *See* COLONIAL UNITS.
Colonial Forces, disbandment of, 25.
Colonial Office, 453–4.
Colonial troops, action of, prolongs campaign, 355.

Colonial Units :—
Ashburner's Light Horse, 416–20.
Australian Bushmen (3rd regiment), 82–4, 142.
Australian Corps, 139, 489, 516.
Beddy's Scouts, 447, 451.
Bethune's Mounted Infantry, 56, 162.
Border Horse, 76.
Brabant's Horse (1st and 2nd), 65.
British South Africa Police, 410, 416–20.
Bushmanland Borderers, 363.
Bushveld Carbineers, 439.
Calvinia District Troops, 351.
Canadian Mounted Rifles, 496.
Cape Mounted Riflemen, 178–9, 232, 241, 279, 304, 369.
Cape Police, 238, 416–20.
Colonial defence forces, 72, 279–80, 283, 286–7, 368.
Colonial division, 55, 369, 462, 466.
Commander-in-Chief's Bodyguard, 55.
Cullinan's Horse, 416–20.
Damant's Horse, 388–91, 496.
Dennison's Scouts, 416–20.
Diamond Fields Horse, 416–20.
District Mounted Rifles, 361.
District troops, 467.
Driscoll's Scouts, 109.
Imperial Bushmen (3rd), 80; (4th), 142, 471.
Imperial Light Horse (brigade), 79–80, 85, 116, 334, 387, 392, 395, 502; (1st regiment), 135, 322, 331, 387, 392, 400, 429; (2nd regiment), 322, 331, 392, 400, 428.
Johannesburg Mounted Rifles, 215, 217–18.
Kaffrarian Rifles, 76, 369.
Kitchener's Fighting Scouts, 70, 440, 443, 445, 448–9, 451; (1st regiment), 437–8; (2nd regiment), 321–3, 330–1, 333, 437, 439.
Kitchener's Horse, 2, 12, 17.
Local fencibles, Cape Colony, 277.
Local volunteers, 471.

Colonial Units—*continued*.
  Menne's Scouts, 212.
  Namaqualand Border Scouts, 470-1.
  Natal Police, 153.
  Natal Volunteers, 154.
  National Scouts, 447-8, 451.
  Nesbitt's Horse, 233.
  New South Wales Bushmen, 262.
  New South Wales Contingent. 101.
  New South Wales Mounted Rifles, 182, 192, 336.
  New Zealand Corps, 139, 489.
  New Zealand Mounted Rifles, 80, 379, 401.
  New Zealand regiment (7th), 262, 427-8.
  Pietersburg Light Horse, 446-7, 451.
  Prince of Wales's Light Horse, 77, 233.
  Queensland Imperial Bushmen, 84, 150, 401.
  Railway Pioneer regiment, 333-4, 346.
  Railway Pioneer regiment (4th), Mounted Infantry, 347.
  Scottish Horse, 185, 210, 215, 293-7, 486, 504; (1st regiment), 408, 500-1; (2nd regiment), 211, 306, 308-14, 500-1.
  South African Constabulary, 170, 194, 255, 264, 304, 315, 324, 327, 333, 338, 346-7, 372, 376, 445, 500, 512-13, 518, 520.
  South African Light Horse, 164, 325, 401.
  South Australian Bushmen, 105-7, 255-7.
  Steinacker's Horse, 447-8, 451.
  Thorneycroft's Mounted Infantry, 51, 159, 318, 488-9.
  Town Guards, 361, 469-70.
  Victorian Imperial Bushmen, 85.
  Victorian Mounted Rifles, 4, 7, 132, 144, 514.; (5th), 203-4, 373.
  West Australian Mounted Infantry, 148, 213.
  Western Province Mounted Rifles, 355, 361, 363.
  Zululand Native Police, 221.
Colonies, Secretary of State for, 230.
Colonists, loyalty of, 69.
Colt gun, 51 ; capture of, 152.
Columns, British—strength of, etc., 22, 59, 92, 110, 127, 138-9, 155, 171, 173, 180 185, 197, 203, 208, 222-3, 225, 228, 244, 269, 290-1, 299, 303, 306, 315, 319, 338, 346-8, 351, 370, 381, 405, 415-16, 422, 434, 437-40, 447, 451-2, 474, 490, 511, 522 ; tied to lines of blockhouses, 462, 472 ; without guns or transport, 492.
Colville, Lieut.-Colonel A. E. W., 28-9, 43-4, 103, 110-13, 116, 127, 147, 153-5, 199, 207, 209-10, 215-16, 218, 222-3, 249, 371, 377, 379, 381, 514, 522.
Colvin, Lieut.-Colonel F. F., 223, 254, 258, 262, 269, 338, 381, 522.
Commadagga, 466-7.
Commander-in-Chief. See LORDS KITCHENER *and* ROBERTS.
Commander-in-Chief's Bodyguard. See COLONIAL UNITS.
Commando Drift (Vaal river), 133, 160, 481, 488, 493.
Commando Nek (north-east of Ficksburg), 54.
Commando Nek (Magaliesberg), 3, 8, 128-9, 193, 292.
Commando Spruit, 481.
Commandos :—328.
  Badenhorst's, 113.
  Bethlehem, 48-9, 336.
  Beyers', 10-13, 19, 75, 113, 437-42, 444-51.
  Bezuidenhout's, 463-5.
  Boksburg, 38, 145.
  C. Botha's, 249.
  C. J. Botha's, 237-9.
  Chris. Botha's, 34, 220.
  P. Botha's, 54-6.
  Bouwers', 264, 278, 364-5, 460.

INDEX.   721

G. Brand's, 67, 89, 429.
Buys', 28.
Carolina, 39.
Celliers', 411–14, 418–20.
Conroy's, 351–2, 367, 468.
De Beer's, 132, 501, 505, 509.
J. H. De la Rey's, 3, 12, 134, 295–301, 411–14.
P. De la Rey's, 194–5.
De Villiers' (rebels), 132, 433.
De Wet's, 45, 49, 53, 76, 88–91, 383–404, 426–9.
Emmett's, 121, 515.
Erasmus', 225, 233–4, 236.
Ermelo, 36, 39.
Fouché's, 172, 174–6, 179, 234–5, 286, 368–9, 458, 463, 465–7.
Fourie's, 54, 76, 89.
Frankfort, 425.
Free Staters, 72, 104, 236, 383, 386.
Froneman's, 76.
Germiston, 40.
Haasbroek's, 76, 88.
Heilbron, 336, 477.
Hertzog's, 67, 87, 89, 94, 166, 430.
Hugo's, 282, 455.
Johannesburg, 38.
Kemp's, 411–14, 418–20.
Kirsten's (or Kerston), 264.
Kritzinger's, 62, 65–6, 71–4, 172–4, 179–80, 225–6, 233, 237–8, 287–8, 317–20, 367.
Krokodil river, 13.
Kroonstad, 336.
Krugersdorp, 10, 13.
Lategan's, 225, 232, 237, 282.
Lemmer's, 418.
Lichtenburg, 412.
Liebenberg's, 194, 325, 411–14.
Lotter's, 237–41.
A. Louw's, 353, 363–4.
Jan Louw's, 468.
Lydenburg, 24, 36.
W. Malan's, 173–6, 178–9, 226–7, 237, 281–2, 364–5, 455–7, 463, 465–7.

S. G. Maritz's (Cape rebels), 224, 228, 271, 350–63, 365, 455, 468, 471.
Mears', 401.
Mentz's, 486–7.
Middelburg, 24, 40.
Muller's, 143, 203–4, 213.
Myburg's, 225, 233–4, 236, 286, 368–9.
Naude's, 366.
Nieuhoudt's (or Nieuwoudt's), 67, 430.
D. Opperman's, 220, 305.
Petrusburg, 96.
Piet Retief, 118.
Potchefstroom, 298, 412.
F. J. Potgieter's, 192, 341–2, 344, 410, 501–3.
H. J. Potgieter's, 220.
Pretoria, 13.
H. Pretorius', 67.
M. G. Pretorius', 439.
A. Prinsloo's, 215.
G. Pyper's, 462.
S. Pypers', 279, 285–6, 364, 462.
Rebels (Cape Colony), 225, 227, 274.
Rustenburg, 412.
Scheepers', 71–4, 172–6, 178–9, 227–9, 237, 242–3, 283–5.
Smit's, 237–40, 365, 462.
J. C. Smuts', 130, 195, 264, 270–9, 455, 469–71.
T. Smuts', 34.
Theron's, 233, 237–9, 243, 283–4, 460, 462.
Theunissen's, 67.
Trichardt's, 28.
Utrecht, 216.
P. Uys', 439.
Van der Venter's, 264, 278–82, 364–5.
G. Van Niekerk's, 431.
Van Reenan's (rebels), 179–80, 225–6, 233, 236, 238, 364, 462.
Van Zyl's, 417.
Van Zyl's, 468, 501, 509.
Vermaas', 143, 341, 418.
Viljoen's, 143, 149, 207–9, 213.

722 THE WAR IN SOUTH AFRICA.

Commandos—*continued*.
Von Tonder's, 501.
Vrede, 336, 485.
Vryheid, 216.
Waterberg, 10, 13, 15.
Wessels', 67.
L. Wessels', 238, 456–7, 462.
P. Wessels', 368–9, 457–8.
W. J. Wessels', 385, 388–91, 396, 401.
Winburg, 51.
Wolmaranstad, 341.
Zoutpansberg, 10, 13.
Commands in the Orange River Colony, 97.
Commissie Bridge (Caledon river), 266, 317–18, 320.
Commissie Drift (Caledon river), 97, 168.
Commissie Drift (Oliphant river), 141–2, 214.
Commissie Hoek, 328.
Commissioners of districts, 29–30.
Compagnies Drift, 359.
Compass Berg, 71.
Compies river, 118, 200–1, 377–8.
Compton, Captain Lord D., 241–2.
Concentration, of Boer forces, Western Transvaal, 184; of British on Natal border, 216.
Concentration camps for refugees. See APPENDIX 12.
Conclusion of peace, 523–63.
Concordia, 469, 471–2.
Conference of Boer leaders, 108, 205–6, 270.
Conference, peace, negotiations, at Middelburg, February 28th, 1901, 119–20, 126; April, 1902, at Klerksdorp, 533; Pretoria, 504, 508, 535; Vereeniging, 471, 473, 487, 541.
Congresses, Dutch, in Cape Colony, 61.
Connaught Rangers. See REGULAR UNITS.
Conoviam, 53.
Conroy, Commandant E., 351–2, 367, 468, 473.

Constable, 54, 279, 360.
Constantia (north-west of Harrismith), 246.
Constantia (north of Rouxville), 164.
Consul, German Imperial, at Pretoria, 74.
Convoys, 3, 113, 115–17, 183; attack on: Anderson's, 410–14; Crabbe's, 364, 455–6; A. C. Hamilton's, 430; Plumer's, 151; Von Donop's, 299; capture of: by Beatson, 144; Benson, 143; B. Campbell, 158; W. P. Campbell, 121; Dawkins, 400; B. Hamilton, 168; E. C. Knox, 122, 128; Methuen, 192, 406; Rawlinson, 195; Rimington, 401; Smith-Dorrien, 116; delay of, French's, 118.
Conway, 226; officer commanding at, column of, 290, 370.
Cookhouse station, 174, 278.
Cookson, Colonel G. A., 14, 492, 494–7, 511.
Cooper, Colonel H., C.M.G., A.D.C., 470–2, 474.
Copeman, Major H. C., 253, 269, 327, 338.
Cornelia, 102, 329, 400.
Cornelius river, 246, 400, 426, 428, 479.
"Corral," 349; definition of, 114.
Correspondence of Boer leaders—*see* LETTERS; between Lord Kitchener, Secretaries of State for the Colonies and War, High Commissioner, and Governor, Cape Colony, 230, 453; for the Army, how dealt with—*see* APPENDIX 9; *re* peace, negotiations for, terms, etc., 524–39.
Cost of the War in South Africa. See APPENDIX 18.
Coulson, Lieutenant G. H. B. (awarded the Victoria Cross), 161.
Council of War, by Boers, 206–7, 334; orders of, 208.
Counter-attack, at Moedwil, 297; Rooiwal, 502; Vlakfontein, 187–8; by du Moulin, 432; by Boers at Vlaklaagte, 513.

INDEX. 723

Country, clearance of, of stock, etc.— see CLEARANCE; Eastern Transvaal, description of, 112; at Bakenlaagte, 307.
Cowan, Major B. W., 342.
Cow-catchers, an army of, 198.
Cox, Lieut.-Colonel F., 427.
Crabbe, Lieut.-Colonel E. M. S., C.B., 65, 80-2, 84, 88-9, 92, 173-4, 179-80, 225-6, 233, 237-8, 244, 279, 284-6, 290, 360-2, 364, 370, 455-6, 459, 474.
Cradock, Lieut.-Colonel M., 78, 80, 92, 94, 110, 138, 272.
Cradock, and district, 71, 173-4, 178, 225-6, 233, 239, 274, 277, 280, 456, 463-4, 466-7, 473; blockhouse line to, 458.
Crandon, Private H. G. (awarded the Victoria Cross), 211.
Crean, Surgeon-Captain T. J. (awarded the Victoria Cross), 387.
Crewe, Lieut.-Colonel C. P., 54-6, 59, 76-7, 92, 94, 96-7, 110, 171, 176, 179-80, 226, 228-9, 231, 244, 290, 370.
Criticism on British strategy, reply to, 435-6.
Crocodile river, 26, 208, 301-2, 443, 445.
Cronje, General A. P., 247.
Cronje, General P., 421.
Crossing of the Orange river, by De Wet, 78, 90, 93.
Crossings of Orange river, assembly of troops at, 231.
Crum, Captain F. M., 310, 314.
Cullinan's Horse. See COLONIAL UNITS.
Cunningham, Trooper A., 313.
Cunningham, Brigadier-General G. G., C.B., D.S.O., 1-2, 6, 75, 128, 130-1, 136, 138, 195, 324, 347-8.
Customs union, 536.
Cyclists, 171, 180, 244, 405, 434, 437, 452, 490.
Cyfergat, 167.

Cyferpoort, 425.
Cypher Gat, 179, 458.
Cypherfontein, 150.
Czar of Russia, 24.

DAGGA, 473.
Daggaboers Nek, 178.
Dalmanutha, 35, 377; attack on, 36-7; casualties at, 44.
Dalzell, Lieut.-Colonel the Hon. A. E., C.B., 347-8.
Damant, Colonel J. H., D.S.O., 252, 263, 266-7, 269, 316-17, 319, 329-35, 338, 383-4, 388-91, 402, 405, 424-5, 434, 475-7, 490, 494-6.
Damant's Horse. See COLONIAL UNITS.
Damhoek, 193.
Damplaats, 486.
Daniel's Kuil, 488.
Darling, 361-2.
Darlington, 174, 278, 466.
Dartnell, Brigadier-General Sir J. G., K.C.B., C.M.G., 111, 113, 116-22, 127, 147, 217, 219, 222-3, 322-3, 331, 333-5, 338, 386-7, 391-2, 404.
Daspoort (east of Dewetsdorp), 46, 48, 52, 328.
Daspoort (north of Villiersdorp), 424.
Dassiefontein (north-west of Nels Poort), 459.
Dassiefontein (south-east of Richmond), 74, 173, 465.
Davel, Commandant, 54, 248.
Davies, Lieut.-Colonel R. H., 511.
Dawkins, Lieut.-Colonel J. W. G., 263, 269, 324-5, 338, 400, 405, 428, 434, 443-5, 452, 511.
De Aar, 65, 80, 87, 176, 225, 238, 243, 281, 351, 366, 462, 473; railway to, 238, 367; supply depôt at, 67.
Dead, robbing of, etc., at Bakenlaagte, 313; Tafel Kop, 390.
De Beer (Tolly), Commandant J., 132, 505, 509; at Rooiwal, 501.
Debts of the Republics, 523, 525, 549.
De Eerste Poort, 89.

VOL. IV. 46*

724   THE WAR IN SOUTH AFRICA.

Deelfontein, 486.
Deep Dene, 319.
Defeat of Boers, effect of, 504.
Defensible posts, 255.
De Grootboom, 140, 142.
De Hoop, 460.
De Jager's Drift, 31, 217–18.
De Kalk, 85–6.
De Kraalen, 121.
Delagoa Bay: attacks on posts, on the railway to, 35; railway, 34, 45, 126, 139, 146–7, 153, 199, 201, 204, 207–8, 210, 214–15, 298, 304, 315, 372–3, 376, 380, 437, 481, 515–16, 520–1; situation on the railway to, 23, 34.
De Lange's Drift (Klip river), 103, 329.
De la Rey, General H. J., 1–4, 6–7, 9–13, 17, 21–2, 105–6, 108, 128–30, 133–6, 182, 184, 190, 205–7, 270, 295–301, 339, 344–5, 366, 383, 407–8, 415–16, 421, 445, 461, 475, 478, 491–8, 501, 504–5, 528; at Tweebosch, 418–20; at Yzerspruit, 410–14; "New Model" of, broken, 503; at the peace conference, 533, 543–7, 556, 560–1, 563.
De la Rey, Commandant P., 194–5.
Delegates, Boer, to Europe, 24, 529–33, 538; attendance at peace conference refused by Lord Kitchener, 540.
Delegates, peace, sixty burghers from commandos to Vereeniging, 541; delay, effect on, 551.
De Lisle, Lieut.-Colonel H. de B., D.S.O., 65, 67, 69–71, 74, 92, 100, 102–7, 110, 168, 171, 173–4, 180, 197, 246–7, 250, 255–9, 261, 264, 269, 315, 321–2, 329, 331, 335, 338, 383–4, 395–6, 399, 405, 423, 426, 434, 475–6, 482, 490, 509, 511.
De Naauwte, 444.
Dennison's Scouts. See COLONIAL UNITS.
Denny, Lieut.-Colonel H. C., C.B., 447, 452.

Depression amongst the commandos 124.
De Put, 79, 88.
Derby, 119.
Derbyshire regiment. See REGULAR UNITS.
De Roodepoort, 113.
De Rust, 256.
Dervishes, a rush of, 501.
Despatches, Lord Kitchener's, 332.
Destruction of blockhouses, systematic attempt at, 483–4.
De Villiers, Commandant P. (Griquatown), 132, 433, 488.
Devondale, 346.
Devonshire regiment. See REGULAR UNITS.
De Wagendrift, 442.
De Wet, Head-Commandant C. R., 1, 42–3, 45–54, 56–8, 62–3, 65–6, 68, 74–90, 93–6, 98–9, 104, 106, 108, 123, 131, 139, 166, 172–3, 205–7, 224, 227, 231, 243, 245, 270–1, 323, 330, 334–7, 350, 354, 357, 366, 383–8, 391–401, 421, 424–30, 461–2, 475–9, 505, 528; breaks up his army, 54, 332, 398; collecting votes on the question of peace, 484; concentration of forces of, 382; escapes from Elliot's cordon, 403–4; plan of British, to surround, 331; at the peace conference, 533, 543–7, 556–7, 560–1, 563; tactics of, 49.
De Wet, Commandant Piet, 356.
Dewetsdorp, and road, 46, 49, 52, 98, 162, 168, 251, 265–6, 320, 327–8.
Diamond Fields Horse. See COLONIAL UNITS.
Diamond Hill, 436, 443.
Diary of a burgher, 125, 198.
Diepkloof, 213.
Difficulties of the campaign, 68, 198–9, 265, 332.
Difficulties of Sir I. Hamilton's great "drive," 509–10; of "drives" generally, 520.
Dingaan's Day, 21.

INDEX. 725

Dipka, 476.
Director of Railways, 65. *See also* APPENDIX 10.
Director of Supplies. *See* APPENDIX 5.
Discussion of terms of peace, and conclusion of, 540–63.
Disloyalty in Cape Colony, 60–63.
Dispersion of Boer forces, 96 ; effects of, 99–100.
Disselfontein, 85–6.
Distance marched by Elliot's troops, 398 ; Jeudwine's column, 354.
Distribution of commands in the Orange River Colony, 97.
District Commissioners, 29–30.
District Mounted Rifles. *See* COLONIAL UNITS.
District troops. *See* COLONIAL UNITS.
Divisions. *See* COLUMNS.
Dixon, Brigadier-General H. G., C.B., A.D.C., 136, 138, 182–4, 189–91, 197 ; at Vlakfontein, 185–8.
Doctors. *See* APPENDIX 7.
Dogs, watch, 35.
Donkerhoek, 117.
Donkerpoort, 443.
Dood's Drift, 326.
Doorn (Hoeks) Berg (north-east of Steynsburg), 180, 226.
Doorn Kloof, 459.
Doorn Kop, 188–9.
Doorn Nek, 178, 464.
Doorn river, 70, 355, 357, 364.
Doornberg, 423.
Doornberg mountain (north-east of Winburg), 58, 75, 91, 93, 159–60.
Doornbult (Brak Spruit), 344, 494, 504.
Doornbult (Orange River Colony), 99.
Doornbult (south of Lichtenburg), 191.
Doornbult siding, 508.
Doornfontein, 159.
Doornhoek (west of Koffyfontein), 262.
Doornhoek (Magaliesberg), 7, 10.
Doornkloof, 403, 479.
Doornkop, 436.
Doornlaagte (east of Kimberley), 167.

Doornlaagte (north of Wolmaranstad), 494, 505.
Dooters Kraal, 85.
Dopper, *régime* of, 124.
Doran, Lieut.-Colonel B. J. C., 130, 178, 226–9, 231–2, 237–40, 244, 272–4, 277–80, 282, 290, 367, 370, 456–7, 459, 463–7, 474.
Doran, Lieut.-Colonel W. R. B., 282, 290, 203–4, 370, 455, 460, 462, 465–6, 474.
Dordrecht (Cape Colony), 225, 234, 236, 272–4, 277, 286–7, 368–9, 457.
Dordrecht (east of P. P. Burg), 122, 179.
Doris, H.M.S., 72.
Dorpsplaats, 202.
Dorsetshire regiment. *See* REGULAR UNITS.
Douglas, Major-General C. W. H., 1.
Douglas, Colonel W., D.S.O., 139, 143–4, 148–9, 155, 199, 204, 207–8, 223.
Douthwaite, Commandant, 505.
Drafts, to South Africa. *See* APPENDIX 14.
Dragoon Guards. *See* REGULAR UNITS.
Dragoons. *See* REGULAR UNITS.
Drakensberg mountains, 103, 219, 286, 368, 424–5, 428–9, 475, 480–2 ; passes of, 217, 323, 423.
Drennan, 178, 463.
Dreyer, Commandant, 320.
Driefontein (west of Bethel), 517.
Driefontein (north-east of Ermelo), 201.
Driefontein (west of Herschel), 267.
Driefontein (north of Middelburg), 143.
Driefontein (south of Somerset East), 277.
Driefontein, battle of (1900), 394.
Driehoek (Komati valley), 148–9.
Driehoek (south of Reitz), 246.
Driekop, 96.
Driekuil, 494, 497–8, 505.
Driespruit, 102.

Drifts of the Vaal, blockhousing of, 346.
Drinkwater, 151.
Driscoll, Major D. P., 109, 340–1, 433–4, 481, 490–1, 511.
Driscoll's Scouts. *See* COLONIAL UNITS.
"Drives": combination of, in Orange River Colony, 326, 485; definition of, 114; difficulties of, 509–10, 520; fortifications thrown up during, 509; in the Eastern Transvaal, 517; on large scale in Western Transvaal, 492, 506–10; Blood's, 140–6; Elliot's, 100–5, 168–9, 196, 246–50, 253, 255–61, 321–3, 383–5, 398–402, 423–29, 475–7, 479–80; Fetherstonhaugh's, 189; French's, 113–22, 236–9, 458, 466; B. Hamilton's, 166–8, 373, 481, 485–7, 520–1; I. Hamilton's, 499–503, 506–10; Kekewich's, 492, 494; F. W. Kitchener's, 492, 494; C. E. Knox's, 166; Lyttelton's, 97, 157; Methuen's, 192; Rawlinson's, 492, 494; Rochfort's, 492; Stephenson's, 459.
Drizzly Hill, 234, 369, 458.
Droogfontein, 319.
Drummond-Hay, Lieut.-Col. J. A. G., 467.
Dublin Fusiliers, The Royal. *See* REGULAR UNITS.
Du Cane, Major H. J., 70, 92, 423–4, 434, 475–6, 490.
Duff, Lieut.-Colonel C. E., 185–8, 302, 485, 487, 490.
Dugdale, Lieutenant F. B. (awarded the Victoria Cross), 119.
Dullstroom, 26–7, 126, 143–4, 210–11, 214, 376–7, 380.
Du Moulin, Lieut.-Colonel L. E., 165, 167–8, 171, 245, 251–3, 263, 269, 319–20, 327, 338, 430, 432, 434.
Dundas, 385, 388–9.
Dundee, 31, 56, 122, 154, 215–18, 222.
Dunlop, Lieut.-Colonel J. W., 399, 405.

Du Preez Lager Drift, 260.
Durban, 350.
Durham Militia artillery. *See* MILITIA UNITS.
Du Toit, Lieutenant, 438.
Dwaal Spruit, 428.
Dwars river (south of Geelhout Kop), 443.
Dwars river (north of Pietersburg), 447.
Dwars river, and valley (north of Roos Senekal), 141, 143.
Dwars Vlei siding (Cape Colony), 173.
Dwarsvlei (Western Transvaal), 2.
Dwyka river, 285.
Dynamite, capture of, by Boers, 469; bombs, 471; mines, 206, 209.
Dysseldorp, 73.

EAST KENT REGIMENT. *See* REGULAR UNITS.
East London, 64, 349; railway to, 467.
East Surrey regiment. *See* REGULAR UNITS.
Eastern Transvaal, blockhouse system in, 371–3; situation in, 371–2. *See also* EVENTS IN.
Eden's Kop, near Heidelberg, 28.
Edenburg, 46, 94, 96–7, 161, 164–5, 167, 245, 251–2, 267, 319, 325–6, 329, 431.
Edward VII., His Majesty the King, 546–7, 551, 561.
Edwards, Lieut.-Colonel A. H. M., C.B., 324, 338.
Eensgevonden, 258–9, 264, 489.
Eerste Geluk, 113.
Eerstefabrieken, 142, 149.
Eerstegeluk, 425.
Effects, of Boer defeat at Rooiwal, 504; of De Wet's inroad into Cape Colony, 172.
Egypt, 279.
Elands Berg (south of Hopetown, Cape Colony), 87.
Elands Berg (north-east of Smithfield), 163, 327.

INDEX. 727

Elands Berg (north of Volksrust), 117-18, 183, 200-3, 216.
Elands Drift (Tarka river), 174, 277, 467.
Elands Kloof (south of Clanwilliam), 362.
Elands Kloof (south of Petrusville), 89.
Elands Kloof Drift (Government Drift, Orange river), 288.
Elands Kop (north of Lindley), 102, 383, 385, 398, 400, 403, 424-5.
Elands Poort (south-west of Richmond), 280.
Elands Poort (north of Tarkastad), 274-6.
Elands river (Cape Colony), 274-5, 277.
Elands river (North-east Transvaal), 142, 214.
Elands river (Western Transvaal), 189, 191, 291, 293, 301-2.
Elands River Bridge, 58, 158, 334, 386-7, 392, 395, 423.
Elands River Drift, 335.
Elands Spruit, 424.
Elands Vallei, 362.
Elandsfontein (north of Bethel), 203-4.
Elandsfontein (south-west of Bethel), 517.
Elandsfontein (east of Boshof), 258.
Elandshoek plateau, 104.
Elandskloof, 268.
Elandskop, 485.
Elandskraal, 8, 193.
Elandslaagte (west of Klerksdorp), 410.
Elandslaagte (Natal), battle of, 394.
Elandsriver station, 210.
Elliot, Major-General E. L., C.B., D.S.O., 97, 100-5, 108, 110, 154-5, 157, 159, 168-9, 171, 196-7, 245-8, 250-1, 253-6, 263-5, 269, 322-3, 325, 328-9, 331, 333-5, 338, 384-6, 388, 395-403, 405, 423-6, 429, 431, 433-4, 475-9, 482, 484-8, 490, 520; " drives " of—*see* " DRIVES "; plans of, 321, 383.
Elliot, Captain H. W. D., 368.

Elliot County, 286.
Elizabethsfontein, 364.
Elsjes Vlakte, 82-3.
Emmaus, and road, 166, 252, 432.
Emmett, General C., 121; capture of, 515.
Endurance of British troops, 242, 379, 399, 449, 493, 521.
Enemy, tenacity of, 327.
Engineers, Royal. *See* REGULAR UNITS.
England, 24, 95, 176, 481.
English, Lieutenant W. (awarded the Victoria Cross), 211.
Enkeldedoorns, 142.
Entonyaneni, district of, 219.
Entrenchments, 365; at Belfast, 37-8; Fort Itala, 219; Ookiep, 471; Pan, 41; during " drives," 402, 509; of the passes, Western Natal, 155.
Enzelberg, 191.
Enzelpoort, 196.
Epitaph, to Scheepers, by President Steyn, 285; to the Spartans at Thermopylæ, 313.
Equator, 75.
Erasmus, Commandant, 225, 233-4, 236, 253, 377.
Ermelo, district, and road, 25, 34, 42-3, 107, 112-14, 116, 123, 126, 130, 140, 146-8, 150, 199-200, 203-5, 209, 214, 305, 373-5, 378-9, 514-15, 527; blockhouse line to, 372, 377-8, 512, 517-18.
Ermelo commando. *See* COMMANDOS.
Erroll, Colonel C. G., The Earl of, K.T., C.B., 133.
Ersterling, 120.
Eshowe, 222.
Essex-Capell, Captain A., 512-13.
Europe, Boer mission to, 206; sympathy of, 230.
European cavalry, a charge of, 501.
Eustace, Major C. L. E., 141, 308, 310.
Evacuation of Wolmaranstad, 415.
Evans, Private C. N., 496.

Evans, Colonel R. W., 154.
Evening Star, 53, 321.
Events in Cape Colony, December, 1900—February 28th, 1901, 60–92; March—April, 172–80; June—September, 224–44; September—October, 270–90; January—May, 1902, 453–74; in the north-west and west of, April—December, 1901, 349–70.
Events in the Eastern Transvaal, December 1st, 1900—January 31st, 1901, 22–44; January—March, 111–27; April—May, 139–55; June—September, 198–223; November, 1901—January, 1902, 371–81; February—May, 512–22; action of Bakenlaagte, 304–15.
Events in the Northern Transvaal, April, 1901—May, 1902, 435–52.
Events in the Orange River Colony, December, 1900—January, 1901, 45–59; February—June, 93–110; April—June, 156–71; July—August, 245–69; August—November, 316–38; December, 1901—February, 1902, 382–405; February, 423–32; March—May, 475–90.
Events in the Western Transvaal, December, 1900, 1–22; January—April, 1901, 128–38; May—August, 181–97; September—November, 291–303; November, 1901—January, 1902, 339–48; January—March, 406–22; March—May, 491–511.
Evidence of Boer misdeeds, at Bakenlaagte, 313.
Expenditure, total, on the War. See APPENDIX 18.
Explosion of dynamite at Ookiep, 472.
Express, 121.

FAIR, MAJOR J., 512.
Fairfax, Thomas, Lord (Parliamentarian General), 382.
Familiehoek, 200.
Families, Boer, 385; rationed and protected by the British, 261.
Fanny's Home, 385, 396, 399, 401–2, 482.
Fanshawe, Lieut.-Colonel H. D., 518–20.
Fanshawe, Lieut.-Colonel R., D.S.O., 102, 110, 171, 395–6, 399, 405, 423–4, 426, 434, 475–6, 482, 490.
Farmer, Sergeant D. (awarded the Victoria Cross), 20.
Farmers, the, of Cape Colony, rising of, 75; British kept at bay by, 411; not liable for war tax, 523; ruined condition of, financial assistance to, 523, 525, 548; subjugating a nation of, 101.
Farms, burning of, 125.
Farrell, Captain H. J., 6.
Fauresmith, 94, 96, 164, 167, 251–2, 266, 317, 325–6, 430, 433.
Fencibles, local, Cape Colony. See COLONIAL UNITS.
Festival, annual, of Boer States, 21.
Fetherstonhaugh, Major-Gen. R. S. R., C.B., 139, 155, 182, 188–92, 194, 197, 250, 291–3, 298, 303, 515–16, 522.
Fever, 58.
Ficksburg, 53–4, 97, 99, 156, 158–9, 321, 431, 477; blockhouse line to, 482.
Field artillery, Royal. See REGULAR UNITS.
"Fiery Cross," The, 216.
Firman, Lieut.-Colonel R. B., 57, 334, 392.
Fish River station, 176, 178, 464.
Flags, Republican, 125, 357.
Florence (north of Lake Chrissie), 148.
Florence (north of Zastron), 318.
Follet, Lieut.-Colonel S. W., 110, 165, 171, 369–70, 457–8, 474.
Food, shortage of, 3, 68, 82, 355, 377; stores of, on the veld, 343.
Forbes, Colonel W., 52.

INDEX. 729

Forbes-Sempill, Captain the Hon. J. (Master of Sempill), 288–9.
Force. *See* COLUMNS.
Forestier-Walker, Lieut.-General Sir F. W. E. F., K.C.B., C.M.G., 63, 69, 176.
Fort Beaufort, 226.
Fort Dahl, 447.
Fort Edward, 446–7.
Fort Itala, attack on, 219–21.
Fort Prospect, attack on, 219–21.
Fort Shelton, 471.
Fort Weeber, 141–3.
Fortescue, Lieut.-Col. The Hon. C. G., C.M.G., D.S.O., 305, 315, 373, 381, 515, 517, 522.
Fortifications on railways, 402; during "drives," 509.
Forts, dismantling of, 536.
Fosbery, Captain F. L., 38.
Fouché, Commandant W. D., 172, 174–6, 179, 225, 234–6, 271–2, 274, 286, 368–9, 457–8, 463–7, 473, 528.
Fourie, Vice-Chief-Commandant P., 51, 54, 76, 78, 81, 89.
Fouriesburg, 157–8, 335, 384, 397; blockhouse line to, 482–3.
Fourteen Streams, 133–5.
France, 24.
Franchise, 536; grant of, to Kaffirs, 523, 526, 548.
Frankfort, 54, 93, 97, 100–2, 108, 249–50, 323, 330–4, 383–4, 397, 399–401, 475, 479, 486, 488; blockhouse line to, 329, 385, 388, 398, 402, 423–4, 476, 482, 485.
Frankfort commando. *See* COMMANDOS.
Franschmans Kop, 367.
Fraserburg (town), 67, 69–70, 455–6.
Fraserburg Road station, 282.
Frederick's Dal, 364.
Frederikstad, 131, 135–6, 194.
Free Staters, 270. *See also* COMMANDOS.
French, Lieut.-General Sir J. D. P., K.C.B., 2, 8, 21–2, 43, 111–17, 120–2, 125, 127–8, 138, 146–8, 151, 156, 199, 225–9, 231–2, 234, 236–9, 260, 265, 272, 274, 278, 280, 282, 286, 290, 317, 359, 368, 370, 443, 454, 461, 472, 474, 528; assumes direction of affairs in Namaqualand, 469; plans of, 228; special efforts to deal with Fouché and Malan, 465–7; tactics of, 358, 363; takes command in Cape Colony, 224, 244.
Froneman, J. F., 350–1.
Froneman, General P., 54, 76; at the peace conference, 556.
Fry, Lieut.-Colonel W., 7, 194, 197.
Fusilier regiments. *See* REGULAR UNITS.

GALLWEY, LIEUT.-COLONEL E. J., C.B., 151–2.
Gamka river, 285.
Gannafontein, 167.
Gans Vlei, 459.
Ganstfontein, 455.
Gansvlei Spruit, 480.
Garies, 469, 472.
Garratt, Lieut.-Colonel F. S., D.S.O., 195–7, 210, 216, 218, 222–3, 249, 254–8, 260–2, 269, 338, 371, 377, 381, 399, 401, 405, 427, 434, 475, 479–81, 485, 488, 490, 520, 522.
Garrison artillery, Royal. *See* MILITIA *and* REGULAR UNITS.
Garrisons, control of, in Cape Colony, 224.
Garrisons of: Aberdeen, 466; Bethlehem, 157, 169; Forts Itala and Prospect, 219; Helvetia, 25; Jamestown, 179; Ladybrand, 321; Ookiep, 470–1; Piquetberg, 361; Tafel Kop, 344; Tontelbosch Kolk, 363.
Garstin, Colonel A. A., C.M.G., 66, 92.
Garstlands Kloof, 178, 233, 239, 280.
Gatberg, 368.
Gatsrand, 2, 75, 128, 131, 136, 196, 268, 271, 346.
Gawne, Lieut.-Colonel J. M., 31.

Geddes, Corporal, gallant conduct of, 106.
Geduld, 135, 194, 341.
Geelhout Kop, 443-4.
Gelderland, 56.
Geluk (south of Hoopstad), 160.
Geluk (south of Lichtenburg), 492.
Geluks Poort, 82, 84, 86.
Gemsbokfontein, 130.
Gemsbokhoek Berg, 250, 425.
George (county), 243.
Gericke, Baron, Netherland Ambassador, 528-31.
German Imperial Consul, Pretoria, 24.
Germans, the, 124.
Germiston, 130.
Germiston commando. *See* COMMANDOS.
Gestopfontein, 492.
Geysdorp, 508.
Ghazis, a rush of, 501.
Gilbert, Brevet-Major A. R., 432-4, 490.
Girdwood, Captain A. C., 300.
Glen, 261, 265, 321.
Glencoe, 122, 216-17.
Godwaan, 208.
Goemans Berg, 164.
Gogarty, Major H. E., 73, 92, 165, 171.
Going, Major G. N., 252, 269, 338.
Golden Gate, 158.
Goldsworthy, Captain C. L., 241.
Goliathskraal, 258.
Goodehoep, 204.
Goodeverwachting, 148.
Gordon, Captain E., 241.
Gordon, Brigadier-General J. R. P., C.B., 22, 128-30, 138.
Gordon Highlanders, The. *See* REGULAR UNITS.
Gorras, 459.
Gorringe, Lieut.-Colonel G. F., C.M.G., D.S.O., 65-6, 72-4, 92, 173-4, 176, 179-80, 225, 233, 236, 238, 244, 272-5, 277-9, 290, 370.
Gottenburg, 477, 485.

Gough, Lieut.-Colonel H. de la P., 32, 216-18, 223.
Gouritz river, 283-4.
Gous Pan, 81.
Government: the British, 119, 230, 261 ; peace terms, negotiations and conclusion of, 523-63 ; of Cape Colony, 230, 272, 369 ; Holland, 528-34 ; Natal, 554 ; Orange Free State, 107 ; peace negotiations of, 523-63 ; South African Republic, 107, 123, 140, 203, 214-15, 305, 376, 380, 515 ; peace negotiations of, 523-63 ; proposed meeting between members of the Boer, 125, 203 ; meeting of, 205-6.
Governor, The, Cape Colony, 230, 272. *See also* HELY-HUTCHINSON, SIR WALTER.
Governor's (or Gouverneur's) Kop, 53, 321-2, 431.
Graaf Water, 359.
Graaff Reinet, 67, 71, 74, 175-6, 178, 226-9, 231-3, 237, 243, 274, 280, 282, 350, 456, 465-6 ; Dutch congress at, 61 ; railway to, 278, 457, 463.
Grahamstown, 354.
Grant, Captain W. L., R.N., 72.
Grant, of a million pounds sterling to meet Boer liabilities, 549 ; of three millions, 550, 552.
Gras Kop, 154.
Gras Vlakte, 82.
Graspan (east of Hoopstad), 256.
Graspan (east of Reitz), 108 ; action at, 105-7.
Grass fires, to cover attack, 105, 151, 167, 186-7.
Great Berg river, 358-62.
Great Fish river (east of Cradock), 175, 277.
Great Fish river (north-west of Sutherland), 353.
Great Harts river. *See* HARTS RIVER.
Great Karroo, 367.
Green Hill (Nooitgedacht), 12, 19.

INDEX. 731

Grenadier Guards. *See* REGULAR UNITS.
Grenfell, Lieut.-Colonel H. M., 46, 59, 62, 65–6, 71–4, 92, 110, 173, 175–6, 180, 409, 415–17, 422, 452, 491, 500–3, 511; commands in the Northern Transvaal, 437–43.
Grey, Lieut.-Colonel R., C.M.G., 199, 209–10, 223.
Greylingstad, 28, 44, 111–12, 149–50, 210, 215, 334, 481, 485, 487; blockhouse line from, 372.
Greytown, 222.
Grierson, Trooper N. H., 313.
Gries, 356.
Griqualand West, 60, 131, 262, 433.
Griquatown, 345, 367, 433, 488.
Grobelaar, Assistant-General, 435.
Grobelaar, Commandant, 10.
Grobelaar, Commandant S., 221.
Grobler's Drift, 424.
Groblers Recht, 148.
Groen Kloof (north-west of Pearston), 240.
Groen Kloof (south of Philippolis), 262.
Groenfontein, 321.
Groenvlei (north-east of Heilbron), 249, 424.
Groenvlei (north of Lindley), 336, 486.
Groenvlei Drift, 246.
Groethoek, 440, 443.
Groot Gannapan, 506.
Groot Letaba river, 450.
Groot (Great) Zwart Berg, 361.
Grootdam, 486–7.
Groote Oliphant River station, 211, 518, 520.
Groote river, 279, 284.
Groote Zwarte Bergen, The, 73, 279.
Grootfontein, 328.
Grootklip, 249.
Grootpan (north-west of Bethel), 150.
Grootpan (east of Vryburg), 416.
Grootvallei, 256–7, 264.
Gruisfontein, action at, 408–9.
Gruisplaats, 425.
Gryze Kop, 238.

Guards, brigade of, 367; regiments of. *See* REGULAR UNITS.
Guerrillas, 28, 124, 182, 184, 198, 227, 265, 343, 348, 357, 397, 421, 461, 504, 514, 519; definition of, 99.
Guinness, Major E., 310–11.
Guinness, Lieut.-Colonel H. W. N., C.B., 141, 381.
Gumbi, Sergeant, 221.
Gun Hill (Bakenlaagte), 310–14, 390.
Gun Hill (Helvetia), 257.
Gunboats, 362.
Guns: Boer—30, 49, 76, 113, 121–2, 134, 141, 144–5, 208–9, 397, 420, 494; destruction of, 141, 145, 438; loss of, 85, 90, 135, 137, 146, 152, 346, 476, 503; British—2, 7, 17–18, 22, 28, 30, 32, 36, 40–1, 43, 51–2, 56–7, 59, 76–7, 80, 92, 110–11, 126–7, 132, 135, 137–9, 151, 155, 157, 180–1, 183, 197, 203, 223, 225, 227, 233, 237, 244, 269, 275, 288, 290, 299–301, 303, 306–15, 346, 348, 351, 370, 381, 389, 392–3, 407, 415–20, 422, 425, 434, 440, 452, 474, 490, 500, 511, 522; at Bakenlaagte, 314; Vlakfontein, 186–7; re-capture of, 318, 375, 401, 493; loss of, at De Jager's Drift, 218; Sannah's Post, 319; Tweebosch, 420; Tweefontein, 394; Wilmansrust, 204; Yzerspruit, 414; **12-prs.**, 32, 36, 40; **4·7-in.**, 2, 17–18, 25–7; **5-in.**, 37, 437, 447; **Howitzers**, 55, 185, 187, 193, 299–300. *See also* COLT, KRUPP, MACHINE, MAXIM, MAXIM-NORDENFELDT *and* VICKERS-MAXIM.
Guns, columns without, 492.

HAAKDOORNFONTEIN, 142.
Haarlem, 73.
Haasbroek, Assistant-Head-Commandant Z. F., 51–2, 76, 86, 88.
Hacket-Thompson, Lieut.-Colonel F., 197, 304, 315, 442.
Haenertsburg, 438 449–50,

Hagenstadt, 95.
Haig, Colonel D., C.B., 71-4, 89, 96-7, 110, 161, 163, 165, 171, 176, 179-80, 224-7, 232-3, 274, 364, 459, 473.
Halfmaan, 486.
Halfmanshof, 359.
Hall, Colonel F. H., C.B., 437.
Halseston, 273.
Hamanskraal, 10, 21, 142, 442, 445.
Hamburg, 102.
Hamelfontein, 79-80, 367.
Hamilton, Major A. C., 319, 327-8, 338, 430, 434.
Hamilton, Major-General Bruce M., 56, 58-9, 80, 84, 87, 92, 97-8, 110, 161, 163-8, 171, 245, 251-3, 255, 262-3, 266, 269, 317, 324, 327, 338; transfer of, to Eastern Transvaal, 219, 221, 319; in command of Eastern Transvaal, south of Delagoa Bay railway, 372, 373-9, 381-2, 481, 512-15, 517, 522; co-operates with Elliot in the Orange River Colony, 485, 490; great "drive" of, 520-1.
Hamilton, Brigadier-General E. O. F., 154, 212, 385, 388, 398-9.
Hamilton, Brigadier-General G. H. C., 109, 188-9, 192, 194, 197, 216, 219, 222-3, 253, 291-2, 303, 315, 379, 381, 513, 518, 522.
Hamilton, Lieut.-General Sir I. S. M., K.C.B., D.S.O., 505, 511; assumes command in the Western Transvaal, 498; at Rooiwal, 499-503; great "drive" of, 506-10; orders of— *see* APPENDIX 4.
Hammonia, 45, 47, 54.
Hanover, and road, 60, 65, 89, 227, 229, 232, 239, 367.
Hantam's Berg, 355.
Harde Heuvel, 354.
Harley, Colonel G. E., C.B., 93, 97, 99, 156-9, 169, 171, 246, 249, 251, 269, 338.
Harmsfontein, 258.
Harris, Major O., 165, 171.

Harrismith, and road, 54, 56-7, 93, 99, 104, 156-8, 169, 217, 219, 246, 249, 251, 322-3, 328, 331, 334-5, 386-7, 392, 401, 423, 434, 482, 485; blockhouse line to, 391, 398, 400, 424-5, 428.
Hart, Major-General A. FitzR., C.B., 1-2, 8, 128, 163, 176, 234-6, 266-9, 286-7, 290, 317, 338, 368, 464.
Hartebeest Kuil, 175.
Hartebeestfontein (south of Brugspruit), 152.
Hartebeestfontein (north-west of Nylstroom), 444.
Hartebeestfontein (north of Paardekop), 200.
Hartebeestfontein, and hills (west of Klerksdorp), 132, 136-7, 181-3, 191, 340-1, 409, 492.
Hartebeestspruit (north of Ermelo), 205.
Hartebeestspruit (north of Rustenburg), 301.
Hartenbosch, 488.
Harts river, and valley, 1, 191, 406, 416, 477, 479, 494, 499, 502, 507. *See also* LITTLE HARTS.
Hartzen Berg, 89.
Hattingh, General J., 336.
Hattingh, Field-Cornet J., 52.
Hay, 60.
Heath, Major F. C., 482, 490.
Heath, Major F. W., 431.
Heen-en-Weers Kop, 430.
Heidelberg (Cape Colony), 283.
Heidelberg (Eastern Transvaal), 21, 28, 43, 101, 108, 127, 153, 188, 205, 210, 250, 317, 423-4, 477, 487, 512-13, 521.
Heilbron, and district, 54, 93, 99-103, 109, 249-50, 323-4, 330-1, 333-4, 336-7, 383-5, 389, 477, 479, 485, 488 · blockhouse line to, 329, 385, 398, 400, 402, 424, 476, 482.
Heilbron commando. *See* COMMANDOS.
Heir to British Throne, at Cape Town, 355.

INDEX.

Hekpoort, district and valley, 21–2, 128–30, 189, 193–4, 442.
Heliographs, 50, 403; capture of De Wet's, 424.
Helpmakaar, 160.
Helvetia (Eastern Transvaal), 25, 34–5; attack on, 26, 42.
Helvetia (Orange River Colony), 45, 163, 168, 251, 316, 319.
Helvetia kopjes, 27.
Hely-Hutchinson, Sir Walter F., G.C.M.G., 272.
Heneage, Major The Hon. H. G., 286, 290.
Henniker, Lieut.-Col. The Hon. A. H., 65, 69–70, 79–82, 84–6, 88–9, 92, 173–4, 176, 178, 180, 226, 244.
Henning, 66, 174.
Henry, Colonel St. G. C., C.B., 118–19, 166–7, 171, 196–7, 245, 253–60, 262–3, 269, 325–6, 338, 345, 348.
Henwoods, 121.
Herbert, Lieut.-Colonel E. B., 45–6, 59, 65–6, 77, 92, 110, 163–4, 171, 173, 180.
Herbert (district), 60.
Herschel, 287.
Hertzog, Assistant-Head-Commandant Judge J. M. Barry, 42–3, 53, 62–3, 65–71, 74–5, 77–9, 87–9, 91, 94, 96, 164, 166, 172–3, 206, 224, 326, 350, 430–1; at the peace conference, 544–6, 560, 563.
Hex river (Orange River Colony), 163.
Hex river (Western Transvaal), 301–2.
Hex Rivier hills, 334.
Hickie, Lieut.-Colonel W. B., 182–3, 189–91, 197, 291–2, 298, 303, 326, 338–40, 345–6, 348, 407, 409, 422.
Hickman, Colonel T. E., C.B., D.S.O., 77, 88–9, 92, 97–8, 110, 161, 164–5, 171.
Hicks, Lieut.-Colonel H. T., C.B., 346, 348.
High Commissioner, the British. *See* MILNER, LORD.

High Veld, 104, 112, 145, 149, 199, 382, 446, 514; problem of, etc., 371–2.
Highland Brigade, 492; change of command of, 176.
Hildyard, Lieut.-General H. J. T., C.B., 31, 117, 120, 153–5.
Hill, Lieutenant H. N., 300.
Hindon, "Captain" J., 282, 442.
Hippisley, Lieut.-Colonel W. H., 474.
History, the present, omissions from, 202.
Hlomohlom, 215.
Hoare, Major R., 474.
Hobbs, Lieutenant R. F. A., 300.
Hoedspruit, 34.
Hoepel, 53.
Hofman's Drift (Vaal river), 160.
Hol Spruit, 400, 426–7.
Holfontein (south of Hoopstad), 258.
Holfontein (west of Klerksdorp), 344, 416.
Holfontein Siding, 75.
Holland, the Government of, 528–33.
Holle Spruit, 179, 273, 457.
Holmes, Major H. G., 269, 331, 338, 402–3, 405, 423, 434, 482, 490.
Holnek (north of Amsterdam), 148.
Holnek (north-west of Roos Senekal), 144.
Hondeblafs river, 79, 88.
Hondeklip Bay, 356.
Honing Spruit, 256, 262.
Honingfontein, 57.
Honingspruit, 102.
Hoopstad, and district, 56, 133, 135, 160, 167, 196, 254–7, 481, 489, 491, 506.
Hopefield, 358, 362.
Hopetown, 64, 84, 86–8, 94, 238.
Hopewell, 440, 443.
Horse artillery, Royal. *See* REGULAR UNITS.
Horses, 45; Boer, supply of, 68, 79, 81–2; capture of, 368–9, 375, 429, 464, 480, 486, 493; casualties among, 107, 115, 191, 204, 233, 277,

Horses—*continued.*
283, 285, 297, 340, 367, 406, 409, 432, 497, 502 ; collection of, in Cape Colony, 63 ; Orange River Colony, 97, 105, 169 ; sickness among, 440 ; stops operations, 445–6 ; stampeding of, 296.
Hospitals. *See* APPENDIX 7.
Hostilities, in Boer territory, to cease during peace negotiations, 508.
Houbaan, 334.
Houd Constant, 457, 463.
Hout Kraal, 80–1, 88, 366.
Hout Nek, 97.
Houwater, 67, 87.
Howard, Major C., 346.
Howitzers, 55, 185, 187, 193, 299–300. *See also* GUNS.
Hughes-Hallett, Lieut.-Colonel J. W., C.B., D.S.O., 77, 92, 204, 212, 223.
Hugo, Assistant-Commandant Judge H. J., 281, 285, 455, 459.
Humans Rust, 327.
Humby, Major J. F., 345.
Hunter-Weston, Lieut.-Colonel A. G., D.S.O., 232, 237–8, 244, 290, 366, 370.
Hussars, regiments of. *See* REGULAR UNITS.
Hut Post (Springhaan Nek), 47–51.

ILLUSTRATIONS OF THE WITKOPPIES, 104.
Imperial Bushmen, Corps of. *See* COLONIAL UNITS.
Imperial Light Horse. *See* COLONIAL UNITS.
Imperial Yeomanry, 2, 65, 73, 227–8, 249, 294–7, 339, 345, 389, 415, 457, 488 ; at Rooiwal, 500 ; Tweefontein, 392–4 ; Vlakfontein, 185–6 ; capture of, 192, 484.
Battalions :—
5th, 132, 181, 299, 410, 416–20.
10th, 132, 181.
11th, 334.
19th, 340.

Companies :—
30th, 390.
31st, 390.
86th, 416–20.
Devon, 16.
Fife, 16.
Scottish, 88.
Welsh, 52.
Other Units :—
Lovat's Scouts, 234–5, 267, 287–9, 368, 465–7.
Paget's Horse, 410–11.
Impilusi. *See* UMPILUSI.
Ind, Shoeing-Smith A. E. (awarded the Victoria Cross), 390.
Independence, declaration of, in Cape Colony, 75 ; of the Republics, 75, 206, 555 ; question submitted to burghers, 541 ; partial surrender of, 544.
India, 25, 97, 355.
Indian Ocean, seaboard of, 74, 350.
Infantry, Mounted, 21, 33, 37, 39, 77, 118, 195, 207, 306, 318–19, 321, 402, 484.
2nd battalion (Legge's), 2, 12.
3rd battalion, 306, 308–14.
4th battalion, 516.
6th battalion, 105–7.
9th battalion, 481.
12th battalion, 437–40, 444.
20th battalion, 439–40.
25th battalion, 306, 308–14.
26th battalion, 371.
28th battalion, 494–6.
Burma, 488.
Unattached Units :—
Vth division, 30, 154, 219.
Connaught Rangers, 267, 287, 368.
Railway Pioneer regiment (4th) *See* COLONIAL UNITS.
Royal Irish Rifles, 347.
South Staffordshire, 392, 394–5.
Gough's, 217–18.
McMicking's, 347.
Pine-Coffin's, 160.
Inglefield, Major N. B., 17–19.

INDEX. 735

Inglis, Captain S. W., 310.
Inhabitants of Cape Colony, attitude of, 60, 230, 453-4.
Inhoek, 316.
Inktpan, 258.
Inniskilling Dragoons. *See* REGULAR UNITS.
Inniskilling Fusiliers, The Royal. *See* REGULAR UNITS.
Intelligence: Boer—24-5, 145, 240; British—19, 32, 42, 75, 81, 177, 204-5, 212, 216, 224, 231, 258, 301, 306, 374, 380, 392-3, 401. 407, 439, 485, 491.
Intermediate Post (Springhaan Nek), 47, 51.
Intombi river, 119, 515.
Invalids, how dealt with—*see* APPENDIX 7; statistics of—*see* APPENDIX 16.
Invasion, of Cape Colony, 42-3, 54, 58, 62, 108, 231; of Natal, 216-21; rumours of, 29.
Irene, 346.
Irish Fusiliers, The Royal. *See* REGULAR UNITS.
Irish regiment, The Royal. *See* REGULAR UNITS.
Irregulars, behaviour of, at Tweebosch, 418-20.
Israels Poort, 46-7, 77.
Itala, fort at, attack on, 219-21.

JACHT LUST, 148.
Jackalsfontein, 413.
Jackson, Stonewall (Confederate General, America), 382.
Jackson, Lieutenant T. D., 313.
Jacobsdal, 166, 252, 262.
Jagersfontein, 96, 433.
Jagersfontein Drift, 252.
Jagersfontein hills, 263.
Jagersfontein Road, 166, 252, 264, 430.
Jagersrust, 333, 335.
Jagtpan, 167.
Jakals Vallei, 455.

Jamestown, and district, 176, 179, 234, 236, 286, 368, 457-8, 464, 473.
Jammersberg Bridge, 327.
Jammersberg Drift, 266, 319-20.
Jan Boers Kraal, 362.
Jansenville, 175-6, 279, 463, 466.
Jardine, Captain W., 408.
Jaskraal, 142.
Jeffreys, Colonel H. B., 79, 92, 94, 110, 223.
Jericho, 445.
Jervis-White-Jervis, Colonel Sir J. H., Bart., 254, 258, 262, 338, 381, 522.
Jeudwine, Major H. S., 225, 244, 351-6, 370.
Johannesburg, and district, 2, 22, 122, 129-30, 304; railway to, 9, 22, 27-8.
Johannesburg commando. *See* COMMANDOS.
Johannesburg Mounted Rifles. *See* COLONIAL UNITS.
Johnson, Lieutenant R. C. M., 221.
Jolly Kop, 169.
Jones, Captain B. J., 484.
Jones, Major-General Inigo R., C.B., 63, 65-6, 233, 367.
Joubert, Commandant-General P., 217.
Juriesfontein, 175.
Jurys Baken, 267.

KAAL SPRUIT, 264.
Kaalfontein (north of Bank), 194.
Kaalfontein (east of Geneva siding), 385, 395.
Kaalpan, 260.
Kaalplaats, 136.
Kaalvley, 258.
Kaffir Kop (north of Fouriesburg), 55, 384-6, 395, 399, 401.
Kaffir river, 166, 327.
Kaffir Spruit, 115.
Kaffirkraal, 321.
Kaffirskraal, 150.
Kaffirstad, 205, 207.
Kaffrarian Rifles. *See* COLONIAL UNITS.
Kakamas, 350, 352, 454, 468.

Kalabas Drift (Riet river), 94.
Kalabas Kraal, 361.
Kalk Kloof (or Kalkkloof), 148.
Kalk Spruit, 388-9.
Kalkfontein (Cape Colony), 88.
Kalkfontein (north of Boshof), 167.
Kalkfontein (north-west of Karee siding), 260.
Kalkfontein (east of Roos Senekal), 211.
Kalkkuil, 160.
Kalklaagte, 252.
Kalkoenkrans, 117, 200.
Kalkrans, 427, 479.
Kambula mountain, 32.
Kameel Drift, 85.
Kameel river, 142.
Kameelfontein (north of Bothaville), 326.
Kameelfontein (east of Kimberley), 99, 254.
Kameelfontein (north-east of Pretoria), 443.
Kamies Berg, 472.
Kammenassie mountains, 72.
Kandos Poort, 279.
Kane, Lieutenant H. R., 219.
Kanon Berg, 361-2.
Kanonfontein, 258.
Karabee, 83.
Kardouws Pass, 262.
Karee Kuil, 89.
Karee siding, 261.
Kareeboomskuil, 410.
Kareeboschfontein, 505, 507.
Kareekuil, 507.
Kareepan, 341-2.
Kareepoort, 341.
Kariega river, and valley, 74, 175, 278.
Karoslaagte, 259.
Karree Bosch, 232.
Karreepan (south by east of Hoopstad), 258.
Karreepoort (north of Odendaal Drift), 164.
Karreepoort (west of Philippolis), 262.
Karroos, The, 435.

Katdoornbult, 258.
Katdoornplaat, 192.
Katkop, 225, 352, 367.
Kattegat, 89.
Kavanagh, Lieut.-Colonel C. T. McM., 237-9, 243-4, 279, 283-6, 290, 360-2, 365, 370, 460, 472, 474.
Keesen Berg, 236, 238.
Keir, Lieut.-Colonel J. L., 158, 171, 402, 405, 424, 434, 475-7, 490, 492-5, 511.
Kekewich, Colonel R. G., C.B., 128-9, 138, 191-4, 197, 291-2, 298-9, 301-3, 329-44, 348, 383, 406-10, 415-16, 422, 491-4, 498, 503-5, 507-8, 511; at Moedwil, 293-7; at Rooiwal, 499-502.
Kelly, Lieutenant J. B., 310.
Kemp, Vecht-General Jan, 136, 184, 186-90, 193, 291-3, 297, 299, 344, 411-14, 418, 445, 505; at Rooiwal, 501; rashness of, at, 504.
Kendrew, 175, 178, 226, 466.
Kenhardt, and district, 60, 70, 224, 350, 352, 467-8.
Kenna, Major P. A., V.C., 430-1, 434, 482, 490.
Kerr's Drift, 347.
Kestell, Rev. J. D., 557.
Khabanyana river, 51.
Khaki clothing, worn by Boers, 275-6, 414, 493.
Kiba Drift (Orange river), 267.
Kikvorsch Berg, 66.
Killed. *See* CASUALTIES, *also* APPENDICES 16 *and* 17.
Kimberley, 65, 252, 260, 433, 488; railway to, 167, 255, 258, 509.
Kimberley column, 84, 99, 166. *See also* PARIS *and* SITWELL.
King's Kopje (Helvetia), 25-6.
King's Liverpool regiment. *See* REGULAR UNITS.
King's Own Royal Lancaster regiment. *See* REGULAR UNITS.
King's Own Yorkshire Light Infantry. *See* REGULAR UNITS.

INDEX.

King's Shropshire Light Infantry. *See* REGULAR UNITS.
Kings Crown, 457.
Kirkpatrick, Major H. P., 472, 474.
Kirsten (or Kerston), Commandant Jan, 264.
Kitchener, General H. H., Lord, G.C.B., G.C.M.G., etc., 1-2, 21, 34, 41-3, 47, 56, 58, 75, 77, 87, 101, 112, 119-20, 123, 126, 132, 136, 139, 146, 157, 163, 165, 198, 205, 214, 222, 251, 265-6, 287, 319, 322, 326-7, 329, 348, 382-3, 392, 398, 401, 404, 417, 429, 465, 487, 491, 493, 498, 506, 508, 512, 515, 519 ; and the Government of Cape Colony, 230-1, 272 ; at the peace conference, terms, etc., 523-63 ; despatches of, 332 ; plans of, to surround De Wet, 331 ; scheme of, for "drives" in the Orange River Colony, 423-4, 475-7 ; to subjugate the Eastern Transvaal, 372 ; takes measures for the safety of Cape Town, 364 ; visits Cape Colony, 229 ; Middelburg, 119-20 ; Klerksdorp, 492.
Kitchener, Major-General F. W., 126-7, 139, 141-4, 148-9, 155, 204-5, 207, 210, 212-14, 216, 218, 221-3, 437 ; in the Western Transvaal, 491-9, 502, 505, 507-9, 511.
Kitchener's Fighting Scouts. *See* COLONIAL UNITS.
Kitchener's Horse. *See* COLONIAL UNITS.
Klaarstroom, and district, 72, 173.
Klaver Vlei, and road, 351-2.
Klein Letaba river, 446.
Klein Marsfontein hills, 316.
Klein Oliphant river, 148.
Klein Sedan, 384.
Klein Waaihoek, 262.
Klein Zevenfontein, 327.
Klein Zwarte Berg, 284.
Kleinfontein (Botha's Berg, Eastern Transvaal), 144.

Kleinfontein (east of Zeerust), 299.
Kleinkop, 102.
Kleinplaats, 340-1.
Klerksdorp, district, and road, 2, 22, 109, 132-7, 181-3, 188-9, 190-2, 194-6, 216, 250-1, 253-5, 291-2, 298, 325, 339-44, 346, 348, 407, 409-11, 413-16, 420, 477-8, 480, 482, 489, 491-3, 498, 505-6 : Boer leaders meet at, to consider peace proposals, 533-4.
Klerksdorp—Pretoria railway, 1, 507.
Klip Bank, 362.
Klip (river) basin, 103.
Klip Drift (Brak river), 83, 462.
Klip Drift (Wilge river), 246.
Klip Gat, 358.
Klip river (Orange River Colony), 101, 103, 154, 250, 424-6.
Klip river (west of Frankfort), 323.
Klip Spruit, 209.
Klipbankspruit, 144, 211.
Klipdam, 437.
Klipdraai hills, 443.
Klipdrift, 340, 499.
Klipfontein (south-east of Bethel), 151.
Klipfontein (south of Ermelo), 116.
Klipfontein (north of Ookiep), 470-2.
Klipgat, 445.
Klipkloof, 140.
Klipkoppies, 150.
Klipkraal, 151.
Klipkrans, 189-90, 194.
Klipoog, 249.
Klippan (south-east of Brugspruit), 152.
Klippan (west of Wolmaranstad), 342.
Klipplaat (Cape Colony), 74, 278, 463.
Klipplaat (north of Rustenburg), 302.
Klipplaatdrift, 143.
Kliprif, 340.
Kliprug, 117.
Klipspruit (north-west of Belfast), 143, 145.

Klipspruit (west of Bothaville), 492.
Klipstapel, 520.
Knapdaar, 175, 225.
Knox, Major-General Sir C. E., K.C.B., 45–6, 48, 52–6, 58–9, 62, 65, 75–8, 80–1, 83–4, 88, 92–3, 96–7, 101–2, 110, 123, 157–60, 166–7, 170–1, 245, 253, 255, 263–4, 269, 327, 338, 402, 429–31, 433–4, 477, 480–1, 490.
Knox, Colonel E. C., 111, 113, 117, 119–20, 122, 127–8, 130, 138, 149–52, 155, 176, 199–203, 223.
Knox, Major-General Sir W. G., K.C.B., 160, 170.
Knysna, 72.
Kobe mountains, 357.
Koedoes Kop, 141.
Koedoesdraai, 196, 255.
Koffyfontein, 96, 262–3, 432.
Kokskraal, affair at, 430.
Komati Poort, and railway, 9, 77, 435. *See also* DELAGOA BAY RAILWAY.
Komati river, and valley, 34, 148–9, 204, 214, 305.
Koms Berg, 357.
Koornfontein, 152.
Koperfontein, 190.
Kopje Alleen, 160, 257.
Kopjes Kraal, 260.
Kopjes station, 109, 324, 485.
Kopjesvlei, 191, 503.
Koppiesfontein, 258.
Koranna Berg, 159, 321, 431.
Korannafontein, 182, 192, 341, 415, 507.
Kordemoersfontein, 364–5.
Korn Spruit, 421.
Kosterfontein, 189, 298.
Koude Heuvel, 240.
Koudeveld Bergen, 175, 227–8, 465.
Kouka river, 279.
Kraai river, 179, 234, 236.
Kraaipan, 420.
Kraal Kop, 258.
Kraankuil, 87–8, 90, 173.

Kraans Pan, 82–3.
Kransfontein, 327.
Kriegars Kraal, 277.
Kritzinger, Commandant P. H., 42–3, 53, 62–3, 65–6, 68, 71–5, 77, 91, 98, 163–5, 172–4, 225–8, 233, 237, 265–7, 271, 287–9, 317–20, 366, 454, 456, 528; driven into Orange River Colony, 238; returns to Cape Colony, 179–80, 367; visits Orange River Colony, 176.
Krogh, J. C., 546, 560, 563.
Krokodil River commando. *See* COMMANDOS.
Krom Spruit, 334, 485, 487.
Kromdraai (south of Ermelo), 115–16, 153, 183.
Kromdraai (east of Springs), 146, 149–50.
Kromhoek, 200.
Krommellboog Spruit, 195.
Kromrivier, 7, 10.
Kromspruit, 55.
Kroonstad, 56, 58, 75, 97, 100, 105, 108, 160–1, 168–70, 216, 250, 254, 257–8, 260–1, 321, 323, 325, 330–1, 333–6, 383–4, 388, 402, 423–4, 431, 475, 477–8, 489; blockhouse line to, 395, 398–9, 426, 479, 485; railway to, 400, 403, 476.
Kroonstad commando. *See* COMMANDOS.
Kruger, H. E., President S. P. J., 453; silence of, 206.
Kruger's Drift, 164, 166.
Krugersdorp, 2–3, 6, 8–11, 20–2, 128–31, 136, 184, 189, 194–5, 346, 447; railway to, 9, 21.
Krugersdorp commando. *See* COMMANDOS.
Krugerspost, 127, 140.
Kruidfontein, 256.
Kruisfontein, 121.
Kruitfontein, 260.
Krupp guns, 144; capture of, 480; shells for, 158.
Kuruman, 131.

INDEX.

LAAGERS, Boer, capture of, 102, 132, 137, 141–2, 152, 154, 182, 192–4, 196, 201, 211, 255–9, 292–3, 302, 305, 326, 329, 371, 410, 430, 438, 443, 506.
Laatstedrift, 143, 211.
Lacedæmonians, 313.
Ladismith, 243, 279, 283–4.
Lady Frere, blockhouse line to, 368.
Lady Grey, 288, 369, 458, 464.
Ladybrand, 97, 157, 253, 321, 331; blockhouse line to, 326, 431.
Ladysmith, 156, 350.
Lagersdrift, 145.
Laing's Nek, 156.
Laingsburg, 283–4, 360.
Lake Chrissie, 114, 123, 147–9, 504, 517.
Laken Vallei, 459.
Lamberts Bay, 42, 70, 359, 362; blockhouse line to, 364–5.
Lambton, Lieut.-Colonel The Hon. C., 16.
Lancaster Hill (Vryheid), 30–1.
Lancaster regiment, The King's Own Royal. *See* REGULAR UNITS.
Lancers. *See* REGULAR UNITS.
Landdrost Monde, 159.
Lang Kloof, 239.
Langberg, 121.
Langdraai, 121.
Lange Berg (Orange River Colony), 387, 391, 395.
Lange Bergen (Cape Colony), 243, 360.
Langgewacht, 117.
Langkloof (Wilge river, Eastern Transvaal), 145, 516.
Langkuil, 257.
Languages, English and Dutch, 523, 525, 536, 547.
Langverwacht (north of Utrecht), 121.
Langverwacht (south of Vrede), 426, 479.
Lansdowne, The Most Hon. H. C. K., Marquis of, K.G., G.C.S.I., etc., 528, 531–4.
Lapfontein, 456, 459.

Lategan, Commandant H. W., 225, 232, 237, 239, 282.
Lauriston, 286.
Lawley, Lieut.-Colonel The Hon. R. T., 423–4, 434, 475, 477, 485, 487, 490, 518–20, 522.
Lawrence, Lieut.-Colonel The Hon. H. A., 474.
Leader, Lieut.-Colonel H. P., 408–9, 422, 500.
Leaders, Republican, 107.
Lean, Major K. E., 253, 266, 269, 272, 290, 327–8, 338.
Leeuw Berg, 80, 84.
Leeuw Hoek, 238.
Leeuw Kop (Orange River Colony), 58, 75, 246.
Leeuw river, 50.
Leeuw Spruit, 246, 482.
Leeuwbank Drift, 108.
Leeuwboschen, 191.
Leeuwdoorn hills, 347.
Leeuwdoorns, 347.
Leeuwfontein (south of Balmoral), 152.
Leeuwfontein (north-west of Klerksdorp), 340, 416.
Leeuwfontein (north of Middelburg), 143.
Leeuwfontein (south-west of Richmond), 456.
Leeuwfontein (north of Tafel Kop, Western Transvaal), 291.
Leeuwfontein (west of Ventersdorp), 182–3, 408.
Leeuwfontein (west of Wolmaranstad), 342.
Leeuwkop (north of Harrismith), 479.
Leeuwkop (north-east of Kimberley), 433.
Leeuwkrantz, 256.
Leeuwkuil (south of Frankfort), 246.
Leeuwkuil (east of Geysdorp), 417, 419.
Leeuwnek, 122.
Leeuwpan (north-east of Geysdorp), 494.

VOL. IV.   47*

Leeuwpan (east of Hoopstad), 256–7.
Leeuwpoort (north of Bethlehem), 169.
Leeuwpoort (west of the Bronkhorst Spruit), 150.
Leeuwspruit (east of Geysdorp), 416–17.
Leeuwspruit (east of Reitz), 246.
Lefroy, Lieutenant B. P., 219.
Legalie's Location, 451.
Legard, Captain D'A., 180.
Legdaar, 207.
Legge, Lieut.-Colonel N., D.S.O., 12–13.
Legislature, Cape Colony, 177, 272.
Leliefontein (north of Garies), 469.
Leliefontein (south-east of Ventersburg), 90, 93, 160.
Lemmer (Senior), General, 418.
Lemmer (Junior), General, 415.
Lemoenfontein Drift, 88.
Lemoenskraal, 424.
Leniency of peace terms, 555.
Lessons of the campaign, 421, 497, 504.
Letjesbosch, 74.
Letskraal siding, 280, 457.
Letters, reports, etc., from Boer leaders, 107, 123–4, 131, 140, 216, 222, 227, 273, 285, 298, 305, 366, 388, 411, 453, 461, 528; for the Army, how dealt with—*see* APPENDIX 9; relating to peace proposals, 524–6, 533–5. *See also* APPENDIX 3.
Leyden, 321.
Leydsdorp, 449–50.
Liabilities, Boer, incurred in the field, 523, 525, 549.
Libenbergs Vlei river, 55, 108, 169, 246, 330–1, 383–5, 388, 396–400, 426, 476–7, 479–80, 482, 485–6.
Licences for firearms, etc., 526, 547.
Lichtenburg, district, and road, 1, 131, 136, 181, 183, 191–2, 292, 344, 406, 409, 416, 421, 475, 508; attack on, 134; blockhouse line to, 407, 492; reinforcements for, 492.

Lichtenburg commando. *See* COMMANDOS.
Lichtenstein, 320.
Liebenberg, General P. J., 1, 194, 325, 340, 411–12.
Light order of columns, neither guns nor transport, 492.
Lilliburn, 116, 148.
Limoen Kloof, 236.
Limpopo river, 435.
Lincelles, 318.
Lincolnshire regiment. *See* REGULAR UNITS.
Lindequee Drift, 195, 324, 333, 346–7.
Lindley, district, and road, 54–7, 101–2, 105, 108, 169, 250, 321, 330–1, 334–7, 383–5, 402–3, 423, 475, 477, 482, 486, 488; blockhouse line to, 395, 398–9, 426, 476, 479, 485.
Lindleys Poort, 291, 293, 298, 339.
Lindsay, Captain M. W., 310.
Lindsell, Lieut.-Colonel R. F., C.B., 173, 180.
Lines of communication, Bloemfontein to Orange river, 176; east of Pretoria (Delagoa Bay railway), 212, 223, 298; attacks on, December 29th, 1900, 24; January 7th, 1901, 35–41; casualties, 44; renewed attacks on, 125, 153; enemy's efforts to destroy, generally, 245; north of Pretoria, 437; Orange River Colony, 170; Standerton railway, 153.
Linyana Spruit, 52–3.
Lisbon, 64.
Little, Brigadier-General M. O., 482, 490.
Little Caledon river, 158.
Little Harts river, 183, 191, 406, 416–17, 492.
Little Salt river, 361.
Liverpool regiment, The King's. *See* REGULAR UNITS.
Lloyd, Major F. C., 253, 269, 338.
Lloyd, Captain T. H. E., 312.

INDEX. 741

Local fencibles and forces. *See* COLONIAL UNITS.
Local volunteers. *See* COLONIAL UNITS.
Loeries Fontein, 352-3, 355.
Lokoala, 53.
Long, Colonel C. J., 45-6, 59, 110.
Los Berg, 195-6, 262, 324, 346.
Loskop, 169.
Lotter (Cape rebel), 225, 237-9, 271 ; capture of, 240-1.
Louis Trichardt, 438-9, 446.
Louw, Commandant A., 353, 363-4.
Louw, Commandant Jan, 468.
Lovat, Major S. J., Lord, D.S.O., 288-9, 457, 464, 466-7, 474.
Lovat's Scouts. *See* IMPERIAL YEOMANRY.
Lowe, Colonel W. H. M., 65-6, 70-2, 74, 89, 92, 102-5, 110, 161, 169, 171, 246, 250, 255-61, 269, 321, 335, 338, 383, 492-3, 497, 511.
Lowry-Cole, Lieut.-Colonel A. W. G. *See* COLE.
Loyal North Lancashire regiment. *See* REGULAR UNITS.
Loyalty, in Cape Colony, 69.
Luckhoff, 94, 96, 166-7, 251, 262-3, 325.
Luipaardsfontein, 54.
Lukin, Lieut.-Colonel H. T., D.S.O., 178-80, 232, 241, 244, 279-81, 290, 369-70, 466-7, 474.
Lund, Captain F. T., 226-7, 231-2, 239, 244, 281, 290, 364, 370, 455-6, 459, 474.
Lüneberg, 117-20, 201.
Luxemburg, 167.
Lydenburg, and district, 25, 126, 140-1, 147-8, 207-8, 211, 216, 250, 304, 376, 381-2, 443.
Lydenburg commando. *See* COMMANDOS.
Lyle, Major H. T., 137.
Lyle, Captain J. C. V., 448-9.
Lynes, Lieutenant W. P., 310-11, 314.

Lyttelton, Lieut.-General The Hon. N. G., C.B., 41, 77-8, 87, 89, 96-7, 110, 126, 161, 163, 171, 174 ; assumes command in Natal, 216.

MAARITSDRIFT, 251.
Mabusa Spruit, 117, 199-200, 379.
McCarthy, Corporal J., 313.
McCracken, Lieut.-Colonel F. W. N., 208.
McCracken's Hill, 40.
McKenzie, Lieut.-Colonel D., 116, 331, 338, 392, 404.
McKinnon's Post, 238.
McLean, Captain A. C., 395.
McMicking, Major H., D.S.O., 346-8, 439-42, 452.
McQueen, Captain, 448-9.
MacAndrew, Lieut.-Colonel J. R., 240, 279-80, 290, 370.
Macbean, Colonel F., 23.
MacDonald, Major-General Sir H. A., K.C.B., D.S.O., 62-3, 65-6, 92, 176.
Macdonald, Captain M., 470.
Machadodorp, 25-6, 35, 148-9, 207-8, 210 ; attack on, 36, 42 ; casualties at, 44.
Machine guns, 22, 59, 92, 110, 127, 138, 155, 171, 180, 197, 223, 244, 269, 290, 303, 315, 348, 370, 381, 422, 434, 452, 474, 490, 511, 522.
MacKenzie, Lieut.-Colonel Colin J., C.B., 176, 373, 375, 378, 381, 485-7, 490, 514, 517, 520, 522.
Mackenzie, Lieut.-Colonel G. F. C., C.B., 345.
Mackenzie, Captain J. R., 408.
Mafeking, 133, 181-3, 191, 292, 298, 348, 443 ; railway to, 443, 461, 494.
Magaliesberg mountains, and valley, 1-2, 4, 7-22, 189-90, 192-3, 293, 295, 437 ; situation in, 128-9.
Magalipsi, 443.
Magato Nek (or Hoek), 291, 293-4, 298, 339.
Magnets Hoogte, 141.

Mahamba, 119, 121, 371.
Mahlabitini, and district, 153.
Mahon, Major Sir W. H., Bart., D.S.O., 283.
Majoors Drift, 423, 425, 428, 475, 482, 488.
Majuba mountain, 9, 125, 393.
Makauws Drift, 431.
Makoiespan, 498.
Makwasi Berg, 341-2, 344, 410.
Makwasi Spruit, 340.
Malan, Fighting-General (Lieutenant) W., 173-6, 178-80, 225-7, 229, 231-2, 237, 281-2, 363-4, 455-9, 462-3, 465-7, 528.
Malips river, 141.
Malipspoort, 446, 448-51.
Malmesbury, 357-8, 360-2.
Mamre, 360.
Manchester regiment. See REGULAR UNITS.
Map, showing physical features of Cape Colony, 358.
Mapoch's Gronden, 145.
Marais, Commandant, 438.
Marais siding, 175, 278.
Maraisburg, 176, 179, 237, 274, 277, 464, 466-7.
Marches, forced, 352, 359-60, 379, 424, 516-17.
Maribogo, 182, 420, 508.
Marico, and district, 301, 416.
Marienthal, 118-19.
Maritz, Commandant S. G., 224, 228, 271, 350-63, 365, 367, 383, 455, 468-9, 471.
Mark's Drift, 86.
Marker, Captain R. J., 85.
Marsala, 402.
Marshall, Major W. R., 402-3, 405, 423, 434, 482, 490.
Marston Moor, 504.
Marten, Second-Lieutenant L. H., 310.
Martial law, absence of, in Cape Town, 177; administration of, in Cape Colony, 230, 272; for Cape ports, 178, 272; for Cape Town, 358.

Martin, Lieut.-Colonel H., C.B., 156.
Martin-Leake, Surgeon-Captain A. (awarded the Victoria Cross), 513.
Maryvale, 117, 375.
Maseru (farm), 53.
Massy, Major W. G., 93-4, 98, 110, 171.
Matala's Location, 446.
Matjesfontein, 69-70, 243, 284-5, 364, 455, 460.
Mauch Berg, 147, 199, 204.
Mausers (Boer rifles), 220, 312.
Maxim gun, 32, 38, 88, 135, 142, 209, 235, 275, 410, 412, 439, 476, 501.
Maxim-Nordenfeldt gun, 387.
Maxwell, Lieut.-Colonel C., 97, 110, 161, 163-5, 171.
Maygar, Lieutenant L. C. (awarded the Victoria Cross), 373.
Mayne, Lieut.-Colonel G. N., 345.
Mears, Commandant, 150, 401.
Measures for subjugation of the Orange River Colony, 326.
Mecca, 9.
Medical arrangements. See APPENDIX 7.
Mediterranean, 255.
Melani Kop, 428, 480.
Melkboschfontein, 35.
Melmoth, and district, 154, 219-20, 222.
Menne's Scouts. See COLONIAL UNITS.
Mentz, Commandant F., 426, 477, 486-7.
Mequatlings Nek, 53, 157, 159, 253, 431.
Methuen, Lieut.-General P. S., Lord, K.C.V.O., K.C.B., C.M.G., 1, 131-5, 137-8, 181-3, 188-92, 194, 197, 291-2, 298-9, 301, 303, 339-45, 348, 383, 406-7, 409, 416, 422, 477, 491-2, 507; at Tweebosch, 417-20.
Meyer, General Lucas J., 206; at the peace conference, 546, 560, 563.
Meyershoop, 117.
Meyerton, 207.
Middel Post (north-west of Kenhardt), 468.

INDEX. 743

Middel Post (north of Sutherland), 460.
Middel Water, 335.
Middelbult, 494, 498, 505.
Middelburg, and road (Eastern Transvaal), 23, 34–5, 41, 111, 113, 125, 143, 146, 148, 203, 207, 209–11, 213–15, 249, 304–6, 373, 515; peace conference at, 119–20, 126, 523–4; peace proposals at, basis for final terms, 540, 545–6, 549.
Middelburg commando. *See* COMMANDOS.
Middeldrift, 153.
Middelkop, 479.
Middelkraal, 152, 207, 209.
Middelplaat, 151.
Middelplaats, 86–7.
Middle Hill (Helvetia), 25–6.
Middle Mount, 463, 465.
Middle Water, 240.
Middleburg (Cape Colony), 64, 67, 71, 176, 224, 226–7, 229, 232, 237–9, 280, 359; blockhouse line to, 458.
Middlesex regiment. *See* REGULAR UNITS.
Military history of Perthshire, 504.
Military railways, system of. *See* APPENDIX 10.
Militia, 63.
Militia Units :—
    Royal Garrison artillery, Durham company, 221.
    The Royal Warwickshire (5th), 470.
    The Prince of Wales's Own (West Yorkshire) (4th), 283.
    The South Wales Borderers (3rd), 410.
Mill (Molen) river, 246, 475.
Millerale, 475.
Mills, Lieut.-Colonel G. A., C.B., 222.
Milne, Lieut.-Colonel R. L., D.S.O., 346, 348.
Milner A., Lord, G.C.B., G.C.M.G., 453–4, 537, 539–40, 544–6, 549–53, 560–3.

Minchin, Lieut.-Colonel C. F., D.S.O., 253, 269, 327, 338.
Mkusi river, 515.
Mobility of Boers, 68.
Modder river, 42, 95, 165–7, 196, 250–2, 254–5, 258, 260, 262, 264, 321, 325, 421, 431–2; Elliot's " drive " to, 257–61.
Modder River station, 254, 257, 262–3, 326.
Modderfontein (Cape Colony), 274–7.
Modderfontein (Gatsrand), 75, 130–1.
Moedwil, 344, 504; action of, 293–8.
Moeras river, 243.
Moeyelykheid, 143.
Mokari Drift, 320.
Molen Spruit, 424.
Molteno, and district, 255–6, 234–5, 272–3, 458, 463.
Money, Lieut.-Colonel C. G. C. (C.E.), C.B., 134.
Monro, Colonel S. C. H., 56–9, 92, 97, 110, 161–5, 171, 179–80, 225–6, 234–6, 244, 271–4, 286–7, 290, 368–70, 457–8, 474.
Montagu, 243, 285, 458.
Monument Hill (Belfast), 37–9.
Mooi Hoek, 457.
Mooi river, blockhouse line to, 345.
Mooifontein (south of Bethel), 151.
Mooifontein (north of Lindley), 384.
Mooigelegen, 246.
Mooihoek, 158.
Mooiklip, 121–2.
Mooimook river, 361.
Mooiplaats (east of Pretoria), 111.
Mooiplaats (north-east of Vryburg), 406.
Mooipoort, 117.
Mooiwater, 159.
Moolmans Spruit, 484.
Moore, Lieut.-Colonel M. G., 234–6, 244, 267, 269, 287, 290, 316, 338, 368–70, 464, 474.
Moorreesburg, 356, 358, 360–2.
Moos river, 144–5, 211, 214, 517.
Morgenzon (north of Blauw Kop), 202.

Morgenzon (east of Reitz), 246, 401.
Morgenzon (west of Warm Bath), 445.
Morgenzon (near Zulu border), 122.
Mortimer, and station, 233, 467.
Mossel Bay, 72, 283.
Mount Prospect, 156.
Mount Stewart, 278.
Mounted Infantry. *See* INFANTRY, MOUNTED.
Mounted Infantry Plateau (Vryheid), 30.
Movement of troops, by railway, 64. *See also* APPENDIX 10.
Mowbray, 104, 487.
Muller, Vecht-General, 38, 143, 203–4, 206, 213, 377, 515–16.
Müllers Pass, 215.
Munitions of war, importation of, for enemy, 177.
Munster Fusiliers, The Royal. *See* REGULAR UNITS.
Murray, Lieut.-Colonel The Hon. A., 110, 163–5, 171, 179–80, 225, 234, 244, 267, 269, 287–90, 316, 338.
Murray, Major F. D., 310, 312.
Murray, Lieut.-Colonel W. H. E., 345.
Murraysburg, 71, 74, 176, 228, 231, 278, 456–7, 459, 463–5.
Myburg, Commandant C., 225, 233–4, 236, 252, 271–2, 274, 286, 368–9.

NAAUWPOORT (Cape Colony), 65, 77; railway to, 367.
Naauwpoort (Botha's Berg, Eastern Transvaal), 143.
Naauwpoort (south of Rustenburg), 129–30, 134, 136, 183–4, 188–9, 191, 193, 292–3, 339, 345.
Naauwpoort Nek (Brandwater basin), 158, 335.
Naboomspruit, 439, 441.
Namaqualand, and district, 224, 455, 462, 467–9, 472–3.
Namaqualand Border Scouts. *See* COLONIAL UNITS.
Namaqualand Field Force, 469.
Napoleon Bonaparte, Emperor, 46–7.

Naseby, 164, 504.
Natal, 34, 56, 117, 125, 129, 147, 153–4, 186, 199, 217, 293, 304–5, 307, 317, 321–3, 328, 350, 377, 423, 425, 478–9, 514; blockhouse line to, 398; borders of, 102, 217–22; Government of, 554; invasion of, rumours of, 29; railway of, 27–8; re-invasion of, plans for, 42, 216; supplies from, for General French's force, 112–13, 117. *See also* APPENDIX 1.
Natal Hill (Machadodorp), 36.
Natal Police. *See* COLONIAL UNITS.
Natal Volunteers. *See* COLONIAL UNITS.
Nation, The British, and military preparedness, 421.
"National Murder," 107.
National Scouts. *See* COLONIAL UNITS.
Native drivers, shot by Boers, 430.
Naude, Commandant, 366.
Ndwandwe district, 219.
Nels Poort station, 173, 231–2, 456, 459, 464–5.
Nelskop, 351.
Nelspruit, 35, 147–8, 207–8.
Nesbitt's Horse. *See* COLONIAL UNITS.
Nesham, Lieutenant T. P. W., 418.
Netherland, The, Government of, 528–33.
New Bethesda, 71, 238, 280–1.
New Holstein, 53, 159.
"New Model," De la Rey's, broken, 503.
New South Wales, contingents from. *See* COLONIAL UNITS.
New Zealand, contingents from. *See* COLONIAL UNITS.
Newcastle, 103, 215.
Newmarket, 476.
Newspapers, Republican, sympathies of, 177.
Ney (French Marshal), 397.
Ngoana, 48, 50–2.
Ngomi forest, 515.
Nicholson, Lieut.-Colonel J. S., D.S.O., 304.

INDEX.

Nicholson's Nek, 27, 186.
Nickalls, Major N. T., 276, 457–8.
Niekerksvlei, 113, 116.
Niet Gedacht, 456.
Nieuhoudt (or Nieuwoudt), Commandant C., 67, 430–1.
Nieuwoudtville, 352–3.
Nieuwveld range, 357, 457.
Nixon, Colonel J. E., 425, 428, 434, 475, 479–81, 485, 488, 490, 520, 522.
Nkandhla, and district, 153–4, 219, 221, 377.
Nondweni, 377.
Nooitgedacht (east of Machadodorp), 35 ; attack on, 40–1 ; casualties at, 44.
Nooitgedacht (Magaliesberg), 8, 11, 193, 295 ; action at, 13–22 ; position at, 12.
Nooitgedacht (north of Poplar Grove), 167.
Nooitgedacht (south of Rooiwal), 503.
Nooitverwacht, 507.
Norfolk regiment. *See* REGULAR UNITS.
Norman castles (Witkoppies), 104.
Northamptonshire regiment. *See* REGULAR UNITS.
Northern Transvaal, 95 ; description of, 435 ; Grenfell's transfer to, 176 ; its occupation and importance, 436–7 ; situation in, 382. *See also* EVENTS IN.
Northumberland Fusiliers. *See* REGULAR UNITS.
Norval's Pont, 63, 78, 93, 96–7, 262 ; railway to, 64, 265.
Notes, issued by South African Republic, 548–9.
Nqutu, and district, 32, 122, 219.
Nurses. *See* APPENDIX 7.
Nylstroom, 439–44.

ODENDAAL, FIELD-CORNET G., 369.
Odendaal Stroom, 62.
Olievenberg, 96.

Olifants Nek, 2–3, 6–8, 10, 22, 128, 191, 193, 195, 292–3, 339.
Olifants river (Clanwilliam, Cape Colony), 359.
Olifants river, and valley (Outdtshoorn, Cape Colony), 72, 279, 284.
Oliphant river, 113, 140–2, 144–6, 149–50, 152, 199, 203, 205, 207, 211, 213–15, 305, 375, 516.
Oliphant River drifts, 437.
Oliphants Kop, 214.
Oliphant's Poort, 141.
Oliver, Second-Lieutenant L. M., 336.
Olivier C., 546, 560, 563.
Oliviers Hoek Pass, 335.
Omdraai Vlei, 462.
Omdurman, battle of, 503.
Omissions from this history, 202.
Omkyk, 468.
Onbekend, 113.
Ongers river, 67, 87, 473.
Onverdacht, action at, 57.
Onverwacht (Cape Colony), 78.
Onverwacht (south-east of Ermelo), 201 ; affair at, 379–80.
Ookiep, 356, 468–9, 473 ; siege of, 470–2.
Oorlogs Poort (north-west of Aberdeen, Cape Colony), 229, 237.
Oorlogs Poort (north-west of Dordrecht, Cape Colony), 236, 457.
Oorlogs Poort (east of Reddersburg, Orange River Colony), 168, 245.
Oorzaak, 2, 7, 193.
Oosthuizen, Acting-Commandant O., 297.
Openbaar, 94.
Oppenheim, Captain L. C. F., 504. *See also* PREFACE.
Opperman, General D., 220, 305, 380.
Orange Free State : army of, 46 ; executive of, meets Transvaal Government, 205–6 ; president of— *see* STEYN, M. T. ; terms of peace for, negotiations, and conclusion of, 523–63.

746   THE WAR IN SOUTH AFRICA.

Orange river, 1, 42, 45, 47, 62–3, 65, 74, 76–8, 81, 83–6, 88–91, 93, 96–8, 163–5, 167, 172–3, 176, 233, 236–9, 261–8, 270, 273, 286–9, 317–18, 366, 462, 468, 473.
Orange River bridge, 94.
Orange River Colony, 65, 68, 75–8, 123, 139, 173, 177–9, 192, 202, 207, 210–11, 216–17, 222, 231, 238, 271–3, 286, 326, 350, 357, 367, 454, 506, 521; "cockpit," the, of the campaign, 475; clearance and subjugation of, 326; commands in, 97; districts of, 263; "drives" in, scheme for, 423–4, 485; Government of, 205–6; B. Hamilton enters, 485; situation in, 382–3, 392–3, 397.
Orange River station, 166.
Order, The, of the Bath, 170, 180, 217, 224.
Orders: by the Commander-in-Chief, 331; to Blood, 205; Clements, 2, 56; Elliot, 323, 335; Fetherstonhaugh, 293; French, 112, 465; Garratt, 195; B. Hamilton, 87, 163, 251; Hart, 267–8, 287; Kekewich, 193; by Benson, 308, 314; Scobell, 240, 242; Elliot, 247; French, 114, 278; I. Hamilton—see APPENDIX 4; Plumer, 94; Wynne, 177; by L. Botha, to attack Benson, 305; for re-invasion of Natal, 217.
Ordnance Department, The Army, and Stores. See APPENDIX 8.
O'Reilly's Pan, 346, 406.
Orr, Major A. S., 381.
Ortlepp's Request, 90.
Oshoek, 495.
Ossenberg, 228.
Otter Spruit, 256.
Otters Hoek, 283.
Otto's Hoop, 1, 131.
Oud Agatha, 450.
Oude Muur, 455.
Oudeberg, 457, 465.
Oudenaarde, 317.

Oudtshoorn, and district, 72, 243, 279, 283–4.
Owen, Lieut.-Colonel H. M., 85, 255–6, 269.
Oxfordshire Light Infantry. See REGULAR UNITS.

PAARDE GRAS VALLEI, 459.
Paarde Vallei, 238.
Paarde Verlies, 369.
Paardeberg, 167, 263, 374.
Paardeberg Drift, 262.
Paardefontein, 150.
Paardehoek, 331, 334.
Paardekop (station), 216, 425, 517.
Paardekraal (south of Vredefort), 100.
Paardenkop, 425.
Paardenkraal, 246.
Paardeplaats (north-west of Klerksdorp), 416.
Paardeplaats (west of Lydenburg), 144.
Paauwpan, 87.
Paget, Major-General A. H., C.V.O., 10, 19, 21, 23, 77, 92–5, 110–11, 128–9, 138.
Paget's Horse. See IMPERIAL YEOMANRY.
Palala, 443.
Palala River valley, 443.
Paling Kloof, 467.
Palmes, Major P., 183.
Palmietfontein (north of Belfast), 143.
Palmietfontein (south-east of Boshof), 254, 259.
Palmietfontein (north by west of Klerksdorp), 182.
Palmietfontein (north of Wolmaranstad), 341–2.
Palmietpan, 254.
Pampasfontein, 327–8.
Pampoen Poort, 459.
Pan, 23, 35, 209, 214, 515; attack on post at, 41; casualties at, 44.
Pandamsfontein, 254.
Paris (France), 24, 124.

INDEX.

Paris, Major A., 84, 86-7, 89, 92, 99, 110, 166-7, 171, 245, 253-5, 258, 261, 269, 338, 416, 422; at Tweebosch, 417-20.
Park, Lieut.-Colonel C. W., A.D.C., 127, 139-44, 147-8, 153, 155, 199, 204, 207-8, 210-12, 214, 223, 304, 376-7, 380-1, 515-17, 520-2.
Parke, Lieut.-Colonel R. K., C.B., 65, 67, 70, 73, 92.
Parsons, Colonel Sir C., K.C.M.G., 46, 53, 59, 65, 67, 69-70, 92, 110, 173, 175, 180.
Parys (south of Villiersdorp), 102.
Parys, and district (west of Wolvehoek station), 100, 109, 249-50, 324, 346-7.
Passage of the Orange river, by De Wet, 78, 90, 93.
Passes of the Drakensberg, closing of, 217.
Patchoana mountain, 47-51.
Patriotism of irregulars, unreliability of, 421.
Patriots Klip, 368-9.
Patten, Captain A., 4-5.
Payne, Lieut.-Colonel R. L., 23.
Peace, 450-1, 474, 510, 521; *Aide-Memoire* from the Netherland Government, as to, 529-31; Articles of, 547-63; Boer proposals for, 544-5; Botha refuses terms of, 119, 126; conclusion of negotiations for, 523-63; conference at Middelburg, 119-20, 126; at Vereeniging, 471, 473, 487; correspondence relating to, 524-39; discussion of terms, etc., 540-63; hostilities to cease during, 508; negotiations for, 107; none without independence, 206; terms of, offered by British Government, 523-4; text of, 560-3.
Pearston, 174-5, 178, 226, 279-80, 457, 463, 466.
Pella, 468.
Peninsula (War), 397.
Pepworth Hill, 141.

Perth, 102, 334.
Perthshire, military history of, 504.
Petersburg, 225-6, 239-40, 463.
Petrusburg, and road, 95-7, 166-7, 251-2, 431.
Petrusburg commando. *See* COMMANDOS.
Petrusville, 65, 86, 88, 173.
Philippolis, 62, 78, 94, 96, 164, 166-7, 252, 262-3, 266, 430-1.
Philipstown, 60, 65, 79-81, 88-9.
Physical features of Cape Colony, 358.
Piccadilly, 3.
Piekeniers Kloof, 362.
Pienaars Pan, 81.
Pienaars River station, 443.
Piet Retief, and road, 117-21, 142, 199-200, 216; blockhouse line to, 372, 377, 379.
Piet Retief commando. *See* COMMANDOS.
Pietermaritzburg, 350.
Pietersburg, 9-10, 95, 139, 141-2, 145-6, 438-9, 441, 443, 446-9; its occupation and importance, 435-7.
Pietersburg Light Horse. *See* COLONIAL UNITS.
Pieterskraal, 142.
Pietersrust, 121.
Pilands Berg, 1.
Pilcher, Colonel T. D., 46, 53-6, 59, 76, 78, 80, 83, 92-3, 96-7, 99, 102, 110, 157-61, 166-7, 171, 176, 245, 250, 253, 265-6, 269, 271-4, 286, 290, 316-17, 327, 329, 338, 368, 430, 434, 481, 488, 490.
Pilgrim's Rest, 380.
Pilson, Major A. F., 36.
Pine-Coffin, Major J. E., 93, 110, 160, 171, 254-5, 257, 259-61, 266, 269, 321, 331, 338.
Pink, Lieut.-Colonel F. J., C.M.G., D.S.O., 103, 110, 154-5.
Piquetberg (town and county), 69-70, 357-64.
Piquetberg mountains, 360, 363.

Piquetberg Road station, 356, 358–9, 361, 455.
Pitsani, 346.
Pitville, 148.
Pivaan river, 120, 201.
Pivaanspoort, 201.
Plan of campaign, and of commanders: Boer—34, 42, 68, 108, 114, 172, 207, 216–17, 270, 357, 359, 383; miscarriage of, 297; in Cape Colony, 461; British—42, 94, 100–1, 112, 139, 146, 228, 237, 242, 255, 265, 326–7, 331, 358, 363, 384, 400, 423–4, 439, 475, 485, 506; marred by railway delay, 516.
Plat Kop Drift (Kraai river), 234.
Plat Nek, 121, 371.
Plat Rust, 229.
Platberg, 262.
Platkop, 334.
Platrand, 147, 152, 154, 200, 202–3, 205; affair at, 212.
Pleasant Gift, 428.
Plesier, 55–6.
Plettenberg Bay, 72.
Plumer, Brigadier-General H. C. O., C.B., 77–89, 92–6, 110, 129–30, 138–42, 145–7, 149–52, 155, 165, 199–203, 222–3, 249–50, 254–5, 257–63, 269, 287, 316–20, 338, 371, 373, 376, 379–81, 435, 437, 514, 522.
Pokwani, 141, 144.
Pompey siding, 78, 265.
Pongola Bosch, and "bush," 200, 202, 320, 371.
Pongola river, 120–1.
Ponies, capture of, 249, 256, 356.
Pont, at Mark's Drift, 86.
Poortje (south of Aberdeen, Cape Colony), 175–6, 231–2.
Poortje (south of Bethlehem), 169.
Poortje (east of Vrede), 425.
Pope, John (Federal General, America), 382.
Poplar Grove, 252, 254, 260.
Port Alfred, railway to, 64.

Port Elizabeth, and railway, 64, 242, 278, 350, 357.
Port Nolloth, 356, 469–70; railway to, 468.
Port Scheiding, 141.
Porterville, 362.
Post office, military, the work of. *See* Appendix 9.
Postal and telegraph union, 536.
Positions, attack on, steepest side most favourable to, 393–4.
Potchefstroom, 2, 128, 131, 133, 136, 183, 192, 195, 298, 324, 491; railway to, 22.
Potchefstroom commando. *See* COMMANDOS.
Potfontein (Cape Colony), 87, 366.
Potgieter, Commandant F. J., 192, 341–2, 344, 410; at Rooiwal, 501.
Potgieter, Commandant H. J., 220–1.
P. P. Burg, 120, 122, 201.
P. P. Rust, 142, 440.
Pram Bergen, 473.
Pram Kop, 105, 329, 426, 485.
Presidents. *See* BURGER, S., *and* STEYN, M. T.
Pretoria, 6–7, 24, 44, 101, 147, 153, 188, 194, 206, 216, 232, 266, 292, 298, 376, 437, 439, 442, 504, 510, 521, 534; peace delegates to, 535; delegates leave, 541; the loss of, its bearing on Boer warfare, 436.
Pretoria commando. *See* COMMANDOS.
Pretoria—Delagoa Bay or Komati Poort railway, 77, 139, 146, 210.
Pretoria—Klerksdorp railway, 1.
Pretoria—Rustenburg road, safety of, 3.
Pretorius, defeat of the Zulus by, in 1838, 21.
Pretorius, Commandant H., 67.
Pretorius, Commandant M. G., 439, 518.
Price, Colonel R. H., C.M.G., 369, 458, 463–5.

INDEX.   749

Price-Davies, Lieutenant L. A. E. (awarded the Victoria Cross), 217.
Prieska, and district, 60, 67, 70, 81, 83, 224, 367, 462.
Prince Albert (town), 243, 279-80, 282-3, 285-6.
Prince Albert Road, 70, 72, 455.
Prince of Wales's Light Horse. *See* COLONIAL UNITS.
Prinsloo, Assistant-Commandant A., 215.
Prinsloo, General M., 48-51, 335-6, 396.
Prinsloo, General M., surrender of, to Hunter, 112.
Priors siding, 78, 164, 263, 316.
Prisoners of war: Boer—52, 85, 88, 97, 102-3, 105, 107-9, 116-19, 121-2, 127, 132, 134-7, 141-4, 146, 149-50, 152-4, 159, 162-4, 166-8, 175, 179-83, 189, 191-3, 195-6, 200-3, 208-9, 211-15, 225, 229, 232, 241, 248-54, 256-60, 262-3, 280, 292-3, 298, 301-2, 304-6, 316, 318, 322-6, 330, 332, 334-5, 339-46, 351, 367-9, 371, 374-81, 397-402, 404, 406-10, 424, 428-31, 438-40, 443-6, 449-51, 457, 460, 463-4, 477, 479-80, 486-7, 493, 503, 505, 509, 513-17, 520-1; return of, 523-4, 547; British—15-16, 26-7, 29, 34, 37-8, 55, 73, 96, 101, 167, 192, 204, 209, 218, 225, 251, 259, 286, 298, 314, 319, 321, 330, 333, 340, 355, 376, 394, 415, 420, 450, 484, 489, 514; brutality of Boers to, 430; deprived of uniform, 497.
Privations endured by troops, 82-3, 118-19, 242, 493.
Problem of the High Veld, 112. *See also* HIGH VELD.
Proclamation by Smuts, for governance of Cape Colony, 462.
Prospect, fort at, attack on, 219-20.
Protection of Boer families, 261.

Pulteney, Colonel W. P., D.S.O., 111, 113, 117, 120-2, 127-8, 138-9, 143-6, 148-9, 155, 204-5, 207, 215, 218, 222-3, 371, 373, 376, 379-81, 514, 522.
Purcell, Captain J. F., 241.
Purchas, Captain E. C., 183.
Pursuit of enemy *versus* clearance of crops, etc., 98.
Putfontein (south of Pretoria), 111.
Putfontein (west of Ventersdorp), 183.
Putters Kraal station, 273-4.
Pylkop, 446-9, 451.
Pyper, Lieutenant G., 455, 462, 473.
Pypers, Commandant S., 279, 285-6, 363, 462, 473.

QUAGGAFONTEIN (west of Lindley), 384, 395, 399.
Quaggafontein (east of Rouxville), 318; action at, 287-8.
Quaggapan, 259.
Quaggas Drift, 228.
Quaggas Nek, 277.
Queen, Her Majesty the, of Holland, 528-31, 534.
Queensland, contingents from. *See* COLONIAL UNITS.
Queenstown, 287.
Quicke, Captain F. C., 256.

RAADEL, 99.
Radclyffe, Captain C. E., 28-9.
Railway Pioneer regiments. *See* COLONIAL UNITS.
Railways, 43, 63, 403-4; attacks on, 36-42, 125; delay on, 516; Bloemfontein, 93, 167-8, 225, 258, 262, 264-5; Buluwayo, 443; Cape Town, 242, 279, 282, 284, 354, 357, 363, 461; De Aar, 238, 367; Delagoa Bay, 23, 139, 146, 199, 201, 204, 207-8, 210, 214-15, 298, 304, 315, 372-3, 376, 380, 437, 481, 515-16, 520-1; East London, 467; fortifications on, 402, 509; Graaff Reinet, 278, 457, 463; importance

Railways—*continued*.
of, 64-5, 77, 243; Johannesburg—Krugersdorp, 9, 21; Johannesburg—Potchefstroom, 22; Johannesburg—Standerton, and Natal, 27-8, 43, 125, 127, 153, 201, 210, 423, 425, 481, 485, 520; Kimberley, 167, 255, 258, 509; Klerksdorp—Pretoria, 1, 507; Kroonstad, 400, 403, 476; Mafeking, 443, 461, 494; military, system of—*see* APPENDIX 10; Naauwpoort, 367; Norval's Pont, 64, 265; Port Elizabeth, 242; Port Nolloth, 468; Sterkstroom—Dordrecht, 273; Stormberg—Rosmead, 66; Vryburg, 507.
Ramagoep's Location, 447.
Ramah, 96, 164, 166, 252, 325.
Ramahutshe, 264.
Rand Berg, 202, 514.
Rations, for Boer families, 261.
Rawlinson, Colonel Sir H. S., Bart., C.B., 135-8, 182-3, 189-91, 195, 197, 222-3, 254-8, 260-1, 265-7, 269, 287, 316-17, 329, 338, 371, 373-5, 377-8, 381, 400, 402, 405, 423-6, 428-9, 434, 475, 478, 480, 490-4, 498-9, 505, 507, 509, 511; at Rooiwal, 502-3.
Rayner station, 179, 236.
Reay, Lieut.-Colonel C. T., C.B., 157-8, 171, 246, 251, 269, 334, 338.
Rebellion in, Cape Colony, 60-1, 68, 172, 224, 349-50, 360; Cape Town, 177.
Rebels, 225, 227, 274, 350-63, 365, 417; penalties in prospect for, 352; recruits, 356, 468-9; strength of, 453; terms to, in Cape Colony, 230; treatment of, under peace terms, 553-4.
Recruiting, tables of. *See* APPENDIX 15.
Reddersburg, 46, 163, 168.
Reeves, Brigadier-General J., 36.
Refugees, 103; concentration camps for—*see* APPENDIX 12.

REGULAR UNITS.
Cavalry :—
1st (King's) Dragoon Guards, 77, 80, 85, 135, 256.
2nd Dragoon Guards (Queen's Bays), 423, 504, 518-19.
3rd (Prince of Wales's) Dragoon Guards, 77.
5th (Princess Charlotte of Wales's) Dragoon Guards, 513.
6th Dragoon Guards (Carabiniers), 194, 210.
7th (Princess Royal's) Dragoon Guards, 65, 486.
1st (Royal) Dragoons, 194.
2nd Dragoons (Royal Scots Greys), 465-7, 513.
5th (Royal Irish) Lancers, 37, 40-1, 232.
6th (Inniskilling) Dragoons, 117, 336.
7th (Queen's Own) Hussars, 423, 518-19.
9th (Queen's Royal) Lancers, 163, 165, 179, 226, 241-2, 369.
10th (Prince of Wales's Own Royal) Hussars, 232, 237-8, 242, 460.
12th (Prince of Wales's Royal) Lancers, 232, 237, 242, 286, 358.
13th Hussars, 371.
16th (Queen's) Lancers, 52, 227, 359, 365, 472.
17th (The Duke of Cambridge's Own) Lancers, 165, 179-80, 225, 227, 233, 272, 274-8, 290, 370, 457-8.
18th Hussars, 211, 213-14, 513.
19th (Princess of Wales's Own) Hussars, 36, 213-14, 513.

Artillery :—
Royal Horse : 233, 390.
G. battery, 77.
J. battery, 21.
O. battery, 495.
P. battery, 2, 14, 17, 137, 495.
Q. battery, 151.
T. battery, 495.
U. battery, 318-19.

INDEX. 751

Serving as cavalry, 402; mounted rifles, 495.
Royal Field :
  4th battery, 299–301, 410, 416–20.
  8th battery, 2, 17–18, 21, 185–8.
  18th battery, 437.
  28th battery, 185–8, 294–7.
  37th (Howitzer) battery, 299–301.
  38th battery, 416–20.
  66th battery, 41.
  69th battery, 32, 219.
  75th battery, 4, 439–40.
  79th battery, 220.
  81st battery, 213.
  83rd battery, 213, 438.
  84th battery, 37, 306, 308–14.
  85th battery, 437, 440.
  Vickers-Maxims, 2 ; XI. section, 390.
Royal Garrison : Eastern division, 17.
Royal Marine : 416.

Engineers :—
  Royal Engineers, 2, 116, 300.
  1st Field troop, 306–14.

Foot Guards :—
  Grenadier Guards (2nd), 392.
  Grenadier Guards (3rd), 80.
  Coldstream Guards (2nd), 79.
  Scots Guards (2nd), 321, 324.

Infantry :—
  The Buffs (East Kent) (2nd) [formerly 3rd Foot], 208, 306, 308–14, 414.
  The King's Own (Royal Lancaster) (2nd) [formerly 4th Foot], 30–2.
  The Northumberland Fusiliers (1st) [formerly 5th Foot], 299–301, 345, 410, 414, 416–20.
  The Northumberland Fusiliers (2nd) [formerly 5th Foot], 2, 11, 14–16.
  The Royal Fusiliers (City of London) (2nd) [formerly 7th Foot], 470.
  The King's (Liverpool) (1st) [formerly 8th Foot], 25–7.
  The Norfolk (2nd) [formerly 9th Foot], 298, 492.
  The Lincolnshire (2nd) [formerly 10th Foot], 439–40.
  The Devonshire (1st) [formerly 11th Foot], 127, 142, 213.
  The Devonshire (2nd) [formerly 11th Foot], 28.
  The Suffolk (1st) [formerly 12th Foot], 345.
  The Prince Albert's (Somersetshire Light Infantry) (2nd) [formerly 13th Foot], 151.
  The Prince of Wales's Own (West Yorkshire) (2nd) [formerly 14th Foot], 4–5, 7, 114, 371.
  The Bedfordshire (2nd) [formerly 16th Foot], 76.
  The Royal Irish (1st) [formerly 18th Foot], 37, 381.
  The Royal Welsh Fusiliers (1st) [formerly 23rd Foot], 345.
  The South Wales Borderers (2nd) [formerly 24th Foot], 131, 183.
  The King's Own Scottish Borderers (1st) [formerly 25th Foot], 185–8, 345.
  The Royal Inniskilling Fusiliers (1st [formerly 27th Foot], 37.
  The Royal Inniskilling Fusiliers (2nd) [formerly 108th Foot], 447–9.
  The Worcestershire (1st) [formerly 29th Foot], 77.
  The East Surrey (2nd) [formerly 70th Foot], 470.
  The Duke of Wellington's (West Riding) (1st) [formerly 33rd Foot], 437.
  The Border (1st) [formerly 34th Foot], 21.
  The South Staffordshire (1st) [formerly 38th Foot], 392.
  The Dorsetshire (2nd) [formerly 54th Foot], 219.
  The Prince of Wales's Volunteers (South Lancashire) (1st) [formerly 40th Foot], 219.
  The Oxfordshire Light Infantry (1st) [formerly 43rd Foot], 324, 347.

Regular Units (Infantry)—*continued*.
The Sherwood Foresters (Derbyshire) (1st) [formerly 45th Foot], 185-8, 293-8.
The Loyal North Lancashire (1st) [formerly 47th Foot], 183, 299-301, 346, 416-20.
The Northamptonshire (2nd) [formerly 58th Foot], 139, 437, 447.
Princess Charlotte of Wales's (Royal Berkshire) (2nd) [formerly 66th Foot], 36, 40-1, 208, 233, 243.
The King's Own (Yorkshire Light Infantry) (2nd) [formerly 105th Foot], 2, 4-6, 12, 16.
The King's (Shropshire Light Infantry) (2nd) [formerly 85th Foot], 37, 39.
The Duke of Cambridge's Own (Middlesex) (2nd) [formerly 77th Foot], 32.
The Duke of Edinburgh's (Wiltshire) (2nd) [formerly 99th Foot], 139, 437-8, 440, 447.
The Manchester (2nd) [formerly 96th Foot], 157.
The York and Lancaster (1st) [formerly 65th Foot], 32.
The York and Lancaster (2nd) [formerly 84th Foot], 32.
The Gordon Highlanders (1st) [formerly 75th Foot], 37, 39.
The Gordon Highlanders (2nd) [formerly 92nd Foot], 139, 437, 439, 441.
The Queen's Own Cameron Highlanders (1st) [formerly 79th Foot], 20, 304, 442.
Princess Victoria's (Royal Irish Fusiliers) (2nd) [formerly 89th Foot], 36.
The Connaught Rangers (1st) [formerly 88th Foot], 234-6.
Princess Louise's (Argyll and Sutherland Highlanders) (1st) [formerly 91st Foot], 4.
The Prince of Wales's Leinster regiment (Royal Canadians) (1st) [formerly 100th Foot], 156.
The Royal Munster Fusiliers (1st) [formerly 101st Foot], 151, 433.
The Royal Dublin Fusiliers (1st) [formerly 102nd Foot], 219.
The Royal Dublin Fusiliers (2nd) [formerly 103rd Foot], 346.
The Rifle Brigade (The Prince Consort's Own) (1st), 28-9, 44.

Army Service Corps. See APPENDICES 1, 5 *and* 6.
Royal Army Medical Corps (including Bearer companies, Field hospitals, etc.). *See* APPENDIX 7.

Reid, Lieutenant G. E., 142.
Reitz, State Secretary F. W., 107, 206 ; at the peace conference, 544, 546, 560, 563.
Reitz (town), 54-6, 58, 97, 101-2, 105, 158-9, 246, 330, 334, 336, 383, 385, 395-6, 398-400, 426, 476, 482 ; surprise of, 247-8.
Reitzburg, and area, 109, 249-50, 256, 324, 326, 347, 478.
Remounts, department of, etc., 224. *See also* APPENDIX 11.
Rensburg Drift (Vaal river), 100, 324, 347.
Rensburghoop, 152.
Reports, etc. *See* LETTERS.
Republican Governments, 24 ; flags of, 124, 357 ; the cause of, in Cape Colony, 61.
Republics, the, 365, 429, 461 ; life of, 271 ; *see also* PEACE NEGOTIATIONS, 523-63.
Retief's Nek, 157-8, 321-2, 485.
Revolution, general, in Cape Colony, 75, 131.
Rexford, 54, 57, 335, 431.
Reynolds, Major P. G., D.S.O., 347, 491, 511.
Rhenoster Berg, 226, 239.

INDEX.

Rhenoster Kop (Cape Colony), 456.
Rhenoster Kop (Eastern Transvaal), 23–4, 42, 516.
Rhenoster Kop (north-west of Kroonstad), 256.
Rhenoster river, 101, 109, 161, 251, 262, 324, 330, 347, 384, 399, 404, 425.
Rhenoster Vlakte, 81.
Rhenosterfontein (north-west of Nels Poort), 459.
Rhenosterfontein (south of Rustenburg), 293.
Rhenosterspruit, 341, 494, 498.
Rhodes, and district, 234, 271–2, 286, 368–9.
Rhodesia, 435.
Richardson, Captain J. J., 347.
Richmond, 71, 74, 226–7, 229, 232, 237, 239, 280, 367, 456, 459, 463, 465.
Richmond Road, 457, 463, 473.
Rickertsdam, 299.
Riebeek Kasteel, 361.
Rienzi, 424.
Riet river, 94, 163, 165–6, 251–2, 255, 263–4, 326, 431–2.
Riet Spruit (Eastern Transvaal), 147.
Riet Spruit (Orange River Colony), 388.
Riet Spruit (Western Transvaal), 136.
Riet valley, 89.
Rietfontein (south-east of Bethel), 113.
Rietfontein (north-east of Carolina), 149.
Rietfontein (west of Klerksdorp), 415.
Rietfontein (east of Lindleys Poort), 299.
Rietfontein (north-west of Lydenburg), 141, 144.
Rietfontein (west of Pretoria), 2, 8, 19–21, 193.
Rietfontein (east of Tafel Kop, Western Transvaal), 291.
Rietfontein (north of Tafel Kop, Western Transvaal), 339.
Rietfontein (south-west of Ventersdorp), 407.
Rietfontein (north of Welverdiend), 190.
Rietfontein (east of Wolvehoek), 330.
Rietfontein Ridge, 90.
Rietgat (south-east of Lichtenburg), 409.
Rietgat (west of Vrede), 246–7.
Rietkuil (north-east of Bethlehem), 482.
Rietkuil (west of Klerksdorp), 416.
Rietpan (east of Bethel), 151.
Rietpan (north of Bethlehem), 56.
Rietpan (south of Doorn Kop, Western Transvaal), 339.
Rietpan (east of Hoopstad), 256.
Rietpoort, 335, 384.
Rietport Pass, 103.
Rietput, 328.
Rietspruit (north of Amersfoort), 200.
Rietspruit (near Ermelo), 123, 125–6.
Rietvlei (north-west of Bethel), 153.
Rietvlei (west of Ermelo), 209.
Rietvlei (west of Klerksdorp), 494.
Rietvlei (south-east of Lichtenburg), 409.
Rietvlei (south-east of Senekal), 54, 322.
Rietvlei (south of Vlakfontein, Standerton railway), 28.
Rietvlei (east of Vryheid), 121.
Rifle Brigade, The. *See* REGULAR UNITS.
Rifle practice, want of, 504.
Rifles, retention of, at conclusion of war, 524, 547; thrown away by burghers, 202.
Rimington, Colonel M. F., C.B., 117, 119–20, 147, 150–2, 155, 199–202, 222–3, 249–50, 269, 321–4, 329–31, 333–8, 383–4, 388–90, 400–2, 404–5, 423–7, 434, 475–7, 479–80, 485, 488, 490, 520, 522.
Rinderpest, 407.
Rising of the farmers, in Cape Colony, 75.
Riversdale, 283.

Robbing the dead and wounded, at Bakenlaagte, 313.
Roberts, Field-Marshal, The Right Hon. F. S., Lord, K.P., G.C.B., V.C., etc., etc., 1, 232, 421, 435–6, 498, 528.
Roberts Drift, 329.
Robinson Pass, 283.
Roche, Lieut.-Colonel The Hon. U. de R. B., C.B., 131.
Rochfort, Colonel A. N., C.B., 165, 167–8, 171, 245, 251–3, 263, 269, 319, 327–8, 338, 416, 422, 423, 429–31, 433–4, 478, 481, 488, 490–3, 502, 505–8, 511.
Rocky Hill (Machadodorp), 36, 42.
Rogers, Sergeant J. (awarded the Victoria Cross), 170.
Roggeveld mountains, 64, 70, 353, 460.
Rolspruit, 113.
Romans, 404.
Rome, 314.
Romilly, Lieut.-Colonel F. W., C.B., D.S.O., 157–8, 171.
Rondavel, 456.
Rondedraai, 246, 476.
Roode Berg (Cape Colony), 238.
Roode Bergen (Orange River Colony), 158, 335.
Roode Hoogte, 173, 280.
Roode Kloof, 235.
Roodekopjes, 246.
Roodekraal, 396.
Roodekrans, 517.
Roodekranz, 144.
Roodepan (east of Belmont), 262.
Roodepan (north-west of Lichtenburg), 407–8.
Roodepoort (south of Dewetsdorp), 328.
Roodepoort (west of Johannesburg), 131.
Roodepoort (north of Kopje Alleen), 161.
Roodepoort (north of Middelburg), 144–5.
Roodepoort (north of Wakkerstroom), 202.
Roodepoortje, 145.
Roodewal (south of Greylingstad), 28.
Roodewal (Orange River Colony), 102, 399, 421.
Roodewal (south-west of Rustenburg), 189–90.
Rooi Berg, and hills, 439, 445.
Rooikraal, 144.
Rooipoort (south-west of Bethel), 113.
Rooipoort (south-west of Ventersdorp), 134.
Rooipoort (north of Wolmaranstad), 340–1.
Rooirantjesfontein, 416, 492, 507.
Rooiwal (Harts river), 406, 504–5; action at, 499–503.
Rooiwal (south-east of Hoopstad), 257.
Roos Senekal, 123, 126, 140, 143–4, 146–7, 152, 211, 213, 380, 515, 521.
Rosmead, and railway, 66–7, 228.
Ross, Commandant, 426.
Ross, Major C., 476.
Rotterdam, 117, 200, 379–80.
Rouxville, and district, 45, 62, 65, 75, 77–8, 164, 179, 267–8, 289, 317–18, 320.
Rowley, Captain C. A., 219.
Royal Artillery. *See* REGULAR UNITS.
Royal Canadian regiment. *See* REGULAR UNITS.
Royal Cavalry regiments. *See* REGULAR UNITS.
Royal Engineers. *See* REGULAR UNITS.
Royal Horse artillerymen, as cavalry, 402.
Royal Infantry battalions. *See* REGULAR UNITS.
Royal Marine artillery. *See* REGULAR UNITS.
Rudolph (Free State officer), 356.
Rundle, Lieut.-General Sir H. M. L., K.C.B., C.M.G., D.S.O., 54, 57–9, 97, 99, 110, 156–8, 169, 171, 217, 219, 245–6, 249–51, 265, 321–2, 329, 331, 334–5, 338, 386, 391–5, 405, 423, 434.
Runnymede, 266, 317.

INDEX.

Rupert, Prince (Royalist General), 382, 504.
Russia, 397 ; Czar of, 24.
Russian cavalry at Balaklava, 501.
Rust, 246, 476.
Rustenburg, district, and road, 1-4, 6-8, 10-11, 19, 21, 128-30, 189, 193-4, 291, 293, 302, 348, 440.
Rustenburg commando. *See* COMMANDOS.
Rustenburg—Pretoria road, safety of, 3.
Rustfontein, 246.
Rustplaats, 119.

SAASI'S DRIFT, 443.
St. Helena (Eastern Transvaal), 200.
St. Helena Fontein, 360.
St. Martin's summer, 61.
St. Petersburg, 24.
Salt river, 278.
Sand Drift, 62, 78, 88-9, 173, 366-7.
Sandcliff, 117.
Sandeman, Captain V. S., 275-6.
Sangars, 221.
Sannah's Post, 321 ; affair at, 318-19.
Sardinia, 255.
Saxony, 463.
Scandinavia, 324.
Scandinavia Drift, 324.
Scarlett, Brigadier-General the Hon. J. Yorke, 501.
Schaapkraal (south of Bethel), 113.
Schaapkraal (north-east of Rustenburg), 292.
Schaapplaats (south-east of Ventersburg), 160.
Schanskopjes, 327.
Scheepers, Commandant, 71-4, 172-6, 178, 224, 227-9, 231-2, 237, 242-3, 271, 279, 283-5, 354, 357-8, 528 ; epitaph to, 285.
Scheepers Nek, affair at, 217-18.
Scheeperslaagte, 122.
Scheerpan, 257-8.
Scheerpoort, 7.
Schiedam, 167.

Schietfontein, 507.
Schietkraal, 465.
Schikhoek, 119.
Schilder Kranz, 369, 457-8.
Schildpad Vallei, 362.
Schmidt's Drift, 488.
Schoeman's Drift, 195, 256, 346, 491.
Scholtz, Commandant, 221.
Schombie, 237.
Schoon Spruit, and district, 136-7, 183, 298 ; blockhouse line on the, 339, 492.
Schoonoord, 507.
Schoonwater, 148.
Schraalfontein, 326.
Schuilhoek, 202.
Schurve Bergen, 292.
Schurvekop, 113, 517.
Schurvepoort (east of Reitz), 105.
Schurwe Berg, 32.
Schweizer Reneke, 132, 191, 344, 346, 502-3, 505, 507-8.
Scobell, Colonel H. J., 110, 171, 173, 175-6, 178-80, 225-6, 228-9, 231-2, 237-42, 244, 274, 278-81, 290, 368-70, 457, 474.
Scots Greys, Royal. *See* REGULAR UNITS.
Scots Guards. *See* REGULAR UNITS.
Scott, Lieut.-Colonel A. B., 192, 377-8, 511.
Scott, Lieutenant W., 389-91.
Scottish Horse. *See* COLONIAL UNITS.
Seacow river, 78, 89-90.
Searchlight, used by armoured trains, 209, 507, 509.
Secretaries of State, for Foreign Affairs, 528 ; for the Colonies, 230 ; for War, 230 ; Boer peace proposals to, 536-9.
Selika Drift, 443.
Selous river, and valley, 189, 293-4, 297.
Selouskraal, 189.
Senekal, 54-7, 101, 159, 169, 253, 424, 431, 433, 477.
Serfontein station, 323.

VOL. IV. 48*

Settle, Major-General Sir H. H., K.C.B., D.S.O., 46, 65-70, 80, 174, 176, 180, 225; covers Cape Town, 69.
Seven Weeks Poort, 284.
Seymour, and district, 237, 277.
Seymour, Lieutenant R. H., 310.
Shea, Major J. S., D.S.O., 255-7.
Shearman, Captain E. R. A., 460.
Sheep, slaughter of, 169.
Sheepskins, used on the feet, by Boers, 33.
Shekleton, Lieut.-Colonel H. P., 134-5, 138, 197.
Shela river, 118, 200-1.
Sheldon station, 174, 277-8.
Shelton, Lieut.-Colonel W., 468, 470-2.
Shepherd, Lieutenant R. E., 312.
Sherborne, 66.
Sherbrooke, Lieutenant N. C. H., 311.
Ships, hospital. *See* APPENDIX 7.
Shooting of British troops at Rooiwal, 503-4.
Shott, Lieutenant H. H., 162.
Shropshire Light Infantry. *See* REGULAR UNITS.
Shute, Major H. G. D., D.S.O., 65-6, 71, 92.
Sicily, 255.
Sick, treatment of, etc. *See* APPENDIX 7.
Sickness, among horses, 440, 445-6.
Siege of: Ookiep, 470-2; Tontelbosch Kolk, 363.
Signal, attack directed by, at Itala, 220.
Signal Hill (Machadodorp), 36.
Silverkop, 149.
Silverton, 149.
Simpson, Lieut.-Colonel G. G., 373, 377-8.
Situation in: Cape Colony, 60-1, 224, 230-1, 271, 349-50, 383, 453-4, 461, 473; the Eastern Transvaal, 371-2; Magaliesberg, 2, 128-9; Northern Transvaal, 383; Orange River Colony, 245, 382-3, 392-3, 397; South Africa, 382; Western Transvaal, 1, 128, 348, 382, 420-1, 491-2; on the Delagoa Bay railway, 23.
Sitwell, Lieut.-Colonel W. H., D.S.O., 433-4, 481, 490, 511.
Slabberts Nek, 321-2.
Sladen, Major J. R. F., 105-6, 108.
Slagboom, 142, 214.
Slaghoek, 144.
Slangapies Berg, 117-18, 200-2.
Slangfontein, 466.
Slik Spruit, 78, 328.
Slyp Steen, 85.
Smaldeel (Orange River Colony), 76, 167.
Smaldeel (north-east of Vryheid), 121.
Smit, Field-Cornet D., 232, 237-40, 364, 459, 462, 473.
Smith, Major S. Bogle, 252, 263, 269, 319, 327-8, 338.
Smith-Dorrien, Major-General H. L., D.S.O., 36-7, 43, 111-21, 126-7, 140.
Smithfield, and district, 62-3, 75, 77, 163-4, 168, 264, 266, 316, 327.
Smithvale, 232.
Smuts, Assistant-Commandant-General J. C. (Attorney-General), 75, 107, 130-1, 195, 231, 262, 264-7, 272-81, 286-9, 316-17, 320, 354, 357-8, 364, 367, 383, 454, 467, 469-71, 473; assumes command of Boer forces in Cape Colony, 363; at the peace conference, 544-6, 556; character of, 271; confidence of, 453; invades Cape Colony, 268, 270; issues proclamation for governance of Cape Colony, 461; tactics of, 455; views of, on the situation in Cape Colony, 365-6, 453, 461.
Smuts, General T., 34-6, 206; deprived of command, 212.
Sneeuw, 228, 278.
Sneeuw Bergen, 64, 71, 74, 172-3, 226, 232, 238.
Snyman's Hoek, 483.
Solomon, Hon. Sir Richard, K.C.M.G., K.C., 546.

Somerset, 485.
Somerset East (county and town), 174–5, 178, 226, 278–80, 463, 467.
Somersetshire Light Infantry. *See* REGULAR UNITS.
Somersfontein, 164, 262.
Somosierra, 46.
Soudan, tribesmen of, 504.
Soult (French Marshal), 397.
South Africa, improved situation in, 382.
South African Constabulary. *See* COLONIAL UNITS.
South African Light Horse. *See* COLONIAL UNITS.
South African Republic, peace terms for, negotiations and conclusion of, 523–63.
South Australian contingents. *See* COLONIAL UNITS.
South Hill (Helvetia), 25–6.
South Lancashire regiment. *See* REGULAR UNITS.
South Staffordshire regiment. *See* REGULAR UNITS.
South Wales Borderers. *See* MILITIA and REGULAR UNITS.
Spandouws Kop, 229.
Spartans, epitaph to, at Thermopylæ, 313.
Spekboom river, 381.
Spelonken mountains, 446.
Spens, Brigadier-General J., C.B., A.D.C., 147–8, 153, 155, 199, 204, 207–8, 210–11, 216, 219, 223, 250, 321–3, 331, 333, 338, 371, 373–4, 376, 378–9, 381, 485, 487, 490, 514, 517, 520, 522.
Spies: Boer—68; British—306.
Spion Berg, 69, 459.
Spion Kop, 394.
Spitz Kop (Bamboes mountains), 464.
Spitz Kop (Sneeuw Bergen), 173, 226, 237, 239, 280, 464.
Spitzkop (south-east of Vryheid), 122.
Spitzkop (north of Wakkerstroom), 380.

Spitzkrans, 169.
Sporting terms, definition of, 114.
Springbok, 469.
Springbok Vlakte, 83.
Springbokfontein, 378.
Springbokspruit, 200.
Springfield Drift, 169, 245–6.
Springfontein, 94, 97–8, 164, 195, 252, 262, 266–7, 319–20, 430.
Springhaan Nek, and Post, 46–52.
Springs, 111, 130, 150, 152, 195, 210, 215, 304, 315, 373, 376, 379, 477, 518, 520; affair near, 513.
Spruit Zonder Drift, 480–1.
Spruitplaats, 192.
Spruyt, General C., 206.
Spytfontein (east of Lindley), 336.
Spytfontein (south of Ventersburg), 160.
Stabbertswaag, 402.
Stampedes, 19, 115, 296, 313, 340, 410, 495, 502.
Standerton, and road, 46, 101, 103, 105, 113, 116, 147, 149–54, 156, 200, 202–3, 215–17, 222, 249, 315, 323, 329, 331, 333, 371, 376, 378, 424, 491, 514; blockhouse line to, 372–3, 378, 517; railway to, 27, 43, 125, 127, 153, 201, 209, 423, 435, 481, 485, 517–18, 520.
Stanhouders Kraal, 262.
Staple Ford, 466.
Statistics, general, Boer and British, 567–705 (APPENDICES).
Steele's Drift, 250.
Steelpoort river, 140–1, 145, 211, 214, 515.
Steenkamp, Commandant Piet, 297, 299.
Steenkool (or Steenbok) Spruit, 150, 152, 199, 203, 210, 215, 306, 517.
Steenkoppies, 194.
Steinacker's Horse. *See* COLONIAL UNITS.
Steinkopf, 469–72.
Stellenbosch Vallei, 175, 232.

Stenekamps Kop, attack on blockhouse at, 483-4.
Stenkamps Berg, 24, 140, 380.
Stephenson, Major-General T. E., C.B., 284, 290, 359-62, 364, 370, 459, 465, 473.
Sterkfontein (east of Boshof), 259.
Sterkfontein (north of Ermelo), 205.
Sterkfontein (north-west of Nylstroom, 444.
Sterkfontein (north-west of Ventersdorp), 339.
Sterkstroom (Cape Colony), 225, 237, 273, 464.
Sterkstroom river, and valley (Western Transvaal), 193, 292-3.
Stewart, Lieut.-Colonel H. K., 217-18, 223, 373, 377-8, 381, 514, 517, 520, 522.
Steyn, H. E. President M. T., 49, 54, 75, 83, 104, 107-8, 124, 140, 205-7, 245-7, 323, 396, 426, 428, 546; addresses Kritzinger's burghers, 367; denounces peace terms, 556; narrow escape of, 248; Scheepers' epitaph by, 285; moves to De la Rey's laager, 478; to peace conference, 533, 535; illness of, compels him to retire from, 541.
Steyn, Field-Cornet, 248.
Steynsburg (Cape Colony), 60, 65, 174, 179-80, 225, 236, 272; blockhouse line to, 458.
Steynsburg (north of Fouriesburg), 322.
Steynsdorp, 148.
Steytlerville, 73.
Stock (cattle and sheep), capture of, by British, 32, 96-7, 99, 101, 103, 107-9, 116, 118-19, 121-2, 133, 136, 141, 146, 149-50, 152-3, 158-9, 161, 163-6, 168-9, 182, 192, 200-3, 208, 211, 249, 251, 253, 255-61, 263, 304, 322-3, 329, 332, 335, 340-5, 352, 371, 376, 429, 443-4, 477, 480, 493.

"Stops," 86, 94, 97, 108, 121, 142, 147, 194, 486; definition of, 114.
Stores, Boer, captured, 476; ordnance—see APPENDIX 8.
Storm Bergen, 64, 272, 473.
Stormberg, and railway, 66, 225, 272, 274, 286, 465; blockhouse line to, 368.
Stormfontein, 238.
Straffontein, 153.
Straker, Lieutenant E. O., 310.
Strategy: Boer—62, 91, 108, 357, 365-6, 383, 461, 528; errors in, 349; British—65, 265; criticisms on, 435.
Strength of: Boer forces—21, 113, 321, 324, 330, 356, 485, 518; Badenhorst's, 444; Beyers', 10, 19, 75, 113; Chris. Botha's, 220; C. Botha's, 249; L. Botha's, 34, 43, 115, 219; Cape rebels, 453; De Beer's, 132; De la Rey's, 3, 134, 297, 411, 418, 499; De Villiers', 132, 433; De Wet's, 45, 49, 53, 76, 94, 384, 393, 397; Emmett's, 121; Fouché's, 179; Hertzog's, 63, 67, 88, 94; Kemp's, 184; Kritzinger's, 63, 174, 179; Lategan's, 232; W. Malan's, 173, 199; Maritz's, 358; Mentz's, 477; Muller's, 143; Myburg's, 368; Opperman's, 220; H. J. Potgieter's, 220; Pretorius', 439; Prinsloo's, 215; Scheepers', 228; Smit's, 462; J. C. Smuts', 130; Theron's, 233; Uys', 439; G. Van Niekerk's, 431; Viljoen's, 26; P. Wessels', 368; W. J. Wessels', 385; in the High Veld, 199; near Carolina, 43; near Vlaklaagte, 43—see also APPENDIX 20; British forces—Alderson's, 21, 111; Allenby's, 111; Babington's, 128; Banon's, 165; Beatson's, 203; Benson's, 306; Bethune's, 77; Broadwood's, 247; Byng's, 47, 165; B. Campbell's, 157; W. P. Campbell's, 111; Chapman's,

377 ; Clements', 2 ; Colenbrander's, 447, 451 ; Colville's, 28, 111 ; Crewe's, 55, 76 ; Cunningham's, 347 ; Dartnell's, 111 ; Denny's, 447 ; Dixon's, 184–5 ; Edwards', 324 ; Elliot's, 100 ; French's, 111, 228 ; Gogarty's, 165 ; Gordon's, 128 ; Gorringe's, 72 ; Grenfell's, 415, 437, 440 ; Harris', 165 ; Hickman's, 77 ; Jeudwine's, 225, 351 ; Kekewich's, 128 ; F. W. Kitchener's, 126 ; E. C. Knox's, 111 ; McMicking's, 440 ; Mills', 222 ; Milne's, 346 ; Monro's, 56 ; Murray's, 288 ; Paris', 416 ; Plumer's, 139 ; Pulteney's, 111, 128 ; Rochfort's, 165 ; Sandeman's, 275 ; Smith-Dorrien's, 43, 111 ; Thorneycroft's, 47 ; Von Donop's, 299 ; W. H. Williams', 165 ; at Helvetia, 25 ; in Cape Colony, 172—*see also* APPENDIX 13 ; of loyalists in Cape Colony, 69 ; on Eastern L. of C., 35 ; states of, 22, 59, 92, 110, 127, 138–9, 155, 171, 180, 197, 203, 223, 244, 269, 290, 303, 315, 338, 348, 370, 381, 405, 422, 434, 452, 474, 490, 511, 522.
Strijdpoort, 246, 423, 425.
Strong, Lieutenant C. P., 107.
Strongholds, Boer, 104, 183–4.
Stryd Poort, 273.
Strydenburg, 67, 81, 84, 87, 462.
Strydkraal, 200.
Strydplaats (south-east of Vrede), 426.
Strydplaats (south of Vryheid), 122.
Subjugation of Orange River Colony, 326.
Successes of Boers, inutility of, 421.
Suffolk regiment, The. *See* REGULAR UNITS.
Sunday river, 175, 466.
Supplies, 67, 169, 193 ; Elliot's, 105 ; for Boers, in Cape Colony, 68–9 ; plenitude of, 199 ; short of, 3, 68, **355, 377** ; for De Wet's force, 76 ;

French's, 112–13, 116–18, 120, 156 —*see also* APPENDIX 1 ; in Cape Colony, 224 ; of the veld, 343 ; Plumer's, 81–3, 95 ; system of— *see* APPENDIX 5 ; Wyndham's, 229.
Surrender : of Boers—118, 143–4, 149, 211, 214, 241, 346, 376, 409, 429, 439, 444, 451, 486, 509, 516–17 ; conditions of, 524–6, 547 ; of British—16, 26–7, 259, 280, 414, 420, 469.
Suspected persons, in Cape Town, 177.
Sutherland, and district, 69–70, 173, 240, 279, 282, 284, 286, 353–6, 358, 362–4, 455, 460–2.
Sutherland, Sergeant, gallant conduct of, 106.
Swanepoerls Poort, 74.
Swartwater, 200.
Swaziland, and border, 43, 116–18, 121, 140, 149, 212, 222, 375 ; blockhouse line to, 371, 377, 379.
Sweetwater, 267.
Swellendam, 243, 283–4.
Swinburne, Lieutenant, 513.
Sybille, H.M.S., 70.
Syferfontein, 306.
Syferkuil, 136.
Sympathy with enemy, 177.
Systematic attempt to destroy blockhouses, 483–4.

TAAIBOSCH SPRUIT, 135–6, 181, 194, 408 ; blockhouse line along the, 407.
Taaiboschfontein, 459.
Taaiboschspruit, 117.
Tabakplaats, 141.
Tabaksberg, the, action on, 76, 159.
Table Bay, 75.
Tactics : Boer—64–6, 89–90, 208, 306, 331, 337, 384, 396, 401, 455, 501, 528 ; British—88, 147, 266, 344, 400 ; central point of, 263 ; in earlier operations, 437.
Tafel Kop (east of Frankfort), 101–2, 249, 399, 423–5, 475–6 ; action near, 389 ; blockhouse line to, 385, 388, 398, 480.

Tafel Kop (Western Transvaal), 136, 182-4, 188-9, 194, 293, 344, 407; blockhouse line to, 344.
Tafelkop (north-west of Ermelo), 378.
Tafelkop (north of Fauresmith), 252.
Tandjes Berg, 225-6, 233, 239-40, 457, 463.
Tanqua river, 357.
Tanqua valley, 355.
Tarka (county), 226.
Tarka river, 174.
Tarkastad, 174, 225-6, 233, 274, 277, 466-7.
Taungs, 131-2, 191-2.
Tax, not to be imposed on landed property, 548.
Taylor, Lieut.-Colonel H. d'A. P., 253, 266, 269, 272-3, 290, 327, 431.
Tenacity of the enemy, 327.
Terms of peace, negotiations for and conclusion of, 523-63.
Ternan, Colonel T. P. B., C.M.G., D.S.O., 431, 434, 481, 488-90.
Thabanchu, and district, 46-51, 53, 76, 97, 99, 170, 253, 264, 385; blockhouse line, 264, 318, 326.
"The Anglo-Boer War," by General B. Viljoen, 35.
The Groote Zwarte Bergen, 73.
The Union of the Boer people from Table Bay to the Equator, 75.
The Willows, 238.
Theatre of war, Cape Colony, the main, 461.
Thebus, 179, 237, 467.
Thermopylæ, epitaph to Spartans at, 313.
Theron, Commandant J., 233, 237-9, 243, 271, 283-4, 356-62, 460, 462, 473.
Theunissen, Commandant H., 67.
Thomas, Lieut.-Colonel Sir Godfrey, Bart., 14, 17-18.
Thompson, Captain T., 318.
Thomson, Major N. A., 438, 444.
Thorndale (Hekpoort valley), 21.

Thorneycroft, Colonel A. W., 46-53, 59, 65, 67, 69-70, 74, 87-9, 92, 97, 110, 158-61, 166-7, 171, 245, 250, 253, 265-9, 287, 289, 316-18, 327, 338, 430-1, 434, 482, 489, 498, 507, 509, 511.
Thorneycroft's mounted infantry. See COLONIAL UNITS.
Thorold, Captain F. T., 310.
Three Sisters station, 457, 459, 464.
"Three Years' War," by C. R. De Wet, 83, 90, 99, 404, 427.
Tiger Kloof Spruit, 386-7, 391.
Tintasdrift, 122.
Tomlin, Major M. H., 481, 490.
Tontelbosch Kolk, 352-3, 355, 462, 473; the siege of, 363.
Toom Nek, 179, 236.
Toovernaarsrust, 121-2.
Torres Vedras, 64.
Touws river, 70, 284-5.
Toverwater river, 228.
Town Guard. See COLONIAL UNITS.
Trains: armoured, 80-1, 209, 228, 238, 362, 366, 402, 442, 467, 507, 509; hospital—see APPENDIX 7; wrecking of, 41, 125-6, 156, 232, 441-2.
Transkei, 234.
Transport, 224; columns without, 492; system of—see APPENDIX 6.
Transvaal, 65, 69, 107-8, 124, 177, 203, 231, 245, 249, 261, 264, 330—see also EVENTS IN EASTERN, NORTHERN and WESTERN; Government of, 205-6, 214-15, 305, 380 515.
Transvaalers, 205-6, 270.
Transvalia, 200.
Travers, Major J. H. du B., 183.
Traynor, Sergeant W. B. (awarded the Victoria Cross), 114.
Treason, in Cape Town, 177.
Trekpoort, 258.
Treurfontein, affair at, 406-7.
Trichardt, Commandant P. T., 28, 515-16.

INDEX. 761

Tucker, Lieut.-General Sir C., K.C.B., 93, 110, 170-1, 327, 434, 481.
Tugela river, 42.
Tulbagh (Cape Colony), 70.
Tulbagh (Orange River Colony), 102.
Tweebosch, 416, 421, 478; action at, 417-20.
Tweedraai, 150.
Tweefontein (north of Amersfoort), 147.
Tweefontein (east of Bethlehem), 169, 232, 392-3, 395, 397, 401; action at, 394.
Tweefontein (north-west of Ermelo), 207.
Tweepannon, 340.
Tweepoort, 54-5.
Twenty-Four river, 359.
Twyfel Poort, 89.
Twyfelkopspan, 260.
Tzamen, 159.

UILEN KRAAL, 361.
Uitenhage (Cape Colony), 74, 278, 466.
Uitenhage (south-east of Serfontein station), 323.
Uitgedacht, 207.
Uitgezocht, 151.
Uithoek, 121.
Uitkomst (west of Graaff Reinet), 228.
Uitkomst (south of Machadodorp), 148.
Uitkyk (south of Heilbron), 102.
Uitkyk (north-east of Standerton), 200, 202.
Uitkyk (north-west of Wolmaranstad), 342.
Uitspan, 116.
Uitspanfontein, 455, 459.
Uitzicht, 151.
Umpilusi river, and valley, 116-17, 149, 377.
Umtali river, 377.
Umvolosi river, 122.
Union of the forces of De Wet and Hertzog, 89.
Union, the, of the Boer peoples from Table Bay to the Equator, 75.

Uniondale, 72-3, 242.
Upington, 468.
Urmston, Lieut.-Colonel E. B., 376-7, 380-1, 515-17, 521-2.
Utrecht, 29-30, 35, 118-20, 201-2, 215-16, 218, 222; attack on, 32-4.
Utrecht commando. *See* COMMANDOS.
Uys, Commandant P., 439.
Uyskraal, 142, 214.

VAAL BASIN, 333.
Vaal Krantz, 121.
Vaal river, 2, 84-6, 100-2, 108-9, 115-16, 133-4, 136, 146, 148, 151, 153, 160, 167, 183, 191, 195-6, 199-200, 202, 206-7, 209-10, 249-51, 253-6, 260, 262, 323-4, 329-30, 333-4, 347, 373, 376, 378-9, 424, 475, 478, 481, 485, 487, 491-3, 505-6, 508; blockhouse line to, 345, 512; drifts of the, blockhouses at, 346.
Vaalbank (north-east of Bethel), 207.
Vaalbank (south-west of Carolina), 205.
Vaalbank (south of Lichtenburg), 492.
Vaalbank (south-east of Reitz), 246.
Vaalbank (north-east of Utrecht), 118.
Vaalbank (west by south of Ventersdorp), 493; blockhouse line to, 407, 492.
Vaalbank (north-east of Vryheid), 122.
Vaalpan, 262.
Vaalspruit, 319.
Vaalwater river, 214.
Val station, 512, 517, 521.
Vallancey, Major H. d'E., 446-7.
Vallentin, Major J. M., 153, 379-80.
Valour, of British, at Bakenlaagte, 310-13.
Valsch river, 160-1, 255-6, 325, 383-4, 404, 424-5, 477, 482.
Valsch River Drift, 257.
Value of railways, for military operations, 64-5.
Van der Merwe, 284.
Van der Merwe, Field-Cornet, 164.

Van der Venter, Commandant, 264, 278–82, 363–4, 368, 455, 460.
Van Dyksdrift, 152, 203–4.
Van Dyksput, 153.
Van Heerden, Commandant J., 297, 465–6.
Van Niekerk, A., 350.
Van Niekerk, Field-Cornet G., 431.
Van Reenan, G. H. P., 179–80, 225–6, 233, 236, 238, 363, 462.
Van Reenen's Pass, 156, 323 ; blockhouse line to, 423–5, 428.
Van Rensburg, Commandant, 438.
Van Rhyns Dorp, 71, 356–7, 365, 453, 460, 462, 468, 472 ; capture of, by Boer force, 355.
Van Stades Drift, 256.
Van Tonder's Drift, 175.
Van Wyks Vlei, 351.
Van Zyl (rebel), Commandant, 468, 501, 509.
Van Zyl (rebel), Commandant, 417–18.
Vant's Drift, 219, 221.
Var Kens Kop, 280.
Varkfontein (north of Boshof), 433.
Varkfontein (north of Victoria West), 473.
Vaughan, Major C. D., 491, 511.
Vaughan, Major J., 457.
Vecht Kop (south of Heilbron), 102, 399.
Vecht Kop (north-east of Zastron), 287–8, 318, 327.
Veld, supplies on, 343 ; blockhouse line across, 364.
Veld fires. See GRASS FIRES.
Venter, Field-Cornet, 439.
Venter, Field-Cornet H. S., 369.
Venter's Poort, 96.
Venters Spruit, 400.
Venter's Valley, 80, 89–90.
Ventersburg, 93, 97, 397, 423.
Ventersburg Road, 160.
Ventersdorp, district of and road, 1, 22, 128–30, 133–6, 183, 189, 192, 194, 291–3, 298, 339 ; blockhouse line to, 345.
Ventershoek, 163, 327.
Venterskroon, and district, 253, 346.
Venterstad, 65, 174, 238, 272.
Verbliden, 159.
Verblyding, 152.
Vereeniging (south-east of Ermelo), 115, 147.
Vereeniging (Vaal river), 102, 109, 195, 207, 210, 249, 346, 485, 521 ; burghers, peace delegates, to, 541 ; peace conference at, 471, 473–4, 487–8, 549, 554–5.
Verkykers Kop, 251, 329, 399, 403.
Verlaten Dam, 86.
Verlaten Kloof, 455.
Verloren Vallei, 362.
Vermaakfontein, 320.
Vermaas, Commandant H. C. U., 134, 341, 418.
Verzamel Berg, 103, 154–5, 212, 425.
Vet river, 159, 254, 256–8.
Vet River station, 161, 166, 257–8.
Veterinary Department, Army, surgeons, etc. See APPENDIX 11.
Vialls, Major H. G., C.B., 82–4, 142.
Vickers-Maxim guns, 2, 14, 22, 28–9, 51–2, 59, 76, 85, 92, 110, 127, 132, 135, 137–8, 144, 151, 155, 162, 171, 180, 185, 187, 197, 203, 213, 223, 244, 269, 290, 294, 299–300, 303, 306, 308, 312, 314–15, 348, 370, 377, 381, 392, 408, 410, 412, 415–18, 422, 434, 437–8, 440, 452, 474, 490, 493, 495, 500, 503, 511, 522. See also APPENDIX 4.
Victoria, 52.
Victoria (Australia), contingents from. See COLONIAL UNITS.
Victoria Crosses, 20, 38, 114, 119, 148, 161, 170, 211, 217, 220, 238, 297, 373, 387, 390, 513. See also APPENDIX 19.
Victoria West, 67, 237, 281 ; blockhouse line to, 364, 459.
Victoria (West) Road, 280, 364, 459.
Victoriaspruit, 336.

INDEX

Viljoen, General B., 23–7, 34–6, 39, 42, 107, 114, 123–4, 126, 140, 143–7, 149–52, 203, 205–11, 213–14, 216, 377, 382, 515 ; capture of, 380–1.
Villiersdorp, 102, 199, 207, 209–10, 329, 333–4, 400, 477, 485–6.
Vinkfontein, 238.
Vinknest, 476.
Virginia siding, 160–1.
Vissers Drift, 88.
Vlak Laagte, 463.
Vlakfontein (Heidelberg railway), 28.
Vlakfontein (north of Lydenburg), 140.
Vlakfontein (north of Reitz), 246.
Vlakfontein (south of Rustenburg), 130, 184–5, 190, 291, 296, 504 ; action at, 186–8.
Vlakfontein (south of Sannah's Post), 318–19.
Vlakfontein (north of Tafel Kop, Western Transvaal), 339.
Vlakfontein (Vaal river), 100.
Vlakhoek, 2, 185–6, 189.
Vlaklaagte, 28, 43, 207 ; affair at, 512–13.
Vlaknek Pass, 103–4.
Vlakplaats, 194.
Vlakpoort, 277.
Vlaktefontein, 236.
Vliegenpan, 447.
Voet Pad, 459.
Vogel river, 174, 280, 457.
Vogel Vlei, 273.
Vogeldraai, 246.
Vogelfontein (east of Bethlehem), 387.
Vogelfontein (east of Hanover), 227.
Vogelstruis Drift, 362.
Vogelstruisfontein, 361.
Volksrust, 46, 120, 147, 153, 222, 320, 373, 380, 477.
Volunteers, 24th Middlesex (Post Office). *See* APPENDIX 9.
Von Donop, Lieut.-Colonel S. B., 292, 299–301, 303, 342, 345, 348, 409–11, 415, 422, 491, 499–501, 511.
Von Tonder, Commandant R., 501.

Voor Sneeuw Berg, 232.
Vosburg, 67.
Vrede, 90, 101–2, 105, 123, 125–6, 140, 156, 205, 246, 249–50, 331, 397, 425, 481 ; blockhouse line to, 377, 398–9, 426–7.
Vrede commando. *See* COMMANDOS.
Vredefort (town), 109, 195, 255–6, 324.
Vredefort Road (station), 101–2, 249, 324, 326, 333.
Vrouw Pan, 82–3.
Vryburg, 131, 192, 345–6, 348, 406, 409, 416, 506–7 ; railway to, 507.
Vryheid, and district, 29, 33, 120–2, 216–17, 219, 221–2, 514 ; attack on, 30–2.
Vryheid commando. *See* COMMANDOS.
Vuurfontein, 505, 507.
Vygehoek, 141.

WAGEN DRIFT, 262–3.
Wagendrift, 143, 146.
Wagon Hill, 188, 394.
Wagons, loss of, 81.
Wakkerstroom, district, and hills, 29, 32, 118–20, 147, 154, 183, 200–1, 216, 222, 249, 380, 514 ; blockhouse line to, 371–2, 379.
Walker, Major H. B., 140.
Walkraal, 255.
Walspruit, 52.
Wanbestuur, 122.
War, cost of—*see* APPENDIX 18 ; prisoners—*see* PRISONERS OF WAR ; Secretary of State for, 230 ; tax, farmers not liable for, 523, 526 ; liabilities incurred by the enemy during, 523.
Warburton, 116.
Warden, Major K. E., 175.
Warfare. *See* GUERRILLAS.
Waring, Sergeant H., 346.
Warm Bath (north of Pretoria), 10, 19, 439–40, 443–5.
Warmbath (Eastern Transvaal), 215.
Warnock, Squadron - Quartermaster Sergeant, 312–13.

Warren, Lieut.-Gen. Sir C., G.C.M.G., K.C.B., 60.
Warrenton, 133, 254.
Warringham, 321.
Warwickshire regiment, The Royal. See MILITIA UNITS.
Wastage, etc., in the Army in South Africa. See APPENDIX 16.
Watch dogs, 35.
Water, scarcity of, 445.
Water Kloof, 225, 239-40, 457.
Waterberg, and district, 436, 439.
Waterberg commando. See COMMANDOS.
Waterberg hills, 445.
Waterbron, 258.
Waterford, 174.
Waterval (east of Fraserburg), 455-6.
Waterval (south-west of Rustenburg), 185-6.
Waterval (north-east of Vryheid), 121.
Waterval Boven, 25-6.
Waterval Drift (Riet river), 421.
Waterval Drift (Wilge river, Eastern Transvaal), 23.
Waterval river (east of Heidelberg), 108, 205, 207, 245, 512.
Waterval river, and valley (north of Lydenburg), 140-1, 143.
Waterval station (east of Greylingstad), 206; blockhouse line to, 372.
Watervaldrift (north-east of Piet Retief), 200.
Watervalhoek, 215.
Watts, Major C. N., 296-7.
Welchman, Second-Lieutenant E. T., 371.
Welgelegen, 200.
Welgevonden (Cape Colony), 84-6.
Welgevonden (Mabusa Spruit), 200.
Welgevonden (north of Vryheid), 120-1.
Welkom, 121-2.
Welsh Fusiliers, The Royal. See REGULAR UNITS.
Welstand, 520.

Weltevreden (south of Bank station), 196.
Weltevreden (south-east of Carolina), 148.
Weltevreden (east of Philipstown), 90.
Weltevreden (east of Springs), 153.
Welverdiend, 128, 136, 183, 191.
Wepener, 49, 98, 168, 251, 317, 319-20, 327.
Wessels, General J. B., 248.
Wessels, Commandant, 67.
Wessels, Commandant L., 238, 367, 456-7, 462, 473.
Wessels, Commandant P., 368-9, 457-8.
Wessels, General W. J., 385, 388-91, 396, 401, 426.
West Australian contingents. See COLONIAL UNITS.
West Riding regiment. See REGULAR UNITS.
West Rietfontein, 433.
West Yorkshire regiment. See MILITIA and REGULAR UNITS.
Western, Lieut.-Colonel W. G. B., 101, 108-10, 171, 192, 196-7, 253, 255-61, 266-7, 269, 286-7, 290, 327, 338, 430, 432-4, 490-1, 511.
Western Province Mounted Rifles. See COLONIAL UNITS.
Western Transvaal, problem of, 190; situation in, 1, 128, 348, 382, 420-1, 491-2; troops from, 265; troops for, 491; Sir I. Hamilton assumes command in the, 494; his great "drive" in the, 506-10. See also EVENTS IN.
Wheat Lands, 463.
White, Lieut.-General Sir George S., G.C.B., G.C.S.I., G.C.I.E., V.C., 186.
White, Lieut.-Colonel The Hon. H. F., 262.
White, Lieutenant H. H. R., 310.
White, Lieut.-Colonel W. L., 45, 52-6, 59, 97, 110, 161, 163-5, 168, 171, 180, 244, 245, 269, 338, 462, 468-9, 472, 474.

INDEX. 765

White flag, 16, 241, 429, 509; misuse of, 201.
Widgeon, H.M.S., 72.
Wiesbaden, 317.
Wiggin, Major E. A., 371.
Wilanspruit, 57.
Wildfontein, attack on, 40; casualties at, 44.
Wildfontein Farm (Cape Colony), 179.
Wildschuts Berg, 274, 277.
Wilge river (Eastern Transvaal), 23, 113, 142, 145–6, 149–50, 152, 183, 214, 305, 315, 371, 513, 516–17.
Wilge river (Orange River Colony), 101, 105–6, 108, 246, 249, 323, 329, 333, 388, 391, 393, 396, 398–400, 423–6, 428–9, 433, 479, 482, 487.
Wilge River station, 153, 372, 516.
Wilgeboomsspruit, 299.
Wilgeboschdrift, 251.
Wilkinson, Lieutenant F. A., 27.
Willemsfontein, 267, 287, 316.
Williams, Captain B., 82.
Williams, Lieut.-Colonel E. C. Ingouville, D.S.O., 93, 98–101, 110, 171, 182–3, 189–92, 197, 291–2, 298, 303, 373, 375, 378, 381, 515–17, 520, 522.
Williams, Major F. A., 392–5, 405.
Williams, Lieut.-Colonel W. H., 45, 52–3, 59, 65–6, 71–2, 74, 89, 92, 110, 161, 163–7, 171, 245, 251–2, 263, 269, 319–20, 325–6, 331, 338.
Williston, 69, 71, 353, 455, 462, 473; blockhouse line to, 364, 459.
Willowmore, 72–4, 175, 227, 237, 242–3, 279, 281–3, 463.
Willson, Major-General M. W., C.B., 136, 138, 181–2, 197, 422.
Wilmansrust, affair at, 203–4.
Wilson, Lieut.-Colonel A. E., 173, 175, 180, 321–3, 330–1, 333–5, 383–5, 402, 405, 424, 434, 437–40, 442, 452, 475–7, 490, 511.
Wiltshire regiment. See REGULAR UNITS.
Winbult, 56.

Winburg, 51, 54–6, 75–6, 95, 97, 159, 170, 253, 259, 321, 325, 331, 335, 384–6, 400, 423–4, 431, 461.
Winburg commando. See COMMANDOS.
Windhoek, 24, 26, 143–5, 380.
Windsorton, 254, 258.
Wing, Lieut.-Colonel F. D. V., 373, 375, 377–8, 485, 513–14, 517, 520, 522.
Winkelhaak (west of Ermelo), 151.
Winkelhaak (north of the Zwart Ruggens), 293.
Winter Berg, 174, 226, 277.
Winterhoek, 238.
Wire, barbed, and entanglements, 33, 35, 38, 40, 221, 257, 360, 403, 480, 484, 495–6, 509.
Witbank (south of Bethel), 151.
Witbank (east of Brugspruit), 142, 149.
Witbank (south of Ermelo), 378.
Witbank (east of Heidelberg), 205.
Witbank (Vaal river), 347.
Witklip (south of Lydenburg), 143.
Witklip (north-east of Springs), 153.
Witklip (north by west of Wolmaranstad), 507.
Witkop, 256.
Witkopjes (or Witkoppies) (south-east of Reitzburg), 109, 347.
Witkoppies (south of Vrede), 104, 251, 329.
Witkrans (south-west of Bothaville), 256.
Witkrans (south-west of Carolina), 148.
Witmoss, and station, 178, 233, 237.
Witpoort (north of Belfast), 213.
Witpoort (north of Wolmaranstad), 341, 478.
Witpoortje, 183.
Witpunt, 115–16, 200.
Witte Bergen (Cape Colony), 285, 454.
Witte Bergen (Orange River Colony), 55, 321–2, 325, 431.
Witte Drift, 364.
Witteputs station, 167.

Witwatersrand range, 9, 129, 183, 194.
Witzies Hoek, 158, 323, 329, 334.
Wodehouse, 60.
Wolfnest, 246.
Wolhuter's Kop, 4, 128, 193.
Wolmarans, Major, 378.
Wolmarans, Field-Cornet F., 298.
Wolmaranstad, 1, 132-4, 182, 192, 341-2, 344, 409-11, 421, 501; evacuation of, 415; President Steyn to, 541.
Wolmaranstad commando. See COMMANDOS.
Wolrige-Gordon, Major J. G., 4-7.
Wolve Hoek Farm, 285.
Wolve Kop, 62, 327.
Wolve Kuil, 80-1.
Wolvehoek, 100-1, 347, 402, 477; blockhouse line to, 385, 400, 423.
Wolvepan, 254.
Wolvespruit, 415.
Women, Boer, spirit of, 206.
Wonderboom, 121-2.
Wonderfontein (Eastern Transvaal), 35, 111, 126, 145, 148, 201, 254, 373; attack on posts at, 40, 43-4; blockhouse line to, 372; casualties at, 44.
Wonderfontein (east of Hoopstad), 256-7.
Wonderfontein (east of Zeerust), 292.
Wonderheuvel, 485.
Wonderkop, 321-2.
Wonderwater Drift, 196, 262.
Woodbush, 438.
Woodman, Lieutenant C., 310.
Woodside, 425.
Wools-Sampson, Colonel A., C.B., 306, 314-15, 374, 407, 491.
Worcester, 243; Dutch congress at, 61.
Worcestershire regiment. See REGULAR UNITS.
Wormald, Major F., 358-60, 362-4, 370, 457, 459, 463, 473-4.
Wounded, at Bakenlaagte, shooting of, etc., 313; at Tafel Kop, outrages on, 390. See also CASUALTIES and APPENDICES 16 and 17.

Wylly, Lieut.-Colonel H. C., 296, 298.
Wyndham, Lieut.-Colonel G. P., 164, 171, 179-80, 225, 227-9, 231-2, 234, 238-9, 244, 283-5, 290, 358-60, 362, 364, 370, 460, 472, 474.
Wynne, Major-General A. S., C.B., 176-8, 224, 243, 363.

YATMAN, CAPTAIN C., 14-15.
Yeomanry. See IMPERIAL YEOMANRY.
Yeomanry Hill (Nooitgedacht), 17-20.
York and Lancaster regiment. See REGULAR UNITS.
Yorkshire Light Infantry, The King's Own. See REGULAR UNITS.
Young, Major A., 314.
Young, Sergeant-Major A. (awarded the Victoria Cross), 238.
Younghusband, Colonel G. J., C.B., 462, 465, 473-4.
Yzerspruit, 196, 341, 410, 416, 418-19, 421, 478; action at, 411-14.

ZAAIFONTEIN, 122.
Zaaiwater, 150.
Zaam Dam, 424.
Zak river, 363.
Zamenkomst (south-west of Standerton), 424.
Zamenkomst (north-east of Thabanchu), 53.
Zamerfontein, 259.
Zand Drift, 360-1.
Zand river, 57, 257.
Zand Spruit (south-east of Ermelo), 378.
Zand Spruit (north of Hoopstad), 256.
Zandbank, 119, 121.
Zandfontein (north of Aliwal North), 287, 327.
Zandfontein (south of Olifants Nek), 291.
Zandheuvel, 258.
Zandrivierspoort, 439-42, 444.
Zandspruit (south-west of Amsterdam), 117.

INDEX.

Zandspruit (Standerton railway), 28, 103, 212, 222.
Zastron, 42, 62, 264-7, 271, 287, 318, 366-7.
Zeekoe Gat, 229, 278.
Zeekoehoek, 10-11.
Zeekoevlei, 425.
Zeerust, and road, 1, 131, 189-91, 250, 292-4, 298-9, 301, 339.
Zekoe Spruit, 149.
Zevenfontein, 200.
Zilikat's Nek, 181.
Zoar, 200.
Zoete Inval, 257.
Zoetendalsvlei, 425.
Zoetwater, 460.
Zondagskraal, 150.
Zonneschyn, 316.
Zorgvleit, 246, 385.
Zout Pan, 82, 84.
Zout river, 362.
Zoutpans Drift, 88.
Zoutpansberg commando. *See* COMMANDOS.
Zoutspruit, 260.
Zuiker Hoek, 200.
Zuikerbosch Rand, 424.
Zuikerboschhoek, 143.
Zuikerkran, 122.
Zulu impis, 15, 376, 402, 501.

Zululand, and border, 43, 120, 122, 153-4, 377; invasion of, 219-22.
Zululand Native Police. *See* COLONIAL UNITS.
Zulus, 9; defeat of, by Pretorius (1838), 21.
Zuur Berg, 66, 176, 179, 238.
Zuur Vlakte, 236; action at, 234.
Zuurberg mountains (north of Port Elizabeth), 277-8, 466.
Zuurberg Poort, 73.
Zuurefontein, 362.
Zuurfontein (Cape Colony), 226.
Zuurfontein (north of Doorn Kop, Western Transvaal), 339.
Zuurfontein (south of Fauresmith), 94.
Zuurfontein (south-east of Kroonstad), 323.
Zuurpoort, and Pass, 74, 228, 465.
Zwagers Hoek (Cape Colony), 178, 233.
Zwagershoek Pass, 143.
Zwart river, 229.
Zwart Ruggens, 1, 190, 291, 293, 339.
Zwartfontein, 385.
Zwartkoppies (near Dullstroom, Eastern Transvaal), 25-7, 126.
Zwartkoppies (Orange River Colony), 252.
Zwartrand, 492.

Printed at The Chapel River Press, Kingston, Surrey.

www.ingramcontent.com/pod-product-compliance
Lightning Source LLC
Chambersburg PA
CBHW052006290426
44112CB00014B/2153